WOMEN, THE FAMILY, AND FREEDOM

THE DEBATE IN DOCUMENTS

Volume Two, 1880-1950

Women, the Family, and Freedom

THE DEBATE IN DOCUMENTS

EDITED BY

Susan Groag Bell & Karen M. Offen

VOLUME TWO, 1880-1950

STANFORD UNIVERSITY PRESS, STANFORD, CALIFORNIA

1983

Acknowledgments will be found on pp. 465-66

STANFORD UNIVERSITY PRESS
Stanford, California
© 1983 by the Board of Trustees of the
Leland Stanford Junior University
Printed in the United States of America
Cloth ISBN 0-8047-1172-0
Paper ISBN 0-8047-1173-9
LC 82-61081

PREFACE

THIS BOOK explores the debate in Western nations over women, their relationship to the family, and their claims to freedom, from the Enlightenment to the mid-twentieth century. Statements of prevailing ideas, all published in their time, are juxtaposed with contemporary challenges to these ideas. The debate is presented in parts and chapters. Each part of the book is introduced by an essay that places the documents in their historical context. Within each thematic chapter, each set of documents is preceded by a headnote establishing context and background. When possible, we have provided selections that can be read in their entirety. When that was impossible, we have cut longer works in a manner that preserves the integrity of the author's argument.

In our presentation of the debate, we balance well-known male and female writers against others who are less well known. We shall introduce texts by a number of forgotten women authors as well as by better-known women, all of whom made significant contributions to this debate. Many of the texts included here have never before been available in English; others are only accessible with great difficulty.

As authors and editors we intend this collection to be a contribution to the study of the history of ideas and to the field of women's studies. It should also provide much-needed material for studies in the humanities, in sociology, in law and political theory, and in comparative literature. As historians, our original intent was to analyze and understand the historical development of this vigorous debate. As our book neared completion, however, we came to view "Women, the Family, and Freedom" as more than a documentary history. For, in fact, the "woman question" still lies embedded in the heart of the Western debate about individual liberty; its resolution is central to the full realization of such liberty within the framework of the democratic state.

This project would not have been possible without the help of many people and institutions. We wish first to thank the libraries in which we worked during the last five years, and their staffs: the Bibliothèque Marguérite Durand, Paris (especially Madame Léautey); the Bibliothèque Nationale, Paris; the Bodleian Library, Oxford; the British Library, London; the Perkins Library and the Medical Center Library, Duke University; the Fawcett Library, London (especially David Dougan); the Georgetown University Library, Washington, D.C.; the Hoover Institution of War, Revolution, and Peace, Stanford University (especially Helen Berman and Agnes Peterson); the Johns Hopkins University Library; the Lane Medical Library, Stanford University Medical Center; the Library of Congress (especially Sarah Pritchard and Kay Blair); the Library of the National Institute of Education, Washington, D.C.; the National Library of Medicine, Bethesda, Md.; the New York Public Library; the Newnham College Library, Cambridge University (especially Ann Phillips); the Stanford University libraries (especially Peter R. Frank, Joanne E. Hoffman, James M. Knox, Mary Jane Parrine, and Elfriede Wiesendanger); the Doe Library, University of California, Berkeley; the McKeldin Library, University of Maryland, College Park; the Louis Round Wilson Library, University of North Carolina, Chapel Hill; the Walter Clinton Jackson Library, University of North Carolina, Greensboro; and the Widener Library, Harvard University.

Those who aided us in procuring particular documents are acknowledged in the source notes. We are also, however, indebted and grateful to the following friends and colleagues, whose interest and assistance made the creation of this work such a pleasure: Renate Bridenthal, Anna Davin, Natalie Zemon Davis, Helene Eisenberg, Stephanie Fierz, Steven C. Hause and Anne R. Kenney, Sondra Herman, Leslie Parker Hume, Claudia Koonz, Carolyn C. Lougee, Claire Goldberg Moses, Winifred A. Myers, Richard K. P. Pankhurst, Agnes F. Peterson, Mollie Schwartz Rosenhan, Jane Slaughter, Bonnie G. Smith, Peter Stansky, Louise Tilly, Nicolas Walter, and Marilyn Yalom. Affiliated and visiting scholars and staff members at the Center for Research on Women, Stanford University, have provided a stimulating environment in which to work. Students in our undergraduate history colloquium on European women, the family, and social thought enriched our insights by their enthusiastic grappling with the documents in this book.

We acknowledge our appreciation to Norris Pope, Stanford University Press, who believed from the start in the potential of this book, and to Madeleine Gleason, who edited the text with uncommon grace and thoroughness. Helen L. Bryson provided enormous help in preparing the Index. Finally, we thank Ronald L. Bell and George R. Offen for their unfailing support.

S.G.B.

K.M.O.

Center for Research on Women,
Stanford University

CONTENTS

DOCUMENTS

Chapter 9. The Revolution in Life and Morals

Chapter 10. The Quest for a Psychology of Womanhood

Chapter 11. Economics, Politics, and the Woman Question

WOMEN, THE FAMILY, AND FREEDOM

THE DEBATE IN DOCUMENTS

Volume Two, 1880-1950

GENERAL INTRODUCTION

See what a record of blood and cruelty the pages of history reveal! . . . The male element has held high carnival thus far, it has fairly run riot from the beginning, overpowering the feminine element everywhere.

Elizabeth Cady Stanton (1869)

Women of France, I tell you here from the loftiness of this podium: . . . we must count on ourselves to achieve our own freedom; we must not abandon our claims. For centuries we have been too much the victims of bad faith to forget ourselves any longer and to believe that by working for the general welfare we will obtain our share.

Hubertine Auclert (1879)

In the last third of the nineteenth century, women orators on both sides of the Atlantic addressed the women in their audiences in ringing tones, urging organization and joint effort to overthrow the "aristocracy of sex."[1] And indeed, the women's movements grew apace, building on the theoretical debate about women that had been fully elaborated during the previous century, and had, by 1880, become a full-blown critique of Western patriarchy.[2] Women's disadvantages in law, in education and economic opportunity, and in political life could no longer be dismissed solely as the problems of a few unusual women. Many more women experienced the tension between family and freedom, and the status of women emerged as a political issue with grave ramifications not only for the psychological climate but also for economic and political institutions in a period of social unrest and of tension between nations. Indeed, evidence abounds that Theodore Roszak is correct in arguing that during this period "the great sex war emerges as the foremost influence upon the cultural character and political style of the Western world."[3]

In the years covered by this book, the basic arguments about women

[1] Introductory quotations from: Elizabeth Cady Stanton, speech before the Woman Suffrage Convention in Washington, D.C., 18 January 1869, as reprinted in the *History of Woman Suffrage*, ed. Elizabeth Cady Stanton, Susan B. Anthony, and Matilda Joslyn Gage, II (Rochester, N.Y., 1881), 351; Hubertine Auclert, *Egalité sociale et politique de la femme et de l'homme, discours prononcé au Congrès ouvrier socialiste de Marseille* (Marseille, 1879), as reprinted in *Romantisme*, no. 13-14 (1976), 126.

[2] See Volume I of this work, covering the period 1750 to 1880.

[3] Roszak 1969.

were refined, sharpened, and expanded by both advocates and opponents of changes in women's civil, political, and economic situation. Organized political movements, formed in support of women's rights, accelerated their activities and their advocacy of women's autonomy. In the face of this agitation, defenders of the existing order asserted with increasing vehemence not only the doctrine of separate male and female spheres but also elaborate concepts of "pure" manliness and womanliness as the sole guarantees of social and political order. Elizabeth Cady Stanton, in her angry outburst at the bloodiness of a history forged without women's consent, set the tone for other writers and speakers who countered with vigorous and highly political analyses and proposed solutions to issues such as sex education, birth control, prostitution, and venereal disease, which seemed to their opponents to be purely intimate matters. Women writers accused patriarchal society of squandering lives and thus abusing female reproductive power. In Austria, Bertha von Suttner was shocked that Western society could so glorify death in battle while at the same time it treated the creation of life as a shameful secret. In Britain, France, and the United States, Helena Swanwick, Nelly Roussel, and Margaret Sanger all accused political leaders of "making life cheap"; in an era of militant nationalism, they looked to the day when women of all nations would "refuse to provide cannon fodder." [4]

In response to such arguments, emperors, popes, presidents, and prime ministers joined forces with playwrights, novelists, essayists, and poets to insist upon the need to keep women in their "proper" place as helpmeets, mothers, and sexual regenerators of men—all in the national interest. In the early twentieth century President Theodore Roosevelt and Kaiser Wilhelm II both insisted that the "primary" task and duty of women was to be domestic and maternal; moreover, the Kaiser emphasized how women's satisfactory performance in this role would serve the "fatherland." Only weeks after the Kaiser had spoken, the British Minister for War, addressing an anti-woman-suffrage rally in Manchester, appealed to his audience in these terms: "The German man is manly, and the German woman is womanly. Can we hope to compete with such a nation as this, if we war against nature, and endeavour to invert the natural roles of the sexes?" [5]

The ominous intensity that pervaded the admonitions of all these speakers from 1880 on suggests the extent to which the debate on the

[4] Bertha von Suttner, *Das Maschinenzeitalter, Zukunftsvorlesungen über unsere Zeit* (Dresden and Leipzig, 1899; Doc. 12); Nelly Roussel, speech protesting the centennial of the French Civil Code, 29 October 1904, as reported in *La Fronde* (1 November 1904; Doc. 29); Helena Swanwick, *Women and War* (London, 1915; Doc. 70); Margaret Sanger, *Woman and the New Race* (New York, 1920; Doc. 81).

[5] Theodore Roosevelt, "Address Before the National Congress of Mothers, Washington, D.C., March 13, 1905," *Presidential Addresses and State Papers*, III (New York, 1910; Doc. 30); Wilhelm II, toast offered at Königsberg, 25 August 1910, *Schulthess' Europäischer Geschichtskalender* (1910), p. 339; Evelyn Baring, First Earl of Cromer, speech at Manchester, as reported in the *Anti-Suffrage Review* (November 1910), p. 10.

woman question[6] had become a central political concern. Yet until recently few historians have addressed this issue. Political historians have clearly been more interested in studying the campaigns of Western governments for territorial expansion and national competition—phenomena that have conventionally been discussed under the rubrics of "nationalism" and "imperialism." Intellectual historians have for the most part skirted the issue of women and the family. Social historians have concerned themselves with the impact of urbanization and industrialization, the causes and effects of the resulting social changes, and the movements for reform that arose in response to these problems. But even when they have treated these issues with respect to the social relationship of the sexes, they have hesitated to connect their findings to the political and cultural context. Few historians have recognized the extent to which the woman question was intrinsic to concerns about national strength—be it demographic or institutional—and to accompanying questions of war and peace. Few have seen that, in the later nineteenth century, every issue concerning women's autonomy raised since 1750 cut across the new political and socioeconomic problems of the patriarchal nation states of the Old World and the New.[7] These states, republics and monarchies alike, confronted one another in a world in which their physical preeminence and moral authority seemed to be rapidly eroding and in which even the future of male-female relations seemed increasingly unpredictable.[8]

[6] We have here adopted the convenient term used by many nineteenth-century Continental writers, mainly French and German, and introduced prominently into English usage in 1884 by Theodore Stanton. Unless they are used by the historical authors themselves, we are deliberately avoiding the terms *feminist, antifeminist, feminism,* and *antifeminism* to characterize challenges and dissenting ideas put forward against entrenched and prevailing points of view on women's position. We aim to circumvent current misunderstandings about the evolution of historical demands made on women's behalf during the last three centuries; most of these misunderstandings arise from present-day efforts to eradicate notions of inherent sexual characteristics and the sexual division of labor and to celebrate the individual. Many of these notions remained unchallenged, however, by eighteenth- and nineteenth-century advocates of women's rights who described themselves, and were in turn described by their contemporaries, as *feminists.* Instead, we have tried to clarify the societal context of those dissenting ideas generally subsumed under the categories of "the emancipation of women," "the women's rights movement," etc., as required to pinpoint the specific character of the demands made by individual women for legal, educational, economic, moral, or political reform and the organized efforts they and their male supporters undertook to achieve them.

[7] The texts on the woman question throughout the period covered by the present volume include not only the works of political leaders and women reformers—speeches, essays, tracts, and government documents—but also works of fiction. As novelists and dramatists became increasingly concerned with social problems during the nineteenth century, they pondered the conundrum of the family and freedom and often addressed the tensions that confronted women. We have drawn liberally, therefore, on the works of socially engaged writers such as Eugène Brieux, Anton Chekhov, Radclyffe Hall, Henrik Ibsen, D. H. Lawrence, George Bernard Shaw, August Strindberg, Leo Tolstoy, Frank Wedekind, Rebecca West, and others, to illustrate the unfolding of the debate.

[8] See references in the Introduction to Part I, note 1, below. Recent works that restore the woman question to the analysis of nationalism and imperialism include Clark 1977, 1982; Davin 1978; Blakeley 1981; Dyhouse 1981; and Offen 1981.

Debate on the woman question during the period 1750-1880 (see Volume I) had developed on two fronts. In Great Britain, where the debate was carried on in a context of liberalism and possessive individualism, values remained essentially aristocratic even as more democratic political institutions emerged. On the Continent, and especially in France, the debate was embedded (both before and after the Revolution) in the conflict between emerging secular republicanism and counterrevolutionary or "traditional" authoritarianism, backed by religious establishments that, although weakened, could still impose their belief system on dissenters. The revolutions and repressions of the later eighteenth and early nineteenth centuries made it abundantly clear that, even among champions of the most radical political positions (for example, Charles James Fox and, later, the Chartists in England, or Etienne Cabet and Pierre-Joseph Proudhon in France), women would be unwelcome as active participants in the new political order, which, as before, was to be based on the male-headed household. Nor were women welcome, despite their already significant presence, as full participants in the new industrial order that was emerging in Western nations. Indeed, their national role was recast in terms of their dependency, as "relative creatures"—citizen-wives and citizen-mothers.[9] Upper-class women were, nevertheless, able to manipulate this role on their own behalf in order to acquire better formal education, some access (for married women) to legal control of property and of their own persons, and legal recourse to divorce.[10]

In the wake of the upheavals of 1848, however, the ideology of "relative" womanhood was once again reformulated, this time by men and women who championed the family-based social structure and the sexual division of labor into male and female spheres. This reformulation emerged as a "pedestal theory," whose promoters, both religious and secular, ranged from Pope Pius IX to Auguste Comte, John Ruskin, and Jules Michelet. These men vested great hope in women's redeeming moral influence over their own kind in a political and economic world that men themselves acknowledged to be corrupt and disheartening and that seemed to be growing increasingly volatile and threatening.[11] This view of women fell far short of universal approbation; indeed, by the 1860's it was fiercely contested throughout the Western world by outspoken critics among both sexes.

Yet, just as Enlightenment conservatives had sought to ground women's subordination in the laws of nature, so a hundred years later the pedestal theory was infused with new life by scientists and educators who sought to rejustify women's subordination and the separation of male

---

[9] The term "relative creatures" originated with Sarah Stickney Ellis, who wrote that women were "from their own constitution, and from the station they occupy in the world . . . relative creatures," in *The Women of England* (London, 1839), p. 155. From Ellis, Françoise Basch imaginatively captured the term for her study, *Relative Creatures: Victorian Women in Society and the Novel* (New York, 1974).

[10] See Volume I of this work, Parts I and II. See also R. Bloch 1978a; Darrow 1979; B. C. Pope 1980; L. Kerber 1980; Hellerstein, Hume & Offen, 1981; and Myers 1982.

[11] See Volume I, Parts II-IV.

and female spheres through the findings of scholarship. Invoking the new disciplines of history, evolutionary biology, and medical physiology, they applied the new tools of academic erudition to the social relationship of the sexes. Scholars and scientists such as Charles Darwin, Herbert Spencer, and Henry Sumner Maine in England, Johann-Jakob Bachofen and Jacob Burckhardt in Switzerland, Paul Broca in France, and Edward Clarke and G. Stanley Hall in the United States, all addressed themselves to the woman question. Educated women like the Anglo-American physician Elizabeth Blackwell, her British counterpart Frances Hoggan, and her American colleague Mary Putnam Jacobi, sought to turn the findings of biological and medical science to women's account in order to counter the much-popularized evolutionary sociobiological determinism of Comte and Spencer.

The academic reinforcement of the pedestal theory, accompanied by unsuccessful attempts to fortify the universities and learned professions against the intrusion of women, was a reaction to the all-fronts campaign launched by women to improve their educational, economic, legal, and political status. Their entry into the medical profession in particular epitomized the difficulties created when prevailing assertions of women's subordinate, domestic place collided with the hard facts of women's need for economic independence and their demonstrated achievements in strongholds of male competence.[12]

Of especial political significance during the nineteenth century prior to 1880 was the centrality of the woman question not only to the conflict between socialist critics of capitalist society and its proponents, but also to fundamental disagreements among those critics. Since the 1830's, when Saint Simonians and Fourierists in France had linked the cause of women with that of the proletariat, the woman question had become a thorny obstacle to socialist doctrinal unity; indeed, few socialist critics writing before 1848 could envision organized society without a sexual division of labor or without men on top, occupying positions of political and economic hegemony. Even Marx and Engels, writing their *Communist Manifesto* in 1848, accused the capitalists of "abolishing" the working class family by appropriating working-class women for factory labor. They treated the advent of women in the industrial labor force not as desirable but as a temporary, and distasteful, expedient destined to be removed with the proletarian revolution. Women's own advocacy of their "right to work" was no better received in socialist and working class circles of the 1830's or the 1860's than among the capitalist bourgeoisie.[13]

The issue of women's paid work loomed even larger after 1880 than it had when the basic issues were formulated in the 1830's. In countries where a cash economy had replaced subsistence economy (in which single women, wives, and widows had played an important role in domestic production), it was becoming increasingly clear that not all women

[12] See Volume I, Part IV.
[13] See Volume I, Parts II-IV: documents on the socialist controversies. See also Tilly & Scott 1978; and Hellerstein, Hume & Offen 1981.

could—or would—marry and become mothers. The problem of "surplus women," especially in the expanding upper and middle classes, grew ever more troublesome to the public consciousness as the century advanced. It was underscored by rising anxiety over the implications for family life of married women's participation in the paid labor force.[14]

The presence of women in the work force was by no means a new phenomenon in the nineteenth century. New only was their increased visibility in paid employment in the expanding urban work force and in the newly mechanized manufacturing sector. From 1850 on, when census takers first began to address the issue, the proportion of employed women in Western European nations was somewhere above one-quarter of all adult women; this proportion continued to rise steadily, into the twentieth century. Such figures alarmed observers not only in Europe but even in the United States, where, except in major cities, the overall proportion was far lower.[15]

Adding to this anxiety was the issue of national population growth. After 1880 leaders of the European nations, and even of the United States (where immigration threatened to upset Anglo-Saxon hegemony on the East Coast), began to express grave concern over a marked and accelerating decline in their respective birthrates. In France it had begun to decline in the late eighteenth century, and by 1830 had fallen below the mark of 30 births per 1,000 women, a turning-point that to demographers signalled the advent of consciously controlled fertility. Census figures in England and in many other nations began to confirm a similar pattern. By the late 1880's, therefore, women's increasing visibility in the labor force was perceived by political leaders, especially in England and Germany, as a direct threat to the birthrate and, thereby, to national strength. The cry of "race suicide" reverberated through the halls of authority. Women's behavior and attitudes concerning their reproductive as well as their productive lives quickly became the business of political leaders in the Western nation-states.[16]

Capturing the cutting edge of a developing debate in documentary form inevitably involves some distortion. For example, the evolutionary

[14] See Volume I, Parts II-IV: documents on women and work.

[15] The best source for comparable labor force figures is Paul Bairoch, *The Working Population and Its Structure*, vol. I of *International Historical Statistics*, ed. T. Deldycke, H. Gelders, J.-M. Limber et al. (Brussels, 1968). For a comparative analysis of women's employment patterns, see Branca 1975.

[16] For overall population growth, see Marcel R. Reinhard and André Armengaud, *Histoire générale de la population mondiale* (Paris, 1961). See also John Hajnal, "European Marriage Patterns in Perspective," *Population in History*, ed. D. V. Glass and D. E. C. Eversley (Chicago, 1965); Ansley Coale, "The Decline of Fertility in Europe from the French Revolution to World War II," in *Fertility and Family: A World View*, ed. S. J. Behrman, Leslie Corsa, and Ronald Freedman (Ann Arbor, Mich., 1969); Edward Shorter, John Knodel, and Etienne Van de Walle, "The Decline of Non-Marital Fertility in Europe, 1880-1940," *Population Studies*, 25 (1971), 375-93; Ansley J. Coale and Melvin Zelnik, *New Estimates of Fertility and Population in the United States* (Princeton, N.J., 1963); and Sheila Ryan Johansson, "Demographic Contributions to the History of Victorian Women," in Kanner 1979.

and economic arguments concerning women introduced by Darwin and his followers in the 1870's (Vol. I, Part IV) do not disappear in the subsequent period but are reiterated and rephrased *ad nauseam* up to and beyond 1914.[17] Although mindful of this highly significant current of social Darwinist thought and its advocates' insistence that the increasing differentiation of the sexes was the hallmark of social progress, we have chosen to focus on newly developing, more highly charged aspects of the debate—accusations of female egotism, the population question with respect to nationalism, and the socialist/liberal rivalry for the political support of women in the prewar period. We focus less, for example, on Charlotte Perkins Gilman's economic analysis, which derived from the European "socialist/feminist" discourse of the early nineteenth century, than on her arguments for the socialization of motherhood, which developed in opposition to the ideas of the Swedish women's rights advocate, Ellen Key. Also, we consider the socialist/liberal controversy over women's work within the framework of national population concerns, a focus absent in previous scholarship on the subject.

It must be stressed, moreover, that certain issues have a longer history of public debate than will be clear to readers first encountering the discussion in this volume. These ideas reach back to the Enlightenment, to the republican ideology of the eighteenth century and even earlier. Among the most important of these concepts, which have been covered extensively in Volume I, was women's growing awareness of their need for economic independence, either through control of property or through employment, in order to achieve autonomy (especially as wives) within the male-headed family in a world in which the cash nexus was becoming dramatically important.

Another highly significant issue discussed in the preceding volume is the philosophic debate juxtaposing nature/culture, sensuality/reason, passivity/activity as the primary female/male dichotomy underpinning male authority in Western society. We have suggested the extent to which men's fear of female sexuality may underlie much of the historic opposition to women's emancipation; this fear was undoubtedly enhanced and frequently elaborated upon during the period 1880-1950. Similarly, we reiterate here the significance of biography and biographical context for understanding the development of the individuals who contributed to the debate over women, the family, and freedom. Because of the personal nature of problems and ideas connected with women's autonomy and rights, the intellectual positions of individuals who wrote on the woman question cannot be understood without reference to their life experiences.[18]

After 1880 a fascinating rivalry developed between bourgeois and socialist advocates of women's rights for the loyalty of women themselves.

---

[17] For assessments of the long shadow cast by Social Darwinist ideology on the woman question debate in Britain and the United States, especially after the publication of *The Evolution of Sex* by Patrick Geddes and J. Arthur Thomson (London, 1889), see Conway 1973; Shields 1975, 1982; Duffin 1978; and Mosedale 1978.

[18] See the General Introduction to Volume I, pp. 8-9.

Pursuing the ideals of liberal individualism, upper-class and bourgeois women and their male supporters sought professional and political equality between the sexes, while socialist revolutionary tacticians concentrated above all on improving the position of proletarian males, promising female equality "after the revolution." By the early twentieth-century, national strength seemed threatened not only by women's employment and the falling birthrate, but also by the twin internationals of revolutionary socialism and women's rights. Both movements were viewed with foreboding by the leaders of the nationalistic and imperialistic nation-states of the Western world.

However different in their emphases, socialist and liberal bourgeois supporters of improvements in women's status and rights nevertheless shared certain common ideas. The first was a commitment to and invocation of "woman's" distinctive "nature"—her nurturing moral character and the deployment in the public sphere of her distinctive womanly qualities in the interest of social reform. Another common idea, an outgrowth and variant of the first, was women's commitment to peace and international understanding rather than to war and force. Perhaps because, historically, these ideas have been used by antagonists as well as champions of women's rights, today's advocates do not always recognize them as being pro-woman. Nevertheless, throughout the period discussed in both volumes of this book, these common ideas of "woman's nature" served both socialist and bourgeois liberal women as a foundation for their efforts to foster cooperation among all women across class and national boundaries.

In 1904, the Swedish author and women's rights advocate Ellen Key made a prophecy that underscored the importance of the woman question in Western nations: "We are here face to face with the profoundest movement of the time, woman's desire of freedom as a human being and as a personality, and in this we are confronted with the greatest tragic conflict the world's history has hitherto witnessed. . . . The struggle that woman is now carrying on is far more far-reaching than any other; and if no diversion occurs, it will finally surpass in fanaticism any war of religion or race."[19] The documents presented here bear witness to the intensity and the tragedy of this conflict and to the enormous importance of the issues at stake.

[19] Ellen Key, *Love and Marriage* (New York, 1911; Doc. 26).

PART I

Nationalism, Materialism, and Motherhood, 1880-1914

Between 1880 and 1914 the problem of women's position in the family and in society troubled the public consciousness as never before. As the sheer bulk of the documents chosen for this period attest, the issue had become central to the critique of the expanding commercial-industrial nation-states of Western Europe and America. On both sides of the Atlantic more women were acquiring the tools of intellect, tools that in a mechanized and fuel-powered society would threaten men's monopoly of power and authority, long based on physical strength. They were exposed to formal education, both primary and secondary, and increasing numbers of women from prosperous families were challenging universities for admission to candidacy for higher degrees. Hundreds of thousands of other women, especially in European countries, were employed in the labor force, as agricultural laborers, as domestic servants or industrial workers, as teachers, and increasingly as white collar workers. Women not obliged to work for pay in the economic interests of their families were organizing themselves for reform work—in the temperance cause, in the fight against government-regulated prostitution, and increasingly in the women's rights movement itself.[1] Meanwhile, the birthrate in all industrializing nations had begun to drop, even as populations continued to increase. This phenomenon seemed to indicate a marked change in the historical pattern of women's behavior.[2]

Nationalism is one of the key themes in the traditional histories of this

[1] There is virtually no trace of these developments in the more traditional surveys covering this period; see C. J. H. Hayes, *A Generation of Materialism, 1871-1900* (New York, 1963); Oron J. Hale, *The Great Illusion, 1900-1914* (New York, 1971); or Gordon A. Craig, *Europe, 1815-1914* (Hinsdale, Ill., 1972). Current scholarship in the new women's history is demonstrating the overwhelming presence of women's issues in the political and intellectual life of the 1880-1914 period.

[2] For references to the population literature, see the General Introduction to this volume, note 16. The connections between women's increased participation—in the labor force, in reform, and in rights movements—and the declining birthrates in Western nations are complex. Contemporary observers were certain that a cause-and-effect relationship existed—although they found it easier to assert than to demonstrate scientifically—and government

period. In the corridors of power "women's issues" were increasingly perceived, especially in the emerging democracies, as threats to prevailing
male-defined concepts of the proper social order. Woman suffrage was,
without doubt, the most explicit and widely acknowledged challenge to
the male monopoly of political and economic power, but it was by no
means the sole challenge to be pressed by women's rights advocates
in national politics. Other challenges addressed divorce, property law,
women's education, the regulation of female employment in industry, and
the regulation of prostitution.

To some extent all these concerns were part of the human problems
affecting both sexes and were connected with the mechanization of labor
and the growth of cities—the "social question" itself. But, as the documents in this volume illustrate, political leaders who attempted to resolve
the social question formulated their responses with an idealized view of a
male-headed family in mind; gender considerations were fundamental to
their policies.[3] As these internal challenges developed, the level of tension
between Western nations was also increasing. Any assessment of diplomatic history between 1900 and 1914 reveals both the growing obsession
with foreign economic competition and alarmist fears over military preparedness and population. The connections between these interlocking
aspects of political life on the domestic and the international fronts surely
deserve further elucidation.

Materialism, too, is a key theme. We see its connection with the
woman question in the increasing attention paid to both the economic
and the sexual aspects of women's lives by reformers and defenders of the
status quo alike. Although in retrospect the economic dimension has attracted more attention, an equally significant development in public discussion of the period was the opening up of the subject of sexuality and
the social ramifications of carnal relationships. Despite vociferous objections from those who preferred not to listen, controversy over such subjects as premarital chastity, ignorance of sexual life, the profligacy of
men, the "double standard" of sexual morality both within and outside
of marriage, and venereal disease—and, finally, the long-proscribed subject of birth control and its relationship to women's emancipation—
gripped the imagination of writers and thinkers, major and minor, female and male. Here women's cause gained a number of champions who
considered that individual liberty and self-realization, even in matters of
sexual expression, were as important for women as for men.

---

policies were frequently based on this contention. For a study that produced a negative cor-
relation between the decline in fertility in nineteenth-century England and the growth of the
women's rights movement, see Banks & Banks 1964. For arguments counter to the hypothesis of Shorter 1973 that high rates of illegitimacy were indicative of nineteenth-century
women's liberated attitudes toward sex, see Tilly, Scott & Cohen 1976. For a perceptive
analysis of the links between women's paid labor and their family concerns in England and
France, see Tilly & Scott 1978. See also General Introduction, note 8.

[3] Recent studies of policies concerning marriage reform, prostitution, wet-nursing, and
child care at the national level include Petrie 1971; Kanipe 1976; Sussman 1977, 1983;
Rothman 1978; Weston 1979; Walkowitz 1980; and Behlmer 1982. The attempt by
R. Evans 1977 to synthesize scholarship on the European and American women's rights
movements is already outdated.

With the growing emphasis on secular solutions to problems of material life, women, like men, increasingly attempted to redress their grievances by appealing to the power of the state rather than by prayers to the Almighty. Where nationalism, materialism, and the woman question intersected, we find a heightened insistence by women's rights advocates on what the state should do to ameliorate the situation of women *as mothers*, whose contribution to the strength, welfare, and future of the national state was politically unarguable. In a society in which "progressive" minds insisted on increasing differentiation of the sexes as a mark of evolutionary progress, this was a powerful argument indeed.[4]

Thus, between 1880 and 1914 a renewed insistence on motherhood—by both the champions and the opponents of expanded rights for women—led to further elaboration of the arguments for women's citizenship on the grounds of their distinctive functional role as mother-educators and arbitrators of moral behavior. This role had taken on national significance in the wake of, and as a reaction to, the American and French revolutions (see Vol. I, Parts I and II). After 1880 the elaboration proceeded, as if by conscious design, as a weapon to counter what many moderate supporters of women's rights perceived as the deadliest threat to the success of their cause—female egotism at the expense of the family. Novelists and dramatists had begun to explore this extreme form of individualism through female characters, as in George Meredith's *The Egoist*, Henrik Ibsen's Nora in *A Doll's House*, and Olive Schreiner's Lyndall in *Story of an African Farm* (Docs. 1, 3). Their unblinking fictional assessments of women's attempts to realize their human potential elicited cries of praise as well as bitter objections. Decrying a self-centeredness and self-cultivation that the French writer Maurice Barrès later celebrated as the "culte de moi" (and that Christopher Lasch has rebaptized, in a more general sense, as the "culture of narcissism"), opponents insisted that such exercises in self-definition could perhaps be tolerated for men, as the life of Barrès itself attests. But for women—never!

Juxtaposed to the Christian concept of spiritual humility, with its emphasis on the unremitting struggle against self, the new secular egotism seemed instead to propound cultivation of self (its opponents argued) with a relentless, unattractive fervor. To the upright public of 1880 there was all the difference in the world between George Sand's heroine Indiana (Vol. I, Doc. 37), who chose to submit to her husband's will, and Ibsen's Nora, who left a husband (however reprehensible) and children (even more unthinkable) in order to pursue autonomy. Worse, women's egoism threatened competition with men on their own ground. The burning artistic ambition revealed by Marie Bashkirtseff's diary (Doc. 4), or the intellectual provocations of Strindberg's Ottilia (Doc. 2) or his Fräulein Julie (not to mention Thomas Hardy's Sue Bridehead), sent shudders through male and female defenders of the established order, for whom the very essence

---

[4]The amelioration-of-motherhood argument predominated in the arguments of American Progressives such as Jane Addams and Frances Willard. See the discussion in Rothman 1978. Before 1914, the same phenomenon was even more evident throughout Europe, thanks to the influence of Ellen Key.

of womanliness was ostensibly other-centeredness, other-mindedness, self-sacrifice. Yet these same writers, through their works, had provoked popular discussion of the "new woman."[5]

One strategic problem facing the organized women's rights movements of every nation was, therefore, especially difficult: how to achieve their desired legal, educational, and economic reforms in the face of growing anxiety over the implications of female egotism among men who wielded political or intellectual power and were now concerned for their own comfort. This vision of egotism seemed only to confirm a more general and widespread sense of cultural despair.[6] To have any chance at all of succeeding, the women had to reassure would-be supporters at the political level that reforms in their status would not produce social chaos or guarantee the demise of Western civilization, but would instead bring a richer dimension to the lives of women and also of men. That their task was not easy is suggested by the hostility they faced from well-known, articulate men ranging from Nietzsche to Zola, Pope Leo XIII to Tolstoy (Docs. 6, 27, 16, 44, 10). These writers, and others like them, perceived any tampering with the male hierarchy, not to speak of female competition with men, as the blow that would shatter not only the social edifice but the male ego as well, the counterarguments of men like George Bernard Shaw (Doc. 5) notwithstanding.[7]

The impact of such concerns could be clearly observed in developments affecting the expansion of formal educational opportunities for women. Indeed, during this period discourse concerning girls' education is grounded in disputes over the sexual division of labor and in repeated restatements of the necessity for separate social functions for each sex. The issues range from the replacement of male teachers in German girls' secondary schools by women (Doc. 35) to problems of curriculum devel-

[5] The literature on the "new woman" during this period was abundant, widely read, and controversial. It clearly deserves a systematic cross-national analysis. Among recent partial assessments of the British "New Woman" novel are A. R. Cunningham 1973; Scanlon 1976; Fernando 1977; and G. Cunningham 1978. There is no comparable survey of this literature for other countries; however, see Kessner 1976 for the New Woman in the New York Yiddish novel. We know, however, from women's diaries and letters of the period that these works aroused great interest. As a girl, Ellen Key read the works of Camilla Collett and Ibsen, as well as those of English women novelists. Among less well known women readers a glimpse of enthusiasm is evident, for example, in a manuscript autobiography by a North Carolina woman who participated in a local woman's book club. "Ibsen," she wrote, "was the first of the newer prophets to fall into our hands. Imagine the intoxication of the thing! Thereafter we read Shaw and Ellen Key and made a headlong leap into the literature of feminism and suffrage agitation then beginning to stir . . ." (quoted in Anne Firor Scott, *The Southern Lady* [1970], p. 160). A British woman, Mrs. Huth Jackson, reported that some girls at Cheltenham Ladies' College "smuggled in *The Story of an African Farm*, then just out. The whole sky seemed aflame and many of us became violent feminists (I was one already)." (Quoted in Amy Cruse, *The Victorians and Their Books* [London, 1935], p. 363.)

[6] On the subject of late-nineteenth-century cultural despair, see Digeon 1959; Mosse 1961; F. Stern 1961; and Swart 1964. Although the woman question did not figure largely in these studies, it now seems conspicuous by its absence.

[7] Most of the writers who expounded their opposition to the organized women's movement and its goals were men. For England, see Harrison 1978. For France, see Offen 1973a, 1981.

opment, as articulated in the renewal of the controversy over sex-specific education between the American educators G. Stanley Hall and M. Carey Thomas (Docs. 37, 38). This era, which witnessed great educational advances for women at the university level, was also the heyday of the home economics movement, which affected educational institutions throughout the Western world. Women must learn to cook, sew, and care for babies, even as they studied philosophy.[8]

Despite the obstacles women's rights leaders faced during this period because of the issue of egotism and the sexual division of labor, a number of significant legal reforms affecting women's position in marriage and as mothers were achieved. In France, despite the vociferous opposition of the Catholic Church, a cautious form of civil divorce was enacted in 1884, and was to be followed by further refinements in the early twentieth century (Docs. 44-46). Women reformers such as the British physician Frances Hoggan and the Swedish writer-educator Ellen Key (Docs. 47, 48) argued for improving women's legal status as mothers. When it came to regulating women's employment in order to improve their lot as mothers, however, even women reformers disagreed, as the contrasting positions of Beatrice Webb, Maria Pognon, and Josephine Goldmark (Docs. 50-52) reveal. Most of them did agree, however, that in the face of mounting concern over the ravages of venereal disease some type of government regulation of personal health prior to marriage was justified in the interests of women and children alike. Not all reformers took as extreme a position on this matter as did Christabel Pankhurst (Doc. 54).

Controversy also emerged over the very matter of women's share in the sexual division of labor within the household. With the advent of a "machine age," as many writers were wont to characterize their times in the late 1880's, both housewifery and motherhood were subjected to analysis and criticism. Visionaries such as the anarchist Kropotkin thought that machines would liberate women from "domestic slavery," while others, such as the Belgian attorney Louis Frank, argued in favor of men's taking on their share of the housework in the conjugal household (Docs. 22, 24). The social organization of motherhood itself became the subject of intense scrutiny, as is suggested by the powerful and diametrically opposed arguments of the American women's rights activist Charlotte Perkins Gilman and the Swedish social radical Ellen Key over the relationship between mothers, their children, and the state (Docs. 25, 26).

Advocacy for sex education and birth control information, especially for young women, was emerging concurrently. This was a new development of extraordinary significance, one that deeply troubled those responsible for formulating national political goals in the face of threatening population declines. The contributions to this discussion of men like the Swiss-Austrian dramatist Frank Wedekind, the French literary critic and political leader Léon Blum (Docs. 41, 43), and the British sexologist

[8] For the new history of the home economics movement in the United States, see Wein 1974a, 1974b; Jenkins 1979; and papers by Berch 1981 and Stage 1981 at the Fifth Berkshire Conference on the History of Women, Vassar College. For England, see Dyhouse 1981.

Havelock Ellis, as well as of women orators like Nelly Roussel in France (Doc. 42) cannot be overestimated.[9]

Finally, we encounter the emotion-fraught debate over women's responsibility for national population problems that emerged, at the highest levels of government and intellectual life, especially in France and the United States. This is illuminated by the literary debate between Zola and Brieux (Docs. 27, 28), by Theodore Roosevelt's cries about "race suicide" (Doc. 30), and by the powerful arguments of activists Nelly Roussel and Anna Howard Shaw, proclaiming women's right to control their own bodies (Docs. 29, 31). The "strike of bellies," as it was then described, was without doubt the most powerful threat women could direct against the male-dominated nation-states of the Western world in the early twentieth century. But it is also apparent that women reformers used such arguments to invoke the aid of the state on behalf of motherhood, as we see in the speeches and articles of Ellen Key, Blanche Edwards-Pilliet, and in the proposals of the German Bund für Mutterschutz (League for the Protection of Mothers) (Docs. 48, 32-34), which were astutely designed to liberate mothers, married or unmarried, from economic dependency on individual, and presumably unreliable, men.[10]

All these issues came together in the critique and defense of maturing industrial capitalism. In the years after 1880 political agitation arose in all Western countries to improve the lot of members of the new urban, industrial working class. A major consideration was whether women workers should be treated as a distinctive group by virtue of their sex. Since the dawn of the modern socialist critique a half-century earlier, the emancipation of women had been linked—in theory at least—to that of the industrial proletariat. Despite this theoretical linkage, however, the notion of emancipating women economically through paid labor faced heavy opposition in the organized workers' movements, as the documents in Volume I have amply illustrated. With the founding of the Second International Workingmen's Association in 1889, Clara Zetkin (Doc. 15) once again found it necessary to chide her socialist colleagues on their failure to appreciate the necessity of paid labor as the touchstone of women's emancipation.[11]

[9] The work of sex education and birth control advocates before 1914 was often linked politically with movements for family limitation and eugenics (or race-improvement). For the U.S., see the differing interpretations of Gordon 1976 and Reed 1978. For England, see McLaren 1978b. For France, see Guerrand 1971 and Ronsin 1980.

[10] Susan B. Anthony's niece Katharine was greatly impressed by European initiatives of this sort. See Anthony 1915; see also Hackett 1975, 1981. French arguments for state support of motherhood are considered by Offen 1981. The less radical mother's pension movement in the U.S. is discussed by Leff 1973 and Weiner 1980.

[11] The discussions of the Second International concerning women have been explored at some length by Sowerwine 1978. On Zetkin's efforts, see Honeycutt 1975, 1976, 1979. See also Sowerwine 1977 for an extensive bibliography of the socialist congresses. The tensions between organized socialism and women's rights advocates during this period have received extensive study. For Germany, see Strain 1964; Thönnessen 1973; Hackett 1976; R. Evans 1976; Quataert 1979; and Niggemann 1981. For French socialist women and the politics of the French section of the International, see Sowerwine 1976 and Boxer 1978. For the Russian case, see Stites 1978. For Italy, see Lavigna 1978.

Socialist criticism of the human costs of laissez-faire capitalism nevertheless provided the impetus for European government efforts to regulate industrial work. Intergovernmental action was swiftly initiated by the governments of Switzerland and imperial Germany, urged on by social Catholics in those countries. The idea, of course, was to stimulate formulation of a unified international approach to worker protection that would diminish the appeal of revolutionary socialism. One of the first targets of such protective regulation was, significantly, the employment of women. Indeed, the thrust of the international effort was clearly to preserve the sexual division of labor in the family by designating women as a special class and "protecting" them from exploitative employment. The ultimate goal was to eliminate women from the labor force altogether.

The year 1890 marked the calling of an intergovernmental congress by the Swiss and German governments that drew up resolutions and stimulated a flurry of subsequent legislative attempts in other countries to restrict night and Sunday work for women aged sixteen or over, to limit their working hours, to restrict women's employment in dangerous and insalubrious industries, and to insist on (unpaid) maternity leave.[12] Not long thereafter, Pope Leo XIII issued his famous encyclical on the condition of the workers (Doc. 16), in which he argued that women's employment was regrettable and insisted on men's responsibility to provide for their families. Among the documents here reprinted are some responses by English, French, and American women to the pope's message and to the national initiatives that ensued (Docs. 17, 50-52). A second international meeting, attended by representatives of most political factions, was convened in Zurich in 1897. It focused attention on the plight of sweated workers, most of whom were women, and resulted in several thorough studies of their situation. In 1905 an intergovernmental congress on workers' protection convened in Berne, and by 1912 an agreement placing formal restrictions on women's work in industry had been ratified by most of the participating nations.[13]

In the shadow of this effort at differential regulation of women's work, and in view of the lack of enthusiasm of either bourgeois or working-class men to endorse agitation for the economic emancipation of women, the issue of political rights for women began to loom increasingly large for its advocates. By 1900 the International Council of Women (ICW, founded in 1889 by the Americans) had declared woman suffrage a worldwide priority. Meeting every five years, in 1899, 1904, 1909,

[12] Historians of women's work have not reexamined the work of these conferences. The minutes of the commission on women's work, as well as of the general discussions, are available, published by the various participating governments. See, for example, France, Ministère des Affaires Etrangères, *Conférence internationale de Berlin, 15-29 Mars 1890: Procès verbaux*, etc. (Paris, 1890), esp. pp. 60-65, 85-86. Prior to 1889 imperial Russia, like imperial Germany, arbitrarily regulated women's industrial work without consulting women workers; see Giffen 1968.

[13] On the Berne Conference and the ensuing conventions, see Marcel Cate, *La Convention de Berne de 1906 sur l'interdiction du travail de nuit des femmes employées dans l'industrie* (Paris, 1911). See also France, Ministère des Affaires Etrangères, *Conférence internationale de Berne 1906: Actes de la conférence diplomatique pour la protection ouvrière réunie à Berne du 17 au 26 septembre 1906* (Berne, 1906). See also Lehmann 1924.

women delegates from every Western nation considered a unified international agenda for political action. In the subsequent campaigns a significant and revealing conflict emerged between leaders of the bourgeois women's movement and the socialist women of the Second International over the issue of political rights. The bourgeois movements, affiliated with the ICW, had gained extraordinary momentum and support. Meanwhile, revisionist thinking on the subject of social reform had made headway among the formerly revolutionary European socialist parties as their members likewise acquired political strength in their respective countries. To the revisionists, universal suffrage appeared increasingly vital. Revisionist socialist women pondered the possibility that, as Herbert Marcuse suggested over a half-century later, "there are no economic reasons why [social, economic, and cultural] equality should not be attainable within the capitalist framework, although a largely modified capitalism." [14]

In 1906, after the first European victory for woman suffrage in the new national state of Finland, socialist women reoriented their tactical position. At the first International Socialist Women's Conference in 1907, the previously exclusive focus on economic emancipation for women gave way to a reconsideration of the question of women's rights. The outcome was an endorsement by the Women's Section of the Second International (Doc. 59) of the pursuit of unrestricted suffrage for women. This purposeful endorsement by Socialist women of the most extreme woman's suffrage position was designed to counter the growing support for gradual advances in woman suffrage advocated by bourgeois women's rights organizations (i.e., beginning with single adult women or widows, unaffected by the complexities of marital property law, or with the pursuit of the municipal rather than the national vote).[15] Meanwhile, world opinion was transfixed by the extraordinary campaign for parliamentary woman suffrage organized in Great Britain by the Women's Social and Political Union (WSPU) (Docs. 60-63). Inspired by Emmeline Pankhurst and her daughters, this campaign set a standard for militant, non-violent action and media attention that has warped public judgment on the entire subject of women's rights activity ever since.[16] By 1913, the American president of the International Woman Suffrage Alliance, Carrie Chapman Catt (Doc. 64), could sense success in the offing. Even though the outbreak of war in 1914 broke the momentum of the suffrage campaigns, women received the vote in many Western countries in the years immediately following the war.

[14] Herbert Marcuse, "Marxism and Feminism," in *City Lights Anthology*, ed. Lawrence Ferlinghetti (San Francisco, 1974), p. 35. See also Eisenstein 1980.

[15] The defensive character of this "offensive" position on the part of the women of the Second International in 1908 has rarely been underscored by scholars, though it is apparent from the texts.

[16] The most comprehensive works on the British suffragettes are D. Mitchell 1967 and Rosen 1974. For the less spectacular, yet highly effective activities of the National Union of Woman Suffrage Societies (NUWSS) headed by Millicent Garrett Fawcett, see Swanwick 1935; Fulford 1956; Rover 1967; and Hume 1979. On the suffrage campaign of Lancashire working women, see also Liddington & Norris 1978 and Chew 1982.

CHAPTER I

The New Woman and the Problem of Egotism

The New Woman of the North

SOURCES
1. Henrik Ibsen, *A Doll's House*. Tr. Henrietta Frances Lord (New York, 1889), pp. 136-48. Originally published as *Et Dukkehjem*, in Copenhagen, 1879.
2. August Strindberg, "A Doll's House," in *Married*, tr. unknown (New York, 1917), pp. 119, 122, 123-33, 135-37. Book originally published as *Giftas*, in Stockholm, 1884.

When Ibsen's Nora first slammed the door on domesticity in 1880, the specter of women's individualism as the arch-enemy of marriage and of the patriarchal concept of womanhood announced itself as a major theme in the debate on women. Pursued obsessively in literature and life from that date until the First World War, this theme threatened to pose a major obstacle to achieving fundamental reforms in the position of women, as the following selections show.

The Norwegian playwright Henrik Johan Ibsen (1828-1906) is considered one of the greatest dramatists of all time, both for his technical mastery of the drama and for his social realism. The second of six children of an unsuccessful businessman on the southeastern coast of Norway, Ibsen left home at fifteen to seek a livelihood. Soon he found a congenial niche in the theatrical world of Christiania (Oslo). In 1864, married and a father, but not successful in any measurable way, Ibsen and his family left Norway. They resided mainly in Rome and Munich during the next twenty-seven years. During this time Ibsen wrote his greatest plays, most of which were fired by his discontent with the narrowness and provincialism of his native country.

During the 1870's Ibsen met and was deeply influenced by the novelist Camilla Collett (Vol. I, Doc. 93) who introduced him to the woman question. Then in early 1880, when Ibsen was in his early fifties, his play *A Doll's House* was produced, first in Copenhagen and then throughout Scandinavia and Germany; wherever it was performed the actions of his heroine Nora provoked scandal. Within the next decade *A Doll's House* was translated into virtually every European language; major productions were mounted in London (1889) and in Paris (1894), with Europe's leading actresses portraying Nora. Here we excerpt the last scene of Act III—controversial because of its shocking attitudes—in which Nora takes charge of her own life, asserting her right to live and think as an independent individual rather than as a reflection of the wishes of men.

Ibsen's Nora soon found her detractors. Among these none was more cunning in his criticism than the Swedish novelist and dramatist August Strindberg

(1849-1912). Some twenty years younger than Ibsen, Strindberg, his actress-wife, and their child likewise left Scandinavia, and his works exuded bitter criticism of the society in which he had grown up. The short story reproduced here, also titled "A Doll's House," was Strindberg's reply to Ibsen. It was first published in an 1884 collection. Another story in the same collection provoked government censors to prosecute Strindberg for blasphemy, thereby reinforcing his growing delusions of persecution and precipitating the rupture of his marriage. An unrepentant patriarch, unable to live apart from women, yet at once fascinated and exasperated by their complexity, Strindberg obsessively explored the social relations of the sexes throughout his career as a dramatist and in his own life.

---

1. Henrik Ibsen (1879)

. . . I have forgiven you, Nora; I swear to you I have forgiven you.

NORA. I thank you for your forgiveness (*goes through the left door*).

HELMER. No, stay (*looks in*). What are you doing in the alcove?

NORA. (*inside*). Taking off my masquerade dress.

HELMER (*in the open door*). Yes, do, dear; try to rest and restore your mind to its balance, my scared little song-bird. You may go to rest in comfort; I have broad wings to protect you (*walks round by the door*). Oh, how beautiful and cozy our home is, Nora! Here you are safe; here I can shelter you like a hunted dove, whom I have saved from the claws of the hawk. I shall soon quiet your poor beating heart. Believe me, Nora, gradually peace will return. To-morrow all this will look quite different to you; I shall not need to repeat over and over again that I forgive you: you will feel for yourself that it is true. How can you think I could ever bring my heart to drive you away, or even so much as reproach you? Oh, you don't know what a true man's heart is made of, Nora! A man feels there is something indescribably sweet and soothing in his having forgiven his wife, that he has honestly forgiven her from the bottom of his heart. She becomes his property in a double sense, as it were. She is as though born again; she has become to a certain extent at once his wife and his child. And that is what you shall really be to me henceforth, you ill-advised and helpless darling. Don't be anxious about anything, Nora: only open your heart to me, and I will be both will and conscience to you. Why, what's this? Not gone to bed? You have changed your dress.

NORA (*entering in her every-day dress*). Yes, Torvald; now I have changed my dress.

HELMER. But why, now it is so late?

NORA. I shall not sleep to-night.

HELMER. But, Nora dear . . .

NORA (*looking at her watch*). It is not so very late. Sit down here, Torvald. We two have much to say to each other (*she sits on one side of the table*).

HELMER. Nora, what does that mean? Your cold, set face!

NORA. Sit down; it will take some time. I have to talk over many things with you.

HELMER (*sitting opposite to her at the table*). Nora, you make me anxious . . . I don't in the least understand you.

NORA. Just so. You don't understand me. And in the same way I have never understood you, till to-night. No, don't interrupt me. Only listen to what I say. . . . This is a breaking off, Torvald.

HELMER. How do you mean?

NORA (*after a short silence*). Does not one thing strike you as we sit here?

HELMER. What should strike me?

NORA. We have now been married eight years. Does it not strike you that to-night for the first time we two, you and I, husband and wife, are speaking together seriously?

HELMER. Well; "seriously," what does that mean?

NORA. During eight whole years and more, since the day we first made each other's acquaintance, we have never exchanged one serious word about serious things.

HELMER. Ought I, then, to have persistently initiated you into difficulties you could not help me by sharing?

NORA. I am not talking of difficulties. All I am saying is, that we have never yet seriously talked any one thing over together.

HELMER. But, dearest Nora, would it have been any good to you if we had?

NORA. That is the very point. You have never understood me. . . . I have been greatly wronged, Torvald. First by father and then by you.

HELMER. What! by us two, by us two—who have loved you more deeply than all others have?

NORA (*shakes her head*). You two have never loved me. You only thought it was pleasant to be in love with me.

HELMER. But, Nora, these are strange words.

NORA. Yes; it is just so, Torvald. While I was still at home with father, he used to tell me all his views, and so of course, I held the same views; if at any time I had a different view I concealed it, because he would not have liked people with opinions of their own. He used to call me his little doll, and play with me, as I in my turn used to play with my dolls. Then I came to live in your house.

HELMER. What expressions you do use to describe our marriage!

NORA (*undisturbed*). I mean—then I passed over from father's hands into yours. You settled everything according to your taste; or I did only what you liked; I don't exactly know. I think it was both ways, first one and then the other. When I look back on it now it seems to me as if I had been living here like a poor man, only from hand to mouth. I lived by performing tricks for you, Torvald. But you would have it so. You and father have sinned greatly against me. It is the fault of you two that nothing has been made of me.

HELMER. How senseless and ungrateful you are. . . . Haven't you been happy here?

NORA. No, never; I thought I was, but I never was.

HELMER. Not . . . not happy?

NORA. No; only merry. And you were always so friendly and kind to me. But our house has been nothing but a nursery. Here I have been your doll-wife, just as at home I used to be papa's doll-child. And my children were, in their turn, my dolls. I was exceedingly delighted when you played with me, just as the children were whenever I played with them. That has been our marriage, Torvald.

HELMER. There is some truth in what you say, exaggerated and over-drawn though it may be. But henceforth it shall be different. The time for play is gone by; now comes the time for education.

NORA. Whose education—mine or the children's?

HELMER. Yours, as well as the children's, dear Nora.

NORA. Oh, Torvald, you are not the man to educate me into being the right wife for you.

HELMER. And *you* say that?

NORA. And I—how have I been prepared to educate the children?

HELMER. Nora!

NORA. Did you not say just now yourself that *that* was a task you dared not intrust to me?

HELMER. In a moment of excitement. How can you lay any stress upon that?

NORA. No; you were perfectly right. For that task I am not ready. There is another which must be performed first. I must first try to educate my-self. In that you are not the man to help me. I must set to work alone: you are not the man to help me with it. I must do it alone. And that is why I am going away from you now.

HELMER (*jumping up*). What—what are you saying?

NORA. I must be thrown entirely upon myself if I am to come to any understanding as to what I am and what the things around me are: so I can not stay with you any longer.

HELMER. Nora, Nora!

NORA. I shall now leave your house at once. Christina will, I am sure, take me in for to-night. . . .

HELMER. You are insane. I shall not allow that; I forbid it.

NORA. From this time it is useless for you to forbid me things. What-ever belongs to me I shall take with me. I will have nothing from you either now or later on.

HELMER. What utter madness this is!

NORA. To-morrow I shall go home—I mean to my birthplace. There it will be easier for me to get something to do of one sort or another.

HELMER. Oh, you blind, inexperienced creature!

NORA. I must try to gain experience, Torvald.

HELMER. To forsake your home, your husband, and your children! And only think what people will say about it.

NORA. I can not take that into consideration. I only know that to go is necessary for me.

HELMER. Oh, it drives one wild! Is this the way you can evade your holiest duties?

NORA. What do you consider my holiest duties?

HELMER. Do I need to tell you that? Are they not your duties to your husband and your children?

NORA. I have other duties equally sacred.

HELMER. No, you have not. What duties do you mean?

NORA. Duties toward myself.

HELMER. Before all else you are a wife and mother.

NORA. I no longer think so. I think that before all else I am a human being just as you are, or at least I will try to become one. I know very well that most people agree with you, Torvald, and what is to be found in books. But I can not be satisfied any longer with what most people say, and with what is in books. I must think over things for myself, and try to get clear about them.

HELMER. Is it possible you are not clear about your position in your own family? Have you not in questions like these a guide who can not err? Have you not religion?

NORA. Oh, Torvald, I don't know what religion is.

HELMER. What are you saying?

NORA. I know nothing but what our clergyman told me when I was confirmed. He explained that religion was this and that. When I have got quite away from here, and am all by myself, then I will examine that matter too. I will see whether what our clergyman taught is true; or, at any rate, whether it is true for me.

HELMER. Who ever heard such things from a young wife's lips? But if religion can not lead you to the right, let me appeal to your conscience; for I suppose you have some moral feeling? Or, answer me, perhaps you have none?

NORA. Well, Torvald, I think I had better not answer you. I really don't know. About those things I am not at all clear. I only know that I have quite a different opinion about them from yours. I have now learnt too that the laws are different from what I thought they were; but I can't convince myself that they are right. It appears that a woman has no right to spare her father trouble when he is old and dying, or to save her husband's life. I don't believe that.

HELMER. You talk like a child. You don't understand the society in which you live.

NORA. No, no more I do. But now I will set to work and learn it. I must make up my mind whether society is right or whether I am.

HELMER. Nora, you are ill, you are feverish; I almost think you are out of your senses.

NORA. I never felt so clear and certain about things as I feel to-night.

HELMER. And feeling clear and certain, you forsake husband and children?

HELMER. Yes; I do.

HELMER. Then there is only one possible explanation of it.

NORA. What is that?

HELMER. You no longer love me.

NORA. No; that is just the thing.

HELMER. Nora . . . Can you bring yourself to say so?

NORA. Oh, I'm so sorry, Torvald; for you have always been so kind to me. But I can't help it. I do not love you any longer.

HELMER (*keeping his composure with difficulty*). Is this another of the things you are clear and certain about?

NORA. Yes, quite. That is why I will not stay here any longer.

HELMER. And can you also explain to me how I have lost your love?

NORA. Yes; I can. It was this evening when the miracle did not happen; for it was then I saw you were not the man I had taken you for.

HELMER. Explain yourself more; I don't understand.

NORA. I have waited so patiently all these eight years; for, indeed, I saw well enough that miracles do not happen every day. Then this trouble broke over my head, and then I was so firmly convinced that now the miracle must be at hand. When Krogstad's letter * lay in the box outside, the thought never once occurred to me that you could allow yourself to submit to the conditions of such a man. I was so firmly convinced that you would say to him, "Pray make the affair known to all the world"; and when that had been done. . . .

HELMER. Well? And when I had given my own wife's name up to disgrace and shame!

NORA. When that had been done, then you would, as I firmly believed, stand before the world, take everything upon yourself, and say, "I am the guilty person."

HELMER. Nora!

NORA. You mean I should never have accepted such a sacrifice from you? No; certainly not. But what would my assertions have been worth compared with yours? That was the miracle that I hoped and feared. And it was to hinder that that I wanted to put an end to my life.

HELMER. I would gladly work for you, day and night, Nora, bear sorrow and trouble for your sake; but no man sacrifices his honor to a person he loves.

NORA. That is what millions of women have done.

HELMER. Oh, you think and talk like a silly child.

NORA. Very likely. But you neither think nor speak like the man I could be one with. When your terror was over—not for what threatened *me*, but for what involved *you*—and when there was nothing more to fear, then it was in your eyes as though nothing whatever had happened. I was just as much as ever your lark, your doll, whom you would take twice as much care of in future because she was so weak and frail (*stands up*). Torvald, in that moment it became clear to me that I had been living here all these years with a strange man and had borne him three children. Oh, I can not bear to think of it. I could tear myself to pieces!

HELMER (*sadly*). I see it, I see it: a chasm has opened between us. . . . But, Nora, can it never be filled up?

---

* Krogstadt had attempted to blackmail Nora for forging her father's signature in order to protect Helmer.—EDS.

NORA. As I now am I am no wife for you.

HELMER. I am strong enough to become another man.

NORA. Perhaps, when your doll is taken away from you.

HELMER. Part—part from you! No, Nora, no; I can not grasp it.

NORA (*going into the right room*). The more reason for it to happen. (*She comes in with her walking things, and a small traveling bag, which she puts on the chair by the table.*)

HELMER. Nora, Nora, not now. Wait till to-morrow.

NORA (*putting on her cloak*). I can not spend the night in the house of a man who is a stranger to me.

HELMER. But can't we live here as brother and sister?

NORA (*tying her bonnet tightly*). You know quite well that would not last long (*puts her shawl on*). Good-by, Torvald. I will not see the children before I go. I know they are in better hands than mine. As I now am I can be nothing to them.

HELMER. But later, Nora—later on?

NORA. How can I tell? I have no idea what will become of me.

HELMER. But you are my wife—both as you are now and as you will become.

NORA. Listen, Torvald. When a wife leaves her husband's house, as I am doing, then I have heard he is free from all duties toward her in the eyes of the law. At any rate, I release you from all duties. You must feel yourself no more bound by anything than I feel. There must be perfect freedom on both sides. There, there is your ring back. Give me mine.

HELMER. That too?

NORA. That too.

HELMER. Here it is.

NORA. Very well. Yes; now it is all past and gone. Here, I lay the keys down. The maids know how to manage everything in the house far better than I do. To-morrow, when I have started on my journey, Christina will come, in order to pack up the few things that are my own. They will be sent after me.

HELMER. Past and gone! Nora, will you never think of me again?

NORA. Certainly. I shall think very often of you and the children and this house.

HELMER. May I write to you, Nora?

NORA. No, never. You must not.

HELMER. But I may send you what . . .

NORA. Nothing, nothing.

HELMER. Help you when you are in need?

NORA. No, I say. I take nothing from strangers.

HELMER. Nora, can I never become to you anything but a stranger?

NORA (*taking her traveling bag sadly*). The greatest miracle of all would have to happen then, Torvald.

HELMER. Tell me what the greatest miracle is.

NORA. We both should need to change so, you as well as I, that—Oh, Torvald, I no longer believe in anything miraculous.

HELMER. But I believe in it. Tell me. We must so change that . . .

NORA. That our living together could be a marriage. Good-by. (*She goes out through the hall.*)

HELMER (*sinks in a chair by the door with his hands before his face*). Nora, Nora! (*He looks round and stands up.*) Empty. She isn't here now. (*A hope inspires him.*) The greatest miracle! (*Below-stairs a door is heard shutting ominously in the lock.*)

2. August Strindberg (1884)

They had been married for six years, but they were still more like lovers than husband and wife. He was a captain in the navy, and every summer he was obliged to leave her for a few months; twice he had been away on a long voyage. But his short absences were a blessing in disguise, for if their relations had grown a little stale during the winter, the summer trip invariably restored them to their former freshness and delightfulness. . . .

In this manner they met for six summers, and always they were just as young, just as mad and just as happy as before. They spent the winter in Stockholm in their little cabins. He amused himself by rigging boats for his little boys or telling them stories of his adventures in China and the South Sea Islands, while his wife sat by him, listening and laughing at his funny tales. It was a charming room, that could not be equalled in the whole world. . . .

This time the corvette was to be away for six months. The captain did not feel easy about it, for the children were growing up and the responsibility of the big establishment was too much for Mama. The captain himself was not quite so young and vigorous as he had been, but—it could not be helped and so he left. . . .

Off Portsmouth the captain received the following letter from his wife:

"Dear old Pal,

"It's horrible here without you, believe me. I have had a lot of worry, too, for little Alice has got a new tooth. The doctor said it was unusually early, which was a sign of (but I'm not going to tell you that). Bob's boots fit him very well and he is very proud of them.

"You say in your letter that I ought to find a friend of my own sex. Well, I have found one, or, rather, she has found me. Her name is Ottilia Sandegren, and she was educated at the seminary. She is rather grave and takes life very seriously, therefore you need not be afraid, Pal, that your Topmast will be led astray. Moreover, she is religious. We really ought to take religion a little more seriously, both of us. She is a splendid woman. She has just arrived and sends you her kind regards.

"Your Gurli."

The captain was not overpleased with this letter. It was too short and not half as bright as her letters generally were. Seminary, religion, grave, Ottilia: Ottilia twice! And then Gurli! Why not Gulla as before? H'm!

A week later he received a second letter from Bordeaux, a letter which was accompanied by a book, sent under separate cover.

"Dear William!"—"H'm! William! No longer Pal!"—"Life is a struggle"—"What the deuce does she mean? What has that to do with us?"—
"from beginning to end. Gently as a river in Kedron."—"Kedron! she's
quoting the Bible!"—"our life has glided along. Like sleepwalkers we
have been walking on the edge of precipices without being aware of
them"—"The seminary, oh! the seminary!"—"Suddenly we find ourselves face to face with the ethical"—"The ethical? Ablative!"—"asserting itself in its higher potencies!"—"Potencies?"—"Now that I am
awake from my long sleep and ask myself: has our marriage been a marriage in the true sense of the word? I must admit with shame and remorse
that this has not been the case. For love is of divine origin. (St. Matthew
xi. 22, 24.)"

The captain had to mix himself a glass of rum and water before he felt
able to continue his reading.—"How earthy, how material our love has
been! Have our souls lived in that harmony of which Plato speaks? (Phai-
don, book vi. Chap. ii. Par. 9). Our answer is bound to be in the negative. What have I been to you? A housekeeper and, oh! the disgrace! your
mistress! Have our souls understood one another? Again we are bound to
answer 'No.'"—"To Hell with all Ottilias and seminaries! Has she been
my housekeeper? She has been my wife and the mother of my children!"—"Read the book I have sent you! It will answer all your questions. It voices that which for centuries has lain hidden in the hearts of all
women! Read it, and then tell me if you think that our union has been a
true marriage. Your Gurli."

His presentiment of evil had not deceived him. The captain was beside
himself; he could not understand what had happened to his wife. It was
worse than religious hypocrisy.

He tore off the wrapper and read on the title page of a book in a paper
cover: *Et Dukkehjem af Henrik Ibsen.* A Doll's House? Well, and—? His
home had been a charming dolls' house; his wife had been his little doll
and he had been her big doll. They had danced along the stony path of
life and had been happy. What more did they want? What was wrong?
He must read the book at once and find out.

He finished it in three hours. His brain reeled. How did it concern him
and his wife? Had they forged bills? No! Hadn't they loved one another?
Of course they had!

He locked himself into his cabin and read the book a second time; he
underlined passages in red and blue, and when the dawn broke, he took
pen and paper and wrote to his wife:

"A well-meant little ablative on the play *A Doll's House*, written by the
old Pal on board the Vanadis in the Atlantic off Bordeaux. (Lat. 45°
Long. 16°.)

"1. She married him because he was in love with her, and that was a
deuced clever thing to do. For if she had waited until she had fallen in
love with someone, it might have happened that *he* would not have fallen
in love with her, and then there would have been the devil to pay. For it
happens very rarely that both parties are equally in love.

"2. She forges a bill. That was foolish, but it is not true that it was done for the husband's sake only, for she has never loved him; it would have been the truth if she had said that she had done it for him, herself and the children. Is that clear?

"3. That he wants to embrace her after the ball is only a proof of his love for her, and there is no wrong in that; but it should not be done on the stage. 'Il y a des choses qui se font mais qui ne se disent point,' as the French say. Moreover, if the poet had been fair, he would also have shown an opposite case. 'La petite chienne veut, mais le grand chien ne veut pas,' says Ollendorf. (Vide the long boat at Dalarö.)

"4. That she, when she discovers that her husband is a fool (and that he is when he offers to condone her offence because it has not leaked out) decides to leave her children 'not considering herself worthy of bringing them up,' is a not very clever trick of coquetry. If they have both been fools (and surely they don't teach at the seminary that it is right to forge bills) they should pull well together in future in double harness.

"Least of all is she justified in leaving her children's education in the hands of the father whom she despises.

"5. Norah has consequently every reason for staying with her children when she discovers what an imbecile her husband is.

"6. The husband cannot be blamed for not sufficiently appreciating her, for she doesn't reveal her true character until after the row.

"7. Norah has undoubtedly been a fool; she herself does not deny it.

"8. There is every guarantee of their pulling together more happily in future; he has repented and promised to turn over a new leaf. So has she. Very well! Here's my hand, let's begin again at the beginning. Birds of a feather flock together. There's nothing lost, we've both been fools! You, little Norah, were badly brought up. I, old rascal, didn't know any better. We are both to be pitied. Pelt our teachers with rotten eggs, but don't hit me alone on the head. I, though a man, am every bit as innocent as you are! Perhaps even a little more so, for I married for love, you for a home. Let us be friends, therefore, and together teach our children the valuable lesson we have learnt in the school of life.

"Is that clear? All right then!

"This was written by Captain Pal with his stiff fingers and slow brain!

"And now, my darling dolly, I have read your book and given you my opinion. But what have we to do with it? Didn't we love one another? Haven't we educated one another and helped one another to rub off our sharp corners? Surely you'll remember that we had many a little encounter in the beginning! What fads of yours are those? To hell with all Ottilias and seminaries!

"The book you sent me is a queer book. It is like a watercourse with an insufficient number of buoys, so that one might run aground at any moment. But I pricked the chart and found calm waters. Only, I couldn't do it again. The devil may crack these nuts which are rotten inside when one has managed to break the shell. I wish you peace and happiness and the recovery of your sound common sense.

"How are the little ones? You forgot to mention them. Probably you were thinking too much of Norah's unfortunate kiddies (which only exist in a play of that sort). Is my little boy crying? My nightingale singing, my dolly dancing? She must always do that if she wants to make her old Pal happy. And now may God bless you and prevent evil thoughts from rising between us. My heart is sadder than I can tell. And I am expected to sit down and write a critique on a play. God bless you and the babies; kiss their rosy cheeks for your faithful old Pal."

When the captain had sent off his letter, he went into the officers' mess and drank a glass of punch. The doctor was there, too.

"Have you noticed a smell of old black breeches?" he asked. "I should like to hoist myself up to the catblock and let a good old N.W. by N. blow right through me."

But the doctor did not understand what he was driving at.

"Ottilia, Ottilia! . . . What she wants is a taste of the handspike. Send the witch to the quarterdeck and let the second mess loose on her behind closed hatches. One knows what is good for an old maid."

"What's the matter with you, old chap?" asked the doctor.

"Plato! Plato! To the devil with Plato! To be six months at sea makes one sick of Plato. That teaches one ethics! Ethics? I bet a marlinspike to a large rifle: if Ottilia were married she would cease talking of Plato."

"What on earth *is* the matter?"

"Nothing. Do you hear? You're a doctor. What's the matter with those women? Isn't it bad for them to remain unmarried? Doesn't it make them . . . ? What?"

The doctor gave him his candid opinion and added that he was sorry that there were not enough men to go round.

"In a state of nature the male is mostly polygamous; in most cases there is no obstacle to this, as there is plenty of food for the young ones (beasts of prey excepted): abnormalities like unmated females do not exist in nature. But in civilised countries, where a man is lucky if he earns enough bread, it is a common occurrence, especially as the females are in preponderance. One ought to treat unmarried women with kindness, for their lot is a melancholy one."

"With kindness! That's all very well; but supposing they are anything but kind themselves!"

And he told the doctor the whole story, even confessing that he had written a critique on a play.

"Oh! well, no end of nonsense is written," said the doctor, putting his hand on the lid of the jug which contained the punch. "In the end science decides all great questions! Science, and nothing else."

When the six months were over and the captain, who had been in constant, but not very pleasant, correspondence with his wife, (she had sharply criticised his critique), at last landed at Dalarö, he was received by his wife, all the children, two servants and Ottilia. His wife was affectionate, but not cordial. She held up her brow to be kissed. Ottilia was as tall as a stay, and wore her hair short; seen from the back she looked like a swab. The supper was dull and they only drank tea. The long boat took in a cargo of children and the captain was lodged in one of the attics. What a change! Poor old Pal looked old and felt puzzled.

"To be married and yet not have a wife," he thought, "it's intolerable!"

On the following morning he wanted to take his wife for a sail. But the sea did not agree with Ottilia. She had been ill on the steamer. And, moreover, it was Sunday. Sunday? That was it! Well, they would go for a walk. They had a lot to talk about. Of course, they had a lot to say to each other. But Ottilia was not to come with them!

They went out together, arm in arm. But they did not talk much; and what they said were words uttered for the sake of concealing their thoughts more than for the sake of exchanging ideas.

They passed the little cholera cemetery and took the road leading to the Swiss Valley. A faint breeze rustled through the pine trees and glimpses of the blue sea flashed through the dark branches.

They sat down on a stone. He threw himself on the turf at her feet. Now the storm is going to burst, he thought, and it did.

"Have you thought at all about our marriage?" she began.

"No," he replied, with every appearance of having fully considered the matter, "I have merely felt about it. In my opinion love is a matter of sentiment; one steers by landmarks and makes port; take compass and chart and you are sure to founder."

"Yes, but our home has been nothing but a doll's house."

"Excuse me, but this is not quite true. You have never forged a bill; you have never shown your ankles to a syphilitic doctor of whom you wanted to borrow money against security *in natura*; you have never been so romantically silly as to expect your husband to give himself up for a crime which his wife had committed from ignorance, and which was not a crime because there was no plaintiff; and you have never lied to me. I have treated you every bit as honestly as Helmer treated his wife when he took her into his full confidence and allowed her to have a voice in the banking business; tolerated her interference with the appointment of an employee. We have therefore been husband and wife according to all conceptions, old and new fashioned."

"Yes, but I have been your housekeeper!"

"Pardon me, you are wrong. You have never had a meal in the kitchen, you have never received wages, you have never had to account for money spent. I have never scolded you because one thing or the other was not to my liking. And do you consider my work: to reckon and to brace, to ease off and call out 'Present arms,' count herrings and measure rum, weigh peas and examine flour, more honourable than yours: to look after the servants, cater for the house and bring up the children?"

"No, but you are paid for your work! You are your own master! You are a man!"

"My dear child, do you want me to give you wages? Do you want to be my housekeeper in real earnest? That I was born a man is an accident. I might almost say a pity, for it's very nearly a crime to be a man now-a-days, but it isn't my fault. The devil take him who has stirred up the two halves of humanity, one against the other! He has much to answer for. Am I the matter? Don't we both rule? Have I ever decided any important matter without asking for your advice? What? But you—you bring up the children exactly as you like! Don't you remember that I wanted you to stop rocking them to sleep because I said it produced a sort of intoxication? But you had your own way! Another time I had mine, and then it was your turn again. There was no compromise possible, because there was no middle course to steer between rocking and not rocking. We got on very well until now. But you have thrown me over for Ottilia's sake!"

"Ottilia! always Ottilia! Didn't you yourself send her to me?"

"No, not her personally! But there can be no doubt that it is she who rules now."

"You want to separate me from all I care for!"

"Is Ottilia all you care for? It almost looks like it!"

"But I can't send her away now that I have engaged her to teach the girls pedagogics and Latin."

"Latin! Great Scott! Are the girls to be ruined?"

"They are to know everything a man knows, so that when the time comes, their marriage will be a true marriage."

"But, my love, all husbands don't know Latin! I don't know more than one single word, and that is 'ablative.' And we have been happy in spite of it. Moreover, there is a movement to strike off Latin from the plan of instruction for boys, as a superfluous accomplishment. Doesn't this teach you a lot? Isn't it enough that the men are ruined, are the women to be ruined, too? Ottilia, Ottilia, what have I done to you, that you should treat me like this!"

"Supposing we dropped that matter.— Our love, William, has not been what it should be. It has been sensual!"

"But, my darling, how could we have had children, if it hadn't? And it has not been sensual only."

"Can a thing be both black and white? Tell me that!"

"Of course, it can. There's your sunshade for instance, it is black outside and white inside."

"Sophist!"

"Listen to me, sweetheart, tell me in your own way the thoughts which are in your heart; don't talk like Ottilia's books. Don't let your head run away with you; be yourself again, my sweet, darling little wife."

"Yours, your property, bought with your labour."

"Just as I am your property, your husband, at whom no other woman is allowed to look if she wants to keep her eyes in her head; your husband, who made a present of himself to you, or rather, gave himself to you in exchange. Are we not quits?"

"But we have trifled away our lives! Have we ever had any higher interests, William?"

"Yes, the very highest, Gurli; we have not always been playing, we have had grave hours, too. Have we not called into being generations to come? Have we not both bravely worked and striven for the little ones, who are to grow up into men and women? Have you not faced death four times for their sakes? Have you not robbed yourself of your nights' rest in order to rock their cradle, and of your days' pleasures, in order to attend to them? Couldn't we now have a large six-roomed flat in the main street, and a footman to open the door, if it were not for the children? Wouldn't you be able to wear silk dresses and pearls? And I, your old Pal, wouldn't have *crows' nests* in my knees, if it hadn't been for the kiddies. Are we really no better than dolls? Are we as selfish as old maids say? Old maids, rejected by men as no good. Why are so many girls unmarried? They all boast of proposals and yet they pose as martyrs! Higher interests! Latin! To dress in low neck dresses for charitable purposes and leave the children at home, neglected! I believe that my interests are higher than Ottilia's, when I want strong and healthy children, who will succeed where we have failed. But Latin won't help them! Goodbye, Gurli! I have to go back on board. Are you coming?"

But she remained sitting on the stone and made no answer. He went with heavy footsteps, very heavy footsteps. And the blue sea grew dark and the sun ceased shining.

"Pal, Pal, where is this to lead to?" he sighed, as he stepped over the fence of the cemetery. "I wish I lay there, with a wooden cross to mark my place, among the roots of the trees. But I am sure I couldn't rest, if I were there without her! Oh! Gurli! Gurli!

"Everything has gone wrong, now, mother," said the captain on a chilly autumn day to his mother-in-law, to whom he was paying a visit.

"What's the matter, Willy, dear?"

"Yesterday they met at our house. On the day before yesterday at the Princess's. Little Alice was suddenly taken ill. It was unfortunate, of course, but I didn't dare to send for Gurli, for fear she might think that it was done on purpose to annoy her! Oh! when once one has lost faith. . . . I asked a friend at the Admiralty yesterday whether it was legal in Sweden to kill one's wife's friends with tobacco smoke. I was told it wasn't, and that even if it were it was better not to do it, for fear of doing more harm than good. If only it happened to be an admirer! I should take him by the neck and throw him out of the window. What am I to do?"

"It's a difficult matter, Willy, dear, but we shall be able to think of a way out of it. You can't go on living like a bachelor."

"No, of course, I can't."

"I spoke very plainly to her, a day or two ago. I told her that she would lose you if she didn't mend her ways."

"And what did she say?"

"She said you had a right to do as you liked with your body."

"Indeed! And she, too? A fine theory! My hair is fast turning grey, mother!"

"It's a good old scheme to make a wife jealous. It's generally kill or cure, for if there is any love left, it brings it out."

"There is, I know, there is!"

"Of course, there is. Love doesn't die suddenly; it gets used up in the course of the years, perhaps. Have a flirtation with Ottilia, and we shall see!" . . .

"On the following day I gave Ottilia a lesson in astronomy. Gurli declared that she was much interested and would like to be present; but Ottilia said we were already too far advanced and she would instruct her in the rudiments later on. This annoyed Gurli and she went away. We had a great deal of sherry for supper. When Ottilia thanked me for a jolly evening, I put my arm round her waist and kissed her. Gurli grew pale. When I buttoned her overshoes, I . . . I . . .'"

"Never mind me," said the old lady, "I am an old woman."

He laughed. "All the same, mother, she's not so bad, really she isn't. But when I was going to put on my overcoat, I found to my astonishment the maid waiting in the hall, ready to accompany Ottilia home. Gurli made excuses for me; she said I had caught a cold on the previous evening, and that she was afraid the night air might do me harm. Ottilia looked self-conscious and left without kissing Gurli.

"I had promised to show Ottilia some astronomical instruments at the college at twelve o'clock on the following day. She kept her appointment, but she was much depressed. She had been to see Gurli, who had treated her very unkindly, so she said. She could not imagine why. When I came home to dinner I found a great change in Gurli. She was cold and mute as a fish. I could see that she was suffering. Now was the time to apply the knife.

"'What did you say to Ottilia?' I commenced. 'She was so unhappy.'

"'What did I say to her? Well, I said to her that she was a flirt. That's what I said.'

"'How could you say such a thing?' I replied. 'Surely, you're not jealous!'

"'I! Jealous of her!' she burst out.

"'Yes, that's what puzzles me, for I am sure an intelligent and sensible person like Ottilia could never have designs on another woman's husband!'

"'No,' (she was coming to the point) 'but another woman's husband might have designs on her.'

"'Huhuhu!' she went for me tooth and nail. I took Ottilia's part; Gurli called her an old maid; I continued to champion her. On this afternoon Ottilia did not turn up. She wrote a chilly letter, making excuses and winding up by saying she could see that she was not wanted. I protested and suggested that I should go and fetch her. That made Gurli wild! She was sure that I was in love with Ottilia and cared no more for herself. She knew that she was only a silly girl, who didn't know anything, was no good at anything, and—huhuhu!—could never understand mathematics. I sent for a sleigh and we went for a ride. In a hotel, overlooking the sea, we drank mulled wine and had an excellent little supper. It was just as if we were having our wedding day over again, and then we drove home."

"And then—?" asked the old woman, looking at him over her spectacles.

"And then? H'm! May God forgive me for my sins! I seduced my own little wife. What do you say now, granny?"

"I say that you did very well, my boy! And then?"

"And then? Since then everything has been all right, and now we discuss the education of the children and the emancipation of women from superstition and old-maidishness, from sentimentality and the devil and his ablative, but we talk when we are alone together and that is the best way of avoiding misunderstandings. Don't you think so, old lady?"

"Yes, Willy, dear, and now I shall come and pay you a call."

"Do come! And you will see the dolls dance and the larks and the woodpeckers sing and chirrup; you will see a home filled with happiness up to the roof, for there is no one there waiting for miracles which only happen in fairy tales. You will see a real dolls' house."

New Women and Their Allies

SOURCES

3. Olive Schreiner, *The Story of an African Farm* (London, 1883), pp. 217, 218-20, 222-30.

4. Marie Bashkirtseff, *Journal of Marie Bashkirtseff*. Tr. Mary Serrano (New York, 1889), pp. 374-75, 402, 407-9, 416-17. Originally published in Paris, 1887.

5. George Bernard Shaw, "The Womanly Woman," from *The Quintessence of Ibsenism* (London, 1913), pp. 47-49, 52-57. Originally published in 1891.

Among the guises in which the "new woman" appeared in the 1880's was that of the exalted adolescent—ambitious, idealistic, yet strangely worldly-wise and ready for adventure; nothing could have been more of a contrast with the ideal of true womanhood cultivated by Victorian society. Here was a type that captivated novelists and dramatists for the next quarter-century.

One of the most celebrated fictional representatives of the new woman was Lyndall, heroine of Olive Schreiner's novel, *The Story of an African Farm* (1883). Olive Emilie Albertina Schreiner (1855-1920) emigrated to England from South Africa, where she had been raised in a German Lutheran missionary family. She herself early exhibited signs of being a free spirit; in her twenties she served as a governess for families in the region near her home, while composing fiction in her spare moments. In 1881 she went to England with the plan of studying medicine. Instead, she successfully published her first novel, under the pseudonym of "Ralph Iron," and embarked on a literary career.

In this excerpt, Schreiner portrays the young Lyndall, who is visiting her married sister Em. Lyndall has just returned from boarding school, which did nothing to dampen her propensity for independent thinking and for sharp criticism of custom and mindlessness; she dreams of Napoleon and the rise of civilization, instead of thinking about her trousseau. Eventually the daring Lyndall leaves the farm with a stranger and bears his child, though she refuses to marry him.

However great the literary scandal created by Schreiner's Lyndall, an even greater sensation was the *Journal* of Marie Bashkirtseff (Mariya Konstantinova

Bashkirtseva, 1860-1884), which was published in Paris in 1887 and quickly thereafter in an abridged English edition. This diary, kept in French by a precocious young Russian noblewoman who lived in high style in France with her adoring family and burned to be a famous artist, was perhaps the most extraordinary woman's document published during the late nineteenth century. Though Bashkirtseff failed to realize her dream through her art, because she died from consumption at the age of twenty-four, she left behind her diary, with the explicit wish that it be published—and indeed, the diary brought her lasting fame. These selections from her journal reveal an adolescent soul bared as no previous writer had dared to do. It sparked heated discussion throughout European intellectual circles about the "true" nature of woman, and gave an enormous boost to discussion of the woman question in the newly developing fields of psychology and psychoanalysis.

Among the most penetrating commentators on the new woman as revealed by Bashkirtseff, Schreiner, and Ibsen was the indomitable English essayist and dramatist George Bernard Shaw (1856-1950). Shaw had become a great admirer of Ibsen and, like the Norwegian writer, used the theater to explore the social questions of the day, including the woman question. In this selection Shaw displays the wit and wisdom that assured his fame, coming out strongly and unequivocally on the side of emancipation of women.

---

3. Olive Schreiner (1883)

"Ah, Lyndall," Em cried, "perhaps you are engaged yourself—that is why you smile. Yes; I am sure you are. Look at this ring!"

Lyndall drew the hand quickly from her.

"I am not in so great a hurry to put my neck beneath any man's foot; and I do not so greatly admire the crying of babies," she said, as she closed her eyes half wearily and leaned back in the chair. "There are other women glad of such work."

Em felt rebuked and ashamed. How could she take Lyndall, and show her the white linen and the wreath and the embroidery? She was quiet for a little while, and then began to talk about Trana and the old farmservants, till she saw her companion was weary; then she rose and left her for the night. But after Em was gone Lyndall sat on, watching the old crone's face in the corner, and with a weary look, as though the whole world's weight rested on these frail young shoulders.

The next morning, Waldo, starting off before breakfast with a bag of mealies slung over his shoulder to feed the ostriches, heard a light step behind him.

"Wait for me; I am coming with you," said Lyndall, adding as she came up to him, "if I had not gone to look for you yesterday you would not have come to greet me till now. Do you not like me any longer, Waldo?" . . .

"Have you learned much?" he asked her simply, remembering how she had once said, "When I come back again I shall know everything that a human being can."

She laughed,—

"Are you thinking of my old boast? Yes; I have learned something, though hardly what I expected, and not *quite* so much. In the first place, I have learned that one of my ancestors must have been a very great fool; for they say nothing comes out in a man but one of his forefathers possessed it before him. In the second place, I have discovered that of all cursed places under the sun, where the hungriest soul can hardly pick up a few grains of knowledge, a girls' boarding-school is the worst. They are called finishing-schools, and the name tells accurately what they are. They finish everything but imbecility and weakness, and that they cultivate. They are nicely adapted machines for experimenting on the question, 'Into how little space can a human soul be crushed?' I have seen some souls so compressed that they would have fitted into a small thimble, and found room to move there,—wide room. A woman who has been for many years at one of those places carries the mark of the beast on her till she dies, though she may expand a little afterwards, when she breathes in the free world."

"Were you miserable?" he asked, looking at her with quick anxiety.

"I?—No. I am never miserable, and never happy. I wish I were. But I should have run away from the place on the fourth day, and hired myself to the first Boer-woman whose farm I came to, to make fire under her soap-pot, if I had had to live as the rest of the drove did. Can you form an idea, Waldo, of what it must be to be shut up with cackling old women, who are without knowledge of life, without love of the beautiful, without strength, to have your soul cultured by them? It is suffocation only to breathe the air they breathe; but I made them give me room. I told them I should leave, and they knew I came there on my own account; so they gave me a bedroom without the companionship of one of those things that were having their brains slowly diluted and squeezed out of them. I did not learn music, because I had no talent; and when the drove made cushions, and hideous flowers that the roses laugh at, and a footstool in six weeks that a machine would have made better in five minutes, I went to my room. With the money saved from such work I bought books and newspapers, and at night I sat up. I read and epitomized what I read; and I found time to write some plays, and find out how hard it is to make your thoughts look anything but imbecile fools when you paint them with ink on paper. In the holidays I learned a great deal more. I made acquaintances, saw a few places and many people, and some different ways of living, which is more than any books can show one. On the whole I am not dissatisfied with my four years. I have not learned what I expected; but I have learned something else. What have you been doing?"

"Nothing."

"That is not possible. I shall find out by-and-by."

They still stepped on side by side over the dewy bushes. Then suddenly she turned on him.

"Don't you wish you were a woman, Waldo?"

"No," he answered readily.

She laughed.

"I thought not. Even you are too worldly-wise for that. I never met a man who did. This is a pretty ring," she said, holding out her little hand, that the morning sun might make the diamonds sparkle. "Worth fifty pounds at least. I will give it to the first man who tells me he would like to be a woman. There might be one on Robben Island* who would win it perhaps, but I doubt it even there. It is delightful to be a woman; but every man thanks the Lord devoutly that he isn't one.". . . "We are cursed, Waldo; born cursed from the time our mothers bring us into the world till the shrouds are put on us. Do not look at me as though I were talking nonsense. Everything has two sides,—the outside that is ridiculous, and the inside that is solemn."

"I am not laughing," said the boy, sedately enough; "but what curses you?"

He thought she would not reply to him she waited so long.

"It is not what is done to us, but what is made of us," she said at last, "that wrongs us. No man can be really injured but by what modifies himself. We all enter the world little plastic beings, with so much natural force, perhaps, but for the rest—blank; and the world tells us what we are to be, and shapes us by the ends it sets before us. To you it says, *Work!* and to us it says, *Seem!* To you it says, As you approximate to man's highest ideal of God, as your arm is strong and your knowledge great, and the power to labor is with you, so you shall gain all that human heart desires. To us it says, Strength shall not help you, nor knowledge, nor labor. You shall gain what men gain, but by other means. And so the world makes men and women.

"Look at this little chin of mine, Waldo, with the dimple in it. It is but a small part of my person; but though I had a knowledge of all things under the sun, and the wisdom to use it, and the deep loving heart of an angel, it would not stead me through life like this little chin. I can win money with it, I can win love; I can win power with it, I can win fame. What would knowledge help me? The less a woman has in her head the lighter she is for climbing. I once heard an old man say that he never saw intellect help a woman so much as a pretty ankle; and it was the truth. They begin to shape us to our cursed end," she said, with her lips drawn in to look as though they smiled, "when we are tiny things in shoes and socks. We sit with our little feet drawn up under us in the window, and look out at the boys in their happy play. We want to go. Then a loving hand is laid on us. 'Little one, you cannot go,' they say; 'your little face will burn, and your nice white dress be spoiled.' We feel it must be for our good, it is so lovingly said; but we cannot understand, and we kneel still with one little cheek wistfully pressed against the pane. Afterwards we go and thread blue beads, and make a string for our neck; and we go and stand before the glass. We see the complexion we were not to spoil, and the white frock, and we look into our own great eyes. Then the curse be-

---

* At that time a leper colony off the coast of Cape Town.—EDS.

gins to act on us. It finishes its work when we are grown women, who no more look out wistfully at a more healthy life; we are contented. We fit our sphere as a Chinese woman's foot fits her shoe, exactly as though God had made both; and yet he knows nothing of either. In some of us the shaping to our end has been quite completed. The parts we are not to use have been quite atrophied, and have even dropped off; but in others—and we are not less to be pitied—they have been weakened and left. We wear the bandages, but our limbs have not grown to them; we know that we are compressed, and chafe against them.

"But what does it help? A little bitterness, a little longing when we are young, a little futile searching for work, a little passionate striving for room for the exercise of our powers,—and then we go with the drove. A woman must march with her regiment. In the end she must be trodden down or go with it; and if she is wise she goes.

"I see in your great eyes what you are thinking," she said, glancing at him; "I always know what the person I am talking to is thinking of. How is this woman who makes such a fuss worse off than I? I will show you by a very little example. We stand here at this gate this morning, both poor, both young, both friendless; there is not much to choose between us. Let us turn away just as we are, to make our way in life. This evening you will come to a farmer's house. The farmer, albeit you come alone and on foot, will give you a pipe of tobacco and a cup of coffee and a bed. If he has no dam to build and no child to teach, to-morrow you can go on your way with a friendly greeting of the hand. I, if I come to the same place to-night, will have strange questions asked me, strange glances cast on me. The Boer-wife will shake her head and give me food to eat with the Kaffirs, and a right to sleep with the dogs. That would be the first step in our progress,—a very little one, but every step to the end would repeat it. We were equals once when we lay newborn babes on our nurse's knees. We shall be equals again when they tie up our jaws for the last sleep."

Waldo looked in wonder at the little quivering face; it was a glimpse into a world of passion and feeling wholly new to him.

"Mark you," she said, "we have always this advantage over you,— we can at any time step into ease and competence, where you must labor patiently for it. A little weeping, a little wheedling, a little self-degradation, a little careful use of our advantages, and then some man will say, 'Come, be my wife!' With good looks and youth marriage is easy to attain. There are men enough; but a woman who has sold herself, even for a ring and a new name, need hold her skirt aside for no creature in the street. They both earn their bread in one way. Marriage for love is the beautifulest external symbol of the union of souls; marriage without it is the uncleanliest traffic that defiles the world." She ran her little finger savagely along the topmost bar, shaking off the dozen little dew-drops that still hung there. "And they tell us we have men's chivalrous attention!" she cried. "When we ask to be doctors, lawyers, lawmakers, anything but ill-paid drudges, they say, 'No; but you have men's chivalrous attention; now think of that and be satisfied! What would you do without it?'"

The bitter little silvery laugh, so seldom heard, rang out across the bushes. She bit her little teeth together.

"I was coming up in Cobb and Co.'s the other day. At a little wayside hotel we had to change the large coach for a small one. We were ten passengers, eight men and two women. As I sat in the house the gentlemen came and whispered to me, 'There is not room for all in the new coach, take your seat quickly.' We hurried out, and they gave me the best seat, and covered me with rugs, because it was drizzling. Then the last passenger came running up to the coach,—an old woman with a wonderful bonnet, and a black shawl pinned with a yellow pin.

"'There is no room,' they said; 'you must wait till next week's coach takes you up'; but she climbed on to the step, and held on at the window with both hands.

"'My son-in-law is ill, and I must go and see him,' she said.

"'My good woman,' said one, 'I am really exceedingly sorry that your son-in-law is ill; but there is absolutely no room for you here.'

"'You had better get down,' said another, 'or the wheel will catch you.'

"I got up to give her my place.

"'Oh, no, no!' they cried, 'we will not allow that.'

"'I will rather kneel,' said one, and he crouched down at my feet; so the woman came in.

"There were nine of us in that coach, and only one showed chivalrous attention,—and that was a woman to a woman.

"I shall be old and ugly too one day, and I shall look for men's chivalrous help, but I shall not find it.

"The bees are very attentive to the flowers till their honey is done, and then they fly over them. I don't know if the flowers feel grateful to the bees; they are great fools if they do."

"But some women," said Waldo, speaking as though the words forced themselves from him at that moment, "some women have power."

She lifted her beautiful eyes to his face.

"Power! Did you ever hear of men being asked whether other souls should have power or not? It is born in them. You may dam up the fountain of water, and make it a stagnant marsh, or you may let it run free and do its work; but *you* cannot say whether it shall be there; *it is there*. And it will act, if not openly for good, then covertly for evil; but it will act. If Goethe had been stolen away a child, and reared in a robber horde in the depths of a German forest, do you think the world would have had Faust and Iphigenie? But he would have been Goethe still—stronger, wiser than his fellows. At night, round their watch-fire, he would have chanted wild songs of rapine and murder, till the dark faces about him were moved and trembled. His songs would have echoed on from father to son, and nerved the heart and arm,—for evil. Do you think if Napoleon had been born a woman that he would have been contented to give small tea-parties and talk small scandal? He would have risen; but the world would not have heard of him as it hears of him now,—a man great and kingly, with all his sins; he would have left one of those names that stain the leaf of every history,—the names of women, who, having power, but being denied the right to exercise it openly, rule in the dark, covertly, and by stealth, through the men whose passions they feed on and by whom they climb.

"Power!" she said suddenly, smiting her little hand upon the rail. "Yes, we have power; and since we are not to expend it in tunnelling mountains, nor healing diseases, nor making laws, nor money, nor on any extraneous object, we expend it on *you.* You are our goods, our merchandise, our material for operating on; we buy you, we sell you, we make fools of you, we act the wily old Jew with you, we keep six of you crawling to our little feet, and praying only for a touch of our little hand; and they say truly, there was never an ache or pain or a broken heart but a woman was at the bottom of it. We are not to study law, nor science, nor art, so we study you. There is never a nerve or fibre in your man's nature but we know it. We keep six of you dancing in the palm of one little hand," she said, balancing her outstretched arm gracefully, as though tiny beings disported themselves in its palm. "There—we throw you away, and you sink to the devil," she said, folding her arms composedly. "There was never a man who said one word for woman but he said two for man, and three for the whole human race."

She watched the bird pecking up the last yellow grains; but Waldo looked only at her.

When she spoke again it was very measuredly.

"They bring weighty arguments against us when we ask for the perfect freedom of women," she said; "but, when you come to the objections, they are like pumpkin devils with candles inside,—hollow, and can't bite. They say that women do not wish for the sphere and freedom we ask for them, and would not use it.

"If the bird *does* like its cage, and *does* like its sugar, and will not leave it, why keep the door so very carefully shut? Why not open it, only a little? Do they know, there is many a bird will not break its wings against the bars, but would fly if the doors were open." She knit her forehead, and leaned farther over the bars.

"Then they say, 'If the women have the liberty you ask for, they will be found in positions for which they are not fitted!' If two men climb one ladder, did you ever see the weakest anywhere but at the foot? The surest sign of fitness is success. The weakness never wins but where there is handicapping. Nature left to herself will as beautifully apportion a man's work to his capacities as long ages ago she graduated the colors on the bird's breast. If we are not fit, you give us to no purpose the right to labor; the work will fall out of our hands into those that are wiser."

She talked more rapidly as she went on, as one talks of that over which they have brooded long, and which lies near their hearts.

Waldo watched her intently.

"They say women have one great and noble work left them, and they do it ill. That is true; they do it execrably. It is the work that demands the broadest culture, and they have not even the narrowest. The lawyer may see no deeper than his law-books, and the chemist see no further than the windows of his laboratory, and they may do their work well. But the woman who does woman's work needs a many-sided, multiform culture; the heights and depths of human life must not be beyond the reach of her vision; she must have knowledge of men and things in many states, a wide catholicity of sympathy, the strength that springs from knowledge, and the magnanimity which springs from strength. *We* bear the world, and *we* make it. The souls of little children are marvellously delicate and tender things, and keep forever the shadow that first falls on them, and that is the mothers, or at best a woman's. There was never a great man who had not a great mother—it is hardly an exaggeration. The first six years of our life makes us; all that is added later is veneer; and yet some say, if a woman can cook a dinner or dress herself well she has culture enough.

"The mightiest and noblest of human work is given to us, and we do it ill. Send a navvy into an artist's studio to work, and see what you will find there! And yet, thank God, we have this work," she added quickly; "it is the one window through which we see into the great world of earnest labor. The meanest girl who dances and dresses becomes something higher when her children look up into her face, and ask her questions. It is the only education we have, and this they cannot take from us."

4. Marie Bashkirtseff (1887)

[1878]

Saturday, April 13th.—At twenty-two years of age I shall be famous or dead.

Perhaps you believe that we work with the eyes and fingers only? You, who are of commonplace intellect, can never know how much unremitting attention, continual comparisons, calculation, sentiment, reflection, is required to obtain success.

Yes, yes, what you say—you say nothing, however; but I swear it to you on the head of Pincio (that seems stupid to you; to me, no) that I shall be celebrated. I swear it to you; I swear it to you seriously; I swear it to you on the Gospel, on the passion of Christ, on myself, that in four years I shall be celebrated. . . .

[*Monday, September 30th.*]—I wrote to Colignon that I wished I were a man. I know that I should become somebody; but with skirts—what can one do? Marriage is the only career for women; man has thirty-six chances, woman has but one, the zero like the Bank. But the Bank gains in any case; we pretend that it is the same with woman; but that is not true. How, then, can you expect that we will not be exceedingly cautious in choosing a *husband?* Never have I rebelled so much against the condition of woman. I am not foolish enough to claim that stupid equality, which is an Utopia (and then, besides, it is bad form) because there can not be equality between two beings so different, as man and woman. I ask nothing, because woman has already all that she should have; but I grumble at being a woman, because I happen to be one only as far as outward appearance goes. . . .

Sunday, October 20th.—I ordered the carriage at 9 o'clock and, accompanied by my maid of honor, Mademoiselle Elsnitz, I went to visit St. Philippe's, the church of Saint Thomas, Aquinas, and Notre Dame. I went up to the top and examined the bells as an English woman might have done. Well, there is an adorable Paris, old Paris, and I can be happy in it; but on the condition that I avoid the boulevards and the Champs Elysées, all the new, the beautiful quarters; in fact, what I execrate, what irritates my nerves. But over there in the Faubourg Saint Germain, I feel quite different.

Afterward we went to the *Ecole des Beaux-Arts*. It is enough to make one cry with rage.

Why can not I go and study there? Where can I get instructions as complete as there? I went to see the Exposition of the *Prix de Rome*. The second prize was won by a pupil of Julian's studio. Julian is very fortunate. If ever I am rich, I will found an art school for women. . . .

Sunday, November 3d.—Mamma, Dina, Madame X—, and I went out together. They wish to marry me, but I told them plainly, in order not to be the means of enriching some gentleman, that I will marry with pleasure, but on condition that the gentleman be rich, occupying a fine position and handsome, or else a man who is intelligent, remarkable, etc. As to his character, he may be Satan, himself; I will manage him.

Madame G— speaks of art in such a trifling manner that I will leave the room if she speaks of it again before me. She mentions ladies who paint at home, who have professors, and says that I can do as much when I am married, and all in that indifferent tone of the woman of the world, of the *bourgeoise*, in which there is something so frightfully low and so insulting to all the artistic and elevated sentiments.

You understand I view matters in a sensible and perfectly just manner.

I shall first try to make the marriage of my dreams. If I do not succeed, I will marry, like all the world, with the aid of my dowry. Now, I am tranquil.

In marrying we must remember that it is not an apartment that we rent by the month, but a house that we buy. We must find in it all our comforts, and we can not overlook the want of a few rooms, as in rented lodgings; and an old Russian proverb says, that "annexes bring misfortune."

Tuesday, November 5th.—There is one old-fashioned idea which is truly beautiful; Annihilation of the woman, before the superiority of the man she loves, must be the greatest enjoyment of self-love that a superior woman can experience. . . .

[1879]

Thursday, January 2d.—What I long for, is the liberty to ramble alone, to come and go, to seat myself on the benches in the garden of the Tuileries, and especially of the Luxembourg, to stop at the artistic shop-windows, enter the churches, the museums, to ramble at night in the old streets, that is what I long for, and that is the liberty without which one can not become a true artist. Do you believe that we profit by what we see when we are accompanied, or when going to the Louvre, we must await our carriage, our *chaperon*, or our family!

Ah! heavens and earth! that is what makes me so angry to be a woman! I will dress myself like a woman of the middle class, wear a wig, and make myself so ugly that I will be as free as a man. There is the liberty that I want and without which I shall never succeed in being anything.

One's thoughts are fettered by this stupid and enervating constraint; even if I disguise myself and make myself homely, I am but half free, for a woman who roams about is imprudent. And in Italy, in Rome?

The idea of going in a landau to visit ruins!

"Where are you going, Marie?"

"To see the Coliseum."

"But you have already seen it! Let us go to the theatre or take a drive, where there will be a crowd."

And that is enough to bind one down to the earth.

That is one of the great reasons why there are no women artists. Oh, sordid ignorance! Oh, savage routine! It is horrible to think of it all!

Even if we said sensible things, we would be assailed by the vulgar and ancient ridicule with which the apostles of woman's emancipation are overwhelmed. However, I think there is certain cause for laughter!

Women will never be anything but women. But, however, if they were brought up in the same manner as men, the inequality which I deplore would not exist, and there would remain only what is inherent in human nature itself. Ah, well! whatever I may say, women will shout and make themselves ridiculous (*I* will leave that to others) in an effort to obtain equality some time during the next century.

I will try to aid the cause by showing myself to society as a woman who has become something, notwithstanding all the disadvantages with which she is overwhelmed by society.

5. George Bernard Shaw (1891)

In 1890 the literary sensation of the day was the Diary of Marie Bashkirtseff. An outline of it, with a running commentary, was given in The Review of Reviews (June 1890) by the editor, the late William Stead, who, having gained an immense following by a public service in rendering which he had to simulate a felony and suffer imprisonment for it in order to prove that it was possible, was engaged in a campaign with the object of establishing the ideal of sexual "purity" as a condition of public life. He had certain Ibsenist qualities: faith in himself, wilfulness, conscientious unscrupulousness, and could always make himself heard. Prominent among his ideals was an ideal of womanliness. In support of that ideal he would, like all idealists, make and believe any statement, however obviously and grotesquely unreal. When he found Marie Bashkirtseff's account of herself utterly incompatible with the picture of a woman's mind presented to him by his ideal, he was confronted with the dilemma that either Marie was not a woman or else his ideal was false to nature. He actually accepted the former alternative. "Of the distinctively womanly," he says, "there is in her but little trace. She was the very antithesis of a true woman." William's next difficulty was, that self-control, being a leading quality in his ideal, could not have been possessed by Marie: otherwise she would have been more like his ideal. Nevertheless he had to record that she, without any compulsion from circumstances, made herself a highly skilled artist by working ten hours a day for six years. Let anyone who thinks that this is no evidence of self-control just try it for six months. William's verdict nevertheless was "No self-control." However, his fundamental quarrel with Marie came out in the following lines. "Marie," he said, "was artist, musician, wit, philosopher, student, anything you like but a natural woman with a heart to love, and a soul to find its supreme satisfaction in sacrifice for lover or for child." Now of all the idealist abominations that make society pestiferous, I doubt if there be any so mean as that of forcing self-sacrifice on a woman under pretence that she likes it; and, if she ventures to contradict the pretence, declaring her no true woman. In India they carried this piece of idealism to the length of declaring that a wife could not bear to survive her husband, but would be prompted by her own faithful, loving, beautiful nature to offer up her life on the pyre which consumed his dead body. The astonishing thing is that women, sooner than be branded as unsexed wretches, allowed themselves to be stupefied with drink, and in that unwomanly condition burnt alive. British Philistinism put down widow-idealizing with the strong hand; and suttee is abolished in India. The English form of it still flourishes; and Stead, the rescuer of the children,* was one of its high priests. Imagine his feelings on coming across this entry in a woman's diary: "I love myself." Or this, "I swear solemnly—by the Gospels, by the passion of Christ, by MYSELF—that in four years I will be famous." The young woman was positively proposing to exercise for her own sake all the powers that were given to her, in Stead's opinion, solely that she might sacrifice them for her lover or child! No wonder he was driven to exclaim again, "She was very clever, no doubt; but woman she was not."

Now observe this notable result. Marie Bashkirtseff, instead of being a less agreeable person than the ordinary female conformer to the ideal of womanliness, was most conspicuously the reverse. Stead himself wrote as one infatuated with her mere diary, and pleased himself by representing her as a person who fascinated everybody, and was a source of delight to all about her by the mere exhilaration and hope-giving atmosphere of her wilfulness. The truth is, that in real life a self-sacrificing woman, or, as Stead would have put it, a womanly woman, is not only taken advantage

---

* It was to force the Government to take steps to suppress child prostitution that Stead resorted to the desperate expedient already alluded to. He succeeded.

of, but disliked as well for her pains. No man pretends that his soul finds its supreme satisfaction in self-sacrifice: such an affectation would stamp him as coward and weakling: the manly man is he who takes the Bashkirtseff view of himself. But men are not the less loved on this account. No one ever feels helpless by the side of the self-helper; whilst the self-sacrificer is always a drag, a responsibility, a reproach, an everlasting and unnatural trouble with whom no really strong soul can live. Only those who have helped themselves know how to help others, and to respect their right to help themselves. . . .

It is not surprising that our society, being directly dominated by men, comes to regard Woman, not as an end in herself like Man, but solely as a means of ministering to his appetite. The ideal wife is one who does everything that the ideal husband likes, and nothing else. Now to treat a person as a means instead of an end is to deny that person's right to live. And to be treated as a means to such an end as sexual intercourse with those who deny one's right to live is insufferable to any human being. Woman, if she dares face the fact that she is being so treated, must either loathe herself or else rebel. As a rule, when circumstances enable her to rebel successfully—for instance, when the accident of genius enables her to "lose her character" without losing her employment or cutting herself off from the society she values—she does rebel; but circumstances seldom do. Does she then loathe herself? By no means: she deceives herself in the idealist fashion by denying that the love which her suitor offers her is tainted with sexual appetite at all. It is, she declares, a beautiful, disinterested, pure, sublime devotion to another by which a man's life is exalted and purified, and a woman's rendered blest. And of all the cynics, the filthiest to her mind is the one who sees, in the man making honorable proposals to his future wife, nothing but the human male seeking his female. The man himself keeps her confirmed in her illusion; for the truth is unbearable to him too: he wants to form an affectionate tie, and not to drive a degrading bargain. After all, the germ of the highest love is in them both; though as yet it is no more than the appetite they are disguising so carefully from themselves. Consequently every stockbroker who has just brought his business up to marrying point woos in terms of the romantic illusion; and it is agreed between the two that their marriage shall realize the romantic ideal. Then comes the breakdown of the plan. The young wife finds that her husband is neglecting her for his business; that his interests, his activities, his whole life except that one part of it to which only a cynic ever referred before her marriage, lies away from home; and that her business is to sit there and mope until she is wanted. Then what can she do? If she complains, he, the self-helper, can do without her; whilst she is dependent on him for her position, her livelihood, her place in society, her home, her name, her very bread. All this is brought home to her by the first burst of displeasure her complaints provoke. Fortunately, things do not remain for ever at this point: perhaps the most wretched in a woman's life. The self-respect she has lost as a wife she regains as a mother, in which capacity her use and importance to the community compare favorably with those of most men of business. She is wanted in the house, wanted in the market, wanted by the children; and now, instead of weeping because her husband is away in the city, thinking of stocks and shares instead of his ideal woman, she would regard his presence in the house all day as an intolerable nuisance. And so, though she is completely disillusioned on the subject of ideal love, yet, since it has not turned out so badly after all, she countenances the illusion still from the point of view that it is a useful and harmless means of getting boys and girls to marry and settle down. And this conviction is the stronger in her because she feels that if she had known as much about marriage the day before her wedding as she did six months after, it would have been extremely hard to induce her to get married at all.

This prosaic solution is satisfactory only within certain limits. It depends altogether upon the accident of the woman having some natural vocation for domestic management and the care of children, as well as on the husband being fairly good-natured and livable-with. Hence arises the idealist illusion that a vocation for domestic management and the care of children is natural to women, and that women who lack them are not women at all, but members of the third, or Bashkirtseff sex. Even if this were true, it is obvious that if the Bashkirtseffs are to be allowed to live, they have a right to suitable institutions just as much as men and women. But it is not true. The domestic career is no more natural to all women than the military career is natural to all men; and although in a population emergency it might become necessary for every ablebodied woman to risk her life in childbed just as it might become necessary in a military emergency for every man to risk his life in the battlefield, yet even then it would by no means follow that the child-bearing would endow the mother with domestic aptitudes and capacities as it would endow her with milk. It is of course quite true that the majority of women are kind to children and prefer their own to other people's. But exactly the same thing is true of the majority of men, who nevertheless do not consider that their proper sphere is the nursery. The case may be illustrated more grotesquely by the fact that the majority of women who have dogs are kind to them, and prefer their own dogs to other people's; yet it is not proposed that women should restrict their activities to the rearing of puppies. If we have come to think that the nursery and the kitchen are the natural sphere of a woman, we have done so exactly as English children come to think that a cage is the natural sphere of a parrot: because they have never seen one anywhere else. No doubt there are Philistine parrots who agree with their owners that it is better to be in a cage than out, so long as there is plenty of hempseed and Indian corn there. There may even be idealist parrots who persuade themselves that the mission of a parrot is to minister to the happiness of a private family by whistling and saying Pretty Polly, and that it is in the sacrifice of its liberty to this altruistic pursuit that a true parrot finds the supreme satisfaction of its soul. I will not go so far as to affirm that there are theological parrots who are convinced that imprisonment is the will of God because it is unpleasant; but I am confident that there are rationalist parrots who can demonstrate that it would be a cruel kindness to let a parrot out to fall a prey to cats, or at least to forget its accomplishments and coarsen its naturally delicate fibres in an unprotected struggle for existence. Still, the only parrot a free-souled person can sympathize with is the one that insists on being let out as the first condition of making itself agreeable. A selfish bird, you may say: one that puts its own gratification before that of the family which is so fond of it—before even the greatest happiness of the greatest number: one that, in aping the independent spirit of a man, has unparroted itself and become a creature that has neither the home-loving nature of a bird nor the strength and enterprise of a mastiff. All the same, you respect that parrot in spite of your conclusive reasoning; and if it persists, you will have either to let it out or kill it.

The sum of the matter is that unless Woman repudiates her womanliness, her duty to her husband, to her children, to society, to the law, and to everyone but herself, she cannot emancipate herself. But her duty to herself is no duty at all, since a debt is cancelled when the debtor and creditor are the same person. Its payment is simply a fulfilment of the individual will, upon which all duty is a restriction, founded on the conception of the will as naturally malign and devilish. Therefore Woman has to repudiate duty altogether. In that repudiation lies her freedom; for it is false to say that Woman is now directly the slave of Man: she is the immediate slave of duty; and as man's path to freedom is strewn with the wreckage of the duties and ideals he has trampled on, so must hers be. She may indeed mask her iconoclasm by proving in rationalist fashion, as Man has often done for the sake of a quiet life, that all these discarded idealist conceptions will be fortified instead of shattered by her emancipation. To a person with a turn for logic, such proofs are as easy as playing the piano is to Paderewski. But it will not be true. A whole basketful of ideals of the most sacred quality will be smashed by the achievement of equality for women and men. Those who shrink from such a clatter and breakage may comfort themselves with the reflection that the replacement of the broken goods will be prompt and certain. It is always a case of "The ideal is dead: long live the ideal!" And the advantage of the work of destruction is that every new ideal is less of an illusion than the one it has supplanted; so that the destroyer of ideals, though denounced as an enemy of society, is in fact sweeping the world clear of lies.

Foes of the New Woman

SOURCES

6. Friedrich Nietzsche, *Beyond Good and Evil*, in *Basic Writings of Nietzsche*, tr. and ed. Walter Kaufmann (New York, 1968), pp. 352-54, 356-59. Originally published as *Jenseits von Gut und Böse*, Leipzig, 1886.

7. Charles Turgeon, "Tendances d'émancipation de la femme nouvelle," in *Le Féminisme français*, 2 vols. (Paris, 1902), I, 33-35. Tr. KMO.

8. Marcel Prévost, "Frédérique," vol. I of Prévost, *Les Vierges fortes*, 2 vols. (Paris, 1900), pp. 80-87, 91-92. Tr. KMO.

In the 1880's the literature of misogyny focuses on the "new woman" and, sensing a deadly threat to male "virility," emits a shrill tone. The earlier prejudices of Proudhon (Vol. I, Docs. 52, 84, 95) cede pride of place to outright hostility and vengeance, as we see in the first selection by Friedrich Nietzsche (1844-1900). Though trained in philology like Bachofen (Vol. I, Doc. 102), the German-born Nietzsche, seeking to smother his ascetic Lutheran heritage in the heady pagan patriarchalism of classical Greece, found among the ancients a different sort of heritage. The central concern in all Nietzsche's prodigious philosophical outpourings was to contemplate the fate of European man and the ideals of European high culture amid what he viewed as the unremitting godlessness and vulgarity (or philistinism, as he called it) of the materialistic society engendered by the industrialization of imperial Germany. At the age of twenty-six he was named full professor at the University of Basel (Switzerland) in recognition of his extraordinary brilliance, but he subsequently resigned the position because of ill health.

The first selection is taken from Nietzsche's *Beyond Good and Evil*, published in the wake of the wreckage of his own relationship with a "new woman," the beautiful, brilliant, and idealistic twenty-year-old Russian-born Lou Salomé. At one point in 1882 Nietzsche had hoped to groom her as his disciple and intellectual heir and, it is reported, had also proposed marriage. As Salomé's most recent biographer, Rudolph Binion, makes clear, Nietzsche was here settling accounts with Salomé (who had first drawn his attention to the woman question with an unpublished essay of her own). His bitter disappointment with her inability to submit without a struggle to his efforts to play Pygmalion, coupled with their mutually idealistic attempts to ignore the force of physical attraction, pushed the older Nietzsche, already a lonely man by temperament and inclination, still further into solitude, pessimism, and—not long afterward—insanity.

The second selection is a turn-of-the century commentary on the new woman by a French law school professor, Charles-Marie-Joseph Turgeon (1855-1934). A Catholic and a professor of social economy at Rennes, Turgeon offers a more complex perspective than does Nietzsche; indeed, his views appear representative of a broad sector of French public opinion, where substantial legal and educational reforms on women's behalf could be tolerated so long as the principle of "equality in difference" was upheld and the customary sexual division of labor was retained. Like many other French social conservatives, including Émile Durkheim, however, Turgeon viewed the family as the "last refuge of social authority." As an economist he especially feared women's economic emancipation, considering it a clear threat to male superiority that might result not only in women's independence but, worse, in their dominance. Like many other Frenchmen, he could not envision realization of women's claims to freedom as anything but a ticket to a topsy-turvy world. This selection illustrates Turgeon's fears—the fears of bourgeois France in 1900—of a possible conjuncture between the issues of sex and class, fears that the single women of lower middle-class origins from which the "professionals of feminism" were recruited might, because of discontent and mischief, begin to swell the ranks of the social revolutionaries.

The third selection is excerpted from a widely read novel by the French writer Marcel Prévost (1862-1941). Parisian by birth, Prévost was educated by the Jesuits and studied civil engineering at the École Polytechnique. But he soon turned from engineering to popular fiction, proclaiming himself a disciple of the romanticism of Sand and Alexandre Dumas *fils* in opposition to the naturalistic school of Zola. Choosing the woman question as his subject, Prévost explored its ramifications in many of his works. In recognition of his literary contributions and his great popularity, he was elected to the French Academy in 1909. His two-volume novel *Les Vierges fortes* [The Stout Virgins] has been acclaimed as his most significant work. This selection, taken from the first volume, presents Prévost's quintessentially masculine perspective on how a young French girl might become converted to "feminism," which he considers to be a secular religion. In these two scenes Frédérique, the elder of two sisters (Léa is the younger), becomes the professed disciple of an older Hungarian woman, Mlle Romaine Pirnitz, who has dedicated her life to achieving the emancipation of women. The reader should note that Prévost portrays as foreign not only the bearer of the new ideology, Mlle Pirnitz, but also the ideology itself, and that he depicts the heroine Frédérique herself as an essentially passive vehicle for receiving the ideological germ.

---

6. Friedrich Nietzsche (1886)

Learning changes us; it does what all nourishment does which also does not merely "preserve"—as physiologists know. But at the bottom of us, really "deep down," there is, of course, something unteachable, some granite of spiritual *fatum*, of predetermined decision and answer to predetermined selected questions. Whenever a cardinal problem is at stake, there speaks an unchangeable "this is I"; about man and woman, for example, a thinker cannot relearn but only finish learning—only discover ultimately how this is "settled in him." At times we find certain solutions of problems that inspire strong faith in *us*; some call them henceforth *their* "convictions." Later we see them only as steps to self-knowledge, signposts to the problem we *are*—rather, to the great stupidity we are, to our spiritual *fatum*, to what is *unteachable* very "deep down."

After this abundant civility that I have just evidenced in relation to myself I shall perhaps be permitted more readily to state a few truths about "woman as such"—assuming that it is now known from the outset how very much these are after all only *my* truths.

Woman wants to become self-reliant, and for that reason she is beginning to enlighten men about "woman as such": *this* is one of the worst developments of the general *uglification* of Europe. For what must these clumsy attempts of women at scientific self-exposure bring to light! Woman has much reason for shame; so much pedantry, superficiality, schoolmarmishness, petty presumption, petty licentiousness and immodesty lies concealed in woman—one only needs to study her behavior with children!—and so far all this was at bottom best repressed and kept under control by *fear* of man. Woe when "the eternally boring in woman"— she is rich in that!—is permitted to venture forth! When she begins to unlearn thoroughly and on principle her prudence and art—of grace, of play, of chasing away worries, of lightening burdens and taking things lightly—and her subtle aptitude for agreeable desires!

Even now female voices are heard which—holy Aristophanes!—are frightening: they threaten with medical explicitness what woman *wants* from man, first and last. Is it not in the worst taste when woman sets about becoming scientific that way? So far enlightenment of this sort was fortunately man's affair, man's lot—we remained "among ourselves" in this: and whatever women write about "woman," we may in the end reserve a healthy suspicion whether woman really *wants* enlightenment about herself—whether she *can* will it—

Unless a woman seeks a new adornment for herself that way—I do think adorning herself is part of the Eternal-Feminine?—she surely wants to inspire fear of herself—perhaps she seeks mastery. But she does not *want* truth: what is truth to woman? From the beginning, nothing has been more alien, repugnant, and hostile to woman than truth—her great art is the lie, her highest concern is mere appearance and beauty. Let us men confess it: we honor and love precisely *this* art and *this* instinct in woman—we who have a hard time and for our relief like to associate with beings under whose hands, eyes, and tender follies our seriousness, our gravity and profundity almost appear to us like folly.

Finally I pose the question: has ever a woman conceded profundity to a woman's head, or justice to a woman's heart? And is it not true that on the whole "woman" has so far been despised most by woman herself—and by no means by us?

We men wish that woman should not go on compromising herself through enlightenment—just as it was man's thoughtfulness and consideration for woman that found expression in the church decree: *mulier taceat in ecclesia!* It was for woman's good when Napoleon gave the all too eloquent Madame de Staël to understand: *mulier taceat in politicis!* And I think it is a real friend of women that counsels them today: *mulier taceat de muliere!*

It betrays a corruption of the instincts—quite apart from the fact that it betrays bad taste—when a woman adduces Madame Roland or Madame de Staël or Monsieur George Sand, of all people, as if they proved anything in *favor* of "woman as such." Among men these three are the three *comical* women as such—nothing more!—and precisely the best involuntary *counterarguments* against emancipation and feminine vainglory.

Stupidity in the kitchen; woman as cook: the gruesome thoughtlessness to which the feeding of the family and of the master of the house is abandoned! Woman does not understand what food *means*—and wants to be cook. If woman were a thinking creature, she, as cook for millennia, would surely have had to discover the greatest physiological facts, and she would have had to gain possession of the art of healing. Bad cooks—and the utter lack of reason in the kitchen—have delayed human development longest and impaired it most: nor have things improved much even today. A lecture for finishing-school girls. . . .

Men have so far treated women like birds who had strayed to them from some height: as something more refined and vulnerable, wilder, stranger, sweeter, and more soulful—but as something one has to lock up lest it fly away.

To go wrong on the fundamental problem of "man and woman," to deny the most abysmal antagonism between them and the necessity of an eternally hostile tension, to dream perhaps of equal rights, equal education, equal claims and obligations—that is a *typical* sign of shallowness; and a thinker who has proved shallow in this dangerous place— shallow in his instinct—may be considered altogether suspicious, even more—betrayed, exposed: probably he will be too "short" for all fundamental problems of life, of the life yet to come, too, and incapable of attaining *any* depth. A man, on the other hand, who has depth, in his spirit as well as in his desires, including that depth of benevolence which is capable of severity and hardness and easily mistaken for them, must always think about woman as *Orientals* do: he must conceive of woman as a possession, as property that can be locked, as something predestined for service and achieving her perfection in that. Here he must base himself on the tremendous reason of Asia, on Asia's superiority in the instincts, as the Greeks did formerly, who were Asia's best heirs and students: as is well known, from Homer's time to the age of Pericles, as their culture *increased* along with the range of their powers, they also gradually became *more severe*, in brief, more Oriental, against woman. *How* necessary, *how* logical, *how* humanely desirable even, this was—is worth pondering.

In no age has the weaker sex been treated with as much respect by men as in ours: that belongs to the democratic inclination and basic taste, just like disrespectfulness for old age. No wonder that this respect is immediately abused. One wants more, one learns to demand; finally one almost finds this tribute of respect insulting; one would prefer competition for rights, indeed even a genuine fight: enough, woman loses her modesty. Let us immediately add that she also loses taste. She unlearns her *fear* of man: but the woman who "unlearns fear" surrenders her most womanly instincts.

That woman ventures forth when the aspect of man that inspires fear—let us say more precisely, when the *man* in man is no longer desired and cultivated—that is fair enough, also comprehensible enough. What is harder to comprehend is that, by the same token—woman degenerates. This is what is happening today: let us not deceive ourselves about that.

Wherever the industrial spirit has triumphed over the military and aristocratic spirit, woman now aspires to the economic and legal self-reliance of a clerk: "woman as clerk" is inscribed on the gate to the modern society that is taking shape now. As she thus takes possession of new rights, aspires to become "master" and writes the "progress" of woman upon her standards and banners, the opposite development is taking place with terrible clarity: *woman is retrogressing.*

Since the French Revolution, woman's influence in Europe has *decreased* proportionately as her rights and claims have increased; and the "emancipation of woman," insofar as that is demanded and promoted by women themselves (and not merely by shallow males) is thus seen to be an odd symptom of the increasing weakening and dulling of the most feminine instincts. There is *stupidity* in this movement, an almost masculine stupidity of which a woman who had turned out well—and such women are always prudent—would have to be thoroughly ashamed.

To lose the sense for the ground on which one is most certain of victory; to neglect practice with one's proper weapons; to let oneself go before men, perhaps even "to the point of writing a book," when formerly one disciplined oneself to subtle and cunning humility; to work with virtuous audacity against men's faith in a basically different ideal that he takes to be *concealed* in woman, something Eternally-and-Necessarily-Feminine—to talk men emphatically and loquaciously out of their notion that woman must be maintained, taken care of, protected, and indulged like a more delicate, strangely wild, and often pleasant domestic animal; the awkward and indignant search for everything slavelike and serflike that has characterized woman's position in the order of society so far, and still does (as if slavery were a counterargument and not instead a condition of every higher culture, every enhancement of culture)—what is the meaning of all this if not a crumbling of feminine instincts, a defeminization?

7. Charles Turgeon (1902)

Both in heart and in mind the professionals of feminism are thorough rebels. By this term I mean the advanced portion who . . . aim straight for free love by suppressing marriage and overthrowing the family. Fortunately, this group of audacious women, a sort of tumultuous and undisciplined advance guard, produces more noise than real evil—this little battalion of exalted women who proclaim the absolute equality of the sexes and, deafening their victims, make all the racket they can in order to convince us of the misfortunes of the "eternal slave" and the "inevitable revolution" of modern women. To this end they profess "integral" feminism.

What shines through the propaganda they spread, along with their unfortunate taste for declamation, is an impatient avidness for advertisement, an unbridled taste for burning notoriety. Impelled by the excellent example we [men] have set for them, it seems, these thickheaded women are dying to fall victim to the unremitting publicity that is compromising family life and the tranquility of upright people these days. The hen is dying of envy to crow like the cock; and the one who can puff herself up the most can display her small self on the highest perch in the henhouse. Following the politician, we now have the *politicienne*. The "new" women require a stage in order to affirm themselves and display themselves to all onlookers. Among their number, no doubt, we will sooner or later see some very good actresses.

It is possible that before long the number of emancipated eccentrics will acquire some important recruits. Until recently our convents took in most of those who were disinherited or defeated by life. But among the upcoming generations, the rapid extension of a freer and broader school-ing will not fail to encourage a growing number of diplomaed young women, of lively and keen intelligence, who will fail, I fear, to find the outlets they seek. Although no one can reasonably oppose the intellectual development of women, it is impossible not to notice that the teaching profession is already overcrowded, and that there are many educated young women, armed with their certificates, who are bored to death with miserable inaction. Too knowledgeable and proud to bend themselves to manual tasks, they can already be seen in the great cities leading a disen-chanted life, quarreling bitterly over a few meager lessons, while in their hearts they nurse bitter resentment against the improvidence of a society that has opened only a dead end to them. Should we not fear that some of these unhappy types, whose superficial knowledge exalts them without nourishing them, will listen to the suggestions of the rebellious spirit and sign on with that auxiliary of the revolutionary army that is already re-ferred to as "the intellectual proletariat of women."

Sprung from the middle classes, misunderstood, isolated, *déclassées*, with tastes, aspirations, and needs that they will be unable to satisfy, what could be more natural than that their sour and disabused souls would be receptive to the ideas of independence that waft through the air, and that, swept up by this excessive preaching that exaggerates the rights of their sex while minimizing its duties, they would become easily per-suaded that they are victims, sacrificial lambs. Diverted from their tradi-tional professions by an ill-considered schooling, they will increasingly lay siege to masculine careers and, faced with the difficulties of finding places and making names for themselves, they will shriek about oppres-sion, calling for absolute equality and total independence.

8. Marcel Prévost (1900)

—My child! my child! said Pirnitz.

Frédérique fell at her feet, her forehead hidden by longing hands that betrayed her misery and were wet with her tears.

—Don't cry. You must speak to me with an open heart. You must be strong—

—Yes, murmured Frédérique, drying her eyes with nervous violence—I don't know what came over me—Please forgive me—I am upset with myself, with my nerves—But I was so troubled this evening when you said you were leaving Paris.

She no longer tried to hide her need for Pirnitz' presence.—And if this departure unites us instead of separating us from one another? Dear child, be brave. The announcement of my trip has already brought us closer; tomorrow, when I leave this house, you will feel that I am still closer. For though I am absent, I will always call you—and you will no longer resist me. Come on, get up. Sit down here.

Frédérique obeyed. She was astonished to hear the foreign woman so easily interpret the state of her own heart. She stammered:

—It is true. I did resist you. Yet you completely preoccupied my thoughts.

—Not only did you resist me, but you also detested me a little!

—I was hurt by the thought that you were taking Léa's heart away from me, that you liked Léa better than me.

—Dear Frédérique! Léa and I spoke only of you. And I did not favor Léa, though I love her like a daughter. I have faith that you will accomplish much greater things.

—Is it possible? murmured Frédérique—me?—me? You had been thinking about me?

She looked at the mysterious face of the foreigner, who replied to her, "Yes!" Joy exalted her, the joy of a young person who, having herself loved with a secret modesty, suddenly discovers that she is loved in turn. It was that and more: for an illumination of her mind coincided with the warming of her heart. Every juvenile soul, experiencing its first affection, brings to it a need to submit, to devote itself. Frédérique immolated herself more than another might have: she sacrificed her prideful thoughts and her fierce sensitivity. Hers was a total abandonment, delicious, a blind sacrifice at once to a being and to an idea, both confounded and indiscernible from one another. She offered herself passionately to the idea and to its apostle, with the unthinkingness of one in love.

She raised her eyes to Pirnitz with a vanquished look:

—I will do whatever you tell me to do. I belong to you. Oh! make me the servant of what is good—I am ignorant—I want so much to learn!

—The road is hard, said Romaine. What was demanded of the first Christians was nothing compared to what the cause of humanity demands. Look at my own life. I have no country, no home—is it not wonderful to be loved, and to have children?

—I will never marry! Frédérique interrupted.

—Why not?—It seems to me that you practice an austerity uncommon among young women. I have never seen you speak to a man. Why is that?

—Because the idea of union with the men that I see, the idea of living with one of them, terrifies me, those of my [social] condition like the others, like the rich. Dear Léa and I can never step into the street without hearing odious words that are saying: Prostitute yourself!—Prostitute yourself!—Oh, Paris! How many times have I thought of fleeing into the depths of the countryside with Léa to be rid of this!

After a pause, she continued:

—Certainly, there is marriage.—To get married, to increase the number of households like those who live in this building and those nearby. Woman, the beast of burden, beaten and crushed—The woman going her own way, the man going his, and this double infamy played out in front of the children. No! I will never get married! I have seen too much, understood too much, since my childhood!—

—I know, said Romaine.

—You know? Léa told you?

—Yes.

Frédérique turned purple.

—She did the right thing, Pirnitz replied, caressing the hands of the girl, whose eyes remained lowered. Do you think that I love and esteem your mother any less?—Far from it.—It is precisely this hard test she has undergone that led me to cherish her.—And since then, I have seen in her a bit of my valiant Frédérique. You yourself have brought her up, in the best sense of the word.

—Alas! said Frédérique, there were some things in the past that I was unable to undo. That my mother was seduced and abandoned was the fault of the miserable man who deceived her. But to have accepted that— for money! Poor mother! No one taught her about the dignity of life. She was prey, like so many working women. And the man responsible for that despicable episode was the same man who, for forty thousand francs, thought he had freed himself from his responsibilities toward her and toward me. To know that this man lives, that he is married, that he has a distinguished position. What kind of a conscience must he have?

She was no longer breathless or timid. She spoke harshly, without emphasis.

—Do not dwell too much on the past, said Pirnitz. The past is dead; it cannot be changed. Let the dead bury the dead! Look rather at the path that is opening before you, and not that trod by your parents. New times are coming. You will not achieve vengeance by condemning your father, but by preventing the same crime from being repeated on other young innocent girls—

—Oh, yes!—To prevent that—To defend such poor girls—But there are no laws!

—One day we will have laws. Today we must attack and reform morals. Yes, here one can achieve something. You are not the first to have suffered from the humiliation of woman, from her subjection. Others before you have seen it, have suffered, and have vowed to fight it. In this corner of old Europe, people ignore or try to ignore the fact that new civilizations are being created, exist, prosper, that recognize the equality of the two sexes, the liberation of woman, and remove her from the odious state of mere flesh for pleasure or for maternity. I assure you, Frédérique, that another Eve is coming who will regenerate the old world and give it back its vigor.

—Speak, go on, said Frédérique.

One corner of the veil that hid from her the felt and hoped-for truth has been torn away. She has dreamed only of rescuing woman from the physical slavery that has menaced poor girls, and likewise preserving her own sister. Then Pirnitz had said: "—A New Eve is coming—the subjection of woman is not eternal—societies exist where the sexes are equal." Now Frédérique understood how narrow and meager her dream had been. The prophecies of the foreign woman had expanded it to include the integral emancipation of womankind.

—Speak, speak!

Pirnitz continued.

She told of the first leaps of feminine emancipation, the history of this coming Eve who was being created at the end of the nineteenth century and whom the twentieth would no doubt see in all the fullness of her strength and grace. The impulse gushed forth in all the new races. Dreamer and mystic, ardent to the point of martyrdom, the Slavic woman was renouncing the privileges accorded her sex in order to struggle with men in their own arena. The Anglo-Saxon woman, well muscled, practical, organized, religious, influenced by Puritanism and Methodism, not content to free only herself, wanted to free men, her former masters, from the low passions whose consequences she had had to suffer. The nervous and hard-working American woman marched over old abolished prejudices full of faith, toward happiness. The Scandinavian woman, on her boreal steppes, tormented especially by problems of conscience, was so to speak overturning customary conventions, constructing a higher, purer morality, exempting the feminine personality from the self-interested laws established by men.

—All this exists, Frédérique; it is not merely a utopia. Women who are independent of men, absolute mistresses of their destiny, are legion in the Anglo-Saxon world; they are numerous in the Slavic and Scandinavian world. Now it is a matter of taking on the old civilizations. Germany is quickly coming over to us: first the Germany of philosophers and sociologists, then popular Germany. London still mocks us; feminism is not appreciated by snobs. What does it matter? Its conquest is certain as of now. Paris—frivolous, ironic, sensual—continues to resist. But we will conquer it. We will vanquish it.

Frédérique listened avidly. Now she understood the role of Pirnitz. Pirnitz was one of the messengers sent to rejuvenate the decaying civilizations. Feminism, whose name—new to her—illuminated and warmed her subtly, appeared to her as a new religion, with apostolic duties and vows.

—The new Eve ought not to marry, is this not true? she asked.

—Why not? Pirnitz replied with a smile. We do not condemn marriage: for a great number of us it surely offers the best situation. There are excellent feminists who have been mothers.

And as Frédérique's face expressed surprise and sadness:

—However, she added, these wives have nearly all known intimate disappointments. Conjugal happiness is egotistical; it cannot benefit humanity. Better, at least during this period of struggle, to enroll as a free individual in the sacred phalange. I have always noticed more self-sacrifice, more ardor and sincerity among those of us who have never known man. The wise virgin can be a strong woman: the stout virgin remains the ideal of woman-to-come. There will always be enough young girls who will marry; humanity is not close to the shrinking-point. A day will come when the aristocracy of women will be composed of stout virgins.

—Neither Léa nor I want marriage, Frédérique replied with pride. Oh, you can count on us, we will be with you. But what must be done?

—For the time being, you must seek instruction in the work that you want to undertake. I am counting a great deal on you, Frédérique, even more than on your sister.

—Who will teach me if you leave?

Pirnitz took the girl's hands into her own slender, cool hands.

—My heart and my thoughts will stay with you. Listen. I am not going to give up my room. My books will remain, the works I have begun, all my humble life here.—I leave it for you; if you want to please me, you will live in it.

—Would you really permit it?

—I wish it. You do not even need to be discreet. On the contrary. I want you to use everything that is mine, just as if it were yours. You will read the same books, surround yourself with the same objects; you will even sleep in the same little bed. From afar it will make me smile to think that your pure and fervent soul is warming this cell, where my solitude was so sweet. Thus will you slowly be penetrated by me.

Never before had Pirnitz spoken so to Frédérique. Her suffering face, her eyes, took on a divine glow. Her features became transparent, offering a glimpse of an angel, a celestial messenger. Frédérique lowered her hands.

—How I do thank you! she said. How I do love you! Alas! I am not worthy of you.

Then, after a pause:

—Why did you choose me?

—It is you, Fédi, who designated yourself. It was not I.—The disciple comes to the faith. I myself, like you, heard the inner call. One day I heard a voice that said to me: "Do not be content with freeing yourself. Live for the liberation of your kind." . . .

[In bidding Frédérique farewell, Pirnitz offers the young woman free run of her library, and designates one book—Mill's *On the Subjection of Woman*—for her to read first and reread, over and over again.—EDS.]

The young woman returned to her room, undressed, prepared herself for the night and went to bed. Before blowing out the light, she opened the book. It said:

"The object of this Essay is to explain as clearly as I am able, the grounds of an opinion which I have held from the very earliest period when I had formed any opinions at all on social or political matters, and which, instead of being weakened or modified, has been constantly growing stronger by the progress of reflection and the experience of life: That the principle which regulates the existing social relations between the two sexes—the legal subordination of one sex to the other—is wrong in itself, and now one of the chief hindrances to human improvement; and that it ought to be replaced by a principle of perfect equality, admitting no power or privilege on the one side, nor disability on the other."

These clear words of Stuart Mill entered Frédérique's mind with such force that she became as though saturated with what they contained and could read no further.

She put out her lamp, closed her eyes, remained motionless, allowing the Idea to penetrate. She felt what seemed like an internal bruise and a sort of sorrowful joy, like that of a wife during the nuptial night.

Her virginal and courageous soul had experienced the first troublings of the heart when she met the apostle; now she became a woman at the touch of the new truth, the new faith, that had fertilized her.

Ego Sublimation Satirized and Applauded

SOURCES

9. Anton Chekhov, "The Darling," in *The Darling and Other Stories*, tr. Constance Garnett (New York, 1916), pp. 3-10, 13, 15-17. Originally published as "The Angel," in 1898.

10. Leo Tolstoy, "Tolstoy's Criticism on 'The Darling,'" in *The Darling and Other Stories*, tr. Constance Garnett (New York, 1916), pp. 23-28. Originally published in 1905.

Central to the critique of the new woman was the issue of whether a woman should be allowed by common consent to exhibit personality or achieve worldly success on her own. This aspect of the debate is exemplified in the following exchange between two of Russia's greatest writers, Anton Pavlovich Chekhov (1860-1904) and Leo Tolstoy (1828-1910).

The brilliant short-story writer and dramatist Anton Chekhov was born the son of a shopkeeper in Taganrog, on the shores of the Sea of Azov. While studying medicine on a scholarship in Moscow, he began to write and publish short stories, earning sufficient reputation to sustain his decision to abandon medicine for literature. During the 1880's he came under the spell of the great Tolstoy and grappled with the latter's idealistic philosophy with its asceticism and dedication to social service. In the early 1890's Chekhov acquired an estate near Moscow and worked diligently to improve the material and moral condition of his peasants, but in 1899 his deteriorating health forced him to sell the land and retire to the Crimea. In the meantime he had begun to cast aside many of his Tolstoian ideas and to produce works for the theater, as well as short stories, in which he explored the situation of women in Russian society. It was during this time also that he met and married the talented actress Olga Knipper, with whom he enjoyed a brief but intense relationship until his death from tuberculosis in 1904.

Chekhov's tongue-in-cheek portrait of Ilenka, a woman whose personal identity is wholly a reflection of the interests of the men in her life, was viewed in quite another fashion by the aging Tolstoy, as the second selection reveals. Tolstoy preferred to see in Ilenka a fictional realization of the supreme "otherness" that he himself had been relentlessly striving to achieve in his own life. While still a young man, Tolstoy had begun to question the universe and the human condition, and to seek the betterment of social conditions in imperial Russia. For over a decade, from 1862 to 1875, however, he found a personal satisfaction in marriage and family life, fathering thirteen children and writing two of his greatest novels, *War and Peace* and *Anna Karenina*. But in 1875 he entered on a period of prolonged spiritual crisis during which he renounced the privileges of his well-born existence to become a sort of Christian anarchist, rejecting material comfort and the pleasures of the flesh in order to better serve God. It is in the context of Tolstoy's obsessive quest for moral perfection, treading the fine line between sainthood and the absurd, that the reader must evaluate his criticism of "The Darling." It is, moreover, revealing that the traits that he admired in others and attributed to his fictional characters—like the Darling, who represents the suppression and loss of self—are uncompromisingly female. When egotism was not suppressed, as in the case of Anna Karenina, his characters come to a bad end. Though Chekhov's portrait of the Darling is a hugely exaggerated portrayal, it is indeed a situation that is both possible and acceptable to the reader's imagination precisely because it does reflect a reality in many women's lives. Chekhov's critical treatment of this situation, as well as Tolstoy's admiration, tells us a great deal about their attitude toward women and the woman question.

---

9. Anton Chekhov (1898)

Olenka, the daughter of the retired collegiate assessor, Plemyanniakov, was sitting in her back porch, lost in thought. It was hot, the flies were persistent and teasing, and it was pleasant to reflect that it would soon be evening. Dark rainclouds were gathering from the east, and bringing from time to time a breath of moisture in the air.

Kukin, who was the manager of an open-air theatre called the Tivoli, and who lived in the lodge, was standing in the middle of the garden looking at the sky.

"Again!" he observed despairingly. "It's going to rain again! Rain every day, as though to spite me. I might as well hang myself! It's ruin! Fearful losses every day."

He flung up his hands, and went on, addressing Olenka:

"There! that's the life we lead, Olga Semyonovna. It's enough to make one cry. One works and does one's utmost; one wears oneself out, getting no sleep at night, and racks one's brain what to do for the best. And then what happens? To begin with, one's public is ignorant, boorish. I give them the very best operetta, a dainty masque, first rate music-hall artists. But do you suppose that's what they want! They don't understand anything of that sort. They want a clown; what they ask for is vulgarity. And then look at the weather! Almost every evening it rains. It started on the tenth of May, and it's kept it up all May and June. It's simply awful! The public doesn't come, but I've to pay the rent just the same, and pay the artists."

The next evening the clouds would gather again, and Kukin would say with an hysterical laugh:

"Well, rain away, then! Flood the garden, drown me! Damn my luck in this world and the next! Let the artists have me up! Send me to prison!—to Siberia!—the scaffold! Ha, ha, ha!"

And next day the same thing.

Olenka listened to Kukin with silent gravity, and sometimes tears came into her eyes. In the end his misfortunes touched her; she grew to love him. He was a small thin man, with a yellow face, and curls combed forward on his forehead. He spoke in a thin tenor; as he talked his mouth worked on one side, and there was always an expression of despair on his face; yet he aroused a deep and genuine affection in her. She was always fond of some one, and could not exist without loving. In earlier days she had loved her papa, who now sat in a darkened room, breathing with difficulty; she had loved her aunt who used to come every other year from Bryansk; and before that, when she was at school, she had loved her French master. She was a gentle, soft-hearted, compassionate girl, with mild, tender eyes and very good health. At the sight of her full rosy cheeks, her soft white neck with a little dark mole on it, and the kind, naïve smile, which came into her face when she listened to anything pleasant, men thought, "Yes, not half bad," and smiled too, while lady visitors could not refrain from seizing her hand in the middle of a conversation, exclaiming in a gush of delight, "You darling!"

The house in which she had lived from her birth upwards, and which was left her in her father's will, was at the extreme end of the town, not far from the Tivoli. In the evenings and at night she could hear the band playing, and the crackling and banging of fireworks, and it seemed to her that it was Kukin struggling with his destiny, storming the entrenchments of his chief foe, the indifferent public; there was a sweet thrill at her heart; she had no desire to sleep, and when he returned home at daybreak, she tapped softly at her bedroom window, and showing him only her face and one shoulder through the curtain, she gave him a friendly smile. . . .

He proposed to her, and they were married. And when he had a closer view of her neck and her plump, fine shoulders, he threw up his hands, and said:

"You darling!"

He was happy, but as it rained on the day and night of his wedding, his face still retained an expression of despair.

They got on very well together. She used to sit in his office, to look after things in the Tivoli, to put down the accounts and pay the wages. And her rosy cheeks, her sweet, naïve, radiant smile, were to be seen now at the office window, now in the refreshment bar or behind the scenes of the theatre. And already she used to say to her acquaintances that the theatre was the chief and most important thing in life, and that it was only through the drama that one could derive true enjoyment and become cultivated and humane.

"But do you suppose the public understands that?" she used to say. "What they want is a clown. Yesterday we gave 'Faust Inside Out,' and almost all the boxes were empty; but if Vanitchka and I had been producing some vulgar thing, I assure you the theatre would have been packed. Tomorrow Vanitchka and I are doing 'Orpheus in Hell.' Do come."

And what Kukin said about the theatre and the actors she repeated. Like him she despised the public for their ignorance and their indifference to art; she took part in the rehearsals; she corrected the actors, she kept an eye on the behaviour of the musicians, and when there was an unfavourable notice in the local paper, she shed tears, and then went to the editor's office to set things right.

The actors were fond of her and used to call her "Vanitchka and I," and "the darling"; she was sorry for them and used to lend them small sums of money, and if they deceived her, she used to shed a few tears in private, but did not complain to her husband.

They got on well in the winter too. They took the theatre in the town for the whole winter, and let it for short terms to a Little Russian company, or to a conjurer, or to a local dramatic society. Olenka grew stouter, and was always beaming with satisfaction, while Kukin grew thinner and yellower, and continually complained of their terrible losses, although he had not done badly all the winter. He used to cough at night, and she used to give him hot raspberry tea or lime-flower water, to rub him with eau-de-Cologne and to wrap him in her warm shawls.

"You're such a sweet pet!" she used to say with perfect sincerity, stroking his hair. "You're such a pretty dear!"

Towards Lent he went to Moscow to collect a new troupe, and without him she could not sleep, but sat all night at her window, looking at the stars, and she compared herself with the hens, who are awake all night and uneasy when the cock is not in the hen-house. Kukin was detained in Moscow, and wrote that he would be back at Easter, adding some instructions about the Tivoli. But on the Sunday before Easter, late in the evening, came a sudden ominous knock at the gate; some one was hammering on the gate as though on a barrel—boom, boom, boom! The drowsy cook went flopping with her bare feet through the puddles, as she ran to open the gate.

"Please open," said some one outside in a thick bass. "There is a telegram for you."

Olenka had received telegrams from her husband before, but this time for some reason she felt numb with terror. With shaking hands she opened the telegram and read as follows:

"Ivan Petrovitch died suddenly to-day. Awaiting immate instructions fufuneral Tuesday."

That was how it was written in the telegram—"fufuneral," and the utterly incomprehensible word "immate." It was signed by the stage manager of the operatic company.

"My darling!" sobbed Olenka. "Vanitchka, my precious, my darling! Why did I ever meet you! Why did I know you and love you! Your poor heart-broken Olenka is all alone without you!"

Kukin's funeral took place on Tuesday in Moscow; Olenka returned home on Wednesday, and as soon as she got indoors she threw herself on her bed and sobbed so loudly that it could be heard next door, and in the street.

"Poor darling!" the neighbours said, as they crossed themselves. "Olga Semyonovna, poor darling! How she does take on!"

Three months later Olenka was coming home from mass, melancholy and in deep mourning. It happened that one of her neighbours, Vassily Andreitch Pustovalov, returning home from church, walked back beside her. He was the manager at Babakayev's, the timber merchant's. He wore a straw hat, a white waistcoat, and a gold watch-chain, and looked more like a country gentleman than a man in trade.

"Everything happens as it is ordained, Olga Semyonovna," he said gravely, with a sympathetic note in his voice; "and if any of our dear ones die, it must be because it is the will of God, so we ought to have fortitude and bear it submissively."

After seeing Olenka to her gate, he said good-bye and went on. All day afterwards she heard his sedately dignified voice, and whenever she shut her eyes she saw his dark beard. She liked him very much. And apparently she had made an impression on him too, for not long afterwards an elderly lady, with whom she was only slightly acquainted, came to drink coffee with her, and as soon as she was seated at table began to talk about Pustovalov, saying that he was an excellent man whom one could thoroughly depend upon, and that any girl would be glad to marry him. Three days later Pustovalov came himself. He did not stay long, only about ten minutes, and he did not say much, but when he left, Olenka loved him—loved him so much that she lay awake all night in a perfect fever, and in the morning she sent for the elderly lady. The match was quickly arranged, and then came the wedding.

Pustovalov and Olenka got on very well together when they were married.

Usually he sat in the office till dinner-time, then he went out on business, while Olenka took his place, and sat in the office till evening, making up accounts and booking orders.

"Timber gets dearer every year; the price rises twenty per cent," she would say to her customers and friends. "Only fancy we used to sell local timber, and now Vassitchka always has to go for wood to the Mogilev district. And the freight!" she would add, covering her cheeks with her hands in horror. "The freight!"

It seemed to her that she had been in the timber trade for ages and ages, and that the most important and necessary thing in life was timber; and there was something intimate and touching to her in the very sound of words such as "baulk," "post," "beam," "pole," "scantling," "batten," "lath," "plank," etc.

At night when she was asleep she dreamed of perfect mountains of planks and boards, and long strings of wagons, carting timber somewhere far away. She dreamed that a whole regiment of six-inch beams forty feet high, standing on end, was marching upon the timber-yard; that logs, beams, and boards knocked together with the resounding crash of dry wood, kept falling and getting up again, piling themselves on each other. Olenka cried out in her sleep, and Pustovalov said to her tenderly: "Olenka, what's the matter, darling? Cross yourself!"

Her husband's ideas were hers. If he thought the room was too hot, or that business was slack, she thought the same. Her husband did not care for entertainments, and on holidays he stayed at home. She did likewise.

"You are always at home or in the office," her friends said to her. "You should go to the theatre, darling, or to the circus."

"Vassitchka and I have no time to go to theatres," she would answer sedately. "We have no time for nonsense. What's the use of these theatres?" . . .

But behold! one winter day after drinking hot tea in the office, Vassily Andreitch went out into the yard without his cap on to see about sending off some timber, caught cold, and was taken ill. He had the best doctors, but he grew worse and died after four months' illness. And Olenka was a widow once more. . . .

Now she was absolutely alone. Her father had long been dead, and his armchair lay in the attic, covered with dust and lame of one leg. She got thinner and plainer, and when people met her in the street they did not look at her as they used to, and did not smile to her; evidently her best years were over and left behind, and now a new sort of life had begun for her, which did not bear thinking about. In the evening Olenka sat in the porch, and heard the band playing and the fireworks popping in the Tivoli, but now the sound stirred no response. She looked into her yard without interest, thought of nothing, wished for nothing, and afterwards, when night came on, she went to bed and dreamed of her empty yard. She ate and drank as it were unwillingly.

And what was worst of all, she had no opinions of any sort. She saw the objects about her and understood what she saw, but could not form any opinion about them, and did not know what to talk about. And how awful it is not to have any opinions! One sees a bottle, for instance, or the rain, or a peasant driving in his cart, but what the bottle is for, or the rain, or the peasant, and what is the meaning of it, one can't say, and could not even for a thousand roubles. When she had Kukin, or Pustovalov, or the veterinary surgeon, Olenka could explain everything, and give her opinion about anything you like, but now there was the same emptiness in her brain and in her heart as there was in her yard outside. And it was as harsh and as bitter as wormwood in the mouth.

Little by little the town grew in all directions. The road became a street, and where the Tivoli and the timber-yard had been, there were new turnings and houses. How rapidly time passes! Olenka's house grew dingy, the roof got rusty, the shed sank on one side, and the whole yard was overgrown with docks and stinging-nettles. Olenka herself had grown plain and elderly; in summer she sat in the porch, and her soul, as before, was empty and dreary and full of bitterness. In winter she sat at her window and looked at the snow. When she caught the scent of spring, or heard the chime of the church bells, a sudden rush of memories from the past came over her, there was a tender ache in her heart, and her eyes brimmed over with tears; but this was only for a minute, and then came emptiness again and the sense of the futility of life. The black kitten, Briska, rubbed against her and purred softly, but Olenka was not touched by these feline caresses. That was not what she needed. She wanted a love that would absorb her whole being, her whole soul and reason—that would give her ideas and an object in life, and would warm her old blood. And she would shake the kitten off her skirt and say with vexation:

"Get along; I don't want you!"

And so it was, day after day and year after year, and no joy, and no opinions. Whatever Mavra, the cook, said she accepted. . . .

10. Leo Tolstoy (1905)

There is a story of profound meaning in the Book of Numbers which tells how Balak, the King of the Moabites, sent for the prophet Balaam to curse the Israelites who were on his borders. Balak promised Balaam many gifts for this service, and Balaam, tempted, went to Balak, and went with him up the mountain, where an altar was prepared with calves and sheep sacrificed in readiness for the curse. Balak waited for the curse, but instead of cursing, Balaam blessed the people of Israel.

Ch. xxiii., v. 11: "And Balak said unto Balaam, What hast thou done unto me? I took thee to curse mine enemies, and, behold, thou hast blessed them altogether. . . .

[Ch. xxiv, v. 11:] "Therefore now flee thee to thy place: I thought to promote thee unto great honour; but, lo, the Lord hast kept thee back from honour."

And so Balaam departed without having received the gifts, because, instead of cursing, he had blessed the enemies of Balak.

What happened to Balaam often happens to real poets and artists. Tempted by Balak's gifts, popularity, or by false preconceived ideas, the poet does not see the angel barring his way, though the ass sees him, and he means to curse, and yet, behold, he blesses.

This is just what happened to the true poet and artist Chekhov when he wrote this charming story "The Darling."

The author evidently means to mock at the pitiful creature—as he judges her with his intellect, but not with his heart—the Darling, who after first sharing Kukin's anxiety about his theatre, then throwing herself into the interests of the timber trade, then under the influence of the veterinary surgeon regarding the campaign against the foot and mouth disease as the most important matter in the world, is finally engrossed in the grammatical questions and the interests of the little schoolboy in the big cap. Kukin's surname is absurd, even his illness and the telegram announcing his death, the timber merchant with his respectability, the veterinary surgeon, even the boy—all are absurd, but the soul of The Darling, with her faculty of devoting herself with her whole being to any one she loves, is not absurd, but marvellous and holy.

I believe that while he was writing "The Darling," the author had in his mind, though not in his heart, a vague image of a new woman; of her equality with man; of a woman mentally developed, learned, working independently for the good of society as well as, if not better than, a man; of the woman who has raised and upholds the woman question; and in writing "The Darling" he wanted to show what woman ought not to be. The Balak of public opinion bade Chekhov curse the weak, submissive undeveloped woman devoted to man; and Chekhov went up the mountain, and the calves and sheep were laid upon the altar, but when he began to speak, the poet blessed what he had come to curse. In spite of its exquisite gay humour, I at least cannot read without tears some passages of this wonderful story. I am touched by the description of her complete devotion and love for Kukin and all that he cares for, and for the timber merchant and for the veterinary surgeon, and even more of her sufferings when she is left alone and has no one to love; and finally the account of how with all the strength of womanly, motherly feelings (of which she has no experience in her own life) she devotes herself with boundless love to the future man, the schoolboy in the big cap.

The author makes her love the absurd Kukin, the insignificant timber merchant, and the unpleasant veterinary surgeon, but love is no less sacred whether its object is a Kukin or a Spinoza, a Pascal, or a Schiller, and whether the objects of it change as rapidly as with the Darling, or whether the object of it remains the same throughout the whole life.

Some time ago I happened to read in the *Novoe Vremya* an excellent article upon woman. The author has in this article expressed a remarkably clever and profound idea about woman. "Women," he says, "are trying to show us they can do everything we men can do. I don't contest it; I am prepared to admit that women can do everything men can do, and possibly better than men; but the trouble is that men cannot do anything faintly approaching to what women can do." . . .

Yes, that is undoubtedly true, and it is true not only with regard to birth, nurture, and early education of children. Men cannot do that highest, best work which brings man nearest to God—the work of love, of complete devotion to the loved object, which good women have done, do, and will do so well and so naturally. What would become of the world, what would become of us men if women had not that faculty and did not exercise it? We could get on without women doctors, women telegraph clerks, women lawyers, women scientists, women writers, but life would be a sorry affair without mothers, helpers, friends, comforters, who love in men the best in them, and imperceptibly instil, evoke, and support it. There would have been no Magdalen with Christ, no Claire with St. Francis; there would have been no wives of the Dekabrists in Siberia; there would not have been among the Duhobors those wives who, instead of holding their husbands back, supported them in their martyrdom for truth; there would not have been those thousands and thousands of unknown women—the best of all, as the unknown always are—the comforters of the drunken, the weak, and the dissolute, who, more than any, need the comfort of love. That love, whether devoted to a Kukin or to Christ, is the chief, grand, unique strength of woman.

What an amazing misunderstanding it is—all this so-called woman question, which, as every vulgar idea is bound to do, has taken possession of the majority of women, and even of men.

"Woman longs to improve herself"—what can be more legitimate and just than that?

But a woman's work is from her very vocation different from man's, and so the ideal of feminine perfection cannot be the same as the ideal of masculine perfection. Let us admit that we do not know what that ideal is; it is quite certain in any case that it is not the ideal of masculine perfection. And yet it is to the attainment of that masculine ideal that the whole of the absurd and evil activity of the fashionable woman movement, which is such a stumbling-block to woman, is directed.

I am afraid that Chekhov was under the influence of that misunderstanding when he wrote "The Darling."

He, like Balaam, intended to curse, but the god of poetry forbade him, and commanded him to bless. And he did bless, and unconsciously clothed this sweet creature in such an exquisite radiance that she will always remain a type of what a woman can be in order to be happy herself, and to make the happiness of those with whom destiny throws her.

What makes the story so excellent is that the effect is unintentional.

I learnt to ride a bicycle in a hall large enough to drill a division of soldiers. At the other end of the hall a lady was learning. I thought I must be careful to avoid getting into her way, and began looking at her. And as I looked at her I began unconsciously getting nearer and nearer to her, and in spite of the fact that, noticing the danger, she hastened to retreat, I rode down upon her and knocked her down—that is, I did the very opposite of what I wanted to do, simply because I concentrated my attention upon her.

The same thing has happened to Chekhov, but in an inverse sense: he wanted to knock the Darling down, and concentrating upon her the close attention of the poet, he raised her up.

Critique of the Double Standard

SOURCES

11. Bjørnstjerne Bjørnson, *A Gauntlet*, in *Three Comedies*. Tr. R. Farquharson Sharp (London, 1912), pp. 162-67. Originally published as *En Hanske*, 1883.

12. Bertha von Suttner, *Das Maschinenzeitalter, Zukunftsvorlesungen über unsere Zeit* (Dresden and Leipzig, 1899), pp. 138-39, 142-44, 156-57, 163-64, 165-66. Originally published in Zurich, 1889. Tr. SGB.

The cultural forms surrounding heterosexual love and the prevailing double standard of sexual morality were subject to increasing criticism by European writers from 1880 on. Writers dealt with such matters with increasing explicitness, though rarely with identical arguments, as two important selections from this literature demonstrate.

The first selection comes from a landmark drama by the distinguished Norwegian playwright Bjørnstjerne Bjørnson (1832-1910). The heroine of Bjørnson's drama, Svava Riis, believes strongly in a single standard of premarital sexual purity, but after her betrothal to Alfred Christensen (the son of a prominent family in the community) she discovers to her dismay that he had once had an affair with another woman. She seeks counsel from her uncle, Dr. Nordan. In this scene from Act II the Christensens have just arrived to pay a call on the Riis family, who are hoping that Svava's idealism will not destroy their chances for social promotion through the match. Though Bjørnson wrote *A Gauntlet* as a comedy, he was deadly serious about its message, and subsequently embarked on a year-long lecture tour, addressing groups throughout northern Europe on the controversial subject of "Monogamy and Polygamy." Wherever *A Gauntlet* was performed, young women followed Svava's example, and in its wake thousands of engagements were reported broken throughout Scandinavia.

The second selection is excerpted from *Das Maschinenzeitalter* (The Machine Age), a social critique written in retrospective style by the Austrian woman's rights advocate, and recipient of one of the first Nobel Peace Prizes in 1905, Bertha von Suttner (1843-1914). In this selection Suttner points out the barbarism of a culture where women are treated solely as sex objects, where "ideal" love is considered the antithesis of physical love, and where death and killing are honored above life and love. Born to a titled family but raised in relative poverty as Bertha Felicie Sophie von Kinsky, Suttner worked in Paris as secretary to the Swedish dynamite magnate and philanthropist Alfred Nobel. Later, during her term as governess in the Suttner household, she scandalized Viennese society by eloping to Russia with the son of the family, who was seven years younger than she. After the couple's return to Vienna and the anonymous publication of her *Maschinenzeitalter*, Bertha von Suttner found herself at a dinner party with a group of deputies to the Austrian Parliament. Drawn into a conversation about the book, her innocent questions were firmly rebuffed: "Oh, no Madame, that is not a book for ladies!"

---

11. Bjørnstjerne Bjørnson (1883)

NORDAN. Here we are! She asked me to come on a little ahead of her.

RIIS. She is not going to keep us waiting any longer, I hope?

NORDAN. She was just behind me.

RIIS. Here she is! (*Goes to the door to meet her;* NORDAN *and* MRS. RIIS *do the same from the other side of the room.*)

CHRISTENSEN. One would think she were the Queen of Sheba.

(SVAVA *comes in, wearing her hat, and with her gloves and parasol in her hand.* CHRISTENSEN *and* MRS. CHRISTENSEN *get up from their seats. She bows slightly to them, and comes to the front of the stage on the right-hand side. All sit down in silence.* NORDAN *is at the extreme left, then* MRS. RIIS, MRS. CHRISTENSEN *and* CHRISTENSEN. *At the extreme right, but a little behind the others, is* RIIS, *who is sitting down one minute and standing the next.*)

MRS. CHRISTENSEN. My dear Svava, we have come here to—well, you know what we have come for. What has happened has distressed us very much; but what is done cannot be undone. None of us can excuse Alfred. But all the same we think that he might be granted forgiveness, especially at the hands of one who must know that he loves her, and loves her sincerely. That makes it a different matter altogether, of course.

CHRISTENSEN. Of course!

RIIS. Of course!

NORDAN. Of course!

MRS. CHRISTENSEN. And, even if you don't quite agree with me about that, I hope you will agree with me about Alfred himself. I mean to say, that we consider his character, my dear Svava, should vouch to you for his fidelity. I know that, if you require it, he will give you his word of honour that—

MRS. RIIS (*getting up*). No! No!

MRS. CHRISTENSEN. What is the matter, my dear Mrs. Riis?

MRS. RIIS. No words of honour! He has to take an oath when he marries, anyway.

NORDAN. But surely two make it all the safer, Mrs. Riis?

MRS. RIIS. No, no! No oath! (*Sits down again.*)

CHRISTENSEN. I was struck with our friend Dr. Nordan's remark. Tell me, my dear sir, do you also take it for granted that the sort of thing my son has done ought to be an absolute bar to marriage with an honourable woman?

NORDAN. Quite the contrary! I am quite sure it never prevents any one getting married—and remarkably well married. It is only Svava that is behaving in an extraordinary manner in every respect.

MRS. CHRISTENSEN. I would not go so far as to say that; but there is one thing that Svava has overlooked. She is acting as if she were free. But she is not by any means free. A betrothal is equivalent to a marriage; at any rate, I am old-fashioned enough to consider it so. And the man to whom I have given my hand is thereby made my master and given authority over me, and I owe to him—as to a superior authority—my respect, whether he act well or ill. I cannot give him notice, or run away from him.

RIIS. That is old-fashioned and sensible. I thank you heartily, Mrs. Christensen!

NORDAN. And I too!

MRS. RIIS. But if it is too late after the betrothal—. (*Checks herself.*)

MRS. CHRISTENSEN. What do you mean, dear Mrs. Riis?

MRS. RIIS. Oh, nothing—nothing at all.

NORDAN. Mrs. Riis means that if it is too late after the betrothal, why do people not speak out before they are betrothed?

RIIS. What a thing to say!

CHRISTENSEN. Well, it wouldn't be such a bad thing, would it? I imagine proposals in future being worded somewhat in this way: "My dear Miss So-and-So, up to date I have had such and such a number of love affairs—that is to say, so many big ones and so many little ones." Don't you think it would be a capital way to lead the conversation on to—

NORDAN. —to assuring her that she is the only one you have ever loved?

CHRISTENSEN. Well, not exactly that, but—

RIIS. Here comes Alfred!

MRS. RIIS. Alfred?

MRS. CHRISTENSEN. Yes, it really is he!

RIIS (*who has gone to the door to meet* ALFRED). Ah, that is right! We are so glad you have come!

CHRISTENSEN. Well, my boy?

ALFRED. When it came to the point, I could not do anything else—I had to come here.

CHRISTENSEN. I quite agree with you.

RIIS. Yes, it was only the natural thing to do. (ALFRED *comes forward and bows respectfully to* SVAVA. *She bows slightly, but without looking at him. He steps back again.*)

NORDAN. Good morning, my boy!

ALFRED. Perhaps I have come at an inconvenient moment.

RIIS. Not a bit of it! Quite the contrary!

ALFRED. At the same time, it seems evident to me that my presence is not welcome to Miss Riis. (*No one answers him.*)

MRS. CHRISTENSEN. But it is a family council we are holding—isn't it, my dear girl?

RIIS. I assure you, you *are* welcome! And we are all particularly anxious to hear what you have to say!

CHRISTENSEN. That is so.

ALFRED. I have not succeeded in getting a hearing yet, you know. I have been refused admittance repeatedly—both in person and when I wrote. So I thought that if I came now, perhaps I should get a hearing.

RIIS. Of course. Who can object to that?

NORDAN. You shall have your hearing.

ALFRED. Perhaps I may take Miss Riis's silence to mean permission? In that case—well—it is nothing so very much that I have to say, either. It is merely to remind you that, when I asked for Miss Riis's hand, it was because I loved her with all my heart—her and no one else. I could not imagine any greater happiness, and any greater honour, than to be loved by her in return. And so I think still. (*He pauses, as if he expected an answer. They all look at* SVAVA.) What explanation I could have given of my own free will—indeed what explanation, under other circumstances, I should have felt impelled to give—I shall say nothing about now. But I *owe* no explanation! My honour demands that I should make a point of that. It is my future that I owe to her. And with regard to that I must confess I have been hurt—deeply hurt—by the fact that Miss Riis could doubt me for a moment. Never in my life has any one doubted me before. With all respect, I must insist that my word shall be taken. (*They are all silent.*) That is all I have to say.

MRS. RIIS (*getting up unwillingly*). But, Alfred, suppose a woman, under the same circumstances, had come and said the same thing—who would believe her? (*They are all silent.* SVAVA *bursts into tears.*)

MRS. CHRISTENSEN. Poor child!

RIIS. Believe her?

MRS. RIIS. Yes, believe her. Believe her if, after a past like that, she came and assured us that she would make an honest wife?

CHRISTENSEN. After a past like that?

MRS. RIIS. Perhaps that is putting it too harshly. But why should you require her to believe a man any more readily than a man would believe her? Because he would not believe her for a moment.

RIIS (*coming up behind her*). Are you absolutely mad?

CHRISTENSEN (*half rising*). Excuse me, ladies and gentlemen; the two young people must settle the affair now! (*Sits down again.*)

ALFRED. I must confess I have never thought of what Mrs. Riis has just said, because such a thing never could happen. No man of honour would choose a woman of whose past he was not certain. Never!

MRS. RIIS. But what about a woman of honour, Alfred?

ALFRED. Ah, that is quite different.

NORDAN. To put it precisely: a woman owes a man both her past and her future; a man owes a woman only his future.

ALFRED. Well, if you like to put it that way—yes.

NORDAN (*to* SVAVA, *as he gets up*). I wanted you to postpone your answer, my child. But now I think you ought to answer at once. (SVAVA *goes up to* ALFRED, *flings her glove in his face, and goes straight into her room.* ALFRED *turns and looks after her.* RIIS *disappears into his room on the right. Every one has risen from their seats.* MRS. CHRISTENSEN *takes* ALFRED *by the arm and goes out with him;* CHRISTENSEN *follows them.* MRS. RIIS *is standing at the door of the room which* SVAVA *has locked after her.*)

NORDAN. That was throwing down a gauntlet, if you like!

MRS. RIIS (*calling through the door*). Svava!

CHRISTENSEN (*coming in and speaking to* NORDAN, *who has taken no notice of him and has not turned round*). Then it is to be war?—Well, I fancy I know a thing or two about war. (*Goes out.* NORDAN *turns round and stands looking after him.*)

MRS. RIIS (*still at the door*). Svava! (RIIS *comes rushing out of his room, with his hat on and his gloves and stick in his hand, and follows the* CHRISTENSENS.) Svava!

12. Bertha von Suttner (1889)

I shall speak of love as it was understood by our ancestors during the Machine Age: reverence would be out of place. This was no queen, but a chained, heavily veiled, slandered, disowned, tortured, despised slave, a slave without rights, who was pushed into the mire.

. . . At that time women and love were generally named in the same breath—a juxtaposition that once again clearly allotted to women the role of object rather than subject in matters of love. This theme provides an opportunity to consider a number of things that were not sufficiently discussed in the previous lecture. Love and marriage were the areas in which the apparent admiration but actual subjection of women were most clearly expressed. To men, love allotted rights and joys; to women, duties—and crimes. This most blessed drive was outlawed and overwhelmed by a heavy curse of sin; however, the curse lay entirely upon the heads of women—it was the "weak" sex that was expected to carry the burden of outlawry. . . .

. . . It is not easy to get a clear impression of the relationship between the sexes in the Machine Age because of the type of evidence transmitted. On the one hand we have moral condemnation—on the other, ecstatic adulation. On the one hand a reserve, a silence as though no such thing as the joys of love existed, while on the other there was a luxurious intoxication of excess. A theory of morals pressed with such weight upon the laws of chastity that they no longer appear to be only a part of morality—but indeed morality itself. Thus, for example, the word *immoral*, particularly when applied to females, did not concern offences against truthfulness, against integrity, against charitableness—it meant simply that the person in question was having a love affair. "Immoral literature" was not literature that aroused hatred of foreigners or attempted to suppress reason, but literature that dealt with the joys of love without condemning them. Had anyone dared to speak out at the time, my present lecture would perhaps also have been considered immoral. . . .

A whole class of people, however, shrugged off the pressure of these laws. They did so not merely by secret violations, but through open insistence that these laws of morality did not apply to them. This was the class of worldly young men. In defiance of the teaching of the catechism, which strictly insists that Christians must follow the sixth commandment, there developed first a silent, then gradually an open consensus that for men a free love-life was neither sinful nor dishonorable—in fact, the very opposite. Even the most deeply believing Christians only smiled at the virtues of the various Josephs of the Old and the New Testament; for the list of 1,003 seductions of Don Juan, there was only admiration. The condemnation connected with the satisfied drive of love was entirely observed for the female partners in the act. In order to produce the wellknown halo of fame surrounding Don Juan, one thousand and three sacrificial victims have had to sink into sin and sorrow, just as we must have the skulls of so many defeated enemies in order to provide the prized adornments of a savage chieftain.

You will understand that the majority of women could not be burdened with the amount of female shame thus created by men's irresponsibility; indeed, they were protected from it by their husbands and brothers. What then happened with this overflow of ignominy? A large group of women—contemptuously and patronizingly referred to as "fallen," and forced into this state by necessity, bad luck, or indiscretion—were destroyed by this disgrace. . . .

The type of love that was considered to be "pure" could be publicly displayed to the world; it received universal esteem and sympathy and was exaggerated in discussion and in poetry. It was boasted about so immoderately and so unjustifiably, its impact on the greatest of all life's questions was considered so important and so absorbing, that all those who had fallen in love felt that they had reached the decisive turning point in their fate.

Possession, the ultimate goal of desire in love, could be openly sought after and openly achieved only in the rarest cases—those cases when every other social condition permitted marriage. It is thus easy to imagine how much disorder this so-called unhappy, and so-called criminal, love bred in society. When we further consider that the achievement of this goal, a fact of nature desired equally strongly by both sexes, was permitted to one sex, but forbidden to the other; that one sex could pursue this goal by all imaginable means, while the other had to avoid it with all imaginable force of renunciation, then we can understand how unequal was the battle between men and women in this world. Pursuit and seduction were prerogatives of the "strong"; resistance, the duty of the "weak."

When the "weak," who were forced to fight not only against their attackers, but at the same time against their own passion, succumbed— who then was despised and punished? Naturally, the seducer, you will answer. Are you still so little able to grasp the spirit of the Machine Age as to assume that what is reasonable, what alone is logically thinkable would prevail? No indeed; senselessness was no reason to brand a concept as illogical; not only in matters of belief but in many other areas as well, absurdity was the rule.

In this case, moreover, it was not the seducer who was accused of a criminal act; she who was seduced was branded the criminal. She alone was forced to do penance—she was the "fallen woman."

He, the "strong," who had caused her, the "weak," to fall, was able to walk away smiling, and was often the first and most bitter among those who despised her. From her yielding, he derived only pleasure, only a gratification of his torturous desire, while she was aware of the extent of her sacrifice and the attendant risk: her honor and life were at stake. However, she loved and knew that she was beloved; from her own longing she knew how much he suffered, how much he also wrestled with the power of nature that overwhelmed them both, and she forgave the lack of love in his passion when he drew her into his arms toward probable destruction. She recognized that he acted not from baseness but under the impact of an irresistible natural force, and she assumed with complete trust that he acknowledged the same process in her. . . .

What, are you ashamed to admit that the basis of your most ecstatic feeling is a drive that you share with the animal world, and so you seek to disavow, if not to suffocate it? Why are you not ashamed of eating—a drive that you also share with animals, or the desire for sunlight that every plant shares with you? Indeed, you have failed to recognize the bond that unites you with the universe, and you persist with the greatest tenacity in your supposed position outside and above nature. And thus you assume a forced sundering of your being; the physical must be associated with the animal—nourishment, breathing, reproduction, these were the functions of matter common to all; but love—which is associated with heroics, sacrifice, enthusiasm, in short with the most noble soaring of the spirit—must not be connected with what is basely physical, not ever! And any sensuality you feel in the process must be fought against or suppressed. You deny love that is noble, that is "pure," the right to strive for physical union; and the higher or more delicate the sensibility, the more you want to tear it from the earthy materialism in which it is rooted. Only those women are considered worthy of this love who would rather die than yield; or those who, of the few with a dowry adequate for marriage, must be so "innocent" that they may not know what awaits them in marriage—. You do not understand that by mutilating spiritual love you have fostered the vice of prostitution, because today this is a vice of which honorable men would be ashamed—as in your day women were condemned to be ashamed of yielding with love but without legality. It was lust (the mere word was not permitted to pass pure lips) that you embraced in secret, to the point of destroying your health, and that you despise with deepest scorn as base animal sensuality. While all the agonies of love are considered as noble and may be bewailed in prose and verse, only the pleasure of love is a disgrace. This pleasure is connected with sensuality, you say scornfully; every animal experiences it; it belongs in the realm of filth and smut, to raw nature in contrast to that divine model after which mankind was created.

Why can you not understand that nature, which you misjudge and revile, is itself divine—as the poet says: perfect wherever man does not infest it with his afflictions. . . .

While the sentence announcing a person's execution for the morrow can be passed only once, the message: "Come (my love) I await you tonight"—as delightful as the other is grimly awful—can be received many times throughout one's life. In all of nature, where you see only the power of destruction, there reigns a stream of constant regenerative joy; for each painful death rattle, a hundred sighs of love ascend to heaven; louder and more irrepressible than the cry of despair uttered by the sacrifice of death, is the jubilant cry of bliss of a pair of lovers engaged in creating life; wherever you have penetrated "with your anguish" you have managed to transform the very joy offered you to counter-balance suffering and death into another source of new suffering. While it is a joy rooted like everything human in corporeality, it nevertheless increases in sensitivity with every refinement of the spirit; it is a joy that contains such a fulfillment of all desires, and such a satisfaction, that it was grasped at whenever possible, even when the penalty was death. Nevertheless, you have managed to turn this joy into a matter of the most painful renunciation or the most shameful vice. You have the deepest distrust of the greatest pleasure because of that unholy and sinister illusion—a remnant of that unreasonable dread of evil spirits and jealous gods—the illusion that even your "God of Love" will be honored by the sorrows of his creatures and insulted by their pleasures. While you glorify death and even murder so much that you know nothing greater and proclaim nothing more loudly than the fame of battles—there exists among you nothing that is more reviled, nothing that must be done more secretly than the creation of life. Death in "man-murdering battle" appears to you the most honorable and enviable, but the children of love are branded as dishonorable! You value death so highly that you find it worthy of having been suffered by God himself—painfully, bleeding and groaning on the cross; but the opposite of death under torture—that is, life created in bliss, is a thing you ascribe to Satan.

CHAPTER 2

Women's Work, Private Property, and the Social Order

The Marxist-Socialist Challenge

SOURCES

13. Friedrich Engels, *The Origin of the Family, Private Property, and the State, in the Light of the Researches of Lewis H. Morgan*, tr. Alick [Alec] West, from the 4th German ed., 1891 (New York, 1942), pp. 5-6, 41-43, 47-51, 54-56, 58, 65-66. Originally published as *Der Ursprung der Familie, des Privateigenthums und des Staats* (Zurich, 1884).

14. Eleanor Marx and Edward Aveling, "The Woman Question: From a Socialist Point of View," *Westminster Review*, 125 (Jan.-Apr. 1886), 207-12, 219-22.

15. Clara Zetkin, "Für die Befreiung der Frau! Rede auf dem Internationalen Arbeiterkongress zu Paris, 19 Juli 1889," *Protokoll des Internationalen Arbeiter-Congresses zu Paris, 14-20 Juli 1889* (Nürnberg, 1890), pp. 80-85. Tr. SGB.

The following selections represent landmarks in the attempt of Marxist socialists to confront the woman question during the 1880's. The first selection is taken from Friedrich Engels' *Origin of the Family*. Engels (1820-1895) made it his job following the death of Karl Marx to interpret—on the basis of Marx's notes and the theory of historical materialism—the contribution of the American anthropologist Lewis Henry Morgan to the discussion of the origins and future of the family. As these excerpts reveal, he also drew on Darwinian concepts of sexual selection and on the work of Bachofen on matriarchy (see Vol. I, Docs. 102, 110) in constructing his arguments. Engels went beyond Marx, as recent analysts have pointed out, in developing Herbert Spencer's juxtaposition (Vol. I, Doc. 112) of production and reproduction. Engels' *Origins* has been translated into many languages and, despite much criticism, continues to attract readers as a classic work of Marxist history and theory.

Only two years after the publication of Engels' work, Eleanor Marx (1855-1898) and Edward Aveling (1851-1898) presented the Marxist understanding of the woman question to the English public. Their essay was presented under the guise of a review of an English translation of the German socialist August Bebel's *Woman under Socialism*, which had recently been banned in Germany. Here Marx's daughter and her life-companion (whose name she had assumed, though they were never married) echo Flora Tristan's and Hubertine Auclert's (see Vol. I, Docs. 60, 142, 143) linkage of the oppression of women with that of the proletariat—insisting, as Engels had, on the economic roots of women's oppression in capitalist society. Condemning mercenary marriage, prostitution, separation of the sexes, "unnatural" chastity, and inadequate sex education, Marx and Aveling recapitulate virtually all the complaints made about women's oppression during the nineteenth century. But they argue that class relations—the consequence of unequal division of property—not sex distinctions, are the problem. They prophesy the inevitable transformation of capitalism into socialism, with the overthrow by the proletariat of the capitalistic system of production. Subsequently, *after* the revolution that will bring about the classless society, the perfect equality of women with men will prevail, and a material independence for women that would enable them to realize their full potential as individuals.

The third selection is from a speech on women's work in the productive sector by Clara Zetkin (1857-1933), given in Paris during the 1889 workers' congress that founded the Second International Workingmen's Association. Zetkin, born Clara Eissner in Saxony, had been encouraged to develop her interest in women's rights by her mother and by meeting the leaders of the German women's movement in Leipzig while she was a student there. During the years when the Social Democratic Party (SPD) was outlawed in Germany, Zetkin lived in Paris with a Russian revolutionary. Though she took his name and bore two children with him, they had never formally married: Zetkin feared losing her German citizenship if she did. During the last three years of her companion's illness, Zetkin supported the entire family. Thus her speech in Paris (and her subsequent career as a women's organizer in the SPD) was informed by her own vivid experiences as a mother, sick-nurse, helpmeet, and wage-earner. After her companion's death and the lifting of the ban on the SPD in 1890, Zetkin returned to Germany and spearheaded the formation of a separate movement for women outside the party framework; her group offered women, until 1908, a way to participate in the socialist movement without violating the German association laws of the 1850's (Vol. I, Doc. 86), which forbade any such participation.

At no time did Zetkin or any of the Marxist socialists of the late nineteenth century seek to alter the traditional division of labor between women and men. Instead, they sought to render women economically independent so that, by setting their own terms, they could become better mothers and more companionable wives while awaiting the revolution. In 1907, however, Socialist women did urge the member parties of the Second International to pursue the revisionist reform of woman suffrage in order to offset the appeal of the bourgeois women's campaign for the vote in England, France, Germany, and Russia (Doc. 59).

---

13. Friedrich Engels (1884)

According to the materialistic conception, the determining factor in history is, in the final instance, the production and reproduction of the immediate essentials of life. This, again, is of a twofold character. On the one side, the production of the means of existence, of articles of food and clothing, dwellings, and of the tools necessary for that production; on the other side, the production of human beings themselves, the propagation of the species. The social organization under which the people of a particular historical epoch and a particular country live is determined by both kinds of production: by the stage of development of labor on the one hand and of the family on the other. The lower the development of labor and the more limited the amount of its products, and consequently, the more limited also the wealth of the society, the more the social order is found to be dominated by kinship groups. However, within this structure of society based on kinship groups the productivity of labor increasingly develops, and with it private property and exchange, differences of wealth, the possibility of utilizing the labor power of others, and hence the basis of class antagonisms: new social elements, which in the course of generations strive to adapt the old social order to the new conditions, until at last their incompatibility brings about a complete upheaval. In the collision of the newly-developed social classes, the old society founded on kinship groups is broken up; in its place appears a new society, with its control centered in the state, the subordinate units of which are no longer kinship associations, but local associations; a society in which the system of the family is completely dominated by the system of property, and in which there now freely develop those class antagonisms and class struggles that have hitherto formed the content of all *written* history. . . .

The history of the family in primitive times consists in the progressive narrowing of the circle, originally embracing the whole tribe, within which the two sexes have a common conjugal relation. The continuous exclusion, first of nearer, then of more and more remote relatives, and at last even of relatives by marriage, ends by making any kind of group marriage practically impossible. Finally, there remains only the single, still loosely linked pair, the molecule with whose dissolution marriage itself ceases. This in itself shows what a small part individual sex-love, in the modern sense of the word, played in the rise of monogamy. Yet stronger proof is afforded by the practice of all peoples at this stage of development. Whereas in the earlier forms of the family men never lacked women, but, on the contrary, had too many rather than too few, women had now become scarce and highly sought after. Hence it is with the pairing marriage that there begins the capture and purchase of women— widespread *symptoms*, but no more than symptoms, of the much deeper change that had occurred. . . .

The pairing family, itself too weak and unstable to make an independent household necessary or even desirable, in no wise destroys the communistic household inherited from earlier times. Communistic housekeeping, however, means the supremacy of women in the house; just as the exclusive recognition of the female parent, owing to the impossibility of recognizing the male parent with certainty, means that the women— the mothers—are held in high respect. One of the most absurd notions ever taken over from eighteenth-century enlightenment is that in the beginning of society woman was the slave of man. Among all savages and all barbarians of the lower and middle stages, and to a certain extent of the upper stage also, the position of women is not only free, but honorable. . . .

The communistic household, in which most or all of the women belong to one and the same gens, while the men come from various gentes, is the material foundation of that supremacy of the women which was general in primitive times, and which it is Bachofen's third great merit to have discovered. The reports of travelers and missionaries, I may add, to the effect that women among savages and barbarians are overburdened with work in no way contradict what has been said. The division of labor between the two sexes is determined by quite other causes than by the position of woman in society. Among peoples where the women have to work far harder than we think suitable, there is often much more real respect for women than among our Europeans. The lady of civilization, surrounded by false homage and estranged from all real work, has an infinitely lower social position than the hard-working woman of barbarism, who was regarded among her people as a real lady (lady, *frowa, Frau*— mistress) and who was also a lady in character. . . .

Bachofen is also perfectly right when he consistently maintains that the transition from what he calls "hetærism" or "*Sumpfzeugung*" to monogamy was brought about primarily through the women. The more traditional sexual relations lost the naïve primitive character of forest life, owing to the development of economic conditions with consequent undermining of the old communism and growing density of population, the more oppressive and humiliating must the women have felt them to be, and the greater their longing for the right of chastity, of temporary or permanent marriage with one man only, as a way of release. This advance could not in any case have originated with the men, if only because it has never occurred to them, even to this day, to renounce the pleasures of actual group marriage. Only when the women had brought about the transition to pairing marriage were the men able to introduce strict monogamy—though indeed only for women.

The first beginnings of the pairing family appear on the dividing line between savagery and barbarism; they are generally to be found already at the upper stage of savagery, but occasionally not until the lower stage of barbarism. The pairing family is the form characteristic of barbarism, as group marriage is characteristic of savagery and monogamy of civilization. To develop it further, to strict monogamy, other causes were required than those we have found active hitherto. In the single pair the group was already reduced to its final unit, its two-atom molecule: one man and one woman. Natural selection, with its progressive exclusions from the marriage community, had accomplished its task; there was nothing more for it to do in this direction. Unless new, *social* forces came into play, there was no reason why a new form of family should arise from the single pair. But these new forces did come into play.

We now leave America, the classic soil of the pairing family. No sign allows us to conclude that a higher form of family developed here, or that there was ever permanent monogamy anywhere in America prior to its discovery and conquest. But not so in the Old World.

Here the domestication of animals and the breeding of herds had developed a hitherto unsuspected source of wealth and created entirely new social relations. Up to the lower stage of barbarism, permanent wealth had consisted almost solely of house, clothing, crude ornaments and the tools for obtaining and preparing food—boat, weapons, and domestic utensils of the simplest kind. Food had to be won afresh day by day. Now, with their herds of horses, camels, asses, cattle, sheep, goats, and pigs, the advancing pastoral peoples—the Semites on the Euphrates and the Tigris, and the Aryans in the Indian country of the Five Streams (Punjab), in the Ganges region, and in the steppes then much more abundantly watered of the Oxus and the Jaxartes—had acquired property which only needed supervision and the rudest care to reproduce itself in steadily increasing quantities and to supply the most abundant food in the form of milk and meat. All former means of procuring food now receded into the background; hunting, formerly a necessity, now became a luxury.

But to whom did this new wealth belong? Originally to the gens, without a doubt. Private property in herds must have already started at an early period, however. It is difficult to say whether the author of the so-called first book of Moses regarded the patriarch Abraham as the owner of his herds in his own right as head of a family community or by right of his position as actual hereditary head of a gens. What is certain is that we must not think of him as a property owner in the modern sense of the word. And it is also certain that at the threshold of authentic history we already find the herds everywhere separately owned by heads of families, as are the artistic products of barbarism—metal implements, luxury articles and, finally, the human cattle—the slaves.

For now slavery had also been invented. To the barbarian of the lower stage, a slave was valueless. Hence the treatment of defeated enemies by the American Indians was quite different from that at a higher stage. The men were killed or adopted as brothers into the tribe of the victors; the women were taken as wives or otherwise adopted with their surviving children. At this stage human labor-power still does not produce any considerable surplus over and above its maintenance costs. That was no longer the case after the introduction of cattle-breeding, metal-working, weaving and, lastly, agriculture. Just as the wives whom it had formerly been so easy to obtain had now acquired an exchange value and were bought, so also with the forces of labor, particularly since the herds had definitely become family possessions. The family did not multiply so rapidly as the cattle. More people were needed to look after them; for this purpose use could be made of the enemies captured in war, who could also be bred just as easily as the cattle themselves.

Once it had passed into the private possession of families and there rapidly begun to augment, this wealth dealt a severe blow to the society founded on pairing marriage and the matriarchal gens. Pairing marriage had brought a new element into the family. By the side of the natural mother of the child it placed its natural and attested father, with a better warrant of paternity, probably, than that of many a "father" today. According to the division of labor within the family at that time, it was the man's part to obtain food and the instruments of labor necessary for the purpose. He therefore also owned the instruments of labor, and in the event of husband and wife separating, he took them with him, just as she retained her household goods. Therefore, according to the social custom of the time, the man was also the owner of the new source of subsistence, the cattle, and later of the new instruments of labor, the slaves. But according to the custom of the same society, his children could not inherit from him. For as regards inheritance, the position was as follows:

At first, according to mother-right—so long, therefore, as descent was reckoned only in the female line—and according to the original custom of inheritance within the gens, the gentile relatives inherited from a deceased fellow member of their gens. His property had to remain within the gens. His effects being insignificant, they probably always passed in practice to his nearest gentile relations—that is, to his blood relations on the mother's side. The children of the dead man, however, did not belong to his gens, but to that of their mother; it was from her that they inherited, at first conjointly with her other blood-relations, later perhaps with rights of priority; they could not inherit from their father, because they did not belong to his gens, within which his property had to remain. When the owner of the herds died, therefore, his herds would go first to his brothers and sisters and to his sister's children, or to the issue of his mother's sisters. But his own children were disinherited.

Thus, on the one hand, in proportion as wealth increased, it made the man's position in the family more important than the woman's, and on the other hand created an impulse to exploit this strengthened position in order to overthrow, in favor of his children, the traditional order of inheritance. This, however, was impossible so long as descent was reckoned according to mother-right. Mother-right, therefore, had to be overthrown, and overthrown it was. This was by no means so difficult as it looks to us today. For this revolution—one of the most decisive ever experienced by humanity—could take place without disturbing a single one of the living members of a gens. All could remain as they were. A simple decree sufficed that in the future the offspring of the male members should remain within the gens, but that of the female should be excluded by being transferred to the gens of their father. The reckoning of descent in the female line and the matriarchal law of inheritance were thereby overthrown, and the male line of descent and the paternal law of inheritance were substituted for them. As to how and when its revolution took place among civilized peoples, we have no knowledge. It falls entirely within prehistoric times. But that it *did* take place is more than sufficiently proved by the abundant traces of mother-right which have been collected, particularly by Bachofen. How easily it is accomplished can be seen in a whole series of American Indian tribes, where it has only recently taken place and is still taking place under the influence, partly of increasing wealth and a changed mode of life (transference from forest to prairie), and partly of the moral pressure of civilization and missionaries. Of eight Missouri tribes, six observe the male line of descent and inheritance, two still observe the female. Among the Shawnees, Miamis, and Delawares the custom has grown up of giving the children a gentile name of their father's gens in order to transfer them into it, thus enabling them to inherit from him.

Man's innate casuistry! To change things by changing their names! And to find loopholes for violating trading while maintaining tradition, when direct interest supplied sufficient impulse.

(Marx.)

The result was hopeless confusion, which could only be remedied and to a certain extent was remedied by the transition to father-right. . . .

The overthrow of mother-right was the *world historical defeat of the female sex*. The man took command in the home also; the woman was degraded and reduced to servitude, she became the slave of his lust and a mere instrument for the production of children. This degraded position of the woman, especially conspicuous among the Greeks of the heroic and still more of the classical age, has gradually been palliated and glozed over, and sometimes clothed in a milder form; in no sense has it been abolished.

The establishment of the exclusive supremacy of the man shows its effects first in the patriarchal family, which now emerges as an intermediate form. Its essential characteristic is not polygyny, of which more later, but "the organization of a number of persons, bond and free, into a family, under paternal power, for the purpose of holding lands, and for the care of flocks and herds. . . . (In the Semitic form) the chiefs, at least, lived in polygamy. . . . Those held to servitude, and those employed as servants, lived in the marriage relation."

Its essential features are the incorporation of unfree persons, and paternal power; hence the perfect type of this form of family is the Roman. The original meaning of the word "family" (*familia*) is not that compound of sentimentality and domestic strife which forms the ideal of the present-day philistine; among the Romans it did not at first even refer to the married pair and their children, but only to the slaves. *Famulus* means domestic slave, and *familia* is the total number of slaves belonging to one man. As late as the time of Gaius, the *familia, id est patrimonium* (family, that is, the patrimony, the inheritance) was bequeathed by will. The term was invented by the Romans to denote a new social organism, whose head ruled over wife and children and a number of slaves, and was invested under Roman paternal power with rights of life and death over them all.

This term, therefore, is no older than the iron-clad family system of the Latin tribes, which came in after field agriculture and after legalized servitude, as well as after the separation of the Greeks and Latins.

Marx adds:

The modern family contains in germ not only slavery (servitus), but also serfdom, since from the beginning it is related to agricultural services. It contains *in miniature* all the contradictions which later extend throughout society and its state.

Such a form of family shows the transition of the pairing family to monogamy. In order to make certain of the wife's fidelity and therefore of the paternity of the children, she is delivered over unconditionally into the power of the husband; if he kills her, he is only exercising his rights. . . .

The monogamous family develops out of the pairing family, as previously shown, in the transitional period between the upper and middle stages of barbarism; its decisive victory is one of the signs that civilization is beginning. It is based on the supremacy of the man, the express purpose being to produce children of undisputed paternity; such paternity is demanded because these children are later to come into their father's property as his natural heirs. It is distinguished from pairing marriage by the much greater strength of the marriage tie, which can no longer be dissolved at either partner's wish. As a rule, it is now only the man who can dissolve it, and put away his wife. The right of conjugal infidelity also remains secured to him, at any rate by custom (the *Code Napoléon* explicitly accords it to the husband as long as he does not bring his concubine into the house), and as social life develops he exercises his right more and more; should the wife recall the old form of sexual life and attempt to revive it, she is punished more severely than ever.

We meet this new form of the family in all its severity among the Greeks. While the position of the goddesses in their mythology, as Marx points out, brings before us an earlier period when the position of women was freer and more respected, in the heroic age we find the woman already being humiliated by the domination of the man and by competition from girl slaves. . . . In the heroic age a Greek woman is, indeed, more respected than in the period of civilization, but to her husband she is after all nothing but the mother of his legitimate children and heirs, his chief housekeeper and the supervisor of his female slaves, whom he can and does take as concubines if he so fancies. It is the existence of slavery side by side with monogamy, the presence of young, beautiful slaves belonging unreservedly to the *man*, that stamps monogamy from the very beginning with its specific character of monogamy *for the woman only*, but not for the man. And that is the character it still has today. . . .

Thus when monogamous marriage first makes its appearance in history, it is not as the reconciliation of man and woman, still less as the highest form of such a reconciliation. Quite the contrary. Monogamous marriage comes on the scene as the subjugation of the one sex by the other; it announces a struggle between the sexes unknown throughout the whole previous prehistoric period. In an old unpublished manuscript, written by Marx and myself in 1846,* I find the words: "The first division of labor is that between man and woman for the propagation of children." And today I can add: The first class opposition that appears in history coincides with the development of the antagonism between man and woman in monogamous marriage, and the first class oppression coincides with that of the female sex by the male. . . .

In the great majority of cases today, at least in the possessing classes, the husband is obliged to earn a living and support his family, and that in itself gives him a position of supremacy, without any need for special legal titles and privileges. Within the family he is the bourgeois and the wife represents the proletariat. In the industrial world, the specific character of the economic oppression burdening the proletariat is visible in all its sharpness only when all special legal privileges of the capitalist class have been abolished and complete legal equality of both classes established. The democratic republic does not do away with the opposition of the two classes; on the contrary, it provides the clear field on which the fight can be fought out. And in the same way, the peculiar character of the supremacy of the husband over the wife in the modern family, the necessity of creating real social equality between them, and the way to do it, will only be seen in the clear light of day when both possess legally complete equality of rights. Then it will be plain that the first condition for the liberation of the wife is to bring the whole female sex back into public industry, and that this in turn demands the abolition of the monogamous family as the economic unit of society. . . .

14. Eleanor Marx and Edward Aveling (1886)

The publication of August Bebel's "Die Frau in der Vergangenheit, Gegenwart, und Zukunft," and the issue of a translation of the work in English, make any attempt to explain the position of Socialists in respect to the woman question timely. The reception that the work has met with in Germany and in England renders such an attempt imperative, unless our antagonists are willing to misunderstand us, and we are willing to remain passive under the misunderstanding. The writers of this article have thought that the English public, with that fairness which is said to be its special prerogative, would give hearing to the views, the arguments, the conclusions of those who call themselves Socialists. Thus, whatever opinions may be held by that English public as to the conclusions, its opinions will at least have a basis of knowledge. And the writers have further considered that the treatment of such a question as this is at its best when it is that of a man and a woman thinking and working together. In all that follows they desire it to be understood that they are giving utterance to their own opinions as two individual Socialists. Whilst they believe that these opinions are shared by the majority of their

*Engels here refers to a work, *Deutsche Ideologie*, that remained unpublished until 1932.—EDS.

fellow-thinkers and fellow-workers in England, on the Continent, and in America, they are in no sense to be understood as pledging their Party to all, or necessarily to any particular one, of the propositions put forward. . . .

Society is, from the point of view of Bebel, and we may fairly say here of Socialists generally, in a condition of unrest, of fermentation. The unrest is that of a mass of rottenness; the fermentation that of putrefaction. Dissolution is at hand, in both senses of the word. The death of the capitalistic method of production, and therefore of the society based on it, is, as we think, within a distance measurable in terms of years rather than of centuries. And that death means the re-solution of society into simpler forms, even into elements, that re-combining will produce a new and better order of things. Society is morally bankrupt, and in nothing does this gruesome moral bankruptcy come out with a more hideous distinctness than in the relation between men and women. Efforts to postpone the crash by drawing bills upon the imagination are useless. The facts have to be faced.

One of these facts of the most fundamental importance is not, and never has been, fairly confronted by the average man or woman in considering these relations. It has not been understood even by those men and women above the average who have made the struggle for the greater freedom of women the very business of their lives. This fundamental fact is, that the question is one of economics. The position of women rests, as everything in our complex modern society rests, on an economic basis. Had Bebel done nothing but insist upon this, his work would have been valuable. The woman question is one of the organization of society as a whole. . . . Those who attack the present treatment of women without seeking for the cause of this in the economics of our latter-day society are like doctors who treat a local affection without inquiring into the general bodily health.

This criticism applies not alone to the commonplace person who makes a jest of any discussion into which the element of sex enters. It applies to those higher natures, in many cases earnest and thoughtful, who see that women are in a parlous state, and are anxious that something should be done to better their condition. These are the excellent and hard-working folk who agitate for that perfectly just aim, woman suffrage; for the repeal of the Contagious Diseases Act, a monstrosity begotten of male cowardice and brutality; for the higher education of women; for the opening to them of universities, the learned professions, and all callings, from that of teacher to that of bag-man. In all this work—good as far as it goes—three things are especially notable. First, those concerned in it are of the well-to-do classes, as a rule. With the single and only partial exception of the Contagious Diseases agitation, scarcely any of the women taking a prominent part in these various movements belong to the working class. We are prepared for the comment that something very like this may be said, as far as concerns England, of the larger movement that claims our special efforts. Certainly,

Socialism is at present in this country little more than a literary move-ment. It has but a fringe of working men on its border. But we can answer to this criticism that in Germany this is not the case, and that even here Socialism is now beginning to extend among the workers.

The second point is that all these ideas of our "advanced" women are based either on property, or on sentimental or professional questions. Not one of them gets down through these to the bed-rock of the eco-nomic basis, not only of each of these three, but of society itself. This fact is not astonishing to those who note the ignorance of economics charac-teristic of most of those that labour for the enfranchisement of women. Judging from the writings and speeches of the majority of women's advo-cates, no attention has been given by them to the study of the evolution of society. Even the orthodox political economy, which is, as we think, mis-leading in its statements and inaccurate in its conclusions, does not ap-pear to have been mastered generally.

The third point grows out of the second. The school of whom we speak make no suggestion that is outside the limits of the society of to-day. Hence their work is, always from our point of view, of little value. We will suppose all women, not only those having property, enabled to vote; the Contagious Diseases Act repealed; every calling thrown open to both sexes. The actual position of women in respect to men would not be very vitally touched. (We are not concerned at present with the results of the increased competition and more embittered struggle for existence.) For not one of these things, save indirectly the Contagious Diseases Act, touches them in their sex relations. Nor should we deny that, with the gain of each or all of these points, the tremendous change that is to come would be more easy of attainment. But it is essential to keep in mind that ultimate change, only to come about when the yet more tremendous so-cial change whose corollary it will be has taken place. Without that larger social change women will never be free.

The truth, not fully recognized even by those anxious to do good to woman, is that she, like the labour-classes, is in an oppressed condition; that her position, like theirs, is one of unjust and merciless degradation. Women are the creatures of an organized tyranny of men, as the workers are the creatures of an organized tyranny of idlers. Even where thus much is grasped, we must never be weary of insisting on the non-understanding that for women, as for the labouring classes, no solution of the difficulties and problems that present themselves is really possible in the present con-dition of society. All that is done, heralded with no matter what flourish of trumpets, is palliative, not remedial. Both the oppressed classes, women and the immediate producers, must understand that their eman-cipation will come from themselves. Women will find allies in the better sort of men, as the labourers are finding allies among the philosophers, artists, and poets. But the one has nothing to hope from man as a whole, and the other has nothing to hope from the middle-class as a whole.

The truth of this comes out in the fact that, before we pass to the con-sideration of the condition of women, we have to speak this word of warning. To many, that which we have to say of the Now will seem exaggerated; much that we have to say of the Hereafter, visionary, and perhaps all that is said, dangerous. To cultured people, public opinion is still that of man alone, and the customary is the moral. The majority still lays stress upon the occasional sex-helplessness of woman as a bar to her even consideration with man. It still descants upon the "natural calling" of the female. As to the former, people forget that sex-helplessness at certain times is largely exaggerated by the unhealthy conditions of our modern life, if, indeed, it is not wholly due to these. Given rational conditions, it would largely, if not completely, disappear. They forget also that all this about which the talk is so glib when woman's freedom is under discussion is conveniently ignored when the question is one of woman's enslavement. They forget that by capitalist employers this very sex-helplessness of woman is only taken into account with the view of lowering the general rate of wages. Again, there is no more a "natural calling" of woman than there is a "natural" law of capitalistic production, or a "natural" limit to the amount of the labourer's product that goes to him for means of subsistence. That, in the first case, woman's "calling" is supposed to be only the tending of children, the maintenance of household conditions, and a general obedience to her lord; that, in the second, the production of surplus-value is a necessary preliminary to the production of capital; that, in the third, the amount the labourer receives for his means of subsistence is so much as will keep him only just above starvation point: these are not natural laws in the same sense as are the laws of motion. . . .

What is it that we as Socialists desire? What is it that we expect? What is that of whose coming we feel as assured as of the rising of to-morrow's sun? What are the evolution changes in society that we believe are already close at hand? And what are the changes in the condition of woman that we anticipate as consequence of these? Let us disclaim all intention of the prophetic. He that, reasoning on a series of observed phenomena, sees the inevitable event to which they lead is no prophet. A man cannot prophesy any more than he has a right to wager, about a certainty. To us it seems clear that as in England the Germanic society, whose basis was the free landholder, gave way to the feudal system, and this to the capitalistic, so this last, no more eternal than its predecessors, will give way to the Socialistic system; that as slavery passed into serfdom, and serfdom into the wage-slavery of to-day, so this last will pass into the condition where all the means of production will belong neither to slaveowner, nor to serf's lord, nor to the wage-slave's master, the capitalist, but to the community as a whole. At the risk of raising the habitual smile and sneer, we confess that into every detail of that Socialist working of society we are no more prepared to enter than were the first capitalists to enter into the details of the system that they founded. Nothing is more common, nothing is more unjust, nothing is more indicative of meagre understanding, than the vulgar clamour for exact details of things under the social condition towards which we believe the world is moving. No expounder of any new great truth, no one of his followers, can hope to work out all the truth into its ultimate ramifications. What would have been thought of those who rejected the gravitation discovery of Newton because he had not, by application of it, found out Neptune? Or of those who rejected the Darwinian theory of Natural Selection because Instinct presented certain difficulties? Yet this is precisely what the average opponents of Socialism do; always with a vacuous calmness, ignoring the fact that for every difficulty or misery they suppose will arise from the socialization of the means of production a score worse are actually existent in the putrescent society of to-day.

What is it that we feel certain is coming? We have wandered so far from Bebel along our own lines of thought, at the entrance of whose ways his suggestive work has generally placed us, that for the answer to this question we return gladly and gratefully to him. "A society in which all the means of production are the property of the community, a society which recognizes the full equality of all without distinction of sex, which provides for the application of every kind of technical and scientific improvement or discovery, which enrolls as workers all those who are at present unproductive, or whose activity assumes an injurious shape, the idlers and the drones, and which, while it minimizes the period of labour necessary for its support, raises the mental and physical condition of all its members to the highest attainable pitch."

We disguise neither from ourselves nor from our antagonists that the first step to this is the expropriation of all private property in land and in all other means of production. With this would happen the abolition of the State as it now is. No confusion as to our aims is more common than that which leads woolly thinking people to imagine that the changes we desire can be brought about, and the conditions subsequent upon them can exist, under a State régime such as that of to-day. The State is now a force-organization for the maintenance of the present conditions of property and of social rule. Its representatives are a few middle and upper-class men contending for places yielding abnormal salaries. The State under Socialism, if indeed a word of such ugly historical associations is retained, will be the organized capacity of a community of workers. Its officials will be no better and no worse off than their fellows. The divorce between art and labour, the antagonism between head and hand work, that grieves the souls of artists, without their knowing in most cases the economic cause of their grief, will vanish.

And now comes the question as to how the future position of woman, and therefore of the race, will be affected by all this. Of one or two things we may be very sure. Others the evolution of society alone will decide positively, though every one of us may have his own idea upon each particular point. Clearly there will be equality for all, without distinction of sex. Thus, woman will be independent: her education and all other opportunities as those of man. Like him, she, if sound in mind and body (and how the number of women thus will grow!) will have to give her one, two, or three hours of social labour to supply the wants of the community, and therefore of herself. Thereafter she will be free for art or science, or teaching or writing, or amusement in any form. Prostitution will have vanished with the economic conditions that made it, and make it at this hour, a necessity.

Whether monogamy or polygamy will obtain in the Socialistic state is a detail on which one can only speak as an individual. The question is too large to be solved within the mists and miasmata of the capitalistic system. Personally, we believe that monogamy will gain the day. There are approximately equal numbers of men and women, and the highest ideal seems to be the complete, harmonious, lasting blending of two human lives. Such an ideal, almost never attainable to-day, needs at least four things. These are love, respect, intellectual likeness, and command of the necessaries of life. Each of these four is far more possible under the system towards which we move than under that in which we now scarce "have our being." The last is absolutely ensured to all. As Ibsen makes Helmer say to Nora, "Home life ceases to be free and beautiful directly its foundations are borrowing and debts." But borrowing and debts, when one is a member of a community, and not an isolated man fighting for his own hand, can never come. Intellectual likeness. The same education for men and women; the bringing up of these twain side by side, until they join hands at last, will ensure a greater degree of this. That objectionable product of capitalism, Tennyson's "In Memoriam" young woman, with her "I cannot understand, I love," will be a myth. Every one will have learnt that there can be no love without understanding. And the love and respect that are wanting or are lost to-day, because of sins and shortcomings, the product of the commercial system of society, will be more easily forthcoming, and vanish almost never. The contract between man and woman will be of a purely private nature, without the intervention of any public functionary. The woman will no longer be the man's slave, but his equal. For divorce there will be no need.

And whether we are right or not in regarding monogamy as the best form for society, we may be sure that the best form will be chosen, and that by wisdoms riper and richer than ours. We may be equally sure that the choice will not be of the barter-marriages, with its one-sided polygamy, of our own sad time. Above all, we may be sure that two great curses that help, with others, to ruin the relations between men and women will have passed. Those curses are the treatment of men and women as different beings, and the want of truth. There will no longer be one law for the woman and one for the man. If the coming society, like European society to-day, regards it as right for man to have mistresses as well as wife, we may be certain that the like freedom will be extended to women. Nor will there be the hideous disguise, the constant lying, that makes the domestic life of almost all our English homes an organized hypocrisy. Whatever the matured and deliberate opinion of the community finds best will be carried out fairly, openly. Husband and wife will be able to do that which but few can do now—look clear through one another's eyes into one another's heart. For ourselves, we believe that the cleaving of one man to one woman will be best for all, and that these will find each in the heart of the other, that which is in the eyes, their own image.

15. Clara Zetkin (1889)

Citizeness Zetkin, delegate of Berlin working women, began to speak on the subject of women's work, accompanied by enthusiastic applause. She explained that she did not intend to report on the condition of female laborers, because it was similar to that of male laborers. However, following the mandate of her colleagues, she would analyze the question of women's work as a theoretical principle. As confusion reigned on the question of women's work, it was essential that an international congress of labor should pronounce clearly on this topic, while considering the question of principle.

The speaker considered it hardly surprising that reactionary elements should view women's work in a reactionary manner. It was, however, most surprising that among socialists one found the strange notion demanding the abolition of women's work.

"Women's emancipation is basically a question of women's work, and one reasonably expects a deeper understanding of economic questions among socialists than that displayed in the attitude just described. Socialists must know that women's work is a necessity for present-day economic development; they must know that women's work will result in shortening the working hours dedicated to society by individuals and will increase that society's wealth; they must know that it is not the competition of women's work per se, but rather capitalistic exploitation of women's labor that depresses the wages of men. Socialists must know, above all, that slavery or freedom depend upon economic dependence or independence.

"Those who have inscribed the liberation of mankind upon their banners must not condemn half of humanity to political and social slavery through economic dependence. As the worker is subjected to the capitalist, so is woman subjected to man; and she will remain subjected as long as she is economically dependent. Work is the essential condition upon which this economic independence of woman is based. If we wish women to be free human beings, to have the same rights as men in our society, women's work must be neither abolished nor limited except in certain quite isolated cases.

"Women workers who aspire to social equality do not expect emancipation through the bourgeois women's movement, which claims to be fighting for women's rights. This structure is built upon sand and has no basis in reality. Working women are absolutely convinced that the question of women's emancipation cannot be isolated and exist in a vacuum, but that it must be seen as part of the great social question. They understand clearly that this question will never be resolved in our society as presently constituted, but only following a complete overthrow of this society. The question of women's emancipation is a child of modern times and is born of the machine. In the period of the Renaissance, women and men were intellectually and socially equal, and no one thought of discussing the question of woman's emancipation.*

"Woman's emancipation means a complete alteration of her basic social position, a revolution of her role in the economy. The old forms of production with unsophisticated tools and machinery chained woman to the family and limited her sphere of activity to the interior of her house. In the bosom of the family women presented an extraordinarily productive work force. They produced almost all the family's necessities. Historic conditions of production and commerce made it difficult, if not impossible, to produce these articles outside the family. While ancient conditions of production existed, women were economically productive. . . . With the change in conditions of production that no longer allowed women productive activity, women became consumers. This turnabout contributed strongly to a decrease in marriages.

"Machine production has killed off women's economic productivity within the family. Large-scale industry produces all articles more cheaply, more quickly, and in larger numbers than was ever possible in individual homes that operated with primitive tools and minuscule output. Women had to pay more for small amounts of raw materials than it cost to buy the finished product of an industrial machine. Added to the price of the raw material was her time and labor. Thus, the productive activity within the family became economic nonsense, a waste of energy and time. While in isolated cases a woman may be usefully employed actively producing goods in the bosom of her family, for society as a whole this type of production signifies a loss.

"This is the reason why the domestically productive woman of the good old days has almost disappeared. Large-scale industry has made it unnecessary to produce articles at home for the family; large-scale industry has nullified the domestic production of women. At the same time it has created a base for women's activity in society. Mechanical production, needing neither muscles nor qualified labor, makes large-scale employment of women possible. Women entered industry desiring to increase the family income. With the development of modern industry, women's labor within industry became essential. And with each modern improvement, male labor became superfluous, thousands of men were dismissed, a reserve army of the poor was thus created, and wages sank to ever-decreasing lows.

"At one time a man's income, together with his wife's productive domestic activity, adequately ensured the family existence; now a man's income barely supports a single laborer. The married laborer must rely on the paid labor of his wife.

"This fact frees women from their economic dependence on men. A woman working in industry, who cannot remain within the family as a mere economic appendage of her husband, learns how to be self-

---

* Zetkin was wrong; the question of women's emancipation was clearly posed by Christine de Pizan in the fifteenth century.—EDS.

sufficient as an economic force, independent of her husband. When, however, a woman is no longer economically dependent upon her husband, there is no sensible reason for her social dependence upon him. As it happens, this economic independence at present is, to be sure, advantageous not for women, but for the capitalist system. Through the force of their monopoly of the means of production, capitalists seized this new economic factor and have used it to their own exclusive advantage. Woman, liberated from economic dependence upon her husband, has become subjected to the economic sovereignty of the capitalist; from being the slave of the husband, she has become the slave of the employer; she has simply changed her master. Nevertheless, she has gained something by the change; she is no longer economically inferior, and economically subject to her husband, but his equal. The capitalist, however, is not content to exploit the woman herself; he makes her doubly useful by exploiting male laborers more and more thoroughly with female assistance.

"From the start, the price of women's labor was less than that of men. Male wages were originally calibrated so that they would cover the needs of the entire family; female wages, from the beginning, accounted only for the subsistence of a single person and then only partially, because it was anticipated that women would continue to labor at home apart from their work in the factory. Further, because of their primitive tools, the products created by women in the home represented only a minuscule quantity, of uncertain social value compared with the products of large-scale industry. It was therefore concluded that women's working capacity was inferior, and this, in turn, led to their being paid lower wages. Added to these reasons for low pay was the idea that women in general have fewer needs than men.

"The most valuable aspect to the capitalist, however, was not the cheap labor of women, but their greater subordination. Capitalists speculated on two specific points: one, to pay women as little as possible, and two, to depress male wages as much as possible as a result of this female competition. Similarly, capitalists used child labor to depress women's wages, and machines to depress human labor in general. The capitalist system alone is responsible for the fact that women's labor has resulted in the very opposite from the natural tendency, since it has led to a longer working day instead of substantially shorter hours. Also, women's work has not meant an increase of societal wealth, that is, a greater well-being of every member of society, but rather an increase in the profits of a handful of capitalists, together with an ever-increasing impoverishment of the masses. The unfortunate effects of women's work, so painfully evident at present, will disappear only with the capitalist system of production.

"In order not to be outdone by his competition, the capitalist must strive to widen as much as possible the gap between the cost of production and the sale of his goods. He therefore produces as cheaply, and sells as expensively, as he can. The capitalist thus is anxious to prolong the working day interminably and to put the worker off with a ludicrous and mean wage. The aim is, of course, directly contrary to the interest of female as well as male laborers. A real polarity of interests between male and female labor does not exist. Very clear, however, is the irreconcilable opposition between the interest of capital and labor.

"Economic reasons argue against the abolition of women's work. The present economic position is one where neither capitalists nor husbands can do without the labor of women. Capitalists must use women's work in order to remain competitive, and husbands must use it if they wish to establish a family. Let us suppose for the moment that women's work were abolished by law—this would not improve the wages of men. Capitalists would soon replace cheap female labor with ever more highly-sophisticated machines, and in a short while, all would be as before.

"After large-scale hiring had benefited the labor force, it was evident to us that with the aid of sophisticated machinery capitalists managed to nullify the workers' achievements.

"If abolition or limiting of women's work is demanded because of women's growing competition, then it would be equally logical to demand the abolition of machinery and the return to medieval guild laws, which decreed the number of workers to be employed in each trade.

"Above all, apart from the economic reasons, there are reasons of principle that argue against the abolition of women's work. It is especially on the basis of principle that women must protest with all their might against every such attempt. They must raise the most ardent and at the same time the most justified protest, because they know that their social and political equality with men depends entirely on their economic self-sufficiency, which they derive from their labor outside the family.

"Thus, we women protest most vehemently against any limitation of women's labor as a matter of principle. Since we do not want to separate our problem from the problem of labor in general, we shall not formulate any particular demands; we ask for no other protection than that demanded in general by labor against capital.

"We suggest only one exception, and that is for pregnant women whose condition requires special protective regulations, both in their own interest and in the interest of the next generation. We recognize no special woman question; we recognize no special female labor question! We expect our full emancipation neither from women's admission to what are known as free trades, nor from equal education with men—although the demand for both of these rights is natural and just—nor from the granting of political rights. Those countries where supposedly free, direct electoral rights exist, have shown us the negligible value of such rights. Electoral rights without economic freedom are neither more nor less than an exchange without currency. If social emancipation depended upon political rights, the social question would no longer exist in those countries offering voting rights to all classes. The emancipation of women, together with that of all humanity, will take place only with the emancipation of labor from capital. Only in a socialist society will female and male workers alike gain complete human rights.

"After considering these facts, women who seriously wish to be liberated have no choice but to join the Socialist Workers' Party, the only party concerned with emancipation of workers.

"Without the assistance of men, yes, often even against the wishes of men, women have rallied to the Socialist banner. . . .

"While women go forward hand in hand with the Socialist Workers' Party, they are prepared to take part in the struggle and sacrifices of the battle. They are, however, also firmly determined to demand all their rights once victory is achieved. Regarding sacrifices and duties as well as rights, they want to be no more and no less than comrades in arms who have been accepted under equal conditions into the ranks of the combatants."

Lively applause, repeated after translation by Citizeness Aveling into English and French.

Catholics Reply to Socialists

SOURCES

16. Leo XIII, *Rerum Novarum*, 15 May 1891; reprinted in Joseph Husslein, ed., *Social Wellsprings*, I (Milwaukee, Wisc., 1940), 167, 168-70, 171-75, 191-92.

17. Marie Maugeret, "Le Féminisme chrétien," *La Fronde*, 11 December 1897, p. 1. Tr. KMO.

In the 1880's the Catholic Church also began to consider the dimensions of the vast social change that was sweeping over Europe, and embarked on a program that exhibited intellectual vigor, spiritual fervor, and social action. This reinvigoration of the Church can be attributed in great part to the successor of Pius IX (Vol. I, Doc. 79), Leo XIII (1810-1903), who had been named Pope in 1878 at the age of 68. Pope Leo, born Vincenzo Giaoacchino Pecci, was Jesuit-educated; he had spent his early years in the priesthood as an apostolic delegate in various Italian cities and as papal nuncio in Brussels, before being named bishop of Perugia and cardinal. After his election to the papacy he encouraged the Church's confrontation with the urban, industrial, and secular world by seeking a *modus vivendi* with anticlerical governments and also with the unsettling findings of the sciences. He encouraged the development of a Catholic press and promoted efforts to arouse social consciousness and activism on the part of clergy and laity alike. He issued a stream of authoritative doctrinal pronouncements to focus Catholic thinking on contemporary conditions and problems. None has received as much praise as his 1891 encyclical *Rerum Novarum*, known in English as "The Condition of the Workingmen." Leo XIII drafted this statement to workers as an explicit counter-challenge to socialist doctrines, asserting the necessity of private property as the foundation of the family, and invoking the "natural right" of personal ownership to counter socialist proposals for the community of goods. He staunchly defended the position that men who are heads of families should toil to support their wives and children, and should pass their accumulated property on to their descendants.

The patriarchal stance of the Pope revealed in the excerpts from the workingmen's encyclical should be contrasted with the second selection, a statement of views by the most outspoken Catholic advocate of women's rights in France, Marie Maugeret (1844-1928). A devout liberal Catholic and bourgeois spinster from Le Mans, Maugeret founded a publication entitled *Le Féminisme chrétien* in 1897, in response to the predominantly socialist flavor of the international women's rights congress held in Paris during April 1896. Her ideas were considered shockingly advanced by more traditional Catholic women, to whom she proposed not only the notion of women's right to work, but substantial reforms in the Civil Code as well, insisting that private property was no less important to women in the modern world than to men. During the early twentieth century Maugeret's campaign led to the formation of several Catholic women's social action groups and, from 1906 on, to increasing Catholic support for the cause of women's suffrage. In this selection Maugeret presents her program to the wider audience of the important new women's daily, *La Fronde*.

---

16. Leo XIII (1891)

The spirit of revolutionary change, long predominant in the nations of the world, when once aroused, gradually passed beyond the bounds of politics and made itself felt in the cognate field of practical economy. The elements of a conflict are unmistakable. We perceive them in the growth of industry and the marvellous discoveries of science; in the changed relations of employers and workingmen; in the enormous fortunes of individuals and the poverty of the masses; in the increased self-reliance and the closer mutual combination of the labour population; and, finally, in a general moral deterioration.

The momentous seriousness of the present state of things, indeed, just now fills every mind with painful apprehension. Wise men discuss it; practical men propose schemes; popular meetings, legislatures, and sovereign princes, all are occupied with it. There is, in fact, nothing which has a deeper hold on public attention.

Hence, Venerable Brethren, as on former occasions, when it seemed opportune to refute false teaching, we addressed you in the interests of the Church and of the commonwealth, and issued letters on Civil Government, Human Liberty, on the Christian Constitution of the State, and on similar subjects, so now We have deemed it well to speak on the Condition of the Workingmen. . . .

All agree, and there can be no question whatever, that some remedy must be found, and quickly found, for the misery and wretchedness which press so heavily at this moment on the large majority of the very poor.

For the ancient workingmen's guilds were destroyed in the last century, and no other organization took their place. Public institutions and the laws have repudiated the ancient religion. Hence by degrees it has come to pass that workingmen have been given over, isolated and defenceless, to the callousness of employers and the greed of unrestrained competition. The evil has been increased by rapacious usury, which, although more than once condemned by the Church, is nevertheless, under a different form but with the same guilt, still practised by avaricious and grasping men. And to this must be added the custom of working by contract, and the concentration of so many branches of trade in the hands of a few individuals, *so that a small number of very rich men have been able to lay upon the masses of the poor a yoke little better than slavery itself.*

To remedy these evils the Socialists, working on the poor man's envy of the rich, maintain that private possessions of goods should be overturned, and that individual possessions should become the common property of all, to be administered by the State or by municipal bodies. They hold that, by thus transferring property from private persons to the community, the present evil state of things will be set to rights, because each citizen will then have his equal share of whatever there is to enjoy. But their proposals are so clearly futile for all practical purposes, that if they were carried out *the workingman himself would suffer.* Moreover they are emphatically unjust, because they would rob the lawful possessor, bring the State into a sphere that is not its own, and cause complete confusion in the community.

It is surely undeniable that when a man engages in remunerative labour the very reason and motive of his work is to obtain property, and to hold it as his own private possession. If one man hires out to another his strength or his industry, he does this for the purpose of receiving in return what is necessary for food and living; he thereby expressly proposes to acquire a full and real right, not only to the remuneration, but also to the disposal of that remuneration as he pleases. Thus, if he lives sparingly, saves money, and invests his savings, for greater security, in land, the land in such a case is only his wages in another form; and, consequently, a workingman's little estate thus purchased should be as completely at his own disposal as the wages he receives for his labour. But it is precisely in this power of disposal that ownership consists, whether the property be movable or immovable goods. The Socialists, therefore, in endeavouring to transfer the possessions of individuals to the community, strike at the interests of every wage earner, for they deprive him of the liberty of disposing of his wages, and thus of all hope and possibility of increasing his stock and of bettering his condition in life.

What is of still greater importance, however, is that the remedy they propose is manifestly against justice. *For every man has by nature the right to possess property as his own. . . . Man is older than the State and he holds the right of providing for the life of his body prior to the formation of any State.*

To say that God has given the earth to the use and enjoyment of the universal human race is not to deny that there can be private property. For *God has granted the earth to mankind in general; not in the sense that all without distinction can deal with it as they please, but rather that no part of it has been assigned to any one in particular, and that the limits of private possession have been left to be fixed by man's own industry and the laws of individual peoples. . . .*

The rights here spoken of as belonging to each individual man, are seen in a much stronger light if they are considered in relation to man's social and domestic obligations.

In choosing a state of life, it is indisputable that all are at full liberty either to follow the counsel of Jesus Christ as to virginity, or to enter into the bonds of marriage. No human law can abolish the natural and primitive right of marriage, or in any way limit the chief and principal purpose of marriage, ordained by God's authority from the beginning. "Increase and multiply" (Gen. i, 28). *Thus we have the family—the "society" of a man's own household; a society limited indeed in numbers, but a true "society," anterior to every kind of State or nation, with rights and duties of its own, totally independent of the commonwealth.* Hence, the right of property, which has been proved to belong naturally to individual persons, must also belong to a man in his capacity of head of a family. Nay, such a person must possess this right so much the more clearly in proportion as his position multiplies his duties.

For it is a most sacred law of nature that a father must provide food and all necessaries for those whom he has begotten. And, similarly, nature dictates that a man's children, who carry on, as it were, and continue his own personality, should be provided by him with all that is needful to enable them honourably to keep themselves from want and misery in the uncertainties of this mortal life. Now, in no other way can a father effect this except by the ownership of profitable property (*fructuosarum possesione rerum*), which he can transmit to his children by inheritance. A family, no less than a State, as we have said, is a true society, governed by a power within itself, that is to say, by the father. Wherefore, provided the limits be not transgressed which are prescribed by the very purposes for which it exists, the family has, at least, equal rights with the State in the choice and pursuit of those things which are needful to its preservation and its just liberty.

We say, at least equal rights; for *since the domestic household is anterior both in idea and in fact to the gathering of men into a commonwealth, the former must necessarily have rights and duties which are prior to those of the latter, and which rest more immediately on nature.* If the citizens of a State, if the families, on entering into association and fellowship, experienced at the hands of the State hindrance instead of help, and found their rights attacked instead of being protected, such association were rather to be repudiated than sought after.

The idea, then, that the civil government should, at its own discretion, penetrate and pervade the family and the household, is a great and pernicious mistake. True, if a family finds itself in great difficulty, utterly friendless, and without prospect of help, it is right that extreme necessity be met by public aid; for each family is a part of the commonwealth. In like manner, if within the walls of the household there occur grave disturbance of mutual rights, the public power must intervene to force each party to give the other what is due; for this is not to rob citizens of their rights, but justly and properly to safeguard and strengthen them. But the rulers of the State must go no further: nature bids them stop here.

Paternal authority can neither be abolished by the State nor absorbed; for it has the same source as human life itself. "Children are in some way part of the father" and, as it were, the continuation of the father's personality. Strictly speaking, the child takes its place in civil society not in its own right, but in its quality as a member of the family in which it is begotten. And it is precisely because "the child belongs to the father," that "before it attains the use of free will, it is in the power and care of its parents" (St. Thomas, *2a, 2ae, q. x, a.* 12). The Socialists, therefore, in setting aside the parent and introducing the providence of the State, act *against natural justice*, and threaten the very existence of family life.

And such interference is not only unjust, but is quite certain to harass and disturb all classes of citizens, and to subject them to odious and intolerable slavery. It would open the door to envy, to evil speaking, and to quarrelling. The sources of wealth would themselves run dry, for no one would have any interest in exerting his talents or his industry. That ideal equality of which so much is said would, in reality, be the leveling down of all to the same condition of misery and dishonour.

Thus it is clear that the main tenet of Socialism, the community of goods, must be utterly rejected; for it would injure those whom it is intended to benefit, it would be contrary to the natural rights of mankind, and it would introduce confusion and disorder into the commonwealth. Our first and most fundamental principle, therefore, when we undertake to alleviate the condition of the masses, must be the inviolability of private property. This laid down, We go on to show where we must find the remedy that we seek. . . .

If we turn now to things exterior and corporal, *the first concern of all is to save the poor workers from the cruelty of grasping men who use human beings as mere instruments for making money.* It is neither justice nor humanity so to grind men down with excessive labour as to stupefy their minds and wear out their bodies. Man's powers, like his general nature, are limited, and beyond these limits he cannot go. His strength is developed and increased by use and exercise, but only on condition of due intermission and proper rest. Daily labour, therefore, must be so regulated that it may not be protracted during longer hours than strength admits. . . .

Finally, work which is suitable for a strong man cannot reasonably be required from a woman or a child. And, in regard to children, great care should be taken not to place them in workshops and factories until their bodies and minds are sufficiently mature. For just as rough weather destroys the buds of spring, so too early an experience of life's hard work blights the young promise of a child's powers, and makes any real education impossible. Women, again, are not suited to certain trades; for a woman is by nature fitted for homework, and it is that which is best adapted at once to preserve her modesty, and to promote the good bringing up of children and the well-being of the family.

17. Marie Maugeret (1897)

Ought one be astonished at this multiplicity of roots thrown out by the feminist idea? No! Ought one to be troubled by it? Even less so! As it is with plants, so it is with ideas—vigor and solidity are acquired in just this way. Indeed, it is immensely important for the success of the feminist party that all milieus be explored and won over—not successively, but simultaneously—to a cause that belongs to no one class of society, to no one part of humanity more than another, but to the entire society and to all humanity.

And this is why, side by side with the groups formed by the partisans of free-thought, socialism, collectivism, of every doctrine and the most diverse philosophies, it was inevitable that one day the great party of Christian feminism would arise, which would adopt, along with the controversial name of feminist, which was at first so poorly understood and looked down on, everything in the various feminist programs that could be reconciled with the teachings of Christian morality.

To dissociate the feminist idea from everything that rendered it unacceptable to the party that represents the immense majority of the nation; to proclaim in all places and upon all occasions that feminism is an independent doctrine, which no party has the right to monopolize; to repeat to our friends that if feminism, spawned by an idea of pure justice, has assumed sectarian airs and put forth other principles that we condemn and combat, the fault lies as much with *those who have not risen to direct it* as with *those who have taken the lead*; to remind them that no one has the right to be apathetic to this current idea, especially those who pretend to be the bearers of Truth; to tell them once and for all that feminism is perhaps the greatest—for it encompasses all the rest—the sole, truly great question of social obligation, from which no one has the right to flee. This has been the *raison d'être*, the constant effort of Christian feminism since the day it entered the arena, respecting every sincere opinion, open to every alliance compatible with its principles, not having nor wishing to have any adversary other than injustice, no other ambition than to conquer by bringing onto the battlefield this immense mass of the nation that, until this moment, has been indifferent, defiant, or hostile.

Here is the program we have submitted to our friends.

At the head of our demands, Christian feminism lists the right to work as the most urgent, the most legitimate, the most incontestably just. We admit no restriction, no limitation, no regulation of this freedom, and we protest with all our energy against any law that, under the fallacious and hypocritical pretext of "protecting" us, takes away our right, the most sacred of all, to earn our living honestly.

For the working woman we demand the right to work wherever, whenever, and as much as she can and is able to—her needs and physical strength, which she alone can judge, being the only authoritative arbiter on this matter. We demand that her salary remain her own personal property, and that this salary be based exclusively on the value of her work and not on the sex of the worker.

For the propertied woman, we demand that she retain control of the property she brings [to marriage] and that the [Civil] Code be modified on this point, in such manner as to safeguard henceforth the interests of the woman as a wife. It is against the husband who so often dissipates the resources of the community property, and not against the fatigues of labor, that women need laws of "protection."

The Women's Movement Organizes

SOURCES

18. The International Council of Women, Call to convention, 1 June 1887, in *Report of the International Council of Women Assembled by the National Woman Suffrage Association, Washington, D.C., March 25 to April 1, 1888* (Washington, D.C., 1888), pp. 10-11.

19. Jeanne-E. Schmahl, "Progress of the Women's Rights Movement in France," *Forum* (Philadelphia and New York), 22 (September 1896), 88-89.

20. Bund Deutscher Frauenvereine, "Programm" (1907), as tr. in Katharine Anthony, *Feminism in Germany and Scandinavia* (New York, 1915), pp. 20-26. Originally published in the *Centralblatt des Bundes Deutscher Frauenvereine* (Berlin, July 1907).

21. Madeleine Pelletier, "La Tactique féministe," *La Revue Socialiste*, 47, no. 280 (April 1908), 318-21, 325. Tr. KMO.

While Socialist and Catholic theoreticians were staking out sweeping ideological positions on the woman question, bourgeois women in various countries were organizing for political action. They were extending the network of local, national, and international associations intended to transform the position of women within the existing social and political institutions. Three of these initiatives are represented here: the founding of the International Council of Women by the leaders of the American suffrage movement; a French reformer's attempt to organize a lobbying effort to accomplish revision of specific articles of the Civil Code; and in Germany an effort by the national women's association to draft a comprehensive platform for demanding changes in the position of German women. The fourth selection, by a French socialist woman doctor, considers the vital question of "feminist tactics" for socialist women, a question that became increasingly pressing in the first decade of the twentieth century.

The first selection is the call to convention issued by the leaders of the National Woman Suffrage Association in 1887. This international gathering was scheduled to commemorate the fortieth anniversary of the Seneca Falls meeting of 1848 by assembling women leaders from many countries; its goal, to promote the coordination of efforts to reform women's legal, educational, and economic position across national boundaries. The founding meeting of the ICW led to the establishment of an international council with representatives from national councils in each member country. This group soon established its own publication and held major congresses every five years in various world capitals to reassess women's progress and to devise strategies for political action.

The second selection is excerpted from an American periodical contribution by the French women's rights advocate Jeanne-Elisabeth Archer Schmahl (1846-1915). The daughter of an Anglo-French couple, Jeanne Schmahl was raised in

England and claimed to have been one of the young Englishwomen who had gone to Edinburgh to study medicine in the wake of Sophia Jex-Blake (Vol. I, Doc. 133). Before the Edinburgh fiasco, she returned to Paris with the intention of continuing medical studies there, but evidently she never completed her medical degree; instead we find her reappearing as a shadowy presence in the Parisian women's movement during the late 1870's under her married name of Madame Henri Schmahl. But Schmahl did not like what she saw in the anticlerical republican women's rights groups of Léon Richer and Maria Deraismes (Vol. I, Doc. 124). She considered that the mixing of politics and religion with the woman question had been "one of the great reasons of the movement's lack of success in France." In the 1890's, therefore, she determined to employ a new strategy for achieving single-issue legal reform, which she describes in the second selection. Her group, L'Avant Courrière (The Forerunner), succeeded in securing passage of the first French married women's property act, as well as legal recognition of women's capacity to testify in official public acts, to sit on juries, etc. Progress was, however, notoriously slow, and the "loi Schmahl" was stalled in the French Senate for nearly a decade after this article was published. As a consequence of these delays, Jeanne Schmahl subsequently devoted her energy to the pursuit of woman suffrage in France; in 1909 she founded the French Union for Woman Suffrage (Union Française pour le Suffrage des Femmes).

The third selection is the 1907 program statement of the Federation of German Women's Associations (Bund Deutscher Frauenvereine). This program, as the admiring American observer Katharine Anthony put it, "fixes the threshold of European feminism. Its demands are the minimum demands of the twentieth-century woman movement." What is perhaps most striking about the Bund's program is its emphasis on the female reproductive role and tasks, which leads straightaway to the formulation of a series of radical reforms potentially realizable within the framework of imperial German society.

As the organization of the women's movement in all countries proceeded and reforms began to be achieved, socialist women began to question their own priorities. Were they to pursue the socialist revolution, predicated on the transformation of property institutions, or should they focus on more immediately-realizable reforms that would, consistent with socialist goals, benefit their sex in the short run? This issue was hotly debated at the 1907 International Socialist Women's Congress in Stuttgart. In the final selection, Dr. Madeleine Pelletier (1874-1939), a young woman of petit bourgeois Parisian origins whose academic success had earned her a medical degree, discusses the question of tactics. Pelletier had imbibed the nectar of revolutionary socialism and syndicalism through her dealings with the left-wing factions of the newly-unified French Socialist party (SFIO), whom she represented on the SFIO's executive committee. In this article, which grew out of her participation in the Stuttgart debates, Pelletier insists on the importance for socialist women of putting the woman question—and especially the question of the vote—before all else. Shortly thereafter, Pelletier became an ardent proponent of woman suffrage, established her own journal *La Suffragiste*, and exhorted French women to adopt the militant tactics of the Women's Social and Political Union (WSPU) in England (see Doc. 61).

18. The International Council of Women (1887)

The first organized demand for equal educational, industrial, professional, and political rights for women was made in a convention held at Seneca Falls, New York (U.S.A.), in the year 1848.

To celebrate the fortieth anniversary of this event, an International Council of Women will be convened under the auspices of the National Woman Suffrage Association, in Albaugh's Opera House, Washington, D.C., on March 25, 1888.

It is impossible to over-estimate the far-reaching influence of such a council. An interchange of opinions on the great questions now agitating the world will rouse women to new thought, will intensify their love of liberty, and will give them a realizing sense of the power of combination.

However the governments, religions, laws, and customs of nations may differ, all are agreed on one point, namely, man's sovereignty in the State, in the Church, and in the Home. In an International Council women may hope to devise new and more effective methods for securing the equality and justice which they have so long and so earnestly sought. Such a Council will impress the important lesson that the position of women anywhere affects their position everywhere. Much is said of universal brotherhood, but, for weal or for woe, more subtle and more binding is universal sisterhood.

Women, recognizing the disparity between their labors and their achievements, will no doubt agree that they have been trammeled by their political subordination. Those active in great philanthropic enterprises sooner or later realize that, so long as women are not acknowledged to be the political equals of men, their judgment on public questions will have but little weight.

It is, however, neither intended nor desired that discussions in the International Council shall be limited to questions touching the political rights of women. Formal invitations requesting the appointment of delegates will be issued to representative organizations in every department of woman's work. Literary Clubs, Art and Temperance Unions, Labor Leagues, Missionary, Peace, and Moral Purity Societies, Charitable, Professional, Educational, and Industrial Associations will thus be offered equal opportunity with Suffrage Societies to be represented in what should be the ablest and most imposing body of women ever assembled.

The Council will continue eight days, and its fifteen public sessions will afford ample opportunity for reporting woman's work and progress in all parts of the world during the past forty years. It is hoped that all friends of the advancement of women will lend their support to this undertaking.

On behalf of the National Woman Suffrage Association.

ELIZABETH CADY STANTON, *President*, 3 W. 40th St., New York.
SUSAN B. ANTHONY, *First Vice-President*, Rochester, N.Y.
MATILDA JOSLYN GAGE, *Second Vice-President*, Fayetteville, N.Y.
MAY WRIGHT SEWALL, *Ch. Ex. Com.*, 343 N. Penn. St., Indianapolis, Ind.

ELLEN H. SHELDON, *Recording Secretary*, 811 9th St. N.W., Washington, D.C.

JANE H. SPOFFORD, *Treasurer*, Riggs House, Washington, D.C.

RACHEL G. FOSTER, *Cor. Sec.*, 748 N. 19th St., Philadelphia, Pa.

June 1, 1887.

19. Jeanne-E. Schmahl (1896)

It came to be pretty generally admitted that women are justified in most of their claims and that there was room outside Maria Deraismes's and M. Léon Richer's societies for some association of no special political or religious tendency: simply groups of men and women united on one point, namely, the amendment of laws concerning women, with perhaps no other point of contact or opinion; Catholics using their own and their friends' influence; Protestants theirs, as well as freethinkers', to help women of all classes and denominations to obtain justice where it is denied them. Unhappily this innovation received neither welcome nor approbation from Mlle. Deraismes, who, with most of her collaborators, looked upon it as disloyalty to herself and as so much energy diverted from what she considered the only true course of action, and likely, therefore, to be detrimental to the Republic itself. For twenty years and more her supremacy had been undisputed, and she could not endure this apparently harmful deviation of the women's movement.

A powerful association was nevertheless gradually forming. Among its earliest members were the leading journalists of Paris, deputies and senators of every shade of opinion, celebrated scientists and jurists, and a few of the best-known female authors, amongst whom was Mme. Adam,[*] now for the first time taking part in the women's movement. Then, as if to give special significance to the new mode of action, a few women of the old French aristocracy, notably the Duchesse d'Uzès, joined the movement. With such a staff the actual work was comparatively easy and I willingly consented to direct the young association; and we started "l'Avant-Courrière" on January 30, 1893.

Taking into consideration that the Civil Code is the one great obstacle to the emancipation of women in France, we decided to attack it. Not, however, in its entirety, as had previously been attempted, but piecemeal, beginning by what appeared to be least defended by our opponents and therefore easiest of conquest; at the same time choosing the point which should logically come first, as the foundation of women's freedom. We were not long in coming to the conclusion that, financial freedom being the root of all liberty, we must first set to work to obtain for married women the right to their own earnings. After having decided what we intended to do, the next decision to be taken was how we should proceed to do it; so, after settling the preliminary questions of membership and

---

[*] Editor of *La Nouvelle Revue* and, as Juliette Lamber, author of *Idées anti-Proudhoniennes* (see Vol. I, Doc. 96).—EDS.

funds, the first point on which we agreed was that each member should be free to choose his or her mode of action, each one working as occasion and situation might permit for the furtherance of the cause in hand. But, as a natural consequence of this freedom of action, each member was to undertake the entire responsibility of his or her acts and pay the cost thereof. Thus free scope would be given for individual initiative; while the society of "l'Avant-Courrière" only took the responsibility of whatever was the common action of the entire association and accepted as such by me.

Next, in consideration of the social odium thrown on the women's rights question, which threatened to deter a great many women from joining us, we stipulated that no name but mine should be published unless by permission. After nearly four years' existence we have every reason to congratulate ourselves on having made our rules so elastic. Each one of us has been able to do the work best adapted to her means and surroundings, and we have found help and encouragement on all sides. One great printing firm after another has printed for us without charge. The press throughout the length and breadth of the land has spoken good things of us. When we decided to placard all Paris and some of the provincial towns, our great, flaming posters cost us nothing but the stamp duty. The artist, A. Lepère, designed our emblem, a dreary barren landscape with the rising sun just visible above the horizon,—woman's land, with the glimmer of hope in the distance,—and one of the best known printers in Paris printed it for us on paper given by another friend. A gang of billposters worked all night, generously giving their help, and on the morning of January 18, 1894, the papers told the Parisians how the walls of their city were covered with an appeal in favor of women. Ever since, our work has continued in the same way. In March [1894], M. Léopold Goirand, a member of the Chamber of Deputies, wrote me expressing sympathy and offering his aid. On July 7 he laid our Married Women's Earnings Bill on the table of the Chamber. In January, 1895, he was nominated *rapporteur* of the parliamentary commission charged with the study of the question, and on February 27, 1896, the bill, conferring upon married women the power of free disposition of their earnings, passed the Chamber of Deputies without opposition—the first time in French history that a women's rights movement has received support from the government. It is difficult to predict what reception we shall get in the Senate, yet even there we have many friends and therefore have the right to be hopeful.

This very important modification of the French marriage laws affects about 4,500,000 workwomen, not to speak of authors, musicians, painters, actresses, teachers, shop-assistants, and domestic servants,—in all about 6,000,000 women-workers who, if married, have, as the law now stands, no right to their own earnings, if that right has not been stipulated for by a legal agreement made at the time of their marriage. Otherwise the French wife may not even work, much less economize, for herself without her husband's leave. The wage of her labor belongs by right of law to her husband, and he alone has the right to spend or otherwise dispose of it as he pleases. The pecuniary position of the Frenchwoman, whose marriage contract is that of the communion of goods, is worse than that of the old Roman slave, for he at least had a right to his *peculium.*

20. Bund Deutscher Frauenvereine (1907)

GOALS AND TASKS OF THE WOMAN'S MOVEMENT

The Woman's Movement has chosen its goals and tasks irrespective of all political and religious parties. It works for the women of all classes and parties.

The demands of the Woman's Movement are based on the existence of thoroughgoing mental and physical differences between the sexes. It deduces from this fact that only by the coöperation of men and women can all the possibilities of cultural progress be realized.

The Woman's Movement, therefore, sets for itself this aim: To bring the cultural influence of women to its complete development and free social effectiveness.

The opportunity for the full development and effectiveness of woman's influence is *not* contained in the social and economic conditions of the present. Much more is it true that modern life has, on the one hand, limited the sphere of influence of the woman within the home, and on the other hand, thrust her into active participation in economic and social life, without providing her with the inward equipment and the outward mobility for it.

The Woman's Movement seeks, therefore, a transformation of ideas and conditions in the fields of:

1. Education.
2. Economic Life.
3. Marriage and the Family.
4. Public Life in Community and State.

EDUCATION

The Woman's Movement holds the opinion that the education of girls in its present form does not show sufficient consideration either for the development of personality in woman or for her future domestic, vocational, and civic duties. It demands from state and community the manifestation of the same interest in the education of girls as in that of boys. It makes especially the following demands:

1. Obligatory continuation schools for girls after their dismissal from the public schools.

2. Reorganization of the secondary schools for girls, so that the latter, without hurt to their special adaptation to women's sphere, shall be made equal to the secondary schools for boys. It must be made possible for girls to prepare themselves, either within the frame-work of their own secondary schools or by admission to the boys' secondary schools, to enjoy their rights in the higher institutions of learning.

3. The unconditional admission of properly qualified and prepared women to all universities and technical schools.

ECONOMIC LIFE

The Woman's Movement regards as the primary and immediate occupation of the married woman the sphere of duties involved in marriage and motherhood. The satisfactory performance of this vocation must be secured in the interest of society by all the means of education, of economic reform, and of legal protection. The work of women in the performance of this vocation shall be valued, economically and legally, as a competent cultural service.

In view of the great number of women who remain unmarried and the still greater number of those who cannot find an adequate provision in marriage, the vocational work of women is an economic and moral necessity. But the Woman's Movement also regards the vocational work of women, in a broader sense and independently of every outward necessity, as a cultural value, for women may be the possessors of a specific talent, and with the full and free development of their capacities may find, in many fields of intellectual and material activity, tasks which by reason of their nature they can perform better than men.

In respect to the economic valuation of women's vocational work, the Woman's Movement stands for the principle: Equal pay for equal work.

In consequence of this view of the economic side of the Woman question, the Woman's Movement makes the following demands:

1. It lays upon parents, and, in a deeper sense, upon society, the obligation to give every girl the opportunity to learn an occupation according to her inclination and capacity.

2. It strives to broaden the range of women's occupations, especially by the furtherance and improvement of the vocational training of girls.

3. It supports all forms of vocational organization as a primary means of elevating women's work, especially its economic valuation.

4. It works towards the continuous broadening and the efficient execution of the laws protecting working women as well as toward the extension of state insurance in the sense of greater economic protection of the mother.

5. It seeks for women participation in the rights which are conferred upon certain classes of business (Merchants' Courts, Trade Courts, and so forth).

MARRIAGE AND THE FAMILY

The Woman's Movement sees in the sacredness of marriage the essential guarantee of the physical and spiritual welfare of posterity and the fundamental condition of public health. With regard to sexual morality, it lays upon men and women alike the same duties and combats the double standard of morals which, on the one hand, grants to the man a sexual freedom fatal in every respect and, on the other hand, strikes the woman with unjust harshness.

It demands for the woman, as the guardian of the home and the educator of the children, that she shall bear, in harmony with the dignity of her obligation and the value of her activities, the same legal responsibility as the man in all the affairs of marriage and of family life.

From the foregoing we derive the following aims:

1. The Woman's Movement combats prostitution with all the means at its command and sees in the legal sanction of vice, expressed by the existing system of regimentation, a social and moral danger.

2. It demands a reform of the marriage laws, by which both parents shall be assured of the same rights of decision in all personal affairs and the same responsibilities and rights in their joint affairs, especially the same share in parental authority. It demands statutory reforms concerning the rights of illegitimate children, reforms which shall lay upon the illegitimate father greater responsibilities toward mother and child.

PUBLIC LIFE, COMMUNITY, AND STATE

The Woman's Movement represents the conviction that our economic, social, and intellectual progress must have as a consequence the increasing participation of women in the public life of community and state. It demands the enlistment of women in the duties and rights of communal and political citizenship. It demands this primarily for the sake of women. For, in the modern state, the economic and cultural interests of women can only be lastingly secured by the acquisition of these rights. Also the exclusion of women from national life and social responsibility, together with the inevitable narrowing of her domestic sphere of influence, must result in the retarding of her development as a personality as well as in the lowering of her social position.

The Woman's Movement makes this demand in the second place for the sake of the public welfare, because the coöperation of women is indispensable to state and community in the solution of all their modern social-political problems.

In particular, the Woman's Movement seeks the following goals, according to the possibilities given by the stage of social development:

1. Admission of women to responsible offices in community and state, primarily to such as stand in a particularly close relation to the interests of women (the education of girls, social-political administration of state and community, the problems concerning working women, courts of law, and so forth).

2. Enlistment of women in the representation of the laity in legal proceedings (justice of the peace and jury members).

3. Removal of all limitations placed on women's right to combine.

4. The extension of the church franchise to women.

5. The extension of the community franchise to women.

6. The extension of the political franchise to women.

21. Madeleine Pelletier (1908)

In order to conquer the right to vote, women should embark along two paths of simultaneous action. They must: (1) create vast feminist organizations; (2) penetrate the existing political parties.

Indeed, every great reform, before seeing the light of day at the tribune of parliament, is elaborated, discussed, examined from all directions and over a number of years in the great associations. The isolated individual has such a sense of weakness that his influence on society seems nonexistent; he limits himself to wishing that things would proceed in the way he would like, but he knows full well that his wish will remain a platonic one. If I were the government, the common people say—but since they are not the government, they think they have no alternative but to suffer and be still. In France, one could certainly find many thousands of women who want political rights; but because they are dispersed, their opinion is drowned in the sea of those who are either hostile or indifferent. If one could succeed in grouping these women together, the nature of the question would be completely changed; that which appeared negligible would become a force to be reckoned with. Ten thousand women battering on the doors of the Chamber of Deputies to reclaim the right to vote would singularly hasten its realization.

All too often women—like many men—do not sufficiently realize the necessity of forming groups when they want to enact a measure of general interest. What am I going to learn, the suffragist thinks, in one more society, that I don't already know? Nobody can teach me anything new about the equality of the sexes and the need for political emancipation of women. Why, then, should I waste my time?

It is certain that in the group a woman who is already a feminist will not learn how to be one; but even so, she should attend in order to reinforce the idea by her words or with her pen, if she is capable of speaking or writing, or by her presence, if she does not possess these other talents. She should feel compelled to be the stone from which the building will be built, the soldier in the army that is marching toward the conquest of political and economic equality of the sexes. Just as the faith that does not lead to action cannot be sincere, so the feminist who derives no pleasure from the society of like-minded persons is not animated by true conviction.

Beyond the fact that it renders action possible, the coming together of persons has as its advantage the unifying of ideas, which though it may be harmful in the domains of philosophy or science is indispensable when it comes to making something happen.

At present it can be said that each feminist has her own brand of feminism; with organization, feminism would become a solidly established doctrine. It is rightly said that revolutions have always been made by minorities; one must add that the minorities that have made them were organized minorities. In the face of an amorphous majority, the voice of an organized and determined minority of persons who know what they want and who all want the same thing is extremely powerful. And with the aid of circumstances, they will very quickly become a majority, swelled by the mass of mediocre minds and characters who are always ready to rally to a cause that shows some strength.

But the role of a suffragist should not be restricted to being a small part of a larger whole. The ideas she has received or comes to define with more precision in our groups should be spread elsewhere and notably in the political parties.

Moreover, the suffragist not only has something to give to a party, but she can benefit greatly from it as well. It should be no secret that most of our supporters are almost completely ignorant in political matters. . . .

At this moment the political parties are scarcely open to women, and suffragists cannot therefore expect to find a warm welcome. But rather than becoming discouraged, they should put even more energy into pushing open the door that is only reluctantly being opened to them. Their slogan should be, "Even so, and in spite of you!"

The Socialist Party program includes the equality of the sexes and, according to its statutes, women ought to be received and treated just as men are. In practice, only the woman who comes on the arm of her husband, her father, or her brother, is welcomed without protest; very often there are protests against the admission of a woman who comes on her own account, because the mass of socialists has not yet come to understand that a woman can think and act for herself. One should not be discouraged; the rules are on your side. . . .

The Radical Party has now opened to women its "Young Republican" groups. Most of those who have joined so far have done so following their husbands or kin, it is true, just as has been the case in the Socialist Party; but this is one more reason why *militantes* should join. On the whole, the radicals are not supporters of women's political emancipation; but the fact of having formed mixed groups from groups that were formerly all-male shows that at least a minority is sympathetic to the feminist idea. This sympathy can only grow by profiting from the access now open and by demonstrating that one can be a devoted party worker. . . .

Under no pretext should a feminist prefer the party she has entered to feminism itself, for while she serves the party, she belongs only to feminism and to no other cause. A woman, like any individual, may be a socialist, a republican, or a monarchist according to her convictions, but before all else she should be a feminist. For under a monarchy, a republic, or socialism, she will not be counted unless the political equality of the sexes becomes a reality.

CHAPTER 3

Women's Duties and the Population Question

Housewifery in the Machine Age

SOURCES

22. Peter Kropotkin, *The Conquest of Bread* (London, 1913), pp. 161-66. This selection was originally published as an anonymous article in *La Révolte—organe communiste-anarchiste* (Paris), no. 21 (8-15 February 1890) and was subsequently incorporated into Kropotkin's book *La Conquête du pain* (Paris, 1892).

23. William Morris, *News from Nowhere; or An Epoch of Rest* (London, 1891), pp. 21-22, 75-79, 101-2, and 174-75. Originally published in *The Commonweal* (London), January-October 1890.

24. Louis Frank, *L'Éducation domestique des jeunes filles; ou la formation des mères* (Paris, 1904), pp. 122-23, 124. Tr. KMO.

Issues concerning the social division of labor invited the renewed attention of socialist and bourgeois critics alike. The three selections that follow present a range of differing views—by men—of the contours of women's household work in the new industrial age. The usefulness of machines, the shoddiness of the life they seemed to produce, compared with the promise they foretold, preoccupied many important nineteenth-century social critics, some of whom also considered their different effects on the two sexes.

Two of these thinkers, the Russian anarchist Peter Kropotkin and the English socialist William Morris, treated this subject directly with reference to housewifery, though they approached it from contrasting points of view. A third, Louis Frank, a Belgian social reformer, offered a totally different approach.

A Russian prince by birth, and a man of great personal charm, Petr Aleksevitch Kropotkin (1842-1921) studied to become a geographer, but his radical anti-statist views soon led him into difficulties with tsarist authorities. In 1872 he left Russia for Switzerland, and from 1882 to 1886 he was imprisoned in France. Following his release, Kropotkin settled in England with his Russian wife, Sophie, herself a writer and social critic, and there was befriended by various socialist groups. In 1886, with Charlotte M. Wilson, a graduate of Newnham College, he founded the anarchist journal *Freedom*, in which an early translation of his views on housework appeared. Kropotkin was not enthusiastic about most socialist proposals for reorganizing society, since they invariably implied a centralized and freedom-restricting authority. For this reason he objected to the then-widely-discussed phalanstery model of communal living where, as he pointed out in his tract on economic emancipation (excerpted below), the women still waited on the men and reared the children. Instead, he pinned his hopes for the liberation of all classes of women from "domestic slavery" on the increased use of labor-saving devices and especially on centralized heating, electricity, and mass kitchens, all of which he had heard existed in the United States. It is difficult to see, however, how the devices and institutions he professed to admire could have functioned adequately without recourse to some variant on the central authority he so abhorred.

During his years in England, Kropotkin was a frequent guest in the hospitable home of the artist, designer-businessman, poet, and socialist William Morris (1834-1896). Morris, who had been born to a comfortable middle-class life, devoted himself to lecturing, writing, and working for the realization of his ideal society. As a student at Oxford he had turned from religious studies to architecture and design, which he then made his business. Following John Ruskin (Vol. I, Doc. 104) in reaction to the harshness and sordid ugliness of industrial mass production, Morris personally practiced, and urged others to return to the practice of, individual craftsmanship, which would combine a love of beauty with pride in work well done. A romantic like other mid-Victorian Pre-Raphaelite artists, architects, and poets, he sought a lost perfection in the Middle Ages, and his designs and his romances were modelled on medieval sources. His wife Jane, who was the most frequent model for his close friend the painter D. G. Rossetti, and his two daughters all took part in his decorative work. Jane Morris was unenthusiastic about politics, and in later years their marriage foundered—one reason, perhaps, why Morris wrote with such perceptive honesty and realism on the subject of sex and marriage.

Morris gradually became convinced that a socialist revolution was necessary to uproot the entrenched capitalist society that surrounded him. Although he adapted Marx's ideas to some extent, Morris's socialism was ultimately aesthetic. He believed with dogged optimism that the perfect society could develop in small voluntary economic and socially cohesive communities rather than through the model of a rigid and centralized bureaucratic state. A belief in human equality pervades all of Morris's work. He was at pains to emphasize that this included equality not only of class but also of sex. Yet while in Morris's vision women are freed from sexual and economic dependence on men's whims, and share with men high intellectual and artistic pursuits, including the *creative* part of domestic work, Morris seemed unable to escape a traditionalist position on the division of labor. In his utopian romance *News from Nowhere*, set ahead in the 1960's, a time after the revolution or "the change" has almost been forgotten, the narrator (a Morris-like character) visits London and those parts of the English countryside Morris knew best. Here he portrays women as graciously performing the menial household tasks and as revered "rearers" of children.

The third selection presents a proposal that has retained its currency to the present day. Its author, Louis Frank (1865-1917), was a Belgian attorney who contributed many works in French to the discussion of woman's position in the law during the 1890's. He served as counsel for the first Belgian woman attorney to seek admission to the bar and was also active in the international peace movement. During the late 1890's Frank campaigned for mutual-aid insurance societies to provide maternity coverage for pregnant working women. In his 1904 treatise *L'Éducation domestique des jeunes filles; ou la formation des mères*, he strongly opposed socialist proposals for communal central kitchens, proposing instead that within the conjugal household both sexes should share responsibility for menial domestic tasks. But, even in Frank's reorganized household, it is still the woman who cooks.

---

22. Peter Kropotkin (1890)

Servant or wife, man always reckons on woman to do the house-work. But woman, too, at last claims her share in the emancipation of humanity. She no longer wants to be the beast of burden of the house. She considers it sufficient work to give many years of her life to the rearing of her children. She no longer wants to be the cook, the mender, the sweeper of the house! And, owing to American women taking the lead in obtaining their claims, there is a general complaint of the dearth of women who will condescend to domestic work in the United States. My lady prefers art, politics, literature, or the gaming tables; as to the work-girls, they are few, those who consent to submit to apron-slavery, and servants are only found with difficulty in the States. Consequently, the solution, a very simple one, is pointed out by life itself. Machinery undertakes three-quarters of the household cares.

You black your boots, and you know how ridiculous this work is. What can be more stupid than rubbing a boot twenty or thirty times with a brush? A tenth of the European population must be compelled to sell itself in exchange for a miserable shelter and insufficient food, and woman must consider herself a slave, in order that millions of her sex should go through this performance every morning.

But hairdressers have already machines for brushing glossy or woolly heads of hair. Why should we not apply, then, the same principle to the other extremity? So it has been done, and nowadays the machine for blacking boots is in general use in big American and European hotels. Its use is spreading outside hotels. In large English schools, where the pupils are boarding in the houses of the teachers, it has been found easier to have one single establishment which undertakes to brush a thousand pairs of boots every morning.

As to washing up! Where can we find a housewife who has not a horror of this long and dirty work, that is usually done by hand, solely because the work of the domestic slave is of no account.

In America they do better. There are already a number of cities in which hot water is conveyed to the houses as cold water is in Europe. Under these conditions the problem was a simple one, and a woman—Mrs. Cochrane—solved it. Her machine washes twelve dozen plates or dishes, wipes them, and dries them, in less than three minutes. A factory in Illinois manufactures these machines and sells them at a price within reach of the average middle-class purse. And why should not small households send their crockery to an establishment as well as their boots? It is even probable that the two functions, brushing and washing up, will be undertaken by the same association.

Cleaning, rubbing the skin off your hands when washing and wringing linen; sweeping floors and brushing carpets, thereby raising clouds of dust which afterwards occasion much trouble to dislodge from the places where they have settled down, all this work is still done because woman remains a slave, but it tends to disappear as it can be infinitely better done by machinery. Machines of all kinds will be introduced into households, and the distribution of motor-power in private houses will enable people to work them without muscular effort.

Such machines cost little to manufacture. If we still pay very much for them, it is because they are not in general use, and chiefly because an exorbitant tax is levied upon every machine by the gentlemen who wish to live in grand style and who have speculated on land, raw material, manufacture, sale, patents, and duties.

But emancipation from domestic toil will not be brought about by small machines only. Households are emerging from their present state of isolation; they begin to associate with other households to do in common what they did separately.

In fact, in the future we shall not have a brushing machine, a machine for washing up plates, a third for washing linen, and so on, in each house. To the future, on the contrary, belongs the common heating apparatus that sends heat into each room of a whole district and spares the lighting of fires. It is already so in a few American cities. A great central furnace supplies all houses and all rooms with hot water, which circulates in pipes; and to regulate the temperature you need only turn a tap. And should you care to have a blazing fire in any particular room you can light the gas specially supplied for heating purposes from a central reservoir. All the immense work of cleaning chimneys and keeping up fires— and woman knows what time it takes—is disappearing.

Candles, lamps, and even gas have had their day. There are entire cities in which it is sufficient to press a button for light to burst forth, and, indeed, it is a simple question of economy and of knowledge to give yourself the luxury of electric light. And lastly, also in America, they speak of forming societies for the almost complete suppression of household work. It would only be necessary to create a department for every block of houses. A cart would come to each door and take the boots to be blacked, the crockery to be washed up, the linen to be washed, the small things to be mended (if it were worth while), the carpets to be brushed, and the next morning would bring back the things entrusted to it, all well cleaned. A few hours later your hot coffee and your eggs done to a nicety would appear on your table. It is a fact that between twelve and two o'clock there are more than twenty million Americans and as many Englishmen who eat roast beef or mutton, boiled pork, potatoes, and a seasonable vegetable. And at the lowest figure eight million fires burn during two or three hours to roast this meat and cook these vegetables; eight million women spend their time preparing a meal which, taking all households, represents at most a dozen different dishes.

"Fifty fires burn," wrote an American woman the other day, "where one would suffice!" Dine at home, at your own table, with your children, if you like; but only think yourself, why should these fifty women waste their whole morning to prepare a few cups of coffee and a simple meal! Why fifty fires, when two people and one single fire would suffice to cook all these pieces of meat and all these vegetables? Choose your own beef or mutton to be roasted if you are particular. Season the vegetables to your taste if you prefer a particular sauce! But have a single kitchen with a single fire, and organize it as beautifully as you are able to.

Why has woman's work never been of any account? Why in every family are the mother and three or four servants obliged to spend so much time at what pertains to cooking? Because those who want to emancipate mankind have not included woman in their dream of emancipation, and consider it beneath their superior masculine dignity to think "of those kitchen arrangements," which they have put on the shoulders of that drudge—woman.

To emancipate woman, is not only to open the gates of the university, the law courts, or the parliaments to her, for the "emancipated" woman will always throw domestic toil on to another woman. To emancipate woman is to free her from the brutalizing toil of kitchen and washhouse; it is to organise your household in such a way as to enable her to rear her children, if she be so minded, while still retaining sufficient leisure to take her share of social life.

It will come. As we have said, things are already improving. Only let us fully understand that a revolution, intoxicated with the beautiful words, Liberty, Equality, Solidarity, would not be a revolution if it maintained slavery at home. Half humanity subjected to the slavery of the hearth would still have to rebel against the other half.

23. William Morris (1890)

[The narrator, "William Guest," describes breakfast upon his arrival at the Guest House, which stands on the site of his former dwelling.]

In this pleasant place, which of course I knew to be the hall of the Guest House, three young women were flitting to and fro. As they were the first of the sex I had seen on this eventful morning, I naturally looked at them very attentively, and found them at least as good as the gardens, the architecture, and the male men. As to their dress, which of course I took note of, I should say that they were decently veiled with drapery, and not bundled up with millinery; that they were clothed like women, not upholstered like arm-chairs, as most women of our time are. In short, their dress was somewhat between that of the ancient classical costume and the simpler forms of the fourteenth-century garments, though it was clearly not an imitation of either: the materials were light and gay to suit the season. As to the women themselves, it was pleasant indeed to see them, they were so kind and happy-looking in expression of face, so shapely and well-knit of body, and thoroughly healthy-looking and strong. All were at least comely, and one of them very handsome and regular of feature. They came up to us at once merrily and without the least affectation of shyness, and all three shook hands with me as if I were a friend newly come back from a long journey: though I could not help noticing that they looked askance at my garments; for I had on my clothes of last night, and at the best was never a dressy person.

A word or two from Robert the weaver, and they bustled about on our behoof, and presently came and took us by the hands and led us to a table in the pleasantest corner of the hall, where our breakfast was spread for us; and, as we sat down, one of them hurried out by the chambers aforesaid, and came back again in a little while with a great bunch of roses, very different in size and quality to what Hammersmith had been wont to grow, but very like the produce of an old country garden. She hurried back thence into the buttery, and came back once more with a delicately made glass, into which she put the flowers and set them down in the midst of our table. One of the others, who had run off also, then came back with a big cabbage-leaf filled with strawberries, some of them barely ripe, and said as she set them on the table, "There, now; I thought of that before I got up this morning; but looking at the stranger here getting into your boat, Dick, put it out of my head; so that I was not before *all* the blackbirds: however, there are a few about as good as you will get them anywhere in Hammersmith this morning."

Robert patted her on the head in a friendly manner; and we fell to on our breakfast, which was simple enough, but most delicately cooked, and set on the table with much daintiness. The bread was particularly good, and was of several different kinds. . . .

[The narrator discusses the new society with Mr. Hammond, a wise old man.]

"Now may I ask you about the position of women in your society?"

He laughed very heartily for a man of his years, and said: "It is not without reason that I have got a reputation as a careful student of history. I believe I really do understand 'the Emancipation of Women movement' of the nineteenth century. I doubt if any other man now alive does."

"Well?" said I, a little bit nettled by his merriment.

"Well," said he, "of course you will see that all that is a dead controversy now. The men have no longer any opportunity of tyrannizing over the women, or the women over the men; both of which things took place in those old times. The women do what they can do best, and what they like best, and the men are neither jealous of it or injured by it. This is such a commonplace that I am almost ashamed to state it."

I said, "O; and legislation? do they take any part in that?"

Hammond smiled and said: "I think you may wait for an answer to that question till we get on to the subject of legislation. There may be novelties to you in that subject also."

"Very well," I said; "but about this woman question? I saw at the Guest House that the women were waiting on the men: that seems a little like reaction, doesn't it?"

"Does it?" said the old man; "perhaps you think housekeeping an unimportant occupation, not deserving of respect. I believe that was the opinion of the 'advanced' women of the nineteenth century, and their male backers. If it is yours, I recommend to your notice an old Norwegian folk-lore tale called How the Man minded the House, or some such title; the result of which minding was that, after various tribulations, the man and the family cow balanced each other at the end of a rope, the man hanging half-way up the chimney, the cow dangling from the roof, which, after the fashion of the country, was of turf and sloping down low to the ground. Hard on the cow, *I* think. Of course no such mishap could happen to such a superior person as yourself," he added, chuckling.

I sat somewhat uneasy under this dry gibe. Indeed, his manner of treating this latter part of the question seemed to me a little disrespectful.

"Come, now, my friend," quoth he, "don't you know that it is a great pleasure to a clever woman to manage a house skillfully, and to do it so that all the house-mates about her look pleased, and are grateful to her? And then you know everybody likes to be ordered about by a pretty woman: why, it is one of the pleasantest forms of flirtation. You are not so old that you cannot remember that. Why, I remember it well."

And the old fellow chuckled again, and at last fairly burst out laughing.

"Excuse me," said he, after a while; "I am not laughing at anything you could be thinking of, but at that silly nineteenth-century fashion, current amongst rich so-called cultivated people, of ignoring all the steps by which their daily dinner was reached, as matters too low for their lofty intelligence. Useless idiots! Come, now, I am a 'literary man,' as we queer animals used to be called, yet I am a pretty good cook myself."

"So am I," said I.

"Well, then," said he, "I really think you can understand me better than you would seem to do, judging by your words and your silence."

Said I: "Perhaps that is so; but people putting in practice commonly this sense of interest in the ordinary occupations of life rather startles me. I will ask you a question or two presently about that. But I want to return to the position of women amongst you. You have studied the 'emancipation of women' business of the nineteenth century: don't you remember that some of the 'superior' women wanted to emancipate the more intelligent part of their sex from the bearing of children?"

The old man grew quite serious again. Said he: "I *do* remember about that strange piece of baseless folly, the result, like all other follies of the period, of the hideous class tyranny which then obtained. What do we think of it now? you would say. My friend, that is a question easy to answer. How could it possibly be but that maternity should be highly honored amongst us? Surely it is a matter of course that the natural and necessary pains which the mother must go through form a bond of union between man and woman, and extra stimulus to love and affection between them, and that this is universally recognized. For the rest, remember that all the *artificial* burdens of motherhood are now done away with. A mother has no longer any mere sordid anxieties for the future of her children. . . . So that, you see, the ordinarily healthy woman (and almost all our women are both healthy and at least comely), respected as a childbearer and rearer of children, desired as a woman, loved as a companion, unanxious for the future of her children, has far more instinct for maternity than the poor drudge and mother of drudges of past days could ever have had; or than her sister of the upper classes brought up in affected ignorance of natural facts, reared in an atmosphere of mingled prudery and prurience."

"You speak warmly," I said, "but I can see that you are right."

"Yes," he said, "and I will point out to you a token of all the benefits which we have gained by our freedom. What did you think of the looks of the people whom you have come across to-day?"

Said I: "I could hardly have believed that there could be so many good-looking people in any civilized country."

He crowed a little, like the old bird he was. "What! are we still civilized?" said he. "Well, as to our looks, the English and Jutish blood, which on the whole is predominant here, used not to produce much beauty. But I think we have improved it. I know a man who has a large collection of portraits printed from photographs of the nineteenth century, and going over those and comparing them with the everyday faces in these times, puts the improvement in our good looks beyond a doubt. Now, there are some people who think it not too fantastic to connect this increase of beauty directly with our freedom and good sense in the matters we have been speaking of: they believe that a child born from the natural and healthy love between a man and a woman, even if that be transient, is likely to turn out better in all ways, and especially in bodily beauty, than the birth of the respectable commercial marriage bed, or of the dull despair of the drudge of that system. They say, Pleasure begets pleasure. What do you think?"

"I am much of that mind," said I. . . .

Said I: "I thought that I understood from something that fell from you a little while ago that you had abolished civil law. Is that so, literally?"

"It abolished itself, my friend," said he. "As I said before, the civil law-courts were upheld for the defence of private property; for nobody ever pretended that it was possible to make people act fairly to each other by means of brute force. Well, private property being abolished, all the laws and all the legal 'crimes' which it had manufactured of course came to an end. Thou shalt not steal, had to be translated into, Thou shalt work in order to live happily. Is there any need to enforce that commandment by violence?"

"Well," said I, "that is understood, and I agree with it; but how about crimes of violence? would not their occurrence (and you admit that they occur) make criminal law necessary?"

Said he: "In your sense of the word, we have no criminal law either. Let us look at the matter closer, and see whence crimes of violence spring. By far the greater part of these in past days were the result of the laws of private property, which forbade the satisfaction of their natural desires to all but a privileged few, and of the general visible coercion which came of those laws. All *that* cause of violent crime is gone. Again, many violent acts came from the artificial perversion of the sexual passions, which caused over-weening jealousy and the like miseries. Now, when you look carefully into these, you will find that what lay at the bottom of them was mostly the idea (a law-made idea) of the woman being the property of the man, whether he were husband, father, brother, or what not. *That* idea has of course vanished with private property, as well as certain follies about the 'ruin' of women for following their natural desires in an illegal way, which, of course, was a convention caused by the laws of private property.

"Another cognate cause of crimes of violence was the family tyranny, which was the subject of so many novels and stories of the past, and which once more was the result of private property. Of course, that is all ended, since families are held together by no bond of coercion, legal or social, but by mutual liking and affection, and everybody is free to come or go as he or she pleases. . . ."

[Later in the novel, the narrator prepares for a boat trip into the countryside.]

It seemed quite early in the morning, and I expected to have the hall to myself when I came into it out of the corridor wherein was my sleeping chamber; but I met Annie at once, who let fall her broom and gave me a kiss, quite meaningless I fear, except as betokening friendship, though she reddened as she did it, not from shyness, but from friendly pleasure, and then stood and picked up her broom again, and went on with her sweeping, nodding to me as if to bid me stand out of the way and look on; which, to say the truth, I thought amusing enough, as there were five other girls helping her, and their graceful figures engaged in the leisurely work were worth going a long way to see, and their merry talk and laughing as they swept in quite a scientific manner was worth going a long way to hear. But Annie presently threw me back a word or two as she went on to the other end of the hall: "Guest," she said, "I am glad that you are up early, though we wouldn't disturb you; for our Thames is a lovely river at half-past six on a June morning; and as it would be a pity for you to lose it, I am told just to give you a cup of milk and a bit of bread outside there, and put you into the boat: for Dick and Clara are all ready now. Wait half a minute till I have swept down this row."

So presently she let her broom drop again, and came and took me by the hand and led me out on to the terrace above the river, to a little table under the boughs, where my bread and milk took the form of as dainty a breakfast as any one could desire, and then sat by me as I ate. And in a minute or two Dick and Clara came to me, the latter looking most fresh and beautiful in a light silk embroidered gown, which to my unused eyes was extravagantly gay and bright; while Dick was also handsomely dressed in white flannel prettily embroidered. Clara raised her gown in her hands as she gave me the morning greeting, and said laughingly: "Look, guest! you see we are at least as fine as any of the people you felt inclined to scold last night; you see we are not going to make the bright day and the flowers feel ashamed of themselves. Now scold me!"

Quoth I: "No, indeed; the pair of you seem as if you were born out of the summer day itself; and I will scold you when I scold it."

"Well, you know," said Dick, "this is a special day—all these days are, I mean. The hay-harvest is in some ways better than corn-harvest because of the beautiful weather; and really, unless you had worked in the hay-field in fine weather, you couldn't tell what pleasant work it is. The women look so pretty at it, too," he said, shyly; "so all things considered, I think we are right to adorn it in a simple manner."

24. Louis Frank (1904)

Nearly everywhere housework is relegated to the diligent hands of women. In various countries of Europe, notably in Corsica, the mother has the humble mission of preparing and serving the meals; she eats in the kitchen with the servants, far from the head of the family, for tradition still refuses her the privilege of sitting down at the father's table.

Should men continue to be exempt from all domestic work? Is it required that they continue to be ignorant of the occupations and tasks of the household, on which the health and happiness of all depend? We do not think so.

Indeed, the question is of especial interest in the case of the petty bourgeois and artisans. There the housewife is obliged to do everything by herself, without help from anyone else. And the smallest details are, for her, complicated by a thousand difficulties.

It is certain that, without reversing roles or wishing to transform husbands into childrens' maids, every man should learn to accept his share of household work. It should easily be possible to establish a rational division of household work. Is it not indecent to see nearly all men and their sons being served, like lords and ruling despots, by the mother of the family, and to make demands of her that are disrespectful, sometimes even disgusting and brutal? Husbands and sons should, for example, shine their own boots, brush their own clothes, help make the beds, turn the mattresses, clean the apartment or residence, and perform some of the heavy, tiring work. Women could then concern themselves especially with purchasing provisions, preparing the meals, serving the table, washing the dishes, and arranging the pots and pans.

Do not raise the objection that a division of domestic labor is impossible to establish, that it is contrary to masculine dignity to accept any part of this burden, or that even the most well-meaning man does not have time to devote part of his leisure time to this.

Such objections have no value. Man will come around to understanding that it is in his interest to help his companion with the housework. For him such cooperation will have the happy result of increasing, through good hygiene, the comfort and well-being of his entire family, of assuring the health of his descendants and prolonging his own life. As for the little bit of time this participation will require, he will easily find it, and happily so, by taking it from the all-too-numerous hours frittered away at gaming, in the cabaret, and in amusement establishments. Moreover, economic evolution tends, according to its laws, toward the progressive shortening of the working day and, also, thanks to motors, to cut down on the amount of energy required of the artisan. Less fatigued from his daily work, man in the future will be able to find more and more leisure time every day. It is only fair that he use some of it for good and not for evil; that he consecrate a part of it to helping his wife in the house, in order to improve both the situation of his companion and the conditions of prosperity for the household.

From another standpoint, the theoretical notions of domestic economy, the laws of general hygiene, the principles of diet, the elements of domestic accounting are equally useful for boys and girls. From this instruction both sexes can derive practical and salutary hints that are useful each day. . . .

In summary, we must combat—beginning with school—the prejudice that household work is strictly women's work. Men must also do their part. Thus we will root out the dangerous prejudice, so destructive to the social interest, that tends to deprecate household work. Later on, according to the principles taught at school, spouses will be able to arrive at a natural division of household work, an equitable allocation of duties, a rational exchange of familial and parental functions.

Motherhood in the Machine Age

SOURCES

25. Charlotte Perkins Gilman, *Women and Economics: A Study of the Economic Relation Between Men and Women as a Factor in Social Evolution* (New York, 1899), pp. 270-73, 276-81, 282-84. Originally published in 1898.

26. Ellen Key, *Love and Marriage*. Tr. Arthur G. Chater (New York, 1911), pp. 201-4, 211-18, 229-33. Originally published in Swedish in 1904 as the opening volume of Key's *Lifslinjer*.

By the turn of the century the significance of motherhood for the stability of national social organization was becoming the focus of much public discussion in all Western countries. What follows are excerpts from two of the most significant contributions to that debate: *Women and Economics*, by Charlotte Perkins Stetson Gilman (1860-1945), and *Love and Marriage*, by Ellen Sofia Karolina Key (1849-1926).

A grandniece of Catharine Beecher, Charlotte Perkins Gilman (who will here be referred to by her best-known name, that of her second husband) was raised in New England by her mother after her father had deserted the family. She attended the Rhode Island School of Design and became self-supporting, married at the age of twenty-four, and bore a daughter the following year. Marriage and motherhood brought her to a state of severe nervous depression and, in 1890, she left her first husband, Walter Stetson, and moved to California with her child. During the 1890's Gilman became acquainted with socialist doctrines. She was particularly influenced by Edward Bellamy's utopian novel *Looking Backwards* (Doc. 49) and by contacts made during several trips to Europe. Her interpretative study of the woman question appeared in 1898 to wide acclaim. Her suggestions for freeing mothers from full-time child care drew on both the Saint-Simonian and Fourierist proposals elaborated in pre-1848 France (Vol. I, Docs. 34-36) and adopted in America at experimental communities like Brook Farm. Gilman elaborated such ideas within an evolutionary Social Darwinist framework, linking the development of new forms of family life (bolstered by communal childcare arrangements and communal kitchens) to her belief in the inevitable progress of humankind toward further individualization and specialization of activities. Unlike many other Social Darwinists, however, she did not accept the notion of increasing differentiation of the sexes. In this selection she declares the bankruptcy of the Western mother-educator ideal and calls for a "less selfish" form of social mothering, supported by trained personnel employed in institutional childcare facilities. Such a system, Gilman believed, would produce less narcissistic children and more freedom for mothers.

The second selection is excerpted from the enormously influential reform tract *Love and Marriage*, by the Swedish writer Ellen Karolina Sofia Key. Key was the eldest child of a Swedish landowner, a political radical of Scottish ancestry, and his wife, a Swedish noblewoman. Educated at home, Key traveled widely throughout Europe with her father during her early adulthood. When the family lost its land during the agricultural crisis of the 1880's, she became a teacher in Stockholm in order to support herself; for many years she lectured at the workers' institute there. Though never married, she had keen insight into the problems of wives and mothers. She was encouraged by the dramatist Bjørnson (Doc. 11) to write, and in middle age she began to publish the controversial works that brought her considerable world fame—*Love and Marriage* and *The Century of the Child*.

In dramatic contrast to Gilman, Ellen Key invokes women's biological nature and the traditional division of labor as foundations for a radical proposal, emphasizing women's duty to take up with joy the obligations and responsibilities of biological and social motherhood. She proposed, however, that formal training for motherhood or for general nursing should be recognized by the state as women's equivalents of military service for men. Throughout her works Key presents a thoroughly secularized, albeit scarcely traditional vision of marriage. She criticized the Catholic and the Lutheran concepts of institutionalized monogamy as well as those of other sects that advocated chastity within marriage except for procreative purposes, and called instead for open acknowledgment of the sexual side of love. In contrast to Gilman, Key argued that women's work in the private home must be accorded adequate social and economic recognition, rather than being communalized. Urging radical reforms in marriage laws that would enhance and dignify women's situation as mothers, Key is in fact advocating the possibility that women could build better homes and raise better children with men with whom they shared a genuinely full and sympathetic relationship. Her ideas found wide support among leaders of the women's movement throughout Northern Europe, especially in imperial Germany.

25. Charlotte Perkins Gilman (1898)

In reconstructing in our minds the position of women under conditions of economic independence, it is most difficult to think of her as a mother.

We are so unbrokenly accustomed to the old methods of motherhood, so convinced that all its processes are inter-relative and indispensable, and that to alter one of them is to endanger the whole relation, that we cannot conceive of any desirable change.

When definite plans for such change are suggested,—ways in which babies might be better cared for than at present,—we either deny the advantages of the change proposed or insist that these advantages can be reached under our present system. Just as in cooking we seek to train the private cook and to exalt and purify the private taste, so in baby-culture we seek to train the individual mother, and to call for better conditions in the private home; in both cases ignoring the relation between our general system and its particular phenomena. Though it may be shown, with clearness, that in physical conditions the private house, as a place in which to raise children, may be improved upon, yet all the more stoutly do we protest that the mental life, the emotional life, of the home is the best possible environment for the young.

There was a time in human history when this was true. While progress derived its main impetus from the sex-passion, and the highest emotions were those that held us together in the family relation, such education and such surroundings as fostered and intensified these emotions were naturally the best. But in the stage into which we are now growing, when the family relation is only a part of life, and our highest duties lie between individuals in social relation, the child has new needs.

This does not mean, as the scared rush of the unreasoning mind to an immediate opposite would suggest, a disruption of the family circle or the destruction of the home. It does not mean the separation of mother and child,—that instant dread of the crude instinct of animal maternity. But it does mean a change of basis in the family relation by the removal of its previous economic foundation, and a change of method in our child-culture. We are no more bound to maintain forever our early methods in baby-raising than we are bound to maintain them in the education of older children, or in floriculture. All human life is in its very nature open to improvement, and motherhood is not excepted. The relation between men and women, between husband and wife, between parent and child, changes inevitably with social advance; but we are loath to admit it. We think a change here must be wrong, because we are so convinced that the present condition is right.

On examination, however, we find that the existing relation between parents and children in the home is by no means what we unquestioningly assume. We all hold certain ideals of home life, of family life. When we see around us, or read of, scores and hundreds of cases of family unhappiness and open revolt, we lay it to the individual misbehavior of the parties concerned, and go on implicitly believing in the intrinsic perfection of the institution. When, on the other hand, we find people living together in this relation, in peace and love and courtesy, we do not conversely attribute this to individual superiority and virtue; but we point to it as instancing the innate beauty of the relation.

To the careful sociological observer what really appears is this: when individual and racial progress was best served by the close associations of family life, people were very largely developed in capacity for family affection. They were insensitive to the essential limitations and incessant friction of the relation. They assented to the absolute authority of the head of the family and to the minor despotism of lower functionaries, manifesting none of those sharply defined individual characteristics which are so inimical to the family relation.

But we have reached a stage where individual and racial progress is best served by the higher specialization of individuals and by a far wider sense of love and duty. This change renders the psychic condition of home life increasingly disadvantageous. . . .

The lines of social relation to-day are mainly industrial. Our individual lives, our social peace and progress, depend more upon our economic relations than upon any other. For a long time society was organized only on a sex-basis, a religious basis, or a military basis, each of such organizations being comparatively transient; and its component individuals labored alone on an economic basis of helpless individualism.

Duty is a social sense, and develops only with social organization. As our civil organization has become national, we have developed the sense of duty to the State. As our industrial organization has grown to the world-encircling intricacies of to-day, as we have come to hold our place on earth by reason of our vast and elaborate economic relation with its throbbing and sensitive machinery of communication and universal interservice, the unerring response of the soul to social needs has given us a new kind of loyalty,—loyalty to our work. The engineer who sticks to his engine till he dies, that his trainload of passengers may live; the cashier who submits to torture rather than disclose the secret of the safe,—these are loyal exactly as was the servitor of feudal times, who followed his master to the death, or the subject who gave up all for his king. Professional honor, duty to one's employers, duty to the work itself, at any cost,—this is loyalty, faithfulness, the power to stay put in a relation necessary to the social good, though it may be directly against personal interest.

It is in the training of children for this stage of human life that the private home has ceased to be sufficient, or the isolated, primitive, dependent woman capable. Not that the mother does not have an intense and overpowering sense of loyalty and of duty; but it is duty to individuals, just as it was in the year one. What she is unable to follow, in her enforced industrial restriction, is the higher specialization of labor, and the honorable devotion of human lives to the development of their work. She is most slavishly bound to her daily duty, it is true; but it does not occur to her as a duty to raise the grade of her own labor for the sake of humanity, nor as a sin so to keep back the progress of the world by her contented immobility.

She cannot teach what she does not know. She cannot in any sincerity uphold as a duty what she does not practise. The child learns more of the virtues needed in modern life—of fairness, of justice, of comradeship, of collective interest and action—in a common school than can be taught in the most perfect family circle. We may preach to our children as we will of the great duty of loving and serving one's neighbor; but what the baby is born into, what the child grows up to see and feel, is the concentration of one entire life—his mother's—upon the personal aggrandizement of one family, and the human service of another entire life—his father's—so warped and strained by the necessity of "supporting his family" that treason to society is the common price of comfort in the home. For a man to do any base, false work for which he is hired, work that injures producer and consumer alike; to prostitute what power and talent he possesses to whatever purchaser may use them,—this is justified among men by what they call duty to the family, and is unblamed by the moral sense of dependent women.

And this is the atmosphere in which the wholly home-bred, mother-taught child grows up. Why should not food and clothes and the comforts of his own people stand first in his young mind? Does he not see his mother, the all-loved, all-perfect one, peacefully spending her days in the arrangement of these things which his father's ceaseless labor has procured? Why should he not grow up to care for his own, to the neglect and willing injury of all the rest, when his earliest, deepest impressions are formed under such exclusive devotion?

It is not the home as a place of family life and love that injures the child, but as the centre of a tangled heap of industries, low in their ungraded condition, and lower still because they are wholly personal. Work the object of which is merely to serve one's self is the lowest. Work the object of which is merely to serve one's family is the next lowest. Work the object of which is to serve more and more people, in widening range, till it approximates the divine spirit that cares for all the world, is social service in the fullest sense, and the highest form of service that we can reach.

It is this personality in home industry that keeps it hopelessly down. The short range between effort and attainment, the constant attention given to personal needs, is bad for the man, worse for the woman, and worst for the child. It belittles his impressions of life at the start. It accustoms him to magnify the personal duties and minify the social ones, and it greatly retards his adjustment to larger life. This servant-motherhood, with all its unavoidable limitation and ill results, is the concomitant of the economic dependence of woman upon man, the direct and inevitable effect of the sexuo-economic relation.

The child is affected by it during his most impressionable years, and feels the effect throughout life. The woman is permanently retarded by it;

the man, less so, because of his normal social activities, wherein he is under more developing influence. But he is injured in great degree, and our whole civilization is checked and perverted.

We suffer also, our lives long, from an intense self-consciousness, from a sensitiveness beyond all need; we demand measureless personal attention and devotion, because we have been born and reared in a very hotbed of these qualities. A baby who spent certain hours of every day among other babies, being cared for because he was a baby, and not because he was "my baby," would grow to have a very different opinion of himself from that which is forced upon each new soul that comes among us by the ceaseless adoration of his own immediate family. What he needs to learn at once and for all, to learn softly and easily, but inexorably, is that he is one of many. We all dimly recognize this in our praise of large families, and in our saying that "an only child is apt to be selfish." So is an only family. The earlier and more easily a child can learn that human life means many people, and their behavior to one another, the happier and stronger and more useful his life will be. . . .

And yet, insidiously, slowly, irresistibly, while we flatter ourselves that things remain the same, they are changing under our very eyes from year to year, from day to day. Education, hiding itself behind a wall of books, but consisting more and more fully in the grouping of children and in the training of faculties never mentioned in the curriculum,—education, which is our human motherhood, has crept nearer and nearer to its true place, its best work,—the care and training of the little child. Some women there are, and some men, whose highest service to humanity is the care of children. Such should not concentrate their powers upon their own children alone,—a most questionable advantage,—but should be so placed that their talent and skill, their knowledge and experience, would benefit the largest number of children. Many women there are, and many men, who, though able to bring forth fine children, are unable to educate them properly. Simply to bear children is a personal matter,—an animal function. Education is collective, human, a social function.

As we now arrange life, our children must take their chances while babies, and live or die, improve or deteriorate, according to the mother to whom they chance to be born. An inefficient mother does not prevent a child from having a good school education or a good college education; but the education of babyhood, the most important of all, is wholly in her hands. It is futile to say that mothers should be taught how to fulfil their duties. You cannot teach every mother to be a good school educator or a good college educator. Why should you expect every mother to be a good nursery educator? Whatever our expectations, she is not; and our mistrained babies, such of them as survive the maternal handling, grow to be such people as we see about us.

The growth and change in home and family life goes steadily on under and over and through our prejudices and convictions; and the education of the child has changed and become a social function, while we still imagine the mother to be doing it all.

26. Ellen Key (1904)

As soon as it is recognised that the individual is also an end in himself, with the right and duty of satisfying in the first place his own demands according to his nature, then it must remain the private affair of the individual whether he will either leave altogether unfulfilled his mission as a member of the race, or whether he will limit its fulfilment.

But as the individual cannot attain his highest life-enhancement or fulfil his own purpose otherwise than in connection with the race, he acquires duties also towards it, and not least as a sexual being. If life has given the individual a lot which renders moral parentage possible, and conditions which are favourable to new lives, then the only moral limitation of the number of children is one which—in and by means of the individual's own life-enhancement and that of the children—is to the advantage of the whole community.

But when only petty and selfish reasons—such as considerations of the children's inheritance, personal good-living and voluptuousness, beauty and comfort—determine fathers and mothers to keep the number of their children below the average required to secure the due increase of population, then their conduct is antisocial. A person, on the other hand, who is content with few or no children, because he or she has a work to perform, may be able to compensate society by the production of another class of value.

To these now moral, now immoral, motives for having few children or none at all, must be added woman's desire to devote her purely human qualities to other tasks. This, however, does not refer to those wives who are obliged to establish their married life upon their own bread-winning labour as well as their husband's; a necessity which for the present hinders them from motherhood although they are continually dreaming of the future child. It is here a question only of women's personal self-assertion.

Women are no longer content to manage their husbands' incomes, but wish to earn their own; they will not use their husband as a middleman between themselves and society, but will themselves look after their interests; they will not confine their gifts to the home but will also put them in public circulation. And in all these respects they are right. But when, in order thus to be able to "live their life," they wish to be "freed from the burden of the child," one begins to doubt. For until automatic nurses have been invented, or male volunteers have offered themselves, the burden must fall upon other women, who—whether themselves mothers or not—are thus obliged to bear a double one. Real liberation for women is thus impossible; the only thing possible is a new division of the burdens.

Those already "freed" declare that, by making money, studying, writing, taking part in politics, they feel themselves leading a higher existence with greater emotions than the nursery could have afforded them. They look down upon the "passive" function of bearing children—and rightly, when it remains only passive—without perceiving that it embodies as

nothing else does the possibility of putting their whole personality in activity. Every human being has the right to choose his own happiness—or
unhappiness.

But what these women have no right to, is to be considered equally
worthy of the respect of society with those who find their highest emotions through their children, the beings who not only form the finest subject for human art, but are at the same time the only work by which the
immortality of its creator is assured. Another thing that these women
who are afraid of children cannot expect is, that their experience should
be considered equally valuable with that of women who—after they have
fulfilled their immediate duties as mothers—employ for the public benefit the development they have gained in their private capacity. . . .

To every thoughtful person, it is becoming increasingly evident that the
human race is approaching the parting of the ways for its future destiny.
Either—speaking generally—the old division of labour, founded in nature, must continue: that by which the majority of women not only bear
but also bring up the new generation within the home; that men—
directly in marriage or indirectly through a State provision for motherhood—should work for women's support during the years they are performing this service to society; and that women, during their mental and
bodily development, should aim, in their choice of work and their habits
of life, at preserving their fitness for their possible mission as mothers.

Or, on the other hand, woman must be brought up for relentless competition with man in all the departments of production—thus necessarily
losing more and more the power and the desire to provide the race with
new human material—and the State must undertake the breeding as well
as the rearing of children, in order to liberate her from the cares which at
present most hinder her freedom of movement.

Any compromise can only relate to the extent, not to the kind, of the
division of labour; for no hygiene, however intelligent, no altered conditions of society with shorter hours of labour and better pay, no new system of study with moderate brainwork can abolish the law of nature: that
woman's function as a mother, directly and indirectly, creates a need of
caution, which at times interferes with her daily work if she obeys the
need; while if, on the other hand, she disregards it, it revenges itself on
her and on the new generation. Nor could any improvements in the care
of children and domestic arrangements prevent what always remains
above these things—if the home is to be more than a place for eating and
sleeping—from taking up time and thought, powers and feelings. If,
therefore, we are to retain the old division of labour, under which the
race has hitherto progressed, then woman must be won back to the
home.

But this involves more than a thorough transformation of the present
conditions of production; for we are here face to face with the profoundest movement of the time, woman's desire of freedom as a human being
and as a personality, and in this we are confronted with the greatest tragic
conflict the world's history has hitherto witnessed. For if it is tragic

enough for an individual or a nation relentlessly to seek out its innermost ego and to follow it even to destruction—how tragic will it not be, when the same applies to half of humanity? Such a tragedy is profound even when it occurs in the struggle between what are usually called the "good" and "evil" powers in man—a form of speech which followers of the religion of Life have given up, since they know that so-called crime may also increase human nature and human worth; that what is profoundly human may appear as evil and yet be healthy and beautiful, since it involves the enhancement of life. But infinitely greater will be the tragedy when the conflict arises between powers unquestionably good—those in the highest sense life-enhancing—and not even between secondary powers of this order, but between the very highest, the fundamental powers themselves, the profoundest conditions of being.

That is how woman's tragic problem now stands, if we leave out of consideration the egoists just alluded to and turn our eyes to the majority: woman's nature against man's nature, exercise of power in order to satisfy the claims of the member of the race or those of the personality. If Shakespeare came back to earth, he would now make Hamlet a woman, for whom the question "to be or not to be" would be full of a double pathos: the eternal terror of the human race and the new terror of the female sex before its own riddle. . . .

The struggle that woman is now carrying on is more far-reaching than any other; and if no diversion occurs, it will finally surpass in fanaticism any war of religion or race.

The woman's movement circles round the periphery of the question without finding any radius to its centre, which is the limitation of human existence to time and space; the limitation of the soul in the power of simultaneously giving itself up to different spheres of thought and feeling, and the limitation of the body in the capacity for bearing a constantly increased burden.

The heaviest cause of degeneration at the present time—the necessity for millions of women of earning their bread under miserable conditions, and the risk that they may lose, some the possibility, some the wish, for motherhood—may disappear, and nevertheless the chief problem will remain unsolved for any woman who has attained individually-human development.

In however high degree a woman may be bodily and mentally competent, this can never prevent the time her outdoor work occupies being a deduction from the time she can bestow on her home, since she cannot simultaneously be in two places; she cannot have her thoughts and feelings simultaneously centred upon and absorbed by her work and her home. And all that is personal in her home life, all that cannot be left to another, will thus necessarily interfere with her individual freedom of movement, in an inward as well as an outward sense.

If the child and the husband mean anything at all in a woman's life, she cannot allow another to have the affection, the care, and the anxiety about them: she must give her own soul to this.

But then, on the other hand, it will interfere with her book, her picture, her lecture, her research, just as infallibly as would the trouble of in her own person nursing and taking care of the child—a trouble which she is really able to renounce, though with a great loss of happiness and of insight into the child's character.

In a word, the most momentous conflict is not between health and sickness, development or degeneration, but between the two equally strong, healthy, and beautiful forms of life: the life of the soul or the life of the family.

Many women, who see the necessity of deciding for one or the other, choose the former and thus avoid or limit their motherhood, since they believe themselves to have another, richer contribution to make to civilisation. But would not the race have gained more by the talents of which these gifted women might have been the mothers?

We may pity for their own sake the barren women of the aristocracy or plutocracy, who from pure selfishness have refused to become mothers. But they do an involuntary service to the race, in that fewer degenerate children are born.

Full-blooded women, in a mental or bodily sense, are, on the other hand, the most valuable from the standpoint of generation. When these are content with one child or none, because they wish to devote themselves to their individual pursuits, then it is their work, not the race, which receives the richness of their blood, the fire of their creative joy, the sap of their thought, and the beauty of their feelings.

But it may be—according to a very moderate calculation—that there are annually produced by the women of the world a hundred thousand novels and works of art, which might better have been boys and girls!

It is nearly always the best women who are confronted by the tragic necessity of choosing one sphere or the other, or of dividing themselves in an unsatisfied way between the two; for, the more they increase their demands upon themselves, the more surely do they feel this partition as a half-measure.

Partly by economical necessity, however, partly by the spirit of the age, the choice is more and more often determined in favour of work, when the two alternatives are evenly balanced in a woman's own feelings; for the emancipation of women has laid the stress of feeling upon independence, social work, creation. This has raised these considerations in the mind of woman to the same extent as it has depreciated those of home life. Want of psychological insight makes the champions of women's rights candid when they declare that they have never depreciated the tasks of the home, but on the contrary have tried to educate woman for them. Schools of housekeeping deserve all recognition, but as regards creating greater enthusiasm for domestic duties they have not hitherto been signally successful. It is because their enthusiasm has been directed to every manifestation of woman's desire to work in man's former sphere, that the calling of wife and mother has now lost in attraction.

Viewed historically, the work of emancipation must be advanced by this one-sided enthusiasm. But now it is a question whether woman, in a new way, will be capable of being inspired by devotion to her purely womanly sphere of activity?

For nothing short of this would in the main be the solution of the question. A return to the old ideal of womanliness would be as unthinkable as it would be unfortunate. A continued struggle to get rid of the ancient division of labour between the sexes is thinkable—and equally unfortunate. That woman should apply her new will to her ancient mission would be the most fortunate solution. But—is this even thinkable? . . .

No, is the answer of Charlotte Perkins Stetson [Gilman] and of many others with her; the solution is State care of children. Look at all the wretched homes, where the children lack the most necessary mental and bodily conditions for healthy development. The collective rearing of all children would be both better and cheaper. Only those women who are liberated from the toils of the nursery and the kitchen are really free. To the woman accustomed to public activity, the tasks of the home are monotonous and tiresome. On the other hand, as a calling freely chosen, the care of children would satisfy those who have the gift for it. The majority of mothers are only ape-mothers to their little children, and, as the latter grow bigger, this vague affection is replaced by an obstinate misunderstanding.

This is what one hears over and over again at the present time. And the more it is repeated, the more certain do women become that all these half-truths are—the truth.

Thus it is the mothers who are not good enough to bring up their own children, that are expected to provide the new illustrious leaders of the community. It is the parents who themselves lack the talent and inclination for bringing up children, that—directly or indirectly—will have to superintend and select the persons who, in their place, will perform the duties of parents. In other words, they are to discover and appreciate qualities that they do not themselves possess. The trouble that a woman cannot take for the children to whom she has herself given life, is to be borne by other women for ten, twenty, or thirty children, who are not their own.

Even to-day, there is sometimes to be found a kind of primitive type of womanliness, so widely maternal, with such a superfluity of strength, of tenderness, of talent for organisation that it is too powerful for a single home; a type which really possesses the immense wealth of spiritual elasticity, joy, and warmth, that is necessary in order that every such child should have its full share of these. But most women probably do not possess any more of these things than is just sufficient for their own children. And with these "elected mothers," quickly worn out as they would be, ten, twenty, or thirty children would be as badly off mentally as they would be bodily if a single mother's milk had to be divided among them all. It is even now a serious loss to society that so many human beings are enfeebled for life by insufficient nourishment in childhood. But according to the plan we have been discussing, which now has so many adherents, everyone would be starved in childhood as regards affection. It is even now a serious loss to culture that school-life makes children uniform. Still more irreparable would be the harm if their fashioning were in the hands of a thorough-going State care of children.

The danger of uniformity is inseparable from the present tendency to a hard-and-fast organisation of society, with an ever greater need of co-operation, an ever closer connection, an ever more intimate feeling of re-lationship between its component parts. The organisation must go on, because, amongst other reasons, it is only in this way that the individual can now gain increased freedom for development and the use of his per-sonal powers. But if these increased possibilities of satisfying personal needs and using personal powers are to be of value to the individual—and through him to the whole community—then we must also have some individualities left who will be capable of taking advantage of their possibilities.

And now it is certain that the home—with its changing conditions of good and evil—is first and foremost the best means of forming an organically developing sense of solidarity with the whole community. Life itself creates in the home an interdependence among its members, a sympathy for others' destiny, a contact with the realities of life, and with the seriousness of work, which no institution can create. It is by the efforts of a father and a mother that the joys of home are provided; it is affection for all which counter-balances the mutual rights of all; which gives to each his weight and his counterpoise in a way so natural that the methodical arrangements of an institution would never be able to imitate it. And furthermore, different homes, with the variety of different impres-sions they offer, are the best means of forming different characters and peculiarities. However straitened and poor in every sense a home may be, it nevertheless, as a rule, provides more personal freedom of movement and results in less uniformity than a collective system of bringing-up.

If this is even true of those homes where there can be no question of education in a higher sense, then in better homes the watchfulness and warmth of affection, its understanding and sensitiveness, will be the forces which will induce and protect individuality of character, and which will most surely discover what ought to be counteracted and what left alone for self-development. To this must be added the insight which the parents' knowledge of themselves and of each other gives into their children's character, an insight which no stranger can possess.

To this it is objected that, if every quarter of a town and every few square miles of country had its "State nursery," parents would often be able to see to their children, as well as to take them home and thus have an opportunity of using their influence. But apart from the circumstance that the relationship would then in most cases resemble that of the French *petite bourgeoisie* visiting their children *en nourrice*—that is to say, that affection would be shown in a desire to amuse and deck out the child, to caress and play with it—the most important point is forgotten.

This is that time, more time, and still more time, is one condition of education, and quiet the other. Souls are not to be tended like maladies, in fixed hours of treatment.

Depopulation and Motherhood in France

SOURCES

27. Émile Zola, *Fruitfulness* (New York, 1900), pp. 481-84. Tr. Ernest Vizetelly. Originally published as *Fécondité* in Paris (1899).

28. Eugène Brieux, *Maternity*, in *Three Plays by Brieux*, ed. and introduced by Bernard Shaw, Tr. Mrs. Bernard Shaw (New York and London, 1911), pp. 54-57. Originally produced in Paris, December 1903.

29. Nelly Roussel, speech given at the women's meeting called to protest the centennial of the Civil Code, 29 October 1904. Published in *La Fronde*, 1 November 1904. Tr. KMO.

France was the first Western nation to experience a sustained decline in its birthrate. In the 1890's public concern over lack of population growth mounted, even as the French women's movement established a firm organizational base. Some commentators went so far as to blame "depopulation" (as it was then called) on female emancipation, even though it was, of course, impossible to prove any causal relationship. The following selections illuminate three widely different perspectives on the intertwining themes of depopulation, nationalism, and women's rights in fin-de-siècle France.

The first selection is taken from *Fruitfulness*, a novel by Émile Zola (1840-1902). Written during his exile in England (following his intervention in the Dreyfus Affair) and published in 1899, *Fruitfulness* ranks among Zola's most widely discussed novels, though it is little known today. In this didactic novel Zola declared war on the idealized, sexless, and infertile image of women that he felt characterized the literary production of the German idealists and their French followers, the symbolists, during the 1880's. In the wake of mounting concern over France's population crisis, Zola expressed his skepticism about achieving greater fertility through legal or fiscal reform. He thought a new moral climate was required and, with his *Four Gospel* (*Les Quatres Evangiles*) sequence of novels, he tried to create one; hence the mystic-religious tone (Zola's rabid anticlericalism notwithstanding) of *Fruitfulness* and its successors, *Work*, *Truth*, and *Justice*. Like the Saint-Simonians, Comte, and Michelet before him, Zola sought to preach a new secular—and patriarchal—religion in which women would play a central role as goddesses of fertility. Indeed, *Fruitfulness* abounds with organic metaphors; the fertility of the land, warmed by the sun and worked by men, symbolically parallels the fertility of the women. Most commentators agree that Zola's personal experiences played a vital role in shaping his literary work. In this case, the critical experience was Zola's own fatherhood late in life, with the births in 1889 and 1891 of his two children by a twenty-year-old mistress, Jeanne Rozerot. Himself an only child whose marriage had been childless (apparently by choice), Zola had nevertheless tasted the fruits of spiritual paternity through the creation of hundreds of characters for his novels; but, like Michelet, Zola at midlife found himself fascinated by the worship of the maternal woman. He became obsessed with the centrality of sex and the creative impulse of physical paternity, and in *Fruitfulness* he presented an immense panorama of bounteous reproduction in loving patriarchal families to inspire the next generation of Frenchmen. This excerpt from the concluding chapter of the novel follows on the celebration of the seventieth wedding anniversary of Zola's prolific hero and heroine, Mathieu and Marianne Froment. Some 158 of their children, grandchildren, and great-grandchildren, with husbands and wives, have come to celebrate with them.

The second selection is from a contemporary play, *Maternity*, by Eugène Brieux (1858-1932). Brieux was the child of Parisian artisans and, in contrast to many of his literary peers, was largely self-educated. He worked as a bank clerk and as a journalist to sustain himself during his early years as a writer. In the 1890's he wrote a series of powerful plays addressing contemporary social issues, many of which explored aspects of the woman question. These plays prompted Bernard Shaw to rank Brieux as "the most important dramatist west of Russia" after Ibsen's death, and earned the playwright election to the Académie Française in 1910. In his 1897 play, *Les Trois Filles de Monsieur Dupont*, Brieux had presented a brief on behalf of women's right to motherhood in the face of men's selfish possessiveness; he followed it with another play indicting the deadly wet-nursing business. These plays so impressed republican political leaders that in 1902 Brieux was appointed to the Extra-Parliamentary Commission on Depopulation. But in 1903 Brieux turned to consider the other side of the question; in *Maternity* he rebuked bourgeois hypocrisy on the subject of unwed motherhood and presented a powerful case for the right of women to control their own bodies against the demands of man and the state for incessant childbearing. Excerpted here is the confrontation scene between Lucie Brignac and her husband, an ambitious and unscrupulous sub-prefect. Lucie has just learned that her younger sister Annette, who lives with the couple and their children, is pregnant by a local notable's son who has no intention of marrying her despite his earlier pledges of undying love.

The third selection comes from an angry speech by Nelly Roussel (1878-1922), given at a meeting of women's movement activists protesting the Civil Code, on the occasion of its centennial celebration. Roussel, married to the sculptor Henri Godet, was in her early twenties the mother of three children and took up writing columns on women's issues for the all-woman staffed daily newspaper *La Fronde*. In 1903 she emerged as a powerful public speaker for Paul Robin's Ligue pour la Régéneration Humaine, which, amid official efforts to deal with the population scare, launched a deliberately provocative campaign to spread birth control propaganda and contraceptive information among working-class women. Roussel toured France, delivering lectures on "the eternal victim" in which she elaborated at length on many of the themes sketched out in this moving indictment.

---

27. Émile Zola (1899)

Then, the banquet ended, they quitted the table and spread freely over the lawn. There was a last ovation around Mathieu and Marianne, who were encompassed by their eager offspring. At one and the same time a score of arms were outstretched, carrying children, whose fair or dark heads they were asked to kiss. Aged as they were, returning to a divine state of childhood, they did not always recognize those little lads and lasses. They made mistakes, used wrong names, fancied that one child was another. Laughter thereupon arose, the mistakes were rectified, and appeals were made to the old people's memory. They likewise laughed, the errors were amusing, but it mattered little if they no longer remembered a name, the child at any rate belonged to the harvest that had sprung from them.

Then there were certain granddaughters and great-granddaughters whom they themselves summoned and kissed by way of bringing good luck to the babes that were expected, the children of their children's children, the race which would ever spread and perpetuate them through the far-off ages. And there were mothers, also, who were nursing, mothers whose little ones, after sleeping quietly during the feast, had now awakened, shrieking their hunger aloud. These had to be fed, and the mothers merrily seated themselves together under the trees and gave them the breast in all serenity. Therein lay the royal beauty of woman, wife and mother; fruitful maternity triumphed over virginity by which life is slain. Ah! might manners and customs change, might the idea of morality and the idea of beauty be altered, and the world recast, based on the triumphant beauty of the mother suckling her babe in all the majesty of her symbolism! From fresh sowings there ever came fresh harvests, the sun ever rose anew above the horizon, and milk streamed forth endlessly like the eternal sap of living humanity. And that river of milk carried life through the veins of the world, and expanded and overflowed for the centuries of the future!

The greatest possible sum of life in order that the greatest possible happiness might result: that was the act of faith in life, the act of hope in the justice and goodness of life's work. Victorious fruitfulness remained the one true force, the sovereign power which alone moulded the future. She was the great revolutionary, the incessant artisan of progress, the mother of every civilization, ever re-creating her army of innumerable fighters, throwing through the centuries millions after millions of poor and hungry and rebellious beings into the fight for truth and justice. Not a single forward step in history has ever been taken without numerousness having urged humanity forward. Tomorrow, like yesterday, will be won by the swarming of the multitude whose quest is happiness. And to-morrow will give the benefits which our age has awaited; economic equality obtained even as political equality has been obtained; a just apportionment of wealth rendered easy; and compulsory work re-established as the one glorious and essential need.

It is not true that labor has been imposed on mankind as punishment for sin; it is on the contrary an honor, a mark of nobility, the most precious of boons, the joy, the health, the strength, the very soul of the world, which itself labors incessantly, ever creating the future. And misery, the great, abominable social crime, will disappear amid the glorification of labor, the distribution of the universal task among one and all, each accepting his legitimate share of duties and rights. And may children come, they will simply be instruments of wealth, they will but increase the human capital, the free happiness of a life in which the children of some will no longer be beasts of burden, or food for slaughter or for vice, to serve the egotism of the children of others. And life will then again prove the conqueror; there will come the renascence of life, honored and worshipped, the religion of life so long crushed beneath the hateful nightmare of Roman Catholicism, from which on divers occasions the nations have sought to free themselves by violence, and which they will drive away at last on the now near day when cult and power, and sovereign beauty shall be vested in the fruitful earth and the fruitful spouse.

In that last resplendent hour of eventide, Mathieu and Marianne reigned by virtue of their numerous race. They ended as heroes of life, because of the great creative work which they had accomplished amid battle and toil and grief. . . . Doubtless, as they themselves jestingly remarked at times, they had been prodigals, their family had been such a large one. But, after all, had they not been right? Their children had diminished no other's share, each had come with his or her own means of subsistence. And, besides, 'tis good to garner in excess when the granaries of a country are empty. Many such improvidents are needed to combat the egotism of others at times of great dearth. Amid all the frightful loss and wastage, the race is strengthened, the country is made afresh, a good civic example is given by such healthy prodigality as Mathieu and Marianne had shown.

28. Eugène Brieux (1903)

LUCIE. If necessary she can stay at home.

BRIGNAC. Stay at home! Rubbish! What would be the good of that? Servants would talk, and the scandal would be all the greater. And you haven't reflected that the consequences would fall upon me. You haven't troubled to consider me, or to remember the drawback this will be to me. I am not alluding to the imbecile jokes people are sure to make about the apostle of re-population. But our respectability will be called in question. People will remark that there are families in which such things don't happen. Political hatred and social prejudice will help them to invent all sorts of tales. And the allusions, the suggestions, the pretended pity! There would be nothing left for me but to send in my resignation!

LUCIE. Send it in.

BRIGNAC. Yes, and what should we live upon then?

LUCIE [*after a silence*] Then *that* is society's welcome to the newborn child!

BRIGNAC. To the child born outside marriage, yes. If it wasn't for that there would soon be nothing but illegitimate births. It is to preserve the family that society condemns the natural child.

LUCIE. If there is guilt, two people are guilty. Why do you only punish the mother?

BRIGNAC. What am I to say to you? Because it's easier.

LUCIE. And that's your justice! The truth is, you all uphold the conventions of society. You do. And the proof is that if Annette stayed here in the town to have her baby, you'd all cry shame upon her; but if she goes to Paris and has it secretly and gets rid of it, nobody will blame her. Let's be honest, and call things by their names: it is not immorality that is condemned, but motherhood. You say you want a larger number of births, and at the same time you say to women "No motherhood without marriage, and no marriage without money." As long as you've not changed *that* all your circulars will be met with shouts of derision—half from hate, half from pity!

BRIGNAC. Possibly. Good-night. I'm going to work.

LUCIE. Listen— Then you drive Annette from your house?

BRIGNAC. I don't drive her from my house. I beg her to go elsewhere.

LUCIE. I shall go with her.

BRIGNAC. You mean, leave me?

LUCIE. Yes.

BRIGNAC. Then you don't love me.

LUCIE. No.

BRIGNAC. Ah! Here's another story. Since when?

LUCIE. I never loved you.

BRIGNAC. You married me.

LUCIE. Not for love.

BRIGNAC. This is most interesting. Go on.

LUCIE. You're another victim of the state of society you are defending.

BRIGNAC. I don't understand.

LUCIE. I was a penniless girl, and so I had no offers of marriage. When you proposed to me I was tired of waiting, and I didn't want to be an old maid. I accepted you, but I knew you only came to me because the women with money wouldn't have you. I made up my mind to love you and be loyal.

BRIGNAC. Well?

LUCIE. But when my first baby came you deceived me. Since then I have only endured you, and you owe my submission to my cowardice. It was only my first child I wanted; the others you forced upon me, and when each was coming you left me. It's true I was unattractive, but that was not my fault. You left me day after day in my ugliness and loneliness, and when you came back to me from those other women, you were full of false solicitude about my health. I begged for a rest after nursing. I asked to be allowed to live a little for myself, to be a mother only with my own consent. You laughed at me in a vain, foolish way. You did not consider the future of your children or the life of your wife, but you forced upon me the danger and the suffering of bringing another child into the world. What was it to you? Just the satisfaction of your vanity. You could jest with your friends and make coarse witticisms about it. Fool!

BRIGNAC. That's enough, thank you. You're my wife—

LUCIE. I'll not be your wife any longer, and I won't have another child.

BRIGNAC. Why?

LUCIE. Because I've just found out what the future of my poor, penniless little girls is to be. It's to be Annette's fate, or mine. Oh, to think I've been cruel enough to bring three of them into the world already!

BRIGNAC. You're mad. And be good enough not to put on these independent airs. They're perfectly useless.

LUCIE. You think so?

BRIGNAC. I am sure of it. If you have had enough of me, get a divorce.

LUCIE. But you would keep the children?

BRIGNAC. Naturally. And let me tell you that as long as you are my wife before the world, you'll be my wife really.

LUCIE. And you will force me to have a child whenever you please?

BRIGNAC. Most certainly.

LUCIE. My God! They think a woman's body is like the clay of the fields; they want to drag harvest after harvest from it until it is worn out and done for! I refuse this slavery, and I shall leave you if you turn out my sister.

BRIGNAC. And your children?

LUCIE. I will take them with me.

BRIGNAC. And their food?

LUCIE. I will work.

BRIGNAC. Don't talk nonsense. You couldn't earn enough to keep them from starving. It's late: go to bed.

LUCIE [*her teeth clenched*] And wait for you?

BRIGNAC. And wait for me. Precisely. [*He goes out.*]

29. Nelly Roussel (1904)

[All] women, in whatever situation they were born, have an interest in a profound [social] upheaval. Among us there are no "ruling classes," no "privileged classes." *All of us* can declare war on today's society, for all of us are more or less ruined, our bodies, our hearts, our consciences brutalized by its laws. Great ladies are mistreated by princely brutes; *bourgeoises* dispossessed of their property; working women frustrated by their meager salaries; active, intelligent women who wish to utilize the resources of their brains, to develop their personalities freely, and who see so many doors closing before them, so many obstacles rising in their path; proud women who are repelled by the idea of being *kept women*, who suffer from not being able to be self-sufficient and having each day to beg their subsistence from some "protector"—legal or illegal—who often makes them pay dearly for his protection. Mothers, especially! Oh, yes indeed, mothers, the noble working women of life, whom Society does not acknowledge and denigrates, even while it dares ask them to multiply their troubles and to work for it unceasingly and without reprieve! And this, my sisters, this is the supreme inequity, among so many others! The most odious aspect of the situation we find ourselves in is that they invoke against us precisely that thing that ought to plead on our behalf. They see as an obstacle to our re-establishment—a pretext for drenching us with sorrow and humiliation in this maternal function—this terrible and sublime function that ought, on the contrary, to assure us every honor and every solicitude!

No honors are too great, no praise too high, for those brave soldiers who are mutilated in battle. But on our own battlefield, we mothers find no glory to be garnered. So-called civilized society has placed the work of death above the work of life by reserving, by some inconceivable aberration, its homage for the destructive soldier, its disdainful indifference for the woman who creates life. And when, revolted by such injustice—in the very name of our *duties*—we dare to reclaim our *rights*, they reply to us, with a shrug of the shoulders:

"Rights? What would you do with them, oh woman? Have you any need of rights? Accomplish without a murmur the sole task that suits you; the task that is your sole reason for existing. Make citizens and soldiers for us; give birth, give birth without pause; destroy your grace and wear away your health by continual gestation. Go! suffer and grieve; weep and wail; submit to your martyr's destiny; but do not count on anyone thanking you. Expect no recompense. You are made to give and not to receive. A married woman—your child will remain the property of his father, of the happy father whose only task in the common work is limited to a few moments of pleasure; and you, the sorrowful and battered *créatrice*, who has paid with your blood, your tears—you will not exist, you will not count! In marriage, annihilated as a *wife*, you will be equally annihilated as a *mother*. [As an] unwed mother, on the other hand, you alone will bear the weight of what bourgeois hypocrisy disdainfully calls your "fault." And it will not be enough to expiate it by bearing the physical tortures that constitute for you, woman, a sort of ransom for love; it will not be enough for you—poor girl—to experience all alone in your attic room, without assistance, without care, without one word of consoling love, without a comforting *squeeze* of the hand, the "sacred torment" of mothers. No! Society, the guardian of "morality," will arrive to add its refinements! For you it reserves—the better to punish you—abandonment, disdain, misery; the impossibility of remaking a happy and free life for yourself through your labor; even the impossibility of obtaining some assistance; and finally, the obligation of making your sad choice between *suicide* and *prostitution*. And if then, panic-stricken, desperate, weary of suffering, you suppress [the life of] this small being that you wanted so much to love, it [society] will find judges to send you away to finish your miserable existence on a bed of prison straw."

Oh, is it not true, *citoyennes*, my sisters; is it not true, you liberated and conscious women, you who have come here this evening to join your protests with our own; is it not true that a woman must be a mother in order to become truly *indignant*? That she must have experienced *all* aspects of a woman's life? that she know how much sorrow and sacrifice there is in this sublime role, to understand just how much is owed her, to measure well the ingratitude of man, and to stand up tall and straight in the face of dogma and codes, in the face of churches that insult her and of social institutions that crush her!!

But beware, oh Society! The day will come—don't doubt it—it has already come for some—when the eternal victim will become weary of carrying in her loins sons whom you will later teach to scorn their mothers, or daughters destined—alas!—to the same life of sacrifice and humiliation! The day when we will refuse to give you, ogres, your ration of cannon-fodder, of work-fodder, and fodder for suffering! The day, at last, when we will become mothers *only when we please*, when we will have resolved, after careful reflection, that we ourselves have good reason to do so; and especially when we will be very certain that we can make of our children beings who are *strong enough so that they will not become your victims*, and *revolted* enough by you so that you will have no reason to take pride over our birthings.

Nationalism and "Race Suicide" in the United States

SOURCES

30. Theodore Roosevelt, "Address Before the National Congress of Mothers, Washington, D.C., March 13, 1905," in *Presidential Addresses and State Papers*, III (New York, 1910), 282-84, 285, 288-90.

31. Anna Howard Shaw, "Presidential Address at the 1905 Convention of the National American Woman Suffrage Association, Portland, Ore., June 29, 1905," *The Woman's Journal* (Boston), 36, no. 28 (22 July 1905), 114-15; "Presidential Address at the 1906 Convention of the National American Woman Suffrage Association, Baltimore, Maryland, February 1906," *The Woman's Journal*, 37, no. 7 (17 February 1906), 26.

The decline in fertility was linked to the woman question in early twentieth-century America as well as in England, France, and Germany. The following selections from the years 1905-6 reveal that the issue was of prime concern both to the newly re-elected president of the United States, Theodore Roosevelt (1858-1919), and to the leadership of the woman suffrage movement, here represented by Dr. Anna Howard Shaw (1847-1919).

Theodore Roosevelt had long been considered a friend of the woman suffrage movement, having actively supported efforts to obtain the franchise in New York state during his term as governor. During his presidency, however, he firmly resisted all attempts to evoke an explicit statement of support for a constitutional suffrage amendment. Roosevelt had been interested in the woman question since his college days; he had argued in his senior thesis at Harvard in favor of equalizing the legal position of women. But both his own later writings and his family life reveal that he was a firm partisan of "equality in difference" for women and a defender of separate spheres for men's and women's daily endeavors. Hence his concern about the rising numbers of women in the labor force and demographic issues (both revealed in the 1890 U.S. census), and the significance of his denunciation of women's selfishness in having fewer children. His 1906 call to Congress for an investigation of the conditions for women in industry resulted in the compiling of an important report and the subsequent passage of protective legislation. In 1906, also, he advocated amending the Constitution to transfer jurisdiction over marriage and divorce law from the states to the federal government, but was unsuccessful in accomplishing this.

Dr. Anna Howard Shaw, the president of the National American Woman Suffrage Association from 1904 to 1915, was considered the movement's most able speaker. Of English ancestry, she had been raised in conditions of severe hardship on the Michigan frontier and, in spite of a childhood dominated by the most rugged physical labor, she acquired sufficient education to enable her to study first for the ministry at Boston University and, a few years later, to obtain a medical degree there as well. But she was soon attracted away from ministering and doctoring on an individual basis, and to political action, first through the WCTU and then by the campaign for woman suffrage, where she became closely associated with Susan B. Anthony. A well-educated, articulate woman who had chosen to remain single in order to accomplish her life's work, Dr. Shaw undoubtedly epitomized to men like Roosevelt the women he viewed as committing "race suicide." Shaw's rejoinders indicate, however, that she was quite capable of defending both the economic and the political interests of all women and mothers, whether single or married.

---

30. Theodore Roosevelt (1905)

Mrs. President:

In our modern industrial civilization there are many and grave dangers to counterbalance the splendors and the triumphs. It is not a good thing to see cities grow at disproportionate speed relatively to the country; for the small landowners, the men who own their little homes, and therefore to a very large extent the men who till farms, the men of the soil, have hitherto made the foundation of lasting national life in every State; and, if the foundation becomes either too weak or too narrow, the superstructure, no matter how attractive, is in imminent danger of falling.

But far more important than the question of the occupation of our citizens is the question of how their family life is conducted. No matter what that occupation may be, as long as there is a real home and as long as those who make up that home do their duty to one another, to their neighbors, and to the state, it is of minor consequence whether the man's trade is plied in the country or the city, whether it calls for the work of the hands or for the work of the head.

But the Nation is in a bad way if there is no real home, if the family is not of the right kind; if the man is not a good husband and father, if he is brutal or cowardly or selfish; if the woman has lost her sense of duty, if she is sunk in vapid self-indulgence or has let her nature be twisted so that she prefers a sterile pseudo-intellectuality to that great and beautiful development of character which comes only to those whose lives know the fulness of duty done, of effort made and self-sacrifice undergone.

In the last analysis the welfare of the state depends absolutely upon whether or not the average family, the average man and woman and their children, represent the kind of citizenship fit for the foundation of a great nation; and if we fail to appreciate this we fail to appreciate the root morality upon which all healthy civilization is based.

No piled-up wealth, no splendor of material growth, no brilliance of artistic development, will permanently avail any people unless its home life is healthy, unless the average man possesses honesty, courage, common-sense, and decency, unless he works hard and is willing at need to fight hard; and unless the average woman is a good wife, a good mother, able and willing to perform the first and greatest duty of womanhood, able and willing to bear, and to bring up as they should be brought up, healthy children, sound in body, mind, and character, and numerous enough so that the race shall increase and not decrease.

There are certain old truths which will be true as long as this world endures, and which no amount of progress can alter. One of these is the truth that the primary duty of the husband is to be the homemaker, the breadwinner for his wife and children, and that the primary duty of the woman is to be the helpmeet, the housewife, and mother. The woman should have ample educational advantages; but save in exceptional cases the man must be, and she need not be, and generally ought not to be, trained for a lifelong career as the family breadwinner; and, therefore, after a certain point the training of the two must normally be different because the duties of the two are normally different. This does not mean inequality of function, but it does mean that normally there must be dissimilarity of function. On the whole, I think the duty of the woman the more important, the more difficult, and the more honorable of the two; on the whole I respect the woman who does her duty even more than I respect the man who does his. . . .

Just as the happiest and most honorable and most useful task that can be set any man is to earn enough for the support of his wife and family, for the bringing up and starting in life of his children, so the most important, the most honorable and desirable task which can be set any woman is to be a good and wise mother in a home marked by self-respect and mutual forbearance, by willingness to perform duty, and by refusal to sink into self-indulgence or avoid that which entails effort and self-sacrifice. Of course, there are exceptional men and exceptional women who can do and ought to do much more than this, who can lead and ought to lead great careers of outside usefulness in addition to—not as substitute for—their home work; but I am not speaking of exceptions; I am speaking of the primary duties, I am speaking of the average citizens, the average men and women who make up the Nation. . . .

There are many good people who are denied the supreme blessing of children, and for these we have the respect and sympathy always due to those who, from no fault of their own, are denied any of the other great blessings of life. But the man or woman who deliberately foregoes these blessings, whether from viciousness, coldness, shallow-heartedness, self-indulgence, or mere failure to appreciate aright the difference between the all-important and the unimportant—why, such a creature merits contempt as hearty as any visited upon the soldier who runs away in battle, or upon the man who refuses to work for the support of those dependent upon him, and who though able-bodied is yet content to eat in idleness the bread which others provide.

The existence of women of this type forms one of the most unpleasant and unwholesome features of modern life. . . . That [she] also exists in American life is made unpleasantly evident by the statistics as to the dwindling families in some localities. It is made evident in equally sinister fashion by the census statistics as to divorce, which are fairly appalling; for easy divorce is now, as it ever has been, a bane to any nation, a curse to society, a menace to the home, an incitement to married unhappiness and to immorality, an evil thing for men and a still more hideous evil for women. These unpleasant tendencies in our American life are made evident by articles such as those which I actually read not long ago in a certain paper, where a clergyman was quoted, seemingly with approval, as expressing the general American attitude when he said that the ambition of any save a very rich man should be to rear two children only, so as to give his children an opportunity "to taste a few of the good things of life." . . .

The way to give a child a fair chance in life is not to bring it up in luxury, but to see that it has the kind of training that will give it strength of character. Even apart from the vital question of national life, and regarding only the individual interest of the children themselves, happiness in the true sense is a hundredfold more apt to come to any given member of a healthy family of healthy-minded children, well brought up, well educated, but taught that they must shift for themselves, must win their own way, and by their own exertions make their own positions of usefulness, than it is apt to come to those whose parents themselves have acted on and have trained their children to act on, the selfish and sordid theory that the whole end of life is "to taste a few good things."

The intelligence of the remark is on a par with its morality, for the most rudimentary mental process would have shown the speaker that if the average family in which there are children contained but two children the Nation as a whole would decrease in population so rapidly that in two or three generations it would very deservedly be on the point of extinction, so that the people who had acted on this base and selfish doctrine would be giving place to others with braver and more robust ideals. Nor would such a result be in any way regrettable; for a race that practiced such doctrine—that is, a race that practiced race suicide—would thereby conclusively show that it was unfit to exist, and that it had better give place to people who had not forgotten the primary laws of their being.

To sum up, then, the whole matter is simple enough. If either a race or an individual prefers the pleasures of mere effortless ease, of self-indulgence, to the infinitely deeper, the infinitely higher pleasures that come to those who know the toil and the weariness, but also the joy, of hard duty well done, why, that race or that individual must inevitably in the end pay the penalty of leading a life both vapid and ignoble. No man and no woman really worthy of the name can care for the life spent solely or chiefly in the avoidance of risk and trouble and labor. Save in exceptional cases the prizes worth having in life must be paid for, and the life worth living must be a life of work for a worthy end, and ordinarily of work more for others than for one's self.

The man is but a poor creature whose effort is not rather for the betterment of his wife and children than for himself; and as for the mother, her very name stands for loving unselfishness and self-abnegation, and, in any society fit to exist, is fraught with associations which render it holy.

The woman's task is not easy—no task worth doing is easy—but in doing it, and when she has done it, there shall come to her the highest and holiest joy known to mankind; and having done it, she shall have the reward prophesied in Scripture; for her husband and her children, yes, and all people who realize that her work lies at the foundation of all national happiness and greatness, shall rise up and call her blessed.

31. Anna Howard Shaw (1905 and 1906)

[1905]

When the cry of race-suicide is heard, and men arraign women for race decadence, it would be well for them to examine conditions and causes, and base their attacks upon firmer foundations of fact. Instead of attacking women for their interest in public affairs and relegating them to their children, their kitchen, and their church, they will learn that the kitchen is in politics; that the children's physical, intellectual, and moral well-being is controlled and regulated by law; that the real cause of race decadence is not the fact that fewer children are born, but to the more fearful fact that, of those born, so few live, not primarily because of the neglect of the mother, but because men themselves neglect their duty as citizens and public officials. If men honestly desire to prevent the causes of race decadence, let them examine the accounts of food adulteration, and learn that from the effect of impure milk alone, in one city 5,600 babies died in a single year. Let them examine the water supply, so impregnated with disease that in some cities there is continual epidemic of typhoid fever. Let them gaze upon the filthy streets, from which perpetually arises contagion of scarlet fever and diphtheria. Let them examine the plots of our great cities, and find city after city with no play places for children, except the streets, alleys, and lanes. Let them examine the school buildings, many of them badly lighted, unsanitary, and without yards. Let them turn to the same cities, and learn that from five to a score or thousand children secure only half-day tuition because there are not adequate schoolhouse facilities. Let them watch these half-day children playing in the streets and alleys and viler places, until they have learned the lessons which take them to evergrowing numbers of reformatories, whose inmates are increasing four times as rapidly as the population. Let them follow the children who survive all these ills of early childhood, until they enter the sweat-shops and factories, and behold there the maimed, dwarfed, and blighted little ones, 500,000 of whom under 14 years of age are employed in these pestilential places. Let them behold the legalized saloons and the dens of iniquity where so many of the voting population spend the money that should be used in feeding, housing, and caring for their children. Then, if these mentors of women's clubs and mothers' meetings do not find sufficient cause for race degeneracy where they have power to control conditions, let them turn to lecturing women. It is infinitely more important that a child shall be well born and well reared than that more children shall be born. It is better that one well-born child shall live than that two shall be born and one die in infancy. That which is desirable is not that the greatest possible number of children should be born into the world; the need is for more intelligent motherhood and fatherhood, and for better born and better educated children. . . .

The great fear that the participation of women in public affairs will impair the quality and character of home service is irrational and contrary to the tests of experience. Does an intelligent interest in the education of a child render a woman less a mother? Does the housekeeping instinct of woman, manifested in a desire for clean streets, pure water, and unadulterated food, destroy her efficiency as a home-maker? Does a desire for an environment of moral and civic purity show neglect of the highest good of the family? It is the "men must fight and women must weep" theory of life which makes men fear that the larger service of women will impair the high ideal of home. The newer ideal, that men must cease fighting and thus remove one prolific cause for women's weeping, and that they shall together build up a more perfect home and a more ideal government, is infinitely more sane and desirable. Participation in the larger and broader concerns of the State, will increase instead of decreasing the efficiency of motherhood, and tend to develop that self-control, that more perfect judgment which is wanting in much of the home training of to-day.

[1906]

In his annual address to Congress, under the heading "Labor," President Roosevelt recommends the Department of Commerce and Labor to make a thorough investigation of the condition of women in industry.

This recommendation will meet with the hearty approval of suffragists everywhere. Realizing as we do its importance to women and to the nation, our Association has been urging it for years, but hitherto our efforts have been futile to direct the attention of the government to it.

The variety of claims and counter-claims which have been made by those interested in the subject of woman's industrial condition and its effect upon the character and the life of the nation, has so confused the ordinary mind that there is little rational thinking upon the subject. It is impossible to draw any definite conclusions, for, as the President points out, "There is an almost complete dearth of data upon which to base any

trustworthy conclusion as regards a subject as important as it is complicated." There is need of full knowledge on which to base action looking
toward "State and municipal legislation for the protection of working
women," and he [Roosevelt] might have justly added, the right of women
to work cannot be denied, when one reads the following statement in the
President's message:

The introduction of women into industry is working change and disturbance in
the domestic and social life of the nation. The decrease in marriage, and especially in the birth rate, have been coincident with it.

This is unquestionably true, but it is also true that this has been coincident with the discovery of gold and the application of steam and electricity to mechanics; and in the last analysis it will be discovered that the
latter facts have had more to do with the present condition of the home
and the birth-rate than has any unreasonable desire on the part of women
to escape from the responsibility of family life or from the joys of domestic felicity.

To draw sweeping and universal conclusions in regard to a matter upon
which there is an "almost complete dearth of data" is never wise. While it
is true that marriage and the birth-rate have decreased within recent
years, before the results are charged to the participation of women in industry, one must answer many questions.

Is it true that there is more "domestic infelicity" to-day than in times
past? Is it true that there is greater "domestic infelicity" in homes where
women are engaged in gainful pursuits than in those homes in which the
strength of women is never taxed by toil, even to the extent of self-
service? Is it true that there is a lower birth-rate among working women
than among those of the wealthy class? Are not the effects of over-work
and long hours in the household as great as are those of the factory or of
the office?

Another point of inquiry would lead the Committee to ask: Is the
birth-rate less among women who are engaged in the new pursuits or occupations unknown to women of the past? Or is the decline alike marked
among those who are pursuing the ancient occupations which women
have followed from time immemorial, but under different conditions?

As a matter of fact, it is no new thing for women to be engaged in industrial pursuits. From primitive times women have been great industrial
factors, and modern economic conditions, instead of introducing them to
industries, have introduced to the world's markets the multiform industries in which women from the earliest times have been engaged, with
ever widening circles of activity, as inventive genius has developed and
civilization progressed.

Woman as an industrial factor and wage-earner is not new. But woman
as an industrial competitor and wage-collector with man is new, not because of woman's revolt against her own industrial slavery, but because
changed economic conditions through inventive genius and industrial
centralization have laid their hands upon the isolated labors and prod-

ucts of woman's toil, and brought them forth from the tent, the cottage, and the farm house, to the shop, the factory, and the marketplace.

If conditions surrounding their employment are such as to make it a "social question of the first importance" it is unfortunate the President had not seen that women, the most deeply interested factor in the problem, should constitute at least a part of any commission authorized to investigate it. No body of men, unaided by women, can be qualified to do so "in a sane and scientific spirit." Such a commission lacks the essential quality of being able to put itself in the position and to understand the character of the very people and conditions it seeks to investigate.

I trust that a resolution will be passed by this convention petitioning the government of the United States to place women upon every commission that investigates the conditions which so deeply affect their lives and the lives of their children.

But if the required investigations were made, even with women upon the committee, what power would the five millions of disfranchised women possess to enact beneficent laws or enforce needed reform?

One can not but wish that with his recognized desire for "fair play" and his policy of "a square deal," it had occurred to the President that, if five millions of American women are employed in gainful occupations, every principle of justice known to a Republic would demand that these five millions of toiling women should be enfranchised to enable them to secure enforced legislation for their own protection.

In all governments, a subject class is always at a disadvantage and at the mercy of the ruling class. It matters not whether its name be Empire, Kingdom, or Republic, whether the rules are one or many; and in a democracy there is no way known among men for any class to protect its interests or to be secure in its most sacred rights, except through the power of the ballot.

The Protection of Motherhood

SOURCES
32. Blanche Edwards-Pilliet, "Rapport de Mme le docteur Edwards-Pilliet, rapporteur," *Congrès international de la condition et des droits des femmes, Paris . . . 1900* (Paris, 1901), pp. 66-68. Tr. KMO.

33. Clara Linzen-Ernst, "Eheliche und uneheliche Mütter in der Mutterschaftsversicherung," *Mutterschutz*, 2, no. 12 (December 1907), 465-69. Tr. SGB.

34. Marie Stritt, "Vorwort" to Dr. Johannes Rutgers, *Rassenverbesserung; Malthusianismus und Neumalthusianismus* (Dresden, 1908; 2d ed. 1911). Published in English in Katharine Anthony, *Feminism in Germany and Scandinavia* (New York, 1915), pp. 101-6. Revised translation SGB.

In the wake of the international alarm over declining birthrates, coupled with shocking rates of infant mortality in the industrializing countries, European women reformers proposed some radical reforms on behalf of mothers. What had begun in Central Europe during the 1880's as rather timid proposals, to include maternity benefits under national health insurance schemes, soon evolved into proposals that would effectively free women from unwanted economic dependence on men, whether in marriage or in prostitution, by means of state subsidies for mothers before and after childbirth.

Among the women who brought such startling proposals to public attention was the French physician and women's rights activist Blanche Edwards-Pilliet (1858-1941). The daughter of a prominent physician and naturalist, A. Milne-Edwards, Blanche Edwards graduated from the Paris Faculty of Medicine in the early 1880's and became one of the first women physicians to break through the all-male competitive examinations for internships and residencies in Paris hospitals. She subsequently served as professor in a Parisian nursing school. Confronting the birthrate crisis, Edwards-Pilliet, now married and herself the mother of a daughter, addressed the inadequacy of Parisian working-class women's preparation for motherhood. This selection is excerpted from a report on hygiene that she presented in 1900 at the International Congress on the Status and Rights of Women, held in Paris. At this time Edwards-Pilliet was optimistic that the French government would support a general measure to subsidize motherhood, insofar as partial measures had already been inaugurated on behalf of pregnant female employees of the state tobacco manufactures, the postal and telegraph administration, and in establishments administered by the French army and navy. In 1901 she helped found (with Augusta Moll-Weiss) the Ligue des Mères de Famille (Mothers' League), a group of women devoted to bringing home help and advice to working-class mothers.

The second selection is from a publication of the German Federation for the Protection of Motherhood (Deutscher Bund für Mutterschutz), founded in 1905 by Helene Stöcker and her associates. This organization made explicit its mandate to protect motherhood not only for married women but for unmarried women as well. Deriving its philosophical justification from the writings of Ellen Key (Docs. 26, 48), the leaders of the Bund repeatedly petitioned the German Reichstag to advocate full governmental recognition that maternity is a national service for which mothers should be duly compensated. Such demands went far beyond earlier measures already incorporated in the national insurance scheme that required partially paid maternity leaves for pregnant working women. The Bund advocated that working women who took maternity leave be able to return to their jobs without penalty, receive full financial compensation for the period they were absent on leave, and receive payments in their own right; the Bund also advocated that *all* mothers, not only wage-earning mothers, be included. In this selection, Clara Linzen-Ernst (dates unknown), an associate of Stöcker, spelled out the Bund position on maternity insurance for *all* mothers.

In the final selection, Marie Bacon Stritt (1855-1928), German reformer and long-time president of the Bund Deutscher Frauenvereine, insists on the importance of making birth-control information available to working-class women in order to enhance the quality of their lives and the lives of their children. That this issue was highly controversial in early twentieth-century Germany is suggested by the fact that Stritt's open advocacy of contraception cost her the presidency of the federation in 1906, when she was defeated by a coalition organized behind a more conservative candidate, Gertrud Baümer (Doc. 66). Stritt, like her colleague Helene Stöcker, was active in the Bund für Mutterschutz. Here she presents to the public an important book by Dr. Johannes Rutgers, a well-known Dutch advocate of eugenics and birth control.

32. Blanche Edwards-Pilliet (1900)

The time will come when woman will be considered a veritable *social functionary* during her gestation and nursing period. At this time she is in the debt of society, which in exchange for the enormous effort of maternity owes her nourishment, lodging, and rest, all of which are indispensable for the creation of a beautiful being, as perfect as she is capable of making. But while we await this time, we must do something more immediate for the mother.

Both here and abroad, prejudice has made pregnancy seem a sort of blemish, a condition to be concealed. If a woman is not married, she knows that the appearance of this proof of her "fault" will prompt her expulsion from the workshop, the place where she earns her living, and often from her family as well—which is to say that poverty awaits her and the coming child.

It is unfortunate to have to say this, but all too often women who are themselves mothers are precisely the ones who turn their backs in disgust on this expectant mother, whose fault (if indeed there be a fault) will be expiated by herself alone.

Thus it is indispensable that new refuges be opened for pregnant women where they can await their delivery in peace, sheltered from want and shame. During this period neither the mother nor the future being, so perfectly innocent, and in which society has an obligation to be interested, should be permitted to suffer deprivation. . . .

Your commission has adopted the following resolution [to be presented to the full Congress]:

The Congress resolves that women, whether [employed] in the administration or the manufacturing facilities of the State, in industrial establishments or commercial establishments, or in civil or other enterprises, be given the opportunity to take a rest-leave of fifteen days before the presumed date of their confinement; that the employing establishments be obliged to give them a four-week leave after their delivery; that for the duration of this leave, a woman has the right to receive a daily allowance of at least two francs from the State; that the State deposit in this maternity fund various revenues to be determined, but including those produced by the State tobacco monopoly.

33. Clara Linzen-Ernst (1907)

Those who have considered the problem closely do not doubt that we shall eventually have insurance protection for mothers. The question that remains is how this insurance will work in practice. Will it be, as in France, a private initiative gradually developing into a solid mandatory insurance; will it be random local authorities that accept the idea and put it into practice; or will the State make insurance for mothers a sound and logical foundation for its overall insurance system? And what of the internal structure of such an insurance? Whenever the problem of insurance for mothers has been publicly discussed, whether in print or in oral debate, the role of the State was unanimously agreed upon; however, there is no unanimity on the internal organization of such insurance.

It is by no means unimportant how this idea will be realized—how long and to what limits and under what conditions the insurance will protect the mothers of the nation. However, this is not what I wish to discuss here; our concern is the treatment of married and unmarried mothers within the framework of this insurance. No sensitive person who has ever worked in the area of social politics could wish to exclude unmarried mothers and illegitimate children, who, on average, would require protection and help from the benefits of this insurance far more than legitimate wives and children.

Yet moralists whom we dare not ignore raise their voices and demand that we differentiate between married and unmarried mothers so that the excellent and practical idea of insurance for mothers should not stimulate irresponsible behavior and immorality. One could easily argue that our state-sanctioned prostitution is far more likely to stimulate immorality and frivolous behavior; that beer-halls, pornographic books, pictures, and exhibits surely do not tend to strengthen weak characters; and above all that miserable homes (the result of landlord exploitation), neglected education, low wages, and hunger, extinguish all morality. Moreover, no attempt has been made by our state to limit alcoholic consumption—we could suggest much more—but this would not produce any positive results. None of these arguments contradict the notion that an otherwise excellent social program might increase immorality. Even though it has been shown (although by a relatively small sample) that a tearing down of so-called protective walls against immorality—we may cite the "récherche de la paternité" [ascertainment of paternity]—has lowered the number of illegitimate births. But even if we admitted that illegitimate births would increase, would this mean that immorality or extramarital sexual intercourse had increased? Not at all. It is more likely that so-called "precautions" (against which much can be said from both ethical and hygienic points of view) would decrease both within and outside of marriage, and that these sad and unnatural crimes against germinating life, and the murder of infants, would probably disappear altogether.

Even the "pure moralist" who carries the scales of justice in his unblemished hands and who dares to weigh and to judge must see and admit that the scale containing the immorality of unmarried mothers carries a relatively light load. How barbarous this hypocrisy is. Particularly on this topic. Certainly there are mothers who are the lowest of creatures—unmarried *and married*. Certainly, there are impure and sordid relationships that beget children outside of marriage and *within marriage*. All married people should ask themselves honestly whether their thoughts, feelings, and actions have always been so full of love that they would dare to cast stones at an unmarried mother, whoever she may be. Have many young married couples not experienced depths never lived through by unmarried mothers? And the men, how will they plead? A joint action forces motherhood only on women and places all the difficulties and consequences upon them, but it does not absolve men. If we insist on attributing "blame" we must attribute blame jointly. In fact, women appear to have paid their share, since they carry not only the natural but also the unnatural consequences that tradition and law have forged for them and their children. Women who give life to illegitimate children are surely far less cunning than those who maintain an extramarital sexual relationship and who do not become mothers. All of them share their "blame" with a partner. Is the attitude of those who want their pleasure, but who do not want children, more pure?

Surely it is only the *attitude* of both persons who approach each other sexually, both outside and within marriage, that counts. We cannot underscore strongly enough how narrow and barbarous it is to be hypocritical in this matter. Both outside and within marriage children are avoided in sexual relationships, their lives suppressed; both outside and within marriage sexual relationships can be deeply sinful. . . . How can we differentiate between a married and an unmarried mother, and especially according to a code of morality and immorality, in developing insurance for mothers! In order to illuminate the absurdity of such a discussion still more sharply, one should appreciate that the attitudes, thoughts, and sensibility of a virgin may be impure and immoral, while an unmarried mother in certain circumstances may be a thoroughly pure, moral, and highly respectable individual. And moreover, what of our men and their relation to prostitution? What of the fact that extramarital and premarital sexual affairs are the rule in the lives of men? Here too, one should refrain from judgment, but take our socio-economic conditions into account. Men have even less right than women to cast stones at unmarried mothers. No one has the right; no one can follow those fine threads that run together and create an individual.

Only the State has rights even regarding the private lives of people who are not guilty of a crime; the State has rights as soon as it introduces State insurance for mothers. When the State recognizes only secular marriage as legitimate and hence the legitimacy only of children resulting from that marriage, the State will have to take another position toward unmarried parents and illegitimate children. I emphasize: *another* position, not the position of an angel of vengeance. I also emphasize the position toward unmarried *parents*, not only toward mothers and children.

34. Marie Stritt (1908)

For those who believe in private and public human rights, one might suppose that the neomalthusian demand that a mother should decide how many children she will bear would be both fundamental and obvious. Furthermore, one might suppose that all adherents of the women's movement would be shocked by the mere thought that they might be expected to abrogate their free will and individual responsibility in this, the most personal of concerns, while permitting blind chance and an ancient sexual slavery to reign unchallenged. To date, unfortunately, neither of these suppositions is true. Very few of us would consider such ideas to be universal principles, let alone have the courage to espouse them publicly. This may be due, first, to inhibitions about discussing such things openly even though they concern the most vital interests of women, indeed, their life or death; second, it may be due to an unfounded fear of offending a wide segment of society, because "chaste ears must not be allowed to hear that which chaste hearts cannot do without." A third reason may be the ignorance and totally unrealistic imaginings of so many unmarried women in our movement about these matters and about the physical and psychological conditions of maternity.

There is another reason, however—the most important of all. We still treat the question of family limitation as a purely academic matter. People exchange opinions at the discussion table without ever considering those most affected—the mothers—who are indeed the most important factor. For the masses family limitation . . . is firmly dismissed, while among the elite, that is, among those who discuss ideas, practical Neomalthusianism makes daily gains. The humorous side of this naïve self-glorification and the strange contradiction between theory and practice seems to be unappreciated by either our male or, unfortunately, our female political leaders. That this should be so among the women is not surprising. The gates of the scientific world have only recently been opened to them. For the present they are neither able to follow, nor dare they follow, their own paths in a foreign terrain; and they are forced to follow gratefully in the footsteps of their leaders—grateful to accept, even in this area [of family limitation], what is offered them by a male perspective in the official world of men. Thus, women politicians today accept the standard of men, which to date has been the sole arbiter in matters of population policies, as the only correct one. Furthermore, these women politicians resign themselves to the deepest suffering of the "comrades of their sex," with the feeble consolation that, although limiting the number of children might be desirable for the individual woman, it would be disastrous for the political economy of society as a whole.

Dr. Rutgers pursues a relentless, yet factual, dignified, and many-sided critique of current population policies—a critique that women, from their standpoint, dare not as yet adopt. With amazing certainty, he unerringly demolishes one weapon after another in the arsenal of those theorists who favor limitless population growth. With a wealth of statistical, historical, and contemporary material he explodes their false conclusions, be they economic or based on race hygiene. Those theorists will have to debate with Dr. Rutgers. It is hardly to be expected that he will convince them, since their contradictory world views will obscure the discussion. This will make mutual understanding more difficult. Still, one may hope that the women theorists at least will be receptive to his analysis, since it will save them from the sad alternative that faces them today. No longer need they sacrifice the individual welfare and autonomy of their sisters to population policies, since these will no longer oppose each other, but will coincide. . . .

For the millions of practitioners (if one may use such an expression for those who have experienced, and continue to experience, in their own bodies, the misery of undesired and unwilling maternity) Dr. Rutgers' book offers redeeming words; indeed, for the women's movement it offers the final word. The woman question is not a "spinster" question, which is how we have previously thought about it: rather, it concerns all of humanity, and it [offers] women an absolute right to autonomy. Only near-sightedness could allow one to accept the erroneous delusion that this latter goal could be attained without relieving woman of her status as a sexual being. All women's other achievements remain illusory, limited, at most, to a comparatively small group, as long as women are not allowed to take responsibility for their own lives in matters of maternity; as long as in this most fundamental area of life they obey the blind power of Nature, which civilized mankind has harnessed and put to work for its own purposes and desires in all other areas. Thus, for those who have learned to follow an idea to its logical conclusion, the questions posed here strike at the innermost core of the woman question. Thus, in a certain sense, the population question is to be understood as the woman question, as well as a question of economics, of social problems, of business, of rights, of morality, and, not least, as a question of education.

"As of now, woman will no longer groan under her fertility as under the curse of paradise lost. Through a knowledge of physiology she has regained power over her own body and her own fate—." Today these proud words of Dr. Rutgers are already partly true, and for educated, property-owning classes they will become more so, thanks to medical discoveries of the past three decades and the Neomalthusianism based on them, which is becoming increasingly accepted. In view of this fact, the middle-class women's movement, which encompasses these circles, has an essential duty that it must not reject. This duty is to make the blessings of Neomalthusianism accessible, first of all through enlightened propaganda, to those who stand in desperate need of them, for whom they are, indeed, a matter of life or death—that is, the struggling and heavy laden mothers of the working people.

CHAPTER 4

The Nation-State and the Education of Women

Two Views of Girls' Secondary Education in Germany

SOURCES

35. Helene Lange, *Die höhere Mädchenschule und ihre Bestimmung*, in Helene Lange, *Kampfzeiten: Aufsätze und Reden aus vier Jahrzehnten*, 2 vols. (Berlin, 1928), II, 14-16, 19-20, 24-26, 31-32. Originally published in Berlin, 1887. Tr. SGB.

36. Hedwig Kettler, "Was ist Frauen-Emanzipation?," in *Bibliothek der Frauenfrage*, ed. Frau J. (Hedwig) Kettler, III (Weimar, 1891), 23-34. Tr. SGB.

During the 1880's the discussion over girls' education in Germany exhibited the same polarization that had marked discussions in England and France decades earlier. At issue was the direction that girls' secondary and higher education should take and the question of who should staff the girls' schools. Education for young men in Prussia and, following the Prussian example, in most other states of the German Empire had developed into a rigorously stratified system of cultural and technical establishments, all of which prepared young men for specialized examinations necessary for entering professional and civil service careers. In contrast, German girls were instructed in public elementary schools (*Volksschulen*); for them there was no equivalent of the boys' humanistic or scientific high schools (*Gymnasium* or *Realschule*). At best, privileged bourgeois girls could attend private "high schools for daughters" (*höhere Töchterschulen*). Even in these schools, male teachers held a virtual monopoly over instruction and administration. Moreover, German universities did not officially permit women to matriculate until 1908. As for curriculum, following German unification in 1870 the imperial government had become even more dictatorial in general educational policy and made a conscious effort to influence the teaching of religion and national consciousness in the schools—through language, history, and literature.

As informed German women became increasingly resentful of their exclusion from educational activities, two differing schools of thought began to crystallize. The majority were influenced by Rousseau, Pestalozzi, and Froebel; they believed that women had a "cultural mission" based upon the principle of "spiritual motherhood," which they were to pursue on two levels—mothering society not only as wives and mothers in the home, but also in public education as the teachers of future mothers. This was the group for whom (like Catharine Beecher some fifty years earlier in America) the ideal of the "mother-educator" offered a powerful weapon for reforming patriarchal education. A minority argued, as had Emily

Davies in England (Vol. I, Doc. 113), that women should be educated exactly like men and, if they so desired, take their places alongside men as career professionals.

At the center of the first group stood Helene Lange (1848-1930), a major propagandist for women's concerns who later became the principal of a seminary for training women teachers. Lange believed firmly in women's unique fitness to instruct and mold others. Her first major contribution to public discussion of German girls' education, the 1887 pamphlet *Die höhere Mädchenschule und ihre Bestimmung* (Girls' High Schools and Their Purpose; popularly known as *Die Gelbe Broschüre* [the Yellow Brochure]) is excerpted in the first selection. Here Lange criticized the conclusions reached at a Weimar congress of male teachers from the German girls' public schools in 1872, upon which the government's subsequent approach to female education had been based; at this meeting the men had argued that "women should be educated so that German men would not be bored at their own hearth by the shortsightedness and narrow-mindedness of their wives." Lange circulated her pamphlet to the Prussian Ministry of Education and to the Prussian House of Representatives and appended to it a petition signed by herself and five other women married to men prominent in Prussian educational circles. The petition demanded (1) greater participation by women in staffing public girls' schools, and, in particular, the appointment of women to teach the core classes in religion and German literature; and (2) the opening of academic teacher-training institutes for women, to qualify them to teach in the upper levels of girls' high schools. Lange's pamphlet and petition challenged the male monopoly in higher education by presenting women not only as competitors for the chance to mold the minds of future generations, but also as potential competitors for teaching posts.

In March 1888, six months after Lange's group had presented their petition to the authorities and the "Yellow Brochure" had been dissected by the press, the pioneering radical German Women's Association "Reform" (Deutscher Frauenverein "Reform") was founded. The organizing committee included members from Dresden, Berlin, Zurich, Weimar, Salzburg, and Vienna, and included Hedwig Dohm (Vol. I, Doc. 139), whose views on woman suffrage had been sharply criticized a few years earlier. Heading the committee was Hedwig Kettler (1851-1937), editor of the journals *Frauenberuf* (Women's Careers) and *Bibliothek der Frauenfrage* (Library on the Woman Question). The radicalism of this group, which Lange's majority group and most other bourgeois Germans found shocking, encompassed the belief that not all German girls would automatically marry and that, therefore, they ought to be prepared for—and admitted to—all professional careers so as to be able to support themselves. Hostilities between the women of the "Reform" Frauenverein and Lange's group broke out into the open in 1889. At that time, Helene Lange, acting with the encouragement and patronage of the German Empress (Queen Victoria's daughter, who had also facilitated Lange's earlier fact-finding visit to the women's colleges at Cambridge) and with the blessing of the Prussian Ministry of Education, opened "special courses" (*Realkurse*) to supplement the curriculum of the *Töchterschulen* by providing a richer intellectual experience for women. The Frauenverein "Reform," led by Kettler, interpreted this step as a crafty move on the part of the imperial government to prevent complete integration of women into higher education, professional careers, and teaching posts. Two years later Kettler denounced such special courses and demanded an education for girls in *Gymnasia* and *Realschulen* identical to the boys' education and, like it, leading to university admission. In 1893 Kettler founded a *Töchterschule* in Karlsruhe that would prepare girls for the university entrance examination—even though university study was not yet an available option for them.

As a result of the Lange group's lobbying, a government decree of May 1894 grudgingly granted certain improvements in girls' secondary education. Women were permitted to teach in the upper grades and could become associate principals in schools headed by men. The course of study was set at nine years (though not at ten, as for boys). Although these schools were administered by state authorities, they were not ranked equally with boys' *gymnasia*; the opinion of the legislators coincided, as one might expect, with that of the majority. Women, they believed, should be prepared for mothering, not for male professional careers.

---

35. Helene Lange (1887)

We cannot shut our eyes to the fact that the most significant mission of a girls' school—that of molding, of producing an inner peace, as Pestalozzi said—is not being fulfilled. Our schools do not mold. They do not educate toward self-direction or moral nobility—they merely instruct. Further, we cannot shut our eyes to the fact that this instruction consists mainly of an unpedagogical overloading of poorly organized material, and that the knowledge of our young girls is therefore disjointed, superficial, and lacking in rigor. We contend that our girls learn only a small part of what men learn thoroughly; and that small part only rarely to the extent that they develop an interest which may lead to later assimilation or independent thought. They learn only positive facts grouped in generalizations or formulas that, not being related to inner experience, quickly disappear from memory, leaving only a vague sensation of knowledge and critical capacity that "once was." This type of instruction explains the unsuitability of our schools for education. What the mind grasps only superficially can hardly contribute to the development of a moral personality; it cannot be related either to the student's inner or external life. In those classes—religion and German literature—where deep absorption would be possible, where a thorough grounding of the material does take place, the hoped-for development again does not occur, for other reasons: male teachers are far too unaware of the sphere of thought and duties of the young girls sitting before them; they cannot usefully connect for them those beautiful passages and sentences harboring infinite wisdom, and many of our young girls therefore accustom themselves to a type of mental double entry bookkeeping. They luxuriate in beautiful thoughts and emotions at school, and enter with a sensitivity, surprising to the male teacher, into his aesthetic and religious reflections. At the same time, with good conscience, they grossly neglect their humble round of domestic and moral duties and, in their spiritual arrogance, even look down upon those members of their family who live in a somewhat less exalted sphere. They will not understand that a close relationship exists between such exalted spheres and real life unless a skillful and experienced hand unsparingly points this out in reference to their own duties. . . .

We must understand this overloading of instruction only as a symptom of a deeper evil. We have already pointed out where we must seek the deeper reason: in the mistaken view of woman's position. . . . As long as woman is not to be educated for her own sake as an individual to become, for better or worse, her own person; as long as in Germany, following Rousseau's very dubious ideas, she is to be educated purely for the sake of man; consequently, as long as an intellectually dependent woman is to be preferred because she guarantees primarily to bring "warmth of emotions" to her future husband (whose interests she cannot possibly envision in advance), the education of German girls will not change. As long as their own comfort is ensured, this will not appear to most men as a great evil. Although a vast amount of talent, potential, happiness, and joy of life will continue to be destroyed, according to a man's view no positive evil will develop.

However, the fact of the matter is quite different. We are not concerned solely with women. Their fate encompasses that of the next generation and is central to the great cultural mission of woman, which is in no way inferior in greatness or beauty to that of man, and which we would not wish to exchange for his. While man discovers and reorganizes that outer world, attempting to mold it and to force time, space, and material according to his ideas and his will, the education of developing humanity lies preeminently in our hands. This includes the care of those noble traits that turn human creatures into human beings; morality, love, and fear of God. We must create the world of the heart and soul in the mind of the child, so that it may recognize the proper values in things, to revere the divine above the temporal, the moral above the sensual; but we must also teach the child to think and to act.

Do we really believe that the fulfillment of this mission is suitably grounded by the instruction given to our girls at school? . . .

Mothers complain that schools do not turn their daughters into self-sufficient, moral women, and that instruction in schools alienates them from, instead of interesting them in, their domestic duties. This is the worst consequence arising from the Weimar theory: the exclusion of women from the educating of older girls. . . . Indeed, women as we would wish to create them *cannot be educated by men only*, since for many reasons this process requires the educational influence of women; in fact, the mother's domestic influence is inadequate, especially when it is constantly eroded [by male influence] at school. There is an imperative need for women teachers, particularly in the upper grades. . . . *In those years when school is more powerful than the home, girls cannot dispense with female leadership and models; not only for the sake of their outward development, in order to accustom girls to good manners, but even more for the sake of their innermost emotional and spiritual life, girls need such support*—a woman counselor in whom they can confide with trust, and who is able to bridge the gap between school and home that often causes such great damage. It is unnecessary to prove that an hour of needlework or gymnastics or an occasional inspection visit are inadequate to provide such female influence.

It is our firm belief that female influence must even outweigh that of men, not by the number of class hours offered by women teachers, but by their impact. It lies in the nature of things that certain hours when women interact with girls can be used quite differently, can produce quite different effects, than the hours when girls interact with men; that in fact a woman has a totally different relationship to a girls' school than a man does, and it is significant for the wrongheadedness of our situation that proof must be furnished for such an assertion.

. . . We know how to meet and counter the foolishness and mistakes that take on such peculiar forms with adolescent girls—in a manner impossible for men—because we see through them and are able to share their feelings because we are of the same sex, which allows us to deal with the problem in a totally different manner of communication by means that male teachers cannot and must not make use of. Even a simple unchaperoned discussion between teacher and girl student, the most important part of education, is one that a tactful male pedagogue will seldom indulge in. . . .

It is further obvious that a woman, out of her womanly mode of thought and sensitivity, will much more easily find the expressions to pursue the clearest line of thought that is to be presented to girls. It is indeed possible only for women to pluck results from the curriculum for daily life, for the range of domestic duties and inner life of her pupils that only a woman can truly know. Particularly is this so with classes in religion and German literature that a man can often make "interesting"—but, as we have already pointed out, his lack of knowledge of female life, female weaknesses and strengths, prevents him from making these subjects meaningful [to girls]. Finally, no one will deny that a woman is more capable than a man of sending girls into the world with a warm religious sensitivity, without which a true female educator cannot be imagined. A great deal more depends upon this point than people think. . . .

With all of this we do not mean that we would entirely forego the contributions of male teachers in a girls' school. We wish to be quite explicit upon this point. In fact we wish to assign to men a far greater place in the instruction of girls than they are willing to assign to us. We want to take part in the instruction for the sake of *true educational development*; therefore it follows that in *those* subjects where educational results are not tied to any particular *quality of care*, instruction can be provided as well by a man. Indeed, we consider that in subjects based entirely upon the *training of the intellect*, such as grammar, arithmetic, natural science, and geography, it is better to assign men than women, and we would not object to handing over these subjects to male teachers, since in these cases there is no question of the drawbacks discussed above. However, these drawbacks are very much in evidence in ethical subjects and these, particularly religion, German—also history, if a suitable person can be found to teach it—these subjects in which not only the human, but also the womanly part of the personality is to be developed and in which every aberration of emotion or thought can be successfully eradicated, belong for this very reason only to the domain of woman. Above all, to woman belongs the leadership of class and school. . . . In leading her own sex she deserves the first and not the fourth place, as offered her in the Weimar decrees.

36. Hedwig Kettler (1891)

. . . There are those who have believed that reform in women's education could be introduced by offering supplementary instruction to girls who are equipped with a good education gained in the regular bourgeois girls' school (*Töchterschule*). This supplementary effort would consist of subjects that were totally neglected in the curriculum of regular girls' schools. Latin, mathematics, etc., were to be made available, in courses lasting two years, to girls who required these subjects for one reason or another.

While we constantly emphasize the fact that through better education we wish to qualify women for academic study and for independent gainful employment, we are not blind to a still broader aim hidden in such a reform. Surely no one who is even slightly concerned with the contemporary women's movement is unaware of the main argument that our opponents bring into play on every occasion, relevant or not—namely, that woman, by virtue of her detachment from intellectual and masculine qualities, is not by nature predestined to the same intellectual development as man and, therefore, should not be offered the same education. (The reverse deduction—the possibility that the same education may advance a like intellectual development—is seldom dignified by serious consideration!)

The whole development of hostility toward our efforts is thus based upon this point of view, which has become a self-evident truth. Therefore we must concern ourselves above all with the point that the principle on which this view is based should no longer exist. This principle has to do with the numerous class hours for schoolgirls during which these girls are forced to indulge their imaginations though they are not forced to think.

The major theme in this regard, discussed in the most diverse variations, is the following: "Woman is unsuited for higher intellectual activity because her emotions are paramount." We know that the word *emotion* is by no means used in the best sense in this instance; it is above all an overwhelming ecstasy of feeling, a sentimentality intruding on every occasion when clear understanding and deliberation alone are required. Throughout a girl's school years these so-called emotions have been allowed to overwhelm all other intellectual qualities of female pupils; indeed, they have been deliberately fostered while all intellectual energy of the awakening young person was prevented from developing except in one area—that of fantasy. To ensure that this excess of fantasy, this romanticism that has no connection whatsoever with real life and that becomes a curse for innumerable women, is not allowed to develop—to ensure this above all—is the most important mission of the defenders of true emancipation for women. As difficult as it is to supplement in two years many years of neglect of intellectual cultivation, it is equally difficult to render harmless the exaggerated cultivation of the imagination acquired over those many years.

Therefore, it will not serve our efforts to build yet another system of supplementary courses onto whatever these years of school instruction have achieved. There is indeed a great danger that failure in such a venture would be attributed not to these courses but to the women students themselves. People will forget that these supplementary courses cannot possibly provide the female students with the same thorough knowledge anchored by years of solid study that would qualify them for careers, just like men. This danger does not exist at present, because the sharp contrast that still exists between the sexes today, both in education and in intellectual qualifications, is obvious to everyone, and therefore any opinion warranting serious consideration must acknowledge these sharp contrasts, not deny them.

For this reason we argue in favor of schools that aim for a different education of the female sex on principle—and not for amalgamation of the present girls' schools with more or less haphazardly added fragments of a classical boys' education. We argue, not for supplementary courses, but for a fully integrated humanistic *Gymnasium* or *Realgymnasium*.

Two American College Presidents Disagree About Girls' Higher Education

SOURCES

37. G. Stanley Hall, *Adolescence: Its Psychology and Its Relations to Physiology, Anthropology, Sociology, Sex, Crime, Religion, and Education,* 2 vols. (New York, 1905), II, 612-14, 617, 619, 627, 632-35, 646. The editors are grateful to Patricia Foster Haines, Ithaca, N.Y., for bringing Hall's arguments to our attention.

38. M. Carey Thomas, "Present Tendencies in Women's College and University Education," *Publications of the Association of Collegiate Alumnae,* ser. 3, no. 17 (February 1908), 45-47, 49-51, 54-58.

By 1900, access to higher education for American women was, for all practical purposes, an accomplished fact. Female college graduates could be counted by the thousands, and females even outnumbered males in U.S. high schools. Perhaps in reaction to this influx, coupled with the new concern over the population issue, certain of the physiological objections to advanced education for women that had arisen in the 1870's found new supporters. One of the most influential spokesmen for these views was G. Stanley Hall (1844-1924), the first president of Clark University in Massachusetts. Hall, whose study of adolescence became required reading in teacher-training institutes all over the country, made his reputation as a pioneer of experimental, or "scientific," psychology; he founded research institutes and journals, and instigated countless investigations in the developing fields of physiological psychology and child study. A New Englander by birth, Hall had nevertheless drunk deeply at the well of European thought during his student years in Germany, where he had immersed himself in philosophical idealism. Yet these enthusiasms were tempered by an equal dose of Yankee empiricism. From reading Comte, Darwin, and Spencer, he had become firmly convinced that increasing differentiation of the sexes was not only desirable but inevitable, and concluded that the respective educations of men and women should therefore differ in both form and content, with that of women preparing them explicitly for motherhood.

In this selection, Hall argues (in opposition to David Starr Jordan, then president of the new coeducational Stanford University in California) that young women should *not* be educated *with* men, and that they should be offered a distinctive curriculum that would favor future motherhood by encouraging their good health, first of all by respecting their need for rest from brain work during menstruation. For "to be a true woman," Hall posited (II, 627), again in response to Jordan, "means to be yet more mother than wife." In the closing paragraphs of this selection, Hall reveals his identity as an unregenerate disciple of the "eternal womanly," following Goethe, Michelet, and Ruskin in at once idealizing and trivializing woman by defining her according to his own desires as the ever self-sacrificing "other."

The second selection is a spirited rejoinder to educators like Hall by M. Carey Thomas (1857-1935), the intrepid president of Bryn Mawr College. Thomas was the eldest of ten children in an affluent Maryland Quaker family. Ambitious and independent-minded from an early age, she convinced her skeptical father to allow her to go to college, and later to finance her graduate studies in Europe. In 1882 she earned a doctorate in English philology (with highest honors) at Zurich, the first woman and the first foreigner to do so. Upon her return to America she obtained a professorship at Bryn Mawr, the newly founded (1885) Quaker women's college outside Philadelphia; by 1894 she had parlayed her initial appointment and deanship into the presidency of the college (her goal from the start). She presided over Bryn Mawr until 1922, shaping it as a rigorously academic institution for undergraduate and graduate women, whose standards were defined according to what she considered to be time-tested standards of excellence. Under M. Carey Thomas's direction, Bryn Mawr achieved a distinguished reputation, despite much contemporary criticism of her aims and methods. In these excerpts from her 1908 speech to the Association of Collegiate Alumnae, Thomas reflects on her own experiences and argues against any sexual specialization, such as home economics, in the education of women.

---

37. G. Stanley Hall (1905)

The long battle of woman and her friends for equal educational and other opportunities is essentially won all along the line. Her academic achievements have forced conservative minds to admit that her intellect is not inferior to that of man. The old cloistral seclusion and exclusion is forever gone, and new ideals are arising. It has been a noble movement and is a necessary first stage of woman's emancipation. The caricatured maidens "as beautiful as an angel but as silly as a goose," who come from the kitchen to the husband's study to ask how much is two times two, and are told it is four for a man and three for a woman, and go back with a happy "Thank you, my dear"; those who love to be called baby, and appeal to instincts half parental in their lovers and husbands; those who find all the sphere they desire in a doll's house, like Nora's, and are content to be men's pets; whose ideal is the clinging vine, and who take no interest in the field where their husbands struggle, will perhaps soon survive only as a diminishing remainder. Marriages do still occur where woman's ignorance and helplessness seem to be the chief charm to men, and may be happy, but such cases are no farther from the present ideal and tendency on the one hand than on the other are those which consist in intellectual partnerships, where there is no segregation of interests but which are devoted throughout to joint work or enjoyment.

A typical contemporary writer* thinks the question whether a girl shall receive a college education is very like the same question for boys. Even if the four K's, *Kirche, Kinder, Kuchen,* and *Kleider,* are her vocation, college may help her. The best training for a young woman is not the old college course that has proven unfit for young men. Most college men look forward to a professional training as few women do. The latter have often greater sympathy, readiness of memory, patience with technic, skill in literature and language, but lack originality, are not attracted by unsolved problems, are less motor-minded; but their training is just as serious and important as that of men. The best results are where the sexes are brought closer together, because their separation generally emphasizes for girls the technical training for the profession of womanhood. With girls, literature and language take precedence over science; expression stands higher than action; the scholarship may be superior, but is not effective; the educated woman "is likely to master technic rather than art; method, rather than substance. She may know a good deal, but she can do nothing." In most separate colleges for women, old traditions are more prevalent than in colleges for men. In the annex system, she does not get the best of the institution. By the coeducation method, "young men are more earnest, better in manners and morals, and in all ways more civilized than under monastic conditions. The women do more work in a more natural way, with better perspective and with saner incentives than when isolated from the influence of the society of men. There is less silliness and folly where a man is not a novelty. In coeducational institutions of high standards, frivolous conduct or scandals of any form are rarely known. The responsibility for decorum is thrown from the school to the woman, and the woman rises to the responsibility." The character of college work has not been lowered but raised by coeducation, despite the fact that most of the new, small, weak colleges are coeducational. Social strain, Jordan thinks, is easily regulated, and the dormitory system is on the whole best, because the college atmosphere is highly prized. The reasons for the present reaction against coeducation are as-

* Hall was referring to David Starr Jordan's article "The Higher Education of Women," *Popular Science Monthly* (December 1902).—EDS.

cribed partly to the dislike of the idle boy to have girls excel him and see his failures, or because rowdyish tendencies are checked by the presence of women. Some think that girls do not help athletics; that men count for most because they are more apt to be heard from later; but the most serious new argument is the fear that woman's standards and amateurishness will take the place of specialization. Women take up higher education because they like it; men because their careers depend upon it. Hence their studies are more objective and face the world as it is. In college the women do as well as men, but not in the university. The half-educated woman as a social factor has produced many soft lecture courses and cheap books. This is an argument for the higher education of the sex. Finally, Jordan insists that coeducation leads to marriage, and he believes that its best basis is common interest and intellectual friendship.

From the available data it seems, however, that the more scholastic the education of women, the fewer children and the harder, more dangerous, and more dreaded is parturition, and the less the ability to nurse children. Not intelligence but education by present man-made ways is inversely as fecundity. The sooner and the more clearly this is recognized as a universal rule, not, of course, without many notable and much vaunted exceptions, the better for our civilization. For one, I plead with no whit less earnestness and conviction that any of the feminists, and indeed with more fervor because on nearly all their grounds and also on others, for the higher education of women, and would welcome them to every opportunity available to men if they can not do better; but I would open to their election another education, which every competent judge would pronounce more favorable to motherhood, under the influence of female principals who do not publicly say that it is "not desirable" that women students should study motherhood, because they do not know whether they will marry; who encourage them to elect "no special subjects because they are women," and who think infant psychology "foolish." . . .

Now that woman has by general consent attained the right to the best that man has, she must seek a training that fits her own nature as well or better. So long as she strives to be manlike she will be inferior and a pinchbeck imitation, but she must develop a new sphere that shall be like the rich field of the cloth of gold for the best instincts of her nature.

Divergence is most marked and sudden in the pubescent period—in the early teens. At this age, by almost worldwide consent, boys and girls separate for a time, and lead their lives during this most critical period more or less apart, at least for a few years, until the ferment of mind and body which results in maturity of functions then born and culminating in nubility, has done its work. The family and the home abundantly recognize this tendency. At twelve or fourteen, brothers and sisters develop a life more independent of each other than before. Their home occupations differ as do their plays, games, tastes. History, anthropology, and sociology, as well as home life, abundantly illustrate this. This is normal and biological. What our schools and other institutions should do, is not to obliterate these differences to make boys more manly and girls more womanly. We should respect the law of sexual differences, and not forget that motherhood is a very different thing from fatherhood. Neither sex should copy nor set patterns to the other, but all parts should be played harmoniously and clearly in the great sex symphony. . . .

We have now at least eight good and independent statistical studies which show that the ideals of boys from ten years on are almost always those of their own sex, while girls' ideals are increasingly of the opposite sex, or also those of men. That the ideals of pubescent girls are not found in the great and noble women of the world or in their literature, but more and more in men, suggests a divorce between the ideals adopted and the line of life best suited to the interests of the race. We are not furnished in our public schools with adequate womanly ideals in history or literature. The new love of freedom which women have lately felt inclines girls to abandon the home for the office. "It surely can hardly be called an ideal education for women that permits eighteen out of one hundred college girls to state boldly that they would rather be men than women." More than one-half of the schoolgirls in these censuses choose male ideals, as if those of femininity are disintegrating. A recent writer, in view of this fact, states that "unless there is a change of trend, we shall soon have a female sex without a female character." In the progressive numerical feminization of our schools most teachers, perhaps naturally and necessarily, have more or less masculine ideals, and this does not encourage the development of those that constitute the glory of womanhood.* . . .

To be a true woman means to be yet more mother than wife. The madonna conception expresses man's highest comprehension of woman's real nature. Sexual relations are brief, but love and care of offspring are long. The elimination of maternity is one of the great calamities, if not diseases, of our age. . . .

Again, while I sympathize profoundly with the claim of woman for every opportunity which she can fill, and yield to none in appreciation of her ability, I insist that the cardinal defect in the woman's college is that it is based upon the assumption, implied and often expressed, if not almost universally acknowledged, that girls should primarily be trained to independence and self-support, and that matrimony and motherhood, if it come, will take care of itself, or, as some even urge, is thus best provided for. If these colleges are as the above statistics indicate, chiefly devoted to the training of those who do not marry, or if they are to educate for celibacy, this is right. These institutions may perhaps come to be training stations of a new-old type, the agamic or even agenic woman, be she aunt, maid—old or young—nun, school-teacher, or bachelor woman. I recognize the very great debt the world owes to members of this very diverse class in the past. Some of them have illustrated the very highest ideals of self-sacrifice, service, and devotion in giving to mankind what was meant for husband and children. Some of them belong to the class of superfluous women, and others illustrate the noblest type of altruism and have

---

* The Evolution of Ideals. W. G. Chambers, Ped. Sem., March 1903, vol. x, p. 101 *et seq.* Also, B. Warner: The Young Woman, &c., New York, 1903, pp. 218.

impoverished the heredity of the world to its loss, as did the monks, who Leslie Stephens thinks contributed to bring about the Dark Ages, because they were the best and most highly selected men of their age and, by withdrawing from the function of heredity and leaving no posterity, caused Europe to degenerate. Modern ideas and training are now doing this, whether for racial weal or woe can not yet be determined, for many whom nature designed for model mothers.

The bachelor woman is an interesting illustration of Spencer's law of the inverse relation of individuation and genesis. The completely developed individual is always a terminal representative in her line of descent. She has taken up and utilized in her own life all that was meant for her descendants, and has so overdrawn her account with heredity that, like every perfectly and completely developed individual, she is also completely sterile. This is the very apotheosis of selfishness from the standpoint of every biological ethics. While the complete man can do and sometimes does this, woman has a far greater and very peculiar power of overdrawing her reserves. First she loses mammary function, so that should she undertake maternity its functions are incompletely performed because she can not nurse, and this implies defective motherhood and leaves love of the child itself defective and maimed, for the mother who has never nursed can not love or be loved aright by her child. It crops out again in the abnormal or especially incomplete development of her offspring, in the critical years of adolescence, although they may have been healthful before, and a less degree of it perhaps is seen in the diminishing families of cultivated mothers in the one-child system. These women are the intellectual equals and often the superiors of the men they meet; they are very attractive as companions, like Miss Mehr, the university student, in Hauptmann's Lonely Lives, who alienated the young husband from his noble wife; they enjoy all the keen pleasures of intellectual activity; their very look, step, and bearing is free; their mentality makes them good fellows and companionable in all the broad intellectual spheres; to converse with them is as charming and attractive for the best men as was Socrates's discourse with the accomplished hetæra; they are at home with the racket and on the golf links; they are splendid friends; their minds, in all their widening areas of contact, are as attractive as their bodies; and the world owes much and is likely to owe far more to high Platonic friendships of this kind. These women are often in every way magnificent, only they are not mothers, and sometimes have very little wifehood in them, and to attempt to marry them to develop these functions is one of the unique and too frequent tragedies of modern life and literature. Some, though by no means all, of them are functionally castrated; some actively deplore the necessity of child-bearing, and perhaps are parturition phobiacs, and abhor the limitations of married life; they are incensed whenever attention is called to the functions peculiar to their sex, and the careful consideration of problems of the monthly rest are thought "not fit for cultivated women."

The slow evolution of this type is probably inevitable as civilization advances, and their training is a noble function. Already it has produced minds of the greatest acumen who have made very valuable contributions to science, and far more is to be expected of them in the future. Indeed, it may be their noble function to lead their sex out into the higher, larger life, and the deeper sense of its true position and function, for which I plead. Hitherto woman has not been able to solve her own problems. While she has been more religious than man, there have been few great women preachers; while she has excelled in teaching young children, there have been few Pestalozzis, or even Froebels; while her invalidism is a complex problem, she has turned to man in her diseases. This is due to the very intuitiveness and naïveté of her nature. But now that her world is so rapidly widening, she is in danger of losing her cue. She must be studied objectively and laboriously as we study children, and partly by men, because their sex must of necessity always remain objective and incommensurate with regard to woman, and therefore more or less theoretical. Again, in these days of intense new interest in feelings, emotions, and sentiments, when many a psychologist now envies and, like Schleiermacher, devoutly wishes he could become a woman, he can never really understand *das Ewig-Weibliche*, one of the two supreme oracles of guidance in life, because he is a man, and here the cultivated woman must explore the nature of her sex as man can not and become its mouthpiece. In many of the new fields opening in biology since Darwin, in embryology, botany, the study of children, animals, savages (*teste* Miss Fletcher), sociological investigation, to say nothing of all the vast body of work that requires painstaking detail, perseverance, and conscience, woman has superior ability, or her very sex gives her peculiar advantages where she is to lead and achieve great things in enlarging the kingdom of man. Perhaps, too, the present training of women may in the end develop those who shall one day attain a true self-knowledge and lead in the next step of devising a scheme that shall fit woman's nature and needs.

For the slow evolution of such a scheme, we must first of all distinctly and ostensively invert the present maxim, and educate primarily and chiefly for motherhood, assuming that if that does not come single life can best take care of itself, because it is less intricate and lower and its needs far more easily met. While girls may be trained with boys, coeducation should cease at the dawn of adolescence, at least for a season. Great daily intimacy between the sexes in high school, if not in college, tends to rub off the bloom and delicacy which can develop in each, and girls suffer in this respect, let us repeat, far more than boys. The familiar *camaraderie* that ignores sex should be left to the agenic class. To the care of their institutions we leave with pious and reverent hands the ideals inspired by characters like Hypatia, Madame de Staël, the Misses Cobb, Martineau, Fuller, Brontë, by George Eliot, George Sand, and Mrs. Browning, and while accepting and profiting by what they have done, and acknowledging every claim for their abilities and achievements, prospective mothers must not be allowed to forget a still larger class of ideal women, both in history and literature, from the Holy Mother to Beatrice,

Clotilda de Vaux, and all those who have inspired men to great deeds, and the choice and far richer anthology of noble mothers. . . .

As a psychologist, penetrated with the growing sense of the predominance of the heart over the mere intellect, I believe myself not alone in desiring to make a tender declaration of being more and more passionately in love with woman as I conceive she came from the hand of God. I keenly envy my Catholic friends their Maryolatry. Who ever asked if the holy mother, whom the wise men adored, knew the astronomy of the Chaldees or had studied Egyptian or Babylonian, or even whether she knew how to read or write her own tongue, and who has ever thought of caring? We can not conceive that she bemoaned any limitations of her sex, but she has been an object of adoration all these centuries because she glorified womanhood by being more generic, nearer the race, and richer in love, pity, unselfish devotion and intuition than man. The glorified madonna ideal shows us how much more whole and holy it is to be a woman than to be artist, orator, professor, or expert, and suggests to our own sex that to be a man is larger than to be gentleman, philosopher, general, president, or millionaire.

But with all this love and hunger in my heart, I can not help sharing in the growing fear that modern woman, at least in more ways and places than one, is in danger of declining from her orbit; that she is coming to lack just confidence and pride in her sex as such, and is just now in danger of lapsing to mannish ways, methods, and ideals, until her original divinity may become obscured. But if our worship at her shrine is with a love and adoration a little qualified and unsteady, we have a fixed and abiding faith without which we should have no resource against pessimism for the future of our race, that she will ere long evolve a sphere of life and even education which fits her needs as well as, if not better than, those of man fit his.

38. M. Carey Thomas (1908)

Anniversaries like this which compel us to pause for a moment and review our progress come with peculiar significance to women of my generation. I doubt if the most imaginative and sympathetic younger women in this audience can form any conception of what it means to women of the old advance guard, among whom you will perhaps allow me to include myself, to be able to say to each other without fear of contradiction that in the twenty-five years covered by the work of the Association of Collegiate Alumnae the battle for the higher education of women has been gloriously, and forever, won.

The passionate desire of the women of my generation for higher education was accompanied throughout its course by the awful doubt, felt by women themselves as well as by men, as to whether women as a sex were physically and mentally fit for it. I think I can best make this clear to you if I refer briefly to my own experience. I cannot remember the time when I was not sure that studying and going to college were the things above all others which I wished to do. I was always wondering whether it could be really true, as everyone thought, that boys were cleverer than girls. Indeed, I cared so much that I never dared to ask any grown-up person the direct question, not even my father or mother, because I feared to hear the reply. I remember often praying about it, and begging God that if it were true that because I was a girl I could not successfully master Greek and go to college and understand things to kill me at once, as I could not bear to live in such an unjust world. When I was a little older I read the Bible entirely through with passionate eagerness, because I had heard it said that it proved that women were inferior to men. Those were not the days of the higher criticism. I can remember weeping over the account of Adam and Eve because it seemed to me that the curse pronounced on Eve might imperil girls' going to college; and to this day I can never read many parts of the Pauline epistles without feeling again the sinking of the heart with which I used to hurry over the verses referring to women's keeping silence in the churches and asking their husbands at home. I searched not only the Bible, but all other books I could get for light on the woman question. I read Milton with rage and indignation. Even as a child I knew him for the woman hater he was. The splendor of Shakespeare was obscured to me then by the lack of intellectual power in his greatest woman characters. Even now it seems to me that only Isabella in *Measure for Measure* thinks greatly, and weighs her actions greatly, like a Hamlet or a Brutus.

I can well remember one endless scorching summer's day when, sitting in a hammock under the trees with a French dictionary, blinded by tears more burning than the July sun, I translated the most indecent book I have ever read, Michelet's famous—were it not now forgotten, I should be able to say infamous—book on woman, *La Femme*. I was beside myself with terror lest it might prove true that I myself was so vile and pathological a thing. Between that summer's day in 1874, and a certain day in the autumn in 1904, thirty years had elapsed. Although during these thirty years I had read in every language every book on women that I could obtain, I had never chanced again upon a book that seemed to me so to degrade me in my womanhood as the seventh and seventeenth chapters on women and women's education of President Stanley Hall's *Adolescence*. Michelet's sickening sentimentality and horrible over-sexuality seemed to me to breathe again from every pseudo-scientific page.

But how vast the difference between then and now in my feelings, and in the feelings of every woman who has had to do with the education of girls! Then I was terror-struck lest I, and every other woman with me, were doomed to live as pathological invalids in a universe merciless to woman as a sex. Now we know that it is not we, but the man who believes such things about us, who is himself pathological, blinded by neurotic mists of sex, unable to see that women form one-half of the kindly race of normal, healthy human creatures in the world; that women, like men, are quickened and inspired by the same great traditions of their race, by the same love of learning, the same love of science, the same love of abstract truth; that women, like men, are immeasurably benefited, physically, mentally, and morally, and are made vastly better mothers, as men are made vastly better fathers, by subordinating the distracting instincts of sex to the simple human fellowship of similar education, and similar intellectual and social ideals.

It was not to be wondered at that we were uncertain in those old days as to the ultimate result of women's education. Before I myself went to college I had seen only one college woman. I had heard that such a woman was staying at the house of an acquaintance. I went to see her with fear. Even if she had appeared in hoofs and horns I was determined to go to college all the same. But it was a relief to find this Vassar graduate tall and handsome and dressed like other women. When, five years later, I went to Leipzig to study after I had been graduated from Cornell, my mother used to write me that my name was never mentioned to her by the women of her acquaintance. I was thought by them to be as much of a disgrace to my family as if I had eloped with the coachman. Now, women who have been to college are as plentiful as blackberries on summer hedges. . . .

We did not know when we began whether women's health could stand the strain of college education. We were haunted in those days by the clanging chains of that gloomy little specter, Dr. Edward H. Clarke's *Sex in Education*. With trepidation of spirit I made my mother read it, and was much cheered by her remark that, as neither she, nor any of the women she knew, had ever seen girls or women of the kind described in Dr. Clarke's book, we might as well act as if they did not exist. Still, we did not *know* whether colleges might not produce a crop of just such invalids. Doctors insisted that they would. We women could not be sure until we had tried the experiment. Now we have tried it, and tried it for more than a generation, and we know that college women are not only not invalids, but that they are better physically than other women in their own class of life. We know that girls are growing stronger and more athletic. Girls enter college each year in better physical condition. For the past four years I have myself questioned closely all our entering classes, and often their mothers as well. I find that an average of 60 per cent. enter college absolutely and in every respect well, and that less than 30 per cent. make, or need to make, any periodic difference whatever in exercise, or study, from year's end to year's end. This result is very different from that obtained by physicians and others writing in recent magazines and medical journals. These alarmists give gruesome statistics from high schools and women's colleges, which they are very careful not to name. Probably they are investigating girls whose general hygienic conditions are bad. The brothers of such girls would undoubtedly make as poor a showing physically when compared to Harvard and Yale men, or the boys of Groton, or St. Paul's, as their sisters make when compared to Bryn Mawr students. Certainly their sisters who have not been to high school or college would in all probability be even more invalided and abnormal. Seventy per cent. of the Bryn Mawr students come from private schools, and from homes where the nutrition and sanitary conditions are excellent. They have undoubtedly been subjected up to the age of nearly nineteen to strenuous and prolonged college preparation, yet their physical condition is far above that of the girls of these other investigations. . . .

We did not really know anything about even the ordinary everyday intellectual capacity of women when we began to educate them. We were not even sure that they inherited their intellects from their fathers as well as from their mothers. We were told that their brains were too light, their foreheads too small, their reasoning power too defective, their emotions too easily worked upon to make good students. None of these things has proved to be so. Perhaps the most wonderful thing of all to have come true is the wholly unexpected, but altogether delightful, mental ability shown by women college students. We should have been satisfied if they had been proved to be only a little less good than men college students, but, tested by every known test of examination, or classroom recitation, women have proved themselves equal to men, even slightly superior. It is more like a fairy story than ever to discover that they are not only as good, but even a little better. When this came to be clearly recognized, as was the case early in the movement, we were asked to remember that those first women students were a picked class, and could not fairly be compared to average men students. But now in many colleges, such as Chicago, the numbers of men and women are practically equal, and many of the women who attend college today have not the bread and butter incentive of men to do well in their classes, yet the slight superiority continues. Year after year, for example, Chicago reports fewer absences and fewer conditions incurred by women than by men in the same classes. This success of women in college-work is producing a curious situation in men's education which is beginning to make itself felt in coeducational colleges.

We are now living in the midst of great and, I believe on the whole beneficent, social changes which are preparing the way for the coming economic independence of women. Like the closely allied diminishing birth rate, but unlike the higher education of women, this great change in opinion and practice seems to have come about almost without our knowledge, certainly without our conscious co-operation. The passionate desire of the women of my generation for a college education seems, as we study it now in the light of coming events, to have been a part of this greater movement. . . .

Women's college education has succeeded too well—that is the whole trouble. And its overwhelming success makes its continuance sure. No institution which has begun to educate women has yet thought of giving up educating them. Instead, each year more colleges for men are assuming fresh responsibilities toward women. Undoubtedly the form of women's college education may change somewhat. Affiliated colleges or annexes will tend to increase, as well as separate colleges for women. Sporadic cases of segregation, as at Chicago, will tend to occur. All forms of education are good, if not equally good. The main thing we are concerned with is to get these thousands of women educated by any method at all.

And just because women have shown such an aptitude for a true college education and such delight in it, we must be careful to maintain it for them in its integrity. We must see to it that its disciplinary quality is not lowered by the insertion of so-called practical courses which are falsely supposed to prepare for life. Women are rapidly coming to control women's college education. It rests with us to decide whether we shall barter for a mess of pottage the inheritance of the girls of this generation which the girls of my generation agonized to obtain for themselves and for other girls. . . .

There is, however, one grave peril which must be averted from women's education at all hazards. . . . [I am] astounded to see the efforts which have been made within the past few years, and perhaps never more persistently than during the past year, to persuade, I might almost say to compel, those in charge of women's education to riddle the college curriculum of women with hygiene, and sanitary drainage, and domestic science, and child-study, and all the rest of the so-called practical studies.

The argument is a specious one at first sight and seems reasonable. It is urged that college courses for women should be less varied than for men and should fit them primarily for the two great vocations of women, marriage or teaching, the training of children in the home, or in the schoolroom. Nothing more disastrous for women, or for men, can be conceived of than this specialized education for women as a sex. It has been wholly overlooked that any form of specialized education, which differs from men's education, will tend to unfit women in less than a generation to teach their own boys at home, as well as of course, other boys in the schoolroom. Women so educated will eventually be driven out of the teaching profession, or confined wholly to the teaching of girls. But there is a more far-reaching answer to this short-sighted demand for specialized women's courses. If 50 per cent. of college women are to marry, and nearly 40 per cent. are to bear and rear children, such women cannot conceivably be given an education too broad, too high, or too deep, to fit them to become the educated mothers of the future race of men and women to be born of educated parents. Somehow or other such mothers must be made familiar with the great mass of inherited knowledge which is handed on from generation to generation of civilized educated men. They must think straight, judge wisely, and reverence truth; and they must teach such clear and wise and reverent thinking to their children. And we have only the four years of the college course to impart such knowledge to women who are to be mothers. If it is true—and it is absolutely true—that all subjects do not train the mind and heart and intellect equally well, it is also true that sanitary and domestic science are not among the great disciplinary race studies. The place for such studies, and they undoubtedly have an important place, is *after* the college course, not during it. They belong with law, medicine, dentistry, engineering, architecture, agriculture in the professional school, not in the college. If they are introduced into the college course of liberal training in any guise whatsoever, our present efficient college woman, like the old-fashioned type of efficient college man, will become a tradition of the past. . . .

But the indications of successive editions of the census in all civilized countries, and many other signs of the times, lead us to believe that in two or three generations practically all women will either support themselves, or engage in some form of civic activity. I have said that about 50 per cent. of college women will marry. We know now that college women marry in about the same proportion, and have about the same number of children as their sisters and cousins who have not been to college. We know also that no one nowadays has more than about two children per marriage—neither college men, nor college women, nor the brothers or sisters of college men and women who have not been to college, nor native white American families, nor American immigrant families in the second generation. This great diminution in the birth rate has taken place notably in the United States, France, Great Britain, and Australia, and is manifesting itself in lesser, but ever increasing degrees, in all other civilized countries. In bringing about this great social change college women have borne no appreciable part. Indeed, only one-half a college woman in every 1,000 women is married, the ratio of college women to other women being as 1 to 1,000. Although this diminishing birth rate is wholly independent of women's college education, it cannot fail to affect it greatly. If it is true, as it seems to be, that college women who marry will have on an average only two children apiece, they could not if they wished, spend all their time in caring for the two rapidly growing-up children, who, moreover, after ten years will be at school, unless they perform also the actual manual labor of their households. In such cases college women will presumably prefer to do other work in order to be able to pay wages to have this manual labor done for them. No college-bred man would be willing day after day to shovel coal in his cellar, or to curry and harness his horses, if by more intellectual and interesting labor he could earn enough to pay to have it done for him. Nor will college women be willing to do household drudgery if it can be avoided. Such married women must, therefore, also be prepared for self-support. Likewise the increasingly small proportion of the married 50 per cent. who will marry men able to support them and their two children in comfort will not wish to be idle. They too must be prepared for some form of public service. Of course, the 50 per cent. of college women who do not marry, that is, all, except the very few who will inherit fortunes large enough to live on throughout life, must be prepared for self-support.

It seems, therefore, self-evident that practically all women, like practically all men, must look forward after leaving college to some form of public service, whether paid, as it will be for the great majority of both men and women, or unpaid, does not matter. Liberally educated women, like liberally educated men, should fit themselves after college for their special work. When their life-work is more or less determined, let those women who expect to marry and keep their own houses (after all, the women householders will be only about half even of those who marry, say 25 per cent., of all college women) study domestic and sanitary science. But it is as preposterous to compel all women to study domestic science and child psychology, irrespective of their future work, as it would be to compel all men to study dentistry, or medicine. It is the same with child-study, pedagogy, and all other special studies. One and all, for women as for men, they belong in the graduate professional school.

Reforming French Secondary Education for Girls

SOURCES

39. Jeanne Crouzet-Benaben, "La Clientèle secondaire féminine et ses be-soins," *Revue Universitaire*, 20, no. 2 (July-December 1911), 282-84. Tr. KMO.

40. Baptiste Roussy, *Education domestique de la femme et rénovation sociale* (Paris, 1914), pp. 2-4. Tr. KMO.

In contrast to the United States, where reformers like G. Stanley Hall had begun to argue adamantly against coeducation and advocated a woman-centered education especially at the secondary level, in France the traditional separation of the sexes persisted in both Catholic and secular institutions of learning for privileged adolescent girls. They continued to offer an "equal but different" curriculum to those families who could afford to send their daughters to school, even at considerable sacrifice. In the early twentieth century, however, the offerings of the girls' *lycées*, designed to turn out companionate wives for the wealthy élite of the new republic, were challenged by women educators and women's rights advocates. This curriculum was considered irrelevant to the needs of the actual clientele—for the most part, girls from less fortunate families who, lacking dowries, might well have to earn their own livings. Such women needed access to the professions, which in France often required proof that candidates had passed the *baccalauréat* (the university entrance examination).

One of the most articulate exponents of curriculum reform in the state lycées for girls was Jeanne Crouzet-Benaben (1870?-1961). A Frenchwoman raised in Algiers, Crouzet-Benaben obtained a "masculine" education (as she put it), preparing the Latin baccalaureate on her own in 1887, and then obtaining a university degree and teaching certificate in the 1890's at the École Sévigné in Paris. After teaching in a girls' lycée in Rouen, she married educator Paul Crouzet (who subsequently held a number of top-level positions in the French educational bureaucracy) and left active teaching for family life. In 1907 Crouzet-Benaben began her monthly chronicle of activities in the girls' lycées for the *Revue Universitaire*, accompanying it with a series of proreform articles, from which the first selection is taken. Crouzet-Benaben seems, in fact, to have held far more radical views on the subject of equalizing women's education than did her husband, whose later views (as expressed in his 1949 work, *Bachelières ou jeunes filles*) more closely resemble those of G. Stanley Hall.

The second selection comes from an influential work by Baptiste Roussy (b. 1856), a physician and assistant director of the École Pratique des Hautes-Études at the Collège de France. Roussy's book-length work was originally composed as a report for the Democratic-Republican Party, then under the leadership of Louis Barthou, who promoted Roussy's views during his brief tenure as prime minister and minister of public instruction in 1913. Although Roussy paid lip service to the notion that the lives of Frenchwomen were being altered irrevocably by major forces of social change, he insisted that the key to revitalizing the nation, both in numbers and in morale, was to improve women's domestic training and to make such training obligatory at all levels of education. "Woman's fundamental profession," he argued, "consists of being a wife, homemaker, mother, and educator of her children." Roussy called for direct state intervention to accomplish this goal, by initiating major curriculum reform in the state schools and by working with industry to provide nursing and day-care facilities for the young children of working mothers who could not afford to quit their jobs and stay at home.

Both these selections highlight the extent to which the woman question had, by the early twentieth century, become a political question that demanded resolution at the highest levels of government.

---

39. Jeanne Crouzet-Benaben (1911)

In his treatise *L'Éducation des filles* [1687], Fénelon wrote: "One must consider, in deciding on the education of a girl, her social status, the surroundings in which she will spend her life, and the vocation she will in all probability choose." The principle is an old one, but it is still timely. Every attempt that has been made during the nineteenth century on behalf of women's education, including the work of the Third Republic—even including the movement for reform that is making itself felt these days—is inspired by this same principle: to give a young woman an education appropriate to her future destination. Despite the fact that these attempts draw inspiration from the same principle, however, they have in the past resulted and still result in the most diverse and even totally contrary consequences.

. . . The founders of girls' secondary education in 1882 did not look at the subject any differently. . . . There was no question in their minds about careers [for women]. If they envisioned a broader and deeper instruction than that conceived by Fénelon, it was because ideas had evolved and the social milieu had been transformed. A tighter family life, a more widespread masculine education had rendered men more demanding than in the seventeenth century about the degree of intellectuality of their companions. No more Racines who would be content with a wife who had not read her husband's tragedies. Because of all this, woman at the end of the nineteenth century needed enough instruction to become the intellectual companion of man. To all her natural gifts she would add the embellishment of knowledge without pedantry, and of grace without frivolity. From this consideration emerged the program they laid out, very different from that for boys—secondary but without classical studies, with five years of instruction instead of six, with non-specialized professors, easier scientific studies, an *intra-muros* diploma, a thoroughly feminine examination, and a useless certificate.

Today, in the name of the same principle, a new conceptualization is in evidence. Girls' secondary instruction, as laid out in 1882, is no longer suited to the needs of its clientele. For a different destination there must be a different education. If the destiny of many women, even today, is to stay at home and raise their children, every day the number grows of those who are obliged to earn their living outside the household or even within it. Women's secondary instruction as currently organized is too feminine, and not secondary enough. It is not secondary enough because it does not lead anywhere and because it is not scientific enough, not prolonged enough. The clientele of the lycées and collèges for girls is not at all, in fact, what its organizers had in mind thirty years ago. Women nowadays have need of diplomas that will open up careers; they need to learn science itself, not a feminine science. Women's secondary education must be reformed.

40. Baptiste Roussy (1914)

From the beginning of my work, I have thought that in order to better conceptualize the desired organization of instruction in home economics [*économie ménagère*] and total child rearing [*puériculture intégrale*], it was necessary to arrive at a full, precise understanding of what these two expressions mean.

After searching in vain for definitions that would satisfy me, I took it upon myself to construct two, as follows:

"Home economics" is the totality of theoretical and practical knowledge that should be applied in order to assure—according to principles of cleanliness and hygiene, economy and good artistic taste, and the moral and social Ideal of the Fatherland (*Patrie*)—the satisfaction of the fundamental needs of one or several members of the same family living together in the same household.

Furthermore, "rational total child rearing" is, likewise, the totality of theoretical knowledge and positive practice that must be applied in order to ensure the uninterrupted growth, development, and improvement in quality of the *body, heart, intelligence,* and *character* or *will* of children, in order to better assure thereafter the necessary extension and perfection of their family and their Fatherland and, consequently, the progressive realization of the great moral and social idea they aspire to realize.

In sum we see, by these two definitions, that both home economics and child rearing can or, logically, should focus their efforts and tendencies toward the same supreme goal, which is not only to protect the individual, the family, the Fatherland, and finally the human species and all of humanity against misery, sickness, degeneration, and death, but also to assure to each of these beings, individually or collectively, the pleasures of existence and [good] health, vigor and strength, free development and self-realization—to guarantee them, in a word, the pleasures of true happiness in all their forms in the infinite perspective of the future.

And it is precisely because our beloved France, like her constituent families and individuals, suffers from the most fearful evils, which weaken her unceasingly and threaten to reduce her, before long, to the status of an increasingly small nation amid rival nations that are increasingly large, if indeed these nations do not suppress her very national existence—it is for these reasons that the restructuring of home economics and child rearing, that is, the regeneration of the family, which ever remains the cornerstone of every society, is clearly seen as necessary today by all foresighted patriots, by all good Frenchmen.

Sex Education for Girls?

SOURCES

41. Frank Wedekind, *Frühlings Erwachen*, ed. Margaret Sander (Waltham, Mass., 1971), pp. 34-38, 71-75. Originally published in 1891. Tr. SGB.
42. Nelly Roussel, "Le Droit des vierges," *La Fronde*, 1 March 1904. Tr. KMO.
43. Léon Blum, *Du Mariage* (Paris, 1907), pp. 87-89. Tr. KMO.

By the early twentieth century (as Carey Thomas's remarks make clear), advocates of institutional schooling in home management and childcare, whether for middle-class college women or working-class girls, were enjoying increasing success. The public agreed that women's understanding of, and satisfactory performance in, their "role" was vital for the future well-being of the nation. The same could hardly be said, however, for another, more controversial aspect of knowledge even more intimately related to motherhood—sex education—the very suggestion of which was sufficient to arouse public anxiety and provoke outbursts of righteous indignation. Here we present three selections from writers, well known in their time, who advocated explicit sex education and responsible sexual freedom for young women: the Swiss-German dramatist Frank Wedekind, the French birth-control enthusiast Nelly Roussel, and the French literary critic (and later statesman) Léon Blum.

The young playwright Frank (Benjamin Franklin) Wedekind (1864-1918) provoked public controversy throughout Europe over the sex education question with his play, *Frühlings Erwachen* (Spring's Awakening), first published in 1891, but not performed until years later. Like Ibsen and Brieux (Docs. 1, 28), Wedekind viewed the theater as a vehicle for social criticism; society's reluctance to allow free discussion of sex was, for him, symptomatic of the repressive nature of civilization in general, especially as concerned women's sexuality. He subsequently developed this theme at length in his two *Lulu* plays. In these two scenes from *Frühlings Erwachen* Wedekind depicts the profound ignorance in which the fourteen-year-old heroine, Wendla Bergmann, is kept, even by her mother and married sister. Curious but unenlightened, Wendla is greatly attracted to a young man of the village and becomes pregnant by him without even realizing the possible consequences of her act of love. Her mother and a cooperative doctor try to induce an abortion by plying Wendla with iron tablets. But the remedy does not work; Wendla dies before the baby can be born, "of anemia," as Wedekind put it, with grim irony. Respectability is preserved, at the cost of an innocent life.

Wedekind was the first playwright to take up the theme of adolescent eroticism and to plead the case for sex education; others soon followed. In France, P.-H. Loyson likewise addressed the issue, in a play entitled *Le Droit des vierges* (1904; The Virgins' Rights). The second selection is a review-essay concerning Loyson's play by Nelly Roussel (Doc. 29), the French advocate of birth control and women's rights.

Only a few years later, the brilliant young French attorney and literary critic, Léon Blum (1874-1950), published *Du Mariage* (On Marriage). Replying to socialist colleagues who denounced marriage as an irremediably corrupt bourgeois institution, Blum upheld the possibility that monogamous marriage might still offer a viable framework for heterosexual relations and the raising of children, despite the recognized propensity of both men and women to be polygamous. But, he insisted, this would be possible only if mores could be radically adjusted. Like Bertha von Suttner (Doc. 12) and Nelly Roussel, Blum condemned the immorality of prevailing bourgeois sexual customs whereby upperclass French men, who had been introduced to sexual activity by prostitutes, in turn brutally and thoughtlessly initiated their uninformed and virginal wives. To Blum such customs could only lead to a lifetime of misunderstanding. How much better it would be, he speculated, if young men and women could marry not only in full awareness of reproductive physiology but with some practical experience that would allow both sexes to appreciate that sexual as well as emotional and intellectual compatibility was required to found an enduring marriage. Such iconoclastic notions would still be held against Blum more than twenty years later when he became the first socialist (and the first Jewish) prime minister of France.

---

41. Frank Wedekind (1891)

SCENE TWO

A Living Room.

FRAU BERGMANN (*enters by the center door. She is beaming. She is wearing a hat, and a mantilla, and has a basket on her arm*). Wendla! Wendla!

WENDLA (*appears in petticoat and corset at the side door, right*). What is it, Mother?

FRAU BERGMANN. You are up already, child? Now, that's a good girl.

WENDLA. You have already been out?

FRAU BERGMANN. Get dressed quickly! You must go down to Ina's at once, and take her this basket.

WENDLA (*dressing herself during the following conversation*). You have been to Ina's?—How is Ina?—Is she still no better?

FRAU BERGMANN. Imagine, Wendla, last night the stork visited her and brought her a little boy!

WENDLA. A little boy?—A little boy!—Oh, how lovely!—So that's the cause of that tiresome influenza.

FRAU BERGMANN. A splendid little boy.

WENDLA. I must see him, Mother. That means I am an aunt for the third time—aunt to a little girl and two little boys!

FRAU BERGMANN. And what little boys!—It always happens that way when one lives so near the church roof!—Just two years ago tomorrow she went up the steps in her muslin gown.

WENDLA. Were you there when he brought him?

FRAU BERGMANN. He had just flown away again.—Won't you pin a rose on?

WENDLA. Why couldn't you have been a little earlier, Mother!

FRAU BERGMANN. I almost believe he brought you something, too—a brooch or something.

WENDLA. It's really a shame!

FRAU BERGMANN. But, I tell you, he brought you a brooch!

WENDLA. I have enough brooches.

FRAU BERGMANN. Then be satisfied, child. What else do you want?

WENDLA. I would love to know whether he flew through the window or down the chimney.

FRAU BERGMANN. You must ask Ina. Yes. You must ask Ina that, dear heart! Ina will tell you exactly. After all, Ina talked with him for half an hour.

WENDLA. I will ask Ina when I go down.

FRAU BERGMANN. Now don't forget, sweet angel! I'm interested myself in knowing if he came in through the window or by the chimney.

WENDLA. Or hadn't I better ask the chimney-sweep? The chimney-sweep must know best whether he flies down the chimney or not.

FRAU BERGMANN. Not the chimney-sweep, child; not the chimney-sweep. What does the chimney-sweep know about the stork? He'd tell you a lot of foolishness he didn't believe himself. Wh—what are you staring at down there in the street?

WENDLA. A man, Mother—three times as big as an ox—with feet like steamboats!

FRAU BERGMANN (*rushing to the window*). Impossible! Impossible!

WENDLA (*at the same time*). He is holding a bedstead under his chin and fiddling *Die Wacht am Rhein*—there, he's just turned the corner.

FRAU BERGMANN. You are, and always will be a foolish child. To scare your simple old mother like that. Go and get your hat. I wonder when you will understand things. I've given you up as hopeless.

WENDLA. So have I, Mother darling, so have I. It's very sad about my understanding. I have a sister who has been married for two and a half years, I myself have been made an aunt for the third time, and I haven't the slightest idea how it all comes about. Don't be cross, darling Mother, don't be cross. Whom in the world should I ask but you. Please tell me, dear Mother. Tell me, dear Mother. I'm ashamed of myself. Please, Mother, speak. Don't scold me for asking you about this. Do give me an answer. How does it happen? How does it all come about? You cannot seriously expect that I, who am fourteen years old, still believe in the stork?

FRAU BERGMANN. Good gracious, child, you are strange. What an idea—I really can't do that.

WENDLA. But why not, Mother? Why not? It can't be anything horrid if everybody is so delighted about it.

FRAU BERGMANN. Oh, Oh, God protect me. I deserve—Go and get dressed child, get dressed.

WENDLA. I am going. And suppose your child went and asked the chimney-sweep?

FRAU BERGMANN. You are enough to drive me mad—But, come here, child, come here, I'll tell you. I'll tell you everything. Oh, great heavens, only not today, Wendla. Tomorrow, the next day, next week—whenever you want, dear heart.

WENDLA. Tell me today, Mother; tell me now. Immediately—Now that I have seen you so horrified, I shall have no peace until you do.

FRAU BERGMANN. I can't do it, Wendla.

WENDLA. Oh, why can't you, Mother dear? See, I shall kneel at your feet and put my head in your lap. You can cover my head with your apron and talk and talk, as if you were completely alone in the room. I won't move, I won't cry, I will bear it all patiently, no matter what it may be.

FRAU BERGMANN. Heaven knows, Wendla, I'm not to blame. Heaven knows. Come here, in God's name. I will tell you, child, how you came into this world.—Listen to me, Wendla.

WENDLA (*beneath the apron*). I'm listening.

FRAU BERGMANN (*beside herself*). It's no use, child. I can't do it. I deserve to be put in prison—to have you taken from me.

WENDLA. Take heart, mother.

FRAU BERGMANN. Listen, then—.

WENDLA (*trembling beneath the apron*). Oh God, Oh God.

FRAU BERGMANN. In order to have a child—do you understand me, Wendla?

WENDLA. Quick, Mother, I can't stand it much longer.

FRAU BERGMANN. In order to have a child—one must love—the man—to whom one is married—love him, I tell you—as one can only love a man. One must love him so much with one's whole heart, so much that one can't describe it. One must love him, Wendla, as at your age you are still incapable of loving—Now you know it.

WENDLA (*getting up*). Great God—in heaven!

FRAU BERGMANN. Now you know what a test lies before you!

WENDLA. And that's all?

FRAU BERGMANN. That's it, God help me. Take your basket now and go down to Ina. You will get chocolate and cakes there. Come, let me look at you—those laced boots, silk gloves, sailor blouse, roses in your hair—your skirt is really becoming much too short for you, Wendla.

SCENE FIVE

A bedroom. Frau Bergmann, Ina Müller, and Doctor von Brausepulver. Wendla in bed.

DOCTOR. How old are you actually?

WENDLA. Fourteen-and-a-half.

DOCTOR. I have been prescribing Blaud's pills for fifteen years and have observed astonishing results in the majority of cases. I prefer them to cod liver oil and iron tonics. Begin with three or four pills a day, and increase the number just as soon as you can tolerate it. I ordered Fräulein Elfriede, Baroness von Witzleben, to increase the dose by one tablet every third day. The Baroness misunderstood me and increased it by three every day. Scarcely three weeks later the Baroness was able to go to Pyrmont with her mother to complete her convalescence. I will spare you from exhausting walks and extra meals; therefore, promise me, dear child, to take frequent exercise and to avoid unwholesome food as soon as your appetite improves. Then these palpitations of the heart will soon stop, and the headache, chills, and dizziness also, as well as this dreadful indigestion. Fräulein Elfriede, Baroness von Witzleben, enjoyed a breakfast of a whole roast chicken with new potatoes, eight days after she began her treatment.

FRAU BERGMANN. May I offer you a glass of wine, Doctor?

DOCTOR. I thank you, dear Lady. My carriage is waiting. Do not take it so to heart. In a few weeks our dear little patient will again be as fresh and bright as a gazelle. Be of good cheer. Good day, Frau Bergmann, good day dear child, good day ladies—good day. (*Frau Bergmann accompanies him to the door.*)

INA (*at the window*). Your plane tree is changing color again. Can you see that from your bed? A short-lived splendor, hardly worth rejoicing over them, they come and go so quickly. I, too, must go right away now. Müller is waiting for me in front of the post office, and I must first go to my dressmaker's. Mucki is to have his first trousers and Karl is getting a new knit-suit for the winter.

WENDLA. Sometimes I feel so happy—all joy and sunshine. I never dreamed one's heart could feel so light. I want to go out, across the meadows in the twilight, and look for cowslips by the river, and sit down on the banks and dream. Then I get a toothache, and I feel as if I would die at dawn; I grow hot and cold; everything is dark before my eyes; and the beast flutters inside me. Whenever I wake up, I see Mother crying. Oh, that hurts me so. I can't tell you how much, Ina.

INA. Shall I lift your pillows?

FRAU BERGMANN (*returning*). He thinks the vomiting will soon stop, and then you can safely get up. I also think it would be better if you got up soon, Wendla.

INA. When I visit you the next time, you will be dancing around the house again. Good-bye, Mother. I simply must go to the dressmaker's. God keep you, Wendla dear. (*Kisses her.*) Get better soon! (*Exit Ina.*)

WENDLA. Good-bye, Ina. Bring me some cowslips the next time you come. My love to the boys.—What did he tell you, Mother, when he was outside?

FRAU BERGMANN. He didn't say anything.—He said Baroness von Witzleben was subject to fainting spells also. It is almost always so with anemia.

WENDLA. Did he say that I have anemia, Mother?

FRAU BERGMANN. You are to drink milk and eat meat and vegetables as soon as your appetite returns.

WENDLA. Oh, Mother, Mother, I don't believe I have anemia.

FRAU BERGMANN. You have anemia, child. Be calm, Wendla, be calm, you have anemia.

WENDLA. No Mother, no! I feel it. I don't have anemia. I have the dropsy—.

FRAU BERGMANN. You have anemia. He said positively that you have anemia. Calm yourself, girl. You will get better.

WENDLA. I won't get better. I have dropsy. I'm going to die, Mother.—Oh, Mother, I am going to die!

FRAU BERGMANN. You will not die, child. You will not die. Great heavens, you will not die.

WENDLA. But then why are you crying so terribly?

FRAU BERGMANN. You are not going to die, child! You don't have dropsy; you are going to have a child, my girl. You are going to have a child.—Oh, why did you do that to me?

WENDLA. I haven't done anything to you.

FRAU BERGMANN. Oh, don't deny it any longer, Wendla.—I know everything. I couldn't bear to say a word to you.—Wendla, my Wendla—!

WENDLA. But it's impossible, Mother. I'm not married yet.

FRAU BERGMANN. Great God Almighty—that's just it, that you are not married. That's the most frightful part of all. Wendla, Wendla, Wendla, what have you done!

WENDLA. God knows I don't know any more. We lay in the hay—I have loved nobody in the world as much as you, Mother.

FRAU BERGMANN. My darling heart—.

WENDLA. Oh Mother, why didn't you tell me everything?

FRAU BERGMANN. Child, child, let us not make each other's hearts any heavier. Get hold of yourself. Don't despair, child. To tell *that* to a fourteen-year-old girl! See, I expected that about as much as that the sun would stop shining. I haven't acted any differently toward you than my dear, good mother did toward me. Oh, let us put our trust in God, Wendla; let us hope for compassion, and do our part. Look, nothing has happened yet, child. And if we are not cowardly now, God won't forsake us. Be brave, Wendla, be brave. One may sit by the window with one's hands in one's lap, while everything seems to change for the better, and then trouble comes, enough to break one's heart.

42. Nelly Roussel (1904)

Decidedly, feminism is making progress—in the theater. For some time now, we have really had little occasion to complain about our dramatic authors.

After Brieux' "Maternity" at the Théâtre Antoine; after the magnificent cry of revolt by this wife whose husband treats her more like a reproductive animal than a conscious human being and condemns her—out of egotism, out of caprice and a stupid desire to be prolific—to the intolerable punishment of continual childbirth without caring in the least about her happiness; after this noble and powerful affirmation of women's

most sacred right, the right to dispose freely of their bodies and to regulate their own fertility, we are offered M. Paul-Hyacinthe Loyson's *Le
Droit des vierges* [The Right of Virgins] at the Théâtre Victor Hugo.

What this play amounts to from the dual perspective of literature and
staging is of little importance. But the sole fact of having dared to undermine the very foundations of this monstrous edifice of stupidity and immorality that we call the "education" of young women ought to suffice to
draw the sympathy of feminists to the author. And I employ the word
"immorality" on purpose, for I can conceive of nothing more profoundly
"immoral" than the marriage of a young woman who is absolutely ignorant of the most elementary laws of physiology, who is thrust, unknowingly, blindly, into this fearful unknown; who is handed over like a toy,
like an object, to a man she doesn't love, whom she is unable to love
because she is ignorant—poor thing—of the very meaning of the word
"love"!

It is terrifying to think that nearly all the women of the generation that
preceded us married under these conditions!—Perhaps we should look
no further for the secret of so many bad marriages, undone as they are
in the very first few weeks. The case of Mme de Simerose, in *L'Ami des
Femmes* [The Women's Friend], existed only in the imagination of Alexandre Dumas. If today's virgins are more enlightened than their mothers
ever were, they owe it—not to the latter, who are obstinately attached, in
spite of everything, to the traditions from which they suffer—but to legitimate curiosity, to the imperious desire to *know* that welled up in their
minds along with the consciousness of their rights, the sense of their dignity, and the weakening of their religious faith. For here again, as everywhere, religions are the real culprits; everywhere and always, we find
them at the root of errors and prejudices.

And while these future wives are being muffled in shadows and shielded
with great care from these things that concern them so directly;—what
about those who, later on, will become their husbands and their "masters"? Very early on, even before puberty, they will be initiated, at least
theoretically—not by the healthy explanations of an educator but by the
clandestine confidences of older or more vicious comrades, by reading
the demoralizing illustrated publications that besmirch and profane Love
—into all the secrets of debauchery. They know too much—and yet they
know nothing. Since childhood they have learned to scorn woman, to
consider her as an object of pleasure. The notion they gain of life will
be neither beautiful nor just. Their sisters know only what is unreal;
they themselves are acquainted only with bestiality. And it is with these
two types that they speak of creating a world of harmony, wisdom, and
beauty!

Ah! when will the day come when sexual questions—so important!—
will cease to be forbidden and to be shrouded in shameful mystery? the
day when schoolbooks will explain to children of both sexes, simply and
scientifically, the reproductive functions, as today they explain digestion
or the nervous system? when nothing that concerns the body, the "mis-

erable rag" that Free Thought wants to rehabilitate, will no longer be neglected or hidden away! when no adolescent will be able to ignore the
laws of Nature and the principles of hygiene? the day when at last everyone will understand the healthful and moralizing influence of Truth?

43. Léon Blum (1907)

The very essence of marriage as it is institutionalized in our morality is
to unite a virgin with an experienced man, and to confide the education
of the virgin to the man's experience. At the basis of this system lies the
principle or rather, in my opinion, the wrong-headed insistence on virginity in brides. But even if we agree that girls should come to marriage in
this state of freshness and ignorance, we should be able to assure that
these novices find good teachers there and that their conjugal preparation
is placed in sure hands. The present system prohibits girls from acquiring
even theoretical experience in love before marriage. Moreover, by indirect effect, it prevents most men from acquiring under acceptable conditions this experience that one of the two spouses must possess. If during
their period of freedom before marriage young men are forced to seek
instruction from prostitutes, is this necessarily a free choice or a preference on their part? Would they not rather find nearby, among those they
know, the mistress whom they must now seek by chance? Instead of
dissipating the ardor of their youth in brief and fortuitous encounters,
would they not prefer to bring it all to a woman friend who is their equal,
who has like them been prepared by a common tenderness for the birth
and exchange of desire? This is precisely what social convention prohibits as the most reprehensible and cowardly of acts, and if this practice
finds justification in the current state of morality, does it not have the
effect of casting young men out in search of venial pleasure, sordid contacts, vicious habits, and such ignoble passivity as this mode of pleasure
carries with it? Under the heaviest penalties you forbid young girls to
come to marriage already instructed in love, but at the same time you
despoil their future masters. This is committing too many errors all at
once.

Consider that these poorly matched marriages take place at the moment when the polygamous instinct attains its full power with women,
when virginity is precisely the only obstacle that, while stimulating its latent ardor, confines its expression—and you can no longer be surprised
that in so many marriages physical disharmony follows so closely on the
wedding night. You can no longer be surprised that after the honeymoon
women experience, not a waning of a happiness they never knew, but the
exhaustion of their already much-tried patience. Our current conception
of marriage leads directly to this. Our error is to build a community existence on a disparity of situations and statuses; our folly is to unite a man
to a virgin, and not a man to a woman. Suppose, instead of a virgin, a
woman who has already had two or three passionate adventures. . . .
Suppose a widow or a divorcee—and the risks of disharmony would di-

minish infinitely, in that the woman could supplement the defects in the man's preparation if she herself were knowledgeable, and if she weren't, she would not expect anything from love that she had not already experienced. Finally, imagine the marriage of a virgin with a man as pure as herself, and whom she knows to be so; this combination, unusual as it might be, nevertheless offers fewer dangers than our customary marriages, in that a period of research and common study would perforce precede harmony, but at least in these initial attempts the responsibility would be shared, and moreover, in love as in many other things, ignorance is easier to overcome than mistakes. Of all the imaginable arrangements, the worst is the one we see ordinarily today and the one that, therefore, seems the most natural. . . .

CHAPTER 5

The Nation-State and Women's Rights

Civil Divorce and the Catholic Church

SOURCES

44. Leo XIII, *Arcanum*, 10 February 1880; reprinted in Joseph Husslein, ed., *Social Wellsprings*, I (Milwaukee, Wisc., 1940), pp. 30-33, 35-39.
45. Alfred Naquet, *Le Divorce*, 2d ed., rev. and enlarged (Paris, 1881), pp. 12-14, 159-60, 161. Originally published in 1877. Tr. KMO.
46. Maria Martin, "Le Divorce," *Journal des Femmes*, no. 172 (March 1907), p. 1. Tr. KMO.

Control of marriage and family law has been a main theme in the struggle between church and state since the sixteenth century, when Henry VIII of England defied Rome in order to divorce Catherine of Aragon. In France, unlike England, the state did not consolidate its hold over marriage until 1792, when the revolutionary convention instituted obligatory civil marriage and enacted divorce legislation. But civil divorce was once again abolished in 1816 by the Catholic-dominated legislature led by Louis de Bonald (Vol. I, Doc. 21). Despite sporadic efforts to reestablish divorce from 1830 on, reformers were unsuccessful until the anticlerical republicans took control of the Third Republic's government in 1879. In Italy, where civil marriage, though available, was never obligatory and civil divorce did not exist, there was similar agitation in the 1870's and 1880's in favor of civil divorce. In both countries, however, legal separation was possible. Significantly, most suits for separations were filed by wives.

The mounting agitation for civil divorce in countries where Catholicism remained strong alarmed leaders at the Vatican. To counter potential Catholic support for such secular legislation and to put civil governments on guard, the new pope Leo XIII (Doc. 16) issued the immensely important encyclical letter *Arcanum*. Here he reaffirmed in no uncertain terms the Church's enduring hostility to the secularization of marriage and to initiatives for divorce legislation. In this view, the maintenance of the sacrament of marriage—and its authoritarian form—takes precedence over any personal inconvenience or unhappiness experienced by individuals of either sex as a result of bad marriages.

In France agitation for the reestablishment of divorce began again in the 1870's, led by republican men such as Léon Richer (Vol. I, Docs. 124, 141) and Alfred Naquet (1834-1916). Naquet was trained as a physician and chemist, but his career in academic medicine was cut short by his radical political activities. In 1869 his book *Religion, Famille, Propriété*, which argued for "free love" (free, that is, from control of either church or state), was condemned by the imperial censors, and Naquet fled to Spain to avoid going to prison. On his return to France he became an active opponent of the Second Empire, and then served as deputy from Vaucluse throughout the 1870's, after the Third Republic was established. In 1879 he spearheaded the campaign to reenact divorce by mutual consent, but his efforts resulted only in the passage of a very cautious law in July 1884, from which mutual consent was clearly absent. This selection is taken from the second edition of his lengthy tract on divorce, which originally appeared in 1877. Although Naquet cites many instances of the injustices created for women by their inability to obtain divorce, it remains clear that the intended audience for this work was the male political establishment.

A woman's perspective on divorce following passage of the Naquet law is given here by Maria Martin (d. 1910), a wife and the mother of four children, who had long been active in the French women's movement. By 1900 the divorce question was again being discussed widely in the press and in literature, and pressure mounted to widen the existing law to include divorce by mutual consent, particularly after the government named a commission to study revision of the Civil Code. In this editorial from Martin's *Journal des Femmes*, she argues in favor of mutual consent. But she has serious reservations about the even more radical demand for divorce on the request of one party only, which she believes would not afford adequate protection for the married woman.

---

44. Leo XIII (1880)

There has been vouchsafed to the marriage union a higher and nobler purpose than was ever previously given to it. By the command of Christ, it not only looks to the propagation of the human race, but to the bringing forth of children for the Church, "fellow citizens with the saints, and the domestics of God" (Eph. ii, 19); so that "a people might be born and brought up for the worship and religion of the true God and our Saviour Jesus Christ" (*Catech. Rom.* viii).

Secondly, the mutual duties of husband and wife have been defined and their several rights accurately established. They are bound, namely, to have such feelings for one another as to cherish always very great mutual love, to be ever faithful to their marriage vow, and to give to one another an unfailing and unselfish help. The husband is the chief of the family, and the head of the wife. The woman, because she is flesh of his flesh, and bone of his bone, must be subject to her husband and obey him; not, indeed, as a servant, but as a companion, so that her obedience shall be wanting in neither honour nor dignity. *Since the husband represents Christ, and since the wife represents the Church, let there always be, both in him who commands and in her who obeys, a heaven-born love guiding both in their respective duties.* For "the husband is the head of the wife; as Christ is the head of the church. . . . Therefore, as the church is subject to Christ, so also let wives be to their husbands in all things" (Eph. v, 23, 24).

As regards children, they ought to submit to the parents and obey them, and give them honour for conscience' sake; while on the other hand, parents are bound to give all care and watchful thought to the education of their offspring and their virtuous bringing up: "Father . . . bring them up [that is, your children] in the discipline and correction of the Lord" (Eph. vi, 4). From this we see clearly that the duties of husbands and wives are neither few nor light; although to married people who are good, these burdens become not only bearable but agreeable, owing to the strength which they gain through the sacrament.

Christ therefore, having renewed marriage to such and so great excellence, commended and entrusted all the discipline bearing upon these matters to His Church. The Church, always and everywhere, has so used her power with reverence to the marriages of Christians, that men have seen clearly how it belongs to her as of native right; no being made hers by any human grant, but given divinely to her by the will of her Founder. Her constant and watchful care in guarding marriage, by the preservation of its sanctity, is so well understood as not to need proof. That the judgement of the Council of Jerusalem reprobated licentious and free love (Acts xv, 29), we all know; as also that the incestuous Corinthian was condemned by the authority of blessed Paul (I Cor. v, 5). Again, in the very beginning of the Christian Church were repulsed and defeated, with the like unremitting determination, the efforts of many who aimed at the destruction of Christian marriage, such as the Gnostics, Manichaeans, and Montanists; and in our own time Mormons, St. Simonians, Phalansterians, and Communists.

In like manner, moreover, a law of marriage just to all, and the same for all, was enacted by the abolition of the old distinction between slaves and free-born men and women; and thus rights of husbands and wives were made equal: for, as St. Jerome says, *"with us that which is unlawful for women is unlawful for men also, and the same restraint is imposed on equal conditions."* The selfsame rights also were firmly established for reciprocal affection and for the interchange of duties; the dignity of the woman was asserted and assured; and it was forbidden to the man to inflict capital punishment for adultery, or lustfully and shamelessly to violate his plighted faith.

It is also a great blessing that the Church has limited, so far as is needful, the power of fathers of families, so that sons and daughters, wishing to marry, are not in any way deprived of their rightful freedom; that, for the purpose of spreading more widely the supernatural love of husbands and wives, she has decreed marriages within certain degrees of consanguinity or affinity to be null and void; that she has taken the greatest pains to safeguard marriage, as much as is possible, from error and violence and deceit; that she has always wished to preserve the holy chasteness of the marriage-bed, personal rights, the honour of husband and wife, and the security of religion.

Lastly, with such power and with such foresight of legislation has the Church guarded this divine institution, that no one who thinks rightfully of these matters can fail to see how, with regard to marriage, she is the best guardian and defender of the human race; and how withal her wisdom has come forth victorious from the lapse of years, from the assaults of men, and from the countless changes of public events.

Yet owing to the efforts of the archenemy of mankind, there are persons who, thanklessly casting away so many other blessings of redemption, despise also or utterly ignore the restoration of marriage to its original perfection. It is the reproach of some of the ancients that they showed themselves the enemies of marriage in many ways; but, in our own age, much more pernicious is the sin of those who would fain pervert utterly the nature of marriage, perfect though it is, and complete in all its details and parts. The chief reason why they act in this way is because very many, imbued with the maxims of a false philosophy and corrupted in morals, judge nothing so unbearable as submission and obedience. They strive with all their might to bring about that not only individual men, but families also, nay indeed human society itself, may in haughty pride despise the sovereignty of God.

Now, since the family and human society at large spring from marriage, these men will on no account allow matrimony to be subject to the jurisdiction of the Church. Nay, they endeavour to deprive it of all holiness, and so bring it within the contracted sphere of those rights which, having been instituted by man, are ruled and administered by the civil jurisprudence of the community. Wherefore it necessarily follows that they attribute all power over marriage to civil rulers, and allow none whatever to the Church. When the Church exercises any such power, they think that she acts either by favour of the civil authority or to its injury. Now is the time, they say, for the heads of the State to vindicate their rights unflinchingly, and to do their best to settle all that relates to marriage according as to them seems good.

Hence are owing civil marriages, commonly so called; hence laws are framed which impose impediments to marriage; hence arise judicial sentences affecting the marriage contract, as to whether or not it has been rightly made. Lastly, all power of prescribing and passing judgement in this kind of cause is, as we see, of set purpose denied to the Catholic Church, so that no regard is paid either to her divine power or to her prudent laws. Yet under these, for so many centuries, have the nations lived on whom the light of civilization shone bright with the wisdom of Christ Jesus. . . .

Let no one then be deceived by the distinction which some court legists have so strongly insisted upon—the distinction, namely, by virtue of which they sever the matrimonial contract from the sacrament, with intent to hand over the contract to the power and will of the rulers of the State, while reserving questions concerning the sacrament to the Church. A distinction, or rather severance, of this kind cannot be approved: *for certain it is that in Christian marriage the contract is inseparable from the sacrament; and that for this reason, the contract cannot be true and legitimate without being a sacrament as well.* For Christ our Lord added to marriage the dignity of a sacrament; *but marriage is the contract itself, whenever that contract is lawfully concluded.*

Marriage, moreover, *is a sacrament, because it is a holy sign which gives grace, showing forth an image of the mystical nuptials of Christ with the Church.* But the form and image of these nuptials is shown precisely by the very bond of that most close union in which man and woman are bound together in one; which bond is nothing else but the marriage itself. *Hence it is clear that among Christians every true marriage is, in itself and by itself, a sacrament;* and that nothing can be further from the truth than to say that the sacrament is a certain added ornament, or outward endowment, which can be separated and torn away from the contract at the caprice of man. Neither, therefore, by reasoning can it be shown, nor by any testimony of history be proved, that power over the marriages of Christians has ever lawfully been handed over to the rulers of the State. If, in this matter, the right of any one else has ever been violated no one can truly say that it has been violated by the Church. . . .

If, then, we consider the end of the divine institution of marriage, we shall see very clearly that God intended it to be a most fruitful source of individual benefit and of public welfare. Not only, in strict truth, was marriage instituted for the propagation of the human race, but also that the lives of husbands and wives might be made better and happier. This comes about in many ways: by their lightening each others' burdens through mutual help; by constant and faithful love; by having all their possessions in common; and by the heavenly grace which flows from the sacrament. Marriage also can do much for the good of families: for, so long as it is conformable to nature and in accordance with the counsels of God, it has power to strengthen union of heart in the parents; to secure the holy education of children; to attemper the authority of the father by the example of the divine authority; to render children obedient to their parents, and servants obedient to their masters. From such marriages as these the State may rightly expect a race of citizens animated by a good spirit and filled with reverence and love for God, recognizing it as their duty to obey those who rule justly and lawfully, to love all, and to injure no one.

These many and glorious fruits were ever the product of marriage, so long as it retained those endorsements of holiness, unity, and indissolubility, from which proceeded all its fertile and saving power. Nor can any one doubt but that it would always have brought forth such fruits, at all times, and in all places, had it been steadily under the power and guardianship of the Church, the trustworthy preserver and protector of these gifts. *But now there is spreading a wish to supplant natural and divine law by human law;* and hence has begun a gradual extinction of that most excellent ideal of marriage which nature herself had impressed on the soul of man, and sealed, as it were, with her own seal. Nay, more, even in Christian marriages this power, productive of such great good, has been weakened by the sinfulness of man. Of what advantage is it if a State can institute nuptials estranged from the Christian religion, when she is the true mother of all good, cherishing all sublime virtues, quickening and urging us to everything that constitutes the glory of a lofty and generous soul? With the rejection and repudiation of the Christian religion, marriage sinks of necessity into the slavery of man's vicious nature and vile passions, and finds but little protection in the help of natural goodness. A very torrent of evil has flowed from this source, not only into private families, but also into states. For when the salutary fear of God is removed, and there remains no longer that refreshment in toil which is nowhere more abounding than in the Christian religion, it very often happens, as indeed is evident, that the mutual services and duties of marriages seem almost unbearable. Thus it comes about that very many yearn to loosen the tie which they regard as woven by human law and made out of their own will, whenever incompatibility of temper, or quarrels, or the violation of the marriage vow, or mutual consent, or other reasons induce them to think that it would be well to be set free. Then, if they are hindered by law from carrying out this shameless desire, they contend that the laws are iniquitous, inhuman, and at variance with the rights of free citizens; adding that every effort should be made to repeal such enactments, and to introduce a more humane code sanctioning divorce.

Now, however much the legislators of these our days may wish to guard themselves against the impiety of men such as here referred to, they are unable to do so, since they profess to hold and defend the very same principles of jurisprudence. Hence they comply with the times, and render divorce easily obtainable. History itself illustrates this. To pass over other instances, we find that at the close of the last century divorces were sanctioned by law in that upheaval, or as we might better call it, conflagration in France, when society was wholly degraded by its abandoning of God. Many at the present time would fain have those laws reenacted, because they wish God and His Church to be altogether exiled and excluded from the midst of human society, madly imagining that in such laws a final remedy must be sought for the moral corruption which is advancing with rapid strides.

Truly, *it is hardly possible to describe the magnitude of the evils that flow from divorce. Matrimonial contracts are by it made variable, mutual kindness is weakened, deplorable inducements to unfaithfulness are supplied, harm is done to the education and training of children, occasion is afforded for the breaking up of homes, the seeds of dissension are sown among families, the dignity of womanhood is lessened and brought low, and women run the risk of being deserted after having ministered to the pleasures of men.* Since, then, nothing has such power to lay waste families and destroy the mainstay of kingdoms as the corruption of morals, it is easily seen that divorces are in the highest degree hostile to the prosperity of families and states, springing as they do from the depraved morals of the people, and, as experience shows us, opening out a way to every kind of evil-doing in public as well as in private life.

Further still, if the matter be duly pondered, we shall clearly see that these evils are the more especially dangerous, because when divorce has once been tolerated, no restraint is powerful enough to keep it within the bounds marked out or presurmised. Great indeed is the force of example, and even greater still the might of passion. With such incitements it must needs follow that the eagerness for divorce which daily spreads in devious ways, will infect the minds of many like a virulent contagious disease, or like a flood of water will burst through every barrier.

45. Alfred Naquet (1881)

[Divorce] is one of those laws that everyone can demand. The republican party can support it, because the republics of Switzerland and the United States have established divorce and because the republicans of 1792 were the first to establish it in our own country. The imperialists can demand it as well, since the empires of Russia and Germany have divorce laws and because the first French empire retained it—indeed, . . . the man who later became Napoleon III wrote, addressing the government of Louis-Philippe: "What have you accomplished? You have not even reestablished divorce, the palladium of family honor."

Not only republicans and imperialists can demand this law on divorce, but Orleanists can demand it as well. The first Chamber of Deputies during the July Monarchy voted four times between 1830 and 1834 in favor of reestablishing it. Even Catholics can support it, that is, all those Catholics who have sincerely accepted civil marriage and who do not wish to return to the situation that existed before 1789. Thus no one can use a vote for divorce as a tool against the Republic. To those who dare to try, the response would be all too easy.

The Republic will never harm itself by enacting useful reforms. Where it will harm itself is by denying its own principles and allowing all the bad institutions of the past to remain standing.

[The Republic] should therefore reestablish divorce without hesitation. It will gain only honor and profit from so doing.

Moreover, it cannot withdraw, after the struggle it has mounted against clericalism.

The law of 8 May 1816 that abolished divorce was dictated by the clerical mentality. Before the Chambers of the Restoration no one argued on its behalf that divorce had produced disorder—for it had produced none—but that it was incompatible with Catholic dogma. It was a first blow against civil marriage, an initial breach made by the past in the edifice of the French Revolution. They hoped to widen this breach and get rid of civil marriage itself, for it is civil marriage that is the true principle that stands in opposition to the pretensions of the Roman [Catholic] court, and not *civil* divorce, which is only its consequence. . . .

The first move of the clerical mentality against the modern democratic mentality was the abrogation of divorce: thus, the first revenge of the democratic spirit against the clerical spirit should be the reestablishment of divorce. This is the inflexible logic that pushes both the parliament and the country. The four years just past have, moreover, brought the problem sufficiently to a head and, after the general elections, parliament will have no more reason to hesitate. The question will assuredly be put to the nation, gathered in its councils, and the verdict of the nation will be favorable. . . .

How, you ask, can religious men accept a law that their dogma condemns?

Indeed, the argument would be very embarrassing if it were a question of laying hands on the sacrament of marriage, of imposing civil law on the domain of conscience, of imposing on the ministers of religion the obligation of blessing, contrary to their faith and to their dogma, the second marriage of divorced persons who demanded the nuptial benediction.

Such has never been the thought of the promoters of the divorce law.

Before 1789, as far as marriage was concerned, the civil and religious laws were one. Marriage was in the hands of the ecclesiastical authorities. Just as in the case of monastic vows, it was a sacrament recognized by the law.

But in 1789, society became secularized. It became laic; the religion of the State was abolished and, reestablished for a short while in 1815, it was again abolished once and for all after the revolution of July 1830.

From that time forth—and without interfering with the religious conscience of the faithful—marriage, viewed from the legal standpoint, ceased to be viewed as a sacrament. It has since been viewed as a simple civil agreement. From that point on, only civil marriage has authority in the eyes of the law, but it in no way prevents the married couple from seeking the nuptial benediction from the ministers of their respective cults. It is true that this benediction is no longer obligatory; by itself, it has no civil effect; but it retains all its sway over the consciences of the faithful.

Thus, at present there are two marriages—civil marriage and religious marriage—whereas before the Revolution there was only one.

Now, the new law [on divorce] concerns civil marriage but does not concern religious marriage in any way, since the latter is the preserve of religious authorities.

If it is true that religious marriage is not coercive in its effects, it is equally true that it is in the very nature of religion to constrain only by means of persuasion.

As long as a Catholic believes in the principles of his religion, he will obey those principles without being physically forced to do so. And on the day he ceases to believe in them, he will cease to be a Catholic. Why, then, should the obligation of obeying ideas that are no longer his be imposed on him?

The divorce that existed in our country under the Revolution and the Empire, which we want to reestablish at this time, is *civil divorce*—the faculty to dissolve civil marriage in certain serious cases foreseen by law.

How then will Catholics, who fulminate unceasingly against civil marriage, possibly be hurt if we dissolve a bond against which they protest and whose validity they do not recognize anyway? . . .

If, in the eyes of Catholics, civil marriage is nothing more than a deplorable concubinage, why should it matter to them if we provide a means of ending this concubinage by divorce? For those who marry with the aid of their religion, the sacrament will remain intact.

46. Maria Martin (1907)

The divorce question is not yet completely resolved. In this regard it resembles many other social questions. Nevertheless, it is becoming clarified, and the obstacles surrounding it are beginning to be removed.

The older persons among us can well remember an era when we were told, in that doctoral tone that was used when no good arguments existed, that divorce was not in accord with the French spirit. M. Naquet has proved the contrary. It will be the same for many other reforms, already adopted in other countries, that we are told are also not in accord with the French spirit. They forget that the French spirit is essentially eclectic and adopts progress more easily than any other.

It is not a question of simplifying the legal procedure for divorce, of putting an end to the scandalous debates that are so painful for the two parties, where the most intimate details are dragged before a public that is all too fond of scabrous subjects, details that sooner or later will inevitably reach the children born of these mal-assorted unions.

Divorce by mutual consent is less of an innovation than is generally believed. It has been practiced for a long time, if not acknowledged in law. The wife has only to consent to let herself be struck in front of witnesses, or the husband to arrange to be discovered *en flagrant délit*, and divorce is easy to obtain. This is, in fact, divorce by mutual consent. Why then not allow entrance by the grand portal of the law to that which so often enters by the small hidden door of subterfuge? Why not suppress these details and these debates that are so unpleasant for everyone and be content with an affirmation—from both parties—that their common life has become intolerable? For what reasons? Is this the business of anyone but the interested parties? If they want to drop a veil over delicate matters, not only for the sake of the couple but also for the sake of the children and the two families, why bring up these disgusting details? Wouldn't it be enough for them to agree to say, "We made a mistake in getting married. We committed a grave mistake that is poisoning our existence. We have come to ask of the law, in its supreme power, to release us from an oath that we made a mistake in taking."

Divorce by the consent of one party alone is another matter and requires serious deliberation before being accepted by the legislators. While it may sometimes liberate a victim, it will more often be the cause of great injustice and great suffering. It leaves too much room for arbitrary action. Man, in general, is by his very nature fickle. Pushed by caprice, and with the instigation of his wife's rival, he could, without giving a reason, install another woman in his household in her place. His moment of aberration past, he would perhaps be the first to regret it, but then the damage would be done and it could not always be easily remedied.

We cannot ignore the fact that the greatest difficulty in the question of divorce is the fate of the children. This is the supreme argument made by those who are opposed to divorce in any form. If a man and woman who have no children decide to lead a common life or to separate, that is their business, but more frequently a third party is involved—the child—and that party is sacred. It is evident that a child cannot develop completely without being with a father and mother who are united by affection in a household where peace and unity reign. But these favorable conditions cannot be assured for all by means of legislation. It remains to be seen whether it is better for a child to see his parents separately (for never is one or the other completely deprived of his society) or to hear them from morning to night arguing, threatening each other, and sometimes even coming to blows. . . .

Divorce is an evil. We agree on that. But of two evils, it may be the lesser one.

Rethinking the Laws on Marriage and Motherhood

SOURCES

47. Frances Elizabeth Hoggan, M.D., "The Position of the Mother in the Family in its Legal and Scientific Aspects," paper read at the annual congress of the National Association for the Promotion of Social Science, Birmingham, 1884 (Manchester, 1884), pp. 10-12, 13-16. British Library 8416 dd 17(3).

48. Ellen Key, "A New Marriage Law," in *Love and Marriage*, tr. Arthur G. Chater (New York, 1911), pp. 359-61, 363-70. Originally published in Swedish in 1904, as the opening volume of Key's *Lifslinjer*.

Between 1880 and 1914 public interest in reforming civil laws governing the position of women broadened in scope. Reformers subsequently considered not only the matter of married women's civil rights and the question of divorce, but also more controversial questions concerning motherhood and the personal health of adults of both sexes, all within the context of increased governmental concern with promoting public health. The selections presented here reveal two aspects of this discussion.

The first excerpt illustrates how recent scientific discoveries in reproductive physiology and evolutionary zoology could be harnessed to reinforce the case for improving the legal status of British women as mothers. The author of this 1884 paper on "The Position of the Mother in the Family," Frances Elizabeth Morgan Hoggan (1843-1927), was the third woman to gain a place on the British Medical Register. After finding all British medical schools closed to her, Frances Morgan had enrolled at the Zurich medical school. On her return to England she established a private practice in London and also worked with Elizabeth Garrett Anderson (Vol. I, Doc. 117) in the New Hospital, staffed for and by women. In 1874 she married Dr. George Hoggan (Vol. I, Doc. 134), a solid supporter of the group that had attempted to open medical studies to women at Edinburgh. From 1882 to 1888 Hoggan was medical superintendent at the North London Collegiate School, which along with Bedford College was one of the first rigorously academic British secondary schools for girls and was greatly concerned about the health of its pupils. Together with her husband, Frances Hoggan published many scientific articles on the lymphatic and nervous systems. She also addressed herself to a variety of topics concerning the woman question, including—as this selection reveals—a fundamental critique of the old Aristotelian view of reproduction itself and the development of a sociobiologic rationale for enhancing women's rights as mothers. Nor did Hoggan hesitate to draw far-reaching sociological conclusions from her scientific findings.

The second excerpt is from the landmark study *Love and Marriage*, by the Swedish writer Ellen Key (Doc. 26). Key, as may be recalled, proposed radical reforms in the legal and economic position of women while respecting the traditional sexual division of labor. In exploring the potential for conflict between the individual's requirements for self-realization and the rights of society, Key proposed that the community itself subsidize motherhood—in the interest of rearing happy, healthy children. By restructuring the economics of child rearing, Key believed, not only mothers but also fathers could be freed to take new joy in the duties and pleasures of parenthood as well as in those of their personal lives. Moreover, the artificial distinction between legitimate and illegitimate children could be eliminated, and the institution of marriage itself would cease to exert such an oppressive form of social control over the relationship of the sexes. Key's proposal aroused enormous interest throughout Europe. Her ideas were constantly invoked, not only by the proponents of motherhood insurance schemes but also by those who, like the leaders of the German Bund für Mutterschutz (Docs. 33, 34), argued for the "nationalization" of motherhood itself.

---

47. Frances Hoggan (1884)

Having seen what the legal position of the mother is in the family—that she has practically no position, except what she owes to the affection and sense of right of her husband, and that she is considered in all respects as secondary, supplementary, subservient to him in the home—let us now turn to the scientific aspect of the question. What is the mother's place in the family, according to science, which, be it remembered, stands for natural law, in so far as we have yet been enabled to discover and interpret it?

The science of the past, with its cut and dried theories, its imperfect deductions and ill-observed facts, had much in common with the masculine systems of legislation under which we live. Starting from the assumption that women were inferior to men, it was argued, sometimes in very curious old phraseology, and fervently believed by men of science, that the mother's part, large though it undoubtedly was and burdensome, was yet distinctly inferior in kind to that of the father. The mother was but the nurse of her child, both before and after birth, her distinct function being to provide it with stores of nutriment. To the father belonged the function of originating a new life. He alone of the two parents had the formative energy required to produce a fresh germ; he alone was the source of a new being. The mother's share in the child was the merely passive one of keeping it alive, by feeding it in all the earlier stages of its existence, first as a germ or embryo, afterwards as an infant. Man, the creator, left to woman, the sustainer, the task of carrying on and finishing the work which he had begun and fully sketched out in all its parts. The woman's work was held to be of long duration, but inferior, mechanical, passive. It is easy to see how this crude physiological theory, fitting in as it did with the newly-awakening desire of men to live over again in their children, and to become the founders of families, gave a species of sanction to the current notion of the inferiority of the mother, and helped to initiate and strengthen the legal enactments which have deprived women of their maternal rights. Here and there some more acute observer and reasoner entered a more or less clear protest against the current views about women, and ventured to suggest that perhaps after all women had some share of function in the formation of the germs from which new beings sprang into life. The other theory was, however, more attractive to the masculine mind, and although unsupported by facts, it held its own, and met with but little opposition, even up to the present century, and it has no doubt been presented to most persons at some time or another with more or less clearness and precision. Recent investigations in embryology have, however, so completely reversed the old theory, that it is time to reconsider the position, and to formulate anew the relation between the two parents.

According to our present knowledge, the mother has incontestably the larger share of function as a parent. She it is, and not the father, who forms the germ of the new being. True, she cannot alone bring it to maturity and found a family. Nature has so ordered it that the co-operation of two parents is necessary to this purpose. In the germ cell produced by the mother, not the father, fusion of a male and female nucleus takes place, and from the resulting combination of force the germ cell is endowed with fresh reproductive energy. The new being is evolved and perfected at the expense of the mother, not the father, and by the mother it is sustained until it is enabled to lead an independent existence, both before and after birth. It has been said, accurately enough, that the mother provides nourishment to the young directly, the father only indirectly, by, in the first instance, supplying the mother with food during the period when she is unable to obtain it for herself, and by being commonly the bread-winner of the household.

The old belief in the father's monopoly of creative force being thus exploded, and exploded in a way which admits of no return to old errors, by careful observation, aided by all the modern appliances for research, who does not see that the whole relation of parents, one to the other, must be revised and made conformable to nature's plan? Man alone, of all created beings, persistently, in his arrogance, disregards, in the arrangements made for the rearing of the young, the clear and unmistakable dictates of nature, the undeniable rights of the mother over the offspring it costs her so much to bear, and to the possession of which she may fairly urge a claim immeasurably exceeding that of the father. To man alone, therefore, had science any message to give on this question.

The instincts of the different animal species have been to them a surer guide, in the relations of the mother to her young, than to man his reason, and it is fitting that his crude theories about the superiority of the male parent over the female should be at last overthrown by more exact knowledge, and henceforth and for ever abandoned.

Nature's plan of parental relations is shadowed forth in the animal world. It is very gradually evolved. In the lowest uni-cellular organisms reproduction takes place, like all the other functions, without any special organs. The cell divides into two, the resulting two cells into two more, and so the process goes on indefinitely. There may be, even in these lowest organisms, a final exhaustion of reproductive energy, only to be revived by the fusion of two individuals exactly alike, or of their two nuclei. We do not know this to be the case with quite the simplest forms of life, but it is probable; and reproduction by means of the fusion of two individuals or cells is a common process a little higher up in both the vegetable and animal world (Zygospores in Algæ and Fungi, and among Protozoa in the Gregarinidæ). Gradually, in the course of evolution towards a higher organisation, function becomes differentiated, and only a part of the individual buds off to form the new being (Basidiomycetes among Fungi, Hydra and Hydroid Zoophytes); or, by a second process, true germ and sperm cells are formed, the former being always larger in size. . . .

Amongst vertebrate animals the reproductive instinct appears to be, as a rule, stronger in the male, as evidenced by the prevalence of polygamy in so many species, but the parental instinct is comparatively feeble, whereas in the female the maternal instinct is highly developed, and may become sublime. Indeed, were it not for the short duration of its exercise towards each brood or litter of young, it might be said to exceed in intensity the maternal instinct of woman. This instinct, so repeatedly called forth in the life of the female animal, is certainly the one which gives colour, force, and dignity to her existence. The male, on the other hand, is often distinguished by greater muscular strength, beauty of colouring or marking, and pugnacity towards other males, accompanied, however, by forbearance towards females. Amongst vertebrate animals there is hardly such a thing known as forcing the inclinations of the female, although great ferocity is often displayed in fighting to obtain possession of her.

The part played by the male in the rearing of the young is almost always a secondary, a subsidiary, and a subordinate one. He may help to provide them with food, and to defend them from external enemies. In the case of animals which live in herds, such as wild cattle, the older males even exhibit great watchfulness, courage, and devotion in their care of the community. Here male animals may reach their highest point of heroism, which in females is generally only reached in the protection of their young. It is only in the lowest classes of Vertebrata (Fishes and Amphibia) that some species are found in which the male makes the nest (sticklebacks) and takes charge of the eggs after they are laid (sticklebacks, seahorses, and *Bufo obstetricians*). Some male birds assist the female actively in making the nest, and in the care of the young, and they even take their turn, and sometimes more than a fair share, in sitting on the eggs (pigeons, ostriches, &c.), and show evident pride and interest in their offspring.

It is noteworthy that it is only at the bottom of the scale of vertebrate animals that anything like an equal division of labour and care for the young between the two sexes is found, and even here it is not constant, but confined to certain species. It would appear that the parental instinct develops in the male in inverse ratio to the polygamous instinct, and that the most favourable condition for its development is that of pairing for the definite purpose of rearing a family, as occurs in so many species of birds. Our knowledge of the habits of animals is still very imperfect, and a closer study of their social peculiarities would be both interesting and instructive.

In the Mammalia, the highest class of vertebrate animals, a still further differentiation of function takes place, which vests the right of property in the young still more unmistakably and unquestionably in the mother. Organs are developed for the elaboration, from the blood of the mother, of food for the helpless newborn animal, and this physical and direct dependence on the mother lasts throughout the whole of the helpless period of life. When it ceases, the animal is freed from all family ties, and begins its own independent career. The new bond between the mother and her young constituted by suckling is the distinguishing characteristic of all the higher animals. The father is more indifferent to his progeny in many species of Mammalia than among the lower orders of the Vertebrata. In some species—rabbits, rats, mice, etc.—the male is so ferocious an enemy of his own offspring that the mother hides them away from him in order to save their life. In general, in the vertebrate kingdom, the mother is the undisputed guardian, the devoted nurse, and the courageous defender of the young, and the father is either wholly indifferent, more or less helpful to the mother, or the protector of the whole community, inclusive of his own offspring; but such a thing as ownership of the young by the father is unknown amongst the higher Vertebrata, and the mother is the parent whose duties and rights predominate throughout the whole animal world.

In the history of the human race it is interesting to find, as it were, an echo of the development of the animal kingdom—first promiscuity, haphazard unions, no parental duties clearly recognised. Next a long period during which maternal predominance is the rule, but only because the father is indifferent to his offspring; partly because he is not sure of the paternity, and partly because his life is too grovelling and sensual for him to find pleasure outside the gratification of his own appetites. The already developed parental instinct in the mother raises her, even then, like the mother animal, into a less ferocious, less self-absorbed existence. Later on in the history of the Aryan race, the paternal instinct asserts itself, humanising in some respects to the father, but arrogant, exclusive, domineering to an extent never observed in the higher animals; where indeed mothers, in the exuberance of maternal instinct, sometimes fight for each other's young to bring them up with their own, as I have observed a very motherly tame rat to do, but where it never seems to enter into the head of the father to dispute the mother's right to her young ones. In the animal kingdom, the paternal instinct gathers strength in an orderly sort of way, seldom becoming very strong, but, on the other hand, not invading the rights of the mother. A buck rabbit may, indeed, devour the whole young family, but this murderous proceeding is the result of complete indifference. He eats them just as he would eat any other dainty morsel, and it does not denote any determination on his part to defraud the mother of her right, or to take her little ones away from her for his own use or pleasure. In the human race, on the contrary, no sooner does the paternal instinct awake, than it becomes aggressive, self-asserting, tyrannical, oppressive. Hence the laws which take the children from the mother, and make them the property of the father; hence the law and custom which place the wife in the dependence and under the control of the husband; hence the opinion that family life is indissolubly bound up with marital supremacy, and that to vest all the rights in the father—who gives and who does so much less for the maintenance of the family, to the exclusion of the mother, who is the natural centre of the family and the mainstay of the home—is the right way to secure family happiness and dignity.

Ars longa, vita brevis. The history of the human race is as yet but a brief span. The organisation of society is incomplete or fragmentary; all our social arrangements require revision, and none require it more obviously, more imperatively than those which relate to the position of the mother in the family. Other nations have gone astray in this particular or in that; the unrepresented sex is everywhere at a legal disadvantage; but in no civilised country in the world are such barbarous enactments still to be found on the statute-book as those which determine the legal position of wives and mothers in this boasted free England of ours. Go where you will, to France, Germany, Italy, nay, even to Russia and Turkey, and you will find, in many important particulars, some recognition of maternal rights which puts to shame our marriage laws, or our laws relating to inheritance and to the care and custody of children. How long, oh, men of England, shall it be that we are scoffed at by all the neighbouring nations for our short-sighted policy in perpetuating the life-long legal minority and non-existence of wives and married mothers, while recognising many rights and privileges in the unmarried, and that, too, in an age characterised by much power, concentration of thought, and vigour of action in English women? How long shall it be that you will consent to usurp the position of masters and oriental despots in your homes, and miss the dignified position, consonant with natural rights and with the highest aspirations of the human mind, which law should respect and incorporate, not trample to the ground; miss the meaning and the beauty of that co-operation in family life, that mutual respect, that union of hopes and aims and labours, so well expressed by the old familiar term of *helpmate*, which embodies the high ideal of human marriage, from which our legislators have so widely and so grievously departed? To be helps meet for one another, equal before the law as husband and wife, equal before each other as dear companions and comrades for life, unequal only in the burden and privilege of bearing and rearing children, which belong of natural right to the mother, and in which the father, unless all natural law be violated, can have but the smaller share—such should be the ideal towards which we tend, such the rule of life to which we all, men as well as women, conform, and such the improved and more truly human standard, according to which we shall call upon the Legislature to remodel and reform the antiquated and inequitable laws which still regulate the relations of English domestic life, and the position of the mother in the family.

48. Ellen Key (1904)

The ideal form of marriage is considered to be the perfectly free union of a man and a woman, who through mutual love desire to promote the happiness of each other and of the race.

But as development does not proceed by leaps no one can hope that the whole of society will attain this ideal otherwise than through transitional forms. These must preserve the property of the old form: that of expressing the opinion of society on the morality of sexual relations—and thus providing a support for the undeveloped—but at the same time must be free enough to promote a continued development of the higher erotic consciousness of the present time. The modern man considers himself supreme in the sense that no divine or human authority higher than the collective power of individuals themselves can make the laws that confine his liberty. But he admits the necessity of a legal limitation of freedom, when this prepares the way for a more perfect future system for the satisfaction of the needs of the individual and a more complete freedom for the use of his powers. Insight into the present erotic needs and powers of individuals must thus be the starting-point of a modern marriage law, but not any abstract theories about the "idea of the family" or juridical considerations of the "historical origin" of marriage.

Since, as already pointed out, society is the organisation which results when human beings set themselves in motion to satisfy their needs and exercise their powers in common, it must also be in a condition of uninterrupted transformation according as new needs arise and new powers are developed. This has now taken place in the erotic sphere, especially since those emotional needs and powers of the soul, which formerly were nourished by and directed towards religion, have been nourished by and directed towards love. Love itself is thus becoming more and more a religion, and one which demands new forms for its practice.

But while the individualist can only be satisfied with the full freedom of love, he is compelled by the sense of solidarity, at least for the present, to demand a new law for marriage, since the majority is not yet ready for perfect freedom.

The sense of solidarity and individualism have equally weighty reasons for condemning the existing institution of marriage. It forces upon human beings, who are seldom ideal, a unity which only an ideal happiness renders them capable of supporting. It fulfils one of its missions—that of protecting the woman—in a way that is now humiliating to her human dignity. It performs its second function—that of protecting the children—in an extremely imperfect fashion. Its third—that of setting up an ideal of the morality of sexual relations—it performs in such a way that this ideal is now a hindrance to the further development of morality. . . .

The marriage law now in force is a geological formation, with stratifications belonging to various phases of culture now concluded. Our own phase alone has left few and unimportant traces in it.

It has been perceived in our time that love ought to be the moral ground of marriage. And love rests upon equality. But the law of marriage dates from a time when the importance of love was not yet recognised. It, therefore, rests upon the inequality between a lord and his dependent.

Our time has given to the unmarried woman the opportunity of making her own living, a legal status, and civil rights. But the marriage law dates from a time when women had none of these things. The married woman, thus, under this law, now occupies a position in sharp contrast to the independence of the unmarried, which has been acquired since that time.

Our time has displaced the ancient division of labour, by which the wife cared for the children and the husband provided maintenance. But the law of marriage dates from a time when this division held full sway and when it was, therefore, almost impossible for a woman to receive protection for herself and her child otherwise than in matrimony. Now society has begun to provide such protection for unmarried mothers, and the renunciation of liberty by which the wife purchases the protection of marriage is seen to be not only more and more unworthy, but also unnecessary.

Our time has recognised more and more the importance of every child as a new member of society and the right of every child to be born under healthy conditions. But the law of marriage was framed at a time when this aspect had not presented itself to the consciousness of mankind; when the illegitimate child was regarded as worthless, however superior in itself, and the legitimate child as valuable, whatever might be its hereditary defects.

Our time has recognised the value to morality of personal choice. It admits as really ethical only such acts as result from personal examination and take place with the approval of the individual conscience.

The marriage system came into being when this sovereignty of the individual was scarcely suspected, much less recognised; when souls were bound by the power of society, and when compulsion was society's only means of attaining its ends. Marriage was the halter with which the racial instinct was tamed, or, in other words, the instinct of nature was ennobled by being brought into unity with social purpose.

Now love has been developed, the human personality has been developed, and woman's powers have been liberated.

On account of woman's present independent activity and self-determination outside marriage, the law must provide that the married woman shall retain her freedom of action by giving her full authority over her person and property.

On account of the individual's dislike of being forced into religious forms that have no meaning for him, the legal form of marriage must be a civil one.

On account of the individual's desire of personal choice in actions that are personally important, the continuance of marriage—as well as its inception—must depend upon either of the parties and divorce be thus free; and this all the more, since the new idea of purity implies that compulsion in this direction is a humiliation.

These are the claims the people of the present day make upon the form of marriage, if it is to express their personal will and further the growth of their personality. The actual institution of marriage, on the other hand, involves forms that have become meaningless and therefore repulsive, and places the parties under the law in a position with regard to one another which, looked at ideally, is as far beneath the merits and dignity of the modern man as it actually is beneath those of the modern woman.

While thus the development of the ideas of personality and of love have resulted in these demands of increased liberty for the individual within marriage, the idea of solidarity and evolutionism, on the other hand, demand great limitations of individual freedom. The knowledge that every new being has a right to claim that its life shall be a real value—as well as knowledge of the right of society that the new life shall be a valuable one—has involved the demand of prohibiting marriages which would be dangerous to the children, and of better protecting the children where there is no marriage or where a marriage has been dissolved.

The economic factor has in modern society an importance for marriage which is felt to be more and more degrading as marriage becomes established on the basis of love.

Marriages inwardly dissolved are now often held together because both the parties would be in a worse financial position after divorce. The husband can not or will not make his wife a sufficient allowance; he is, perhaps, unable to realise her fortune, which he has invested in his business, or perhaps he has spent it; the wife at marriage has abandoned an occupation which she cannot now take up again in order to support herself—and so on to infinity.

But even happy marriages suffer through the wife's subordinate position, economically as well as judicially.

It is, therefore, of great importance both in happy and unhappy marriages that the wife should retain control over her property and her earnings; that she should be self-supporting in so far as she can combine this with her duties as a mother, and that she should be maintained by the community during the first year of each child's life. Similar proposals have been made from the socialist side, but also in other quarters.

A woman ought to be able to claim this subsidy if she can prove:

That she is of full legal age;

That she has performed her equivalent of military service by undergoing a one year's training in the care of children and in hygiene, and—if possible—in nursing the sick;

That she will, herself, care for the children or provide other efficient care;

That she is without sufficient personal means or earnings to provide for her own and half of the children's support, or that she has given up work for the sake of looking after the children.

Those who are unwilling to conform to the above conditions will not apply for the subsidy, which naturally cannot be greater than what is strictly necessary, and which will only in exceptional cases be distributed for longer than a child's *three* first and most important years.

Those who renounced the subsidy would thus be as a rule the well-to-do, or those who wished to devote themselves to self-support and thus gave up, either altogether or after the first year, this help from the community. The arrangement would fulfil its purpose in those classes of society where at present the mother's outdoor work, both in country and town, involves equally great dangers to herself and the children. The charges for this most important of defensive taxes ought, like other similar ones, to be graduated and thus to fall most heavily upon the rich, but upon the unmarried in the same degree as the married.

Inspection should be carried out by commissioners to be appointed in every commune, varying in number according to the size of the commune, but always composed of two-thirds women and one-third men. These would distribute the subsidy and supervise the care not only of young children but also of older ones. The mother who neglected her child would, after three cautions, be deprived of the subsidy and the child would be taken from her. The same would also apply to other parents who subjected their children to bodily or mental ill-treatment.

The mother's maintenance would always amount to the same sum per annum, but for every child she would receive in addition the half of its maintenance, until the number of children was reached that the community might consider desirable from its point of view. Any children born beyond that number would be the affair of the parents. Every father would have to contribute a corresponding half of the child's maintenance from its birth up to the age of eighteen. At present the community affords a man help as breadwinner for a family in the form of higher wages calculated to that end and a rising scale according to age, which, however, he receives whether he is married or single, childless or the father of a family. But by paying the subsidy to the mother, all need of unequal wages for the two sexes would cease, and the subsidy would really further the purpose that is of importance to the community: the rearing of the children.

The present system, on the other hand, maintains that most crude injustice, the difference between legitimate and illegitimate children; it frees unmarried fathers from their natural responsibility; it drives unmarried mothers to infanticide, to suicide, to prostitution.

All these conditions would be altered by a law which prescribed that every mother has a right, under certain conditions, to the support of the community during the years in which she is bearing the burden most important to the community; and that every child has a right to maintenance by both its parents, to the name of both and—so far as there may be property—to the inheritance of both.

Since the mother must now, with increasing frequency, be a breadwinner as well as the husband, it is just, even from this point of view, that she should share with him authority over the children. But since, furthermore, she has suffered more for them, thus loves them more and understands them better—and thus, as a rule, not only does more for them but also means more to them—it is likewise just that, whereas the mother now has to be satisfied with what power the father allows her, the conditions should be reversed, so that the mother should receive the greatest legal authority.

Women's Employment and Protective Legislation

SOURCES

49. Edward Bellamy, *Looking Backward, 2000-1887* (Boston, 1889), pp. 357-65.

50. Beatrice Webb, *Women and the Factory Acts*, Fabian Tract no. 67 (London, 1896), pp. 3-5, 10-13, 14-15.

51. Maria Pognon, "La Loi néfaste de 1892," *La Fronde*, 3, no. 743 (20 December 1899). Tr. KMO.

52. Josephine C. Goldmark, "The Necessary Sequel of Child-labor Laws," *American Journal of Sociology*, 11, no. 3 (November 1905), 312-13, 313-15, 322, 324-25.

The question of women's participation in the labor force and the problems it posed for their family life also attracted renewed public interest—and prompted government intervention—in most industrializing nations. Concern focused primarily on women employed in industries where increased capitalization and mechanization were transforming the production process itself. Certain handwork skills were rendered obsolete, and both men and women were forced to seek their living away from their households. Of course, the removal of processing operations from the home gravely affected married women's ability to combine productive labor with childbearing and childraising activities, but—as we have seen in Volume I, Part II—it also influenced thinking about the wage-earning activities of single women. The selections included here represent conflicting views about the desirability of government legislation designed specifically to protect women employed in extra-domestic industries. Should women's labor-force participation be subjected to different rules from that of men? This question was relentlessly debated during the 1890-1914 period by employers, labor reformers, women's movement leaders, and social revolutionaries, during congresses on worker protection and women's rights, and in the periodical press. Their debate was heavily influenced by role expectations and by concern over national population strength.

The first selection comes from a best-selling anticapitalist novel, *Looking Backward, 2000-1887,* by the American writer Edward Bellamy (1850-1898). The speakers in the dialogue excerpted here are the narrator, a young nineteenth-century Bostonian gentleman who has awakened from a deep sleep to find himself in the year 2000, and Dr. Leete, the late twentieth-century inhabitant of the narrator's house. Here Dr. Leete describes to his surprised guest Bellamy's vision of the way in which women's employment would be organized—quite separately from that of men—in the industrial army of the next century.

The second selection is from Fabian Tract no. 67 by Beatrice Potter Webb (1858-1943). The independent-minded daughter of an English "captain of industry," she spurned the genteel lifestyle of the new plutocracy, married the scholarly reformer Sidney Webb, and became a social reformer in her own right. Together with George Bernard Shaw and H. G. Wells, she and her husband were founding members of the Fabian Society; their philosophy for social change was the "inevitability of gradualness" through state intervention as opposed to violent revolution. Beatrice Webb was a firm supporter of women's employment and its professionalization; she was convinced that under adequate laws women's work need be treated no differently than men's. Such a philosophy was in keeping with the general socialist view that once the problems of the working class were resolved, the woman question would solve itself. In this pamphlet Webb examined the confrontation that had arisen between working-women's representatives and women's rights advocates over several provisions of the new Factory and Workshop Act of 1895. This act was intended to regulate the hours and working conditions of women in the sweated trades, much as had been done earlier for women employed in the textile mills. A staunch partisan of factory employment for women and of trade unionism, Webb subsequently argued that "the factory system which provides the great market for women's labor" in England must replace sweated labor. Moreover, she insisted, effective trade unionism for women could be developed only in a well-regulated factory setting. Webb deftly sidestepped the issue of women's special functions raised earlier by so many others.

The split between the regulators and women's rights advocates is illuminated by the third selection. This article by Maria Pognon (1844-1925), then president of the Ligue Française pour le Droit des Femmes (French League for Women's Rights), appeared in the Parisian women's daily paper *La Fronde* in 1899. The French law of 2 November 1892, to which Pognon refers, limited the working hours of women and children in all industrial establishments, thereby effectively prohibiting night work for women in many industrialized trades—including those that directly affected the all-female production staff of *La Fronde* itself.

Cited for violation of the 1892 law, *La Fronde*'s editor-in-chief, Marguerite Durand, had contested its provisions in court, only to be ruled against; thus, the sharpness in Pognon's remarks must be understood in the context of this particular incident. It should be further noted that Pognon, unlike Beatrice Webb, does address the issue of women's work with reference to the population question, an issue that in 1896 was utterly absent from the concerns of reformers such as Webb.

The fourth selection is excerpted from an important article by the American social reformer Josephine Clara Goldmark (1877-1950). The daughter of a well-to-do liberal Jewish family (her father had been a refugee from the failed Austrian revolution of 1848 and had made a fortune from U.S. Civil War munitions patents), Goldmark had studied at Barnard College and subsequently worked closely with the reformer Florence Kelley at the National Consumers' League. Goldmark's broadly conceived background studies of American women's labor force participation later provided fuel for the conclusive arguments of her brother-in-law, Louis Brandeis, in his briefs for the U.S. Supreme Court's 1908 landmark ruling for the constitutionality of Oregon's protective legislation for working women. In this article Goldmark adopts an argument that initially seems analogous to that of Beatrice Webb. But, writing ten years after Webb and in an intellectual climate conditioned by the social Darwinist views of men like G. Stanley Hall and Theodore Roosevelt (Docs. 37, 30), Josephine Goldmark is less sanguine about the positive effects of factory labor for the thousands of young single women, potential mothers all, who were pouring into the American labor force during this period.

---

49. Edward Bellamy (1889)

"I suppose," I said, "that women nowadays, having been relieved of the burden of housework, have no employment but the cultivation of their charms and graces."

"So far as we men are concerned," replied Dr. Leete, "we should consider that they amply paid their way, to use one of your forms of expression, if they confined themselves to that occupation, but you may be very sure that they have quite too much spirit to consent to be mere beneficiaries of society, even as a return for ornamenting it. They did, indeed, welcome their riddance from housework, because that was not only exceptionally wearing in itself but also wasteful in the extreme, of energy, as compared with the co-operative plan; but they accepted relief from that sort of work only that they might contribute in other and more effectual, as well as more agreeable ways, to the common weal. Our women, as well as our men, are members of the industrial army, and leave it only when maternal duties claim them. The result is that most women, at one time or another of their lives, serve industrially some five or ten or fifteen years, while those who have no children fill out the full term."

"A woman does not, then, necessarily leave the industrial service on marriage?" I queried.

"No more than a man," replied the doctor. "Why on earth should she? Married women have no housekeeping responsibilities now, you know, and a husband is not a baby that he should be cared for."

"It was thought one of the most grievous features of our civilization that we required so much toil from women," I said; "but it seems to me you get more out of them than we did."

Dr. Leete laughed. "Indeed we do, just as we do out of our men. Yet the women of this age are very happy, and those of the nineteenth century, unless contemporary references greatly mislead us, were very miserable. The reason that women nowadays are so much more efficient co-laborers with the men [and at] the same time are so happy, is that, in regard to their work as well as men's, we follow the principle of providing every one the kind of occupation he or she is best adapted to. Women being inferior in strength to men, and further disqualified industrially in special ways, the kinds of occupation reserved for them, and the conditions under which they pursue them, have reference to these facts. The heavier sorts of work are everywhere reserved for men, the lighter occupations for women. Under no circumstances is a woman permitted to follow any employment not perfectly adapted, both as to kind and degree of labor, to her sex. Moreover, the hours of women's work are considerably shorter than those of men's, more frequent vacations are granted, and the most careful provision is made for rest when needed. The men of this day so well appreciate that they owe to the beauty and grace of women the chief zest of their lives and their main incentive to effort, that they permit them to work at all only because it is fully understood that a certain regular requirement of labor, of a sort adapted to their powers, is well for body and mind, during the period of maximum physical vigor. We believe that the magnificent health which distinguishes our women from those of your day, who seem to have been so generally sickly, is owing largely to the fact that all alike are furnished with healthful and inspiriting occupation."

"I understood you," I said, "that the women-workers belong to the army of industry, but how can they be under the same system of ranking and discipline with the men when the conditions of their labor are so different."

"They are under an entirely different discipline," replied Dr. Leete, "and constitute rather an allied force than an integral part of the army of the men. They have a woman general-in-chief and are under exclusively feminine regime. This general, as also the higher officers, is chosen by the body of women who have passed the time of service, in correspondence with the manner in which the chiefs of the masculine army and the president of the nation are elected. The general of the women's army sits in the cabinet of the president and has a veto on measures respecting women's work, pending appeals to Congress. I should have said, in speaking of the judiciary, that we have women on the bench, appointed by the general of the women, as well as men. Causes in which both parties are women are determined by women judges, and where a man and a woman are parties to a case, a judge of either sex must consent to the verdict."

"Womanhood seems to be organized as a sort of *imperium in imperio* in your system," I said.

"To some extent," Dr. Leete replied; "but the inner *imperium* is one from which you will admit there is not likely to be much danger to the nation. The lack of some such recognition of the distinct individuality of the sexes was one of the innumerable defects of your society. The passional attraction between men and women has too often prevented a perception of the profound differences which make the members of each sex in many things strange to the other, and capable of sympathy only with their own. It is in giving full play to the differences of sex rather than in seeking to obliterate them, as was apparently the effort of some reformers in your day, that the enjoyment of each by itself, and the piquancy which each has for the other, are alike enhanced. In your day there was no career for women except in an unnatural rivalry with men. We have given them a world of their own with its emulations, ambitions, and careers, and I assure you they are very happy in it. It seems to us that women were more than any other class the victims of your civilization. There is something which, even at this distance of time, penetrates one with pathos in the spectacle of their ennuied, undeveloped lives, stunted at marriage, their narrow horizon, bounded so often, physically, by the four walls of home and morally by a petty circle of personal interests. I speak now not of the poorer classes who were generally worked to death, but also of the well to do and rich. From the great sorrows, as well as the petty frets of life, they had no refuge in the breezy outdoor world of human affairs, nor any interests save those of the family. Such an existence would have softened men's brains or driven them mad. All that is changed to-day. No woman is heard nowadays wishing she were a man, nor parents desiring boy rather than girl children. Our girls are as full of ambition for their careers as our boys. Marriage, when it comes, does not mean incarceration for them, nor does it separate them in any way from the larger interests of society, the bustling life of the world. Only when maternity fills a woman's mind with new interests does she withdraw from the world for a time. Afterwards, and at any time, she may return to her place among her comrades, nor need she ever lose touch with them. Women are a very happy race nowadays, as compared with what they ever were before in the world's history, and their power of giving happiness to men has been of course increased in proportion."

"I should imagine it possible," I said, "that the interest which girls take in their careers as members of the industrial army and candidates for its distinctions, might have an effect to deter them from marriage."

Dr. Leete smiled. "Have no anxiety on that score, Mr. West," he replied. "The Creator took very good care that whatever other modifications the dispositions of men and women might with time take on, their attraction for each other should remain constant. The mere fact that in an age like yours when the struggle for existence must have left people little time for other thoughts, and the future was so uncertain that to assume parental responsibilities must have often seemed like a criminal risk, there was even then marrying and giving in marriage, should be conclusive on this point. As for love nowadays, one of our authors says that the vacuum left in the minds of men and women by the absence of care for one's livelihood, has been entirely taken up by the tender passion. That, however, I beg you to believe, is something of an exaggeration. For the rest, so far is marriage from being an interference with a woman's career that the higher positions in the feminine army of industry are intrusted only to women who have been both wives and mothers, as they alone fully represent their sex."

"Are credit cards issued to the women just as to the men?"

"Certainly."

"The credits of the women I suppose are for smaller sums, owing to the frequent suspension of their labor on account of family responsibilities."

"Smaller!" exclaimed Dr. Leete, "O, no! The maintenance of all our people is the same. There are no exceptions to that rule, but if any difference were made on account of the interruptions you speak of, it would be by making the woman's credit larger, not smaller. Can you think of any service constituting a stronger claim on the nation's gratitude than bearing and nursing the nation's children? According to our view, none deserve so well of the world as good parents. There is no task so unselfish, so necessarily without return, though the heart is well rewarded, as the nurture of the children who are to make the world for one another when we are gone."

"It would seem to follow, from what you have said, that wives are in no way dependent on their husbands for maintenance."

"Of course they are not," replied Dr. Leete, "nor children on their parents either, that is, for means of support, though of course they are for the offices of affection. The child's labor, when he grows up, will go to increase the common stock, not his parents', who will be dead, and therefore he is properly nurtured out of the common stock. The account of every person, man, woman, and child, you must understand, is always with the nation directly, and never through any intermediary, except, of course, that parents, to a certain extent, act for children as their guardians. You see that it is by virtue of the relation of individuals to the nation, of their membership in it, that they are entitled to support; and this title is in no way connected with or affected by their relations to other individuals who are fellow members of the nation with them. That any person should be dependent for the means of support upon another, would be shocking to the moral sense, as well as indefensible on any rational social theory. What would become of personal liberty and dignity under such an arrangement?"

50. Beatrice Webb (1896)

The discussion on the Factory Act of 1895 raised once more all the old arguments about Factory legislation, but with a significant new cleavage. This time legal regulation was demanded, not only by all the organizations of working women whose labor was affected, but also by, practically, all those actively engaged in Factory Act administration. The four women Factory Inspectors unanimously confirmed the opinion of their male colleagues. Of all the classes having any practical experience of Factory legislation, only one—that of the employers—was ranged against the Bill, and that not unanimously. But the employers had the powerful aid of most of the able and devoted ladies who have usually led the cause of women's enfranchisement, and whose strong theoretic objection to Factory legislation caused many of the most important clauses in the Bill to be rejected.

The ladies who resist further legal regulation of women's labor usually declare that their objection is to special legislation applying only to women. They regard it as unfair, they say, that women's power to compete in the labor market should be "hampered" by any regulation from which men are free. Any such restriction, they assert, results in the lowering of women's wages, and in diminishing the aggregate demand for women's work. I shall, later on, have something to say about this assumed competition between men and women. But it is curious that we seldom find these objectors to unequal laws coming forward to support even those regulations which apply equally to men and to women. Nearly all the clauses of the 1895 Bill, for instance, and nearly all the amendments proposed to it, applied to men and women alike. The sanitary provisions; the regulations about fire-escapes; the pre-eminently important clause making the giver-out of work responsible for the places where his work is done; the power to regulate unhealthy trades or processes: all these made no distinction between the sexes. Yet the ladies who declared that they objected only to inequality of legislation, gave no effective aid to the impartial sections of the Bill. If we believe that legal regulation of the hours and conditions of labor is found, in practice, to promote the economic independence and positively to add to the industrial efficiency of the workers concerned, why should we not help women workers in unregulated trades to gain this superior economic position, even if Parliament persists in denying it to the men? It is clear that there lurks behind the objection of inequality an inveterate scepticism as to the positive advantages of Factory legislation. Indeed, the most energetic and prominent opponents of women's Factory Acts openly avow as much. Mrs. Henry Fawcett and Miss Ada Heather-Bigg, for instance, usually speak of legal regulation as something which, whether for men or for women, decreases personal freedom, diminishes productive capacity, and handicaps the worker in the struggle for existence. I need not recall how firmly and conscientiously this view was held by men like Nassau Senior and John Bright in the generation gone by. To-day there are evidently many ladies of education and position superstitiously clinging to the same belief. Therefore before discussing whether any particular Factory Act is good for women or not, we had better make up our minds on the general question. Does State regulation of the hours and conditions of labor increase or decrease the economic independence and industrial efficiency of the workers concerned?

Now those who object to further Factory legislation are right in asserting that the issue cannot be decided by harrowing accounts of factory tyranny, or particular cases of cruelty or hardship. I shall not trouble you with the long list of calamities in the unregulated trades, on which the official report of the Chief Inspector of Factories lays so much stress— the constitutions ruined by long hours in dressmakers' workrooms or insanitary laundries, the undermining of family life by the degradation of the home into a workshop, the diseases and deaths caused by white lead and lucifer matches. And, I hope, no one in the discussion will think it any argument against Factory Acts that some poor widow might find it more difficult to get bread for her starving children if she were forbidden to work at the white lead factory; that some sick man's daughter would not be allowed to earn the doctor's fee by taking extra work home after her factory day; or that some struggling laundress might find it impossible to make a living if she could not employ her girls for unlimited hours. Either way there must be hard cases, and individual grievances. The question is whether, taking the whole population and all considerations into account, the evils will be greater under regulation or under free competition.

Let us concede to the opponents of Factory legislation that we must do nothing to impair or limit the growing sense of personal responsibility in women; that we must seek, in every way, to increase their economic independence, and their efficiency as workers and citizens, not less than as wives and mothers; and that the best and only real means of attaining these ends is the safeguarding and promoting of women's freedom. The only question at issue is how best to obtain this freedom. When we are concerned with the propertied classes—when, for instance, it is sought to open up to women higher education or the learned professions—it is easy to see that freedom is secured by abolishing restrictions. But when we come to the relations between capital and labor an entirely new set of considerations come into play. In the life of the wage-earning class, absence of regulation does not mean personal freedom. Fifty years' experience shows that Factory legislation, far from diminishing individual liberty, greatly increases the personal freedom of the workers who are subject to it. Everyone knows that the Lancashire woman weaver, whose hours of labor and conditions of work are rigidly fixed by law, enjoys, for this very reason, more personal liberty than the unregulated laundrywoman in Notting Hill. She is not only a more efficient producer, and more capable of associating with her fellows in Trade Unions, Friendly Societies, and Co-operative Stores, but an enormously more independent and self-reliant citizen. It is the law, in fact, which is the mother of freedom. . . .

First let us realize the exact amount of the inequality between the sexes in our Factory Acts. All the regulations with respect to safety, sanitation, employers' liability, and age apply to men and women alike. The only restriction of any importance in our Labor Code which bears unequally on men and women is that relating to the hours of labor. Up to now there has been sufficient influence among the employers, and sufficient prejudice and misunderstanding among legislators, to prevent them expressly legislating, in so many words, about the hours of labor of adult men. That better counsels are now prevailing is shown by the fact that Parliament in

1892 gave power to the Board of Trade to prevent excessive hours of work among railway servants, and that the Home Secretary has now a similar power in respect of any kind of manual labor which is injurious to health or dangerous to life and limb. I need hardly say that I am heartily in favor of regulating, by law, the hours of adult men, wherever and whenever possible. But although the prejudice is breaking down, it is not likely that the men in the great staple industries will be able to secure for themselves the same legal limitation of hours and prohibition of overtime that the women in the textile manufactures have enjoyed for nearly forty years. And thus it comes about that some of the most practical proposals for raising the condition of the women in the sweated trades must take the form of regulations applying to women only.

It is frequently asserted as self-evident that any special limitation of women's labor must militate against their employment. If employers are not allowed to make their women work overtime, or during the night, they will, it is said, inevitably prefer to have men. Thus, it is urged, any extension of Factory legislation to trades at present unregulated must diminish the demand for women's labor. But this conclusion, which seems so obvious, really rests on a series of assumptions which are not borne out by facts.

The first assumption is, that in British industry to-day, men and women are actively competing for the same employment. I doubt whether any one here has any conception of the infinitesimal extent to which this is true. We are so accustomed, in the middle-class, to see men and women engaged in identical work, as teachers, journalists, authors, painters, sculptors, comedians, singers, musicians, medical practitioners, clerks, or what not, that we almost inevitably assume the same state of things to exist in manual labor and manufacturing industry. But this is very far from being the case. To begin with, in over nine-tenths of the industrial field there is no such thing as competition between men and women: the men do one thing, and the women do another. There is no more chance of our having our houses built by women than of our getting our floors scrubbed by men. And even in those industries which employ both men and women, we find them sharply divided in different departments, working at different processes, and performing different operations. In the tailoring trade, for instance, it is often assumed that men and women are competitors. But in a detailed investigation of that trade I discovered that men were working at entirely separate branches to those pursued by the women. And when my husband, as an economist, lately tried to demonstrate the oft-repeated statement that women are paid at a lower rate than men, he found it very difficult to discover any trade whatever in which men and women did the same work. As a matter of fact, the employment of men or women in any particular industry is almost always determined by the character of the process. In many cases the physical strength or endurance required, or the exposure involved, puts the work absolutely out of the power of the average woman. No law has hindered employers from engaging women as blacksmiths, steel-smelters, masons, or omnibus-drivers. The great mass of extractive, constructive, and transport industries must always fall to men. On the other hand, the women of the wage-earning class have hitherto been distinguished by certain qualities not possessed by the average working man. For good or for evil they eat little, despise tobacco, and seldom get drunk; they rarely strike or disobey orders; and they are in many other ways easier for an employer to deal with. Hence, where women can really perform a given task with anything like the efficiency of a man, they have, owing to their lower standard of expenditure, a far better chance than the man of getting work. The men, in short, enjoy what may be called a "rent" of superior strength and endurance; the women, on their side, in this preference for certain employments, what may be called a "rent" of abstemiousness.

I do not wish to imply that there are absolutely no cases in British industry in which men and women are really competing with each other. It is, I believe, easy to pick out an instance here and there in which it might be prophesied that the removal of an existing legal restriction might, in the first instance, lead to some women being taken on in place of men. In the book and printing trade of London, for instance, it has been said that if women were allowed by law to work all through the night, a certain number of exceptionally strong women might oust some men in bookfolding and even in compositors' work. We must not overlook these cases; but we must learn to view them in their proper proportion to the whole field of industry. It would clearly be a calamity to the cause of women's advancement if we were to sacrifice the personal liberty and economic independence of three or four millions of wage-earning women in order to enable a few hundreds or a few thousands to supplant men in certain minor spheres of industry.

The second assumption is, that in the few cases in which men and women may be supposed really to compete with each other for employment, the effect of any regulation of women's hours is pure loss to them, and wholly in favor of their assumed competitors who are unrestricted. This, I believe, is simply a delusion. Any investigator of women's work knows full well that what most handicaps women is their general deficiency in industrial capacity and technical skill. Where the average woman fails is in being too much of an amateur at her work, and too little of a professional. Doubtless it may be said that the men are to blame here: it is they who induce women to marry, and thus divert their attention from professional life. But though we cannot cut at the root of this, by insisting, as I once heard it gravely suggested, on "three generations of unmarried women," we can do a great deal to encourage the growth of professional spirit and professional capacity among women workers, if we take care to develop our industrial organization along the proper lines. The first necessity is the exclusion of illegitimate competitors. The real enemies of the working woman are not the men, who always insist on higher wages, but the "amateurs" of her own sex. So long as there are women, married or unmarried, eager and able to take work home, and do it in the intervals of another profession, domestic service, we shall never disentangle ourselves from that vicious circle in which low wages lead to bad work, and bad work compels low wages. The one practical remedy for this disastrous competition is the extension of Factory legislation, with its strict limitation of women's hours, to all manufacturing work wherever carried on. It is no mere coincidence that the only great industry in which women get the same wages as men—Lancashire cotton weaving—is the one in which precise legal regulation of women's hours has involved the absolute exclusion of the casual amateur. No woman will be taken on at a cotton mill unless she is prepared to work the full factory hours, to come regularly every day, and put her whole energy into her task. In a Lancashire village a woman must decide whether she will earn her maintenance by working in the mill or by tending the home: there is no "betwixt and between." The result is a class of women wage-earners who are capable of working side by side with men at identical tasks; who can earn as high wages as their male competitors; who display the same economic independence and professional spirit as the men; and who are, in fact, in technical skill and industrial capacity, far in advance of any other class of women workers in the kingdom. If we want to bring the women wage-earners all over England up to the level of the Lancashire cotton weavers, we must subject them to the same conditions of exclusively professional work. . . .

[Webb's third assumption is that the mechanical evolution of industry itself and the resulting division and specialization of labor "leads inevitably to an increased demand for women's labor."]

We can now sum up the whole argument. The case for Factory legislation does not rest on harrowing tales of exceptional tyranny, though plenty of these can be furnished in support of it. It is based on the broad facts of the capitalist system, and the inevitable results of the Industrial Revolution. A whole century of experience proves that where the conditions of the wage-earner's life are left to be settled by "free competition" and individual bargaining between master and man, the worker's "freedom" is delusive. Where he bargains, he bargains at a serious disadvantage, and on many of the points most vital to himself and to the community he cannot bargain at all. The common middle-class objection to Factory legislation—that it interferes with the individual liberty of the operative—springs from ignorance of the economic position of the wage-earner. Far from diminishing personal freedom, Factory legislation positively increases the individual liberty and economic independence of the workers subject to it. No one who knows what life is among the people in Lancashire textile villages on the one hand, and among the East End or Black Country unregulated trades on the other, can ever doubt this.

All these general considerations apply more forcibly to women wage-earners than to men. Women are far more helpless in the labor market, and much less able to enforce their own common rule by Trade Unionism. The only chance of getting Trade Unions among women workers lies through the Factory Acts. We have before us nearly forty years' actual experience of the precise limitation of hours and the absolute prohibition of overtime for women workers in the cotton manufacture; and they teach us nothing that justifies us in refusing to extend the like protection to the women slaving for irregular and excessive hours in laundries, dressmakers' workrooms, and all the thousand and one trades in which women's hours of work are practically unlimited.

Finally, we have seen that the fear of women's exclusion from industrial employment is wholly unfounded. The uniform effect of Factory legislation in the past has been, by encouraging machinery, division of labor, and production on a large scale, to increase the employment of women, and largely to raise their status in the labor market. At this very moment the neglect to apply the Factory Acts effectively to the domestic workshop is positively restricting the demand for women workers in the clothing trades. And what is even more important, we see that it is only by strict regulation of the conditions of women's employment that we can hope for any general rise in the level of their industrial efficiency. The real enemy of the woman worker is not the skilled male operative, but the unskilled and half-hearted female "amateur" who simultaneously blacklegs both the workshop and the home. The legal regulation of women's labor is required to protect the independent professional woman worker against these enemies of her own sex. Without this regulation it is futile to talk to her of the equality of men and women. With this regulation, experience teaches us that women can work their way in certain occupations to a man's skill, a man's wages, and a man's sense of personal dignity and independence.

51. Maria Pognon (1899)

On this very day that unfortunate law of so-called protection is returning to the Chamber of Deputies from the Senate. It is so badly written that it is impossible to apply, and on behalf of women we have a duty to protest against it.

On the pretext of protecting women against exploitation by their employers, on the pretext of safeguarding the future of the race through the women, our legislators decided that all night work should be prohibited and that the number of working hours of a female worker should be limited to eleven hours a day.

In practice it was quickly realized that, on the one hand, the mixed workshops [i.e., sexually integrated] could not function without shared work and that with the departure of the women who ran a machine, for instance, the men could not continue with their own tasks. On the other hand, it appeared that there were certain types of work such as folding newspapers, binding periodical reviews, lighting lamps in the mines, which were so badly paid that no man wanted the jobs. Now, however lowly certain tasks may seem, they are nonetheless indispensable and pressure was brought on the law to allow night work at these newspapers, journals, and mines.

A decree issued on July 15, 1893, authorized the employment of women on a permanent basis in these types of work for seven hours per night.

In addition to the newspaper folders, who are now authorized to wear themselves out for very little gain, it was noted that certain morning newspapers employed female compositors and that these women were well able to support themselves and their children.

At that point came an about-face! Women folders could be permitted, but not women compositors. The inspectors received strict orders, and everywhere the women compositors were replaced by men. In the meantime, one printer in the provinces resisted; on the basis of the law that prohibited night work by minor girls and married women, he alleged that adult single women were not included under this prohibition. In consequence he dismissed the married women he had employed and replaced them with single women who were of age, affirming that this put him right with the law. The court found against him; he lost his appeal and was obliged to dismiss the adult single women along with the others.

Are we supposed to believe that this law was made in the interest of women? Quite the contrary: it is protection in reverse. What! For seven years we have witnessed new decrees authorizing night work in certain industries, such as pouring and drying starch; in the glassworks women are permitted to sort and arrange bottles—in a word, to execute such tasks as men refuse because they are not sufficiently lucrative.

The 1892 law was made by antifeminists, who were concerned with reserving all the well-paying work for their constituents: this is the real truth!

We have nothing against the protection of children. But we find the law much too harsh for them; they are not allowed to work in factories or workshops more than six hours per day before the age of sixteen, and are supposed to use the remaining hours for their instruction and their physical development. As for a woman, she is an adult being who should be free to govern herself just as much as a man. If the end result is to limit the workday to a certain number of hours for all workers, so be it, but there should be no unfavorable exceptions for one sex to the profit of the other. In all the industries such as the cotton spinneries of the Vosges, the wool-combing establishments of the Nord, the 1892 law had the effect of opening up jobs for men, whose hours were not restricted. The poor children were plunged into utmost misery as a result of the forced unemployment of their mothers.

Since then many, many exemptions have been granted, on the demand of employers who said they could not do without their female workers. The hatmakers, the *couturières* have all arranged a certain number of authorized night-work sessions.

But wherever the night work is well-paid, someone has found it too tiring for women, or unhygienic, or even dangerous!

Many thanks for your protection, *Messieurs les députés*. From now on leave women free to work or to rest as they see fit, according to the circumstances. Get used to considering them as responsible beings, capable of directing their own lives and of taking responsibility for their own actions; do not confuse them with their children, whose reasoning powers are not yet fully developed, and, if you want to protect the little ones, let their mothers work in their places.

Help these women to unionize so that they can themselves arrange their terms of work with the employers, but do not deprive them of their jobs on the pretext of safeguarding their health. If the father's health is not good, the children will not be much to brag about either.

We can improve the race by requiring of workers only a reasonable expenditure of physical strength. But since both sexes are called upon to procreate, we must be prudent and kind to both; otherwise it is lost labor.

52. Josephine Goldmark (1905)

Recent agitation against the abuses of child-labor has been confined to the needs of children to the age of fourteen or at most sixteen years. This vital issue should not obscure the imperative need of relief from overwork of young girls above that age. For obvious reasons, girls between sixteen and twenty-one years stand in need of protective legislation, primarily a limitation upon their hours of labor. That women *as women* should have certain safeguards secured by law, that women need special legislation, is a proposition adopted and acted upon by all enlightened states. In view of the fact that practically one-half of the working-women in the United States (49.3 per cent. in 1900) are girls—young women under the age of twenty-five years—such special legislation is specially needed.

In the census of 1900 the section on "Occupations" shows very clearly in what direction the employment of women has been tending during the last twenty years. Two striking facts stand out vividly: (1) the increase in the percentage of working-women over the percentage of men between 1880 and 1900; (2) the large percentage of young women (sixteen to twenty years) in the total number of working-women, as compared with the small percentage of young men of the same ages in the total number of working-men.

In 1880 the percentage distribution *by sex* of all persons engaged in gainful occupations was: working-men, 84.8; working-women, 15.2. By 1900 this ratio had changed as follows: working-men, 81.8; working-women, 18.2—an increase of 3 per cent. of women workers, with a corresponding decrease of 3 per cent. of men workers.

In every geographic division, and in every state and territory except three, females formed an increased proportion from 1890 to 1900 of the total number of persons gainfully employed, and in the three states excepted—Georgia, Florida, and Louisiana—the proportion remained practically stationary.

To illustrate the increase in the percentage of working-women over working-men in particular industries, the figures given for manufacture and trade are of striking interest: In 1880 the percentage of working-men in manufacture was 83.8; by 1900 this figure had sunk to 81.5. The percentage of working-women in manufacture, on the contrary, rose from 16.7 in 1880 to 18.5 in 1900.

In trade and transportation—a division of industry including the employment of women as "stenographers, typewriters, telegraph and telephone operators, bookkeepers, clerks, and saleswomen"—the percentage of women rose from 3.4 in 1880 to the surprising figure of 10.5 in 1900: while the percentage of men sank from 96.6 to 89.5 in the same twenty years.

Thus the rapid increase in the number of working-women, and the rate at which they are gaining upon men, comparatively, in the industries that call for the labor of women, warrant a careful study of the results of such employment, and of the status of the working-woman before the law, in the various states, as a means of obtaining more adequate protection. . . .

Legislation for working-men has been most advanced in the western mining states. The eight-hour day is no longer an ideal, but has been obtained as a legal maximum for all laborers in mines in Arizona, Colorado, Missouri, Montana, Nevada, Utah, and Wyoming. Eighteen states, both east and west, restrict to an eight-hour day all work contracted for by the state.

If it is recognized as desirable that men should not be obliged to work more than eight hours in a day in certain industries, the work of women should, without question, be limited to that maximum. If a working-day of ten, twelve, or fourteen hours reduces a man to the level of a mere machine, it leaves a woman in a more unhappy plight—in imminent danger of physical breakdown.

The new strain in industry.—From the point of view of health, two particular hardships exist for the woman worker: the extreme length of the working-day and the requirement of night work. The former is the more widespread evil, and directly affects the larger number.

The industries of today differ most markedly from those of the past in the relentless speed which they require. This speed is acquired in various ways: by mechanical devices which "speed up" the individual machines; by increasing the number of machines attended by each worker; by the specialization which trains a worker to one detail of production year after year; and by other methods. . . .

One of the most conspicuous examples of trades which have vastly increased their output during the last few years—and an example most pertinent to the discussion of women's employment—is the stitched-underwear trade. A brief description of this industry may illustrate the conditions under which a large and rapidly increasing class of young girls are employed. The machines have been so improved that they set twice as many stitches as they did five years ago, the best machines, driven by dynamo power, now setting 4,400 stitches a minute.

The operative cannot see the needle; she sees merely a beam of light striking the steel needle from the electric lamp above her head. But this she must watch, as a cat watches a mousehole; for one variation means that a broken needle is cutting the fibers of the garment, and a different variation means that the thread is broken and the seam is having stitches left unsewn. Then the operative must instantly touch a button and stop the machine. Such intent watching wears out alike nerves and eyes.

The result of speed so greatly increased tends inevitably to nervous exhaustion. Machines may be revolved more and more swiftly, but the endurance of the girl workers remains the same. No increase in vitality responds to the heightened pressure. A constant drain of nervous energy follows—particularly deplorable in the case of young women, whether they are to marry after a few years of overstrain, or to continue through longer years of such employment. . . .

The Supreme Court on labor legislation.—For all these workers, those partly protected and those unprotected, any future legislation must be broad and inclusive, to afford real relief. Labor legislation prohibiting certain employments or restricting the hours of labor has in some instances been wrecked upon the Fourteenth Amendment to the Constitution of the United States, which assures to every man liberty of contract. This liberty of the individual, however, to contract for such purposes and under such conditions as he pleases, must yield to superior considerations of life, health, and safety. Under the police powers of the state, specific measures can be enacted from time to time against clearly proved abuses. When laws restricting the hours of labor have been declared unconstitutional by the federal Supreme Court, the state legislatures have been held to infringe upon the individual right of contract *without good cause*; or, in other words, the evil against which legislation was aimed was held *not evil enough* to justify the interference with individual rights. On the other hand, the labor laws which have been upheld as constitutional by the Supreme Court have been regarded as legitimate measures, conspicuously necessary for health or safety, and therefore not in conflict with the Fourteenth Amendment. . . .

Labor legislation for women.—Protection ampler and more far-reaching than exists, enacted under the police powers of the state, is now claimed for women as necessary for health and safety. All the arguments which apply in favor of the restriction of the hours of working-men apply with a hundred-fold power to the restriction of women's hours of labor. Their youth, their helplessness, their increasing numbers, the conditions under which they are employed, all call for uniform and enforceable statutes in their behalf. Eight hours were deemed by the Supreme Court a "reasonable" period for men's employment in an industry liable to injure the health. Eight hours cannot be called an unreasonable period for the young girls who constitute so large a proportion of the army of working-women.

To obtain this restriction will require a campaign of education. The National Consumers' League is asking co-operation for this next great step in protective legislation from the General Federation of Women's Clubs, an organization whose wide influence has done much to secure the gradually improving child-labor laws of the nation.

There is needed, first, the co-operation and sympathy of all who have at heart the welfare of the industrial state. "The whole is no greater than the sum of all the parts, and when the individual health, safety, and welfare are sacrificed or neglected, the state must suffer."

Women's Health and Protective Legislation

SOURCES

53. Dr. Alfred Mjøen, "Legal Certificates of Health Before Marriage; Personal Health-Declaration versus Medical Examination," tr. Dr. Bergen, in *The Eugenics Review*, 4, no. 4 (January 1913), 360-62. Originally published in the Norwegian journal of women's rights, *Nylaende* (New Land), April 1912.

54. Christabel Pankhurst, "A Woman's Question," in *Plain Facts About a Great Evil* (London, 1913), pp. 13, 16-21, 22-23. Originally published in *The Suffragette* (London), 1, no. 43 (8 August 1913), 737.

A second type of state intervention encouraged on women's behalf was the effort to legislate required medical certification as a precondition for marriage—and parenthood. The impetus for such intervention came from members of the medical profession closely associated with public health concerns and from women reformers sensitized to the ravages of venereal disease—especially syphilis—through their efforts to combat regulated prostitution and the white slave trade. The selections that follow illustrate the discussion that took place over such intervention during 1913, by which time both the first truly effective treatment for syphilis and Wassermann's diagnostic blood test were just coming into use.

The first selection is the text of a petition presented to the Norwegian parliament, or *Storthing*, in 1913 by Dr. Alfred Mjøen (1860-1939). Mjøen, one of three sons of a landed Norwegian family, owned a leading pharmacy in Christiania (Oslo) and was a founder of the international eugenics movement. He had established a private institute for race-hygiene research, and in 1915 published a controversial treatise on race hygiene that earned him the enmity of the Norwegian left. Dr. Mjøen had concluded that the correct approach to the marriage regulation issue was to require each party to declare his or her physical fitness before a registered physician, as a condition for contracting marriage. He had ruled out as unacceptable to public opinion the alternative concept of a required physical examination. In this petition he advocated that a series of such health declarations be made obligatory by amending the marriage laws of Norway.

A more uncompromising position on the subject of women's personal health is found in the writings of Christabel Harriette Pankhurst (1880-1958). The eldest daughter of the progressive-minded Pankhurst family from Lancashire, Christabel Pankhurst was precociously political. She studied law and received a degree in 1906, although she could not be admitted to the bar. In the meantime she became the chief theorist and tactician for the militant British woman suffrage organization, the Women's Social and Political Union (WSPU), which she, her sister Sylvia (Doc. 74) and her mother Emmeline (Doc. 61) had founded in 1903. In 1912-13 Christabel Pankhurst was living in self-imposed exile in Paris to avoid capture under the nefarious "Cat and Mouse Act," aimed at muzzling the militant suffragettes. Nevertheless, she remained a presence in London through her weekly articles in the WSPU newspaper, *The Suffragette.* In mid-1913 the disclosure of a London sex scandal involving high-ranking political figures who frequented sado-masochistic brothels—and opposed woman suffrage—provoked Christabel Pankhurst to publish a scathing series of articles decrying male vice and underscoring its evil consequences for innocent women. She prescribed a single standard—"Votes for Women and Chastity for Men."

53. Alfred Mjøen (1912)

The following suggested amendment to the Norwegian marriage law was subsequently drawn up by Dr. Mjøen, and will be sent in the form of a petition to the Storthing of 1913.

"That [in addition to the provisions at present embodied in the marriage law] there should be a declaration by each of the two contracting parties, made at a date not exceeding six months before the marriage, as to whether either is subject to a disease or weakness which might have an injurious effect on the health of the other or of the offspring; and, further, that each declaration should be accompanied by a document signed by the parents or guardians of both parties, stating that it had been submitted to their notice and that consequently they had been given an opportunity to raise any necessary objections or to make representations to the one or the other of the couple intending marriage. The declarations should be made before a physician authorised by the State."

In support of this suggestion it was pointed out by the petitioner, "that there are diseases and tendencies to disease, as well as mental and physical defects, which experience has shown are either congenital or inherited. Children who are subject to defects of this nature, unless they die in infancy, are a source of great care to their parents and a burden to the public. If they subsequently marry, the evil is only carried further, often through generations, affecting an ever-widening circle of individuals. Consequently, in order to protect the family and the home, a movement to adopt a new form of marriage law has arisen in America, New Zealand, and in several European countries, where many authorities are inclined to favour a medical examination before marriage. The chief object of this examination is to discover whether, in either of the contracting parties, or their families, there are diseases or tendencies to disease, such as alcoholism, tuberculosis, scrofula, insanity, criminal inclinations (as a result of defective mental development) or venereal diseases. Especially the latter, by reason both of the unpleasant consequences and dangers which result from them, no less than their excessive prevalence, are of greater significance than most other diseases.

"The legislative adoption of a medical examination would, however, be attended by certain disadvantages which are of such a nature as to render inadvisable the introduction of an *obligatory* medical examination before marriage. The disease from which society would especially endeavour to protect itself through such legislation, namely, syphilis, frequently cannot be detected in its latent state, even by the most observant and skilled physician; and it would also seem to be a mistake to introduce the obligatory medical examination of young women at a time when the examination of prostitutes for venereal disease is almost everywhere being allowed to fall into disuse. To my mind, an obligatory medical examination should not be suggested until bio-chemical methods of research have been so improved, that the presence or absence of such diseases as must be considered in relation to marriage can be ascertained without the necessity of a physical examination. In doubtful cases—and there are many such—the medical certificate would, nevertheless, have to be issued; and it would certainly have an effect contrary to its purpose and bring both the law and the physician into discredit. And if obligatory medical examinations became statutory (especially in case they were to lead to the prohibition of the union of those considered unfit to marry) they would bring the physician into conflict with his duty of professional secrecy, and easily drive the patient into illegitimate sexual relations.

"On the other hand, a personal health-declaration, such as is described above, made on one's honour before a physician authorised by the State, would have the great advantage of being actually of greater validity than the obligatory certificate on the basis of a medical examination and much less rigorous in form. False declarations would hardly ever be made; or, at the worst, their number would be exceedingly small. The circumstance that the declaration must be made before a physician would also tend to deter many who might otherwise be tempted to make a false statement in the hope of being able to shift the responsibility to the 'medical certificate' and to the examining physician himself.

Among the many advantages that would result from such health-declarations made before a physician and submitted to parents or guardians for their consideration may be included the awakening of the sense of individual moral responsibility and the national conscience in regard to marriage and the health of the race; for no one of either sex could marry without first having to ask himself the question, whether or not he is physically fitted for marriage. The result would be that a large number of defective individuals, especially such as those whose offspring are now supported by the community, would renounce the idea of founding a family. The burdens borne by the public in the form of Poor Law rates, prosecutions, prisons, inebriate homes, schools for the feeble-minded, and the like, would be lightened, and there would be a not inconsiderable improvement in the genetic qualities of the race, bringing with it health and strength and more national happiness, without any interference whatever with personal freedom. There would be a direct stimulus to the promotion of good health, and encouragement to keep one's body clean and inviolable; and the authorities would be given an admirable opportunity for watching over the physical welfare of the nation, especially during the youth of its inhabitants. In other words, a legal health-declaration before marriage would be the first step towards a practical system of "national hygiene."

54. Christabel Pankhurst (1913)

The Prime Minister has been holding forth on the subject of the prevention of tuberculosis. A most desirable thing, but it is even more desirable that the Prime Minister shall talk about another and even more terrible form of disease, and that he shall try to prevent it—that he shall strike at the cause of sexual disease.

The cause of sexual disease is the subjection of women. Therefore to destroy the one we must destroy the other. Viewed in the light of that fact, Mr. Asquith's opposition to votes for women is seen to be an overwhelming public danger. . . .

For women the question of venereal disease has a special and a tragic interest. It strikes at them in their own person and through their children. A woman infected by syphilis not only suffers humiliation and illness which may eventually take the most revolting form, but is in danger of becoming the mother of deformed, diseased, or idiot children. Why are such children born into the world? women have often cried in despair. The answer is—Syphilis! Miscarriage is frequently caused by the same disease. Indeed nothing, as one doctor says, is so murderous to the offspring as syphilis.

Rather different, though hardly less terrible where women are concerned, is the effect of gonorrhœa. . . .

Gonorrhœa is one of the most prevalent of all diseases. It is acquired before marriage by 75 per cent. or 85 per cent. of men, and it is very often contracted after marriage by such men as are not entirely faithful to their wives. To men the disease gives comparatively little trouble, and in the old days the doctors made very light of it.

But to women, owing to their physiological structure, it is one of the gravest of all diseases. A very large number of married women are infected by their husbands with gonorrhœa. The common result is sterility, which prevents the birth of any child, or may prevent the birth of more than one child. Race Suicide!

Generally speaking, the female ailments which are urged by some ignoble men as a reason against the enfranchisement of women are not due to natural weakness, but—to gonorrhœa. Women—and there are so many of them—who "have never been well since they married," are victims of gonorrhœa.

An enormous percentage of the operations upon women are necessitated by this disease, which in many cases so affects the organs of maternity as to necessitate their complete removal. Race Suicide again.

These are awful truths, so awful that the woman's instinct is to keep them hidden, until she realises that only by making these truths known can this appalling state of affairs be brought to an end.

Women have suffered too much from the conspiracy of silence to allow that conspiracy to last one minute longer. It has been an established and admitted rule in the medical profession to keep a wife in ignorance of the fact that she has become the victim of venereal disease. A bride struck down by illness within a few days, or within a few weeks, of her wedding day is told by her husband and the doctor that she is suffering from appendicitis, and under cover of this lie her sex organs are removed without her knowledge. Women whose husbands contract syphilis, and are in turn infected, are kept in ignorance of this, and are thus unable to protect themselves and to do their duty by the future generation.

Here we have the woman question in perhaps its most urgent and acute form. Have the Anti-Suffragist women any idea of what the wrongs of women really are? We beg them to realise that so long as the subjection of women endures and is confirmed by law and custom, so long will the race be injured and degraded, and women be victimised.

Sexual disease, we say again, is due to the subjection of women. It is due, in other words, to the doctrine that woman is sex and beyond that nothing. Sometimes this doctrine is dressed up in the saying that women are mothers and beyond that nothing. What a man who says that really means is that women are created primarily for the sex gratification of men, and secondarily, for the bearing of children if he happens to want them, but of no more children than he wants.

As the result of this belief the relation between man and woman has centred in the physical. What is more, the relation between man and woman has been that of an owner and his property—of a master and his slave—not the relation of two equals.

From that evil has sprung another. The man is not satisfied to be in relation with only one slave; he must be in relation with many. That is to say, sex promiscuity has arisen, and from that has in its turn come disease.

And so at the beginning of this twentieth century in civilised Britain we have the doctors breaking through the secrecies and traditions of long years, and sounding the note of alarm. This canker of venereal disease is eating away the vitals of the nation, and the only cure is Votes for Women, which is to say the recognition of the freedom and human equality of women. . . .

The outcome of enfranchisement will be to make women hate more than anything else in the world the very thought of selling themselves into slavery as under the conditions of the present day so many of them do sell themselves. The weapon of the vote will enable them to break down existing barriers to honest livelihood.

Upon men the effect of women's enfranchisement will be to teach them that women are their human equals, and not the sub-human species that so many men now think them; not slaves to be bought and soiled and degraded and then cast away.

We know to what bodily and spiritual corruption the subjection of women has brought humanity. Let us now see to what cleanness and nobility we can arrive through her emancipation!

CHAPTER 6

The Nation-State and Woman Suffrage

Woman Suffrage in England Before 1900

SOURCES

55. *Female Suffrage, a Letter from the Right Hon. W. E. Gladstone to Samuel Smith, M.P., 11 April 1892.* Reprinted by the American Women Remonstrants to the Extension of Suffrage to Women (n.p., n.d.), pp. 3-8. Originally published in London, 1892.

56. Susan Elizabeth Gay, *A Reply to Mr. Gladstone's Letter on Woman Suffrage* (London, 1892), pp. 3-8.

Ever since John Stuart Mill had broached the subject of female suffrage in the House of Commons (Vol. I, Docs. 135, 136), this issue had occupied a growing number of Liberal Party supporters both in and out of Parliament. However, the supremely influential party leader, William Ewart Gladstone (1809-1898), was fundamentally opposed to giving women the parliamentary vote. A complex man, who struggled throughout his long political career to reconcile his deep-rooted religious convictions and the expediency demanded of a politician, Gladstone was convinced that the political arena would besmirch women's God-given nature and destroy her role "at the hearth." Although his wife Catherine lent her name as a figurehead supporter to the female-suffrage oriented Women's Liberal Federation (the women's auxiliary of the Liberal Party), and his daughter Helen—one of eight children, four of whom were daughters—was one of the first women students and later vice-principal of Newnham College, Cambridge, Gladstone still considered his family life a haven from his preoccupations with thorny and unpopular causes. The latter ranged from home rule for Ireland to the rehabilitation of prostitutes through personal concern and persuasion, an unconventional avocation fully supported by Gladstone's wife. Helen, the only remaining unmarried daughter, gave up her Cambridge post in 1896 in order to look after her aging parents.

In 1892, just before the still vigorous eighty-two-year-old Gladstone became prime minister for the fourth time, and twenty-five years since the House had first discussed J. S. Mill's amendment, he circulated a printed letter to all members of parliament to urge them to prevent a second reading of a bill that recommended extension of the parliamentary franchise to unmarried women. The issue had been thoroughly aired three years earlier (1889) in the *Nineteenth Century* in several articles, the first written by Mary (Mrs. Humphry) Ward and signed by 104 well-known women, rejecting suffrage. The responding articles were by Millicent

Garrett Fawcett, leader of the women's suffrage movement, and Lady Dilke, a prominent writer and women's trade-union organizer.

A Reply to Mr. Gladstone came two months later, published by the Women's Printing Society and written by a member of the Women's Liberal Federation, Susan Elizabeth Gay (c.1840-c.1920). Gay, born in Oswestry, Shropshire, was the daughter of a surveyor. In her youth she had published articles in the *Victoria* and other magazines. She had lectured in the United States and there published a volume, *Spirit of the New Testament*, in 1885. After writing her letter to Gladstone she published *Womanhood and the Bible*. In the latter part of her life she settled near Falmouth, in Cornwall, where she occupied herself with the town's history and wrote several books on the subject. As is apparent from her published works and from the letter reprinted here, Gay was preoccupied with a religious approach to the woman question comparable to that of the Grimké sisters and of Lucretia Mott in the United States some fifty years earlier. This orientation, coupled with her appeal to justice, made her refutation of Gladstone's "religious" arguments all the more persuasive.

---

55. William E. Gladstone (1892)

1. Carlton Gardens,
Dear Mr. Samuel Smith   April 11, 1892.

In reply to your letter, I cannot but express the hope that the House of Commons will not consent to the second reading of the Bill for Extending the Parliamentary Suffrage to Women, which will come before it on the 27th instant.

The Bill is a narrow Bill, inasmuch as it excludes from its operation the entire body of married women; who are not less reflective, intelligent, and virtuous, than their unmarried sisters, and who must I think be superior in another great element of fitness, namely the lifelong habit of responsible action. If this change is to be made, I certainly have doubts, not yet dispelled, whether it ought to be made in the shape which would thus be given to it by a halting and inconsistent measure.

But it is a change which obviously, and apart from disputable matter, ought not to be made without the fullest consideration and the most deliberate assent of the nation as well as of the Parliament. Not only has there been no such assent, but there has not been even an approach to such consideration. The subject has occupied a large place in the minds of many thoughtful persons, and of these a portion have become its zealous adherents. Just weight should be allowed to their sentiments, and it is desirable that the arguments on both sides should be carefully and generally scrutinised: but the subject is as yet only sectional, and has not really been taken into view by the public mind at large. Can it be right, under these circumstances, that the principle of a change so profound should be adopted? Cannot its promoters be content with that continuance and extension of discussion, which alone can adequately sift the true merits of their cause?

I offer this suggestion in the face of the coming Election. I am aware that no legitimate or effectual use can be made of it for carrying to an issue a question at once so great and so novel; but I do not doubt, considering the zeal and ability which are enlisted in its favour, that the occasion might be made available for procuring an increase of attention to the subject, which I join with them in earnestly desiring.

There are very special reasons for circumspection in this particular case. There has never within my knowledge been a case in which the franchise has been extended to a large body of persons generally indifferent about receiving it. But here, in addition to a widespread indifference, there is on the part of large numbers of women who have considered the matter for themselves, the most positive objection and strong disapprobation. Is it not clear to every unbiassed mind that before forcing on them what they conceive to be a fundamental change in their whole social function, that is to say in their Providential calling, at least it should be ascertained that the womanly mind of the country, at present so largely strange to the subject, is in overwhelming proportion, and with deliberate purpose, set upon securing it?

I speak of the change as being a fundamental change in the whole social function of woman, because I am bound in considering this Bill to take into view not only what it enacts, but what it involves. The first of these, though important, is small in comparison with the last.

What the Bill enacts is simply to place the individual woman on the same footing in regard to Parliamentary elections, as the individual man. She is to vote, she is to propose or nominate, she is to be designated by the law as competent to use and to direct, with advantage not only to the community but to herself, all those public agencies which belong to our system of Parliamentary representation. She, not the individual woman, marked by special tastes, possessed of special gifts, but the woman as such, is by this change to be plenarily launched into the whirlpool of public life, such as it is in the nineteenth, and such as it is to be in the twentieth century.

So much for what the Bill enacts: now for what it involves, and involves in the way of fair and rational, and therefore of morally necessary, consequence. For a long time we drew a distinction between competency to vote and competency to sit in Parliament. But long before our electorate had attained to the present popular proportions, this distinction was felt to involve a palpable inconsistency, and accordingly it died away. It surely cannot be revived: and if it cannot be revived, then the woman's vote carries with it, whether by the same Bill or by a consequential Bill, the woman's seat in Parliament. These assertions ought to be strictly tested. But, if they cannot be confuted, do not let them be ignored.

If the woman's vote carries with it the woman's seat, have we at this point reached our terminus, and found a standing ground which we can in reason and in justice regard as final? Capacity to sit in the House of Commons now legally and practically draws in its train capacity to fill every office in the State. Can we alter this rule and determine to have two categories of Members of Parliament, one of them, the established and the larger one, consisting of persons who can travel without check along all the lines of public duty and honour; the other, the novel and the smaller one, stamped with disability for the discharge of executive, administrative, judicial, or other public duty? Such a stamp would I apprehend be a brand. There is nothing more odious, nothing more untenable, than an inequality in legal privilege which does not stand upon some principle in its nature broad and clear. Is there here such a principle, adequate to show that when capacity to sit in Parliament has been established, the title to discharge executive and judicial duty can be withheld? Tried by the test of feeling, the distinction would be offensive. Would it stand better under the laws of logic? It would stand still worse, if worse be possible. For the proposition we should have to maintain would be this. The legislative duty is the highest of all public duties; for this we admit your fitness. Executive and judicial duties rank below it: and for these we declare you unfit.

I think it impossible to deny that there have been and are women individually fit for any public office however masculine its character; just as there are persons under the age of twenty-one better fitted than many of those beyond it for the discharge of the duties of full citizenship. In neither case does the argument derived from exceptional instances seem to justify the abolition of the general rule. But the risks involved in the two suppositions are immeasurably different. In the one, individual judgment and authority plainly would have to distinguish between childhood and manhood, and to specify a criterion of competency in each case, which is now more conveniently fixed by the uniformity of law. In the other, a permanent and vast difference of type has been impressed upon women and men respectively by the Maker of both. Their differences of social office rest mainly upon causes, not flexible and elastic like most mental qualities, but physical and in their nature unchangeable. I for one am not prepared to say which of the two sexes has the higher and which has the lower province. But I recognize the subtle and profound character of the differences between them, and I must again, and again, and again, deliberate before aiding in the issue of what seems an invitation by public authority to the one to renounce as far as possible its own office, in order to assume that of the other. I am not without the fear lest beginning with the State, we should eventually be found to have intruded into what is yet more fundamental and more sacred, the precinct of the family, and should dislocate, or injuriously modify, the relations of domestic life.

As this is not a party question, or a class question, so neither is it a sex question. I have no fear lest the woman should encroach upon the power of the man. The fear I have is, lest we should invite her unwittingly to trespass upon the delicacy, the purity, the refinement, the elevation of her own nature, which are the present sources of its power. I admit that we have often, as legislators, been most unfaithful guardians of her rights to moral and social equality. And I do not say that full justice has in all things yet been done; but such great progress has been made in most things, that in regard to what may still remain the necessity for violent remedies has not yet been shown. I admit that in the Universities, in the professions, in the secondary circles of public action, we have already gone so far as to give a shadow of plausibility to the present proposals to go farther; but it is a shadow only, for we have done nothing that plunges the woman as such into the turmoil of masculine life. My disposition is to do all for her which is free from that danger and reproach, but to take no step in advance until I am convinced of its safety. The stake is enormous. The affirmation pleas are to my mind not clear, and, even if I thought them clearer, I should deny that they were pressing.

Such being the state of the evidence, and also such the immaturity of the public mind, I earnestly hope that the House of Commons will decline to give a second reading to the Woman's Suffrage Bill.

I remain, dear Mr. S. Smith,
Very faithfully yours,
W. E. Gladstone.

56. Susan Elizabeth Gay (1892)

Sir,

I have been one of those women—perhaps altogether in the minority —who have refrained, in the course of our work for a great cause, from taking sides on the question of Woman Suffrage, with the hope that some clearer light might be thrown upon it by one whom we regard as a great leader. But now that we women have received your expression of opinion upon it, I for one feel it may not be amiss to offer a reply, and on the large ground that no consideration of expediency, no temporary end, however important, should ever be allowed to lead us aside from principles which are based, not upon caprice, prejudice, or momentary conditions, but eternal justice.

Permit me, Sir, briefly to review your arguments.

"The Bill does not include married women." The conferring of the franchise has always been progressive in character; there has been some substantial opposition to conferring the vote on married women, an opposition in which I do not share, and with which I have no sympathy, which is entirely absent in the cases for which that Bill would have provided. Moreover, the "lifelong habit of responsible action" is surely exercised by those women who are alone and have been widows for years, who have had to provide for and bring up families, and [by] single women who are working for a living, and have the sole management of their property, and not infrequently the care of relatives' children.

Again, when you assert that there has been not only no assent to this reform, but no approach to it, you certainly very seriously overstate the facts. The question of Woman Suffrage has been before the nation for the last twenty-five years, and frequently before Parliament, and has been steadily supported by intelligent women and men, and by the press in an increasing degree. But for the pains taken to suppress its discussion in Parliament of late—all the more easy to arrange from the fact that *no* class of women is represented—the public education would have been far more complete even than it is. The change can hardly be termed "profound" either. Measures involving far more positive and extensive action on the part of women have been passed, and have been found to be both useful and beneficial to the community. For a striking example of a woman to whom ideas of this kind are never applied, we need only refer to our Queen.

You assert that a certain proportion of women are hostile to the franchise. Probably they are. Probably they are also excellent women in many respects, although lacking in that growing appreciation of the just and right as such, which marks the women no less than the men of a younger generation, and is one of the most hopeful signs of our day. But are they obliged to use their vote if they possess it? And should they be permitted to coerce other women by their own narrower views? If the possession of the franchise involves what you describe as a "fundamental change in the whole social function of woman," how is it that the women of Wyoming, in the United States, are quite as womanly as Englishwomen, and that the State in question has shown such a marked social and electoral improvement since women were nobly included among its electors, even at the risk—found to be groundless—of the State being excluded from representation in the Union?

Even if the act of voting plunged women into the "whirlpool of public life," just as much may be said with regard to the stage, ballet-dancing, and other occupations, which not only actually do this, but bring women into direct and frequent contact with objectionable men, and publicly expose them to the gaze of those who are generally far from exalted in mind or morals. But to tell the truth, the association of which your esteemed wife herself is the President, presents aspects in its public work and meetings far more in accordance with your description than the simple exercise of the franchise. Of this you must certainly be aware. And does any thinking person consider this an objection to the valuable work of that association?

The assertion that the woman's vote carries with it the woman's seat, is pure speculation. It is outside the domain of practical politics in our day altogether, and need not even be discussed. The time may eventually come when natural capacity and high principle may count for something more than difference of sex with regard to any office; but we are very far from such an ideal state of human life, and I might add, far below it. Using your own words in other relations, it may well be said that "nothing is more odious, nothing more untenable, than an inequality in legal privilege," which is based on the mere physical differences of man and woman, and which disregards all those higher qualities of mind and soul which both possess in common.

I take it, the aim of all politics—unfortunate term!—should be the amelioration of human life, the growth of progress and reform, the breaking down of selfish and unfraternal privileges and barriers, whether of race, caste, creed, or sex—and in this woman must share with man.

You add, Sir, in the close of your letter, that a "permanent and vast difference of type has been impressed upon women and men respectively by the Maker of both," and state that their "differences of social office" are "physical and unchangeable." But they are also temporary, and not only temporary as regards the individual, but as regards the race. Evolution clearly shows us that even physical nature is plastic, and that man himself becomes at a certain stage of his evolution creative, and that he has been at all times a creative force, and a producer of environments on our planet. Sex may embrace not only one plane, but many planes, until we ascend from the physical to the spiritual, where it ceases to operate. For the spiritual is eternal; there is no sex in soul, and therefore, "In *Christ Jesus* (or the divine nature), there is neither male nor female." And men and women, as such, and now, possess infinitely more in common, than apart. No, Sir, it is not by depriving woman, or any portion of womanhood, of just rights, that you can preserve "her delicacy, purity and refinement," it is not by accentuating sex that you can promote the "elevation of her own nature"; it is by upholding that which makes her a human being in its full sense, free of choice, with issues as vast as those you possess yourself; a soul as divine; an immortality as profound. If "delicacy and refinement" are the results of the old system of regarding womanhood, what are we to say of our music-halls, our casinos, of such a spectacle as the Strand presents any night in London, and of the various diversions which are brought forward for the dubious amusements of men? In these sex is the supreme and central attraction, and unfortunately "the present sources of its power" are very far from being on the plane which would make man noble and woman free.

In carrying the idea of womanly dependence beyond the domain of sentiment, which is its sole legitimate expression, and converting it into a system of religious and legal oppression and moral inequality, a foul wrong has been perpetrated, not only on womanhood but on the entire race, whose excessive and perverted sexual instincts show the natural consequences. We have no quarrel with sentiments of nature expressed in *freedom*; we oppose that repressive system which deprives woman of her spiritual birthright, and is subversive of all that is exalted in life.

There remains no further argument in your letter deserving of pressing notice, and in furnishing what may be justly considered logically unanswerable rejoinders to the statements and opinions given in its pages, I earnestly trust you may be led at no distant date to remove a growing stain upon the Liberal cause, to reconsider the question of Woman Suffrage, and to look at it in the clear and simple light of Justice.

I remain, Sir,

Yours very respectfully,

The Rt. Hon. W. E. Gladstone, M. P.   S. E. G.
June, 1892.

The First European Success for Woman Suffrage

SOURCES

57. Alexandra Gripenberg, "The Great Victory in Finland" (29 June 1906) in *The Englishwoman's Review*, n.s. 38, no. 3 (16 July 1906), 155-57.

58. Maria Martin, "L'Union fait la force," *Journal des Femmes*, no. 167-68 (July-August 1906), p. 1. Tr. KMO.

59. International Socialist Women's Conference, Resolution on woman suffrage, Stuttgart, 1907. From *Dokumente und Materialien zur Geschichte der deutschen Arbeiterbewegung* IV (Berlin, 1967), 206-7; tr. Alfred G. Meyer, in *Women in Russia*, ed. D. Atkinson, A. Dallin, and G. Lapidus (Stanford, Calif., 1977), pp. 93-94.

The first European victory for unrestricted woman suffrage and eligibility for public office was realized in 1906 in Finland, where advocates of national independence had just won significant concessions from the tsar after nearly a century of Russian rule. The women of Finland had played a vital role in this struggle, especially through their work in combating the russification campaign of the 1890's by teaching the Finnish language to their children. With independence they claimed their reward. Finland's woman suffrage victory was enthusiastically announced to her envious European and American counterparts by Baroness Alexandra Gripenberg (1857-1913), novelist and long-time women's rights advocate, who was subsequently elected to the Finnish parliament. This victory served as a rallying point for the intensification of suffrage campaigns by women's rights advocates throughout the Western world. Ultimately, it stimulated the reorientation of socialist and Catholic policy on the question as well.

In France, Maria Martin (Doc. 46), editor of the *Journal des Femmes* and a fervent champion of woman suffrage since the days of her collaboration with Hubertine Auclert (Vol. I, Docs. 142, 143), published Gripenberg's letter and celebrated the Finnish women's triumph. Martin, English by birth but a French national through her marriage to Jules Martin, was closely attuned to developments in the women's rights movements in England and the United States. A pacifist and an internationalist, Martin insisted on the importance of international women's associations in pressing the suffrage initiative throughout the world.

The third selection is an analysis of the suffrage issue prepared by the European socialist women in August 1907, when they held their own conference during the Stuttgart congress of the Second International. Their resolution underscores the importance of property ownership and class as barriers to complete equality among individuals, male or female. But its authors (among whom Clara Zetkin [Doc. 15] doubtless figured) also cleverly argue that the socialists ought to join in the reformist struggle for unrestricted woman suffrage as a means of furthering the cause of the proletariat. Shortly thereafter, the delegates to the Second International Congress adopted a more general resolution in support of women's issues—pledging their various national sections to work on behalf of political, as well as legal, equality for women within the existing social order.

---

57. Alexandra Gripenberg (1906)

The miracle has happened! On May the 29th the Finnish Diet agreed to an Imperial proposal from the Czar concerning changes in the constitution of Finland, which changes also include political suffrage and eligibility to the Diet for Women, married and unmarried, on the same conditions as for men. The earlier history of this wonderful reform is related in the April Review. I will now only add that the constitution committee in the Diet recommended Women's Suffrage and eligibility for the following reasons: the women in Finland get now-a-days exactly the same education as men, even in the same schools as men, since co-education has been adopted in wide circles. Women are in our time employed side by side with men in different lines of work. The experience from these dominions, as well as from women's participation in social work and philanthropy, is such that there is no reason to fear that women would not use their suffrage and fulfil their duties as citizens as well as men. Finally, the women themselves have shown a strong desire to get the suffrage.

It would be impossible to explain to foreign readers all the reasons which have led our law-makers to a decision, which will all at once place our little insignificant people—in a certain way—above the great countries of an old culture in Europe. But one thing is clear: the universal suffrage reform has made it easier for the women to bring forward their claims. Many men, who would not have agreed to a proposal for Women's Suffrage, have now supported it when it came in connection with a proposal for universal suffrage for men, because the injustice against women showed itself clearer in this way. Even the women themselves would not so universally have manifested their desire to be enfranchised, if the reform had not been based on universal suffrage for men. For—as I wrote in an earlier letter to the Review—there was in the beginning a strong feeling among large groups of women that they wanted suffrage only in case that universal suffrage for men was established.

As this word with us is not understood exactly in the same way as in several other countries, I will shortly mention the following. According to the new law we shall henceforward in Finland have only one house in the Diet, to which members are elected by universal suffrage. Every man and woman above 24 years of age, married and unmarried, has the right to vote, with the following exceptions: soldiers, minors (that is, those who for some reasons have been put under guardianship although they are 24 years of age), those who, for other reasons than poverty, have not paid their taxes to the government the last two years, those who have not the last three years been registered as Finnish subjects, those who are inmates of workhouses or get aid from the Poor Law Guardian funds, those who have been committed to prison for crimes or for vagrancy, those who are in bankruptcy, who are condemned for a certain time "to be without the confidence of their fellow-citizens," and finally, those who have behaved dishonestly in the elections. All who have the right to vote are also eligible to the Diet.

The new election law is said to be very difficult to understand, so there are already objections against it. The social democrats are opposed to the reform because the age for voters is made 24, not 21, as they wanted. Whether the women belonging to this party will vote because of this objection is, I think, not yet settled. These and other difficulties are in our way, but of course no reform can be set in motion without disturbances in the beginning.

Our victory is in all cases great, and the more so as the proposal has been adopted almost without opposition. The gratitude which we women feel is mingled with the knowledge that we are much less worthy of this great success than the women of England and America, who have struggled so long and so faithfully, with much more energy and perseverance than we. I use this occasion to bring the thanks from the women of Finland to our sisters all over the world who have, by their untiring work, educated public opinion and thus enabled us to gain our rights. May we be worthy of them!

58. Maria Martin (1906)

At no time has the question of woman suffrage aroused so much attention as at present. People still remember the feminist demonstrations that took place during this year's general elections. Though some people objected to them, their criticism was directed more to the form than to the principle. Generally speaking, public opinion favors giving women the right to vote. Only—there are always "onlys" and "buts"—some would prefer that they [the women] not ask for it. According to these persons it would be preferable to wait in silence for the socialists, or the Catholics, or the radicals, to offer women the vote on a silver platter. This would be much more gracious than making a fuss. Others would ask for nothing more than to let women vote—certainly—except for the fact that their political education is not yet complete. They need more time to learn, from men's example, the sound and true manner of voting. When they have sufficiently studied the models of wisdom and virtue, of tolerance, of calm and disinterestedness offered them by the elections in which only men vote, perhaps then we women will be allowed to try it in our turn.

The women of England have made even more fuss than the women of France. Like the latter, they have promenaded in flag-draped carriages, and beyond that they have made speeches to large audiences, both in public halls and out-of-doors, as is so often done in England. Many members of the English Parliament have taken part in these only slightly boisterous demonstrations. A delegation of women wished at all costs to obtain an audience with the prime minister, and laid siege to the front door of his residence. The minister refused to receive the women, no doubt because it would have been too painful for him not to accede immediately to their desires. Some of these ladies were put in prison—out of generosity, of course—to prevent them from encountering trouble in the streets. Mme Montfiore refuses to pay her taxes because, she says, she didn't vote in favor of them. . . . What is most remarkable about this movement—most distressing, according to the antisuffragists—is that not one of these ladies, whether sentenced to prison or to paying a fine, has promised not to begin it all over again.

In Finland another spectacle presents itself to our view. In this tiny favored country a truly universal suffrage, suffrage for all without distinction of either class or sex, has been obtained through the combined efforts of men and women. We will never forget the happiness and pride with which the Finnish delegates present at the [June meeting of the] International Council [of Women] announced this great news to us, though [they seemed] almost ashamed to have arrived at this result while their sisters in France, England, and America, who have fought so hard, still find themselves classified with the insane, with criminals, and with children. . . .

Now the Universal Alliance for Woman Suffrage has convoked us to meet in Copenhagen from August 6th to 11th. There we will once again encounter many of the delegates to the conference of the International Council who could not come to Paris in June. The International Council, like the national councils, has accepted three points as the basis of its principles: the right to vote, peace, and the abolition of regulated prostitution. Beyond these three points, which all the councils agree to pursue and which are, indeed, international in character, each council is completely autonomous and can tailor its demands to the ideas and requirements of its own country.

The entente of all the women of Europe to demand the vote is complete. Here we see one of the fortunate results of that coordination of strength born of the institution called the International Council and its branches. . . . No one can say that women cannot agree with one another. We have proof to the contrary in this organization, and we can state that every time women join together for common action, it is to advance the most just and humanitarian causes, those most necessary to the progress of humanity.

59. International Socialist Women's Conference (1907)

The demand for women's right to vote is the result of economic and social transformations engendered by the capitalist mode of production, but especially the revolutionary change in the nature of work as well as in the position and the consciousness of women. Essentially it is a derivative of the bourgeois-democratic principle demanding the abolition of all social distinctions not based on property and proclaiming the full legal equality of all adults in private and public life to be the right of every individual. Hence individual thinkers have demanded women's suffrage in connection with all struggles in which the bourgeoisie fought for the democratization of political rights as a precondition of its political emancipation and domination as a class. However, it has acquired driving and compelling power as a mass demand only through the rising wage labor of the female sex, and especially through the inclusion of proletarian women into modern industry. Women's suffrage is the correlate of the economic emancipation of women from the household and of their economic independence from family owing to their professional work. . . .

The class differences that are effective for women as much as for men cause the value and chief purpose of the franchise to be different for women of the different classes. The value of the franchise as means of social struggle is inversely proportional to the amount of property and the social power it imparts. Depending on the class situation, its chief purpose is either the full legal equality of the female sex or the social emancipation of the proletariat through the conquest of political power with the aim of abolishing class rule and bringing about a socialist society which alone guarantees the full human emancipation of women.

Because of the class contradictions within the female sex the bourgeois women's movement does not fight for the general female suffrage in total unity and with maximal possible force. Hence in fighting for their full citizen's rights the female proletarians have to rely on their own resources and on the resources of their class. The practical requirements of its fight for emancipation as well as its historical insight and that sense of justice which springs from its class position—all these make the proletariat into the most consistent fighter for complete equality of political rights for the female sex. Hence in principle as well as in practice, the socialist parties, the political fighting organizations of the class-conscious proletariat, fight for women's suffrage.

With the sharpening of the class struggle, the question of women's suffrage rises in importance. In the ruling reactionary classes, there is a growing tendency to strengthen the political power of property by introducing a limited franchise for women. One must, today, understand the limited women's suffrage less as a first step toward the equality of political rights for the female sex than, rather, the last step in the social emancipation of property. It emancipates the woman not as an individual but as the carrier of property and income; hence it functions as the plural franchise of the possessing classes, leaves broad masses of proletarian women without political rights, and consequently does not, in fact, signify the equality of political rights for the entire female sex. For the proletariat there is an increasing necessity to revolutionize the minds and to place its adult members into the battlefront well armed, without regard to sex differences. The fight for universal female suffrage is the most suitable means to use this situation in the interest of the proletarian struggle for liberation.

Militant Tactics in England and Their Reception

SOURCES

60. Carrie Chapman Catt, *Mrs. Catt's International Address* (pamphlet), pp. 5-7. Address delivered as president of the International Woman Suffrage Alliance at the Amsterdam Congress, 15 June 1908.

61. Emmeline Pankhurst, "Speech from the Dock [Police Court]," in *Votes for Women*, 29 October 1908, p. 1.

62. Millicent Garrett Fawcett, *Women's Suffrage: A Short History of a Great Movement* (London, 1912), pp. 60-67.

63. Helene Lange, "Die Taktik der Suffragettes" (Sonderheft, Frauenstimmrechtverband für Westdeutschland, 1913), in *Kampfzeiten: Aufsätze und Reden aus vier Jahrzehnten*, II (Berlin, 1928), 118-20, 123. Tr. SGB.

64. Carrie Chapman Catt, Address to the Seventh Congress of the International Woman Suffrage Alliance at Budapest, 15 June 1913, in IWSA, *Report of the Seventh Congress, Budapest, Hungary, June 15-21, 1913* (Manchester, Eng., 1913), p. 85.

With the achievement of woman suffrage in Finland in 1906, the woman suffrage movements in all countries entered a new phase. No movement, however, was more startling to the public than that in England, where in an election year the Woman's Social and Political Union (WSPU), headed by Emmeline Pankhurst and her lawyer-daughter Christabel, embarked on a systematic program of militant activity in pursuit of votes for women. The selections reprinted here reveal the varied reactions that WSPU civil disobedience, intended to provoke arrest and imprisonment, received from other women active in suffrage work between 1908 and 1914.

The first selection is from a speech given in Copenhagen in 1908 by the American suffrage leader Carrie Chapman Catt (1859-1947). Catt, then president of the International Woman Suffrage Alliance, here invokes parallels between the women's campaign then under way in England and that of the first campaign for written legal rights in England some seven hundred years earlier. On this anniversary of Magna Carta, she is optimistic about the impending triumph of the suffrage cause.

In the second selection Emmeline Goulden Pankhurst (1858-1928), the widow of political activist Dr. Richard Pankhurst, and the mother of several grown children, spells out before the police court judge—and the public—the reasons that led her and other WSPU women to adopt the controversial tactics that were earning them increasing notoriety. Indeed, the transition from passive to active militancy, which the suffragettes then followed up by hunger strikes, had ensured the WSPU enormous and invaluable visibility in both the English and the international press. In this particular case, the women had distributed a leaflet urging their supporters "to rush the House of Commons." For refusing to "bind themselves over"—that is, to pledge good behavior in the future, Emmeline Pankhurst, her daughter Christabel, and another colleague were sentenced to serve two months in Holloway Prison as common criminals, in spite of their insistence that they be tried as political offenders.

The third selection presents the response to WSPU militancy of Millicent Garrett Fawcett (1847-1929), president of Britain's National Union of Women Suffrage Societies (NUWSS), younger sister of pioneer physician Elizabeth Garrett Anderson (Vol. I, Doc. 117), and widow of Henry Fawcett, who as a member of parliament had supported Mill's woman suffrage bill in 1867 (Vol. I, Doc. 136). By the time Fawcett wrote this piece in 1912, the repertoire of WSPU tactics had expanded from civil disobedience to calculated acts of violence against property, with the 1911 window-breaking raid in London that led to the arrest of some 150 women, who promptly embarked on hunger strikes in jail. Finally, even the more moderate NUWSS made the difficult decision to respond to the Liberal Party's betrayal of the woman suffrage cause in Parliament by adopting, in 1912, the line long advocated by the WSPU—to hold the party in power responsible on the woman suffrage issue and to campaign against all its candidates—irrespective of the fact that many among the staunchest supporters of suffrage were found among the men of that divided party. A similar campaign policy was soon adopted in the United States by Alice Paul's Congressional Union.

The fourth selection is a view from a German suffragist, Helene Lange (Doc. 35), long a staunch advocate of improved education for German women. At the time she wrote, the WSPU had escalated its tactics to include even more ingenious (some thought reprehensible) acts of guerilla warfare against property (though not against persons). To this the English Liberal government had responded by passing the infamous Cat and Mouse Act. By the terms of the act, hunger-striking suffragettes could be released from prison long enough to recover their strength, only to be subject to immediate reimprisonment upon their recovery. Clearly, Lange considered the WSPU tactics to be beyond the pale, preferring the NUWSS approach even though it drew only half the publicity. Some German suffragists disagreed with Lange, however, and followed the Pankhursts' example.

In contrast to Helene Lange, Carrie Chapman Catt (Doc. 60) celebrated the impact of the English campaign in her presidential address to the International Suffrage Alliance in 1913, excerpted in the fifth selection. In 1915 Catt took over the presidency of the National American Woman Suffrage Association, devising and executing a brilliant tactical campaign that resulted in the passage of the Nineteenth Amendment by Congress in 1919 and its ratification in 1920.

---

60. Carrie Chapman Catt (1908)

Although from Occident to Orient, from Lapland to sunny Italy, and from Canada to South Africa the agitation for woman suffrage has known no pause, yet, after all, the storm-centre of the movement has been located in England. In other lands there have been steps in evolution; in England there has been a revolution. There have been no guns, nor powder, nor bloodshed, but there have been all other evidences of war. There have been brave generals, well-trained armies, and many a well-fought battle; there have been tactics and strategies, sorties, sieges, and even prisoners of war. There are those who have criticised the methods employed; but until we know the whole truth concerning what the women of England have actually done, why they did it, and how they did it, we have no right to criticise. It must be admitted that the English campaign stands out clearly by comparison not only as the most remarkable ever conducted for woman suffrage, but as the hardest fought campaign ever waged for any reform. There have been several organizations, and these have differed widely as to methods, yet no time has been wasted in disputing over them, and the main object has never been lost sight of for a moment. The so-called suffragettes have displayed an amazing amount of energy, of persistency and executive force. Yet the older and more conservative body of workers has been no less remarkable. Human nature is so constituted that most leaders would have "sulked in their tents," or joined the general stone-throwing at the new comers, whose methods were declared to be "setting the cause backward hundreds of years." These English leaders did nothing of the kind. Instead, with forbearance we may all do well to imitate, they quadrupled their own activities. Every class, including ladies of the nobility, working girls, housewives and professional women, has engaged in the campaign, and not a man, woman or child in England has been permitted to plead ignorance concerning the meaning of woman suffrage. Together, suffragists and suffragettes have carried their appeal into the byways and most hidden corners of the kingdom. They have employed more original methods, enlisted a larger number of women workers, and grasped the situation in a bolder fashion than has been done elsewhere. In other countries persuasion has been the chief, if not the only, weapon relied upon; in England it has been persuasion plus political methods.

"By their fruits shall ye know them." Already these English women have made woman suffrage a political issue. No one can understand the meaning of this achievement so well as those who have borne the brunt of hard fought suffrage battles. It has been the dream of many a suffrage campaign, but no other women have made it a realization. When the deputation of 60 members of Parliament paid a visit to the Prime Minister a few days ago to ask his support for woman suffrage, the zenith of the world's half-century of woman suffrage campaigning was reached.

English women have effected another result, which is likewise an unfailing sign of coming triumph. A new movement is invariably attacked by ridicule. If the movement is a poor one, it is laughed out of existence, if it is a good one, it waxes strong under attack. In time the laugh is turned upon its early opponents, and when ridicule sets in that direction, it is a sign that the strife is nearly finished.

The laugh has now been turned upon the English government. What may have been its effect upon England, only those who know that country from the inside can tell; but there has been a change of sentiment toward the English suffrage campaign on the outside, and of this we may speak.

First, the world joined in loudly expressed disgust at the alleged unfeminine conduct of English suffragists. Editorial writers in many lands scourged the suffrage workers of their respective countries over the shoulders of these lively English militants. Time passed; comment ceased; and the world, which had ridiculed, watched the contest in silence, but with never an eye closed. It assumed the attitude of the referee who realizes he is watching a cleverly played game, with the chances hanging in the balance. Then came the laugh. The dispatches flashed the news to the remotest corners of the globe that English Cabinet Ministers were "protected" in the street by bodyguards; the houses of Cabinet Ministers were "protected" by relays of police, and even the great Houses of Parliament were "protected" by a powerful cordon of police. Protected! and from what? The embarrassing attack of unarmed women! In other lands, police have protected emperors, czars, kings and presidents from the assaults of hidden foes, whose aim has been to kill. That there has been such need is tragic; and when, in contrast, the vision was presented of the Premier of England hiding behind locked doors, skulking along side streets, and guarded everywhere by officers, lest an encounter with a feminine interrogation point should put him to rout, it proved too much for the ordinary sense of humor.

Again, the dispatches presented another view. Behold, they said, the magnificent and world-renowned Houses of Parliament surrounded by police, and every woman approaching that sacred precinct, halted, examined, and perhaps arrested! Behold all this elaborate precaution to save members of Parliament from inopportune tidings that women would have votes; yet, despite it all, the forbidden message is delivered, for over the House floats conspicuously and defiantly a huge "Votes for Women" kite. Perhaps England did not know the big world laughed then; but it did, and more, from that moment it conceded the victory to the suffragists. The only question remaining unanswered, is: How will the government surrender, and at the same time preserve its dignity and consistency?

I have no wish to defend, or condemn, the tactics which have been employed in England; but let me ask a question. Had there been newspapers and cables in 1215, do you not think the staid and dignified nobility of other lands would have been scandalized at the unruly behaviour of the English Barons? They certainly would. Yet we have forgotten the names of those barons, and we have forgotten the methods by which they wrested the Magna Charta from King John; we only remember that they did it, and that all mankind has enjoyed larger liberties and opportunities ever since. History repeats itself, and I venture the second prediction: For the English suffragists, final triumph is near at hand. When it comes, the world will forget the details of the campaign it has criticized, and will remember only that woman suffrage is an established fact in one of the greatest governments of the world. Nay, more, as the English Barons fought a battle for the rights of all mankind in the thirteenth century, so do I conscientiously believe that these English women of the twentieth century, suffragists and suffragettes, are striking a tremendously effective blow in behalf of the political liberty of the women of all the nations. Let those who will, criticise. English women are making history today, and coming generations will pronounce it nobly made. When they have won their cause, all women should understand that their proper relation to these plucky, self-sacrificing English women is not that of critic, but of debtor.

61. Emmeline Pankhurst (1908)

Ever since my girlhood, a period of about 30 years, I have belonged to organisations to secure for women that political power which I have felt was essential to bringing about those reforms which women need. I have tried constitutional methods. I have been womanly. When you spoke to some of my colleagues the day before yesterday about their being unwomanly, I felt that bitterness which I know every one of them felt in their hearts. We have tried to be womanly, we have tried to use feminine influence, and we have seen that it is of no use. Men who have been impatient have invariably got reforms for their impatience. And they have not our excuse for being impatient.

You had before you in this court yesterday a man who has a vote, a man who had been addressing other men with votes, and he advised action which we would never dream of advising. But I want to say here and now, as a woman who has worked in the way you advised, that I wonder whether this womanly way is not a weakness that has been taken advantage of. I believe that Mr. Will Thorne was right when he said that no action would have been taken against him, if his name had not been mentioned in this court, because it is a very remarkable thing that the authorities are only proceeding against him when goaded to it by the observations which women made here.

Now, while I share in the feeling of indignation which has been expressed to you by my daughter, I have lived longer in the world than she has. Perhaps I can look round the whole question better than she can, but I want to say here, deliberately, to you, that we are here to-day because we are driven here. We have taken this action, because as women—and I want you to understand it is as women we have taken this action—it is because we realise that the condition of our sex is so deplorable that it is our duty even to break the law in order to call attention to the reasons why we do so.

I do not want to say anything which may seem disrespectful to you, or in any way give you offence, but I do want to say that I wish, sir, that you could put yourself into the place of women for a moment before you decide upon this case. My daughter referred to the way in which women are huddled into and out of these police-courts without a fair trial. I want you to realise what a poor hunted creature, without the advantages we have had, must feel.

I have been in prison. I was in Holloway Gaol for five weeks. I was in various parts of the prison. I was in the hospital, and in the ordinary part of the prison, and I tell you, sir, with as much sense of responsibility as if I had taken the oath, that there were women there who have broken no law, who are there because they have been able to make no adequate statement.

You know that women have tried to do something to come to the aid of their own sex. Women are brought up for certain crimes, crimes which men do not understand—I am thinking especially of infanticide—they are brought before a man judge, before a jury of men, who are called upon to decide whether some poor, hunted woman is guilty of murder or not. I put it to you, sir, when we see in the papers, as we often do, a case similar to that of Daisy Lord, for whom a great petition was got up in this country, I want you to realise how we women feel, because we are women, because we are not men, we need some legitimate influence to bear upon our law-makers.

Now, we have tried every way. We have presented larger petitions than were ever presented for any other reform; we have succeeded in holding greater public meetings than men have ever had for any reform, in spite of the difficulty which women have in throwing off their natural diffidence, that desire to escape publicity which we have inherited from generations of our foremothers; we have broken through that. We have faced hostile mobs at street corners, because we were told that we could not have that representation for our taxes which men have won unless we converted the whole of the country to our side. Because we have done this, we have been misrepresented, we have been ridiculed, we have had contempt poured upon us. The ignorant mob at the street corner has been incited to offer us violence, which we have faced unarmed and unprotected by the safeguards which Cabinet Ministers have. We know that we need the protection of the vote even more than men have needed it.

I am here to take upon myself now, sir, as I wish the prosecution had put upon me, the full responsibility for this agitation in its present phase. I want to address you as a woman who has performed the duties of a woman, and, in addition, has performed the duties which ordinary men have had to perform, by earning a living for her children, and educating them. In addition to that, I have been a public officer. I enjoyed for 10 years an official post under the Registrar, and I performed those duties to the satisfaction of the head of the department. After my duty of taking the census was over, I was one of the few Registrars who qualified for a special bonus, and was specially praised for the way in which the work was conducted. Well, sir, I stand before you, having resigned that office when I was told that I must either do that or give up working for this movement.

I want to make you realise that it is a point of honour that if you decide—as I hope you will not decide—to bind us over, that we shall not sign any undertaking, as the Member of Parliament did who was before you yesterday. Perhaps his reason for signing that undertaking may have been that the Prime Minister had given some assurance to the people he claimed to represent that something should be done for them. We have no such assurance. Mr. Birrell told the women who questioned him the other day that he could not say that anything would be done to give an assurance to the women that their claims should be conceded. So, sir, if you decide against us to-day, to prison we must go, because we feel that we should be going back to the hopeless condition this movement was in three years ago if we consented to be bound over to keep the peace which we have never broken, and so, sir, if you decide to bind us over, whether it is for three or six months, we shall submit to the treatment, the degrading treatment, that we have submitted to before.

Although the Government admitted that we are political offenders, and, therefore, ought to be treated as political offenders are invariably treated, we shall be treated as pickpockets and drunkards; we shall be searched. I want you, if you can, as a man, to realise what it means to women like us. We are driven to do this, we are determined to go on with agitation, because we feel in honour bound. Just as it was the duty of your forefathers, it is our duty to make this world a better place for women than it is to-day. . . .

This is the only way we can get that power which every citizen should have of deciding how the taxes she contributes to should be spent, and how the laws she has to obey should be made, and until we get that power we shall be here—we are here to-day, and we shall come here over and over again. You must realise how futile it is to settle this question by binding us over to keep the peace. You have tried it; it has failed. Others have tried to do it, and have failed. If you had power to send us to prison, not for six months, but for six years, for 16 years, or for the whole of our lives, the Government must not think that they can stop this agitation. It will go on.

I want to draw your attention to the self-restraint which was shown by our followers on the night of the 13th, after we had been arrested. It only shows that our influence over them is very great, because I think that if they had yielded to their natural impulses, there might have been a breach of the peace on the evening of the 13th. They were very indignant, but our words have always been, "be patient, exercise self-restraint, show our so-called superiors that the criticism of women being hysterical is not true; use no violence, offer yourselves to the violence of others." We are going to win. Our women have taken that advice; if we are in prison they will continue to take that advice.

Well, sir, that is all I have to say to you. We are here not because we are law-breakers; we are here in our efforts to become law-makers.

62. Millicent Garrett Fawcett (1912)

At the end of 1905 the general public first became aware of a new element in the suffrage movement. The Women's Social and Political Union had been formed by Mrs. and Miss Pankhurst in 1903, but the "militant movement," with which its name will always be associated, had not attracted any public notice till the end of 1905. Its manifestations and multifarious activities have been set forth in detail by Miss Sylvia Pankhurst in a book, and are also so well known from other sources that it is unnecessary to dwell upon them here. It is enough to say that by adopting novel and startling methods not at the outset associated with physical violence or attempts at violence, they succeeded in drawing a far larger amount of public attention to the claims of women to representation than ever had been given to the subject before. These methods were regarded by many suffragists with strong aversion, while others watched them with sympathy and admiration for the courage and self-sacrifice which these new methods involved. It is notorious that differences of method separate people from one another even more acutely than differences of aim. This has been seen in the history of religion as well as in politics:—"Christians have burnt each other, quite persuaded / That the apostles would have done as they did."

It was a most anxious time for many months when there seemed a danger that the suffrage cause might degenerate into futile quarrelling among suffragists about the respective merits of their different methods, rather than develop into a larger, broader, and more widespread movement. This danger has been happily averted, partly by the good sense of the suffragists of all parties, who held firmly to the sheet anchor of the fact that they were all working for precisely the same thing, the removal of the sex disability in Parliamentary elections, and, therefore, that what united them was more important than that which separated them. The formation of the anti-suffrage societies was also from this point of view most opportune, giving us all an immediate objective. It was obvious to all suffragists that they should turn their artillery on their opponents rather than on each other. Therefore, while recognising fully all the acute differences which must exist between the advocates of revolutionary and constitutional methods, each group went on its own way; and the total result has undoubtedly been an extraordinary growth in the vigour and force of the suffrage movement all over the country. The most satisfactory feature of the situation was that however acute were the differences between the heads of the different societies, the general mass of suffragists throughout the country were loyal to the cause by whomsoever it was represented, just as Italian patriots in the great days of the *Risorgimento* supported the unity of Italy, whether promoted by Cavour, Garibaldi, or Mazzini.

The National Union of Women's Suffrage Societies endeavoured to steer an even keel. They never weakened in their conviction that constitutional agitation was not only right in itself, but would prove far more effective in the long run than any display of physical violence, as a means of converting the electorate, the general public, and, consequently, Parliament and the Government, to a belief in women's suffrage. But the difficulties for a long time were very great. A few of our own members attacked us because we were not militant; others resigned because they disapproved of the militantism which we had repudiated. On one such occasion a high dignitary of the Church of England, who is also a distinguished historian, wrote to resign his position as vice-president of one of our societies because he highly disapproved of the recent action of the members of militant societies. The honorary secretary replied, asking him if he was also relinquishing his connection with Christianity, as she gathered from his writings that he strongly disapproved of what some Christians had done in the supposed interests of Christianity. It is to the credit of both that the threatened resignation was withdrawn. We tried to comfort and help the weak-hearted by reminding them, in the words of Viscount Morley, that "No reformer is fit for his task if he suffers himself to be frightened by the excesses of an extreme wing."

Personally it was to myself the most difficult time of my forty years of suffrage work. I was helped a good deal by recalling a saying of my husband's about the Irish situation in the 'eighties, when he was heard saying to himself, "Just keep on and do what is right." I am far from claiming that we actually accomplished the difficult feat of doing what was right, but I believe we tried to. The tensity of the situation was somewhat relieved by the brutal severity with which some of the militant suffragists were treated. It gave suffragists of all parties another subject on which they were in agreement.

Minor breaches of the law, such as waving flags and making speeches in the lobbies of the Houses of Parliament, were treated more severely than serious crime on the part of men has often been. A sentence of three months' imprisonment as an ordinary offender was passed in one case against a young girl who had done nothing except to decline to be bound over to keep the peace which she was prepared to swear she had not broken. The turning of the hose upon a suffrage prisoner in her cell in a midwinter night, and all the anguish of the hunger strike and forcible feeding are other examples. All through 1908 and 1909 every possible blunder was committed with regard to the suffrage prisoners. A dead set was made upon law-breakers, real or supposed, who were obscure and unknown; while people with well-known names and of good social position were treated with leniency, and in some cases were allowed to do almost anything without arrest or punishment.

The militant societies split into two in 1907, when the Freedom League was formed under the Presidency of Mrs. Despard. Shortly after this both the militant groups abandoned the plan upon which for the first few years they had worked—that of suffering violence, but using none. Stone-throwing of a not very formidable kind was indulged in, and personal attacks upon Ministers of the Crown were attempted. These new developments necessitated, in the opinion of the National Union of Women's Suffrage Societies, the publication of protests expressing their grave and strong objection to the use of personal violence as a means of political propaganda. These protests were published in November 1908 and October 1909. The second, and shortest, was as follows:—"That the Council of the National Union of Women's Suffrage Societies strongly condemns the use of violence in political propaganda, and being convinced that the true way of advocating the cause of Women's Suffrage is by energetic, law-abiding propaganda, reaffirms its adherence to constitutional principles, and instructs the Executive Committee and the Societies to communicate this resolution to the Press." To this was added:—"That while condemning methods of violence the Council of the N.U.W.S.S. also protests most earnestly against the manner in which the whole Suffrage agitation has been handled by the responsible Government."

The National Union has not thought it necessary publicly to protest against every individual act of violence. Having definitely and in a full Council, where all the societies in the Union are represented in proportion to their membership, put upon record that they "strongly condemn the use of violence in political propaganda," it appears unnecessary to asseverate that they condemn individual acts of violence. There is a remarkable passage in one of Cromwell's letters explaining why that which is gained by force is of little value in comparison with that which is conceded to the claims of justice and reason. "Things obtained by force," he wrote, "though never so good in themselves, would be both less to their honour and less likely to last than concessions made to argument and reason." "What we gain in a free way is better than twice as much in a forced, and will be more truly ours and our posterity's." The practical example of male revolutionists is often cited to the contrary; but with all due respect to the other sex, is not their example too often an example of how not to do it? The Russian revolution [of 1905], for instance, seems to have thrown the political development of Russia into a vicious circle: "we murder you because you and your like have murdered us," and thus it goes on in an endless vista like one mirror reflecting another. I admit fully that the kind and degree of violence carried out by the so-called "suffragettes" is of the mildest description; a few panes of glass have been broken, and meetings have been disturbed, but no one has suffered in life or limb; our great movement towards freedom has not been stained by serious crime. Compared with the Irish Nationalist movement in the 'eighties, or the recent unrest in India, the so-called "violence" of the suffragettes is absolutely negligible in degree, except as an indication of their frame of mind.

Far more violence has been suffered by the suffragettes than they have caused their opponents to suffer. The violence of the stewards at Liberal meetings in throwing out either men or women who dared to ask questions about women's suffrage has been most discreditable. . . .

Mark Twain once wrote of the women suffragists in his own country, "For forty years they have swept an imposingly large number of unfair laws from the statute books of America. In this brief time these serfs have set themselves free—essentially. *Men could not have done as much for themselves in that time without bloodshed*, at least they never have, and that is an argument that they didn't know how."

Perhaps the mild degree of violence perpetrated by the suffragettes was intended to lower our sex pride; we were going to show the world how to gain reforms without violence, without killing people and blowing up buildings, and doing the other silly things that men have done when they wanted the laws altered. Lord Acton once wrote: "It seems to be a law of political evolution that no great advance in human freedom can be gained except after the display of some kind of violence." We wanted to show that we could make the grand advance in human freedom, at which we aimed without the display of any kind of violence. We have been disappointed in that ambition, but we may still lay the flattering unction to our souls that the violence offered has not been formidable, and that the fiercest of the suffragettes have been far more ready to suffer pain than to inflict it. What those endured who underwent the hunger strike and the anguish of forcible feeding can hardly be overestimated. Their courage made a very deep impression on the public and touched the imagination of the whole country.

Of course a very different measure is applied to men and women in these matters. Women are expected to be able to bear every kind of injustice without even "a choleric word"; if men riot when they do not get what they want they are leniently judged, and excesses of which they may be guilty are excused in the House of Commons, in the press, and on the bench on the plea of political excitement. Compare the line of the press on the strike riots in Wales and elsewhere with the tone of the same papers on the comparatively infinitesimal degree of violence shown by the militant suffragists. No one has been more severe in his condemnation of militantism than Mr. Churchill, but speaking in the House of Commons in August 8, 1911, about the violent riots in connection with Parliamentary Reform in 1832, he is reported to have said: "It is true there was rioting in 1832, *but the people had no votes then, and had very little choice as to the alternatives they should adopt.*" If this is a good argument, why not extend its application to the militant suffragists?

63. Helene Lange (1913)

Once again the German newspapers are full of the suffragettes. . . .

[The] question whether their "militant" tactics are tenable must be considered.

We must admit at the outset that the suffragettes' methods cannot be judged by German conceptions of public life, and especially not by German standards for the political temperament of women. Two facts must be considered at the outset. Macaulay once said that the basis of English liberty and the pride of Britons is "immediate self-help for every superimposed wrong." This consciousness of a "right to revolution" is in their blood, its practice is a random test for the passion and vehemence with which a wrong is felt. This is, no doubt, the attitude upon which Winston Churchill based his frivolous comment about women not being serious because they were unable even to foment a proper revolution; the suffragettes answered him with their actions. Moreover, political demonstrations by women have a long history in England. As early as the seventeenth century women demonstrated against Archbishop Laud, and a contemporary couplet describes their excursion into Parliament: "The Oysterwomen lock'd their fish up / and trudg'd away to cry: no bishop!"

But even when we force ourselves to see the tactics of the suffragettes in the spirit of English custom in public life, one thing still counts against them: their *failure*. For we can hardly doubt any longer that militant methods have spoiled the mood for woman's suffrage instead of enhancing it. . . .

This leads to a further question: what is the reason for using "militant" methods? Are they merely demonstrations of mood—that is, of indignation, or are they means of agitation and of pressure? Is it a means of expressing desperation about not having and not being given the vote, or is it a way of making people inclined to award the suffrage to women? Perhaps the chief political mistake of the suffragettes lies in their confusion of these two ideas, or in their expectation of achieving both by the same means. Or do they believe that there simply was no other means of effective agitation and that therefore from every point of view only the one remained?

The question is whether conditions in England were truly such as to justify this understanding of the matter and hence the extreme use of force. In England itself opinion on this topic is divided. Who will say whether the friends of women's suffrage in Parliament are really betraying women, whether all seemingly hopeful prospects are in truth only illusory? If so, the behavior of the suffragettes would signify an outburst of desperation and disappointment. Those whose rights are betrayed move outside the law, refuse to acknowledge social order, ignore the protection of property and public safety, allow themselves to be imprisoned and mistreated and thereby provide evidence of their indomitable spirit and their bitterness. However, such a demonstration demands some sort of solution. Either the extreme *must* be followed by even greater extreme— that is, a bloodletting, or the matter will end with that single protest. Workers have a short, demonstrative strike, the aim of which is just such a declaration of political conviction.

However, the suffragettes pursue yet another aim by their methods. They want to bring the country to desperation by their disturbances; they want to rob the ministers of every moment of pleasure; and in this manner they hope to force admission to suffrage purely as a means of eliminating an altogether intolerable situation. Thus would suffrage be tossed at their feet in rage by those from whom they have forced it. Is this a proper way to win a political right? We instinctively reply—a thousand times *no!* . . .

One could consider it a particular merit of the suffragettes that they have heroically rejected the aesthetics of behavior in the interest of their great aim. The question of "dignity" is, however, not merely a question of aesthetics, but also one of morals and, in a conspicuous sense, of politics. It demands that we should not place ourselves in situations in which we are not comfortable and where we are therefore not the masters of our conduct. It is a *political* mistake to make oneself ridiculous—and the greatest mistake of all from a political point of view is to exhibit powerlessness in an act intended as a test of strength. English women have found such *good* forms of propaganda for their interests in their massive demonstration marches and in their huge public meetings. These forms are good because they express the meaning of the problem as well as the energy of women's collective will. From this point of view the guerilla tactics of the suffragettes can also be misunderstood. They easily give the impression that a minority must compensate through noise and violence for the majority's lack of energy. Large numbers of women will not be attracted by these methods; even less will those classes of women be attracted who are effective in winning the suffrage through the weight of their respectability and their achievements. These women are mostly connected with the non-militant suffrage movement and reject participation in the desperado politics of the suffragettes. Moreover, by these noisy means, attention is diverted from the more important and positive, but less noisy, manifestations. The fact that here in a foreign country the press is interested only in the suffragettes is surely also a symptom of what is happening in England.

64. Carrie Chapman Catt (1913)

When movements are new and weak, Parliaments laugh at them; when they are in their educational stages, Parliaments meet them with silent contempt; when they are ripe and ready to become law, Parliaments evade responsibility. Our movement has reached the last stage. The history of the past two years has demonstrated that fact beyond a shadow of a doubt. Parliaments have stopped laughing at woman suffrage, and politicians have begun to dodge! It is the inevitable premonition of coming victory.

PART II

Women and the Politics of the Family, 1914-1950

T HROUGHOUT the first half of the twentieth century the controversy over woman's relationship to the family and her rights as an individual was embedded in preoccupations with war, revolution, economic depression, and population. The cumulative consequences of two world wars, the Russian Revolution, the worldwide depression of the 1930's, and fascist dictatorships permeated every discussion, whether of women's right to work, women's social role, or women's nature. Both war and revolution present societies with concrete emergencies—situations where taboos on gender can be lifted, sanctions violated, and rules temporarily suspended, as indeed they repeatedly were. During the 1914-18 war, for the first time in history, the governments of both the Allied and Central powers mobilized an enormous pool of female labor to keep vital war production going; these women workers were promptly dismissed at war's end. A similar sequence of events occurred during the Second World War. As for revolution, the initial hopes that in Soviet Russia women's position in the family would be substantially altered were soon disappointed by the family law of 1918 that sustained parental retention of financial responsibility for children. Indeed, it appears that, after war or revolution, traditional sanctions and taboos concerning gender could be all too quickly reimposed in even more rigid forms than before, in the name of social stability.

The years from 1918 to 1950 witnessed the revival in yet another guise of the centuries-old debate over women's nature, this time from the standpoints of labor economics and psychology, the newest of the behavioral sciences. The financial and psychological difficulties following the Treaty of Versailles helped to place women on a continuous economic seesaw; resolution of claims to women's right to employment became increasingly dependent not only upon national conditions but also on international crises beyond their control. It appears also as though the backlash against the gains women had achieved was exacerbated by the evident contrast between the maimed and decimated male populations on the one hand and the comparatively flourishing female populations on the other.[1] Particularly in the fascist states, official policy was directed to reducing women's autonomy and to prescribing a quasi-official definition of gender roles, based on the subordination of women, that reemphasized their reproductive role. Meanwhile, the postwar climate of uncertainty stimulated the behavioral scientists' interest in the old question of woman's nature. The discussion was elaborated with sophistication in the developing field of psychoanalytical theory, where Freud had established sexuality as central to all psychological development. This, in turn, had an impact on the arts and on the exploration of the psychosexual dimension of female identity in literature.

Competition between nations and empires had propelled the Western powers into the awesome and tragic Great War of 1914-18. National fears of loss of industrial and military strength, which often manifested themselves in the alarm over "race suicide" (discussed in Part I), appeared to have played a significant part in precipitating the conflict.[2] Once war was declared in 1914, governments of combatant nations all called on women to support the war, which everyone believed would be short and swiftly concluded. Most leaders of the women's rights movements rallied to the cause (Docs. 65-67). As the months dragged on, however, each nation entered a state of total war; thereafter, governments appealed to women to contribute actively to the war effort wherever needed, as was appropriate to their social class (Docs. 73-76), and with the understanding that the wartime utilization of female labor was a temporary measure. The assumption by those in power was that women would, and must, return to domestic roles as soon as the war ended, so that male veterans reentering civilian life would be reinstated in their proper positions in the labor force.[3]

Yet wartime propaganda applauded women's contribution and efficiency, seconded by what soon became a superficial and highly romanticized treatment of the woman question by the press of all nations. This propaganda succeeded to such an extent that some historians have been misled into ascribing far-reaching changes in women's formal position and status to the immediate influence of the war.[4] Similarly, the high visi-

[1] Casualty figures for the First World War have been placed at ten million men dead and twenty million wounded. See *An Encyclopedia of World History*, ed. William L. Langer (Boston, 1952), p. 951.
[2] Standard histories of the war and the prewar period, e.g., Oron J. Hale, *The Great Illusion* (New York, 1970), do not raise this aspect of the population issue. Even more recent syntheses, e.g., Robert Paxton, *Europe in the Twentieth Century* (New York, 1975) and H. S. Hughes, *Contemporary Europe: A History*, 4th ed. (Englewood Cliffs, N.J., 1976) do not discuss the concern over population on the governmental level as we are doing here. The argument we make is based on a return to the published sources. It is intended to provoke further examination of generalizations about the origins of the war from the perspective of women's history. See Offen 1973a, 1981.
[3] On women and the war effort in France, see Hause & Kenney 1979 and McMillan 1981. For England, see Braybon 1981 and H. Smith 1978.
[4] See, for example, Gollancz 1917 and Marwick 1977. For a critique of this position, see McMillan 1981.

bility given to militant British suffragettes by the international press of the period once led scholars to view the militants as the single most important political force responsible for obtaining women's suffrage at war's end.[5] No doubt, the militant suffrage campaign on the eve of the war and the war itself accelerated the pace of women's entry into public life; no doubt, the drama of militancy and of women's war effort also heightened public awareness of their contribution to the economic and political life of their countries. As we have seen, however, both here and in Volume I, women's extensive participation in the labor force and their quest for active participation in the governments of the democratizing nation-states long predated the outbreak of war in 1914. Indeed, as Carrie Chapman Catt had put it so aptly that very year, "Parliaments have stopped laughing at woman suffrage, and politicians have begun to dodge!"

In England, the groundwork for woman suffrage had been so firmly established by 1914 that the first British Electoral Reform Bill giving women the vote at the age of thirty passed the House of Commons in April 1917—in the midst of the hostilities. Across the Channel in France, by contrast, the war did not erode the deep-seated cultural prejudice against women in politics. Even though the Chamber of Deputies passed four woman suffrage bills between 1918 and 1936, the Senate refused to ratify them. Thus, French women, who had been the first to demand formal political rights during the Revolution of 1789, had to wait until 1945—after the Second World War—to be admitted to the polls. In 1918, however, German women in the new Weimar Republic reaped the rewards of socialist women's earlier commitment to achieving unrestricted suffrage. They were empowered to vote and to sit in the new parliament (the Reichstag) of the German republic. Owing to the Weimar constitution's policy of proportional representation, they achieved representation in far greater numbers than was possible for women in older democracies such as Britain and the United States, where generations of women had been visibly active in pursuing political rights. As in the case of Finland earlier (Doc. 57), granting the vote to women had accompanied a major national political change. In the wake of this development, the intense political activity of German socialist women (under the continuing leadership of Clara Zetkin) forced hesitant bourgeois-liberal German women to become politically active in their turn in order to prevent a socialist landslide at the polls (Doc. 79).[6]

Journalistic attention to suffragette militancy in the prewar period had yet another unfortunate effect—the vote had come to be seen as both the substance and the symbol of women's demands for equality. When, at the

[5] See Dangerfield 1931; and D. Mitchell 1966, 1967. This view has since been contested by Morgan 1974; Pugh 1974; and Liddington & Norris 1978.

[6] For a general assessment on granting of suffrage in European nations, see R. Evans 1977. For England, see Fulford 1956; Rover 1967; Rosen 1974; and Hume 1979. For France, see Hause 1977 and Hause & Kenney 1981. For Germany, see Puckett 1930; Koonz 1976; R. Evans 1976 (ch. 8); Bridenthal 1979; and Greven-Aschoff 1981 (pt. D). For an analysis of the postsuffrage status of women's rights in the United States, see Chafe 1972 and Freedman 1974. For England, see Lewis 1973, 1980a.

end of the war, women were enfranchised in most Western countries and in the new communist Soviet Union, some observers assumed that all goals of women reformers had been met. The vote alone, however, could not and did not resolve the woman question. This fact was emphasized in the 1920's both by revolutionaries such as Aleksandra Kollontai in Russia and by reformers such as Alva Myrdal in Sweden and, in Britain, Eleanor Rathbone (Docs. 89, 91) and the "Six Points Group" (Doc. 87), which included Winifred Holtby (Docs. 104, 108). Rathbone conceived the phrase *the new feminism* and insisted that women should become politically and economically conscious of their needs as mothers and wives within the family, not solely as professionals and workers in the public sphere (Doc. 91). The proposals developed by women's rights advocates well before the war were thus visibly incorporated in the programs of social democrats throughout the postwar world.

The war itself did not create important changes in the family-bound reality of women's position in postwar Europe. This much is clear despite the granting of suffrage and the incorporation into the Treaty of Versailles and international law of certain equal rights provisions, such as equal pay for equal work and the inclusion of women in the committees set up by the Versailles Peace Conference.[7] Even so, the cataclysmic impact of a war that had totally destroyed the basic stability of older systems of society was to heighten public apprehension of the revolutionary potential of true equality and self-determination for women. In the immediate postwar period there were a number of changes apparent in the outward lives of women. In many countries they had become enfranchised and were nominally exercising their right to vote. They had won the right to higher education; some entered traditional male professions; the fashionable clothing, hair-styles, cigarette smoking, and public behavior of the flapper produced an image of daring liberation and a new, less passive and therefore threatening, sexuality that was highlighted by the press and cinema. Although some of these gains (notably higher education and entry into professions) had been won decades before the war, and the flappers' daring was only superficial, the combination of them all was highly visible during the 1920's and contrasted unfavorably with the psychological depression of the remnant of the men who had survived the trauma and carnage of the battlefields. The fear that women would impinge upon the established patriarchal order and lose their womanliness was evident in literature and in the psychological writings of the twenties. Particularly in France, where populationist concerns were paramount, the war appears only to have solidified resistance to any fundamental change in the way the sexes were perceived or in the relationship between them. Even the British novelist Radclyffe Hall (Doc. 97), writing her lesbian novel, *The Well of Loneliness*, in Paris reflected this conservative emphasis.[8]

[7] Treaty of Versailles: see, in particular, the Preamble, and Articles 389 and 427.
[8] For France, see Sohn 1972; McMillan 1981; and Offen 1982. On Hall, see Zimmerman 1981.

In effect, the war did add a new and highly politicized dimension to the debate over women. In wartime many women's rights activists set aside their own goals in order to serve the overriding interests of national survival being fought for by their husbands, lovers, brothers, and sons. In so doing, however, these women—and many of their less activist sisters as well—became ever more deeply aware of their impotence and, in particular, of the ways in which patriarchal mores and traditions circumscribed them. This in turn may have introduced a recognition, by women who were politically aware, of their own inability to influence decisions concerning war or peace; this recognition increased throughout the thirties and forties. Winifred Holtby and Virginia Woolf both expressed this despair during the 1930's as they confronted fascism and the prospect of yet another war (Docs. 108, 109); in the late 1940's Simone de Beauvoir and Margaret Mead (Docs. 119, 120) both wrote under the shadow of the atomic bomb exploded at Hiroshima, and were keenly aware of the capacity for total societal destruction developed by a male-dominated Western civilization. These four women nevertheless insisted that women must become deeply involved in political as well as social causes, in order to confront and reverse the direction in which public policy directed by men seemed to be leading the West.

Nor is it surprising that politically aware women should have despaired when confronted with the totality of twentieth-century war. Ever since the Hundred Years' War in the fifteenth century, when Christine de Pizan wrote *Le Livre de la paix* (1413; The Book of Peace), women thinkers, concerned with the subordination of women and aware of the close connection between recurrent militarism and the deployment by men of women solely as breeders and servants, have argued eloquently against military might and force. Bertha von Suttner (Doc. 12) wrote her path-breaking and internationally best-selling novel *Die Waffen Nieder* (Lay Down Your Arms) after witnessing the horrors of the battlefields during the Austro-Prussian war of 1866; she then began a pacifist crusade that brought her international renown and a Nobel Peace Prize. While many women openly supported the war effort in the 1914-18 period in the national interest, many more—as Helena Swanwick (Doc. 70) pointed out—silently deplored the war but felt restrained from speaking out while the men they cared about were fighting for their lives in the trenches.[9]

A small but vocal minority of women was nevertheless in the vanguard of international pacifist activity throughout the war itself (Docs. 69-72). Some of the bourgeois members of the International Women's Suffrage Alliance converted this group into an international women's league for peace in 1915. Led by the American reformer, Jane Addams, and drawing heavily on the program of the British Union for Democratic Control, with which Swanwick was closely associated, the league's goal was to ter-

[9]McMillan 1981 makes this point for France. See also *Women's Poetry and Verse of the First World War*, collected by Catherine Reilly (London, 1981).

minate the war by "continuous mediation" (the concept of Julia Grace Wales) rather than by force. While women pacifists could be found in all major political parties, the most highly visible were clearly the women affiliated with splinter groups of the Left. The "Red Countess" (Lady Warwick) and Helena Swanwick (Doc. 70) in Britain, Hélène Brion (Doc. 71) in France, and Clara Zetkin (Doc. 15), Luise Zietz (Doc. 80), and Rosa Luxemburg in Germany, continued to sustain a belief in the tradition of an international unity of workers, women and men alike, that necessarily opposed war. These independents were at odds with majority socialists who supported the war effort.[10]

Internationalism continued after the war as a driving and sustaining force, not only with respect to pacifism but also with respect to efforts to improve women's formal status. Not only had women activists opposed the war; they were also active in drafting the terms of the peace, and they had cultivated the support of the American president Woodrow Wilson to make sure that their concerns were not ignored during the treaty negotiations. It was no accident that the Treaty of Versailles, which had established the League of Nations, included articles that mandated equal pay for equal work and the promotion of women both in the government labor inspectorate and among technical experts of the new International Labour Office (ILO). A remnant of the same international organization of women that had turned from suffrage to pacifism in 1915 remained, after 1918, as a lobbying organization for women's concerns, with an office in Geneva, the headquarters for the new League of Nations. From this base, international women's organizations, such as the International Council of Women and the Women's International League for Peace and Freedom, monitored the ILO and the activities of the League itself, to ensure that women's interests were recognized, publicized, and thereby protected (Docs. 110, 111).[11]

Totalitarian extremism in the inter-war period—whether Nazi fascism under Hitler in Germany (1933-1945) or Soviet communism under Stalin in the USSR (1936-1956)—clearly revealed the efforts expended to reinforce and restructure patriarchal control over women. Leaders of these militaristic empires repeatedly restated and insisted upon the ideological primacy of women's function as breeders and as nurturers of the family on behalf of the patriarchal nation-state. They did so even when the urgent need for women's services in productive labor brought women into the labor force of the fascist and communist states in large numbers and, sometimes, into ostensible leadership positions. Hitler offered a *Mutterkreuz* (mothers' medal) and Stalin a "glory of motherhood" award. The initiatives of both leaders reflect precedents set by the Roman Em-

---

[10] For various perspectives on women and pacificism and on women pacifists, see Addams 1916; Degen 1939; Herman 1969 (ch. 5); Conway 1971; Sowerwine 1979; and S. Bell 1982, 1983.

[11] On the activities of these groups, see Hurwitz 1977 and Whittick 1979.

peror Augustus or, more recently, by the postwar leaders of the French Third Republic in the early 1920's (Doc. 84).[12]

Twentieth-century fascism had emerged in the early 1920's in Italy with the rise of Mussolini (Doc. 103); it also triumphed in Spain with General Franco's victory in the Civil War of 1935-37, in Portugal with Salazar, and in various countries in Eastern Europe.[13] Yet it is the German case that offers especially clear insight into the fascist mentality regarding women's position. German fascism developed within the young and fragile democratic Weimar Republic, where women were suddenly visible in political life and Jewish women were conspicuous in prestigious professions.[14] Since women were voters as well as members of the Weimar republican assembly, the Nazi leadership, from Adolf Hitler to Gertrud Scholtz-Klink (Docs. 105, 106), addressed the problems of women's family responsibilities with empathetic efficiency. In the process they also effectively coopted many of the proposals for state intervention that had been put forward on women's behalf by radicals in the prewar German women's movement.

The success of Hitler's German National Socialist Worker's (NSDAP or Nazi) party illustrates the fascist potential that lurks below the surface of every mass society. In the decade following the devastating upheaval of the Great War, European nations experienced disillusionment with the consequences of peace and of democracy. They also suffered from economic dislocation—widespread unemployment, financial boom followed by bust, and hunger. All this discontent might have been mobilized in support of revolution. The victors—Great Britain and France both insisting on huge reparation payments from defeated Germany, and the United States on the repayment of its loans to its European allies—were somewhat less painfully affected, at least during the 1920's. But the losers, particularly Germany, whose new regime had to walk an economic tightrope, soon reached a point of psychological debility that spawned support for the counter-revolutionary "new order" of national socialism, racism, and aggressive masculinity promised by Hitler. By the end of the

[12] On the French precedents, see Offen 1981. For Germany, see the collective work of the Frauengruppe Faschismusforschung 1981. For the Stalinist shift in Soviet policy encouraging motherhood, see Lapidus 1978.

[13] For comparative treatment of fascism and other radical right-wing groups, see Hans Rogger and Eugen Weber, eds., *The European Right* (Berkeley and Los Angeles, Calif., 1965); Ernst Nolte, *Three Faces of Fascism* (London, 1965); A. James Gregor, *The Ideology of Fascism* (New York, 1969); Henry A. Turner, Jr., *Reappraisals of Fascism* (New York, 1975); Walter Laqueur, *Fascism: A Reader's Guide* (Berkeley and Los Angeles, Calif., 1976); and S. J. Woolf, ed., *Fascism in Europe* (London and New York, 1968). Few discussions of fascism consider the woman question. Among notable exceptions are Virginia Woolf, *Three Guineas* (London, 1938); Peter Nathan, *Psychology of Fascism* (London, 1943); and recent works on French fascism by Robert Soucy, including his *Fascist Intellectual: Drieu la Rochelle* (Berkeley and Los Angeles, Calif., 1979). For Italy, see also Grand 1976 and Pieroni-Bortolotti 1978. For Germany, see also Schoenbaum 1967; Millet 1969; Stephenson 1975; Koonz 1977; and Rupp 1977.

[14] See especially Rupp 1977 and Kaplan 1981.

decade, all Western nations, victors and losers alike, were painfully stricken by what appeared to some to be the death-agony of the capitalist order itself—the interrelated transatlantic financial and trade involvements, the Wall Street crash of 1929, and the failure of European banks. Industrial and primary production slowed down appreciably, and the opportunities for paid employment, for men as well as women, were drastically reduced. The Great Depression of the 1930's had begun.[15]

Hitler's national socialism appealed particularly to members of the German and Austrian lower-middle classes, those most vulnerable to and most fearful of sinking to the level of the proletariat. Already during the 1920's the NSDAP had expressed the frustrations experienced by millions of defeated and unemployed German men. The strong-arm paramilitary suppression of rival socialist parties that later characterized Hitler's dictatorship gained for National Socialists an increasing political following in the late 1920's. These elements of Nazi success are well known.

Less well known are the techniques and appeals that the Nazis, once in power, used to attract support from women. The techniques they used to identify, and the measures they used to exploit, the needs and concerns of women are worth examination. They are enlightening in the context not only of the specific success of the Nazis but also of the broader appeal of fascist dictatorships and the mechanics of social revolution in general. First, National Socialist party leaders did address women; they raised women's consciousness in small and large gatherings and made them feel needed, and a part of the communal effort. Nazi leaders stressed the importance of women's unity with men in the new enterprise, but they also insisted on women's own unique potential. Moreover, by promising carefully and efficiently organized day-care facilities for their children (Docs. 105, 106), they attempted to provide the means that might enable working-class and lower middle-class women to improve their economic and social situation. National Socialists, in fact, adopted many of the measures promoted before the war by the radicals of the Bund für Mutterschutz (Docs. 33, 34), and applied them in their own perverse way. These measures included legal abortion (acceptable only in cases of what the Nazis considered "unfit" elements), state benefits for unmarried "Aryan" mothers as well as for legally married women, and improved state maternity benefits in the all-important drive to increase the birthrate. The Nazis appropriated some of the most radical proposals from the prewar bourgeois women's movement, as well as from the German socialist and communist parties. Combining these proposals with a generalized anti-intellectualism and a highly specific racism, they presented and carried them out as their own program.[16]

Reaction to the dangers of fascism, which threatened to destroy the gains made by partisans of republican liberalism and political democracy

[15] See Maier 1975.
[16] On the prewar precedents, see Hackett 1981.

since the revolutions of the eighteenth century, came swiftly. Protests were forthcoming from critics at both the journalistic and the philosophical level, and most vociferously from the socialist and communist Left. Here again, ideals of liberal and socialist internationalism came to the fore—and women who adhered to the liberal aspirations of social democracy were understandably fearful that women's drive for independence and equality would be eclipsed in any victory of a militaristic and race-conscious dictatorial nationalism (Docs. 102, 103, 107-109). Virginia Woolf's much-misunderstood contribution to this debate in her polemic *Three Guineas* (Doc. 109) was especially perceptive. She recognized that the roots of fascism lay in patriarchy and must be eradicated in the family; no patriarchal society—however liberal—was immune, she argued, from fascist tendencies.[17]

Virginia Woolf's analysis of patriarchal interference with the process of women's emancipation in liberal Western democracies was all too well corroborated by experiences in the Soviet Union, where some radical women had hoped to establish a truly egalitarian, nonsexist society. Only a tiny minority of the Russian revolutionaries, here represented by the writings of Aleksandra Kollontai (Docs. 77, 83), genuinely understood and believed that family structure and attitudes needed to be changed in order for women's complete emancipation to occur. However, the effectiveness of oft-advocated organizational panaceas for women—communal kitchens, nurseries, legalized abortion—as well as of those concerning equalization of education and women's entry into professional and political life, was greatly diminished in the absence of a parallel radical transformation in the psychological and structural underpinnings of social relationships between men and women.[18]

A recent analysis has shown that primary-school readers used since the 1920's in Soviet schools invariably depicted men and boys as active all-round producers and in political and military leadership roles; women and girls by contrast were portrayed as followers or as nurturing mothers. This is a measure of the degree to which (despite the West's fears) the rulers of the new socialist Soviet state were opposed to effecting a thorough-going revolution within the family, even as they attempted to transform the political and economic superstructure.[19] Without transformation of the patriarchal family, revolution of a political system and of its economic class-base was not sufficient to build a truly new, nonexploitative society. It is therefore not wholly surprising to find that in the 1940's, at the end of the Second World War, Stalin's embattled regime offered "glory of motherhood" medals to "heroine mothers" of large families, even as it recognized women's heroic efforts both as combatants in the Russian army and as workers in the economic sector while men were being slaughtered in the millions.[20] Nor is it surprising that at this

---

[17] See Showalter 1977; Carroll 1978; Rose 1978; and Marcus 1981, 1982.
[18] Lapidus 1978; Stites 1978; Rosenhan 1981 (ch. 2); and Sargent 1981.
[19] Rosenhan 1977, 1981.
[20] U.S. Army Center of Military History 1978, pp. 19-62.

time of military and demographic crisis the Soviet regime should have re-segregated boys and girls in Moscow schools in order to train them re-spectively for military and domestic careers (Doc. 115). The manpower needs of the nation took precedence over the Soviet socialist program for emancipating Russian women.

The failure of the Soviet state to achieve any fundamental restructuring of the patriarchal Russian family is thrown into relief by the partially successful—if less widely recognized—inter-war achievements of women reformers in the noncommunist democracies. In Britain Eleanor Rath-bone (Docs. 89, 91), and in Sweden Alva Myrdal (Docs. 112, 117), both bolstered by their university educations and their elected political posi-tions, achieved legal changes in family relationships by instituting state subsidies, payable directly to mothers rather than to the male heads of household. Alva Myrdal, albeit in the interest of population growth, was able to modify the Swedish 1937 population policy to allow married women to be employed and to legalize birth control and sex education. Swedish, like American, women's advocates focused their attention on ways to aid economically underprivileged mothers. In England, however, Eleanor Rathbone's aim in her "family allowance" scheme was more comprehensive. She sought for women of all classes a measure of eco-nomic—and therefore psychological—autonomy within the family.[21]

In the same vein, advocacy of contraception, which had emerged as a full scale social reform movement after the First World War, became a highly charged political issue in the inter-war period. Women like the American Margaret Sanger (Doc. 81) and her British counterpart, Marie Stopes, argued for the lifting of restrictions on birth control information; they couched their case in terms of producing healthier children as well as healthier, more responsible, and more loving mothers. But their argu-ments were persistently—and perhaps willfully—misinterpreted as ef-forts to promote female promiscuity, beyond male control and at the ulti-mate expense of the nation. Unfortunately, these birth control reformers' chances at success were impeded by public reaction to Soviet Russia's re-cent legalization of abortion on demand (Doc. 82), which was being uni-versally condemned as the epitome of Bolshevik godlessness and anarchy in a world shocked and frightened not only by the excesses of the Russian Revolution, but by the major powers' awesome losses of men on the bat-tlefields. Although none of the birth control advocates in the West dared to suggest so radical a measure as legalized abortion on demand, they still encountered heavy opposition from many quarters. In France (Docs. 84, 85, 88), where the war had intensified anxiety over a declining birth-rate, both Catholic and secular spokesmen mounted campaigns against birth control. American states with large Catholic populations secured state laws against dissemination of birth control information. In Italy, Pope Pius XI himself (Doc. 86) spoke out against the freedom that

---

[21] For Sweden, see Hatje 1974 and Carlson 1974, 1980. For Britain, see Stocks 1950 and Lewis 1980a, 1980b.

women would acquire through control over their own fertility, which he perceived not only as a theological issue but also as a dangerous threat to the patriarchy and the family.[22]

Upholders of the status quo who viewed contraception as a violation of woman's nature soon found new arguments to buttress their opinion. Their support came from new developments in psychology and from the field of psychoanalysis. We have seen in Volume I how successive new social scientific developments throughout the nineteenth century, such as Bachofen's anthropology, Darwin's evolutionary biology, and Spencer's socio-economics, all firmly reiterated and reemphasized an ever-starker male/female dichotomy, with the positive emphasis on the male pole. Thus it should hardly be surprising that the new scientific psychology of the unconscious did likewise. Its proponents emphasized the uniqueness of the individual and the historical importance of formative familial relationships in shaping that individual's personality and sexual orientation. Insofar as these ideas grew from the methodical enquiries of the Viennese physician, Sigmund Freud, psychoanalysis developed as a masculine science par excellence. Analysis of both male and female sexuality from a male perspective permitted its creator to state flatly in 1933 that "the purpose of shame in women is the concealment of genital deficiency" (Doc. 94) and that every human being, born with androgynous propensities, resolves this ambivalence by developing a male or female orientation by means of his or her own resolution of the Oedipus complex. Freud's close disciple Carl Gustav Jung developed a break-away theory that, even in its disagreement with Freud, further reinforced the dichotomy between male and female (Doc. 98). It was left to a woman psychoanalyst, Karen Horney (Doc. 93), to argue that, among men, childbearing and womb-envy might play just as important a role in shaping manliness as penis-envy in the Freudian theory of womanliness.[23]

As the controversies within psychoanalysis effectively opened up discussion of sexuality even to women practitioners, literary pioneers on the topics of sexuality and gender began to address the subject in purely male terms. Thus we find that prophet of sex, D. H. Lawrence, glorifying the phallus (Doc. 95); and, almost simultaneously, the tortured lesbian novelist Radclyffe Hall (Doc. 96) was clothing in fictional form the immature theories of male sexologists who viewed female homosexuality as the unnatural result of an exaggerated case of penis-envy. Though Hall's novel remained an illegal publication in her native Britain, it was extensively reprinted in the United States and on the Continent, and left a literary legacy of a model manly/womanly lesbian "couple" that persisted for the next five decades.[24]

[22] See Talmy 1962; Kennedy 1970; Guerrand 1971; Gordon 1976; Hall 1977; and Duden 1981.

[23] For Freud's terminology and translation problems, see Bettelheim 1982 and editors' note (Doc. 92). On psychoanalysis, see particularly J. Miller 1973; Lasch 1974; J. Mitchell 1974; Strouse 1974; Garrison 1981; and Van Herik 1982.

[24] Cook 1979; Fassler 1979; Faderman 1981; Schwarz 1981; Smith-Rosenberg 1981; Vicinus 1981; and Zimmerman 1981.

The politics concerned with women and the family did not diminish after World War II. In the wake of Hiroshima, two world-famous, university-trained women writers, Simone de Beauvoir and Margaret Mead, summed up two conflicting approaches, deeply divisive even now, to the matter of women, the family, and freedom. Each based her theories on an amalgam of her own research and her unique personal experience. On the one side was the philosopher Beauvoir's angry, and now classic, analysis and denunciation of a patriarchal system that patronized women, and in which, philosophically speaking, to be female was to be in a state of perpetual retreat from self-realization. On the other side was anthropologist Mead's insistence on the universality of a sexual division of labor, based on complementarity, in all organized human societies. Mead maintained that this division should not and need not necessarily result in discrimination against women. Beauvoir's and Mead's statements (Docs. 119, 120) epitomize the conflicting perspectives that still persist. Beauvoir's polemical analysis inspired women writers and activists after mid-century to explore in greater depth the European existentialist vision of women as "other," which she had dissected with such passion. Mead's more pragmatic view, based on her study of a wide range of sexual and familial relationships in human societies far beyond Europe, gave other reformers a basis on which to argue for readjustments that would make the relations between the sexes in Western societies more truly equitable, without resorting to revolution.[25]

In the twentieth century the breadth and the depth of the woman question in patriarchal society were fully exposed. Women were finally permitted a stake in the democratic political process, and significant changes occurred in their legal and educational status. But these changes were not enough to resolve the woman question. To some degree, the fear and hostility exhibited in the past by those who argued that woman's place was in the home, and who opposed allowing women either freedom of choice in childbearing or economic independence, was exacerbated by women's entry into political life. One thing has become clear, however: the woman question could not be resolved without addressing the personal, reproductive, and economic relationship between men and women, as manifested institutionally in the family, the patriarchal structure of which has been repeatedly reinforced by church and state alike. Dissenters and activists gradually began to appreciate that only if this relationship could be fundamentally readjusted would women be able to participate on equal terms in the economic, intellectual, and political world. Dissenters also became aware that such a fundamental change would by no means come easily. Yet, the history of the past two hundred years clearly documents women's persistence in claiming their right to self-determination. Proponents of such claims insist that their objectives will only be realized when both women and men are convinced that equality will mean a happier human existence for both sexes.

[25] On Beauvoir, see Eisenberg 1979; Dijkstra 1980; and Felstiner 1980. On Mead, see Rosenberg 1982.

CHAPTER 7

The Great War, 1914-1918

Women and Patriotism

SOURCES

65. Millicent Garrett Fawcett, "To the Members of the National Union," *The Common Cause* (London), 7 August 1914, p. 376. Dated 5 August 1914. The editors wish to thank Leslie Parker Hume, Stanford University, for furnishing this document.

66. Gertrud Bäumer, "Wir Frauen," in *Weit hinter den Schützengräben* (Jena, 1916); reprinted in *Dr. Gertrud Bäumer, Aus ihren Schriften, Aufsätzen, und Reden* (Berlin, 1924), pp. 8-10. Originally published in *Die Frauenbewegung: Revue für die Interessen der Frauen*, 16 (14 August 1914), 96. Tr. SGB.

67. Helene Lange, "Die Dienstpflicht der Frau," in *Kampfzeiten, Aufsätze und Reden aus vier Jahrzenten*, II (Berlin, 1928), 165-67. Originally given as a speech before the Congress of the Union of German Women Teachers, Whitsun 1915. Tr. SGB.

The outbreak of war in Europe on August 4, 1914, brought about a realignment of women's movement leaders in support of their countries' diplomatic commitments at the expense of earlier endeavors to achieve legal emancipation, suffrage, educational, economic, and sexual rights for women. Although notable exceptions existed among strong-minded women in all the combatant nations— women who continued to put peace ahead of patriotism throughout the war years—the great majority of women did follow the example set by the leaders of the women's movements. Such women devoted their emotional, mental, and physical energy to the war effort by encouraging, and sometimes even replacing, their fathers, husbands, brothers, and sons in men's normal peacetime activities. The following selections illustrate the calls to action and support of the war effort by three leaders of the now-enemy British and German women's movements.

In the first selection the president of the British National Union of Women's Suffrage Societies (NUWSS), Millicent Garrett Fawcett (Doc. 62), addressed her membership on the day after the outbreak of war. Fawcett's concern and distress at the failure of diplomatic efforts to avert war is evident in the wording of her call to action. Despite her seeming abandonment of the women's suffrage cause, however, Fawcett continued to lobby male politicians on its behalf throughout the four years of hostilities, even as she continued to urge NUWSS members to support the war effort. She lived to see the achievement of woman suffrage in England, which was granted in 1919.

In comparison to Fawcett the president of the Federation of German Women's Associations (Bund Deutscher Frauenvereine, or BDF), Dr. Gertrud Bäumer (1873-1954), strikes a more emotional and chauvinistic chord of patriotism. Her call to action and her emphasis, in keeping with the German public's belief at the time that war had been forced upon their country, offers a good example of the political astuteness that won her a seat in the Reichstag after the war and gained woman suffrage from the new Weimar Republic, and her subsequent appointment as counsellor for education and youth in the Weimar government's ministry of the interior.

Throughout her life Gertrud Bäumer worked for women's economic independence. Personal circumstances doubtless contributed to this interest, for upon her father's death when Bäumer was ten, her impoverished mother was forced to move, with her three fatherless children, back into her own mother's highly authoritarian household as a dependent. Bäumer subsequently became a distinguished teacher, benefiting from Helene Lange's earlier efforts (Doc. 35) to improve female education and the status of women teachers. However, going beyond Lange (whose devoted follower and friend she became), in 1904 Bäumer became one of the first German women to earn a doctorate in Germanic language and literature and philosophy at the University of Berlin. In 1910 she had been elected president of the BDF, the largest of the bourgeois women's organizations; as a left Liberal she underscored the federation's solidarity against more radical members such as former president Marie Stritt, Helene Stöcker, and Lida Augusta Heyman, who had urged endorsement of such controversial issues as pacifism and the legalization of abortion.

Throughout the war Bäumer, in her capacity as president of the BDF, supported the hotly debated issue of a "service duty" for women, as expounded in the third selection by her friend and colleague Helene Lange (Docs. 35, 63). This 1915 speech is one of many statements, articles, and pamphlets Lange prepared on the subject of women's compulsory war service (e.g., *Frauen Dienstpflicht* and *Weibliches Dienstjahr*). The proposal that training and service duty to the state be compulsory for women as a complement to obligatory male military service had become a major subject of discussion in the German women's movement in 1911. The key argument of the *Dienstpflicht* advocates was that women of all classes should improve their domestic training and housekeeping capabilities so they would be able to deploy their domestic skills not only in the privacy of their own homes, but also in the wider sphere of social welfare, for the general good of the nation-state, and, in the event of war, for military purposes.

---

65. Millicent Garrett Fawcett (1914)

The greatest crisis known in all our national history is upon us. Nearly all Europe is at war, and our country is involved.

I have often made appeals to you to render services involving much hard work and self-sacrifice for the sake of the great cause which binds us all together. I have never asked in vain. I now make another and a different appeal. Let us members of the National Union bind ourselves together for the purpose of rendering the greatest possible aid to our country at this momentous epoch.

As long as there was any hope of peace most members of the National

Union probably sought for peace and endeavoured to support those who were trying to maintain it. But we have another duty now. Now is the time for resolute effort and self-sacrifice on the part of every one of us to help our country; and probably the way in which we can best help it is by devising and carrying through some well thought out plan which can be worked at continuously over many months, to give aid and succour to women and children brought face to face with destitution in consequence of the war.

We have already appealed to our 500 Societies to make suggestions as to how best work of this kind could be done, and we have received many letters from individual members of the N.U. expressing a hope that some plan on these lines will be devised and recommended by the N.U. as a whole.

The Executive Committee will be considering these plans to-morrow, and our Societies will be communicated with as soon as possible.

In the midst of this time of terrible anxiety and grief, it is some little comfort to think that our large organisation which has been carefully built up during past years to promote Women's Suffrage, can be used now to help our country through this period of strain and sorrow. "He that findeth his life shall lose it, and he that loseth his life for My sake shall find it." Let us show ourselves worthy.

66. Gertrud Bäumer (1914)

We women feel the fatefulness of days to come perhaps even more deeply than the men, who are themselves concerned with these actions and decisions. We feel more strongly and more deeply how future decisions will elude human calculation and human efforts during the conflict of such powerful forces. Whatever world-view we profess, we must all have faith in those spiritual properties that will help us to remain strong and calm during these days. . . .

The phrase "we women" has always had a deep and meaningful sound for us. We have felt united in a movement that would raise the value of our sex and give us wider scope for activity in the battle for the freedom of our powers and our aspirations. Today this union indicated by the phrase "we women" has still another meaning. Over and above political parties and world-views our nation is unified at this moment as a nation struggling for its existence. Every one of the young men presently marching through our streets defends neither his party, nor his class, but all of us—the great mass of all people.

We women recognize the greatness and power of this national unity, a unity of those whose special efforts were usually performed under the pressure of personal goals. We are swept up in this great, serious unification of all national endeavor into a great consensus: that is, to defend the power and greatness of our nation in this war that has been forced upon us.

The present moment does not kindle a mood of battle in us. Many thousands have to part from their husbands, their sons, and their brothers; none of us can watch the departure of a host of glowing manly youth without fearing the somber fate that they themselves approach with such firmness. Our feeling cannot go beyond the immeasurable sacrifices that the war will exact, whatever happens.

Therefore we are unified in our determination to do all we can in order to ease these sacrifices. If at this moment we feel a great unity, it is this determination that unifies us. When, during the hurried organization of our efforts, we feel in every word and every action how strong our unity has become—this is because we see clearly that our unity is created by our national duty. All of us are determined to devote our efforts to whatever we can do now. This determination possesses us all.

67. Helene Lange (1915)

The national service of men reaches its ultimate destiny only in times of war, while the national service of women is essentially destined for constant duties throughout times of peace. The efforts of women in war are basically the same as their efforts in peace. These efforts consist of nursing and all sorts of organized welfare work. Thus we see that women need no special preparation for war. Peace offers them duties of service in all areas of social work. Through the introduction of a female service duty with preparation and training, we would gain forces for voluntary social service who would be truly qualified.

Female national service consists of voluntary management of social services, of boards of guardians, of care of the poor, of orphans, of youth services, etc. This civic duty should be delegated to women in the same way as it is delegated to men. Women should only be excused from carrying out these duties for the same reasons that apply also to men. With the exception of women with small children, or domestic conditions that allow them no free time for voluntary activities, this also applies to gainfully employed housewives.

Nursing the wounded is a particular service duty for women in wartime. This should be done as far as possible by professional nurses. However, volunteers must be used as aides in military hospitals. These volunteers must serve as part of their official female service duty.

The educational basis for all forms of female service duty is the capacity to manage a simple household. This must therefore be a prerequisite for further training, or it must form the content of the female service or training period.

Physical training must also be a major part of the female service year, since it has proved to be a considerable advantage in men's training.

Based upon these different prerequisites, it is clear that a different type of education is required for girls who will graduate from elementary schools and those who will graduate from secondary schools. These different types of education are analogous to different types of service duties for men.

(a) Girls who have graduated from elementary schools ought to receive one year of free education between their 17th and 20th years. This year should offer them a thorough grounding in home economics, with heavy emphasis on the national economic responsibilities of housewives: health-care, infant care, and a knowledge of civic affairs. Only with such an ar-rangement would the service year achieve its goals completely.

(b) A general introduction of such a service duty is not feasible for pri-vate and for national economic reasons at this time. However, a begin-ning in this direction could be attempted as follows: (1) a general ex-tension of one-half year of the education of girls, devoted entirely to the practice of household management; (2) introduction of academic in-stitutions modeled on Danish high schools, which offer older girls with an elementary education the opportunity to have a year's free service-education in the format suggested under (a) above; (3) an increase in the establishment of agricultural schools for household management.

Like voluntary soldiers who are doing their year of service, girls who have graduated from secondary schools must pay the costs of their own training. Before entering the service duty they must present proof of the household management training they have received either at home or in a designated institution of household management. Their service training time—between the ages of 17 and 20—will be taken up with training for some social service. This could be a specialized training for infant care, care of the poor, nursing, etc.

By developing the women's schools we can prepare for compulsory in-troduction of the female service duty for this class of women.

Women and Pacifism

SOURCES

68. International Woman Suffrage Alliance, "To His Excellency, the President of the United States," letter signed by Carrie Chapman Catt and Rosika Schwim-mer, IWSA, 7 Adam St., Adelphi, London, 14 September 1914; reprinted in *The Woman Voter*, October 1914, p. 8.

69. "Manifesto Issued by Envoys of the International Congress of Women at The Hague to the Governments of Europe and the President of the United States," in *Women at The Hague. The International Congress of Women and Its Results*, by Jane Addams, Emily G. Balch, and Alice Hamilton (New York, 1915), pp. 160-66.

70. Helena Maria Swanwick, *Women and War*, pamphlet no. 11, published by the Union of Democratic Control (London, 1915), pp. 1-11. Reprinted, with an introduction by Blanche Wiesen Cook, in the Garland Library of War and Peace (New York, 1971).

71. "L'Affaire Hélène Brion au 1ᵉ Conseil de Guerre," *Revue des Causes Célè-bres*, no. 5 (2 May 1918), pp. 152-54. Tr. KMO.

While the majority of women in both the combatant and the neutral nations were swept up in the war effort, either for ideological or economic reasons or simply as victims, an outspoken minority worked insistently for peace throughout the four years of the war. In most European countries the outbreak of the war had called a halt to agitation on behalf of woman suffrage; as we have seen, suffrage leaders urged members to channel all their effort into supporting the nation during the war crisis. To a large degree this call to action had been heeded. From the first days of the war, however, an antimilitarist and internationalist minority of women continued to pursue both individual and organized political efforts on behalf of women's suffrage and world peace. No simple, clear-cut division by political alliance or social class can be established; bourgeois reformers as well as socialist revolutionary women could be pacifists, though perhaps most women were attracted to the cause of social democracy. The following selections offer insights into the reasoning of women who outspokenly refused to be drawn into active support of the war in spite of governmental rhetoric and even coercion.

The first two selections present statements by women active in the international women's organizations. A few weeks after the outbreak of war, on September 18, 1914, the American Carrie Chapman Catt (Docs. 60, 64) and the Hungarian Rosika Schwimmer (1877-1948), acting as president and secretary of the International Woman Suffrage Alliance, presented a petition to the President of the United States, Woodrow Wilson. They asked that he, as the leader of the most important non-aligned nation, head a combined effort by neutral nations to end hostilities in Europe. A year later, in 1915, a group of delegates representing the International Congress of Women, headed by Jane Addams (1860-1935), traveled through Europe meeting with government representatives seeking ways to end the war. The manifesto of the peace delegates, drafted after the completion of their tour, again called on neutral nations for action in an effort to end the war through peaceful negotiation.

The third selection is excerpted from a pamphlet by Helene Maria Sickert Swanwick (1864-1939). Swanwick, the child of a Danish father and an English mother, and the sister of the well-known artist Walter Sickert, attended Girton College in its early years. She subsequently became a journalist, writing for the *Manchester Guardian*, and a tireless worker for women's political and economic emancipation. For many years she worked with Millicent Garrett Fawcett (Docs. 62, 65, 90) and edited the British constitutional woman suffrage publication, *The Common Cause*. With the outbreak of the war, however, Swanwick severed her long and close association with Fawcett because of their opposing views, views which on the occasion of the 1915 Hague Congress of the International Council of Women, split the British National Suffrage executive body into two nearly equal halves. After resigning the editorship of *The Common Cause*, Swanwick chaired the Women's International League for seven years and helped found the Union of Democratic Control (UDC), an organization that urged international democratic control of foreign policy. She later became the editor of its journal, *Foreign Affairs*. Under the auspices of the UDC, Swanwick lectured throughout England and published *Women and War*. In her pamphlets, Swanwick wrote in her autobiography, she gave vent to "the pity, grief, and patriotism" with which she had discovered "the truth about war in general and this war in particular."

The final selection is a statement read by the accused French pacifist Hélène Brion (1882-1962) at her own trial for treason. Brion was the only woman among many pacifists prosecuted during a series of French treason trials held during the spring months of 1918. A state-employed nursery school teacher in the Paris suburb of Pantin, Brion had long been active in a left-wing teachers' union and in the Parisian women's movement. In 1917 she had been dismissed from her teaching post because of her pacifist activities, specifically for distributing antiwar brochures. She was prosecuted under a law curtailing freedom of speech, which the French government had enacted immediately after the outbreak of the war, and received a suspended sentence of three years' imprisonment. Brion's statement on the relationship between the status of women and pacifism offers an important counterpoint to Helena Swanwick's discussion of the same issue.

---

68. International Woman Suffrage Alliance (1914)

[Rosika Schwimmer's Preface:] Our thoughts turn to your free and happy country. No one else in the world but your Nation, your Government, your President, can lead the action to save Europe. The Woman Suffrage Associations of the World turned spontaneously to Mrs. Carrie Chapman Catt, as the President of the International Woman Suffrage Alliance, imploring her to organize a movement for mediation. Although international communication is terribly restricted, those suffrage associations which could be reached by cables and letters immediately responded to a call to send a European suffragist to the United States in behalf of peace.

Following the instruction of this commission Mrs. Catt and the writer of this report went to Washington to see President Wilson and Secretary of State Bryan. Senator Thomas and Mr. Bryan kindly arranged for an interview with the President on the 18th of September.

To an audience which lasted nearly twenty minutes the European envoyee presented the following petition to President Wilson:

To His Excellency, the President of the United States.
Sir:

We come to you representing the women of many lands who have sent to our London headquarters urgent appeals that our officers should urge the United States Government to lead a movement to end the present European war.

We entreat you, therefore, in the name of our common civilization to combine the neutral nations under your own wise leadership in an insistent demand to all belligerent powers to call an immediate armistice until mediation has been given a fair opportunity to find a just settlement of international differences.

Let the demand be repeated again and again until it is heeded. If at first such action calls forth criticism, an international sentiment will surely be created which will transform criticism into gratitude, and it will at least bring courage and hope to the millions whose hearts are breaking with despair.

Men of the families of our leaders in fifteen countries are at the front. We learn that the homes of some are now hospitals for the wounded, and all European suffrage headquarters are transformed into relief stations. The stories which these women tell us of suffering, want, destruction of property, disease, atrocities and brutal attacks upon women are well nigh unbelievable in this twentieth century.

We accept these scattered testimonials of women we know well as certain indications that civilized Europe has relapsed into barbarism. Under these circumstances no diplomatic conventions should be allowed to stand in the way of the most expeditious means of securing mediation.

The women of the world are looking to you, the leader of the only great neutral nation, to find a way of mediary interference.

The petitions which we present have been voluntary and unorganized. Not less significant than the entreaties which we have received is the absence of appeals from Austria, Servia, Finland, Galicia, and Bohemia. These countries are silent only because they cannot speak, but we know their sentiment so well that we dare to assure you that mediation hastened by outside intervention will be as welcome to the women of these lands as to those whose names are hereto appended.

That the petitions of these women might reach you quickly and surely Madam Rosika Schwimmer, of Hungary, has come to this country for the express purpose of presenting them to you.

> Carrie Chapman Catt,
> President.
> Rosika Schwimmer,
> Secretary.

The following countries have signed the petition:

Australia
    Vida Goldstein for Women's National Political Union.
Canada
    Mrs. Flora McD. Dennison for National Suffrage Association.
Denmark
    Miss Elene Hansen, Fru Elna Munch. Three associations numbering 30,000 women. (Fru Munch's husband is the Danish Minister of War.)
France
    Mme. DeWitt Schlumberger for French Woman Suffrage Association.
Holland
    Dr. Aletta Jacobs for Dutch Woman Suffrage Society.
Hungary
    Fraulein Vilma Glucklich for three associations numbering 20,000 women.
Italy
    Mme. Anita Dobelli Zampetti for Italian Woman Suffrage Association.
Norway
    Froken Gina Krog for Norwegian Council of Women, Mme. Randi Blehr for Norwegian Women's Peace Society.
Russia
    Mme. Schischkina Yavein, M. D.
Sweden
    Froken Signe Bergman for 300,000 Swedish women.
United States
    Dr. Anna Howard Shaw for National American Woman Suffrage Association.

Great Britain

E. Fell for the Civil Union for the Right Understanding of International Interests.

Germany

Frieda Perlen Stadtpfarrar Umfried for West German Woman Suffrage Association.

69. International Congress of Women (1915)

Here in America, on neutral soil, far removed from the stress of the conflict we, the envoys to the Governments from the International Congress of Women at The Hague, have come together to canvass the results of our missions. We put forth this statement as our united and deliberate conclusions.

At a time when the foreign offices of the great belligerents have been barred to each other, and the public mind of Europe has been fixed on the war offices for leadership, we have gone from capital to capital and conferred with the civil governments.

Our mission was to place before belligerent and neutral alike the resolutions of the International Congress of Women held at The Hague in April; especially to place before them the definite method of a conference of neutral nations as an agency of continuous mediation for the settlement of the war.

To carry out this mission two delegations were appointed, which included women of Great Britain, Hungary, Italy, the Netherlands, Sweden, and the United States. One or other of these delegations were received by the governments in fourteen capitals, Berlin, Berne, Budapest, Christiania, Copenhagen, The Hague, Havre (Belgian Government), London, Paris, Petrograd, Rome, Stockholm, Vienna, and Washington. We were received by the Prime Ministers and Foreign Ministers of the Powers, by the King of Norway, by the Presidents of Switzerland and of the United States, by the Pope and the Cardinal Secretary of State. In many capitals more than one audience was given, not merely to present our resolutions, but for a thorough discussion. In addition to the thirty-five governmental visits we met—everywhere—members of parliaments and other leaders of public opinion.

We heard much the same words spoken in Downing Street as those spoken in Wilhelmstrasse, in Vienna, as in Petrograd, in Budapest, as in the Havre, where the Belgians have their temporary government.

Our visits to the war capitals convinced us that the belligerent Governments would not be opposed to a conference of neutral nations; that while the belligerents have rejected offers of mediation by single neutral nations, and while no belligerent could ask for mediation, the creation of a continuous conference of neutral nations might provide the machinery which would lead to peace. We found that the neutrals on the other hand were concerned, lest calling such a conference might be considered inopportune by one or other of the belligerents. Here our information from the belligerents themselves gave assurance that such initiative would not be resented. "My country would not find anything unfriendly in such action by the neutrals," was the assurance given us by the foreign Minister of one of the great belligerents. "My Government would place no obstacle in the way of its institution," said the Minister of an opposing nation. "What are the neutrals waiting for?" said a third, whose name ranks high not only in his own country, but all over the world.

It remained to put this clarifying intelligence before the neutral countries. As a result the plan of starting mediation through the agency of a continuous conference of the neutral nations is to-day being seriously discussed alike in the Cabinets of the belligerent and neutral countries of Europe and in the press of both.

We are in a position to quote some of the expressions of men high in the councils of the great nations as to the feasibility of the plan. "You are right," said one Minister, "that it would be of the greatest importance to finish the fight by early negotiation rather than by further military efforts, which would result in more and more destruction and irreparable loss." "Yours is the sanest proposal that has been brought to this office in the last six months," said the Prime Minister of one of the larger countries.

We were also in position to canvass the objections that have been made to the proposal, testing it out severely in the judgment of those in the midst of the European conflict. It has been argued that it is not the time at present to start such a process of negotiations, and that no step should be taken until one or other party has a victory, or at least until some new military balance is struck. The answer we bring is that every delay makes more difficult the beginnings of negotiations, more nations become involved, and the situation becomes more complicated; that when at times in the course of the war such a balance was struck, the neutrals were unprepared to act. The opportunity passed. For the forces of peace to be unprepared when the hour comes, is as irretrievable as for a military leader to be unready.

It has been argued that for such a conference to be called at any time when one side has met with some military advantage, would be to favor that side. The answer we bring is that the proposed conference would start mediation at a higher level than that of military advantage. As to the actual military situation, however, we quote a remark made to us by a foreign Minister of one of the belligerent Powers. "Neither side is to-day strong enough to dictate terms, and neither side is so weakened that it has to accept humiliating terms."

It has been suggested that such a conference would bind the neutral governments coöperating in it. The answer we bring is that, as proposed, such a conference should consist of the ablest persons of the neutral countries, assigned not to problems of their own governments, but to the common service of a supreme crisis. The situation calls for a conference cast in a new and larger mould than those of conventional diplomacy, the governments sending to it persons drawn from social, economic, and scientific fields who have had genuine international experience.

As women, it was possible for us, from belligerent and neutral nations alike, to meet in the midst of war and to carry forward an interchange of question and answer between capitals which were barred to each other. It is now our duty to make articulate our convictions. We have been convinced that the governments of the belligerent nations would not be hostile to the institution of such a common channel for good offices; and that the governments of the European neutrals we visited stand ready to coöperate with others in mediation. Reviewing the situation, we believe that of the five European neutral nations visited, three are ready to join in such a conference, and that two are deliberating the calling of such a conference. Of the intention of the United States we have as yet no evidence.

We are but the conveyors of evidence which is a challenge to action by the neutral governments visited—by Denmark, Holland, Norway, Sweden, Switzerland, and the United States. We in turn bear evidence of a rising desire and intention of vast companies of people in the neutral countries to turn a barren disinterestedness into an active good-will. In Sweden, for example, more than 400 meetings were held in one day in different parts of the country, calling on the government to act.

The excruciating burden of responsibility for the hopeless continuance of this war no longer rests on the wills of the belligerent nations alone. It rests also on the will of those neutral governments and people who have been spared its shock but cannot, if they would, absolve themselves from their full share of responsibility for the continuance of war.

Signed by

Aletta Jacobs [Holland]
Chrystal Macmillan [Great Britain]
Rosika Schwimmer [Austro-Hungary]
Emily G. Balch [United States]
Jane Addams [United States]

70. Helena M. Swanwick (1915)

"We do not war upon women and children!" This is a commonplace of British rhetoric at the present moment. But it is not true. War is waged by men only, but it is not possible to wage it upon men only. All wars are and must be waged upon women and children as well as upon men. When aviators drop bombs, when guns bombard fortified towns, it is not possible to avoid the women and children who may chance to be in the way. Women have to make good the economic disasters of war; they go short, they work double tides, they pay war taxes and war prices, like men, and out of smaller incomes.

There are in this country seven millions of "gainfully occupied" women and girls, and yet it is curious how officialism generally overlooks this large body of wage and salary earners and assumes that all is well if there is not extensive unemployment of men. The sea and land forces draw off a million men and thus a shortage of male labour is created and (what we are very apt to forget) a shortage of the useful things which that male labour would have created for the benefit of the country; but men and women so largely still do different work that this withdrawal of men does not create any considerable demand for female labour, and the curtailment of men's work often causes the dismissal of the women whose labour dovetails with men's. To take only the clerks and typists, we have seen how the reduction of business by the withdrawal of men has hit the women. Again, the effect of war upon all the luxury trades, in which so many women are employed, is sudden and disastrous, throwing out thousands of dressmakers, milliners, embroidresses, and so forth, while teachers, artists, and many classes of professional women suffer terribly also. One half of these earning women have relatives dependent on them, making the strain and the suffering heavier. And, if we take the other half of the working women of the country—those who are humorously reckoned as not being "employed persons," the working housewives—it does not take much imagination to realise what a rise in the prices of necessaries amounting to 25 per cent. means of pinching and penury to the woman who is trying to housekeep on a sum which is round about a pound a week in the towns and far less in the rural districts.

But, far more heavy than the burden which they share with men, is the burden more particularly their own, which war lays upon women. Two pieces of work for the human family are peculiarly the work of women: they are the life-givers and the home-makers. War kills or maims the children born of woman and tended by her; war destroys "woman's place"— the home. Every man killed or mangled in war has been carried for months in his mother's body and has been tended and nourished for years of his life by women. He is the work of women: they have rights in him and in what he does with the life they have given and sustained. . . .

Another obvious fact is that a constant state of preparedness for war requires a tremendous yearly sacrifice of the fruits of toil; wealth, which might be used to nourish and enlarge and make beautiful the life which is women's charge, is wasted in the competitive increase of armaments, yearly scrapped and replaced by fresh inventions of destruction. Men cannot afford to protect motherhood adequately and to start their children well in life, because they must expend so much wealth in making engines to destroy the children of foreign nations. Again, homicidal wars tend greatly to reduce the proportion of young men to young women, and this disproportion must result either in polygamy or in the establishment of a very large class of celibate women, or of a combination of both, such as we are at present familiar with. There are, besides, all the deep injuries to women created by the barrack system and the corrupting effect of the breaking up of homes. Moreover, when men are called upon to waste their lives in war, women are called upon to spend (and frequently to give up) their lives in child-bearing to make good the waste; the greater the waste of life the greater the waste of women in repairing life. Militarist states always tend to degrade women to the position of breeders and slaves.

In all these ways the possibility of war, the preparation for war, the militarist basis of States (whether "civilised" or "uncivilised") affect the position of women and affect it altogether evilly.

WHEN MIGHT IS RIGHT.

There are, however, other less-obvious ways in which women, and through women the causes of civilisation and democracy, suffer from militarism. The fact that so many people do not clearly apprehend these injuries makes them particularly insidious. They are, however, the inevitable result of a barbarous conception of the foundations of government. In militarist states, women must always, to a greater or less degree, be deprived of liberty, security, scope, and initiative. For militarism is the enthronement of physical force as the arbiter of nations, and under such an arbitrament women must always go under. Women, whose physical force is specialised for the giving and nurture of life, will never be able to oppose men with destructive force. If destructive force is to continue to dominate the world, then man must continue to dominate woman, to his and her lasting injury. The sanction of brute force by which a strong nation "hacks its way" through a weak one is precisely the same as that by which the stronger male dictates to the weaker female. Not till the idea of public right has been accepted by the great nations will there be freedom and security for small nations; not till the idea of moral law has been accepted by the majority of men will there be freedom and security for women. . . .

We British have invented the name of "Prussianism" for a doctrine which we are finding very ugly and hateful. But we should not forget that it is the doctrine with which our British Anti-Suffragists have made us very familiar during the past ten years and which has been enunciated even by the Prime Minister. Suffragists call it "the Physical Force Argument." It runs:—Political power (which alone gives freedom) must always be in the hands of those who can enforce their will; women can never enforce their will as against men; therefore women can never have political power (which alone gives freedom). Once you admit the validity of the major premise, you have proved much more than the necessity for the eternal subjection of women to men; you have proved the necessity for the eternal subjection of small nations and the necessity for the eternal strife of nations, to determine which is the stronger, and the eternal necessity for competitive armaments and shifting alliances and the eternal necessity of wars like this one. It is time that British men realised that anti-suffragism is "Prussianism"; it is time that women suffragists realised what their denial of the major premise of the anti-suffragist entails.

People who desire the enfranchisement of women will only be effective workers if they work for pacifism, or the control of physical by moral force. Pacifists will only be effective if they admit that woman's claim to freedom is based on the same principle as the claim of small nations. The anti-suffragist's major premise of force as the basis of political power is not argument; it is man's knock-out blow. We have no right to assume that what has been always will be; that men are incapable of development; that they must always worship the god of brute force. There is no reason whatever why men should not gradually learn that they get no good, but much evil, from the uncontrolled domination of force. They have shown already in countless ways that they are learning the lesson. They will learn it much faster when women have studied the causes of war and set themselves against them; when women cease to idealise pugnacity in men and see it in its true light as fretful egotism; when, finally, women who demand citizenship join with democratic men and thus show that they understand the very foundation of their own claim and can teach men to understand better the democratic creed which they profess. . . .

As for honour. It is one of the tragic results of the intellectual subjection of women that they should have been willing to accept the association of the notion of honour with that of physical force. If honour were a thing that could be taken away by force and only defended by force, it would be clear that women must always hold their honour at the mercy of men: must always, that is to say, be slaves in the spirit as well as in the flesh; have honour only lent to them by men—never possess it. Women who thought their own thoughts and men of sufficient enlightenment and sympathy to put themselves into the place of a woman have never held this view. But if it be not true of women, why then of men or nations? Women who think their own thoughts will, at any rate, ask themselves whether these points of honour for which men have waged so many public and private quarrels down all the ages are not a relic of the barbarous past, of the superstitious remnant of belief in ordeal by battle.

Perhaps an angry militarist will say: "You have picked out all the ugly motives and none of the beautiful ones. Men fight for love of their country, for patriotism." This is perfectly true. Probably, in all countries, certainly in this, men fight for love of their country, for the ashes of their fathers and the temples of their gods, and for their wives and children. This is why it is so difficult in war time to say anything against war. (Yet it must be said in war time, first because of the peace that has to be made, if possible without the seeds of future wars, and second because it is so difficult to get people in peace time to think seriously and continuously of the causes of war; it seems such "insensate devilry" that men in their peace minds find it inconceivable.) . . .

There remain the people who venture to doubt whether women's influence or vote would really be for peace. They will tell you that they have heard more bloodthirsty and violent talk from women than from men. These comparisons are always very difficult to check, but it would seem natural that, in militarist circles, the women should be more violent in speech than the men, because they can only relieve their feelings by words, whereas the men can go and fight. Professors and journalists and other sedentary men are notoriously more bloodthirsty in their language than the fighting men. But it does not follow that even these women would be anxious to go to war, and we must further remember that it is the conversation of such women which sticks in the memory; the millions of heart-sore women are, for the most part, silent. They have a deep sense of loyalty to their men and are acutely aware of their sufferings and sacrifices. Not for the world will they say anything which would seem to undervalue these, or suggest that they are offered for a wrong or a mistaken cause. So that, in backing their men in the war in which they are actually engaged, many women seem to be backing warfare itself, although in their hearts they abhor it.

There are, again, among suffragist women, two groups which hold aloof from widely different causes. One says she will take no part in "men's politics" until men have enfranchised her: the other fears that, by adopting a definitely pacifist attitude, women would "antagonise" militarist men. We may think both these views wrong, but men, at least, should be tolerant of a state of mind created by their own neglect to do justice. They cannot have it all ways, and the unfree will not all have all the virtues of the free. Women have learned by bitter experience that, unless they concentrate upon winning their own liberty, they are very apt to be made merely the catspaws of political parties, and that, when the party for which they have worked is triumphant, it pushes aside the women's claim with more or less polite circumlocution. But to work for a right foundation of government; to endeavour to establish public right in control of physical force, is not to work merely for a party victory; it is to work for the very foundation of a free and secure existence for women. Every suffrage society ought to be a pacifist society and realise that pacifist propaganda is an integral part of suffrage propaganda. If there are some suffragists who do not yet see this, they are matched by some pacifists who do not see that their creed removes the only real obstacle to the enfranchisement of women.

The difficulty in seeing these connections is due to mere muddleheadedness, but there is something a little contemptible about the fear of antagonising the militarist men. No one ought to wish to get the vote on false pretences. The timid may, however, be recommended to consider this: these men who would not give women the vote if they believed women would vote pacifist are the men who would not give women the vote at any price; these are the relics of barbarism; these are the men with whom it is no use reasoning at all. It is the civilised men who are going to enfranchise women, and it is with such men that women should ally themselves.

71. Hélène Brion (1918)

I appear before this court charged with a political crime; yet I am denied all political rights.

Because I am a woman, I am classified *de plano* by my country's laws, far inferior to all the men of France and the colonies. In spite of the intelligence that has been officially recognized only recently, in spite of the certificates and diplomas that were granted me long ago, before the law I am not the equal of an illiterate black from Guadeloupe or the Ivory Coast. For *he* can participate, by means of the ballot, in directing the affairs of our common country, while *I* cannot. I am outside the law.

The law should be logical and ignore my existence when it comes to punishments, just as it is ignored when it comes to rights. I protest against its lack of logic.

I protest against the application of laws that I have neither wished for nor discussed.

This law that I challenge reproaches me for having held opinions of a nature to undermine popular morale. I protest even more strongly and I deny it! My discreet and nuanced propaganda has always been a constant appeal to reason, to the power of reflection, to the good sense that belongs to every human being, however small the portion.

Moreover, I recall, for form's sake, that my propaganda has never been directed against the national defense and has never called for peace at any price: on the contrary, I have always maintained that there was but one duty, one duty with two parts: for those at the front, to hold fast; for those at the rear, to be thoughtful.

I have exercised this educational action especially in a feminist manner, for I am first and foremost a *feminist*. All those who know me can attest to it. And it is because of my feminism that I am an enemy of war.

The accusation suggests that I preach pacifism under the pretext of feminism. This accusation distorts my propaganda for its own benefit! I affirm that the contrary is true, and it is easy for me to prove it. I affirm that I have been a militant feminist for many years, well before the war; that since the war began I have simply continued; and that I have never reflected on the horrors of the present without noting that things might have been different if women had had a say in matters concerning social issues. . . .

I am an enemy of war because I am a feminist. War represents the triumph of brute strength, while feminism can only triumph through moral strength and intellectual values. Between the two there is total contradiction.

I do not believe that in primitive society the strength or value of woman was inferior to that of men, but it is certain that in present-day society the possibility of war has established a totally artificial scale of values that works to women's detriment.

Woman has been deprived of the sacred and inalienable right given to every individual to defend himself when attacked. By definition (and often by education) she has been made a weak, docile, insignificant creature who needs to be protected and directed throughout her life.

Far from being able to defend her young, as is the case among the rest of creation, she is [even] denied the right to defend herself. In material terms she is denied physical education, sports, the exercise of what is called the noble profession of arms. In political terms she is denied the right to vote—what Gambetta called "the keystone of every other right"—by means of which she could influence her own destiny and have at least the resource to try to do something to prevent these dreadful conflicts in which she and her children find themselves embroiled, like a poor unconscious and powerless machine. . . .

You other men, who alone govern the world! you are trying to do too much and too well. Leave well enough alone.

You want to spare our children the horrors of a future war; a praiseworthy sentiment! I declare that as of now your goal has been attained and that as soon as the atrocious battle that is taking place less than a hundred miles from us has been brought to a halt, you will be able to speak of peace. In 1870 two European nations fought—only two, and for scarcely six months; the result was so appalling that throughout all of Europe, terrified and exhausted, it took more than forty years before anyone dared or was able to begin again. Figure that as of now we have fought, not six months, but for forty-four long months of unbelievable and dreadful combat, where not merely two nations are at odds, but more than twenty—the elite of the so-called civilized world—that almost the entire white race is involved in the melee, that the yellow and black races have been drawn into the wake. And you say, pardon me, that as of now your goal has been achieved!—for the exhaustion of the world is such that more than a hundred years of peace would be instantaneously assured if the war were to end this evening!

The tranquility of our children and grandchildren is assured. Think about assuring them happiness in the present and health in the future! Think about some means of providing them bread when they need it, and sugar, and chocolate to drink! Calculate the repercussions that their present deprivation will have on this happiness that you pretend to offer them by continuing to fight and making them live in this atmosphere, which is unhealthy from every possible point of view.

You want to offer freedom to enslaved people, you want—whether they like it or not—to call to freedom people who do not seem ready to understand it as you do, and you do not seem to notice that in this combat you carry on for liberty, all people lose more and more what little they possess, from the material freedom of eating what they please and traveling wherever they wish, to the intellectual liberties of writing, of meeting, even of thinking and especially the possibility of thinking straight—all that is disappearing bit by bit because it is incompatible with a state of war.

Take care! The world is descending a slope that will be difficult to remount.

I have constantly said this, have written about it incessantly since the beginning of the war: if you do not call women to your rescue, you will not be able to ascend the slope, and the new world that you pretend to install will be as unjust and as chaotic as the one that existed before the war!

Women and War Work

SOURCES

72. Magda Trott, "Frauenarbeit, ein Ersatz für Männerarbeit?," *Die Frau: Propaganda-Ausschuss der Frauen der nationalliberalen Partei*, 3, no. 43 (1915). Tr. SGB.

73. Emma Stropp, "Frauen als landwirtschaftliche Beamtinnen," *Die Frau: Propaganda-Ausschuss der Frauen der nationalliberalen Partei*, 4, no. 5 (1916). Tr. SGB.

74. E. Sylvia Pankhurst, "How to Meet Industrial Conscription," *The Woman's Dreadnought*, 2, no. 2 (20 March 1915).

75. Helena M. Swanwick, *The War in its Effect upon Women* (August 1916), reprinted from the *Annual* of the Co-operative Wholesale Societies Limited, and published by the Women's International League (London, 1917), pp. 3-4, 5-6, 7-9.

While war fever swept the belligerent nations of the Western world and pacifism was pursued by a thoughtful but unpopular minority, women's war work and the wider issues of women's employment became the key to the debate on the woman question. The mobilization of men in turn propelled women of all classes into a new range of activities, whether as volunteers in routine administrative activities behind the military effort; as paid workers and supervisors in positions previously held by men in the civil service, commerce and industry; or most visibly as workers in government munitions factories. It is no oversimplification to say that women's efforts on behalf of their countries and as a replacement for the men at the front could be duly applauded as long as everyone understood that women's war work was a temporary solution to a crisis, and that their permanent place in peacetime was not in the work force but at home. Nevertheless, there were intellectual radicals, and others not completely overwhelmed by the patriotic emotional turmoil of the war, who were troubled by the prospect that when the war ended not all women would have a "home" in which to remain, *unless* they were employed outside of it. Added to this was dissent over the principle of women's right to work and the charge that women were simply a surplus labor force waiting in the wings, to be deployed only in times of crisis. Moreover, there were problems of women's guilt over usurping the position of men who had staked their lives and often forfeited their health on behalf of their country, and in defense of "the women and children."

The selections below illuminate the conflicts arising from the need for women's labor in wartime. The first two selections, written by frequent contributors to German women's newspapers—Magda Trott (dates unknown) and Emma Stropp (dates unknown)—who were associated with the conservatively oriented national liberal party (Nationalliberale Partei), emphasize the transitory nature and expectations of conservative women who were nevertheless concerned with improving women's position.

The third selection is by Estelle Sylvia Pankhurst (1882-1960), the second daughter of Emmeline Pankhurst (Doc. 61), artist, socialist, pacifist, and founder of the East London Women's Suffrage Federation, who had dissociated herself and her growing organization from the political conservatism and bellicose enthusiasm of her mother's and her sister Christabel's suffragettes in the Women's Social and Political Union (WSPU). In this selection from an editorial in her weekly newspaper, *The Woman's Dreadnought,* Sylvia Pankhurst promoted two goals: first, continuing demands for woman suffrage so that women could not be ordered by the government into war work without proper representation of their views—a notable contrast to the position of other leaders of women's suffrage societies, who officially dropped suffrage demands for the duration of the war; and, second, the need for women's equal pay with men in the industrial labor force, in order to prevent both exploitation of women and discrimination against men whose trade unions had negotiated higher wages. Pankhurst's discussion of the wage issue contrasts pointedly with Magda Trott's in her article on German women's clerical employment.

The final selection is from a pamphlet by the British author, suffragist, and pacifist Helena Maria Swanwick (Doc. 70). As in all of her writings Swanwick here exhibits her depth of vision into human problems and relationships. Her concern was for men and women's interaction after the war. She stands out from others writing about the impact of the war, by her analysis of its longer-range effects upon the situation of men and women whose lives have been deeply disturbed and uprooted. But Swanwick never lost sight of the fact that women would be dealt a double blow, since having tasted "the exhilaration of being brought in to work for the good of the whole" they might again have to retreat into a secondary position. Her premonitions were realized when governments set an example to industry by abruptly dismissing women in their employ at the end of the war, even offering bonuses to those who withdrew before a certain date.

---

72. Magda Trott (1915)

With the outbreak of war men were drawn away from the management of numerous organizations and, gradually, the lack of experienced personnel made itself felt. Women working in offices were therefore urged not to waste the opportunities offered them by the war, and to continue their education so that they would be prepared to take on the position once held by a male colleague, should the occasion arise.

Such occasions have indeed arisen much sooner than anticipated. The demand for educated women has risen phenomenally during the six months since the war began. Women have been employed in banks, in large commercial businesses, in urban offices—everywhere, in fact, where up till now only men had been employed. They are to be tested in order to see whether they can perform with equal success.

All those who were certain that women would be completely successful substitutes for men were painfully disappointed to discover that many women who had worked for years in a firm and were invited to step up to a higher level, now that the men were absent, suddenly handed in their resignations. An enquiry revealed that, especially in recent days, these notices were coming with great frequency and, strange as it may seem, applied mostly to women who had been working in the same company from four to seven years and had now been offered a better and even better-paid job. They said "no" and since there was no possibility for them to remain in their old jobs, they resigned.

The enemies of women's employment were delighted. Here was their proof that women are incapable of holding down responsible positions. Female workers were quite successful as clerks, stenographers, and typists, in fact, in all those positions that require no independent activity—but as soon as more serious duties were demanded of them, they failed.

Naturally, we enquired of these women why they had given up so quickly, and then the truth of the matter became plain. All women were quite ready, if with some trepidation, to accept the new positions, particularly since the boss made it clear that one of the gentlemen would carefully explain the new assignments to them. Certainly the work was almost entirely new to the young ladies since till now they had only been concerned with their stenography, their books, and so forth. However, they entered their new duties with enthusiasm.

But even on the first day it was noticeable that not everything would proceed as had been supposed. Male colleagues looked askance at the "intruder" who dared to usurp the position and bread of a colleague now fighting for the Fatherland, and who would, it was fervently hoped, return in good health. Moreover, the lady who came as a substitute received exactly half of the salary of the gentleman colleague who had previously occupied the same position. A dangerous implication, since if the lady made good, the boss might continue to draw on female personnel; the saving on salaries would clearly be substantial. It became essential to use all means to show the boss that female help was no substitute for men's work, and a united male front was organized.

It was hardly surprising that all the lady's questions were answered quite vaguely. If she asked again or even a third time, irritated remarks were passed concerning her inadequacy in comprehension, and very soon the male teacher lost patience. Naturally, most of his colleagues supported him and the lady found it difficult, if not impossible, to receive any instruction and was finally forced to resign.

This is what happened in most known cases. We must, however, also admit that occasionally the fault does lie with the lady, who simply did not have sufficient preparation to fill a difficult position. There may be male colleagues who would gladly share information with women; however, these women are unable to understand, because they have too little business experience. In order to prevent this sort of thing, we would counsel all women who are seeking a position in which they hope to advance, to educate themselves as much as possible. All those women who were forced to leave their jobs of long standing might not have been obliged to do so, had they been more concerned in previous years with understanding the overall nature of the business in which they were employed. Their colleagues would surely and generously have answered their questions and given them valuable advice, which would have offered them an overview and thereby avoided the total ignorance with which they entered these advanced positions when they were offered. At least they would have had an inkling and saved themselves the questions that betrayed their great ignorance to their colleagues. They might even have found their way through all the confusion and succeeded in the new position.

Therefore, once again: all you women who want to advance yourselves and create an independent existence, use this time of war as a learning experience and keep your eyes open.

73. Emma Stropp (1916)

The wider circle of careers that has opened up for women because of the changes in the male labor market by the war included work as secretaries on country estates and as agricultural bookkeepers and accountants. Until now this type of work had been reserved for male employees. The gaps caused by the war are now to be filled by women.

In due recognition of this fact, the Chambers of Agriculture of the provinces of Brandenburg and Breslau are offering courses for commercially trained girls and women that will acquaint them with the knowledge essential to understanding the special conditions of agricultural concerns. These arrangements should also be considered by women whose background in the country inclines them to remain in their familiar environment and who wish to take up a career that seems especially suited to them, since they, more than urban women, have been preconditioned for it from youth.

We must, however, point out that an excessive rush to these careers must be avoided, since we have to assume that a number of the positions now vacant will be filled by men returning after the war.

Readers may therefore be interested in the curriculum offered by the courses from the 9th January to the 4th March 1916 by the province of Brandenburg in Berlin. The classes will be held in the auditorium of the Agricultural Institute [*Hochschule*], no. 42 Invalidenstrasse, Berlin, on Tuesdays and Fridays from 8-10 p.m. Fees are 20 marks for members of the Union of Commerce; and 15 marks for female employees. The curriculum will include simple agricultural bookkeeping, beginning with taking of inventories; practice with books on accounting, cultivation, and animals, as well as other reference works. Insurance for workers and employees will be thoroughly studied as will accounts dealing with taxable income and property management. If there is interest, students will also be offered an opportunity to study other systems. After earlier three-week-long courses, the Brandenburg Chamber of Agriculture was able to find jobs in agricultural establishments for a number of well-prepared women who had been introduced to agricultural accounting, commerce, and office procedure.

Concerning salaries—we reckon on an annual starting salary of 400-600 marks. Experienced employees will certainly not be less well paid (considering their expense-free support) than women employees in urban commercial establishments. Since we are dealing mostly with private employment it is difficult to give exact figures. Salaries higher than 800-900 marks per annum have not generally been noted in private places, which does not necessarily exclude the possibility that especially well-qualified women who are able to work independently could be offered duties of great responsibility and would then receive higher amounts.

There are indeed splendid opportunities for commercially trained women, particularly when we consider that for many of them a sojourn in the country is most desirable for reasons of health. We can also welcome these opportunities for careers in the country as a means of easing the pressure on the urban labor market, since we are likely to witness an overcrowding (especially in commercial careers) by men who have been invalided out of the war. It would seem desirable that the daughters of owners of agricultural estates not swell these urban crowds, but rather have the chance to be gainfully employed in the familiar surroundings of their youth.

However, as I have already indicated, these opportunities for employment must not be overrated. The Chamber of Agriculture itself has emphasized that training of female estate-secretaries and accountants must be kept within narrow limits in order to avoid later disappointments. Nevertheless, these career branches are recommended to these women who are suited to them.

74. E. Sylvia Pankhurst (1915)

To the women whom they have refused to grant the rights of enfranchised citizens, the Government, through the President of the Board of Trade, has issued an appeal to enlist for War service.

The Women's Societies which the Government has so often flouted are urged to lend their aid in marshalling the volunteers.

Registers of women who are prepared to undertake any kind of paid work, industrial, agricultural, clerical, etc., are to be kept at the Labour Exchanges, and registration forms are being sent out to the women's organisations. Those who register must state their ages and whether they are married, widowed or unmarried: if they have ever done any paid work, and if so, what and when, and in whose employ: if they are free to work whole or part time, or to leave their homes; whether there is any kind of work that they are willing or able to do, and whether they are willing to train for work which they have not previously done.

In view of this appeal, which is being made to women by the Government—appeals by Governments usually tend to become irresistible demands—it is surely time that all the women's organisations, trade union, political, educational and social, should come together to discuss this important matter and formulate their demands to safeguard the position of women of all ranks in the labour army.

The men who signed the Army forms that were sent round to the householders, found themselves called up for service, sometimes much to their surprise. The women who sign their names on the War Service Register will probably find themselves called up too, whether they wish or not. Shall we allow them to go without fair conditions first being assured?

The Government, through Mr. Lloyd George and Lord Kitchener, has announced that it is about to take extensive control of industry.

The Government makes it plain that it is determined that the provisions of munitions of war, both for Great Britain and the Allies, shall absorb all our entire national energies, so that all our people may become part of a great war machine engaged either in fighting, supplying the wherewithal to fight, or in providing necessaries of food, clothing, housing and transport for the soldiers or armament makers.

In order to conciliate the British workmen (who, by their votes, have been made the ultimate arbiters of the nation's destiny, though they scarcely realize their power), Mr. Lloyd George has held conference with the Great Trade Unions which, as yet, are almost entirely controlled by men. The Government has promised that limits shall be set to the profits of employers, and that good wages and fair conditions of labour shall be ensured.

Various increases in wages have been made, and negotiations are taking place in regard to demands for much larger increases. The Trade Union leaders and Labour Members of Parliament occupy a position of grave and anxious responsibility at this time, for on their handling of the situation the position of millions of workers largely depends.

Perhaps an even vaster responsibility rests on the shoulders of women who are leaders of women at this time. As yet, the working women, the sweated drudges of the world, are but poorly organised, and all the women's suffrage and other political and social organisations must lend their aid at this crisis, in securing the best possible terms for the masses of women workers, on whom the future of our race so largely depends.

It is more urgently imperative than ever that every woman who works for her living should join a Trade Union, in order that she may have a strong organisation to protect her interests, and that she may help to protect the interests of other women.

A national conference of women should be called immediately to formulate demands for the regulation of this industrial enlistment of women. Here are some of the demands which would, undoubtedly, be adopted by such a conference:—

(1) As the Government is already by far and away the largest employer of labour in the country, and may soon be almost the sole employer, it is absolutely imperative that *women who are to be enlisted as recruits in the National War Service shall have the Vote at once.*

(2) That fair wages shall be assured to women. *That where a woman is employed on work hitherto done by men she shall receive the wage hitherto paid to men, in addition to any war bonus or increase in wages which might have been paid for the work now, in the case of men employees. That in no case shall an unskilled woman be employed at a lower wage than the current rate to men unskilled labourers.*

(3) The Government has announced its determination to put an end to industrial disputes, and proposes that, where the parties concerned fail to come to an agreement:—

"The matter shall be referred to an impartial tribunal, nominated by his Majesty's Government, for immediate investigation and report to the Government with a view to a settlement."

The Women's Conference would undoubtedly demand that *women should have strong representation on this tribunal, and that in all disputes in regard to women's employment, a woman of standing and experience (the nation has many such to draw upon) should be the chairman of the tribunal, or in case of the appointment of a sole arbiter, a woman should be the arbiter of the dispute.*

(4) That proper safeguards in regard to hours, wages, and conditions be arranged in conjunction with representatives of the women concerned, and that no woman shall be compelled to work under conditions which the representative of the organisation to which she belongs, reports to be unsatisfactory.

This is a moment of very vital importance to women, calling for all our energy and resource, all our earnestness, all our solidarity.

Let us band ourselves together—sinking our differences—to build up a position of dignity and security for our sisters, in order that as free citizens they may give their services to the nation willingly and with enthusiasm.

75. Helena M. Swanwick (1916)

How has the war affected women? How will it affect them? Women, as half the human race, are compelled to take their share of evil and good with men, the other half. The destruction of property, the increase of taxation, the rise of prices, the devastation of beautiful things in nature and art—these are felt by men as well as by women. Some losses doubtless appeal to one or the other sex with peculiar poignancy, but it would be difficult to say whose sufferings are the greater, though there can be no doubt at all that men get an exhilaration out of war which is denied to most women. When they see pictures of soldiers encamped in the ruins of what was once a home, amidst the dead bodies of gentle milch cows, most women would be thinking too insistently of the babies who must die for need of milk to entertain the exhilaration which no doubt may be felt at "the good work of our guns." When they read of miles upon miles of kindly earth made barren, the hearts of men may be wrung to think of wasted toil, but to women the thought suggests a simile full of an even deeper pathos; they will think of the millions of young lives destroyed, each one having cost the travail and care of a mother, and of the millions of young bodies made barren by the premature death of those who should have been their mates. The millions of widowed maidens in the coming generation will have to turn their thoughts away from one particular joy and fulfilment of life. While men in war give what is, at the present stage of the world's development, the peculiar service of men, let them not forget that in rendering that very service they are depriving a corresponding number of women of the opportunity of rendering what must, at all stages of the world's development, be the peculiar service of women. After the war, men will go on doing what has been regarded as men's work; women, deprived of their own, will also have to do much of what has been regarded as men's work. These things are going to affect women profoundly, and one hopes that the reconstruction of society is going to be met by the whole people—men and women—with a sympathetic understanding of each other's circumstances. When what are known as men's questions are discussed, it is generally assumed that the settlement of them depends upon men only; when what are known as women's questions are discussed, there is never any suggestion that they can be settled by women independently of men. Of course they cannot. But, then, neither can "men's questions" be rightly settled so. In fact, life would be far more truly envisaged if we dropped the silly phrases "men's and women's questions"; for, indeed, there are no such matters, and all human questions affect all humanity.

Now, for the right consideration of human questions, it is necessary for humans to understand each other. This catastrophic war will do one good thing if it opens our eyes to real live women as they are, as we know them in workaday life, but as the politician and the journalist seem not to have known them. . . .

Women are, through the war, becoming good "copy." But women have not suddenly become patriotic, or capable, or self-sacrificing; the great mass of women have always shown these qualities in their humble daily life. Now that their services are asked for in unfamiliar directions, attention is being attracted to them, and many more people are realising that, with extended training and opportunity, women's capacity for beneficent work would be extended. The fiction of women's incapacity must have indeed bitten deep, when it could be supposed that it required a "super-woman" to clip a ticket! *

There never was any justification for that sort of sentimentalism, but we are now in some danger of sentimentalism of the opposite kind. Extravagant writers are filling the papers with assertions that women in engineering works can do two or three times as much work as men, and that raw female hands can plough a straighter and deeper furrow in heavy soil than practised men are able. All this does nothing but harm. If unpractised women have turned out more work at a lathe than practised men, it is most assuredly not because the men could not have turned out more than they did; we must seek for other reasons. The problem of the readjustment of men's and women's work after the war is going to be so difficult and so great that we want none of this frivolous sentimentality in dealing with it. We want facts. We want a sober judgment. We want an alert mind, which will meet the problems with no dead obstructive preju-

* A published snapshot of the first women ticket collectors on English buses had been captioned "Superwomen."—EDS.

dices, but with the single intention to make the very best use of the men and women who will emerge from this ghastly catastrophe. To condemn any section of the people to inaction, to restrict or cramp their powers of production and of healing, is going to cripple the nation and be the most unpatriotic course conceivable.

It is often forgotten that for full prosperity a country needs to be producing as much wealth as possible, consistently with the health, freedom, and happiness of its people. To arrive at this desired result, it is quite clear that as many people as possible should be employed productively, and it is one of the unhappy results of our economic anarchy that employers have found it profitable to have a large reserve class of unemployed and that wage-earners have been driven to try and diminish their own numbers and to restrict their own output. To keep women out of the "labour market" (by artificial restrictions, such as the refusal to work with them, or the refusal to allow them to be trained, or the refusal to adapt conditions to their health requirements) is in truth anti-social. But it is easy to see how such anti-social restrictions have been forced upon the workers, and it is futile to blame them. A way must be found out of industrial war before we can hope that industry will be carried on thriftily. Men and women must take counsel together and let the experience of the war teach them how to solve economic problems by co-operation rather than conflict. Women have been increasingly conscious of the satisfaction to be got from economic independence, of the sweetness of earned bread, of the dreary depression of subjection. They have felt the bitterness of being "kept out"; they are feeling the exhilaration of being "brought in." They are ripe for instruction and organisation in working for the good of the whole. . . .

The return of millions of men to civil life and work will tax the goodwill and organising capacity of the whole nation. The change from war production to peace production will possibly be even greater. The readjustments required must necessarily be slow and difficult, and unless there can be co-operation between employers and employed, and between all sections of employed, there will be friction to the raw and many disastrous mistakes.

Because it will obviously be impossible for all to find work quickly (not to speak of the right kind of work), there is almost certain to be an outcry for the restriction of work in various directions, and one of the first cries (if we may judge from the past) will be to women: "Back to the Home!" This cry will be raised whether the women have a home or not. All who care for the good of the whole must meet this cry and all that it implies with a sympathetic understanding of all sides of the problem, and a grasp, not only of present difficulties, but of the needs of the future, and there must be no hurried rushing into emergency measures which will seriously cripple future development. We must understand the unimpeachable right of the man who has lost his work and risked his life for his country, to find decent employment, decent wages and conditions, on his return to civil life. We must also understand the enlargement and enhancement of life which women feel when they are able to live by their own productive work, and we must realise that to deprive women of the right to live by their work is to send them back to a moral imprisonment (to say nothing of physical and intellectual starvation), of which they have become now for the first time fully conscious. And we must realise the exceeding danger that conscienceless employers may regard women's labour as preferable, owing to its cheapness and its docility, and that women, if unsympathetically treated by their male relatives and fellow workers, may be tempted to continue to be cheap and docile in the hands of those who have no desire except that of exploiting them and the community. The kind of man who likes "to keep women in their place" may find he has made slaves who will be used by his enemies against him. Men need have no fear of free women; it is the slaves and the parasites who are a deadly danger.

The demand for equal wage for equal work has been hotly pressed by men since the war began, and it is all to the good so far as it goes. But most men are still far from realising the solidarity of their interests with those of women in all departments of life, and are still too placidly accepting the fact that women are sweated over work which is not the same as that of men. They don't realise yet that starved womanhood means starved manhood, and they don't enough appreciate the rousing and infectious character of a generous attitude on the part of men, who, in fighting the women's battles unselfishly and from a love of right, would stimulate the women to corresponding generosity. There are no comrades more staunch and loyal than women, where men have engaged their truth and courage. But men must treat them as comrades; they must no longer think only of how they can "eliminate female labour"; they must take the women into their trade unions and other organisations, and they must understand that the complexities of a woman's life are not of her invention or choosing, but are due to her function as mother of men.

The sexual side of a woman's life gravely affects the economic side, and we can never afford to overlook this. As mothers and home-makers women are doing work of the highest national importance and economic value, but this value is one which returns to the nation as a whole and only in small and very uncertain part to the women themselves. The fact that a woman is a wife and mother diminishes her value in the "labour market," and even the fact that she is liable to become a wife and mother has done so in the past. Unless men are prepared to socialise the responsibilities of parenthood, one does not see how women's labour is ever to be organised for the welfare of the whole, nor does one see how women are to perform their priceless functions of motherhood as well as possible if they are to be penalised for them in the future as they have been in the past. I do not overlook the complexity of the problem of the reconcilement of women's work as mothers with their work as home-makers and wage-earners, but I plead that the problem should be treated as a whole and not in scraps, as hitherto.

CHAPTER 8

War's End and the Revolutions

The Russian Revolution

SOURCES

76. Lenin, Speech at the First All-Russian Congress of Women, 19 November 1918, reprinted in Lenin, *Women and Society* (New York, 1938), pp. 11-13.

77. Aleksandra Kollontai, "The Labour of Women in the Evolution of the Economy" (1923), translated and reprinted in *The Family in the U.S.S.R.*, ed. Rudolf Schlesinger (London, 1949), pp. 45-48. Originally published in Russian.

78. *The Woman Patriot*, 1, no. 11 (6 July 1918), 4: "Germany's Strongest Allies."

The appalling death toll, the dislocations of work and private lives, caused in the Western world by the war were paralleled, if not overshadowed, during 1917 by the collapse of the Russian empire and the Revolution. The reality and magnitude of the upheaval, and the specter it cast upon Western Europe and the United States with respect to the woman question, are reflected in the selections from two major Russian revolutionary figures, Aleksandra Kollontai and Lenin, and an American anti-suffrage newspaper of the period.

Equality for women and their position in the family had been a constant theme in radical thought since the eighteenth century. Having read Russian, French, and German literature on the woman question, middle-class and aristocratic women in Tsarist Russia had also organized to achieve equal rights. The theorist, short-story writer, and political leader Aleksandra Kollontai (1872-1952), who will be introduced first, exemplified the combination of Marxist thought and the bourgeois women's movements. Moreover, she was keenly aware of the conflicts caused by freeing women not merely from household drudgery, but also from emotional and sexual dependence on male breadwinners. A general's daughter, born into a family of Russian-Finnish and Ukrainian background, Kollontai grew up in a milieu of the liberal intelligentsia. At the age of twenty-six she left her husband and four-year-old son to study Marxism in Zurich. She published the first of her many works of fiction and non-fiction, *The Social Bases of the Woman Question*, in 1903. In exile from 1909 to 1917, Kollontai wrote her most important articles on the relationship between female sexuality and female subjugation. Like Ellen Key (Docs. 26, 48), who may have influenced her thinking, Kollontai stands out from most other writers on women's issues of her period, because she never lost sight of the need to stress the psychological importance of economic independence for women as well as their biological service to society as mothers.

Although Kollontai had become convinced that Marxism and revolution offered the only hope for achieving women's emancipation, she had great difficulty in convincing either of the opposing Russian revolutionary factions—Bolsheviks or Mensheviks—of the importance of the woman question as a distinct and primary goal. She finally committed herself to the Bolsheviks led by Lenin in 1915, and on being elected to the Central Committee a few months before the October Revolution in 1917, succeeded in establishing a women's bureau in the party. When Lenin formed his first cabinet after the revolution in 1917, he appointed Kollontai, the only woman in this group, to the post of People's Commissar for Public Welfare.

The two-fold and interdependent aims of Kollontai and her associates in the Women's Bureau, backed by Lenin and Trotsky, were to rally women to the support of the new regime and to attend to their special interests. Reorganization of society, they argued, necessitated the active and enthusiastic participation of all Russian women—no mean task in a vast country containing millions of illiterate, isolated, and conservative peasants. Kollontai and her co-workers in the Women's Bureau or, as it soon became known, the Zhenotdel, organized both small meetings and large congresses to introduce Russian women to the questions of legal and social equality of women and men.

Over a thousand people crowded the first All-Russian Congress of Women on 19 November 1918, just a year after the revolution. Only three hundred had been expected. There, for the first time in history, a head of state, the already legendary Lenin, called for an end to women's domestic slavery and drudgery, to the double standard of sexual morality, and to prostitution.

Lenin (born Vladimir Il'ich Ulianov; 1870-1924) was one of the first Russian revolutionaries to become converted to Marxism. He was the central figure of the Bolshevik party, which advocated revolution by force, and he lived to become the founder and guiding spirit behind the new Soviet state. While in exile in Siberia he married another revolutionary, Nadezhda Krupskaya, who in the course of serving as her husband's research associate (gathering information on the condition of Russian laborers) found material for her own book, *The Woman Worker* (1900), the first Russian-Marxist treatment of the problems of female labor. During the war years Lenin, then exiled in Switzerland, worked closely with Krupskaya and with the German socialist Clara Zetkin (Doc. 15) to oppose the war and to bring about the victory of international socialism. Meanwhile Kollontai continued her own revolutionary work from Sweden.

The selections in this section include Lenin's rallying call to the All-Russian Women's Congress, summarizing the goals of the Bolshevik women's bureau as formulated by Kollontai and others, and Kollontai's critique of the "bourgeois feminist" movement in Tsarist Russia and the Western democracies, contrasting it with Bolshevik intent in revolutionizing women's position. The final selection is an article from *The Woman Patriot*, a newspaper published in Washington, D.C., that was explicitly devoted to combating "woman suffrage, feminism, and socialism." Both the *Woman Patriot* article and Kollontai attack the suffragists, but from diametrically-opposed understandings of the suffragist position.

---

76. Lenin (1918)

Comrades, in a certain respect this congress of the feminine section of the proletarian army is of particularly great significance, since in all countries women have been the slowest to stir. There can be no socialist revolution, unless a vast section of the toiling women takes an important part in it.

In all civilized countries, even the most advanced, the position of women is such as justifies their being called domestic slaves. Not in a single capitalist country, not even in the freest republic, do women enjoy complete equality.

The aim of the Soviet Republic is to abolish, in the first place, all restrictions of the rights of women. The Soviet government has completely abolished the source of bourgeois filth, repression, and humiliation—divorce proceedings.

For nearly a year now our completely free divorce laws have been in force. We issued a decree abolishing the difference in the status of children born in wedlock and those born out of wedlock, and also the various political disabilities. In no other country have the toiling women achieved such complete freedom and equality.

We know that the entire burden of the obsolete rules is borne by the women of the working class.

Our law wiped out, for the first time in history, all that made women inferior. But it is not a matter of law. In our cities and factory settlements this law on the complete freedom of marriage is taking root, but in the countryside it very frequently exists only on paper. There, church marriage still predominates. This is due to the influence of the priests, and it is more difficult to fight this evil than the old laws.

Religious prejudices must be fought very cautiously: a lot of harm is caused by those who carry on this struggle in such a way as to offend religious feelings. The struggle must be carried on by means of propaganda, by means of enlightenment. By introducing acrimony into the struggle we may antagonize the masses; this kind of struggle contributes to the division of the masses according to religion, but our strength is in unity. The deepest source of religious prejudice is poverty and ignorance; it is with these evils that we must contend.

Up to the present the position of women has been such that it is called a position of slavery. Women are crushed by their domestic drudgery, and only socialism can relieve them from this drudgery, when we shall pass on from small household economy to social economy and to social tilling of the soil.

Only then will women be fully free and emancipated. It is a difficult task. Committees of poor peasants are now being formed, and the time is at hand when the socialist revolution will be consolidated.

It is only now that the poorer section of the population in the villages is organizing, and in these organizations of the poor peasants socialism is acquiring a firm foundation.

It has often happened before that the cities became revolutionary and the countryside took action afterwards.

The present revolution has the countryside to rely on, and therein is its significance and strength. It has been observed in the experience of all liberation movements that the success of a revolution depends on the extent to which women take part in it. The Soviet government is doing everything to enable women to carry on their proletarian socialist activity independently.

The position of the Soviet government is difficult inasmuch as the imperialists of all countries hate Soviet Russia and are preparing to wage war against her for the reason that she has kindled the flame of revolution in a number of countries and that she has made resolute steps towards socialism. At present, while they are bent on defeating revolutionary Russia, the ground is beginning to get hot under their feet in their own countries. You know that the revolutionary movement is gaining momentum in Germany, that in Denmark a struggle is going on between the workers and the government, and Holland is about to be transformed into a Soviet republic. The revolutionary movement in these small countries has no independent significance, but it is particularly symptomatic because of the fact that these countries have not been at war and that they have maintained a perfectly "lawful" democratic order. When countries such as these are getting into motion, that is an assurance that the revolutionary movement is embracing the whole world.

Up to the present not a single republic has been capable of emancipating the women. The Soviet government will help them. Our cause is invincible, for in all countries the invincible working class is rising. This movement signifies the growth of the invincible socialist revolution.

77. Aleksandra Kollontai (1923)

During the whole of the nineteenth century the bourgeois feminist movement developed independently of the political movements of bourgeois men, showing only slight traces of the similarity of social level. The movement made great strides towards the end of the century, having cast a well-knit net of feminist organizations over all the bourgeois countries of West and East. Its main objective was the achievement of equal rights for women, equal rights with men in all spheres of life within the limits of a bourgeois capitalist society. From the start these advocates of feminine rights in the bourgeois camp never even thought of a new social order as offering women the widest and only firm basis of their emancipation. Socialism was alien to them. And when towards the end of the century some of the bourgeois "suffragettes" put forward demands borrowed from the Socialists, they did so only in order to woo the support of the female proletariat, to bribe their sympathy and thereby enhance their own political significance.

A second characteristic aspect of the bourgeois "suffragettes" lay in their imagining themselves to be the advocates and spokesmen of the demands and aspirations of all women, believing themselves placed above all class differences, when in fact they were but the very mouthpieces for the needs and interests of women of the bourgeois class, even if of various social groupings.

The movement had its third hall-mark in the fact that the adherents of feminism, while endeavouring to imitate the men in every possible way, kept strictly apart and opposed the interests of women to those of men. The feminists made yet another mistake: they absolutely refused to take into account that woman bears a twofold responsibility towards society and that the "natural right" which they were so fond of quoting not only demands that women should effectively contribute to society but also that they should provide society with healthy offspring. Motherhood and its defence, the safeguarding of woman's interests as mother, were in no way included in the aims and programme of the bourgeois "equal-righters," and the bourgeois women who late in the nineteenth and early in the twentieth century found the problem of safeguarding motherhood attracting their attention were not of those who had been drawn into the feminist camp. The bourgeois feminist organizations were very reluctant to include in their programmes the demands for safeguarding motherhood and protecting female labour; they hesitated a great deal and began to include them only towards the twentieth century, when without these points they risked losing the support of the great masses of proletarian women, who came forward as active defenders of these demands.

The feminists naïvely attempted to transfer the struggle for women's equal rights from the firm basis of class relationships into the realm of a struggle between the sexes. The result was a distorted caricature.

Lacking a flair for politics, the feminists strayed from the true path of their struggle. Where they might have assured themselves of success and gained the support of the men of their own class, they lost both by proclaiming at every juncture, heedless of appropriateness, those onesided feminist catchwords which urged equal rights for women, instead of putting forward the demands common to their class which would by themselves have resulted in a claim for women's rights. Only in the twentieth century did the more politically minded women's movements join hands with some definite political party, becoming a part or a complement of it. It was in this way that in pre-revolutionary Russia the "Female Kadets" (Constitutional Democratic Party) worked in the "Union of Equal Rights for Women" and later in the "League for Equal Rights for Women." A similar policy was pursued by some German and English societies.

In their zeal to establish equal rights and prove woman in every respect equal to man, the feminists were bound to disregard the natural characteristics of women which mark them out for a special place in the collective.

In the primitive communist society women were respected by the tribe as being the mainstay of the household and giving birth to new life for sustaining the growth of the tribe. Motherhood, i.e., woman's ability to bear children, is not in itself a sufficient reason for society to support her on an equal footing with the men who bear all the responsibility of maintenance. But if the women share with the men in doing work useful for the society, their additional social responsibilities—child-bearing and child-feeding—undoubtedly entitle them to extra care and special treatment from the society. The bourgeois feminists, in their enthusiasm for equal rights as an overriding principle, failed to recognize this. They made their greatest mistake in believing that to acknowledge feminine rights is the same thing as to give women equal rights with men. The more hard-bitten feminists adopted a male style of clothing "on principle," cut their hair short not for comfort but in imitation, walked along the streets with long masculine strides. . . . When the feminists found out that, driven by necessity, women were working as dockers in ports and lugging impossible weights, these naïve advocates of equal rights brimmed over with triumph and wrote in their newspapers and periodicals: "Women score yet another victory for equal rights! Women dockers carry four hundredweight, hold their own with men!" It did not enter their heads that in the interest both of society and of the women dockers they should have written an article to the contrary, pointing out that in its greed for profit capitalism was undermining the nation's health, ruining the female organism by unsuitable and unbearable work, and thus destroying the welfare of the people. The feminists could not understand that women's different physique would always set them apart, but that this by no means affects the acknowledgment of their rights or their value to the community. Women should do not the same kind of work as men, but work that contributes equally to the welfare of the community, if the community is to give them recognition and guarantee them equal rights. The feminists did not grasp this; hence the onesidedness and narrowness of their movement.

78. The Woman Patriot (1918)

Woman suffrage and socialism, which always go hand in hand, are proving themselves Germany's strongest allies. In Finland, woman suffrage brought socialism, then pacifism; anarchy followed, and then German rule. In Russia, woman suffrage and socialism came in together and brought ruin to Russia and triumph to Germany. Australia is the one part of the British Empire which has had woman suffrage long enough to learn how it works. Australia is completely in the hands of the socialists, and is the one part of the British Empire, except Ireland, which refuses to adopt conscription. At the recent election in South Australia, with women voting, the Vaughn party (which seceded from the Socialist Party because of the latter's opposition to conscription) was unable to elect a single candidate. In Queensland too the socialists have had a sweeping victory, and the control of the next Federal Government will be in the hands of militant International Socialists. Could Germany ask anything better?

England, without allowing the people any voice in the matter, has made the appalling mistake of enfranchising 6,000,000 women in war-time. The socialists, knowing well what a rich harvest that promises for them, are putting up between 300 and 400 candidates for Parliament. One of these is Mrs. Philip Snowden, the Socialist, who has adorned many suffrage platforms in this country. If Germany can prolong the war until the Socialists in England, strengthened by woman suffrage, have had time to get in their deadly work, Germany can hope to annex England as she annexed Finland and Russia.

Germany's last and greatest victory would come with the passage of the Susan B. Anthony amendment by the Senate of the United States. At the very beginning of the war, Germany sent a clever agent to the United States, Frau Rozsika Schwimmer, to work for woman suffrage in this country. Why?

The pro-German Socialists in New York City worked so hard for woman suffrage that they fastened it on the State. Why? They declared that by 1920, when the foreign Socialist women have had time to be naturalized, Socialism in New York will be unbeatable. What could Germany ask better?

Every anti-American element in the country favors woman suffrage. Why?

Every man and woman arrested and convicted of disloyalty is an ardent advocate of woman suffrage. Why?

There is reason to believe that woman suffrage has been part of the German propaganda in Finland, Russia and England, as we know it has been in America. Will the Senate walk into the trap? With America and England in the grip of the suffrage-Socialist-pacifist element—and Socialism and pacifism follow woman suffrage as certainly as night follows day—Prussia can rule the world.

The Politicization of German Women

SOURCES

79. Emma Stropp, "Die deutschen Frauen und ihr neues Recht," *Land und Frau*, 2, no. 50 (14 December 1918), 394-95. Tr. SGB. The editors are grateful to Renate Bridenthal for drawing their attention to this document.

80. Luise Zietz, "Die Frauen im Reichsparliament," *Die Kämpferin*, 1/2 (1919-20), no. 8 (29 April 1920), 59-60. Tr. SGB.

At the time of Germany's defeat in 1918, the country's economy was in total disarray. The imperial government and the right wing and center parties feared a combined workers' and soldiers' revolution similar to that of Russia in 1917. To forestall such an event, the cabinet forced the Kaiser to abdicate, and a democratic republic with a social democratic majority was established at Weimar on 9 November 1918. The constitution of the so-called Weimar Republic, ratified in August 1919, incorporated emancipating measures for women in order to pacify and to some extent outmaneuver the militant socialist left. These measures were included in Article 128, which stipulated equality of the sexes before the law and the admission of women as well as men to all public functions irrespective of sex. Thus, German women were given not only the vote but the right to serve in the National Assembly (the Reichstag) as well.

Because the Weimar Republic established a system of proportional representation of political parties with lists of candidates, the electorate voted for the party list, rather than for individual office-seekers. Thus, in the first decade of political emancipation, forty-one German women found themselves elected to the Reichstag. Their numbers offered a stunning contrast to the situation in both the United States Congress and the British Parliament, where the requirement for individual candidacy limited the number of women elected to a handful, even though Anglo-American women had sought to participate in political life far more actively than had their German counterparts.

The first selection is by Emma Stropp (Doc. 73), a frequent contributor to *Land und Frau*, the journal of the National Federation of Agricultural Housewives' Associations. Stropp's article appeared almost immediately after the dramatic toppling of the imperial regime and exemplifies the mood of rural conservatism forced to come to terms with a new world in which, it was assumed, urban industrial workers would play a prominent political role. Stropp makes clear that traditional socialist emphasis on women's involvement in political action was well understood, when she insisted on the need to overcome conservative German women's inertia regarding politics.

The second selection is an article by Luise Korner Zietz (1865-1922). Zietz was the editor of *Die Kämpferin* (The Woman Fighter), a journal that represented independent socialist women from 1919 till Zietz's death in 1922. Zietz, who had been trained as a Froebel kindergarten teacher, had been active in social democratic politics since 1892, when she was twenty-seven years old, and had served as a writer, agitator, and organizer. She joined the Socialist Party in 1908, as soon as it was legally possible for a woman to do so, and soon became a member of the Party Executive Committee. She was, however, expelled from the committee early in 1916 because, like other prominent socialist women, she disagreed with the majority's support of the war and allied herself with Rosa Luxemburg's Independent Socialist Democratic Party (USDP) when it split off from the majority socialists who had the backing of the trades unions. Zietz became the USDP party secretary, and from January 1919 until June 1920 she represented the party in the Reichstag. Thus, her analysis of women's parliamentary participation (in the article from the *Kämpferin*, reprinted as the second selection) is an eyewitness account based on her own personal experience. It also reflects the ideas she had developed on the 104 occasions when, in contrast to most other female representatives, she spoke her mind in the Reichstag. Finally, this article exhibits Zietz's familiarity with the multiple aspects of the woman question, such as the employment of women, protection of mothers and infants, and the complexity of political struggles with agricultural female labor in a socialist state, about which she had published a number of books.

---

79. Emma Stropp (1918)

A new era has arrived; the storms of November have swept away everything we honored and held dear. In these weeks, many of our companions face the crumbling of hopes that seemed certain of fulfillment; they look into a country that is shrouded by heavy veils of mist. Will the sun ever again shine upon Germany? Will any new shoots and young blossoms follow this pitiless winter's night? Such anxious questions make our hearts tremble.

Surely Longfellow's great image "that above the clouds the sun is shining" is true also for us, the more so since all German forces in both country and city are prepared to work upon the land which is now so barren and lies before us in ruins. New fruit must and will thrive upon the land, but it will require hard and devoted labor to prepare the land, the hard and devoted labor of men and women.

Yes, women too, because through the collapse of the old regime women have gained a new right—a right that thrusts a new responsibility upon their shoulders. They now have a duty to participate in the elections and vote upon the constitutional organization of the National Assembly and upon the future parliament and the basic form and development of the building of the new state, which will ensure our care and safety and that of our children.

Some country women who lived far from politics and found full satisfaction in their domestic activity will say: "What is the new right to us? We didn't want it!" And they add indignantly: "Politics is men's business."

No, it is no longer men's business. That dream has been dreamed long enough, that dream of a protected and sheltered womanhood, concerned only with its domestic duties involving the family and the care of the sick and needy. The delicate veil that screened big events from your view and shielded your ears from the conflicts of the day has been whisked away. That veil was torn away from the dreamers most harshly and violently on the ninth of November. The twenty-one and a half million women who will go to the polls to determine the future of Germany, with only eighteen million men, find themselves in a new era. The figures speak for themselves and emphasize the great excess of women's votes over men's. And there is another figure. At the last election 40% of all votes were cast for the Social Democrats. Who will not admit that since that time the followers of this party have multiplied infinitely, owing to their support of many past occurrences and to a most dedicated and effective canvassing. This canvassing was conducted not only by men, but by social democratic women who have long been politically organized and who have used the full weight of their extremely important influence in their homes and families in order to fill the ranks of their party members ever more solidly.

Meanwhile, what have bourgeois women done in politics? Almost nothing at all. Only about 800,000 of them who are incorporated in the Union of Women's Federations are politically organized. This is not to offer reproaches, but merely to answer the question: "Why should I be concerned with politics?"

Whoever asks this question today does not recognize the seriousness of the times; she lays upon herself a heavy burden of guilt which neither can nor will ever be forgiven. Red flames leap sky-high from the devastated house. And in the light of these flames, who dares to say, "How does this concern me?"

Whether women have previously opposed or approved of female suffrage is now irrelevant. Today *all* bourgeois women must vote; we cannot have elections that *strengthen our political opponents.*

The time remaining to us before the great day of the battle between two world views must be used by German women in preparation for that day. So that they may be armed, not as "voting beasts"—forgive this crude expression—but as far as possible in this short time to vote from their own convictions, with their votes as women.

Opportunities to educate oneself for that day are being promoted in the cities and in the country. The great women's organizations are tirelessly at work stimulating and spreading discussion and understanding of the most important current economic and political questions, through education courses, through civic and political lectures. We must take advantage of these opportunities.

Housewives and mothers should avail themselves of these opportunities; they should try to take along their female domestics as well as those young people who are not yet of voting age. What women have missed, whether through their own fault or not, must not be neglected in their daughters, for they will soon be citizens with full political rights. Unfortunately, the good intentions of the present government have set the voting-age limit extremely low. Twenty-year-old women comrades in working circles know very well for which party they will vote. However, among rural domestic servants we shall find many girls who are completely naïve politically, but whose ballots have the same impact as those of more knowledgeable women. Therefore, they should not be contemptuously neglected but rather one should try to persuade them and to counsel them tactfully, and through friendly discussion awaken their understanding of the great duty they must discharge.

Wives of owners of country estates and their daughters must also not neglect to find political and economic instruction in the newspapers. They must read leading articles in the news section, before the short stories and miscellaneous material; they must get to know and think through the programs of individual parties; they must become members of whatever bourgeois party speaks to their own interpretation of what must be pursued and what can be achieved. This entry into a specific political organization must not be undervalued; it offers a feeling of belonging that strengthens and vitalizes. This is especially necessary for women who are newcomers to political life and who are still largely prey to emotions that might influence purely practical evaluation of thought. In addition, the economic strength and thus the power and sphere of the party's canvassing activity grows even through minimal membership dues. One should consider what the working woman has done for her party with her annual contribution of 12 marks or more, and should ask oneself what one has done personally to further one's political conviction.

Thus, through their new rights, German women are charged with a number of duties. They may be compared to tools for sharpening the plough that will furrow the desolated acres so that fruitful seeds may take root. The seeds themselves, however, are the votes cast by men and women for the national assembly—there must be no empty kernels. It is the duty of German women in city and country to ensure this; in their hands lies the future of Germany. Let them be fully aware of the great responsibility that their new rights have laid on them.

80. Luise Zietz (1920)

All political parties, even those fundamentally opposed to women's suffrage, added women to their list of candidates for the National Assembly in preferred areas.

Thus women members represent all political perspectives. And in this manner, those political parties which were (and still are) opposed to women's suffrage are forced to recognize the fact, if not the principle, of both active and passive female suffrage. [That is, to have the vote and to be a candidate for office.—EDS.]

In order to make the best possible use of women's suffrage, that is in order to win as many women's votes outside the narrow circle of party membership as possible, they [the anti-female-suffragists] were obliged to put potentially successful women of their parties on their slate of candidates, against their principles and thus [in spite of themselves, helping] women to achieve their right to representation.

Little or nothing has been gained for social laws or for the actual achievement of equal rights for women by electing female representatives of bourgeois parties or even of right-wing socialists.

We now see very clearly how mistaken was the view that the introduction of limited women's suffrage for proletarian women would achieve the minimum—the first step for equality of suffrage. The contrary has happened.

Bourgeois women have used limited suffrage as a weapon to deprive proletarian women of their right and thus to weaken social democratic influence. It was impossible either to create a union of all female representatives in order to bring about some improvements for their "poorer sisters," or to reform civic rights, now cut from capitalist cloth, for all women.

Only twice have all female representatives worked together; both times, the interests of capitalism were unaffected: once, when it was a matter of expediting the repatriation of prisoners of war (and then we had to ensure that the resolution was not used for nationalistic purposes), and on another occasion, when we protested against the ruthless expulsion of female workers and employees from their jobs as a result of the demobilization law. However, when we attempted to abolish existing laws of exception against *illegitimate children* and their mothers, bourgeois female representatives voted against our motion as did their male colleagues.

Understandably enough!

The definitions of bourgeois laws, according to which an illegitimate child and its mother have diminished rights, reflect the moral double-standard for men and women. This standard is rooted in *private property* which developed an institution based on monogamy and the family, the force of which ensures the father's property for his legitimate children.

Just as Abraham chased Hagar and Ishmael into the desert when in old age he fathered a legitimate son to whom he wished to leave his property, so today exceptional laws in the bourgeois codes erect fences that imprison the illegitimate child and its mother in the desert of social outlawry and economic need, while they protect the property of the father and his legitimate family. In this matter the entire bourgeoisie stands together.

In these cases female members of the Reichstag belonging to the bourgeois parties do not consider themselves as representatives of women's interests, but as protectors of capital.

We experienced the same thing when we proposed the abolition of special laws against prostitutes that were becoming a danger even for decent women—laws through which prostitutes, who are sacrifices to our social order, sink ever more deeply into the mire of our moral degeneracy. No one in the rarefied atmosphere of the Upper House wanted to hear of such matters. Men as well as women of the bourgeoisie declined to discuss our proposal.

Even our proposal to abolish the law that female teachers and civil servants must leave the work force when they marry was defeated. Women of the Center, of the National, and of the Democratic parties polarized against us from the most diverse motives. The vague resolution that all laws of exception against female civil servants and teachers were to be abolished served these women as a fig-leaf to hide their reactionary position. In practice, everything has remained as before in every state of the republic.

The wildest results occurred when the law concerning federal aid to women in child-bed was discussed and dismissed.

Bourgeois and right-wing socialist female representatives polarized and voted against our proposals to provide the following for women during pregnancy and childbirth:

(1) Welfare payments during 8 weeks of pregnancy, at the basic minimum wage (that is, twice the usual sickness benefit).

(2) Childbirth support for 8 weeks at the minimum wage.

(3) Free and obligatory midwifery services and, when necessary, medical assistance during pregnancy problems and delivery.

(4) Maternity benefits for 26 weeks at the same level as sickness benefits.

(5) Obligatory family care for the insured.

Instead of the obligatory midwifery services, a sum of 50 marks was decided upon; childbed support at the level of sickness benefits only, and recovery support for only 13 weeks at a totally inadequate level of half the usual sickness benefits; added to which, insurance premiums were increased enormously. Here the most important questions of the life of mother and child were being gambled with, and all the female representatives voted them down—because the state has no funds!

The interests of capitalism are prized more highly than the life of human beings.

All these things must become common knowledge as widely as possible in women's circles so that female voters may draw the proper conclusions before the approaching elections.

In your meetings, in your workplace conferences, and among your friends, you comrades must discuss these problems.

Therefore, go forth and sow the seeds of socialism and rally around our banner of independent social democrats all those who are troubled and suffering in their struggle against capitalism and for their own liberation.

Tell them: wherever the banners of independents are hoisted, there you will find fighters for women's rights and women's protection.

CHAPTER 9

The Revolution in Life and Morals

The Improvement of Motherhood

SOURCES

81. Margaret Sanger, *Woman and the New Race*, with a preface by Havelock Ellis (New York, 1920), pp. 4-8.

82. "The Soviet Decree on the Legalization of Abortion, 18 November 1920," in N. A. Semashko, *Health Protection in the U.S.S.R.* (London, 1934), pp. 82-84.

83. Aleksandra Kollontai, "The Labour of Women in the Evolution of the Economy" (1923), tr. and reprinted in *The Family in the U.S.S.R.*, ed. Rudolf Schlesinger (London, 1949), pp. 51-55. Originally published in Russian.

Nineteenth-century attacks on the sexual double standard (Docs. 11, 12, 41-43, 54), coupled with the influential writing of psychologists like Havelock Ellis who insisted on the normalcy of female sexuality, and of eugenicists whose concern was to eradicate the low standard of living of the poor, promoted the notion of voluntary and quality motherhood. In the United States, in western Europe, and in Russia the war and the revolution had brought to a head public concern over the plight of orphaned and illegitimate children, and of widowed and deserted mothers who were incapable of, or too poor to, support their offspring. This issue was soon taken up by writers who popularized the psychological aspect of the problem as well as practical and legal ways of dealing with it. Romantic and idealistic sex manuals like Dr. Marie Stopes' *Married Love* (1918), which for the first time described the sexual act in clear and simple language, sold millions of copies on both sides of the Atlantic. Such books were soon followed by others offering simplified instructions on birth-control methods, since it had become clear that a growing acceptance of women's sexuality must be accompanied by recognition of the likelihood of conception. Dr. Aletta Jacobs had opened the world's first successful birth-control clinic in Amsterdam as early as 1882, but it was not until 1916 that the American Margaret Sanger (1883-1966) founded— and was promptly arrested for opening—the first birth-control clinic in the United States.

Margaret Higgins Sanger was one of eleven children of an Irish stonecutter's family in upstate New York. She suggested in her autobiography that her mother had died, worn out with the bearing of children conceived in consequence of her father's unchecked passion. Nevertheless, Sanger herself inherited from her father a stubborn iconoclasm that enabled her to fight vigorously to realize her controversial goals, even against tremendous opposition. Too poor to attend medical school as she had hoped, Sanger trained as a nurse. She married an artist and, after the birth of their three children, the Sangers moved to New York City. While associating with anarchists and socialists in the metropolis, she was introduced to the works of Kropotkin and Key (Docs. 22, 26, 48) and to the psychosexology of Krafft-Ebing, Freud, Edward Carpenter, and Havelock Ellis. The ideas of these writers, coupled with Sanger's own experiences as an obstetric nurse in the overcrowded slums of New York's Lower East Side (where she had witnessed many deaths among women who had sought illegal abortions), propelled her into a lifelong mission to promote effective and easily available contraceptive methods.

The first selection, from Sanger's *Woman and the New Race*, presents her impassioned plea for women's creation, in full freedom and knowledge, of loved and desired children who by their very scarcity would rid the world of war. Paralleling Sanger's work are two selections from Soviet Russia. The Soviet government's 1920 decree legalizing abortion was grounded in the belief that concern for the improvement of motherhood would eventually make abortions unnecessary, but that in the meantime it was important to safeguard women's health by eradicating incompetent and unhygienic clandestine abortions. The chief proponent of this measure, Nikolai A. Semashko (1874-1949) was an ardent Russian revolutionary who had gone to Paris with Lenin in 1911. After his return in 1917 he was appointed the first People's Commissar of Health. In the 1920's he became the first professor of social hygiene at Moscow University and editor of the Soviet *Medical Encyclopedia*. One of the features of Semashko's decree, it should be noted, was to transfer control of abortion from village midwives to the male-dominated medical profession.

The selection from Aleksandra Kollontai, the Bolshevik government's first Commissar of Public Welfare (Doc. 77), presents the Soviet regime's view of improved motherhood which, like that of Margaret Sanger, stressed women's indispensable contribution as mothers to the newly revolutionized state. It is important to emphasize that these counsels for birth control, whether they came from men or women, whether they originated from the English scientist Marie Stopes, the American nurse Margaret Sanger, the Soviet People's Commissar of Health Nikolai Semashko, or the Soviet writer and revolutionary activist Aleksandra Kollontai, all posited that the ultimate social goal was to foster the birth of improved and healthier children for the nation, and not—as it was so often mistakenly thought—to license individual female promiscuity.

---

81. Margaret Sanger (1920)

The creators of over-population are the women, who, while wringing their hands over each fresh horror, submit anew to their task of producing the multitudes who will bring about the *next* tragedy of civilization.

While unknowingly laying the foundations of tyrannies and providing the human tinder for racial conflagrations, woman was also unknowingly creating slums, filling asylums with insane, and institutions with other defectives. She was replenishing the ranks of the prostitutes, furnishing grist for the criminal courts and inmates for prisons. Had she planned deliberately to achieve this tragic total of human waste and misery, she could hardly have done it more effectively.

Woman's passivity under the burden of her disastrous task was almost altogether that of ignorant resignation. She knew virtually nothing about her reproductive nature and less about the consequences of her excessive childbearing. It is true that, obeying the inner urge of their natures, *some* women revolted. They went even to the extreme of infanticide and abortion. Usually their revolts were not general enough. They fought as individuals, not as a mass. In the mass they sank back into blind and hopeless subjection. They went on breeding with staggering rapidity those numberless, undesired children who become the clogs and the destroyers of civilizations.

To-day, however, woman is rising in fundamental revolt. Even her efforts at mere reform are, as we shall see later, steps in that direction. Underneath each of them is the feminine urge to complete freedom. Millions of women are asserting their right to voluntary motherhood. They are determined to decide for themselves whether they shall become mothers, under what conditions and when. This is the fundamental revolt referred to. It is for women the key to the temple of liberty.

Even as birth control is the means by which woman attains basic freedom, so it is the means by which she must and will uproot the evil she has wrought through her submission. As she has unconsciously and ignorantly brought about social disaster, so must and will she consciously and intelligently *undo* that disaster and create a new and a better order.

The task is hers. It cannot be avoided by excuses, nor can it be delegated. It is not enough for woman to point to the self-evident domination of man. Nor does it avail to plead the guilt of rulers and the exploiters of labor. It makes no difference that she does not formulate industrial systems nor that she is an instinctive believer in social justice. In her submission lies her error and her guilt. By her failure to withhold the multitudes of children who have made inevitable the most flagrant of our social evils, she incurred a debt to society. Regardless of her own wrongs, regardless of her lack of opportunity and regardless of all other considerations, *she* must pay that debt.

She must not think to pay this debt in any superficial way. She cannot pay it with palliatives—with child-labor laws, prohibition, regulation of prostitution and agitation against war. Political nostrums and social panaceas are but incidentally and superficially useful. They do not touch the source of the social disease.

War, famine, poverty and oppression of the workers will continue while woman makes life cheap. They will cease only when she limits her reproductivity and human life is no longer a thing to be wasted.

Two chief obstacles hinder the discharge of this tremendous obligation. The first and the lesser is the legal barrier. Dark-Age laws would still deny to her the knowledge of her reproductive nature. Such knowledge is indispensable to intelligent motherhood and she must achieve it, despite absurd statutes and equally absurd moral canons.

The second and more serious barrier is her own ignorance of the extent and effect of her submission. Until she knows the evil her subjection has wrought to herself, to her progeny and to the world at large, she cannot wipe out that evil.

To get rid of these obstacles is to invite attack from the forces of reaction which are so strongly entrenched in our present-day society. It means warfare in every phase of her life. Nevertheless, at whatever cost, she must emerge from her ignorance and assume her responsibility.

She can do this only when she has awakened to a knowledge of herself and of the consequences of her ignorance. The first step is birth control. Through birth control she will attain to voluntary motherhood. Having attained this, the basic freedom of her sex, she will cease to enslave herself and the mass of humanity. Then, through the understanding of the intuitive forward urge within her, she will not stop at patching up the world; she will remake it.

82. The Soviet Decree on the Legalization of Abortion (1920)

During the past decades the number of women resorting to artificial discontinuation of pregnancy has grown both in the West and in this country. The legislation of all countries combats this evil by punishing the woman who chooses to have an abortion and the doctor who makes it. Without leading to favourable results, this method of combating abortions has driven the operation underground and made the woman a victim of mercenary and often ignorant quacks who make a profession of secret operations. As a result, up to 50 per cent of such women are infected in the course of operation, and up to 4 per cent of them die.

The Workers' and Peasants' Government is conscious of this serious evil to the community. It combats this evil by propaganda against abortions among working women. By working for socialism, and by introducing the protection of maternity and infancy on an extensive scale, it feels assured of achieving the gradual disappearance of this evil. But as the moral survivals of the past and the difficult economic conditions of the present still compel many women to resort to this operation, the People's Commissariats of Health and of Justice, anxious to protect the health of the women and considering that the method of repressions in this field fails entirely to achieve this aim, have decided:

(1) To permit such operations to be made freely and without any charge in Soviet hospitals, where conditions are assured of minimising the harm of the operation.

(2) Absolutely to forbid anyone but a doctor to carry out this operation.

(3) Any nurse or midwife found guilty of making such an operation will be deprived of the right to practise, and tried by a People's Court.

(4) A doctor carrying out an abortion in his private practice with mercenary aims will be called to account by a People's Court.

83. Aleksandra Kollontai (1923)

The reduction of woman's fruitless labour in the household is only one side of her emancipation. Care of children and their upbringing was no less a burden, chaining her to the house, enslaving her in the family. This burden is completely lifted from women's shoulders by the Soviet government and its communist policy of safeguarding motherhood and of social upbringing and is placed on the social collective, on the working country.

In its pursuit of new forms of life, morals and economy which should correspond to the interests of the proletariat, the Soviet Republic inevitably made a number of mistakes and revised, straightened out its line. But in the realm of safeguarding motherhood and social upbringing the Workers' Republic immediately found the right approach. And it is precisely in this field that the greatest, the most far-reaching revolution of morals and views is taking place. Problems which in a bourgeois system are incapable of solution are solved naturally and simply in a country where private property is abolished and where policy is prompted by a desire to raise the nation's economy.

Soviet Russia approached the question of safeguarding motherhood from the angle of the chief problem of the Workers' Republic: the problem of developing the country's productive power, of establishing and increasing production. If this is to be brought about it is first of all necessary to release as much man-power as possible from fruitless labour, to utilize properly all available working hands for the country's production; secondly, to assure the Workers' Republic of an incessant flow of fresh workers in the future, i.e., to safeguard the natural increase of population.

As soon as this point of view is adopted, the problem of freeing women from the burden of motherhood is automatically solved. The working country establishes an entirely new principle: the care of the new generation of children is no longer a task confined to the family, but rests on the community, the country. Motherhood must be safeguarded not only in the interest of women, but even more so to meet the difficulties of the national economy in its transformation into a workers' system: it is necessary to save women's strength from being wasted on the family in order to employ it more reasonably for the benefit of the collective; it is necessary to preserve their health in order to guarantee a steady stream of fit workers for the Workers' Republic in the future. In a bourgeois country such an attitude towards the motherhood problem would be impossible; the class-struggle and lack of agreement between private and national economic interests would make it so. In a Workers' Republic, on the other hand, where the individual economic effort is absorbed by the national economy and where the classes disintegrate, disappear—such a solution of the motherhood problem is dictated by life and sheer necessity. The Workers' Republic treats women primarily as participants in its production efforts; the mother's function is held to be a highly important but complementary obligation, not only towards the private family, but to society.

"Our policy in safeguarding motherhood and babyhood," as Comrade Vera Pavlovna Lebedeva says quite rightly, "is guided by the fact that we always look upon woman as a worker."

But in order to enable woman to participate in productive work without forcing her nature, without abandoning motherhood, a second step was necessary: the removal of all cares connected with motherhood from the individual woman's shoulders, transferring them to the collective and thus recognizing that the rearing of children transcends family limits and is a social, a State institution.

Motherhood is looked at from a new angle: the Soviet government regards it as a social obligation. With this principle in mind the Soviet government outlines a number of reforms tending to lift the burden of motherhood from woman's shoulders and to place it on the State. Care of babies, economic protection of children, proper establishment of social education—the Soviet government undertakes all this through the Subdepartment of Safeguarding Motherhood and Babyhood (headed by Comrade V. P. Lebedeva) and through the Narkompros (People's Commissariat for Education) Department for Social Education.

To remove the cares of motherhood but leave untouched the joyous smile which is born of woman's contact with her child—such is the Soviet government's principle in solving the motherhood problem. Naturally this principle is far from being fully implemented. In practice we lag behind our intentions. In our endeavours to create new forms of life and morals which would free the working woman from family obligations, we are stumbling over the same old obstacles: our poverty and economic distress. But the foundations have been laid, the signposts pointing the road to the solution of the motherhood problem erected; it remains to follow the road indicated determinedly and firmly.

The Workers' Republic does not limit itself to safeguarding motherhood financially and giving the mother the sort of help we discussed in the last lecture. It intends above all to change the system and to reform living conditions in a manner which will give women every chance to combine motherhood with rearing the baby for the Republic, to surround it with the necessary care and attention.

Since the first months of the existence of the dictatorship of the proletariat in Russia the government of peasants and workers has been engaged in an attempt to cover working Russia with a network of institutions for safeguarding motherhood and for social education. The mother and the baby became objects of special care for Soviet policy. When I was People's Commissar of Social Security during the first months of the Revolution my first job was to map out the course which the Workers' Republic was to follow in its policy of safeguarding the interests of women both as units of man-power and as mothers.

It was then that the College for Safeguarding Motherhood was set up and work begun on the exemplary "Palace of Motherhood." Since then, under the direction of that able and energetic worker, Comrade V. P. Lebedeva, the enterprise of safeguarding motherhood has grown in scope and taken firm root.

The Soviet government hastens to help working women from the moment of their pregnancy. Facilities for medical consultation for expectant and nursing mothers are available all over Russia. In Imperial Russia there were only six centres for consultation—now there are 200 of them, and 138 milk kitchens.

But, of course, the chief task is to relieve the working mother of her unproductive worries concerning physical care for the baby. Motherhood does not by any means necessarily consist in changing napkins, washing the baby, and being chained to the cradle. The social obligation of motherhood consists primarily in producing a healthy and fit-for-life child. To make this possible the working society must provide the most suitable conditions for pregnant women; while the woman herself must observe all the requirements of hygiene during the period of pregnancy, remembering that during these months she does not belong to herself, that she is working for the collective, that from her own flesh and blood she is "producing" a new unit of labour, a new member of the Workers' Republic. Her second obligation, from the point of view of the mother's social task, is to feed the baby at her own breast. Only after having done this has the woman, as member of the working collective, the right to say that her social obligation towards the child is fulfilled. The remaining cares for the growing generation can be passed on to the collective. Naturally the maternal instinct is strong and we should not let it die out. But why should this instinct be confined exclusively to narrow love and care for one's own baby? Why not let this instinct, so precious for working humanity, branch out and rise to its highest level—that of caring about other children, equally helpless though not one's own, and of devoting love and attention to other babies?

The watchword which the Workers' Republic proclaims to the wide masses of women—"Be the mother not only of your own child, but of the children of the peasants and workers"—should teach working women a new approach to motherhood. Is it conceivable, for instance, that a mother, who may in many cases be a Communist, should refuse her breast to another's baby ailing for shortage of milk, merely because it is not her own child? Humanity of the future, communist in its feelings and conceptions, will be as surprised by such an act of egotism and unsociableness as we are to-day when we read that a native woman who loves her own baby tenderly has with great relish consumed the baby belonging to a woman of another tribe.

Or another perversion: is it conceivable that a mother should deprive her own baby of her milk, so as not to burden herself with looking after the infant? But the fact is that the number of foundlings in Soviet Russia is increasing at an intolerable rate. True, this state of affairs is made possible by the fact that the motherhood problem, though on the way to solution, is as yet unsolved. Hundreds of thousands of women during this difficult period of transition succumb under the double burden of daily work and motherhood. The number of crèches, nurseries, and maternity homes is insufficient; financial assistance cannot keep pace with the rise in prices for goods on the open market: all this makes working women, women in employment, afraid of motherhood and makes mothers leave their children at the State's doorstep. But this increase in the number of foundlings also shows that the women of the Workers' Republic have not yet fully realized that motherhood is not a private matter but a social obligation.

State, Church, and the Population Question

SOURCES

84. The French Decree Establishing Medals for Mothers, *Journal Officiel de la République Française*, 28 May 1920, p. 7815: Letter from the Minister of Hygiene, Jules-Louis Breton, 26 May 1920. Tr. KMO.

85. "Loi de 31 Juillet 1920," as reprinted in Roger Guerrand, *La Libre Maternité, 1896-1969* (Tournai, 1971), p. 149. Tr. KMO.

86. Pius XI, "Casti Connubii," 31 December 1930 (On Christian Marriage in Our Day; De matrimonio christiano spectatis praesentibus familiae et societatis conditionibus, necessitatibus, erroribus, vitiis). English text in Joseph Husslein, ed., *Social Wellsprings: Eighteen Encyclicals of Social Reconstruction, by Pius XI*, II (Milwaukee, Wisc., 1949), 143-45, 146-49, 150-51.

87. Winifred Holtby, "The Pope and Female Modesty," in Holtby, *Women and a Changing Civilization* (London, 1934), pp. 170-74.

Toward the end of the Great War some nations and individuals in Western society attempted to institutionalize progressive approaches to sexuality and reproduction by legalizing birth control and by setting up public birth control and abortion clinics. Reaction was swift and far-reaching, especially from the Catholic Church and from nations who feared for their status in the international power sweepstakes as a consequence of population stagnation. In France alarm over population figures had grown steadily throughout the nineteenth century (Docs. 27-29); the loss of lives in the First World War aggravated the problem still more. France was therefore one of the first nations to attempt to encourage births through legislation. Meanwhile, in Italy leaders of the Catholic Church grew increasingly concerned about the swelling membership of the Italian Communist party. The example of the secular pragmatism of the new Bolshevik state in Russia, in legalizing birth control and abortion, was not lost on the economically depressed and increasingly hungry Italian proletariat. Therefore the pope, representing the church, spoke out against an international trend that challenged some two thousand years of Christian dogma on human procreation and family life.

As the first two selections in this section, we have chosen documents illustrating the efforts of the French government in the year 1920 to bolster the birthrate. The first, an official letter to the president of the Republic, accompanied the text of a governmental decree establishing a series of awards for worthy mothers, known as "Medals of the French Family." The author of this letter and of the accompanying decree, the French minister of hygiene Jules-Louis Breton (1872-

1940), was born in Courrières (Pas-de-Calais). Breton had studied chemistry and retained an active interest in science and scientific policy throughout his career as a journalist and, later on, as a legislator. In political life he always identified himself with the "far left" and the staunchly anticlerical Groupe Républicain Socialiste. He served as minister of health in three ministries and became well known as "minister of natality" because of his efforts to encourage large families; indeed, the motherhood medals of 1920 became known as Breton's Medals. The concept of offering awards to worthy mothers of large families was later adopted by Mussolini, Hitler, and Stalin in their respective programs to encourage population growth.

The second selection, the French anti-abortion and anti-contraception law (referred to by its opponents as the "abominable law") was enacted two months after Breton's decree for the medals of the French family. This law, prohibiting the dissemination of contraceptive methods, was the first of a series of ever more stringent laws (1923, 1939) that set down heavy prison sentences for women convicted of undergoing abortions and could deprive physicians performing abortions of their licenses to practice.

The third selection is excerpted from one of the most famous and still most quoted papal encyclicals, the "Casti Connubii" of Pius XI. This pope, Ambrose-Damien-Achille Ratti (1857-1939), gained favor for his scholarship in Christian history and for his social programs. His papacy is remembered for his resolution (in cooperation with Mussolini) of the breach between church and state in Italy, for his uncompromising opposition to communism (he had experienced the Bolshevik invasion of Poland in 1919 while he was papal nuncio in Warsaw), and for his support for Franco during the Spanish Civil War. In the encyclical "On Christian Marriage," Pius XI updated the statements on Christian doctrine elaborated in 1880 by Leo XIII (Doc. 44), in light of the growing political and eugenic attacks on traditional doctrine. While the French government's laws and decrees had concerned themselves only implicitly with female liberty as a by-product of individual choice through birth control and family limitation, the pope, writing ten years later, alluded explicitly to the advances made in female emancipation following the war and in the granting of suffrage in several Western countries, and to the entry of women into the professions and politics. His reaction to these developments was clearly exacerbated by the Bolshevik legislation on sexual morality (Doc. 82) and by Anglo-American proponents of birth control like Marie Stopes and Margaret Sanger (Doc. 81).

The final selection is from the British novelist and journalist Winifred Holtby (1898-1935). Holtby was born in Yorkshire, the daughter of middle-class parents. Her mother was an active member of the elected county council. Holtby had joined the Women's Army Auxiliary Corps (WAACS) at the end of the war. In 1919, at the age of twenty-one, she took up her scholarship at Somerville College, Oxford, alongside returning undergraduate servicemen. This preparation gave her an experience of life unusual among earlier members of the Oxbridge women's colleges. After graduation she set up house with a former college friend, Vera Brittain. Together they joined the newly founded "Six Points Group," an organization chaired by Lady Rhondda, the publisher of the weekly *Time and Tide*. The Six Points Group pledged to work for six closely connected objectives concerning the status of women: (1) pensions for widows; (2) equal right of guardianship for married parents; (3) improvement of the laws dealing with child assault; (4) improvement of the laws dealing with the position of the unmarried mother; (5) equal pay for male and female teachers; and (6) equal opportunities for men and women in the civil service.

Soon thereafter Holtby joined *Time and Tide* as a roving reporter. In 1926, after a lecture tour in South Africa, she became one of the youngest directors on the board of the journal, and a colleague of Rebecca West (Doc. 96).

One of Holtby's last works before her untimely death at the age of thirty-seven was her book, *Women and a Changing Civilization*, from which this selection is excerpted. In this book she analyzed economic and political events from a historical perspective. As is clear from her remarks about Pius's encyclical, Holtby understood the continuing fragility of women's new-found opportunities in a male-dominated society; moreover, she was keenly concerned about the all-too-evident connection between Catholic dogma and the opportunistic, dictatorial authoritarianism over the family that had been cast in concrete by the pope's 1929 concordat with Mussolini.

---

84. The French Decree Establishing Medals for Mothers (1920)

Monsieur le Président,

The raising of the birthrate, which our country must undertake in order to retain the rank in which victory has placed us and to permit us to harvest all its fruits, is above all a moral question.

Therefore we must neglect nothing that can encourage French mothers to give maternity the place it ought to have in the ideals of those who found a home. Mothers should be honored as they ought to be; they should feel surrounded by the pious respect and the deferential solicitude of their co-citizens, instead of colliding with the indifference—not to say the spite—of the public; the importance and grandeur of her social role should be apparent to everyone's eyes; and the mother—far from regarding as intolerable the trials, suffering, even the dangers that are inseparable from childbirth, and rejecting them as if they contradicted her destiny—would nobly accept them with legitimate pride as a part of her patrimony as a spouse.

Between these two sentiments—the one egotistical, where the individual thinks only of her own well-being, the other altruistic, where she hopes to perpetuate her race and her country beyond her own life—the state does not have the right to remain neutral. The Republic ought to testify in a striking manner to her gratitude and respect toward those who contribute the most to maintaining, through their descendants, the genius and civilization, the influence and radiance of France.

The decree we have the honor of presenting for your signature, which expresses the unanimous resolution of the Supreme Council on Natality, establishes under the name of "medal of the French family" an order of honorary compensations for mothers who have undertaken the task of raising numerous children in a dignified manner. For this work a testament of public esteem is due to them and will be given to them along with a bronze medal if they have raised at least five living children, the last of which has reached the age of one. The medal will be silver if this number is eight, and gold, if it reaches ten.

We insist on the point that, in order to be worthy of this award, it is not sufficient just to bear children, but it is necessary to know how to raise them and to make a point upon every occasion, by counsel and by example, of inculcating in them a healthy moral education.

Naturally it is not a question of the State, which respects all philosophies and all beliefs, intervening in the domain reserved for the freedom of parents, nor meddling in their manner of understanding the education given to their children.

We do not intend to judge this matter except from outside, and by taking an exclusively objective stance, based on facts observable to everyone. Do the parents live an honorable life? Do their children, on the whole, show signs of conforming to this good example, as is natural for children whose mother has watched over them? We must not go beyond this test; but we cannot retreat from it either. The testimony of merit and esteem that we have in mind will be applicable only to truly meritorious families, esteemed as such by their co-citizens.

Thus will their value be understood; and we like to think that the humble ribbon, which will remind everyone of this testimony of respect and national recognition, will have the greatest value in the eyes of the mothers who vest all their pride in the number and value of their children.

Therefore I ask you, *monsieur le Président*, to render to mothers of large families the homage that is their due, by adding your signature to the following decree which, we know in advance, responds fully to your own sentiments.

85. "Loi de 31 Juillet 1920"

Article 1. A sentence of six months to three years in prison and a fine of one hundred to three thousand francs will be levied against any person who advocates the crime of abortion, even when such advocacy does not achieve a specific result, whether by means of speeches given in public places or assemblies, or by the selling, placing on sale, or by private offering, or by the display, posting, or distribution in the public throughfare or in public places, or by the distribution at home, or through the mails, whether sealed or unsealed, or by any other means of distribution or transportation, of books, writings, printed matter, announcements, posters, drawings, pictures, or emblems, or by means of advertising of medical or so-called medical clinics.

Article 2. The same penalties will be levied against whomsoever sells, places for sale or allows to be sold, distributes or allows the distribution in whatever manner, of remedies, substances, instruments, or any objects in the knowledge that they are destined for use in committing the crime of abortion, even if such abortion is neither completed nor attempted, and even when such remedies, substances, instruments, or other objects proposed as efficacious means for abortion are, in reality, unsuitable for its accomplishment.

Article 3. A sentence of one to six months in prison and a fine of one hundred to five thousand francs will be levied against any person who, for the purpose of contraceptive propaganda, describes, divulges, or offers to reveal, by one of the means specified in Articles 1 and 2, the procedures for preventing pregnancy or facilitates the use of such procedures. The same penalties will apply to any person who actively engages in propagandizing in favor of contraception or against having children by any of the means designated in Article 23 of the law of 29 July 1881.

86. Pius XI (1930)

And now, Venerable Brethren, we shall explain in detail the evils opposed to each of the benefits of matrimony.

First consideration is due to the offspring, which many have the boldness to call the disagreeable burden of matrimony. This, they say, is to be carefully avoided by married people, not through virtuous continence (which Christian law permits in matrimony when both parties consent), but by frustrating the marriage act. Some justify this criminal abuse on the ground that they are weary of children and wish to gratify their desires without their consequent burden. Others say that they cannot on the one hand remain continent, nor on the other can they have children, because of the difficulties whether on the part of the mother or on the part of family circumstances.

But no reason, however grave, can be put forward by which anything intrinsically against nature may become conformable to nature and morally good. *Since, therefore, the conjugal act is destined primarily by nature for the begetting of children, those who in exercising it deliberately frustrate its natural power and purpose sin against nature and commit a deed which is shameful and intrinsically vicious.*

Small wonder, therefore, if Holy Writ bears witness that the Divine Majesty regards with greatest detestation this horrible crime and at times has punished it with death. As St. Augustine notes, "Intercourse even with one's legitimate wife is unlawful and wicked where the conception of the offspring is prevented. Onan, the son of Juda, did this and the Lord killed him for it."

Since, therefore, openly departing from the uninterrupted Christian tradition some recently have judged it possible solemnly to declare another doctrine regarding this question, the Catholic Church, to whom God has entrusted the defense of the integrity and purity of morals, standing erect in the midst of the moral ruin which surrounds her, that so she may preserve the chastity of the nuptial union from being defiled by this foul stain, raises her voice in token of her divine ambassadorship and through Our mouth proclaims anew: *any use whatsoever of matrimony exercised in such a way that the act is deliberately frustrated in its natural power to generate life is an offense against the law of God and of nature, and those who indulge in such are branded with the guilt of a grave sin.*

We admonish, therefore, priests who hear confessions and others who have the care of souls, in virtue of Our supreme authority and in Our solicitude for the salvation of souls, not to allow the faithful entrusted to them to err regarding this most grave law of God; much more, that they keep themselves immune from such false opinions, in no way conniving in them. . . .

Holy Church knows well that not infrequently one of the parties is sinned against rather than sinning, when for a grave cause he or she reluctantly allows the perversion of the right order. In such a case, there is no sin, provided that, mindful of the law of charity, he or she does not neglect to seek to dissuade and to deter the partner from sin. Nor are those considered as acting against nature who in the married state use their right in the proper manner although on account of natural reasons either of time or of certain defects, new life cannot be brought forth. For in matrimony as well as in the use of the matrimonial rights there are also secondary ends, such as mutual aid, the cultivating of mutual love, and the quieting of concupiscence which husband and wife are not forbidden to consider so long as these are subordinated to the primary end and so long as the intrinsic nature of the act is preserved.

We are deeply touched by the sufferings of those parents who, in extreme want, experience great difficulty in rearing their children.

However, they should take care lest the calamitous state of their external affairs should be the occasion for a much more calamitous error. *No difficulty can arise that justifies the putting aside of the law of God which forbids all acts intrinsically evil. There is no possible circumstance in which husband and wife cannot, strengthened by the grace of God, fulfill faithfully their duties and preserve in wedlock their chastity unspotted.*
. . .

But another very grave crime is to be noted, Venerable Brethren, which regards the taking of the life of the offspring hidden in the mother's womb. Some wish it to be allowed and left to the will of the father or the mother; others say it is unlawful unless there are weighty reasons which they call by the name of medical, social, or eugenic "indication." Because this matter falls under the penal laws of the state by which the destruction of the offspring begotten but unborn is forbidden, these people demand that the "indication," which in one form or another they defend, be recognized as such by the public law and in no way penalized. There are those, moreover, who ask that the public authorities provide aid for these death-dealing operations, a thing which, sad to say, everyone knows is of very frequent occurrence in some places.

As to the "medical and therapeutic indication" to which, using their own words, we have made reference, Venerable Brethren, *however much we may pity the mother whose health and even life is gravely imperiled in the performance of the duty allotted to her by nature, nevertheless what could ever be a sufficient reason for excusing in any way the direct murder of the innocent?* This is precisely what we are dealing with here. Whether inflicted upon the mother or upon the child, it is against the precept of God and the law of nature: "Thou shall not kill": The life of each

is equally sacred, and no one has the power, not even the public authority, to destroy it. It is of no use to appeal to the right of taking away life,
for here it is a question of the innocent, whereas that right has regard
only to the guilty. Nor is there question here of defense by bloodshed
against an unjust aggressor (for who would call an innocent child an unjust aggressor?). Again there is no question here of what is called the
"law of extreme necessity" which could even extend to the direct killing
of the innocent. *Upright and skillful doctors strive most praiseworthily to
guard and preserve the lives of both mother and child;* on the contrary,
those show themselves most unworthy of the noble medical profession
who encompass the death of one or the other, through a pretense of practising medicine or through motives of misguided pity.

All of which agrees with the stern words of the Bishop of Hippo in
denouncing those wicked parents who seek to remain childless, and failing in this, are not ashamed to put their offspring to death: "Sometimes
this lustful cruelty or cruel lust goes so far as to seek to procure a baneful
sterility, and if this fails the foetus conceived in the womb is in one way or
another smothered or evacuated, in the desire to destroy the offspring before it has life, or if it already lives in the womb, to kill it before it is born.
If both man and woman are party to such practices they are not spouses
at all; and if from the first they have carried on thus they have come together not for honest wedlock, but for impure gratification; if both are
not party to these deeds, I make bold to say that either the one makes
herself a mistress of the husband, or the other simply the paramour of his
wife" (*De Nupt. et Concup.*, xv).

What is asserted in favor of the social and eugenic "indication" may
and must be accepted, provided lawful and upright methods are employed within the proper limits; but to wish to put forward reasons based
upon them for the killing of the innocent is unthinkable and contrary to
the divine precept promulgated in the words of the Apostle: Evil is not to
be done that good may come of it (Rom. iii, 8).

Those who hold the reins of government should not forget that it is the
duty of public authority by appropriate laws and sanctions to defend the
lives of the innocent, and this all the more so since those whose lives are
endangered and assailed cannot defend themselves. Among whom we
must mention in the first place infants hidden in the mother's womb. And
if the public magistrates not only do not defend them, but by their laws
and ordinances betray them to death at the hands of doctors or of others,
let them remember that God is the Judge and Avenger of innocent blood
which cries from earth to heaven (Gen. iv, 10).

Finally, that pernicious practice must be condemned which closely
touches upon the natural right of man to enter matrimony but affects also
in a real way the welfare of the offspring. For there are some who, over-
solicitous for the cause of "eugenics," not only give salutary counsel for
more certainly procuring the strength and health of the future child—
which, indeed, is not contrary to right reason—but put "eugenics"
before aims of a higher order. By public authority they wish to forbid

marriage to all those who, even though naturally fit for marriage, are regarded, in accordance with the norms and conjectures of their investigations, as persons who through hereditary transmission would bring forth defective offspring. And more, they wish to legislate to deprive these of that natural faculty by medical action, despite their unwillingness. And this they propose to do, not as an infliction of grave punishment under the authority of the state for a crime committed, nor to prevent future crimes by guilty persons, but against every right and good they wish the civil authority to arrogate to itself a power over a faculty which it never had and never can legitimately possess.

Those who act in this way are at fault in losing sight of the fact that the family is more sacred than the state and that men are begotten not for the earth and for time, but for heaven and eternity. Although often these individuals are to be dissuaded from entering into matrimony, certainly it is wrong to brand men with the stigma of crime because they contract marriage, on the ground that, despite the fact that they are in every respect capable of matrimony, they will give birth only to defective children, even though they use all care and diligence.

Public magistrates have no direct power over the bodies of their subjects; therefore, where no crime has taken place and there is no cause present for grave punishment, they can never directly harm, or tamper with the integrity of the body, either for the reasons of eugenics or for any other reason. St. Thomas teaches this when, inquiring whether human judges for the sake of preventing future evils can inflict punishment, he admits that the power indeed exists as regards certain other forms of evil, but justly and properly denies it as regards the maiming of the body. "No one who is guiltless may be punished by a human tribunal either by flogging to death, *or mutilation,* or by beating" (*2a, 2ae, q.* 108, *a.* 4 *ad* 2).

Furthermore, Christian doctrine establishes, and the light of human reason makes it most clear, that private individuals have no other power over the members of their bodies than that which pertains to their natural ends; and they are not free to destroy or mutilate their members, or in any other way render themselves unfit for their natural functions, except when no other provision can be made for the good of the whole body. . . .

The same false teachers who try to dim the luster of conjugal faith and purity do not scruple to do away with the honorable and trusting obedience which the woman owes to the man. Many of them even go further and assert that such a subjection of one party to the other is unworthy of human dignity, that the rights of husband and wife are equal; wherefore, they boldly proclaim, the emancipation of women has been or ought to be effected. This emancipation in their ideas must be threefold, in the ruling of the domestic society, in the administration of family affairs, and in the rearing of the children. It must be social, economic, physiological— *physiological,* that is to say, the woman is to be freed at her own good pleasure from the burdensome duties properly belonging to a wife as companion and mother (We have already said that this is not an emancipation but a crime); *social*, inasmuch as the wife being freed from the care of children and family, should, to the neglect of these, be able to follow her own bent and devote herself to business and even public affairs; finally, *economic*, whereby the woman even without the knowledge and against the wish of her husband may be at liberty to conduct and administer her own affairs, giving her attention chiefly to these rather than to children, husband, and family.

This, however, is not the true emancipation of woman, nor that rational and exalted liberty which belongs to the noble office of a Christian woman and wife; it is rather the debasing of the womanly character and the dignity of motherhood, and indeed of the whole family, as a result of which the husband suffers the loss of his wife, the children of their mother, and the home and the whole family of an ever watchful guardian. More than this, this false liberty and unnatural equality with the husband is to the detriment of the woman herself, for *if the woman descends from her truly regal throne to which she has been raised within the walls of the home by means of the Gospel, she will soon be reduced to the old state of slavery* (if not in appearance, certainly in reality) and become as among the pagans the mere instrument of man.

This equality of rights which is so much exaggerated and distorted must indeed be recognized in those rights which belong to the dignity of the human soul and which are proper to the marriage contract and inseparably bound up with wedlock. In such things undoubtedly both parties enjoy the same rights and are bound by the same obligations; in other things there must be a certain inequality and due accommodation, which is demanded by the good of the family and the right ordering and unity and stability of home life.

As, however, the social and economic conditions of the married woman must in some way be altered on account of the changes in social intercourse, it is part of the office of the public authority to adapt the civil rights of the wife to modern needs and requirements, keeping in view what the natural disposition and temperament of the female sex, good morality, and the welfare of the family demands, and provided always that the essential order of the domestic society remain intact, founded as it is on something higher than human authority and wisdom, namely on the authority and wisdom of God, and so not changeable by public laws or at the pleasure of private individuals.

87. Winifred Holtby (1934)

The quality of thought dominating both Fascist Italy and Southern Ireland is Catholic. Even where men and women are nominally agnostic or protestant, the social philosophy of Catholicism inevitably affects them in areas geographically or even historically influenced by the Holy See. The cult of the cradle is a feature not only of nationalism. It is a policy of modern Catholicism as it was a policy of ancient Hebraicism. Wherever a people, a church, a race or a cult believes itself to have been specially chosen by the Living God, it is its obvious business to increase and multiply until its seed covers the earth. Since Communism is wiping out Greek Orthodoxy quite effectively on its own, the Pope has only to prohibit all methods of birth control while Protestants and Agnostics are scientifically reducing their families, and then, by sheer force of numbers, Catholicism can recapture Christendom.

To-day Rome is fighting, in Western Europe and America, a stern and hitherto pretty successful battle. It is fighting against the claim of women to choose their own time and circumstances for conception, pregnancy and childbirth. It is fighting against the masculine attempt to escape the economic risk threatening satisfaction of passion. (The liability of imprisonment for non-payment of maintenance remains, for those to whom methods of contraception are prohibited or unknown, a rod in pickle for impetuous lovers.) It is fighting against the social experiment to control population by deliberate will and foresight rather than by the unpredictable orderings of an omnipotent Providence.

Catholic philosophy may have been ambiguous in former pronouncements about individual methods of averting conception. Its present policy of encouraging large families and discountenancing birth-control propaganda is unquestionable.

This matter is fundamental to women's position. But Catholic influence to-day does not end there.

When the Apostle Paul pronounced in his Epistle to the Galatians that in Jesus Christ there was no room for Jew nor Gentile, no room for male nor female, no room for bond nor free, he gave to the Christian Church its mandate of equality. That gospel of spiritual democracy still stands. But the social policy of Catholicism has followed a different model.

The Papal Encyclical upon Christian Marriage significantly entitled "Casti Connubii" and dated December 31, 1930, is a social document of immense importance. Naturally it upholds the view that matrimony is an indissoluble sacrament, divorce an unmitigated evil, birth control a sin, and the subservience of wives a divine principle.

The subjection of the wife to the husband, states the Encyclical, "does not deny or take away the liberty which belongs to the woman both in view of her dignity as a human being and in view of her most noble office as wife and mother and companion." But it does exclude that "exaggerated licence which is not for the good of the family" and it forbids that "in this body which is the family, the heart be separated from the head, to the great detriment of the whole body and the proximate danger of ruin."

The attitude is clear enough. In marriage the position of husband and of children is positive; that of the wife is dependent and ancillary.

After that theory of marriage it is logical that the Pope should warn his flock against "false teachers" who from "idle opinion" advocate the emancipation of women. Acceptance of their theories would not entail "true emancipation . . . nor that rational and exalted liberty which belongs to the whole office of the Christian woman and wife." This "false liberty and unnatural equality with the husband is to the detriment of the woman herself, for if she descends from her truly regal throne she will soon be reduced to her former state of slavery."

The reaction of the non-Catholic is to ask why there should be this inevitable alternation between throne and fetter. What is there about women that should force them to become either queens or slaves? The history of social evolution, the evidence of contemporary life, do not suggest this inexorable alternative. Why is there no room in the Catholic mind for comradeship and equality?

Again we are driven back to consider the origin of that fear which haunted Tertullian and which led even that artist of genius, Saint Augustine, to curious observations about the nature of women. To accept as authoritative the maxims upon marriage of a brilliant neurotic, whose own relationships to his mother, concubine and betrothed wife were far from exemplary and not even honourable, hardly inspires confidence, in the non-Catholic observer. But the theory governing the Marriage Encyclical is not merely a legacy from Early Fathers.

In February 1934 the veteran Cardinal Bourne issued a Lenten Pastoral Letter to his English flock. In it he deplored "a kind of modernism which gives a certain toleration to departures from the traditional modesty reserve and reticence which are characteristic of Christianity," and he blamed particularly "the writers of books and painters of pictures, the actors on the stage and for the Screen, the women, by the fashion of their dress, who render self-control more difficult for the average normal man or woman."

It is the old cry of fear of the body, fear of the mysterious feminine power to disturb masculine equilibrium. The harsh breath from the desert that blew over pagan Africa to Imperial Rome stings with its fierce consciousness of danger through the prim restraint of the language. In the month when the Cardinal was writing, Europe, Christendom, indeed the whole world from West to East, were most gravely menaced by the threat of uncontrolled lusts and passions. The lust for power, the lust for possession, the lust for imposing opinion upon those who would resist it, were causing torture in Germany, bloodshed in Vienna, rioting in Paris, kidnapping and murder in the United States, conspiracy, hatred, fear and insecurity in every Christian country. There had rarely before been a profounder need for those values of mercy, courage, faithfulness, and love preached by the Founder of the Christian faith. Yet the Cardinal expressed himself as chiefly concerned about the extravagances of women's dress.

It is this timid poking restlessness about the body, about sex, about modesty, about women as dangerous animals whose flesh must be hidden under ankle-length skirts and flowing sleeves in order to be rendered innocuous, that defaces Catholic Social theory. The superb metaphysic of its theological philosophy has little but dignity and reassurance to offer the human mind; but its nervous preoccupation with the body is inevitably disastrous to social sanity and explains the backwardness of women in every nation ruled by Catholic thought.

Freedom is not only a question of the law; it is a habit of the mind. To be free from the domination of the body is not possible to those afraid of it. Only when physical needs, feelings, actions and preoccupations become less important and less significant than intellectual and spiritual life, does the individual really escape from the "body of this death" which is mortality. The Catholic emphasis upon chastity, fidelity, maternity, and dignity destroys its own true object. Wherever in the modern world Catholic influence is in the ascendancy, women are subjected to this perpetual reminder of their sexual distinction, its dangers, its disadvantages and its precarious privileges. It is impossible that thus handicapped the majority of them should achieve full human maturity.

Family Endowment and the "New Feminism"

SOURCES

88. "Déclaration des Droits de la Famille" (December 1920), reprinted in Robert Talmy, *Histoire du mouvement familial en France, 1896-1939,* 2 vols. (Paris, 1962), I, 236-37. Tr. KMO.

89. Eleanor Florence Rathbone, *The Disinherited Family* (London, 1927), pp. vii-xi. Originally published in 1924.

90. Millicent Garrett Fawcett, "The Case Against Family Endowment," in *The Woman's Leader,* 30 January 1925, pp. 3-4.

91. Eleanor Rathbone, "The Old and the New Feminism," in *The Woman's Leader,* 13 March 1925, p. 52.

A growing concern for the stability and well-being of the patriarchal family as a pillar of the state developed during the post-war debate over depopulation, birth control, and the new morality, as was shown in the previous section. In the excerpts that follow, this concern is evident in diametrically opposed views relating to male authority and woman's position within the family.

The "Déclaration des droits de la famille" is a document drafted by a leading Catholic professor of Law, Eugène Duthoit (1869-1944) for the first Congress on the Family held at Lille, France, in December 1920. This congress, blessed with official patronage of the French Ministry of Health, initiated a major organizational effort by advocates of large families. The declaration, prepared and publicized by a group of conservative, high-ranking lawyers, political personalities, and civil servants in the North of France, claims to advocate the "rights of the family." What they meant, however, was the reassertion of patriarchal authority over the other members of the family, which even advocated weighting a father's vote by the number of his minor children.

In England, by contrast, the 1920's debate on the family was brought into focus through Eleanor Rathbone's plan for "family allowances." The descendant of a wealthy family of Liverpool shipbuilders and political liberals with a long tradition of public service, Eleanor Florence Rathbone (1872-1946) became one of the first women members of Parliament, and a highly distinguished one. A graduate of Somerville College, Oxford (where as a student she was known as "the philosopher"), she concerned herself throughout her life with a variety of causes, attempting always to improve the position of the disadvantaged—be they British children, Indian women, African victims of female circumcision rites, or Nazi refugees. Through all her concerns, however, there runs a thread of clear-sighted understanding of the position of women as dependents in contemporary society—a position Rathbone was determined to change. For some of these changes she worked actively, through the National Union of Suffrage Societies, where she succeeded Millicent Garrett Fawcett as the second president. Under Rathbone, this organization became the National Union of Societies for Equal Citizenship (NUSEC).

Beginning in 1908, when Eleanor Rathbone was elected to the Liverpool City Council, and throughout her parliamentary career from 1929 to 1945, she opposed the idea of a "family wage," advocating instead a plan for family allowances whereby the husband's employer or, in case of his unemployment, the state, would pay a separate allowance for each child to his *wife*. By this means she hoped to enhance the oppressed and narrow lives of working-class wives and mothers. Rathbone characterized her plan as a practical development of what she described as the "New Feminism," dealing with women's needs in women's terms. Now that the vote had been won and the professions opened to women, Rathbone argued that women no longer had to fight for the right to equality in the public sphere, but could concentrate on eliminating basic inequalities, which clearly began in the family.

Her book, *The Disinherited Family* (1924), presented her views on the woman question in the guise of an appeal to the nationalist and imperialist sentiments of those who were concerned about the low birthrate and the shrinking power of the nation in the post-war period. Rathbone's insistence that the family allowance must be paid to the wife rather than to the wage-earning husband and father evoked the greatest resistance; however, she stood firm and rejected a parliamentary proposal that would instead have paid the money to the father. Rathbone's family endowment plan was ultimately incorporated (June 1945) into a "Family Endowment Act" by the Labour Government immediately after the end of the Second World War.

Resistance to Rathbone's family allowance plan was strong in all quarters. The plan quite clearly undercut the economic roots of patriarchal power and was thus feared as likely to undermine the family breadwinner's drive to earn a living; moreover, even although Rathbone clearly advocated employer—not state—participation, her suggestions smacked dangerously of socialism.

A significant statement of opposition came from Millicent Fawcett (Docs. 62, 65), Rathbone's predecessor as leader of the largest British group of organizations fighting for women's rights. True to her nineteenth-century Liberal principles, Fawcett cautioned that payment to the wife and mother would undermine the sense of responsibility of men—husbands and fathers—by degrading their role as economic providers, and would thereby destroy, rather than stabilize, the family. Fawcett's attitude exemplifies the view of the "bourgeois women's movement" criticized in 1923 by Aleksandra Kollontai (Docs. 77, 83), when she accused the movement of concerning itself only with equality with men in public—i.e., political and professional—affairs, while ignoring the economic roots of women's oppression as sexual and maternal beings.

The final selection, from Eleanor Rathbone's rejoinder to Fawcett, "The Old and the New Feminism," restates clearly her belief that family endowment would provide the essential means for women to attack the root causes of their societal oppression and inequality, now that they were in possession of the right to vote.

---

88. "Déclaration des Droits de la Famille" (1920)

The family, founded upon marriage and hierarchically constituted under paternal authority, has as its goal to transmit, to uphold, to develop, and to perpetuate human life. To this end it has at its disposal rights that are irrevocable, anterior to and superior to all positive law.

Art. 1: The family has the right to multiply. From the family the fatherland (*patrie*) acquires its citizens, soldiers, artisans, missionaries, and pioneers. Whatever interferes with the transmission of life—moral propaganda, the disorganization of work, the bad distribution of profits, or public expenses—strikes at the family in the most basic of its rights.

Art. 2: The family has rights concerning education. It must shape the body, the intelligence, and the soul of the child. Thus it has the right to put in motion all legitimate practices that contribute to this triple goal, and especially to carry on a continuous relationship of collaboration and control with the school.

Art. 3: The family has the right to be protected against the various scourges that menace it with dissolution: licentious behavior in the streets and at public events, and by a certain type of press, and by alcoholism, tuberculosis, slums, and the multiplication of divorces.

Art. 4: The family has the right to own property. As a living and concrete society, born in and living amid the external possessions that surround it, [the family] has the right not only to a decent home but to the easy acquisition of a familial property or domain, and to the cultivation of a parcel of the national soil.

Art. 5: The family has the right to perpetuate itself. It no more dies along with the temporary representatives of domestic authority than the State dies when the holders of political authority disappear. The hereditary transmission of the patrimony should be guaranteed, without family property being truncated by excessive transfer taxes or pulverized by forcible division.

Art. 6: The family has the right to live from its work. Any scheme of production that is harmful to the life forces of the father, the mother, the child, or that troubles family life should be prohibited. A salary sufficient for the family to live on should be guaranteed by the appropriate organizations, under the sponsorship of the [respective] professions and the law.

Art. 7: The family has a right to distributive justice. Taxes, expenses, tariffs, subsidies, and allocations for *la vie chère* should be calculated as a function of the family, not as a function of the single individual.

Art. 8: The family, the true social cell, has the right to elect its representatives to the assemblies of the commune, the department, the region, and the nation. In addition to his own personal vote, the father should dispose of the number of votes equal or proportional to those of unemancipated minor children who are under his power. The mother will vote in the name of a dead or absent father or one who has forfeited or has been stripped of his [civil] rights.

Art. 9: Inasmuch as the family is the source of all national glory and all economic prosperity, it is the property of the family that ought to serve both as inspiration for and coordinator of social laws. Every law, every decree, all jurisprudence, every administrative regimen that is judged, on the basis of experience, as harmful to or perilous to the family, should be revised. The family must have its own part in influencing all organisms whatever that have as their function the preparation of the laws or their execution.

In a word, the Family comes first! If the family is strong, united, and prosperous, the rest will follow.

89. Eleanor Rathbone (1924)

I doubt whether there is any subject in the world of equal importance that has received so little serious and articulate consideration as the economic status of the family—of its members in relation to each other and of the whole unit in relation to the other units of which the community is made up. I say "articulate consideration" because what appears haphazard in our present arrangements for the family is probably the result of more deliberate purposing and choosing than appears on the surface, but it has been a sub-conscious and therefore inarticulate purpose and choice. The reasons for this we shall come to later on. For the present we are only concerned with the fact itself. If the reader doubts it, let him consider any of the other units or classifications that have to be taken into account in framing the economic structure of society, that is in providing material means for its maintenance—capital and labour; rent, profits and wages; production and distribution; collective and private enterprise, and so forth. Not one of them but has been the subject, in general and in detail, of a never-ending stream of writing among economists, industrial experts, politicians and pressmen. The family too has, of course, been written about—as a problem of population by Imperialists; of breeding by eugenists; in relation to endless problems of health, housing and child welfare. But of the family as an economic unit—something which has its own claim, based on its own value to the nation, to its own share in the nation's wealth—there has been next to no consideration at all. The claim has been not so much disparaged or negatived as ignored. In saying this I do not forget the work, to which this book itself owes much, of Mr. Seebohm Rowntree and of the sociologists and labour leaders who have followed him in pleading for the claim of the wage-earner to "a living wage" based on the needs of a family. But unfortunately their plea assumes acceptance of a supposition which it is one of the main objects of this book to refute—that all men are heads of families and that all families are of the same size, or rather can justifiably be assumed to be so for the purpose of regulating wages. As I shall try to shew, this fiction bears so little relation to the real facts that the attempt to base a wage system upon it inevitably breaks down. Or rather it does worse than break down. It exerts just enough pull on the industrial machine to drag it off the high road of a remorseless but efficient commercialism into a morass of confused thinking and frustrated, because impracticable, humanitarian purpose.

Further, those who have put forward this theory of the "living wage" regard the family not as it really is—an aggregate of individual human beings, each with an actual or potential value to the community—but as "the dependants" of the wage-earner. The very word suggests something parasitic, accessory, non-essential. A wife and children, and the wherewithal to keep them, are conceded to the wage-earner as though they were part of the "comforts and decencies promotive of better habits" for which he may reasonably ask as necessary to his development as a full human being. But if he prefers to use the margin thus allowed him for breeding pigeons or racing dogs or for some other form of personal gratification, instead of for keeping a family, that is assumed to be his affair, not the State's or his employer's. His wages are his remuneration, earned by the sweat of his brow or the travail of his brain, and how he spends them is no one's business but his own.

Yet when we are considering society from any other point of view than the economic, we can all see well enough that, of all its institutions, the family is after all the institution that matters most. It is at once indispensable as a means to all the rest and, in a sense, an end in itself. Pluck from under the family all the props which religion and morality have given it, strip it of the glamour, true or false, cast round it by romance, it will still remain a prosaic, indisputable fact, that the whole business of begetting, bearing and rearing children, is the most essential of all the nation's businesses. If it were not done at all, the world would become a desert in less than a century. To the extent that it is done badly, a nation finds itself confronted, in war time, with the problem of making an A.1 army out of a C.3 population; in peace time with the competition of rivals that manage better. To do it superlatively well, so that the rank and file of citizens should be well born and well bred, would go further than anything else to ensure national greatness, intellectual prestige, material prosperity, efficiency, productivity—everything that appeals most to the mind of the plain business man. It is another indisputable fact—bordering on a platitude—that the strongest emotions, the most enduring motives, the most universally accessible sources of happiness, are concerned with this business of the family; perhaps (though here we are straying from platitude into conjecture) because it is in self-reproduction that the average man finds the surest satisfaction for the instinct of immortality, for the desire to be quite certain that death will not end everything for him.

It being so generally recognized that the well-being of the family concerns the community as a whole, there seems something strange in the assumption so commonly made, that the question of the maintenance of families concerns only individual parents and can be safely left to them; or that, at most, society need only take cognizance of the matter by, as it were, mixing a little philanthropy with its business and influencing employers to pay wages which will enable their male employees to indulge in the praiseworthy leisure-time occupation of keeping families. The mere magnitude of the economic problem involved might have preserved it from so haphazard a treatment. When we remember that wives and dependent children constitute nearly half of the entire population, surely it is worth considering whether the problem of rationing this vast National Reserve cannot be solved in a more economic and efficient fashion than through the above-mentioned conception of "a living wage," based on the needs of a family, and ladled out indiscriminately to all male wage-earners of average capacity and industry.

One object of this book is, as it were, to put the present method of providing for families on the dissecting table and subject it to a thorough examination. I have set myself to trace its history; to examine its implications in theory and its consequences in practice; to discuss its effect on the distribution of wealth; on the character of national expenditure; on the efficiency of the workers; on the well-being of their homes, their wives and their children; on the quantity and quality of the birth-rate; on the status of women as mothers and as wage-earners.

The second object of this book is to discuss alternative methods of providing for the family; to describe the experiments, projected or actually in being, which other nations are making in the endowment of families; to consider how far these experiments are applicable to the conditions of this country, and how the difficulties and objections which impede them can best be met.

But behind these two definite objects lies an even larger, if vaguer, aim. This book will have failed if it does not convince the reader that Family Endowment involves something much greater than a scheme of child welfare, or a device of wage distribution—that it offers a hope, not dependent for achievement on a revolution or a scientific miracle but realizable here and now, of making attainable by every family, even the lowest on the industrial ladder, the material means for healthy living, and of placing the service of motherhood in the position of security and honour which it merits but can never reach under the present system.

90. Millicent Garrett Fawcett (1925)

I hope none of my readers will imagine that in opposing schemes of what is called "Family Endowment" I am animated by any want of appreciation of the magnificent work done for our cause and for the country at large by Miss Rathbone and those who share her views on this subject. But just before our late hon. sec., Miss Macadam, went to Canada in the autumn, she urged me to write for publication in *The Woman's Leader* a statement of the reasons which cause me to differ fundamentally from Miss Rathbone in regard to the tremendous step she is advocating in the direction of practical Socialism. I promised Miss Macadam to do this, and am now endeavouring to fulfil my promise.

Miss Rathbone has written an able and scholarly book on the subject, but she has not shaken my objections or made me feel that it would be a good thing for the State, or for the individual men and women who compose it, to relieve parents of the legal obligation of maintaining their children. I look upon the family as the unit of the State, and regard the proportional number of families leading industrious, self-sustaining, and self-respecting lives, not in one class only, but in all classes, as a not unsatisfactory test of the general well-being of the State. To remove from parents the necessity of maintaining their children would, in my judgment, withdraw the financial keystone of the family arch, would moreover in innumerable instances weaken or perhaps destroy some of the best influences in the lives of men and women, undermine their sense of responsibility, and relax the inducements to daily self-denying toil and industry.

The phrase "Family Endowment" is moreover, to my mind, in itself misleading. Where is the endowment? We do not usually speak of an endowment when we mean an income compulsorily raised by rates and taxes. Hospitals and schools are "endowed" when they derive their income, or a substantial part of it, from private benefactions voluntarily bestowed, but the so-called "endowed family" would derive its income in quite another manner, and from a totally different source. If the word "Endowment" is used in this inverted sense, we should, I suppose, soon be speaking of our richly endowed army and navy, meaning merely that the tax-payers have to provide for purposes of defence something like £100,000,000 annually. "Family Endowment" is quite a case of living on taking in each other's washing.

The care and perpetual solicitude which quite average parents show for their children are in themselves an education, and could not, in my opinion, but be weakened if they (and the children also) knew that the latter were being maintained at the public expense. In some instances it is difficult not to perceive that under "family endowment" even the parents may be living on the allowances granted by the State for the maintenance of the children. Suppose the allowance to be 10s. per head, per week (it could hardly be less) and that there were a family of five to be provided for, or six if the wife is also to be "endowed"; in this case the family would be receiving £3 a week, without the father bringing in a single shilling. Is it not obvious that this would materially weaken the motive for continuous exertion on his part? Miss Rathbone herself speaks in her book of this possibility, and suggests also that the Australian unmarried working man might be tempted to back his favourite in the races with the price of his suppositious wife's "one gossamer 5s. 6d. or two winter bloomers 8s."

It may be that Plato, three thousand years ago, or Mr. H. G. Wells and the Bolsheviks to-day, advocate the removal from parents of the financial responsibility for their children's maintenance, but I cannot see that the average British parent of to-day has anything to learn from them. The Athenians, with all their wonderful achievements in art and literature, practised infanticide in a wholesale fashion, leaving unwanted children exposed in pots to perish of cold and hunger. Of course, there was no freedom for women (other than Courtesans) in the ancient civilization of Athens. Mr. H. G. Wells has a brilliant imagination, but I do not think he has much to teach his contemporaries in the matter of the maintenance of a high standard of domestic life. The Bolshevik experiment has not had time to work itself out; but what we hear of it has not encouraged a general desire to imitate it. The noble freedom of women in family life, as improved and strengthened by Christianity and the women's movement, probably reaches a higher level here and now than has ever before been reached in the social history of the world; the reverse of all this, the fundamental degradation of women in the ancient classical societies, was probably the festering sore which finally rotted to the very heart the wonderful but short-lived civilization of Athens.

The late Dr. Arthur Verrall, whose opinion as an eminent scholar and a good feminist I venture to quote, stated in one of his essays that "the radical disease of which more than of anything else the ancient civilizations perished was their fundamentally imperfect ideal of womanhood." The predominance of the wife and mother in the home has been a source of strength and vitality which counts enormously for good in our type of civilization. How far the dependence of children on their parents forms an essential part of the structure of our society I think can perhaps hardly be measured. I have already referred to its influence for good on parents, forming [*illegible*] times the very strongest influence in their lives. The children, too, in their turn, while in their infancy they accept all the sacrifices of their parents as a matter of course, remember them later with gratitude and reverence, sometimes, perhaps, almost with remorse, knowing how little they appreciated these services while they were being rendered. When this is the case, the impression made very often only deepens with the years, and causes parents to resolve that as they cannot in many cases repay the debt they owe their own forebears, they will at least carry on the tradition by doing for their own children what their parents had done for them. There is a beautiful French proverb which says: "When le bon Dieu found He could not be everywhere, He invented mothers."

I now pass to another aspect of the subject. This so-called "Endowment" would add to the already tremendously heavy taxation of the country, a sum variously estimated at between £200,000,000 and £400,000,000 annually. . . .

With regard to the criticism that "Family Endowment" would diminish or even destroy the incentive to industry, Miss Rathbone's reply is that this type of objection is usually applied by well-to-do people to the working classes, but never by well-to-do people to themselves. I cannot accept this criticism as justified by the facts. I certainly have heard it applied without the least trace of class distinction where the circumstances seemed to warrant it. I could myself cite within my own small experience cases in which well-educated young professional men, after an expensive training, absolutely declined the daily drudgery which the opening years of professional life often call for. They preferred being kept by their wife's family or to live in comfortable idleness on the slender earnings of sisters who were high-school mistresses. . . . I confess that until recently I had looked upon the proposals for "Family Endowment" throwing upon the Exchequer an additional annual charge of some three or four hundred millions a year as fantastic, simply from its own inherent disadvantages, but it seems to me now that I was mistaken and that it may become a real danger. I recognize, of course, that Miss Rathbone, Mr. H. G. Wells, and other distinguished advocates of throwing the financial burden of the bringing up of children on the national exchequer, argue that this would not be a new burden, but rather a new way of meeting existing charges. I believe, however, that this source of consolation is highly illusory. No allowance is made for the cost of administration and distribution. Each General Election as it came round would offer great opportunities for pressing for the increase of the weekly or monthly family allowance. All economies would be represented as contemptible cheeseparing, and constant pressure would be exerted to get larger and larger allowances guaranteed by the State.

I have lately been looking over a paper I wrote about two years ago on the changes in the law favourable to women which have been effected since we got the vote. One of the most significant of these was the raising of the maximum sum which could be charged under an affiliation order on the father of an illegitimate child. For as many years as I can remember the maximum that such a father (whatever his wealth) could be ordered to pay was 5s. a week. Immediately that women became voters this was raised without any agitation whatever to 10s. a week, and in 1922 the maximum was again raised to 20s. a week. Imagine what use could be made of these facts by a clever agitator who was pressing for the raising of the sum allowed by the State under the plan of "family endowment." How outrageous that respectable children, members of an honourable family, should only have 8s. or 10s. a week, while the base-born might have as much as 20s. There would be a constant, and a constantly successful, pressure brought to bear on the Guardians of the Public Purse to give larger and larger allowances.

But I end as I began: my deepest and most irremovable objection to the whole scheme is based on the irreparable injury done to parents and children alike by withdrawing from parents the financial responsibility for the upbringing of their children.

The strongest and most universal element in the education of all of us is responsibility. What should be aimed at in our public institutions, as well as in our private life, is the combination of responsibility with liberty. Of course, there can be no responsibility without liberty. It rests with us in this, as in other great issues, to make the right choice and to see that extended liberty is not used to undermine responsibility.

91. Eleanor Rathbone (1925)

We believe that the inferior status of women in industry and the jealousy which works against them in the professions are only partly the fruit of sex prejudice; that they have deep-rooted economic causes and that the only effective method of attack is to penetrate to and remove these causes, or at least modify and bring them under control.

Whatever view we take of those questions, I think that everyone who is thinking ahead must realize that the National Union is approaching a stage in its existence when its work will be less obvious and clearly defined and ready to hand than it has been during the last five years. The time has come to take stock and decide what next. It seems to me that, broadly speaking, there are two lines of possible development. We may complete the task of removing from the Statute Book the remaining traces of legal inequality; we may continue to chant the gospel of sex equality to the inattentive ears of employers and Trades Unionists, comforting ourselves that the fault is theirs if they fail to listen. But it must be confessed that this is a programme not likely to arouse much enthusiasm or attract new recruits, and if that is all, we must be prepared to see the once broad river of the N.U.S.E.C. dwindle till it becomes a trickle and loses itself in the sands. Or we may say: "Now the legal barriers are down; there is still some débris left which we must clear away. But we need not give ourselves up entirely to that, for women are virtually free. At last we have done with the boring business of measuring everything that women want, or that is offered them by men's standards, to see if it is exactly up to sample. At last we can stop looking at all our problems through men's eyes and discussing them in men's phraseology. We can demand what we want for women, not because it is what men have got, but because it is what women need to fulfil the potentialities of their own natures and to adjust themselves to the circumstances of their own lives. We can do this without any sense of yielding to sex selfishness or antagonism, because we know that it is only in this way that women can make a contribution of real value to the common stock of human good; can throw on its problems a light which shines from within; can refute the gibe that while women are clever as imitators, they are deficient in initiative and originality."

Does this all sound rather vague and wordy? Let me try to give it concreteness by applying it to a particular problem—the problem of Equal Opportunities and Pay. Hitherto we have contented ourselves with demanding that in the economic sphere women shall be free to attempt the same tasks as men and shall be paid at the same rates *when they are doing men's work*. But under what conditions are they to labour and at what rates are they to be paid when they are doing work which only women can do or for which they have a special fitness? So far the National Union have made no pronouncement about that. Yet surely it is as important a question as the other. Is it only the women who have adopted callings glorified by the presence in them of men who need security for adequate remuneration and suitable conditions? Is it not possible that, just because these economic problems have been thought out by men with special reference to the conditions of their own lives, there are spheres of service just as important to the community which have been neglected, left at the mercy of ruthless economic forces without any consideration of the well-being of the human beings concerned in them, though on their efficiency must depend in the long run the efficiency of the service itself? There is the dangerous service of maternity, the delicate and skilled task of rearing children. There are the services of midwifery and nursing, there are all the questions of houses fit to be workshops for women as well as dormitories for men. Where in this sphere are the equivalents of the Factory Legislation, the Trades Boards and Industrial Councils, the Trades Unions and Employers' Federations which regulate and protect the services which employ men? Can anyone who begins to contemplate these facts wonder any longer why it is that such questions as Family Endowment, Birth Control, Housing, crop up ubiquitously and irresistibly in the programmes of Women's Conferences? Whatever the rights and wrongs of these questions, whether we are on the one side or the other, who can doubt that they are questions which women must think out for themselves and mould to their own patterns. When we are trying to do this, let us not forget that the path in which we are treading is a path which has been trod in by others before us who have been pioneers in asserting the rights of self-determination for their own group or class. When working men first began to struggle for their liberties their demands were at first limited to political privileges and to breaking down of legal disabilities. Only gradually they realized that the privileges and the formulae that had been shaped to meet the needs of the classes that had hitherto held dominion were not necessarily sufficient in themselves to bring real freedom, real equality of opportunity, to the manual workers, that these must work out for themselves a whole new science and art of living that would enable them not merely to copy the manners and customs of their betters, but to shape their own destinies. We, like they, have to learn that the achievement of freedom is a much bigger thing than the breaking off of shackles. First strike off the shackles, but afterwards give the released prisoner just the kind of nourishment, just the scientific gymnastic, just the free exercise in the open air and sunshine that will enable him to grow to the full measure of the stature which Nature has destined for him.

CHAPTER 10

The Quest for a Psychology of Womanhood

Psychoanalysis and Woman's Character

SOURCES

92. Sigmund Freud, "Some Psychological Consequences of the Anatomical Distinction Between the Sexes," in *The Standard Edition of the Complete Psychological Works of Sigmund Freud*, ed. James Strachey, XIX (London, 1964), 249-50, 251-54, 255-56, 257-58. Originally published in German as "Einige psychische Folgen des anatomischen Geschlechtsunterschieds," 1925; first English translation, by James Strachey, published in the *International Journal of Psycho-Analysis*, 8, no. 2 (1927).

93. Karen Horney, "The Flight from Womanhood: The Masculinity Complex in Women as Viewed by Men and Women," *International Journal of Psycho-Analysis*, 7, pts. 3-4 (July-October 1926), 324, 328-31, 333, 335-36, 337-39.

94. Sigmund Freud, "Femininity," in *New Introductory Lectures on Psychoanalysis*, tr. and ed. by James Strachey (New York, 1965), pp. 131-35. Originally published in German as "Die Weiblichkeit," 1933.

In the 1920's the practitioners of the controversial new field of psychoanalysis, developed through years of patient experiment by the Viennese physician Sigmund Freud, addressed themselves to the woman question. They focused on what Freud and most of his English-speaking contemporaries called womanliness, or, as Strachey translated it, "femininity." What follows are selections from two of the ranking contributors to this debate—Sigmund Freud himself and the German psychoanalyst Karen Horney.

Sigmund Freud (1856-1939) was nearly seventy when in 1925 he finally addressed himself specifically to the subject of feminine psychology. He was, however, no stranger to the European discussion of the woman question; indeed, during his years of military service—well before he went to Paris to study with Charcot or made the series of important psychiatric discoveries that were to establish his fame as the father of psychoanalysis—he had translated Harriet Taylor Mill's 1851 essay on the enfranchisement of women (Vol. I, Doc. 88) for a German edition of the collected works of John Stuart Mill. And he had written to his then fiancée, Martha Bernays, criticizing Mill's assumption (he believed that John Stuart Mill, not Harriet Taylor Mill, had composed the piece) that a married woman might earn as much as her husband. "We surely agree," he told Martha in 1883 (in a letter published by his biographer Ernest Jones), "that the management of a house, the care and bringing up of children, demand the whole of a human being and almost excludes any earning. . . ." "It is really a still-born thought to send women into the struggle for existence exactly as men." And he closed his remarks by affirming that "nature has determined women's destiny through beauty, charm, and sweetness. . . ."

We see from these brief passages that young Freud's ideas about women's place conformed to the conventions of his time and place, though he did acknowledge that changes in their legal and educational situation might be in order. Some forty years later, Freud's dedication to a secular, scientific knowledge led him to admit that a male model was not adequate to elucidate the formation of the female psyche. In the important paper excerpted here (and first presented to the 1925 International Psycho-Analytical Congress by his daughter and disciple Anna Freud) Sigmund Freud argued that the individual psyches of young children—both girls and boys—contain "bisexual" potentialities at birth. The problem, then, for psychoanalytical theory was to determine through what process of psychodynamic interaction with father and mother a girl will develop toward womanhood differently than a boy toward manhood—"womanliness" and "manliness" being concepts that Freud was careful to qualify as ideal constructs corresponding to notions of "passivity" and "activity." It is here that Freud's concept of penis-envy assumed its centrality, leading him to posit the existence of a "masculinity complex" in women. Freud drew evidence for all his hypotheses, of course, from case studies of individuals who had grown up in central European patriarchal families, the dynamics of which were epitomized for him in the symbolism of the Oedipus myths of ancient Greece. Although Freud's theory of the sexual origins of a distinctively female psychopathology is more complex than the crude biological determinism of Comte or Proudhon (Vol. I, Docs. 62, 95), it did nothing to dispel a fatalistic diagnosis of the female condition as "passive" that not all of his followers were willing to accept. Clearly, his dichotomization of manly and womanly traits made more of an impression on his listeners than did his qualifying ideas concerning the intrinsic bisexuality of the individual.

One of Freud's most perceptive challengers was Karen Danielsen Horney (1885-1952), a woman of Norwegian and Dutch parentage, born near Hamburg. At the age of twenty-four, while a medical student, she married an aspiring young lawyer, Oscar Horney, and bore three daughters, meanwhile completing her medical degree and psychiatric training in Berlin. Horney's speculations and therapeutic casework concerning women, coupled with her own experiences as a mother and partner in an unhappy marriage, soon led her to question, then reject, Freud's theories of the centrality of the libido in favor of a less instinctual, somewhat more cultural, yet still biologically deterministic interpretation of female psychological development. Emphasizing the centrality of motherhood to any definition of the female psyche, she countered Freud's concept of penis-envy by producing evidence for the existence of womb-envy on the part of men. In the paper excerpted below, Horney spelled out the disagreements with Freud on which she later constructed her theory of the neurotic personality. In 1932 Horney sharpened her attack by asserting that the male's castration anxiety was caused by his dread of woman and by his sense of physical inferiority resulting from his incapacity as childbearer. That same year she emigrated to the United States, settling first in Chicago and then in New York, where she broke definitively with the Freudian psychoanalytic school.

In 1933, the year after Horney's publication of her stronger attack, "The Dread of Woman," and her departure for the United States, Freud published his lecture "Die Weiblichkeit," in which he summarized much of his earlier thinking on the psychology of women. In our excerpt from this lecture Freud reinterpreted and refined his analysis with regard to subsequent theoretical statements concerning ego psychology and in the context of his own ever-increasing fascination with the psychological theory of culture. Here he extended his remarks to consider the personality of the mature woman within the cultural context of the times.

The important issues raised by Horney's approach were almost ignored by theorists for at least forty years, while Freud's view of female psychology set the tone for the psychoanalytical profession and popularizers. Only gradually did Horney's concept of womb-envy find its way into the works of others, such as Erich Neumann, Bruno Bettelheim, and Wolfgang Lederer.

---

92. Sigmund Freud (1925)

In examining the earliest mental shapes assumed by the sexual life of children we have been in the habit of taking as the subject of our investigations the male child, the little boy.* With little girls, so we have supposed, things must be similar, though in some way or other they must nevertheless be different. The point in development at which this difference lay could not be clearly determined.

In boys the situation of the Oedipus complex is the first stage that can be recognized with certainty. It is easy to understand, because at that stage a child retains the same object which he previously cathected with his libido—not as yet a genital one—during the preceding period while he was being suckled and nursed. The fact, too, that in this situation he regards his father as a disturbing rival and would like to get rid of him and take his place is a straightforward consequence of the actual state of affairs. I have shown elsewhere how the Oedipus attitude in little boys belongs to the phallic phase, and how its destruction is brought about by the fear of castration—that is, by narcissistic interest in their genitals. The matter is made more difficult to grasp by the complicating circumstance that even in boys the Oedipus complex has a double orientation, active and passive, in accordance with their bisexual constitution; a boy

---

* Sigmund Freud Copyrights Ltd. have denied our request to substitute a revised and, in our minds, more accurate English rendering for the authorized James Strachey translation. For the reader's information, the significant modifications and clarifications we would have introduced to enhance English readers' understanding of what Freud said in nontechnical German are as follows:

(1) *Bisexualität* and *bisexual*. Freud used these words to denote a combination of "manly" and "womanly" character traits in an individual. In the passages included here at least, he did not intend to suggest that "bisexuality" denoted homosexual as well as heterosexual drives combined in one person (a more recent use of the word). Strachey rendered "Bisexualität" as "bisexuality." We believe the reader ought to be alerted to Freud's meaning in this regard.

(2) *Männlich, Weiblich, Männlichkeit*, and *Weiblichkeit*. We had planned to translate these terms as, respectively, "manly," "womanly," "manliness," and "womanliness," which were common in English usage in the 1920's and 1930's. We still believe this rendering captures Freud's meaning better than "masculine," "feminine," "masculinity," and "femininity," the terms Strachey used.

also wants to take his *mother's* place as the love-object of his *father*—a fact which we describe as the feminine attitude. . . .

In little girls the Oedipus complex raises one problem more than in boys. In both cases the mother is the original object; and there is no cause for surprise that boys retain that object in the Oedipus complex. But how does it happen that girls abandon it and instead take their father as an object? In pursuing this question I have been able to reach some conclusions which may throw light precisely on the prehistory of the Oedipus relation in girls.

Every analyst has come across certain women who cling with especial intensity and tenacity to the bond with their father and to the wish in which it culminates of having a child by him. We have good reason to suppose that the same wishful phantasy was also the motive force of their infantile masturbation, and it is easy to form an impression that at this point we have been brought up against an elementary and unanalysable fact of infantile sexual life. But a thorough analysis of these very cases brings something different to light—namely, that here the Oedipus complex has a long prehistory and is in some respects a secondary formation. . . .

The genital zone is discovered at some time or other, and there seems no justification for attributing any psychical content to the first activities in connection with it. But the first step in the phallic phase which begins in this way is not the linking-up of the masturbation with the object-cathexes of the Oedipus complex, but a momentous discovery which little girls are destined to make. They notice the penis of a brother or playmate, strikingly visible and of large proportions, at once recognize it as the superior counterpart of their own small and inconspicuous organ, and from that time forward fall a victim to envy for the penis.

There is an interesting contrast between the behaviour of the two sexes. In the analogous situation, when a little boy first catches sight of a girl's genital region, he begins by showing irresolution and lack of interest; he sees nothing or disavows what he has seen, he softens it down or looks about for expedients for bringing it into line with his expectations. It is not until later, when some threat of castration has obtained a hold upon him, that the observation becomes important to him: if he then rec-

---

(3) *Seele* and *Seelenleben*. We had planned to translate these words as "soul" and "emotional life," in contrast to Strachey's "mind" and "mental life." Because "the soul-life of the woman" is a clumsy phrase, we would prefer "emotional life" as the closest approximation to *Seelenleben*; it is certainly the emotions rather than the mind that concerned Freud. *Psyche* is indeed the Greek word for soul, and Freud's whole concern was the analysis of the psyche or the soul, or psychoanalysis; yet, we prefer "emotional life" to "psychic life," on the grounds that an expression like "psychic life" would be untrue to Freud's intention of making himself easily understood by his lay audience.

(4) *Kultur*. We would have preferred the word "culture" (in place of Strachey's word "civilization") to incorporate Freud's meaning of the combination of both "high" culture (including both learning and art), and culture in the anthropological sense. Freud clearly recognized (Doc. 99) that both types of culture surround women in a world shaped by men.

On the general problem of translating Freud, see Bettelheim 1982.—EDS.

ollects or repeats it, it arouses a terrible storm of emotion in him and forces him to believe in the reality of the threat which he has hitherto laughed at. This combination of circumstances leads to two reactions, which may become fixed and will in that case, whether separately or together or in conjunction with other factors, permanently determine the boy's relations to women: horror of the mutilated creature or triumphant contempt for her. These developments, however, belong to the future, though not to a very remote one.

A little girl behaves differently. She makes her judgement and her decision in a flash. She has seen it and knows that she is without it and wants to have it.

Here what has been named the masculinity complex of women branches off. It may put great difficulties in the way of their regular development towards femininity, if it cannot be got over soon enough. The hope of some day obtaining a penis in spite of everything and so of becoming like a man may persist to an incredibly late age and may become a motive for strange and otherwise unaccountable actions. Or again, a process may set in which I should like to call a 'disavowal', a process which in the mental life of children seems neither uncommon nor very dangerous but which in an adult would mean the beginning of a psychosis. Thus a girl may refuse to accept the fact of being castrated, may harden herself in the conviction that she *does* possess a penis, and may subsequently be compelled to behave as though she were a man.

The physical consequences of envy for the penis, in so far as it does not become absorbed in the reaction-formation of the masculinity complex, are various and far-reaching. After a woman has become aware of the wound to her narcissism, she develops, like a scar, a sense of inferiority. When she has passed beyond her first attempt at explaining her lack of a penis as being a punishment personal to herself and has realized that that sexual character is a universal one, she begins to share the contempt felt by men for a sex which is the lesser in so important a respect, and, at least in holding that opinion, insists on being like a man.

Even after penis-envy has abandoned its true object, it continues to exist: by an easy displacement it persists in the character-trait of *jealousy*. Of course, jealousy is not limited to one sex and has a wider foundation than this, but I am of opinion that it plays a far larger part in the mental life of women than of men and that that is because it is enormously reinforced from the direction of displaced penis-envy. . . .

There is yet another surprising effect of penis-envy, or of the discovery of the inferiority of the clitoris, which is undoubtedly the most important of all. In the past I had often formed an impression that in general women tolerate masturbation worse than men, that they more frequently fight against it and that they are unable to make use of it in circumstances in which a man would seize upon it as a way of escape without any hesitation. Experience would no doubt elicit innumerable exceptions to this statement, if we attempted to turn it into a rule. The reactions of human individuals of both sexes are of course made up of masculine and feminine traits. But it appeared to me nevertheless as though masturbation were further removed from the nature of women than of men, and the solution of the problem could be assisted by the reflection that masturbation, at all events of the clitoris, is a masculine activity and that the elimination of clitoridal sexuality is a necessary precondition for the development of femininity. Analyses of the remote phallic period have now taught me that in girls, soon after the first signs of penis-envy, an intense current of feeling against masturbation makes its appearance, which cannot be attributed exclusively to the educational influence of those in charge of the child. This impulse is clearly a forerunner of the wave of repression which at puberty will do away with a large amount of the girl's masculine sexuality in order to make room for the development of her femininity. It may happen that this first opposition to auto-erotic activity fails to attain its end. And this was in fact the case in the instances which I analysed. The conflict continued, and both then and later the girl did everything she could to free herself from the compulsion to masturbate. Many of the later manifestations of sexual life in women remain unintelligible unless this powerful motive is recognized.

I cannot explain the opposition which is raised in this way by little girls to phallic masturbation except by supposing that there is some concurrent factor which turns her violently against that pleasurable activity. Such a factor lies close at hand. It cannot be anything else than her narcissistic sense of humiliation which is bound up with penis-envy, the reminder that after all this is a point on which she cannot compete with boys and that it would therefore be best for her to give up the idea of doing so. Thus the little girl's recognition of the anatomical distinction between the sexes forces her away from masculinity and masculine masturbation on to new lines which lead to the development of femininity.

So far there has been no question of the Oedipus complex, nor has it up to this point played any part. But now the girl's libido slips into a new position along the line—there is no other way of putting it—of the equation 'penis-child'. She gives up her wish for a penis and puts in place of it a wish for a child: and *with that purpose in view* she takes her father as a love-object. Her mother becomes the object of her jealousy. The girl has turned into a little woman. . . .

In girls the motive for the demolition of the Oedipus complex is lacking. Castration has already had its effect, which was to force the child into the situation of the Oedipus complex. Thus the Oedipus complex escapes the fate which it meets with in boys: it may be slowly abandoned or dealt with by repression, or its effects may persist far into women's normal mental life. I cannot evade the notion (though I hesitate to give it expression) that for women the level of what is ethically normal is different from what it is in men. Their super-ego is never so inexorable, so impersonal, so independent of its emotional origins as we require it to be in men. Character-traits which critics of every epoch have brought up against women—that they show less sense of justice than men, that they are less ready to submit to the great exigencies of life, that they are more often influenced in their judgements by feelings of affection or hostility—all these would be amply accounted for by the modification in the formation of their super-ego which we have inferred above. We must not allow ourselves to be deflected from such conclusions by the denials of the feminists, who are anxious to force us to regard the two sexes as completely equal in position and worth; but we shall, of course, willingly agree that the majority of men are also far behind the masculine ideal and that all human individuals, as a result of their bisexual disposition and of cross-inheritance, combine in themselves both masculine and feminine characteristics, so that pure masculinity and femininity remain theoretical constructions of uncertain content.

93. Karen Horney (1926)

In some of his latest works Freud has drawn attention with increasing urgency to a certain one-sidedness in our analytical researches. I refer to the fact that till quite recently the mind of boys and men only was taken as the object of investigation.

The reason of this is obvious. Psycho-analysis is the creation of a male genius, and almost all those who have developed his ideas have been men. It is only right and reasonable that they should evolve more easily a masculine psychology and understand more of the development of men than of women. . . .

Now, if we try to free our minds from this masculine mode of thought, nearly all the problems of feminine psychology take on a different appearance.

The first thing that strikes us is that it is always, or principally, the genital difference between the sexes which has been made the cardinal point in the analytical conception and that we have left out of consideration the other great biological difference, namely, the different parts played by men and by women in the function of reproduction.

The influence of the man's point of view in the conception of motherhood is most clearly revealed in Ferenczi's extremely brilliant genital theory. His view is that the real incitement to coitus, its true, ultimate meaning for both sexes, is to be sought in the desire to return to the mother's womb. During a period of contest man acquired the privilege of really penetrating once more, by means of his genital organ, into a uterus. The woman, who was formerly in the subordinate position, was obliged to adapt her organization to this organic situation and was provided with certain compensations. She had to 'content herself' with substitutes of the nature of phantasy and above all with harbouring the child, whose bliss she shares. At the most, it is only in the act of birth that she perhaps has potentialities of pleasure which are denied to the man.

According to this view the psychic situation of a woman would certainly not be a very pleasurable one. She lacks any real primal impulse to coitus, or at least she is debarred from all direct—even if only partial—fulfilment. If this is so, the impulse towards coitus and pleasure in it must undoubtedly be less for her than for the man. For it is only indirectly, by circuitous ways, that she attains to a certain fulfilment of the primal longing—i.e., partly by the roundabout way of masochistic conversion and partly by identification with the child which she may conceive. These, however, are merely 'compensatory devices.' The only thing in which she ultimately has the advantage over the man is the, surely very questionable, pleasure in the act of birth.

At this point I, as a woman, ask in amazement, and what about motherhood? And the blissful consciousness of bearing a new life within oneself? And the ineffable happiness of the increasing expectation of the appearance of this new being? And the joy when it finally makes its appearance and one holds it for the first time in one's arms? And the deep pleasurable feeling of satisfaction in suckling it and the happiness of the whole period when the infant needs her care?

Ferenczi has expressed the opinion in conversation that in that primal period of conflict which ended so grievously for the female, the male as victor imposed upon her the burden of motherhood and all that it involves.

Certainly, regarded from the standpoint of the social struggle, motherhood *may* be a handicap. It is certainly so at the present time, but it is much less certain that it was so in times when human beings were closer to nature.

Moreover, we explain penis-envy itself by its biological relations and not by social factors; on the contrary, we are accustomed without more ado to construe the woman's sense of being at a disadvantage socially as the rationalization of her penis-envy.

But from the biological point of view woman has in motherhood, or in the capacity for motherhood, a quite indisputable and by no means negligible physiological superiority. This is most clearly reflected in the unconscious of the male psyche in the boy's intense envy of motherhood. We are familiar with this envy as such, but it has hardly received due consideration as a dynamic factor. When one begins, as I did, to analyse men only after a fairly long experience of analysing women, one receives a most surprising impression of the intensity of this envy of pregnancy, child-birth, and motherhood, as well as of the breasts and of the act of suckling.

In the light of this impression derived from analysis one must naturally enquire whether an unconscious masculine tendency to depreciation is not expressing itself intellectually in the above-mentioned view of motherhood? This depreciation would run as follows: In reality women do simply desire the penis; when all is said and done motherhood is only a burden which makes the struggle for existence harder, and men may be glad that they have not to bear it.

When Helene Deutsch writes that the masculinity-complex in women plays a much greater part than the femininity-complex in man, she would seem to overlook the fact that the masculine envy is clearly capable of more successful sublimation than the penis-envy of the girl, and that it certainly serves as one, if not as the essential, driving force in the setting-up of cultural values.

Language itself points to this origin of cultural productivity. In the historic times which are known to us this productivity has undoubtedly been incomparably greater in men than in women. Is not the tremendous strength in men of the impulse to creative work in every field precisely due to their feeling of playing a relatively small part in the creation of living beings, which constantly impels them to an over-compensation in achievement?

If we are right in making this connection we are confronted with the problem why no corresponding impulse to compensate herself for her penis-envy is found in woman? There are two possibilities; either the envy of the woman is absolutely less than that of the man or it is less successfully worked off in some other way. We could bring forward facts in support of either supposition.

In favour of the greater intensity of the man's envy we might point out that an actual anatomical disadvantage on the side of the woman exists only from the point of view of the pregenital levels of organization. From that of the genital organization of adult women there is no disadvantage, for obviously the capacity of women for coitus is not less but simply other than that of men. On the other hand, the part of the man in reproduction is ultimately less than that of the woman.

Further, we observe that men are evidently under a greater necessity to depreciate women than conversely. The realization that the dogma of the inferiority of women had its origin in an unconscious male tendency could only dawn upon us after a doubt had arisen whether in fact this view were justified in reality. But if there actually are in men tendencies to depreciate women behind this conviction of feminine inferiority, we must infer that this unconscious impulse to depreciation is a very powerful one. . . .

It was natural to conclude—and especially natural because of the male orientation of our thinking—that we could link these impressions on to the primary penis-envy and to reason *a posteriori* that this envy must possess an enormous intensity, an enormous dynamic power, seeing that it evidently gave rise to such effects. Here we overlooked the fact, more in our general estimation of the situation than in details, that this desire to be a man, so familiar to us from the analyses of adult women, had only very little to do with that early, infantile, primary penis-envy, but that it is a secondary formation embodying all that has miscarried in the development towards womanhood.

From beginning to end my experience has proved to me with unchanging clearness that the Oedipus complex in women leads (not only in extreme cases where the subject has come to grief, but *regularly*) to a regression to penis-envy, naturally in every possible degree and shade. The difference between the outcome of the male and the female Oedipus complexes seems to me in average cases to be as follows. In boys the mother as a sexual object is renounced owing to the fear of castration, but the male rôle itself is not only affirmed in further development but is actually over-emphasized in the reaction to the fear of castration. We see this clearly in the latency and prepubertal period in boys and generally in later life as well. Girls, on the other hand, not only renounce the father as a sexual object but simultaneously recoil from the feminine rôle altogether. . . .

The girl now takes refuge in a fictitious male rôle. . . . The fiction of maleness enabled the girl to escape from the female rôle now burdened with guilt and anxiety. It is true that this attempt to deviate from her own line to that of the male inevitably brings about a sense of inferiority, for the girl begins to measure herself by pretensions and values which are foreign to her specific biological nature and confronted with which she cannot but feel herself inadequate.

Although this sense of inferiority is very tormenting, analytical experience emphatically shews us that the ego can tolerate it more easily than the sense of guilt associated with the feminine attitude, and hence it is undoubtedly a gain for the ego when the girl flees from the Scylla of the sense of guilt to the Charybdis of the sense of inferiority. . . .

Now these typical motives for flight into the male rôle—motives whose origin is the Oedipus complex—are reinforced and supported by the actual disadvantage under which women labour in social life. Of course we must recognize that the desire to be a man, when it springs from this last source, is a peculiarly suitable form of rationalization of those unconscious motives. But we must not forget that this disadvantage is actually a piece of reality and that it is immensely greater than most women are aware of.

Georg Simmel says in this connection that 'the greater importance attaching to the male sociologically is probably due to his position of superior strength', and that historically the relation of the sexes may be crudely described as that of master and slave. Here, as always, it is 'one of the privileges of the master that he has not constantly to think that he is master, whilst the position of the slave is such that he can never forget it'.

Here we probably have the explanation also of the under-estimation of this factor in analytical literature. In actual fact a girl is exposed from birth onwards to the suggestion—inevitable, whether conveyed brutally or delicately—of her inferiority, an experience which must constantly stimulate her masculinity complex.

There is one further consideration. Owing to the hitherto purely masculine character of our civilization it has been much harder for women to achieve any sublimation which should really satisfy their nature, for all the ordinary professions have been filled by men. This again must have exercised an influence upon women's feelings of inferiority, for naturally they could not accomplish the same as men in these masculine professions and so it appeared that there was a basis in fact for their inferiority. It seems to me impossible to judge to how great a degree the unconscious motives for the flight from womanhood are reinforced by the actual social subordination of women. One might conceive of the connection as an interaction of psychic and social factors. But I can only indicate these problems here, for they are so grave and so important that they require a separate investigation.

The same factors must have quite a different effect on the man's development. On the one hand they lead to a much stronger repression of his feminine wishes, in that these bear the stigma of inferiority; on the other hand it is far easier for him successfully to sublimate them.

In the foregoing discussion I have put a construction upon certain problems of feminine psychology which in many points differs from the views hitherto current. It is possible and even probable that the picture I have drawn is one-sided from the opposite point of view. But my primary intention in this paper was to indicate a possible source of error arising out of the sex of the observer, and by so doing to make a step forward towards the goal which we are all striving to reach: to get beyond the subjectivity of the masculine or the feminine standpoint and to obtain a picture of the mental development of woman which shall be truer to the facts of her nature—with its specific qualities and its differences from that of man—than any we have hitherto achieved.

94. Sigmund Freud (1933)

It is not my intention to pursue the further behaviour of femininity through puberty to the period of maturity.* Our knowledge, moreover, would be insufficient for the purpose. But I will bring a few features together in what follows. Taking its prehistory as a starting-point, I will only emphasize here that the development of femininity remains exposed to disturbance by the residual phenomena of the early masculine period. Regressions to the fixations of the pre-Oedipus phases very frequently occur; in the course of some women's lives there is a repeated alternation between periods in which masculinity or femininity gains the upper hand. Some portion of what we men call 'the enigma of women' may perhaps be derived from this expression of bisexuality in women's lives. But another question seems to have become ripe for judgement in the course of these researches. We have called the motive force of sexual life 'the libido'. Sexual life is dominated by the polarity of masculine-feminine; thus the notion suggests itself of considering the relation of the libido to this antithesis. It would not be surprising if it were to turn out that each sexuality had its own special libido appropriated to it, so that one sort of libido would pursue the aims of a masculine sexual life and another sort those of a feminine one. But nothing of the kind is true. There is only one libido, which serves both the masculine and the feminine sexual functions. To it itself we cannot assign any sex; if, following the conventional equation of activity and masculinity, we are inclined to describe it as masculine, we must not forget that it also covers trends with a passive aim.

* See the note on translation of Doc. 92 above.—EDS.

Nevertheless the juxtaposition 'feminine libido' is without any justification. Furthermore, it is our impression that more constraint has been applied to the libido when it is pressed into the service of the feminine function, and that—to speak teleologically—Nature takes less careful account of its [that function's] demands than in the case of masculinity. And the reason for this may lie—thinking once again teleologically—in the fact that the accomplishment of the aim of biology has been entrusted to the aggressiveness of men and has been made to some extent independent of women's consent.

The sexual frigidity of women, the frequency of which appears to confirm this disregard, is a phenomenon that is still insufficiently understood. Sometimes it is psychogenic and in that case accessible to influence; but in other cases it suggests the hypothesis of its being constitutionally determined and even of there being a contributory anatomical factor.

I have promised to tell you of a few more psychical peculiarities of mature femininity, as we come across them in analytic observation. We do not lay claim to more than an average validity for these assertions; nor is it always easy to distinguish what should be ascribed to the influence of the sexual function and what to social breeding. Thus, we attribute a larger amount of narcissism to femininity, which also affects women's choice of object, so that to be loved is a stronger need for them than to love. The effect of penis-envy has a share, further, in the physical vanity of women, since they are bound to value their charms more highly as a late compensation for their original sexual inferiority. Shame, which is considered to be a feminine characteristic *par excellence* but is far more a matter of convention than might be supposed, has as its purpose, we believe, concealment of genital deficiency. We are not forgetting that at a later time shame takes on other functions. It seems that women have made few contributions to the discoveries and inventions in the history of civilization; there is, however, one technique which they may have invented—that of plaiting and weaving. If that is so, we should be tempted to guess the unconscious motive for the achievement. Nature herself would seem to have given the model which this achievement imitates by causing the growth at maturity of the pubic hair that conceals the genitals. The step that remained to be taken lay in making the threads adhere to one another, while on the body they stick into the skin and are only matted together. If you reject this idea as fantastic and regard my belief in the influence of lack of a penis on the configuration of femininity as an *idée fixe*, I am of course defenceless.

The determinants of women's choice of an object are often made unrecognizable by social conditions. Where the choice is able to show itself freely, it is often made in accordance with the narcissistic ideal of the man whom the girl had wished to become. If the girl has remained in her attachment to her father—that is, in the Oedipus complex—her choice is made according to the paternal type. Since, when she turned from her mother to her father, the hostility of her ambivalent relation remained with her mother, a choice of this kind should guarantee a happy marriage. But very often the outcome is of a kind that presents a general threat to such a settlement of the conflict due to ambivalence. The hostility that has been left behind follows in the train of the positive attachment and spreads over on to the new object. The woman's husband, who to begin with inherited from her father, becomes after a time her mother's heir as well. So it may easily happen that the second half of a woman's life may be filled by the struggle against her husband, just as the shorter first half was filled by her rebellion against her mother. When this reaction has been lived through, a second marriage may easily turn out very much more satisfying. Another alteration in a woman's nature, for which lovers are unprepared, may occur in a marriage after the first child is born. Under the influence of a woman's becoming a mother herself, an identification with her own mother may be revived, against which she had striven up till the time of her marriage, and this may attract all the available libido to itself, so that the compulsion to repeat reproduces an unhappy marriage between her parents. The difference in a mother's reaction to the birth of a son or a daughter shows that the old factor of lack of a penis has even now not lost its strength. A mother is only brought unlimited satisfaction by her relation to a son; this is altogether the most perfect, the most free from ambivalence of all human relationships. A mother can transfer to her son the ambition which she has been obliged to suppress in herself, and she can expect from him the satisfaction of all that has been left over in her of her masculinity complex. Even a marriage is not made secure until the wife has succeeded in making her husband her child as well and in acting as a mother to him.

A woman's identification with her mother allows us to distinguish two strata: the pre-Oedipus one which rests on her affectionate attachment to her mother and takes her as a model, and the later one from the Oedipus complex which seeks to get rid of her mother and take her place with her father. We are no doubt justified in saying that much of both of them is left over for the future and that neither of them is adequately surmounted in the course of development. But the phase of the affectionate pre-Oedipus attachment is the decisive one for a woman's future: during it preparations are made for the acquisition of the characteristics with which she will later fulfil her role in the sexual function and perform her invaluable social tasks. It is in this identification too that she acquires her attractiveness to a man, whose Oedipus attachment to his mother it kindles into passion. How often it happens, however, that it is only his son who obtains what he himself aspired to! One gets an impression that a man's love and a woman's are a phase apart psychologically.

The fact that women must be regarded as having little sense of justice is no doubt related to the predominance of envy in their mental life; for the demand for justice is a modification of envy and lays down the condition subject to which one can put envy aside. We also regard women as weaker in their social interests and as having less capacity for sublimating their instincts than men. The former is no doubt derived from the dissocial quality which unquestionably characterizes all sexual relations. Lovers find sufficiency in each other, and families too resist inclusion in more comprehensive associations. The aptitude for sublimation is subject to the greatest individual variations. On the other hand I cannot help mentioning an impression that we are constantly receiving during analytic practice. A man of about thirty strikes us as a youthful, somewhat unformed individual, whom we expect to make powerful use of the possibilities for development opened up to him by analysis. A woman of the same age, however, oftens frightens us by her psychical rigidity and unchangeability. Her libido has taken up final positions and seems incapable of exchanging them for others. There are no paths open to further development; it is as though the whole process had already run its course and remains thenceforward insusceptible to influence—as though, indeed, the difficult development to femininity had exhausted the possibilities of the person concerned. As therapists we lament this state of things, even if we succeed in putting an end to our patient's ailment by doing away with her neurotic conflict.

That is all I had to say to you about femininity. It is certainly incomplete and fragmentary and does not always sound friendly. But do not forget that I have only been describing women in so far as their nature is determined by their sexual function. It is true that that influence extends very far; but we do not overlook the fact that an individual woman may be a human being in other respects as well. If you want to know more about femininity, enquire from your own experiences of life, or turn to the poets, or wait until science can give you deeper and more coherent information.

Breaking the Sexual Taboo in Literature

SOURCES

95. D. H. Lawrence, "Sun," in *The Complete Short Stories*, 3 vols., II (London, 1976), 528, 529-31, 535. Originally published in 1926.

96. Rebecca West, *The Judge* (London, 1980), pp. 284-88. Originally published in 1922.

97. Radclyffe Hall, *The Well of Loneliness* (New York, 1932), pp. 4-5, 163, 171, 210-11, 226-33. Originally published in London, 1928.

Throughout the 1920's, as Freudian psychoanalysts were addressing the issue of women and femininity, a growing number of creative writers insisted on the centrality of sexual identity in their fiction, incorporating a more general Freudian outlook into their best-selling novels and short stories. The shock-value of this topic surely stimulated sales, but what was more significant was the serious attempt to grapple with the increasingly polarized psychology of manliness and womanliness that emerged in the inter-war period. Three important British authors whose works apply such psychosexual insights to women's lives are excerpted below.

The best known literary exponent of Freud's theory of penis-envy was David Herbert Lawrence (1885-1930), the sickly son of a Nottinghamshire coal-miner's family who brilliantly transposed his own grandiose dreams of sexual and social power into fictional form. Lawrence had been introduced to Freud's insistence on sexuality as the central motivating force for all human behavior by Frieda von Richthofen, a German aristocrat who divorced her pedantic English husband in order to marry the fascinating Lawrence. As he explored the relationships between the sexes, Lawrence insisted in his postwar book *Fantasia of the Unconscious* (1922) that the sexes must be kept pure—"pure maleness in a man, pure femaleness in a woman"—and that men's transcendent purpose was the key to their dominance over women. He interpreted women's longings alternately as a quest for men's roles and endeavors—that is, as a phallic substitute—or as an explicitly phallic quest for sexual union. The latter approach characterizes his highly-charged short story "Sun," in which an American heroine from the Northeast is sent off to Greece by her doctors to recapture her primitive female identity, a vehicle for Lawrence's exultation in phallic symbolism. In "Sun," the grandeur and cruelty of maleness totally overwhelms the passive receptive demands of the woman.

A contemporary of D. H. Lawrence and, like him, an early enthusiast for Freudian insights, was the novelist and journalist Rebecca West (born 1892). Born Cicily Isabel Fairfield and educated in Edinburgh, the youngest of three sisters, she chose Rebecca West as her pseudonym after Ibsen's free-thinking "new woman" heroine in *Rosmersholm*. West burst upon the London literary scene in 1911 while still in her teens as a fearless and incisive reviewer for a newly founded weekly entitled *Freewoman*. Here she displayed her interests in philosophy, politics, and literature which, when coupled with woman suffrage and socialism, placed her in the vanguard of thinking about the woman question. In drawing on psychological theories of sexuality, West clearly emphasized a female perspective, and celebrated the creative aspects of female sexuality and maternity. She acknowledged later that she had "soon become disenchanted with Freudian thought, particularly as imported into England, because of its anti-feminism."

As a twenty-year-old staff member she wrote in *Freewoman* of the fifty-five-year-old H. G. Wells, who in 1912 was at the height of his literary fame: "He is the Old Maid among novelists, even the sex obsession lay clotted . . . like cold white sauce . . ."—a challenge the philandering Wells could not resist. Their encounter resulted in a stormy ten-year liaison and the birth of a son out of wedlock. The passages in our second selection are excerpted from West's novel *The Judge* (1922), which she wrote toward the end of her relationship with Wells. They reveal West's grappling with the still tabooed topic of unmarried motherhood and with the mother's complex quasi-sexual Oedipal bond with her infant son, both of which offended the sensibilities of male reviewers. In the story the heroine contracts a marriage of convenience with the butler Peacey—on the understanding that it would be a token marriage only—in order to give her illegitimate child a name.

Our third selection presents the courageous attempt of a woman writer, Radclyffe Hall (1886-1943), to seek public acceptance and understanding for the phenomenon of lesbianism. Although the double standard and women's sexuality in heterosexual relationships had only recently become acceptable topics in Western literature, serious discussion of homosexuality or "sexual inversion," as it was then called, was still confined to medical textbooks. Even though an English avant-garde writer, Edward Carpenter, had published a nontechnical work on homosexuality in 1908 (in which he attempted to justify homosexuality by compiling examples of unusually talented representatives), it was left to a woman to precipitate a literary *cause célèbre* in the 1920's by considering this subject at length in fiction.

The novelist and self-styled "sexual invert" Radclyffe Hall, who had early dropped her given name Marguerite, published her novel *The Well of Loneliness* in 1928, with the express purpose of making the subject of lesbianism "available to the general public who did not have access to technical treatises." Interpreting her own personal experience and that of her acquaintances in the well-known artistic lesbian circle of Natalie Barney in Paris, Hall's characters embody a psychosexual stereotype of the lesbian women traceable to Krafft-Ebing and other early sexologists. According to this stereotype, these women's "abnormal" instincts are larger than life; they are physically strong, active, ambitious, and protectively "masculine"—while their "normal" female mistresses are characterized by all the stereotypical instincts of soft, clinging, confused "womanliness." The point that Radclyffe Hall was most anxious to impress upon her reluctant public was that sexual inverts had a deep capacity for love, that they were moral, law-abiding human beings who were unfortunately physically, and therefore psychically, abnormal. In affirming the misconceptions of early sexologists and the stereotypes of the masculinized "new women," however, she mirrored the received wisdom of her time. Even the British sexologist Havelock Ellis, who wrote an approving preface to Hall's novel, considered homosexuality "a highly abnormal aberration." Hall's concern with the moral strength and good character of lesbians notwithstanding, *The Well of Loneliness* was quickly banned in England under the Obscene Publications Act of 1857. However, English editions published in France and America continued to sell in large quantities, and the novel was soon translated into most European languages, thereby imprinting the stereotype of the "male/female" lesbian couple upon the minds of its many twentieth-century readers.

---

95. D. H. Lawrence (1926)

"Take her away, into the sun," the doctors said.

She herself was sceptical of the sun, but she permitted herself to be carried away, with her child, and a nurse, and her mother, over the sea. . . .

"You know, Juliet, the doctor told you to lie in the sun, without your clothes. Why don't you?" said the mother.

"When I am fit to do so, I will. Do you want to kill me?" Juliet flew at her.

"To kill you, no! Only to do you good."

"For God's sake, leave off wanting to do me good."

The mother at last was so hurt and incensed, she departed.

The sea went white—and then invisible. Pouring rain fell. It was cold, in the house built for the sun.

Again a morning when the sun lifted himself naked and molten, sparkling over the sea's rim. The house faced southwest. Juliet lay in her bed and watched him rise. It was as if she had never seen the sun rise before. She had never seen the naked sun stand up pure upon the sea-line, shaking the night off himself.

So the desire sprang secretly in her to go naked in the sun. She cherished her desire like a secret.

But she wanted to go away from the house—away from people. And it is not easy, in a country where every olive tree has eyes, and every slope is seen from afar, to go hidden.

But she found a place: a rocky bluff, shoved out to the sea and sun and overgrown with large cactus, the flat-leaved cactus called prickly pear. Out of this blue-grey knoll of cactus rose one cypress tree, with a pallid, thick trunk, and a tip that leaned over, flexible, up in the blue. It stood like a guardian looking to sea; or a low, silvery candle whose huge flame was darkness against light: earth sending up her proud tongue of gloom.

Juliet sat down by the cypress trees and took off her clothes. The contorted cactus made a forest, hideous yet fascinating, about her. She sat and offered her bosom to the sun, sighing, even now, with a certain hard pain, against the cruelty of having to give herself.

But the sun marched in blue heaven and sent down his rays as he went. She felt the soft air of the sea on her breasts, that seemed as if they would never ripen. But she hardly felt the sun. Fruits that would wither and not mature, her breasts.

Soon, however, she felt the sun inside them, warmer than ever love had been, warmer than milk or the hands of her baby. At last, at last her breasts were like long white grapes in the hot sun.

She slid off all her clothes and lay naked in the sun, and as she lay she looked up through her fingers at the central sun, his blue pulsing roundness, whose outer edges streamed brilliance. Pulsing with marvellous blue, and alive, and streaming white fire from his edges, the sun! He faced down to her with his look of blue fire, and enveloped her breasts and her face, her throat, her tired belly, her knees, her thighs and her feet.

She lay with shut eyes, the colour of rosy flame through her lids. It was too much. She reached and put leaves over her eyes. Then she lay again, like a long white gourd in the sun, that must ripen to gold.

She could feel the sun penetrating even into her bones; nay, farther, even into her emotions and her thoughts. The dark tensions of her emotion began to give way, the cold dark clots of her thoughts began to dissolve. She was beginning to feel warm right through. Turning over, she let her shoulders dissolve in the sun, her loins, the backs of her thighs, even her heels. And she lay half stunned with wonder at the thing that was happening to her. Her weary, chilled heart was melting, and, in melting, evaporating.

When she was dressed again she lay once more and looked up at the cypress tree, whose crest, a flexible filament, fell this way and that in the breeze. Meanwhile, she was conscious of the great sun roaming in heaven.

So, dazed, she went home, only half-seeing, sun-blinded and sun-dazed. And her blindness was like a richness to her, and her dim, warm, heavy half-consciousness was like wealth. . . .

It was not just taking sunbaths. It was much more than that. Something deep inside her unfolded and relaxed, and she was given. By some mysterious power inside her, deeper than her known consciousness and will, she was put into connection with the sun, and the stream flowed of itself, from her womb. She herself, her conscious self, was secondary, a secondary person, almost an onlooker. The true Juliet was this dark flow from her deep body to the sun.

She had always been mistress of herself, aware of what she was doing, and held tense for her own power. Now she felt inside her quite another sort of power, something greater than herself, flowing by itself. Now she was vague, but she had a power beyond herself.

96. Rebecca West (1922)

The evening when it all happened she had been so utterly given up to happiness. She had taken the most preposterously long time to put Richard to bed. He had had a restless day, and had been so drowsy when she went to feed him in the evening that she had put him back in his cradle in his day clothes, but about half-past eight he had awakened and called her, and she found him very lively and roguish. She had stripped him and then could not bear to put his night-clothes on, he looked so lovely lying naked in her lap. He was not one of those babies who are pieces of flesh that slowly acquire animation by feeding and sleeping; from his birth he had seemed to be charged with the whole vitality of a man. He was minute as a baby of three months is, he was helpless, he had not yet made the amazing discovery that his hand belonged to him, but she knew that when she held him she held a strong man. This babyhood was the playful disguise in which he came into the world in order that they might get on easy terms with one another and be perfect companions. Never would he be able to feel tyrannous because of his greater strength, for he would remember the time when she had lifted him in her weak arms, and that same memory would prevent her from ever being depressed into a sense of inferiority, so that they would ever move in the happy climate of a sense of equality. And every moment of this journey towards that perfect relationship was going to be a delight.

She bent over him, enravished by the brilliant bloom of his creamy skin and the black blaze of his eyes, which had been black from birth, as hardly any children's are; turned him over and kissed the delicate crook of his knees and the straight column of his spine and the little square wings of his shoulderblades, and then she turned him back again and jeered at him because he wore the phlegmatic, pasha-like smile of an adored baby. She became vexed with love for him, and longed to clasp him, to crush him as she knew she must not. She put on his night-clothes, kissing him extravagantly and unsatedly, and when she finished he wailed and nuzzled to her breast. "Oh, no, you greedy little thing," she cried, for it was a quarter of an hour before he should have been fed again, but a wave of love passed through her and she took him to her. They were fused, they were utterly content with one another. He finished, smacking his lips like an old epicure. "Oh, my darling love!" she cried and put him back into the cot and ran downstairs. If she stayed longer she would keep him awake with her kisses and play. She was brightened and full of silent laughter, like a girl who escapes from her sweetheart.

Grandmother sat very quietly at her sewing and soon went upstairs. Grandmother was getting very old. When she said "Good-night" she seemed to be speaking out of the cavern of some preoccupation, and when she went upstairs her shawl fell from her shoulders and trailed its corner on the ground. Marion hoped that the old lady had not worn herself out by worrying about her, and she pulled out the sewing that had been shut up in the work-basket and meditated finishing it, but she was too tired. Nowadays she knew a fatigue which she could yield to frankly, as it was honourable to her organism, and meant that her strength was going into her milk and not into her blood. She folded her arms on the table and laid her head on them and thought of Richard. It was his monthly birthday to-day. He was three months old. She grieved to think that she could feed him for only six months more. How could she endure to be quite separate from him? Sometimes even now she regretted that the time had gone when he was within her, so that each of her heartbeats was a caress to him, to which his little heart replied, and she would feel utterly desolate and hungry when she could no longer join him to her bosom. But she would always be able to kiss him. She imagined herself a few years ahead, calling him back when he was running off to play, holding his resistant sturdiness in her arms while he gave her hasty, smudged kisses and hugged his ball for more loving. But she reflected that, while the character of those kisses would amuse her, they would not satisfy her craving for contact so close that it was unity with his warm young body, and she must set herself to be the most alluring mother that ever lived, so that he would not sruggle in her arms but would give her back kiss for kiss. She flung her head back, sighing triumphantly because she knew she could do it, but as her eyes met her image in the mirror over the mantelpiece she was horrified to see how little like a mother she was looking. Lips pursed with these long imaginary kisses were too oppressive for a child's mouth; she had lost utterly that sacred radiating lethargy which hushes a house so that a child may sleep: on a child's path her emanations were beginning to cast not light but lightning.

She called out to herself: "You fool! If you really love Richard you will let him run out to his game when he wants to, that he shall grow strong and victorious, and if you call him back it must be to give him an orange and not a kiss!" But it seemed to her that this would be a sacrifice until, staring into the glass, she noticed that she was now more beautiful than she had ever been, and then she saw the way by which she could be satisfied. Harry must come back; she knew he was coming back, for they had intercepted his letter to her, and they would not have done that if it had been unloving. After she had weaned Richard she must conceive again and let another child lift from him the excessive burden of her love: then her mind and soul could go on in his company without vexing him with these demands that only the unborn or the nursling could satisfy. Then this second child would become separate from her, and she must conceive again and again until this intense life of the body failed in her and her flesh ceased to be a powerful artist exulting in the creation of master-pieces. It must be so. For Richard's sake it must be so. Her love would be too heavy a cloak for one child, for it was meant to be a tent under which many should dwell. Again as in the wood she laid her hand on her body and felt it as an inexhaustible treasure. Again she was instantly mocked.

There had come, then, a knock at the door. She had felt a little fright-ened, for since her stoning in Roothing High Street she had felt fear at any contact with the external world; she knew now that rabies is endemic in human society, and that one can never tell when one may not be bitten by a frothing mouth. But it was not late, and it was as likely as not that this was Cousin Tom Stallybrass come to say how the Frisian calf had sold at Prittlebay market, so she opened it at once.

Peacey stood there. He stood quite still, his face held obliquely, his body stiff and jointless in his clothes, like a huge, fat doll. There was an appearance of ceremony about him. His skin shone with the white lac-quer of a recent washing with coarse soap, he was dressed very neatly in his Sunday broadcloth, and he wore a black-and-white check tie which she had never seen him wear before, and his fingers looked like varnished bulging pods in tight black kid gloves.

He did not speak. He did not answer her reluctant invitation that he should enter. She would have thought him drunk had not the smell that clung about him been so definitely that of soap. From the garden behind him, which was quilted by a thick night fog, came noises as of roosting birds disturbed. His head turned on the thick hill of his neck, his lids, with their fringe of long but sparse black lashes, blinked once or twice. When the sound had passed, his face again grew blank and moonish and he stepped within. He laid his bowler hat on the table and began to strip off his gloves. His fleshy fingers, pink with constriction, terrified her, and she clapped her hands at him and cried out: "Why have you come?"

But he answered nothing. Speech is human, and words might have fo-mented some human relationship between them, and he desired that they should know each other only as animals and enemies. He continued to take off his gloves, while round him fragments of fog that had come in with him hung in the warm air like his familiar spirits, and then bent over the lamp. She watched his face grow yellow in the diminishing glare, and moaned, knowing herself weak with motherhood. Then in the blackness his weight threshed down on her. Even his form was a deceit, for his vast bulk was not obesity but iron-hard strength. All consciousness soon left her, except only pain, and she wandered in the dark caverns of her mind.

Her capacity for sexual love lay dead in her. She saw it as a lovely naked boy lying with blue lips and purple blood pouring from his side, where it had been jagged by the boar who still snuffled the fair body, sitting by with its haunches in a spring. She cried out to herself: "You can rise above this! This is only a physical thing," but her own answer came: "Yes, but the other also was only a physical thing. Yet it was a sacrament and gave you life. There is white magic and black magic. This is a black sacrament, and it will give you death." Her soul fainted into utter nothingness.

97. Radclyffe Hall (1928)

Sir Philip never knew how much he longed for a son until, some ten years after marriage, his wife conceived a child; then he knew that this thing meant complete fulfilment, the fulfilment for which they had both been waiting. When she told him, he could not find words for expression, and must just turn and weep on her shoulder. It never seemed to cross his mind for a moment that Anna might very well give him a daughter; he saw her only as a mother of sons, nor could her warnings disturb him. He christened the unborn infant Stephen, because he admired the pluck of that Saint. He was not a religious man by instinct, being perhaps too much of a student, but he read the Bible for its fine literature, and Stephen had gripped his imagination. Thus he often discussed the future of their child: "I think I shall put Stephen down for Harrow," or: "I'd rather like Stephen to finish off abroad, it widens one's outlook on life."

And listening to him, Anna also grew convinced; his certainty wore down her vague misgivings, and she saw herself playing with this little Stephen, in the nursery, in the garden, in the sweet-smelling meadows. "And himself the lovely young man," she would say, thinking of the soft Irish speech of her peasants: "And himself with the light of the stars in his eyes, and the courage of a lion in his heart!"

When the child stirred within her she would think it stirred strongly because of the gallant male creature she was hiding; then her spirit grew large with a mighty new courage, because a man-child would be born. . . .

But: "Man proposes—God disposes," and so it happened that on Christmas Eve, Anna Gordon was delivered of a daughter; a narrow-hipped, wide-shouldered little tadpole of a baby, that yelled and yelled for three hours without ceasing, as though outraged to find itself ejected into life.

Anna Gordon held her child to her breast, but she grieved while it drank, because of her man who had longed so much for a son. And seeing her grief, Sir Philip hid his chagrin, and he fondled the baby and examined its fingers.

"What a hand!" he would say. "Why it's actually got nails on all its ten fingers: little, perfect, pink nails!"

Then Anna would dry her eyes and caress it, kissing the tiny hand.

He insisted on calling the infant Stephen, nay more, he would have it baptized by that name. "We've called her Stephen so long," he told Anna, "that I really can't see why we shouldn't go on—" . . .

Through the long years of life that followed after, bringing with them their dreams and disillusions, their joys and sorrows, their fulfilments and frustrations, Stephen was never to forget this summer when she fell quite simply and naturally in love, in accordance with the dictates of her nature.

To her there seemed nothing strange or unholy in the love that she felt for Angela Crossby. To her it seemed an inevitable thing, as much a part of herself as her breathing; and yet it appeared transcendent of self, and she looked up and onward towards her love—for the eyes of the young are drawn to the stars, and the spirit of youth is seldom earth-bound.

She loved deeply, far more deeply than many a one who could fearlessly proclaim himself a lover. Since this is a hard and sad truth for the telling; those whom nature has sacrificed to her ends—her mysterious ends that often lie hidden—are sometimes endowed with a vast will to loving, with an endless capacity for suffering also, which must go hand in hand with their love.

But at first Stephen's eyes were drawn to the stars, and she saw only gleam upon gleam of glory. Her physical passion for Angela Crossby had aroused a strange response in her spirit, so that side by side with every hot impulse that led her at times beyond her own understanding, there would come an impulse not of the body; a fine, selfless thing of great beauty and courage—she would gladly have given her body over to torment, have laid down her life if need be, for the sake of this woman whom she loved. And so blinded was she by those gleams of glory which the stars fling into the eyes of young lovers, that she saw perfection where none existed; saw a patient endurance that was purely fictitious, and conceived of a loyalty far beyond the limits of Angela's nature. . . .

Pacing restlessly up and down her bedroom, Stephen would be thinking of Angela Crossby—haunted, tormented by Angela's words that day in the garden: "Could you marry me, Stephen?" and then by those other pitiless words: "Can I help it if you're—what you obviously are?"

She would think with a kind of despair: "What am I in God's name— some kind of abomination?" And this thought would fill her with very great anguish, because, loving much, her love seemed to her sacred. She could not endure that the slur of those words should come anywhere near her love. So now night after night she must pace up and down, beating her mind against a blind problem, beating her spirit against a blank wall—the impregnable wall of non-comprehension: "Why am I as I am—and what am I?" Her mind would recoil while her spirit grew faint. A great darkness would seem to descend on her spirit—there would be no light wherewith to lighten that darkness. . . .

Terrible, heart-breaking months. She grew gaunt with her unappeased love for Angela Crossby. And now she would sometimes turn in despair to the thought of her useless and unspent money. Thoughts would come that were altogether unworthy, but nevertheless those thoughts would persist. Roger was not rich; she was rich already and some day she would be even richer.

She went up to London and chose new clothes at a West End tailor's; the man in Malvern who had made for her father was getting old, she would have her suits made in London in future. She ordered herself a rakish red car; a long-bodied, sixty horse power Métallurgique. It was one of the fastest cars of its year, and it certainly cost her a great deal of money. She bought twelve pairs of gloves, some heavy silk stockings, a square sapphire scarf pin and a new umbrella. Nor could she resist the lure of pyjamas made of white crêpe de Chine which she spotted in Bond Street. The pyjamas led to a man's dressing-gown of brocade—an amazingly ornate garment. Then she had her nails manicured but not polished, and from that shop she carried away toilet water and a box of soap that smelt of carnations and some cuticle cream for the care of her nails. And last but not least, she bought a gold bag with a clasp set in diamonds for Angela.

All told she had spent a considerable sum, and this gave her a fleeting satisfaction. But on her way back in the train to Malvern, she gazed out of the window with renewed desolation. Money could not buy the one thing that she needed in life; it could not buy Angela's love.

That night she stared at herself in the glass; and even as she did so she hated her body with its muscular shoulders, its small compact breasts, and its slender flanks of an athlete. All her life she must drag this body of hers like a monstrous fetter imposed on her spirit. This strangely ardent yet sterile body that must worship yet never be worshipped in return by the creature of its adoration. She longed to maim it, for it made her feel cruel; it was so white, so strong and so self-sufficient; yet withal so poor and unhappy a thing that her eyes filled with tears and her hate turned to pity. She began to grieve over it, touching her breasts with pitiful fingers, stroking her shoulders, letting her hands slip along her straight thighs— Oh, poor and most desolate body! . . .

Two days later Anna Gordon sent for her daughter. Stephen found her sitting quite still in that vast drawing-room of hers, which as always smelt faintly of orris-root, beeswax and violets. Her thin, white hands were folded in her lap, closely folded over a couple of letters; and it seemed to Stephen that all of a sudden she saw in her mother a very old woman—a very old woman with terrible eyes, pitiless, hard and deeply accusing, so that she could but shrink from their gaze, since they were the eyes of her mother.

Anna said: "Lock the door, then come and stand here."

In absolute silence Stephen obeyed her. Thus it was that those two confronted each other, flesh of flesh, blood of blood, they confronted each other across the wide gulf set between them.

Then Anna handed her daughter a letter: "Read this," she said briefly. And Stephen read:

DEAR LADY ANNA,

With deep repugnance I take up my pen, for certain things won't bear thinking about, much less being written. But I feel that I owe you some explanation of my reasons for having come to the decision that I cannot permit your daughter to enter my house again, or my wife to visit Morton. I enclose a copy of your daughter's letter to my wife, which I feel is sufficiently clear to make it unnecessary for me to write further, except to add that my wife is returning the two costly presents given her by Miss Gordon.

I remain, Yours very truly,
RALPH CROSSBY.

Stephen stood as though turned to stone for a moment, not so much as a muscle twitched; then she handed the letter back to her mother without speaking, and in silence Anna received it. "Stephen—when you know what I've done, forgive me." The childish scrawl seemed suddenly on fire, it seemed to scorch Stephen's fingers as she touched it in her pocket—so this was what Angela had done. In a blinding flash the girl saw it all; the miserable weakness, the fear of betrayal, the terror of Ralph and of what he would do should he learn of that guilty night with Roger. Oh, but Angela might have spared her this, this last wound to her loyal and faithful devotion; this last insult to all that was best and most sacred in her love— Angela had feared betrayal at the hands of the creature who loved her!

But now her mother was speaking again: "And this—read this and tell me if you wrote it, or if that man's lying." And Stephen must read her own misery jibing at her from those pages in Ralph Crossby's stiff and clerical handwriting.

She looked up: "Yes, Mother, I wrote it."

Then Anna began to speak very slowly as though nothing of what she would say must be lost; and that slow, quiet voice was more dreadful than anger: "All your life I've felt very strangely towards you;" she was saying, "I've felt a kind of physical repulsion, a desire not to touch or to be touched by you—a terrible thing for a mother to feel—it has often made me deeply unhappy. I've often felt that I was being unjust, unnatural—but now I know that my instinct was right; it is you who are unnatural, not I. . . ."

"Mother—stop!"

"It is you who are unnatural, not I. And this thing that you are is a sin against creation. Above all is this thing a sin against the father who bred you, the father whom you dare to resemble. You dare to look like your father, and your face is a living insult to his memory, Stephen. I shall never be able to look at you now without thinking of the deadly insult of your face and your body to the memory of the father who bred you. I can only thank God that your father died before he was asked to endure this great shame. As for you, I would rather see you dead at my feet than standing before me with this thing upon you—this unspeakable outrage that you call love in that letter which you don't deny having written. In that letter you say things that may only be said between man and woman, and coming from you they are vile and filthy words of corruption— against nature, against God who created nature. My gorge rises; you have made me feel physically sick—"

"Mother—you don't know what you're saying—you're my mother—"

"Yes, I am your mother, but for all that, you seem to me like a scourge. I ask myself what I have ever done to be dragged down into the depths by my daughter. And your father—what had he ever done? And you have presumed to use the word love in connection with this—with these lusts of your body; these unnatural cravings of your unbalanced mind and un-disciplined body—you have used that word. I have loved—do you hear? I have loved your father, and your father loved me. That was *love*."

Then, suddenly, Stephen knew that unless she could, indeed, drop dead at the feet of this woman in whose womb she had quickened, there was one thing that she dared not let pass unchallenged, and that was this ter-rible slur upon her love. And all that was in her rose up to refute it; to protect her love from such unbearable soiling. It was part of herself, and unless she could save it, she could not save herself any more. She must stand or fall by the courage of that love to proclaim its right to toleration.

She held up her hand, commanding silence; commanding that slow, quiet voice to cease speaking, and she said: "As my father loved you, I loved. As a man loves a woman, that was how I loved—protectively, like my father. I wanted to give all I had in me to give. It made me feel terribly strong . . . and gentle. It was good, good, *good*—I'd have laid down my life a thousand times over for Angela Crossby. If I could have, I'd have married her and brought her home—I wanted to bring her home here to Morton. If I loved her the way a man loves a woman, it's because I can't feel that I am a woman. All my life I've never felt like a woman, and you know it—you say you've always disliked me, that you've always felt a strange physical repulsion. . . . I don't know what I am; no one's ever told me that I'm different and yet I know that I'm different—that's why, I suppose, you've felt as you have done. And for that I forgive you, though whatever it is, it was you and my father who made this body—but what I will never forgive is your daring to try and make me ashamed of my love. I'm not ashamed of it, there's no shame in me." And now she was stam-mering a little wildly, "Good and—and fine it was," she stammered, "the best part of myself—I gave all and I asked nothing in return—I just went on hopelessly loving—" she broke off, she was shaking from head to foot, and Anna's cold voice fell like icy water on that angry and sorely tor-mented spirit.

"You have spoken, Stephen. I don't think there's much more that needs to be said between us except this, we two cannot live together at Mor-ton—not now, because I might grow to hate you. Yes, although you're my child, I might grow to hate you. The same roof mustn't shelter us both any more; one of us must go—which of us shall it be?" And she looked at Stephen and waited.

Morton! They could not both live at Morton. Something seemed to catch hold of the girl's heart and twist it. She stared at her mother, aghast for a moment, while Anna stared back—she was waiting for her answer.

But quite suddenly Stephen found her manhood and she said: "I understand. I'll leave Morton." . . .

As though drawn there by some strong natal instinct, Stephen went straight to her father's study; and she sat in the old armchair that had survived him; then she buried her face in her hands.

All the loneliness that had gone before was as nothing to this new loneliness of spirit. An immense desolation swept down upon her, an immense need to cry out and claim understanding for herself, an immense need to find an answer to the riddle of her unwanted being. All around her were grey and crumbling ruins, and under those ruins her love lay bleeding; shamefully wounded by Angela Crossby, shamefully soiled and defiled by her mother—a piteous, suffering, defenceless thing, it lay bleeding under the ruins.

She felt blind when she tried to look into the future, stupefied when she tried to look back on the past. She must go—she was going away from Morton: "From Morton—I'm going away from Morton," the words thudded drearily in her brain: "I'm going away from Morton." . . .

Getting up, she wandered about the room, touching its kind and familiar objects; stroking the desk, examining a pen, grown rusty from long disuse as it lay there; then she opened a little drawer in the desk and took out the key of her father's locked book-case. Her mother had told her to take what she pleased—she would take one or two of her father's books. She had never examined this special book-case, and she could not have told why she suddenly did so. As she slipped the key into the lock and turned it, the action seemed curiously automatic. She began to take out the volumes slowly and with listless fingers, scarcely glancing at their titles. It gave her something to do, that was all—she thought that she was trying to distract her attention. Then she noticed that on a shelf near the bottom was a row of books standing behind the others; the next moment she had one of these in her hand, and was looking at the name of the author: Krafft Ebing—she had never heard of that author before. All the same she opened the battered old book, then she looked more closely, for there on its margins were notes in her father's small, scholarly hand and she saw that her own name appeared in those notes— She began to read, sitting down rather abruptly. For a long time she read; then went back to the book-case and got out another of those volumes, and another. . . . The sun was now setting behind the hills; the garden was growing dusky with shadows. In the study there was little light left to read by, so that she must take her book to the window and must bend her face closer over the page; but still she read on and on in the dusk.

Then suddenly she had got to her feet and was talking aloud—she was talking to her father: "You knew! All the time you knew this thing, but because of your pity you wouldn't tell me. Oh, Father—and there are so many of us—thousands of miserable, unwanted people, who have no right to love, no right to compassion because they're maimed, hideously maimed and ugly—God's cruel; He let us get flawed in the making."

And then, before she knew what she was doing, she had found her father's old, well-worn Bible. There she stood demanding a sign from heaven—nothing less than a sign from heaven she demanded. The Bible fell open near the beginning. She read: "And the Lord set a mark upon Cain. . . ."

Then Stephen hurled the Bible away, and she sank down completely hopeless and beaten, rocking her body backwards and forwards with a kind of abrupt yet methodical rhythm: "And the Lord set a mark upon Cain, upon Cain. . . ." she was rocking now in rhythm to those words, "And the Lord set a mark upon Cain—upon Cain—upon Cain. And the Lord set a mark upon Cain. . . ."

That was how Puddle [her former governess] came in and found her, and Puddle said: "Where you go, I go, Stephen. All that you're suffering at this moment I've suffered. It was when I was very young like you—but I still remember."

Stephen looked up with bewildered eyes: "Would you go with Cain whom God marked?" she said slowly, for she had not understood Puddle's meaning, so she asked her once more: "Would you go with Cain?"

Puddle put an arm round Stephen's bowed shoulders, and she said: "You've got work to do—come and do it! Why, just because you are what you are, you may actually find that you've got an advantage. You may write with a curious double insight—write both men and women from a personal knowledge. Nothing's completely misplaced or wasted, I'm sure of that—and we're all part of nature. Some day the world will recognize this, but meanwhile there's plenty of work that's waiting. For the sake of all the others who are like you, but less strong and less gifted perhaps, many of them, it's up to you to have the courage to make good, and I'm here to help you to do it, Stephen."

Civilization and Women's Discontents

SOURCES

98. Carl Gustav Jung, "Woman in Europe," in *Contributions to Analytical Psychology*, tr. H. G. and Cary F. Baynes (London, 1928), pp. 167-71. Originally published in the *Europäische Revue* (Leipzig) in October 1927.

99. Sigmund Freud, *Civilization and Its Discontents*, tr. James Strachey (New York, 1962), pp. 50-51. Originally published in German as *Das Unbehagen in der Kultur* (Vienna, 1930); first English edition, 1930.

100. Virginia Woolf, *Three Guineas* (London and New York, 1938), pp. 92-97, 100-101, 105-6, 113.

While literary exponents were busy popularizing the latest scientific theories on "manliness" and "womanliness" in the 1920's, psychoanalysts began to extend their own theories to encompass a broader interpretation of civilization itself, partly in consequence of political developments on the European continent. In the late 1920's and early 1930's the assertively patriarchal character of Mussolini's fascist authoritarian regime fully revealed itself, a development underscored by the coming to power in 1933 of Adolf Hitler in Germany. As instances of political and economic aggrandisement by these two regimes multiplied, and thus posed the likelihood of yet another war, other psychologists and social critics were likewise impelled to connect their analysis of personality formation to a diagnosis of the plight of European culture. Karen Horney (Doc. 93) was by no means the only commentator to insist on the intimate relationship between patriarchal culture and the problems of female personality. The following selections illustrate the ways in which the issue of women and culture was addressed by Carl Gustav Jung, Sigmund Freud, and Virginia Woolf.

The founder of "analytical psychology," Carl Gustav Jung (1875-1961) was raised in Basel, Switzerland. Until 1912, Jung, by then established in Zurich, was considered the most promising disciple of Freud. He broke with his mentor when he elaborated a competing theory of the unconscious that did not depend, as did Freud's, on the primacy of sexual concerns and family dynamics. In this 1927 article from the *Europaische Revue*, Jung considered the adverse psychic impact that "male careers" seemed to be having upon the educated women of his time. It should be kept in mind that Jung, like Freud, considered the human personality to be initially androgynous. However, Jung argued that as personality inevitably developed, according to the sex of the individual, in the direction of "manliness" or "womanliness," the opposing traits (which he refers to as the "animus" and the "anima") remain latent within the individual, occasionally reasserting themselves in troubling ways. Psychological health, then, depended on keeping these latent and opposing traits firmly in check. Jung's scholarly elaborations of these concepts reveal his firm commitment to the cultural necessity for sexual dimorphism—to the gender dichotomy expressed in such opposing pairs as rationality/intuition, abstract/concrete, active/passive. Woman's psychological destiny, Jung argued, is inevitably the pursuit of eros—of relationships, of wholeness—not of logos, or the pursuit and dissection of the facts of objective reality.

In *Das Unbehagen in der Kultur*, Sigmund Freud (Docs. 92, 94) extended his theory of personality formation to the development of culture, or civilization itself. In the paragraphs that precede the selection here he argued that, historically speaking, "love comes into conflict with the interests of culture," while, unavoidably, "culture threatens love with substantive restrictions." Woman, in this view, becomes hostile to the man-made social structures that surround her.

The phenomenon is viewed in a radically different light by the English novelist and critic Virginia Stephen Woolf (1882-1941). The daughter of one of the most eminent Victorian literary scholars, Leslie Stephen, and the wife of a Jewish socialist author and journalist, Virginia Woolf (together with her sister Vanessa Bell) formed the nucleus of a group of artists and intellectuals later known as the Bloomsbury Group. Recognized today as a path-breaking novelist for her imaginative exploration of consciousness and time, Woolf was equally well known in the thirties for her literary criticism—and for her eloquent questioning of the position of women. In *A Room of One's Own* (1928), Woolf had argued that economic self-sufficiency was the sole foundation for women's emancipation. In 1931 she decided to explore further the situation of the "daughters of educated men." But only in 1936 did she begin the book *Three Guineas*, in the shadow of Hitler's occupation of the Rhineland and Mussolini's invasion of Abyssinia; before she finished it, her favorite nephew, the poet Julian Bell, who had left to fight for liberty in Spain, had met his death there.

Thus, in addressing the philosophical question of how the daughters of educated men could work effectively for the prevention of war, Woolf injected an element of concreteness into the discussion about women's discontent with Western culture by drawing illustrative material from biography and the daily press. She questioned whether the very characteristics of the professions newly opened to women were themselves inimical to the preservation of peace, or whether, indeed, the entire superstructure of Western society as represented and led by an educated male elite ought not to be revolutionized from within. In this she differed fundamentally from those women who, in the nineteenth century, had assumed that, merely by taking part in politics, women could and would alter society for the better.

Before Woolf was willing to contribute one of the hypothetical three guineas (of the title of her book) to an association devoted to assisting women, she drafted a response asserting that "we are not going to send you a guinea to help you to help women to enter the professions unless you can assure us that they will practise those professions in such a way as to prevent war." Her closing remarks seem particularly chilling in light of her subsequent suicide, after war in Europe had indeed broken out.

---

98. Carl Gustav Jung (1927)

All the problems of the present form a knot; so that it is scarcely permissible to detach a single problem by itself, and treat it independently of the rest. There is, for instance, no problem of the 'woman in Europe' which omits man and his world. If she is married, then in the great majority of cases she is economically dependent upon man; if unmarried and earning her livelihood, then she is working in a profession already initiated and established by man. Unless there is a voluntary sacrifice of her whole erotic life, she must again stand in an essential relation to man. In manifold ways woman is indissolubly bound up with the man's world and therefore is exposed, as he is, to all the shocks and concussions of this world. The war, for example, has affected woman just as deeply as it has man, and she has to adapt to its consequences as he must. What the upheavals of the last twenty or thirty years mean for the world of men is displayed roundly on the surface; it is reported every day in the journals. But what it means for woman is not at first visible. For woman as woman is neither politically, nor economically, nor spiritually a visible factor of any importance. If she were she would stand more plainly in man's field of vision, and then would be taken into account as a competitor. Sometimes she does do this; but in doing so she becomes visible only as a man who, so to speak, is accidentally a woman. But since, as a rule, she stands on the intimate side of man, on the side where he only feels; that side for which either he has no eyes or will not see, woman appears as a sort of opaque mask, behind which everything possible and impossible can be assumed. Not only does he assume, he thinks he actually sees, and yet he somehow fails to hit upon the essential thing. The elementary fact, that a man always presupposes another's psychology as being identical with his own, aggravates the difficulty and hinders a correct understanding of the feminine psyche. This circumstance finds a purposive accommodation, viewed biologically, in the unconsciousness and indefiniteness of the woman. She allows herself to be convinced by projected masculine feelings. This is, of course, a general human characteristic; but with woman it has an especially dangerous nuance, since in this respect she is not naïve, for only too often her aim is to allow herself to be convinced. It fits in with her nature to remain in the background as an independently willing and responsible ego, in order not to hinder the man, but rather to invite him to make real his aims with respect to herself. This is a sexual pattern, but it has far-reaching ramifications in the feminine mind. By maintaining a passive attitude with an invisible purpose in the background, she aids a man towards his realization, and in that way holds him. At the same time she weaves a web of fate for herself, because whoever digs a pit for others falls himself therein. . . .

When we observe the way in which women, since the second half of the nineteenth century, have begun to learn masculine callings, to become active in politics, to found and lead societies, etc., we can see that woman is in the process of breaking with the purely feminine sexual schema in which apparent unconsciousness and passivity play a leading role. She begins to concede something to masculine psychology by establishing herself as a visible member of society; not merely hiding behind the mask of Mrs. So-and-So, with the obliging intention of having all her wishes fulfilled by the man, or to make him feel it if things don't go as she wishes.

This step towards social independence is a symptom even though it be only a response to compelling economic facts, and due to causes, other than the actual need itself. The courage and capacity for self-sacrifice of such women is certainly to be marvelled at, and only the blind could fail to see the good that has come out of these efforts. But no one can evade the fact, that in taking up a masculine calling, studying, and working in a man's way, woman is doing something not wholly in agreement with, if not directly injurious to, her feminine nature. She is doing what would be scarcely possible for a man to do, even were he a Chinaman. Could he, for example, take a place as a governess, or be in charge of a kindergarten? When I speak of injury, I do not mean physiological merely, but above all psychic injury. It is a woman's understanding characteristic that she can do everything for the love of a man. But those women who can achieve something important for the love of a thing are most exceptional, because this does not really agree with their nature. The love of a thing is a man's prerogative. But, since the nature of the human being unites masculine and feminine elements, a man can live the feminine in himself, and a woman the masculine in herself. None the less in man the feminine is in the background, as is the masculine in woman. If one lives out the opposite sex in oneself, one is living in one's own background, and that restricts too much the essential individuality. A man should live as a man, and a woman as a woman. The part belonging to the opposite sex is always in the dangerous neighbourhood of the unconscious. It is even typical that the effects in consciousness that emanate from the unconscious have the opposite-sex character. Thus, for example, the soul (anima, psyche) is of the feminine sex, since this concept, as concepts in general, proceeds from the mind of man. . . . What comes to the woman from the unconscious is a sort of opinion, that only perverts her mood secondarily. These opinions lay claim to being valid truth, and hold their own all the more solidly and durably the less they are subjected to conscious criticism. Like the moods and feelings of man, they are somewhat veiled and often quite unconscious. Hence they are seldom recognized in their true colours. They are in fact collective, having the character of the opposite sex, as though a man, the father for example, had thought them.

Thus it can happen, and does almost regularly, that the mind of a woman who follows a masculine calling is influenced by her unconscious masculinity in a way not noticeable to herself, but quite obvious to her environment. From this there comes a certain rigid intellectuality concerning so-called principles, and a whole host of argumentative biases which always go a little beside the point in the most irritating way, and which, furthermore, always inject a little something into the problem that is not really there. Unconscious assumptions or opinions are the worst enemy of woman; they can even grow into a downright dæmonic passion that irritates and disgusts men, and that does the woman herself the greatest injury by gradually smothering the charm and meaning of femininity, and driving it into the background. Such a development naturally ends in a deep, psychological division, in short, a neurosis.

Naturally, things need not go to this length, but long before this point is reached the mental masculinization of the woman has unwelcome results. She may indeed become a good comrade to the man, without having access to his feelings. The reason is that her animus (that is, her masculine rationalism, assuredly not true reasonableness!) has stopped up the entrance to her own feeling. She can even become frigid, as a defence-reaction to the type of masculine sexuality that corresponds to her masculine type of mind. Or, if the defence-reaction is not successful, instead of the receptive sexuality of woman, there develops an aggressive, urgent form of sexuality that is characteristic of man. This reaction is also a purposeful phenomenon, intended to throw a bridge across by main force to the slowly vanishing man. A third possibility, especially favoured in Anglo-Saxon countries, is a facultative homosexuality in the masculine rôle.

99. Sigmund Freud (1930)

Furthermore, women soon come into opposition to civilization and display their retarding and restraining influence—those very women who, in the beginning, laid the foundations of civilization by the claims of their love.* Women represent the interests of the family and of sexual life. The work of civilization has become increasingly the business of men, it confronts them with ever more difficult tasks and compels them to carry out instinctual sublimations of which women are little capable. Since a man does not have unlimited quantities of psychical energy at his disposal, he has to accomplish his tasks by making an expedient distribution of his libido. What he employs for cultural aims he to a great extent withdraws from women and sexual life. His constant association with men, and his dependence on his relations with them, even estrange him from his duties as a husband and father. Thus the woman finds herself forced into the background by the claims of civilization and she adopts a hostile attitude towards it.

100. Virginia Woolf (1938)

There they go, our brothers who have been educated at public schools and universities, mounting those steps, passing in and out of those doors, ascending those pulpits, preaching, teaching, administering justice, practising medicine, transacting business, making money. It is a solemn sight always—a procession, like a caravanserai crossing a desert. Greatgrandfathers, grandfathers, fathers, uncles—they all went that way, wearing their gowns, wearing their wigs, some with ribbons across their breasts, others without. One was a bishop. Another a judge. One was an admiral. Another a general. One was a professor. Another a doctor. And some left the procession and were last heard of doing nothing in Tasmania; were seen, rather shabbily dressed, selling newspapers at Charing Cross. But most of them kept in step, walked according to rule, and by hook or by crook made enough to keep the family house, somewhere, roughly speaking, in the West End, supplied with beef and mutton for all, and with education for Arthur. It is a solemn sight, this procession, a sight that has often caused us, you may remember, looking at it sidelong from an upper window, to ask ourselves certain questions. But now, for the past twenty years or so, it is no longer a sight merely, a photograph, or fresco scrawled upon the walls of time, at which we can look with merely an esthetic appreciation. For there, trapesing along at the tail end of the procession, we go ourselves. And that makes a difference. We who have looked so long at the pageant in books, or from a curtained window watched educated men leaving the house at about nine-thirty to go to an office, returning to the house at about six-thirty from an office, need look

* See the note on translation of Doc. 92 above.—EDS.

passively no longer. We too can leave the house, can mount those steps, pass in and out of those doors, wear wigs and gowns, make money, administer justice. Think—one of these days, you may wear a judge's wig on your head, an ermine cape on your shoulders; sit under the lion and the unicorn; draw a salary of five thousand a year with a pension on retiring. We who now agitate these humble pens may in another century or two speak from a pulpit. Nobody will dare contradict us then; we shall be the mouthpieces of the divine spirit—a solemn thought, is it not? Who can say whether, as time goes on, we may not dress in military uniform, with gold lace on our breasts, swords at our sides, and something like the old family coal-scuttle on our heads, save that that venerable object was never decorated with plumes of white horsehair. You laugh—indeed the shadow of the private house still makes those dresses look a little queer. We have worn private clothes so long—the veil that St. Paul recommended. But we have not come here to laugh, or to talk of fashions—men's and women's. We are here, on the bridge, to ask ourselves certain questions. And they are very important questions; and we have very little time in which to answer them. The questions that we have to ask and to answer about that procession during this moment of transition are so important that they may well change the lives of all men and women for ever. For we have to ask ourselves, here and now, do we wish to join that procession, or don't we? On what terms shall we join that procession? Above all, where is it leading us, the procession of educated men? The moment is short; it may last five years; ten years, or perhaps only a matter of a few months longer. But the questions must be answered; and they are so important that if all the daughters of educated men did nothing, from morning to night, but consider that procession, from every angle, if they did nothing but ponder it and analyse it, and think about it and read about it and pool their thinking and reading, and what they see and what they guess, their time would be better spent than in any other activity now open to them. But, you will object, you have no time to think; you have your battles to fight, your rent to pay, your bazaars to organize. That excuse shall not serve you, Madam. As you know from your own experience, and there are facts that prove it, the daughters of educated men have always done their thinking from hand to mouth; not under green lamps at study tables in the cloisters of secluded colleges. They have thought while they stirred the pot, while they rocked the cradle. It was thus that they won us the right to our brand-new sixpence. It falls to us now to go on thinking; how are we to spend that sixpence? Think we must. Let us think in offices; in omnibuses; while we are standing in the crowd watching Coronations and Lord Mayor's Shows; let us think as we pass the Cenotaph; and in Whitehall; in the gallery of the House of Commons; in the Law Courts; let us think at baptisms and marriages and funerals. Let us never cease from thinking—what is this 'civilization' in which we find ourselves? What are these ceremonies and why should we take part in them? What are these professions and why should we make money out of them? Where in short is it leading us, the procession of the sons of educated men?

But you are busy; let us return to facts. Come indoors then, and open the books on your library shelves. For you have a library, and a good one. A working library, a living library; a library where nothing is chained down and nothing is locked up; a library where the songs of the singers rise naturally from the lives of the livers. There are the poems, here the biographies. And what light do they throw upon the professions, these biographies? How far do they encourage us to think that if we help the daughters to become professional women we shall discourage war? The answer to that question is scattered all about these volumes; and is legible to anyone who can read plain English. And the answer, one must admit, is extremely queer. For almost every biography we read of professional men in the nineteenth century, to limit ourselves to that not distant and fully documented age, is largely concerned with war. They were great fighters, it seems, the professional men in the age of Queen Victoria. There was the battle of Westminster. There was the battle of the universities. There was the battle of Whitehall. There was the battle of Harley Street. There was the battle of the Royal Academy. Some of these battles, as you can testify, are still in progress. In fact the only profession which does not seem to have fought a fierce battle during the nineteenth century is the profession of literature. All the other professions, according to the testimony of biography, seem to be as bloodthirsty as the profession of arms itself. It is true that the combatants did not inflict flesh wounds; chivalry forbade; but you will agree that a battle that wastes time is as deadly as a battle that wastes blood. You will agree that a battle that costs money is as deadly as a battle that costs a leg or an arm. You will agree that a battle that forces youth to spend its strength haggling in committee rooms, soliciting favours, assuming a mask of reverence to cloak its ridicule, inflicts wounds upon the human spirit which no surgery can heal. Even the battle of equal pay for equal work is not without its time-shed, its spiritshed, as you yourself, were you not unaccountably reticent on certain matters, might agree. Now the books in your library record so many of these battles that it is impossible to go into them all; . . . they all seem to have been fought on much the same plan, and by the same combatants, that is by professional men *v.* their sisters and daughters. . . . It seems as if there were no progress in the human race, but only repetition. We can almost hear them, if we listen, singing the same old song, "Here we go round the mulberry tree, the mulberry tree, the mulberry tree," and if we add, "of property, of property, of property," we shall fill in the rhyme without doing violence to the facts.

But we are not here to sing old songs or to fill in missing rhymes. We are here to consider facts. And the facts which we have just extracted from biography seem to prove that the professions have a certain undeniable effect upon the professors. They make the people who practise them possessive, jealous of any infringement of their rights, and highly

combative if anyone dares dispute them. Are we not right then in thinking that if we enter the same professions we shall acquire the same qualities? And do not such qualities lead to war? In another century or so if we
practise the professions in the same way, shall we not be just as possessive, just as jealous, just as pugnacious, just as positive as to the verdict of
God, Nature, Law and Property as these gentlemen are now? . . .

There it is then, before our eyes, the procession of the sons of educated
men, ascending those pulpits, mounting those steps, passing in and out of
those doors, preaching, teaching, administering justice, practising medicine, making money. And it is obvious that if you are going to make the
same incomes from the same professions that those men make you will
have to accept the same conditions that they accept. Even from an upper
window and from books we know or can guess what those conditions
are. You will have to leave the house at nine and come back to it at six.
That leaves very little time for fathers to know their children. You will
have to do this daily from the age of twenty-one or so to the age of about
sixty-five. That leaves very little time for friendship, travel or art. You will
have to perform some duties that are very arduous, others that are very
barbarous. You will have to wear certain uniforms and profess certain
loyalties. If you succeed in those professions the words 'For God and the
Empire' will very likely be written, like the address on a dog-collar, round
your neck. . . .

We, daughters of educated men, are between the devil and the deep sea.
Behind us lies the patriarchal system; the private house, with its nullity,
its immorality, its hypocrisy, its servility. Before us lies the public world,
the professional system, with its possessiveness, its jealousy, its pugnacity,
its greed. The one shuts us up like slaves in a harem; the other forces us to
circle, like caterpillars head to tail, round and round the mulberry tree,
the sacred tree, of property. It is a choice of evils. Each is bad. Had we not
better plunge off the bridge into the river; give up the game; declare that
the whole of human life is a mistake and so end it?

CHAPTER II

Economics, Politics, and the Woman Question

The Great Depression and the Threat to Women's Employment

SOURCES

101. Second Reichskongress of Working Women, "Kampfappell," Berlin, 22-23 November 1930. Published in the *Sächsiche Arbeiterzeitung* (Leipzig), 26 November 1930. Reprinted in *Dokumente der revolutionären deutschen Arbeiterbewegung zur Frauenfrage, 1848-1974: Auswahl* (Leipzig, 1975), pp. 122-24. Tr. SGB.

102. Teresa Noce [Estella], "The Life and Struggles of the Toiling Women of Italy," *International Press Correspondence* (World News and Views, Special Number on International Women's Day), 14, no. 13 (1 May 1934), 326-27.

103. Benito Mussolini, "Macchina e donna," *Opera omnia*, XXVI (Rome, 1958), 310-11. Originally published in *Il Popolo d'Italia*, 31 August 1934. The editors are grateful to Jane Vaden, Green Library, Stanford University, for the translation of this document.

104. Winifred Holtby, *Women and a Changing Civilization* (London, 1934), pp. 111-16.

The Great Depression of the 1930's posed a serious threat to women's employment, not only to women in the industrial labor force but also, especially, to the gains made by women in the professions during the 1920's. The following documents, incorporating testimony from mass meetings, political speeches, and other publications of the early 1930's, illustrate the nature of women's economic discontent, as well as the ways in which political leaders of that generation used the woman question to bolster their own political positions.

Married women were most gravely affected by the conflict between what society expected from them and their own need to be gainfully and productively employed, as our selections show. In the United States, because of "states' rights," no across-the-board federal solution to the problem of female labor was forthcoming (as was attempted in European nations). Yet public opinion might well have supported such a solution; the Gallup poll, conducted in August 1935 in the midst of the Depression, showed that a majority of 82 percent of those interviewed felt that a married woman should not work for pay if she had a husband capable of supporting her.

In England and on the European continent, the trend was to force married women out of the work-place once the Depression had set in. The issue was complicated, however, by the fact that the scale of women's wages, traditionally lower than that for men, still made it attractive to employers to hire women rather than men whenever they could.

In all nations stricken by the Depression, the Communist party spearheaded efforts to counter unemployment and exhibited special concern for the employment of women. To a large extent it was this effort that brought many intellectuals, the "Marxists of the heart," into the communist camp throughout the Western world.

The first two selections in this section show Communist women appealing to women and men of the (as yet non-fascist) Western world to unite against the quadruple threat of unemployment, antifeminism, fascism, and war. In 1929, the year before the second Reichskongress of working women in Berlin published its battle cry against hunger and need, two million German men were unemployed, compared with three hundred thousand women. Within three years, by 1932, the number of unemployed men had increased by about 124 percent and the number of unemployed women by over 200 percent, underscoring the metaphor of "misery increasing like an avalanche," but also illustrating that women's unemployment was increasing far more rapidly than men's in this period.

The author of the second selection, Teresa Noce (1900-1980), became an active member of the Italian Communist Youth Federation at the age of eighteen as a result of her experience as a factory worker in Northern Italy. Born in Turin, she began to work at the age of six delivering bread. Later she worked as a laundress and then as a textile mill operative. Through her activities in the Communist Youth Federation, she met Luigi Longo, well known as a former secretary of the Italian Communist Party. Noce had three children with Longo and married him in 1925.

In the 1930's Noce found herself in Paris, one of many Italian Communist women exiled from Mussolini's Italy. Working as a journalist under the pseudonym "Estella," she published a variety of tracts and articles dealing with oppression of Italian women, both as workers in the labor force and in the home. She also attacked the alliance of the Italian Catholic Church and the fascist state, both of whom she claimed were manipulating women for reproductive purposes. She left Paris for Spain to join the International Brigade, but after a period as a correspondent in the Spanish Civil War she returned to France. During the Second World War she was imprisoned in the Nazi women's concentration camp at Ravensbrück together with a group of other "undesirable" anti-fascist French women. Her marriage to Longo did not survive this separation. After the war, in 1948, Noce was elected to the Italian Chamber of Deputies as a member of the Communist party.

Noce's prime target was, of course, the Italian dictator Benito Mussolini (1883-1945), the author of the third selection. Mussolini epitomized fascism not only in the eyes of the women of the German Working Women's Reichskongress, but for everyone in the remaining Western democracies. The son of a blacksmith, Mussolini had been a schoolteacher, day laborer, and editor of a socialist newspaper. In 1914 he broke with the Italian Socialist party over Italy's entry into the First World War. Soon thereafter he established his own paper, *Il Popolo d'Italia*, which continued to serve as his propaganda organ after his foundation in 1919 of the Fasci di Combattimento (Fighting Bands)—one of the many small political groups to spring up in Italy after the war. Through Mussolini's powerful oratory and opportunistic leadership, this group swept aside all competitors and established a dictatorial hold over the nation's political life that endured from October 1922 until 1943. His methods provided an example for other would-be dictators and, in the process, gave the world a new political concept: fascism. Mussolini's fascist principles of militarism and statism underlay his emphasis on women's importance as mothers of soldiers, and on their "proper" place in the home, rather than in the work-place or the political arena. Few were as outspoken as he, however, in delineating the dichotomy between the work-place and the home in terms of their differing moral and physical impact on the virility and reproductive capacity of the sexes.

The final selection, by Winifred Holtby (Doc. 87), was published the same year as the articles by Noce and Mussolini. Here Holtby summed up the effects of the Depression, the loss of idealism, and the bitter rivalry for jobs between men and women that had replaced the postwar atmosphere of optimism regarding equality and achievements of women in a new democratic society. Holtby wrote from a British perspective, but as a political journalist and traveller she was keenly aware of both the national and the international impact of the Italian and German fascist ideologies and developments.

---

101. Second Reichskongress of Working Women (1930)

To Our Working Sisters in City and Countryside!

We—the thousand delegates of the second Reichskongress of working women in Berlin, we who are responsible to working women, to workers' wives, to agricultural laboring women, to the unemployed, to office workers and civil servants, to women of the middle classes and to young working girls from all parts of Germany—direct our revolutionary battle cry to you, our laboring sisters.

Dire need and misery grows like an avalanche sweeping down the mountainside: the grimly swelling numbers of the famished unemployed, the mounting exploitation of factory workers to the limits of physical collapse, the painful suffering of sick and undernourished children, the frightful prospect of further increase in our misery through the execution of the government's hunger program this winter, and the threatening danger of fascism—all these hard facts forcefully and relentlessly confront us with the question: *How can we escape hunger and misery?*

The Reichskongress makes clear that there is no escape from the capitalist attacks through silent suffering and retreat, as the bourgeois women's organizations have suggested. Nor is there any escape in a vain belief in a better "hereafter," as preached by the Church and the Center Party. Nor does escape lie in peaceful reconciliation with the rich—of workers' unions with the employers, as the Social Democrats would have you believe. Never will the owners voluntarily offer up their factories, their estates, or their magnificent villas simply because the majority of the laboring masses demand it. Nor does escape lie in the "Third Reich," that fascist dictatorship which the National Socialists, following the Italian example, want to create in a last-ditch attempt to save capitalism.

Escape from hunger and misery means a concerted battle for libera-

tion, to be fought by millions of workers. This battle must annihilate the rich, the exploiters, and the parasites who feed on the body of the working people; it must declare all industries and the land as the property of the workers; it must offer labor and bread to all; and, following the shining example of the Soviet Union, it must build Socialism.

The Second Reichskongress summons all working women in city and countryside to fight with us for this great aim—and to struggle for the advancement of women, through

full equality for women,
higher wages, equal wages for equal work,
a seven hour day at full wages,
adequate protection for mother and child,
revocation of the abortion restriction, in article no. 218.

The Second Reichskongress calls upon working women to join the ranks of the army of millions of battle-ready proletarians:

for the offensive against Fascism,
against the threatened danger of war,
against a government of hunger and slavery,
for a free Socialist Germany.

The only leader in this fight, as discovered by the delegates of the Second Reichskongress through practical daily struggles and through the lectures and discussion at this congress: *the one and only leader in this struggle is the K.P.D.* [the Communist Party of Germany]!

The organizer of our economic struggle in industry is the revolutionary opposition of the unions.

Follow the leaders of the Proletariat!

Follow the heroic example of fighting women metal-workers of Berlin, the women metal-workers of Mansfeld, the women miners of the Ruhr district, the Russian strikers, the Red women's armies, the women textile workers in all parts of Germany and China, the Indian women freedom-fighters, all of whom have demonstrated that working women have enlisted in the Red class front, that they are already fighting in the front ranks of the battle, and that in the Soviet Union they are working with the same rights as men to build Socialism!

Long live the struggle to liberate women from exploitation and slavery!

Long live the unified revolutionary struggle of workers in town and countryside!

Long live the struggle for liberation of the exploited of the world!

102. Teresa Noce (1934)

Even before Hitler, Italian fascism put forward the slogan that "the woman must go back to the home" and that "jobs should be given to the men who have to support their families." In reality, however, the fascist campaign against the employment of women in the factories coincides with the sharpening of the economic crisis and the growth of unemployment, which developed simultaneously with the crisis.

At the present time, there are in Italy 1,132,000 registered unemployed, which constitutes an increase, in comparison with last year. Among them are 241,000 women. These, however, are only the figures of the "official" fascist statistics. In fact, the number of unemployed is much larger, in particular of unemployed women.

In waging its campaign against the employment of women in the factories, fascism pursues the aim of (1) decreasing the value of female labour and cutting down wages to the extreme minimum; and (2) throwing the burden of unemployment mainly on the shoulders of the women, because, as a rule, unemployed women do not receive any benefit. On the other hand, the low wages for women make it easier to attack wages in general, and thus the employers are able to pay lower wages to those workers who are being taken on instead of the dismissed women, according to the principle "Back to the home," giving those workers the same or even lower wages than the dismissed women.

In those cases, however, where it is more advantageous for the fascist industry to use female labour instead of male labour, the men are dismissed—in spite of all the demagogy about the necessity of giving the jobs, in the first place, to the supporters of families—and are replaced by women or even children.

The conditions of starvation and misery into which fascism has forced the Italian toiling masses, weigh particularly on the proletarian women. From official, i.e., fascist statistics, it may be gathered that wage-cuts on the basis of collective agreements in the time from 1927 to 1932, amounted to 30-40 per cent. in the main branches of industry, employing mostly men. In those industries where mainly women are employed, the wage-cuts amount to 50-60 per cent. and even more.

Thus, for instance, the wages of the women cleaning rice (more than 180,000 agricultural women workers who work only during the season) fell from 25 liras in 1925 to 9.60 liras in 1933. As to the agricultural women workers in the South of Italy, their wages were cut down to 2.50 liras a day. (In order to judge the real value of wages in Italy, one must take into consideration that a kilo of bread costs 1.50 up to 1.90 liras, according to quality.)

This concerns only the "official" wage cuts laid down in the fascist wage agreements. In reality, however, as has been admitted by the fascist trade union officials themselves, wages have fallen much more.

Besides all this, the wages of women workers are reduced still further because the wage agreements contain a number of points which enable the employers to exploit them to the utmost. Thus, the fascist wage agreement for the cotton industry (the textile industry employs the largest amount of workers in Italy, up to 600,000) lays down that fines may amount to 25-50 per cent. of the wages, that improvements in the cloth have to be paid for through reductions from the wages of the women workers, and finally, that the wages of young workers, which really constitute the majority of the workers in the mills, may not exceed 60 per cent. of the wages of an adult worker, although the norm of a young worker must be at least 70 per cent. of the ordinary norm.

The inhuman exploitation to which the women workers are subjected is admitted by the fascist trade union officials themselves (obviously for demagogic reasons) who express themselves on the subject as follows:—

The necessity to maintain cut-throat and often ruinous competition compels the employer to resort to various means in order to cut down production costs. Besides wage-cuts and demands for increased labour productivity on the part of the workers, etc., the employers resort to a great extent to the replacement of men by women, youth and children. The same production norm is demanded from these categories as had been given before by adult men, the result being that about 50 per cent. is saved on wages. ("Lavora Mascista" of July 2, 1933.)

Against these conditions of starvation, exploitation and terror into which the Italian working masses are being forced by fascism, the women workers react by marching in the front ranks of the struggle against fascism and against the exploitation by the employers, shoulder to shoulder with the men.

In the numerous unemployed demonstrations, protest meetings, demonstrations against taxes and fascism, in the strikes and during stoppages of work in the factories and mills, in the course of the actions and struggles against the employers inside the fascist trade unions, the Italian women workers are in the front ranks, which can be proved by a number of examples:—

In Sassano and Monte-San-Giacomo, the whole of the population took part in a demonstration aiming at occupying the Town Hall. In the fight with the gendarmes, the demonstrators answered with stones and gunfire. Eight demonstrators, men and women, were killed, and two gendarmes wounded.

In Asiago women with their children organised a demonstration against compulsory joining of the fascist party for the workers. The demonstration was held under the slogan: "Down with taxes!"

In San-Osvaldo (Udine) a large group of women who had been deprived of winter relief, went to the "Podesta" to protest. Before the demonstration leaflets had been distributed. In spite of the tremendous police apparatus, the workers succeeded in carrying through the demonstration and in winning their demands.

In the textile mill of Albina Botto (Trona Biellese) the workers were agitating against the compulsory operation of two machines. The fascist trade unions try to induce the workers to operate two machines instead of one, while accepting a wage-cut of 0.50 liras per 1,000 revolutions, when working on one machine, and of 1.33 liras per 1,000 revolutions when operating two machines. The Italian Federation of Trade Unions issued an illegal appeal. The workers refused, in an organised way, to operate two machines. Two workers were dismissed and taken home, guarded by gendarmes. The others were threatened with dismissal. The factory was occupied by a troop of gendarmes, who threatened to arrest the women workers unless they started work. Thereupon, the women workers in the spinning department stopped all machines and carried out a stay-in strike.

Many more examples could be given.

In the course of the difficult, stubborn, and heroic struggle against fascism and the employers, a great number of workers have been killed on the front of the class struggle. Many of them have been exiled to one of the Italian islands or condemned to long prison sentences. From the ranks of the Italian proletarian women, new fighters come forward to take their place.

The Italian women workers are determined to follow the example of their Russian comrades, and to fight for liberation as they have done. Under the leadership of the Communist Party of Italy and the revolutionary Trade Union Federation, the Italian women workers will continue their struggle against fascism and capitalism.

103. Benito Mussolini (1934)

We bring to your attention the questionnaire concerning unemployment and what to do about it, sent by the National Federation of Unions for the Chemical Industries (Federazione nazionale dei sindacati industrie chimiche) to the unions in the provinces (Unioni provinciali). Certainly, to pose the problem is not to solve it, but without clarifying the particulars of the problem we can hardly hope to find a solution.

Among the eight points covered by the questionnaire, two are of primary importance: the limiting of female employment and the ratio of machine work to manual labor. It is useless to bury our heads in the sand; the problem of mechanization affects us all equally. It is pointless to say that machines impede progress, that man is something less than civilization but something more than mechanized progress. The life of nations stands above and beyond that of mechanization. It is indeed significant that the very organizations of workers who, in the past, made use of this idea on behalf of the well-known emancipation of workers from manual labor are the ones who are now sounding the alarm. It is the worker who is now demanding to return to the much-hated and tedious manual labor.

Female labor is the second major aspect of the thorny problem of unemployment. And in addition, the woman factory worker and the woman worker in general bears directly on the demographic question. Work, though not a direct impediment, does distract from reproduction; it encourages an independence and consequent physical and moral habits that are incompatible with childbearing. The man, disoriented and, above all, "unemployed" in every sense of the word, ultimately renounces the family.

All things considered, machines and women are the two major causes of unemployment. In some cases, the woman herself often saves the family after the man has abandoned it but, on the whole, her work is the source of moral and political bitterness. The salvation of a few individuals is paid for by the blood of multitudes.

There can be no victory without death. The exodus of women from the work force would, without a doubt, have economic repercussions on many families, but legions of men would be able to raise their heads high and hundreds of new families would suddenly enter national life. It is necessary to convince ourselves that the same work that causes woman to lose her reproductive attributes furnishes man with an extremely powerful physical and moral virility. Such a virility the machine should sustain.

104. Winifred Holtby (1934)

The effect of the slump upon women's economic position is most obvious, not only in the problems of unemployment among both industrial and professional women, but still more in the bitterness surrounding the question of married women's paid employment, "pin money" office girls, unorganised casual female factory labour, and claims to alimony, maintenance and separation allowances. These are the dilemmas of scarcity. It is here that the shoe pinches when national purchasing power has failed to distribute adequately the products of industry.

During the War, women entered almost every branch of industry and most of the professions. Even the Diplomatic Service, still, when this book is written, closed to women (though a committee is inquiring into future possibilities) was temporarily invaded by the adventurous Gertrude Bell who, under the modest title of Temporary Assistant Political Officer, really acted as British representative in Iraq. In transport, engineering, chemicals, textiles, tailoring and woodwork, women took the places which, ever since the sorting-out process which followed the first disorganised scramble of the Industrial Revolution, had been reserved to men. They took and they enjoyed them.

Then the men returned, and on demobilisation demanded again the jobs which they had left. The position was not simple.

Some of the men had received promises that their work should be kept for them; but of these, some did not return. Some women surrendered their shovels, lathes and hoes without a grievance. Their work had been "for the duration of the war" and they had no desire to retain it.

But others thought differently. Women, they told themselves, had been excluded from the more highly-skilled and better-paid industrial posts for two or more generations. They had been told that certain processes were beyond their power. It was a lie. During the war they had proved it to be so, by their own skill and efficiency. Why surrender without a word opportunities closed to them by fraud and falsehood? They had as much right to wheel, loom or cash-register as any man. Why then pretend that they were intruders in a world which was as much their own as their brothers'?

Some of these malcontents were nevertheless driven out; some stayed because their employers found them cheaper, and became unwilling blacklegs. One notable example of this was the case of "writing assistants" in the Civil Service, the lowest-graded category of clerks, engaged on purely mechanical and routine tasks. Organisations of ex-service men repeatedly petitioned that men should be admitted to this work; but the refusal was justified on the grounds that the work—besides being inadequately paid—was "too mechanical" for men.

The boom came; the new industries of the South sprang up like mushrooms; cities grew. For six or seven years it seemed as though production was infinite in expansion and the presence of women at unfamiliar tasks, though arousing occasional local criticism, not nationally disturbing.

The slump changed all that. After 1928, jobs became not duties which war-time propaganda taught girls that it was patriotic to perform, but privileges to be reserved for potential bread-winners and fathers of families. Women were commanded to go back to the home.

The bitterness began which has lasted ever since—the women keeping jobs and the men resenting it—the men regaining the jobs and the women resenting it.

On November 14th, 1933, the Central Hall, Westminster, was crowded for a mass meeting of women's organisations to proclaim the right of married women to paid employment. The crowds, the banners, the enthusiasm, echoed, faintly but unmistakably the spirit of pre-war suffrage meetings. The following March the Hall was nearly filled again when a similar demand was made for "Equal Pay for Equal Work."

In January 1934 the *News-Chronicle* published an article on Women Secretaries by a well-known writer, pleading the advantages of higher payment in order that the girls might not only be better fed and housed, but neater in appearance, more self-respecting and therefore more efficient. On the next day a correspondent had written in to the paper, bitterly complaining: "Better pay and smarter clothes for women: unemployment and patched pants for men."

The men have a real grievance. So long as women are content to accept lower wages, to remain unorganised, and to regard wage-earning as a "meanwhile" occupation till marriage, their cheap labour will continue to blackleg; and during any widespread contraction of trade, under a system of competitive capitalism, employers will deliberately use them for this purpose.

But the trouble is complex. The slump did not only depress the economic life of the country; it depressed its political, its intellectual and spiritual life.

Just after the war, society was infected by a rush of idealism to the head. Democracy and reason, equality and co-operation were acclaimed as uncontested virtues. In the new constitutions of Europe and America were incorporated splendid statements about the freedom of opinion, equality of the sexes, accessibility of education. We were about to build a brave new world upon the ruins of catastrophe.

The children who to-day are young men and women were assured at school of a good time coming. Everything evil was the result of four years' war; that horror had passed; they were to inherit the benefits purchased by sacrifice. Old hampering conventions had broken down: superstitions were destroyed; the young had come into their kingdom.

It was under the influence of this optimism that young women cherished ambitions for the wider exercise of their individual powers, and saw no limit to the kind and quality of service which they might offer to the community.

About 1926, after the General Strike in England and its failure, after the entry of Germany into the League of Nations, and the delay by the Powers in making good their promises, the slump in idealism began to set in. Reason, democracy, the effort of the individual human will, liberty and equality were at a discount. As economic opportunities shrank, so the hopefulness and idealism of the early post-war period dwindled.

In Italy, Germany and Ireland a new dream of natural instinctive racial unity was arising, which designed for women a return to their "natural" functions of house-keeping and child-bearing; while in the English-speaking countries a new anti-rational philosophy combined with economic fatalism, militated against the ebullient hopes which an earlier generation had pinned to education, effort, and individual enterprise.

All generalisations are false. In every civilised country are little groups of older women with memories of suffrage struggles, and young women who grew up into the post-war optimism, and whose ideas remain unchanged by the fashions of the hour. It is they who still organise protests against reaction; who in national and international societies defend the political, civil, and economic equality of men and women; who invade new territories of achievement; who look towards a time when there shall be no wrangling over rights and wrongs, man's place and woman's place, but an equal and co-operative partnership, the individual going unfettered to the work for which he is best suited, responsibilities and obligations shared alike.

But these groups of professional women, organisers, artists, writers, members of societies like the Equal Rights International, the Open Door Council, the National Women's Party of America, the Women's International League of Peace and Freedom, are now in a minority and they know it.

The younger women more closely resemble a description recently given of the newly-adult generation in modern France. "They are fatalists. They are sensible. They are not interested in ideas. They believe that a war is coming against Germany which will destroy all individual plans, and they say 'Que Faire?' They do not choose their work. They have to take what they can get and be glad of that. They marry early, feeling that life being so short and uncertain they must make sure of posterity while they can. They are completely indifferent to large general principles or long-distance hopes of social amelioration. They have stoical courage but no enterprise, no hope, and no idealism. They ask for discipline, not freedom; for security, not for opportunity. Many of them are returning to orthodox religion; but few of them seem to have experienced religious ardour."

One man I know, an ex-minister of the Crown in this country, gave an explanation that the young generation just recently adult has grown up in a time of huge impersonal events—the War, the Boom, the Slump. News is reported daily of immense catastrophes over which they can have no control, the Japanese and Indian earthquakes, Chinese famine, African drought. The cheap daily press and wireless bring these facts vividly home to them in a way their ancestors never knew. The individual will seems unimportant, the individual personality is dwarfed, by happenings on so large a scale. The world is too much for them. They give it up, content to be passive passengers in a vehicle which they cannot steer.

This is the slump complex—this narrowing of ambition, this closing-in alike of ideas and opportunities. Somewhere, a spring of vitality and hope has failed. As though it required too great an effort against such odds to assume responsibility for their own individual destiny, they fall back upon tradition, instinct, orthodoxy. The slump is really a general resignation by humanity of its burden of initiative, and women fall under its influence as much as men.

German Fascism Seeks Women's Support

SOURCES

105. Adolf Hitler, Speech to the Nationalsozialistische Frauenschaft, 8 September 1934, Nuremberg; reprinted in *Hitler, Reden und Proklamationen*, ed. Max Domarus, 2 vols. (Würzburg, 1962), I, 449-54. Tr. SGB.

106. Gertrud Scholtz-Klink, Speech to the Nationalsozialistische Frauenschaft, 10 September 1935, reprinted in *Der Parteitag der Freiheit 1935, Officieller Bericht über den Verlauf des Reichsparteitages mit sämtlichen Kongressreden* (Munich, 1935), pp. 165-69, 171-72. Tr. SGB.

The postwar political and economic instability of the defeated nations provided singular opportunities for strong, uncompromising leaders who vowed to set things right once more. Following Adolf Hitler's coming to power in Germany in 1933 as the leader of National Socialism, German fascists addressed women's needs as mothers, wives, and workers in a time of dire poverty and economic despair; Nazi orators raised women's political consciousness but also—and more importantly—appealed to their self-esteem as *women*. Only then did the Nazis impress upon women the state's need for their sacrifices.

Two selections from speeches by National Socialist leaders—the dictatorial chancellor, Adolf Hitler, and his National Women's Leader, Gertrud Scholtz-Klink—provide the essence of German fascist ideology concerning women in the early days of Hitler's Third Reich.

The son of a minor state official, Adolf Hitler (1889-1945) had an unsettled childhood on the Austro-Bavarian border. In later life he dramatized his youth and his poor scholastic performance as years of poverty and privation. His youth in fact presents a chronicle of frustrations, rejection, and defiance of figures of male authority. Unemployed, and supported by his widowed mother, he acquired a political and ideological education with the Christian Socialist Party in Vienna, where he was profoundly impressed by the German nationalism and anti-semitism then flourishing in Austria's capital.

At the end of the First World War, soon after demobilization from the German army as a corporal, he joined the group that later became the National Socialist German Workers' Party, attracted by its platform of nationalism, imperialism, and anti-semitism, and by its strong-arm terrorist methods. By 1923 Hitler had emerged as one of the party's chief propagandists. While imprisoned for his part in an unsuccessful rising in Munich in that year, he wrote his ideological testa-ment, *Mein Kampf* (My Struggle). By 1933, his hypnotic personality, coupled with his political skill and the fanaticism of his followers, brought him, as leader (*Führer*) of the party, to the office of chancellor of the Reich, which was soon transformed into a dictatorship resembling that of Mussolini in Italy.

The National Socialist or German Fascist position on the woman question was expressed by Hitler in his many speeches to mass meetings of German women, as illustrated by our first selection. His hypnotic effect on large groups (both female and male) extended to many women who met him in person. However, Hit-ler's own close relationships with women exemplify the submissiveness expected from their sex in Nazi ideology. His two long-standing relationships both in-volved women who were about twenty years younger than he. The first was his seventeen-year-old niece, Geli Raubal, whose slightest friendship with other men precipitated Hitler's jealous rage. She was his constant companion from 1925 un-til she was found shot in their apartment in 1931, apparently a suicide. The sec-ond, his mistress Eva Braun, was at first kept at a discreet distance; Hitler made no secret of the fact that he felt marriage would hinder his career and his effec-tiveness as a charismatic leader. He finally married Braun after twelve years of intimacy, on the day before they took their own lives, with the Nazi empire shat-tered, and advancing American and Soviet armies at their door.

One of the women whom Hitler inspired to extraordinary efforts on behalf of his plans for the Third Reich was Gertrud Scholtz-Klink (born 1902) upon whom he conferred the title "National Women's Leader" in November 1934. The daughter of a small-town surveyor in the province of Wuerttemberg, and herself a trained social worker, Scholtz-Klink was married three times and raised eleven children. In *Die Frau im dritten Reich* (Woman in the Third Reich), she described the impact Hitler had made on her. She explained how, in her impressionable ad-olescent years after the first war, defeated Germans lived in a world of "hatred, darkness, and hopelessness. Until one day the name of a soldier who had been at the front—Adolf Hitler—awakened our people . . . and gave us what we needed more desperately than all else: self-confidence, faith in a future, and the courage for this faith." Her first husband, also a soldier returned from the front, joined the National Socialists; in 1930, when he died of a heart attack during an election meeting, she (at the suggestion of a party district leader) replaced him as a politi-cal speaker, specifically to encourage women's political participation.

Scholtz-Klink's experience as a social worker and mother of a large family, combined with her organizational acumen and oratorical flair, were effective as-sets in her rise to the nominal leadership of women in the Third Reich. Given Fascist philosophy, however, which placed women in a polarized (but submissive) role to men as breeders and nurturers of the pure Aryan race, and despite her imposing title, Scholtz-Klink's position was that of supporter—never one of cre-ative independent authority. This distinction became especially apparent in the Nazi doctrine that "women's" place was in the work force whenever the economy so demanded, a tenet that was emphasized as Hitler began to prepare for war and that became even more essential when military production depended increasingly on female labor after war was declared in 1939. As the war progressed, Scholtz-Klink herself became less concerned with the social work that had interested her earlier, and more with directing women's efforts out of the "Reichs maternity service" and into the industrial labor force, assisted by the 32,000 day nurseries her organization had established, which cared for over a million children.

Her 1935 speech to the Nazi Women's organization is a splendid illustration of the range of psychological appeals developed to ensure women's participation in building a cohesive National Socialist State by focusing reforms on areas of their greatest concern.

---

105. Adolf Hitler (1934)

Today, for the first time in many years, I am taking part in a meeting of National Socialist women and am therefore also taking part in the work of National Socialist women. I am aware that the preparations for this are the work of innumerable individual women and especially the work of your leader. Ever since its inception the National Socialist movement has not only recognized woman as its most loyal helpmeet but has also found her to be so.

I remember those difficult years of the movement's struggles, particularly those times when luck seemed to turn its back on us; those times when many of us lingered in jail, and others were in flight to alien lands, when many of us lay wounded in hospitals or were being murdered. I remember the time when the German spirit believed overwhelmingly that problems could be resolved only through reason and that this attitude caused many to abandon us for lack of faith. I know that at that time there were innumerable women who remained unshakably faithful to the movement and to myself.

At that time strength of emotion was demonstrably both the more forceful and the correct response. We saw that subtle intellect can too easily be led astray, that apparent intellectual arguments can make men of subtle intellect hesitate, and that at just such times the deepest instinct of self- and national preservation awakens in woman. Woman has proved to us that she knows best! In those times when the great movement appeared to many to be faltering and everyone was sworn against us, depth and certainty of feeling proved to be more stable factors than refined intellect and reputed learning. It is after all only a small minority who can advance beyond superficiality to innermost knowledge. However, the deepest knowledge is in effect rooted in the world of feeling. Those things that few philosophically endowed spirits are able to analyze scientifically, the mind of an unspoiled person will know instinctively. The feelings and, above all, the soul of woman have always complemented the mind of man.

When, as has occasionally happened in human affairs, the division of labor between man and woman has become blurred along an unnatural line, it was not because woman strove to dominate man, but because man was no longer in a position to fulfill his mission. The great wonder of nature and Providence lies in the fact that there is no possibility of conflict between the sexes as long as each sex fulfills its natural mission.

The phrase "emancipation of woman" is the product of Jewish intellect, and its content is stamped with that same intellect. During those truly good times in German life the German woman never found it necessary to emancipate herself. She controlled exactly that which nature freely gave her as her due to administer and preserve—just as the man in good times did not have to fear that woman would oust him from his position. Woman was quite uninterested in threatening man's position. Only when he became uncertain about his own mission did woman's eternal instinct for self- and national preservation enter into revolt. And following this revolt a reversal began that went against nature and that lasted until both sexes returned to the places assigned to them by eternal Providence.

When we say that man's world is the state, that man's world is his battle, his stake in the community, we could perhaps also say that woman's world is a smaller world. Because her world is her husband, her family, her children, and her home. But where would the greater world be without someone to care for that smaller world? How could that greater world survive if there were none who considered the cares of the smaller world their life's work? Indeed, the great world can only be built upon this smaller world! The great world cannot exist unless the small world is solidly established. Providence has appointed woman to care for this, her own world, so that man's world may be constructed from and upon it.

These two worlds never conflict. They complement each other, they belong together just as man and woman belong together.

We feel it is not correct for a woman to invade man's world—his chief sphere; to the contrary, we believe it is natural for these two worlds to remain divided from one another. The power of the heart and the soul dominates the one; the other is reserved for the power of vision, of hardiness, of decision making and the will to take command. In the first case this power demands woman's willingness to preserve and increase this important cell; and in the other case it demands man's willingness to sustain life.

Whatever sacrifices man makes in the struggle for his People, woman offers an equal amount in the struggle to preserve the individuals of the nation. Whatever man offers in the way of heroic courage on the battlefield, woman offers in ever-patient service and ever-patient pain and suffering. Every time a woman gives birth she fights a battle for the existence or disappearance of her people. Both partners must therefore honor and respect one another when they realize that each helps to fulfill the mission entrusted to them by nature and Providence. Thus, out of this position of both missions arises a reciprocal respect.

It is not true—as Jewish intellect would have us believe—that mutual respect is based upon the overlapping of sexual spheres of activity. On the contrary, such respect demands that neither sex encroach upon the sphere of the other. After all, this respect lies in the knowledge of each party, that the other is doing everything necessary to preserve the whole society!

Thus woman has ever been the helpmeet of man and his most faithful friend, and man has ever been the protector of woman and thus her best friend. And both of them recognized in this conduct of life the mutual basis for the existence of what they loved, and of its continuation. Woman is selfish about the preservation of her small world so that man may be in a position to protect the greater world, and man is selfish in the preservation of the greater world because it is inseparably bound to the other. We must resist that greatly depraved intellectualism that intends to tear asunder what God has joined together.

Because woman always operates from the deepest root, she is the most stable element for the preservation of a people. It is woman who has an infallible understanding of what is essential so that the race will not be destroyed, because it is her children who would be the first to suffer.

Men are usually far too intellectually changeable to recognize the truth of such basic knowledge. Only with time and proper education will men recognize their mission. It is for this reason that we National Socialists have argued for many years against women's participation in political life, which we consider unworthy of them. Once a woman said to me: "you must ensure that women become members of Parliament because only they will ennoble it." "I do not believe," I answered her, "that a person can ennoble that which in itself is evil. A woman who finds her way into this parliamentary business will not ennoble it; on the contrary, it will disgrace and profane her. I would not allow to women what I intend to take away even from men." My opponents believed that this view would prevent women from joining our movement. However, we attract more women than all other parties combined, and I am sure that we would win over the very last German woman once she has the opportunity to study the Parliament and the degradation of the women who are active in it.

Therefore, we have incorporated woman into the struggle for the people's community in such a manner as nature and providence have determined. We do not envision our women's movement as one that inscribes a program for the battle of the sexes upon its banners; on the contrary, we ensure a woman's movement that will struggle jointly with men. It is upon this very basis—the coming to us of millions of faithful, fanatical, female comrades-in-arms—that we have founded the new National Socialist people's community. These are sisters-in-arms for a mutual life in the service of the mutual preservation of life. These sisters-in-arms are not concerned with "rights" mirrored for them by Jewish intellectualism, but with duties that nature has assigned to us all.

In contrast to the many, many points in the program of the earlier liberal, intellectual women's movement based upon so-called intellect, the program of our National Socialist women's movement contains only one point—and this is: the child. It is this small being who must grow and develop and for whom alone the entire struggle for life makes sense. After all, what are we battling and struggling for if there were no one to come after us who would benefit from it and pass it on to the next generation? . . .

You, my women comrades, are here as leaders, organizers, and helpers in this struggle. You have taken on a glorious mission. For that which we desire to create on a broad scale for our people, you must offer a solid and sturdy inner foundation. You must give it an inner, spiritual, and emotional support and stability. In this struggle that we carry on today for our people's freedom, equality, honor and peace, you must be the complement of man so that, with a view to the future, we may take our places as true fighters for our people and before our people!

Only then will it be impossible for quarrels and disputes to flare up between the sexes; instead they will go hand in hand through life, combating together, just as Providence has ordained and for which purpose Providence created them both. Then only will the blessings of such joint labor be granted. Then only will there be no wrong-headed fight concerning theories; then only will man and wife not be divided by false ideas, but the blessing of the Almighty be bestowed upon their joint struggle in life.

106. Gertrud Scholtz-Klink (1935)

A year has passed since the day we met here for the first time as a unified group of German women, to demonstrate our willingness to cooperate in our Führer's work of reconstruction.

This year has been inspired by the desire to mark our times with our best efforts so that our descendants will be able to forget our nation's fourteen years of weakness and sickness. We women knew, quite as well as German men, that we had to teach a people, partially sunk in self-despair, attitudes requiring those very qualities that had been deliberately suppressed in our nation. In order to carry out our intention to unite and to march shoulder to shoulder, we demanded honor and loyalty, strength and sincerity, humility and respect—such virtues appeal to the soul of a people. In matters of the soul, however, it is no longer the majority who decide, but the strength and inner freedom of upright individuals. Therefore, we could only fulfill our task if it enabled us to penetrate the soul of the individual. . . .

When we came to the point of recognizing that the human eye reflected a nation's soul, we had to reach the women of our nation, once and for all, through our labor on women's behalf. Because as mothers our women have carried the heavy burden of the past fourteen years—and the ruins of the war and post-war period—in their hearts; and as future mothers other women must presently develop an understanding of the demands of our times—to both of these groups we dedicated the first important path that we built to the hearts of German women: our Reichs-Maternity Service.

Urged on by the tired eyes of many overburdened mothers and the responsibility for the coming generation of mothers, we joined together under the leadership of the National Socialist Women's Association [*N. S. Frauenschaft*] and appealed to the German women especially trained for this work. When I tell you today that, between the 1st of October 1934 and the 1st of April 1935, we enrolled more than 201,700 women in 7,653 maternity school courses in about 2,000 locations throughout the German Reich, it may not seem much at first glance. But we must not forget that we had no funds and met with much opposition, and that we had no patronage since we were quite unknown. But we did have absolute and unshakable faith. None of our traveling teachers asked: How much will I earn? or, What are my pension rights? We have done this work out of a sense of duty to our nation—and our nation has responded. On Mothers' Day this year we were presented with 3.5 million marks for this work of maternity training. Moreover, on this day of honor for the mothers of Germany, when we all collected money in the streets, we found that our humblest fellow-countrymen were the most generous. This was surely the most wonderful reward for all of us, but it also gave practical evidence of where our major efforts must be directed. And when, only one or two months from now, we open our Reichs-Maternity School in Wedding, formerly one of the most solidly "red" quarters of Berlin, we will be able to congratulate ourselves on having prepared a place, on behalf of our Party and our State, that will reveal to all of you how we are solving our problems.

In this place, mothers of all ages and classes discuss their problems and their needs. Here they will become acquainted with the aims of the National Socialist state and will receive inspiration to pass them on from woman to woman, and thus to recover our national faith in ourselves. If by means of the Reichs-Maternity Service we gradually succeed in brightening the eyes of our mothers and in bringing some joy into their often difficult lives, perhaps even a song to their lips, we may consider that we have accomplished our task, because happy mothers will raise happy children. But our Reichs-Maternity Service must also make a point of teaching our young and future mothers those things that a liberal era did not teach them—for the omission of which our nation has had to pay dearly—namely, that through marriage we consciously become mothers of the nation; that is, we understand and share every national requirement laid upon German men, and that, therefore, as wives we must unconditionally become the companions of our men—not merely in personal terms, but in all national requirements.

First we pursued our task by appealing to the mothers of the nation, and then to that generation closest to the mothers, the girls between eighteen and twenty-five years of age. We called upon them to join voluntarily in the chain of helping hands and to create a relationship of unbreakable trust among German women. And they came, our girls of the German Women's Labor Service.

You, my girls, who have now spent two years with me in the struggle for the autonomy of the German people, have learned to carry every responsibility and have become the inspiration of our mothers. No matter whether our girls are cheerfully helping German settlers on the moors in their difficult work of creating new homes; or whether they are working in Rhön, Spessart, or in eastern Bavaria, hand in hand with the National Socialist Welfare Organization in giving help to careworn adults and joyless children, in reawakening a taste for beauty and a belief in themselves; or whether they are helping German peasant women harvest from dawn to dusk—one thing unites them all, for they know: We are needed, we are of some use, and we are playing our part in the rebirth of our nation. And what is perhaps even more important, they come to know themselves, because the German land or the German plight confronted them with inexorable demands. Faced with the realities of life, neither beauty nor examinations, neither wealth nor connections suffice—only the value of personal character will stand the test. Because we have experienced all of this so deeply, we have demanded compulsory labor service for girls exactly as for German men.

Since at present we cannot satisfy all these demands, owing to financial and organizational difficulties, we have begun by making only those demands that professional and university women can take the lead in supporting. German women students have accepted the demand for compulsory labor service with the utmost readiness. But in spite of this, for the next few years our principal task will be to keep German women students constantly in touch with the vital realities of our nation, in contrast to the detachment of their private academic existence that was formerly so common. At one time, it was considered the height of achievement in Germany to know everything and thereby to lose the simplemindedness of childhood. We wish to impress on our women at the universities that, as university students, they must place the intellectual abilities entrusted to them at the disposal of their nation with the same humility as that with which women workers and mothers fulfill their duties. . . . This summer our women students began to live in this manner and thereby joined the chain of helping hands we have created among ourselves. They went into German factories and replaced working women and mothers, enabling them to have a real vacation in order to regain strength for their hard day-to-day existence. For it is these women, these mothers of families, who are hardest hit by the short working hours or unemployment of their husbands, because at home their children sap their strength. We were able to carry out this work of mutual assistance without great expenditure, owing to the solidarity of German women students and the cooperation of industrial management, the Labor Front, the National-Socialist Welfare Organization, and the National-Socialist Women's League.

This brings us to the point where we must consider the millions of German women who perform heavy labor in factories day in and day out. If we consider the human eye as the measure of a people's soul, it is here that we find the deepest imprints of that fourteen-year-long attempt to strangle our national soul. We know that a great deal of industrial work must always be done by women, but it is essential that the woman at the machine should feel that she, in her position, represents her nation, in common with all other women. That is to say, we awaken her consciousness so that she will say to herself: "This is my responsibility, my attitude determines the attitude of the nation." In recent times, this very basic consciousness of recognition of the importance of the tight mesh of joint national labor of individuals was not instilled. For this reason, we in the Women's Section of the German Labor Front have given the women workers their own women trustees and their own district and regional superintendents chosen from their own ranks, in order that they too may play their part in the labor of the nation. We are well aware that it is most difficult to include the working woman in the general scheme of responsibilities, because she is hardest hit by problems of unemployment and reduced working hours. But since we women are not directly concerned with financial relief, the help we can give must be indirect, though equally effective. We begin by giving advice to women and girls in the form of courses in cooking, sewing, and child-care in the maternity schools. In this way we have given considerable assistance to over 80,000 women workers and workers' wives in the past year. . . .

Our most important effort, however, toward the education of working women for a national socialist life-style has been our appointment of female social workers among the women working in factories. These female social workers (upon whom we are forced to make extraordinary demands, both human and political) must stand by the side of the factory managers and counsellors responsible for the welfare of the workers and, as comrades of the women workers, they must help to introduce them to all other women's organizations and to ensure that the individual woman factory worker feels truly committed to her own labor. . . .

I must deal briefly with a question that is constantly brought to our attention, that is, how our present attitude toward life differs from that of the previous women's movement. First, in principle we permit only Germans to be leaders of German women and to concern themselves with matters of importance to Germans. Second, as a matter of principle we never have demanded, nor shall we ever demand, equal rights for women with the men of our nation. Instead we shall always make women's special interests dependent upon the needs of our entire nation. All further considerations will follow from this unconditional intertwining of the collective fate of the nation.

Anti-fascism and the Woman Question

SOURCES

107. Reichskomitee of Working Women, "Aufruf." Published in *Die rothe Fahne*, Berlin, 5 June 1932. Reprinted in *Dokumente der revolutionären deutschen Arbeiterbewegung zur Frauenfrage, 1848-1974: Auswahl* (Leipzig, 1975), pp. 126-27. Tr. SGB.

108. Winifred Holtby, *Women and a Changing Civilization* (London, 1934), pp. 158-63.

109. Virginia Woolf, *Three Guineas* (London and New York, 1938), pp. 76-81, 155-57.

Women critics responded at various levels to fascist threats to their hard-won, and still delicate, political and professional toeholds. The nature and extent of their criticism varied according to their proximity to events and also to their particular political and personal world-view.

The German Reichskongress of working women, which in 1930 had produced the "Battle Cry" to their "sisters" to fight against the political dangers of unemployment and hunger (Doc. 101), elected a committee to consider their own special problems. This committee, closely associated with the women's department of the Central Committee of the German Communist Party, published an appeal to German laboring women and laborers' wives on 5 June 1932, four days after the reactionary government of Franz von Papen was installed and nine months before Hitler established his dictatorship in March 1933. In their appeal, published in the German Communist newspaper *Die Rothe Fahne* (The Red Flag) they protested against a Nazi takeover, publicizing the brutal Nazi harassment of workers and especially of working women in their neighborhoods.

The second and third selections, by two English women, Winifred Holtby (Docs. 87, 104) and Virginia Woolf (Doc. 100), were inspired by events on the European continent, but also by demonstrations of the British Union of Fascists and National Socialists under Oswald Mosley in London. Holtby and Woolf analyzed the danger of fascism from a radically philosophical point of view. Holtby, writing in 1934—the year after Hitler took power—recognized that the flight to a false security in the form of traditionalism and dictatorial leadership symbolized nothing less than a failure of nerve and of reason. She argued that a society that no longer believes in the power of reason must necessarily revert to mystery as well as to physical repression. Women in such a society are doomed to sexual subordination and have no chance of obtaining or retaining equal rights.

Virginia Woolf, painfully clear-sighted, went to the heart of the matter in a witty and subtle essay, which even some of her most admiring recent biographers have treated as an uncharacteristic aberration, related perhaps to the psychotic episodes that overcame her periodically. Woolf perceived that fascism and dictatorship, publicly accepted in Germany, Italy, and Spain, though viewed with horror by the Western democracies, in fact shared the same ideological basis on which the Western family and patriarchy were founded. She pointed out that such an understanding of Western civilization was not new, but that earlier activists like Josephine Butler in the nineteenth century had recognized that women could only obtain justice, liberty, and equality if these principles were understood to apply universally, as *human* requirements. Perhaps, she speculated, inasmuch as continental European dictatorships were threatening equality and liberty for men, men themselves would empathize with women and would henceforth appreciate that the two sexes had a common cause.

---

107. Reichskomitee of Working Women (1932)

Wives, mothers, girls of the Working Class! We appeal to you at this critical time: join together in anti-fascist action!

No longer can you permit Nazi gangs to murder your husbands and your sons. Think of Mrs. Bassy whose husband was brutally slain by the Nazis before her very eyes. Her fate may become your own tomorrow if you do not enroll in anti-fascist action against Nazi terror and class justice.

Anti-fascist fighters in the Niederrhein region were given ten- to twelve-year jail sentences. The Nazi murderer Kienast who killed worker Bassy received a ridiculous sentence of three years and three months in jail. Such class-oriented sentences provoke us.

Protest against these class distinctions! Demand the release of all anti-fascist fighters!

The Nazis tell you that they want to save the family. In Braunschweig where a Nazi—Klagges—governs, all regulations concerning the indigent are brutally enforced against working people. Klagges has cancelled all plans for mothers' homes and nurseries. In Klein-Twülpstedt Klagges gave orders to evict a tubercular unemployed worker, his pregnant wife, and their two small children. The mother was forced to deliver her baby in a windowless room six meters square with the rain pouring through the roof.

The Nazis demand the death sentence for abortion. They want to turn you into compliant birth-machines. You are to be servants and maids for men. Your human dignity is to be trampled underfoot. Your families will be driven to desperation from ever greater hunger.

The Nazis are the deadly enemies of liberation and equal rights of women. You must refuse to deal with them!

Social-democratic working women—Union colleagues! You were told: Vote for Hindenburg. Then you will beat Hitler! The very same Hindenburg has put the generals and the barons into the saddle of government and has thereby prepared Hitler's road to power. Whatever party or world-view you favor—come and join together in anti-fascist action. Arouse all the laggards in the factories, in government offices, in residential neighborhoods! Prevent the establishment of a bloody fascist dictatorship by your revolutionary activity! Respond with strikes against fascist terror, lowering of wages and social security services! Join the self-protection efforts of the red masses. Form unified committees for the joint battle against hunger, fascism, and war!

Fight for Freedom, Bread, Peace, and Socialism! Become anti-fascist women fighters for a free Socialist Germany!

At the Reichstag elections vote for the Communist Party, the only party that is waging the battle to free the working class, against fascism and against the ruling capitalist system!

Reichskomitee of Working Women

108. Winifred Holtby (1934)

Events in contemporary Germany would be less important did they not march with fashionable and world-wide theory. The passionate protests of Sieburg, the grave sententious mysticism of Count Keyserling, the inarticulate apologists for National Socialism strike a note which had already become familiar to Europe and America.

The insistence upon racial solidarity, instinctive unity, "blood-thought" and intuitive functionalism preached to-day from Munich to Posen is only one expression of a revolt against reason which has affected the intellectual life of the entire Western World. It has been traced to a dozen different sources—to a resurgence of the subconscious intuitive self from long suppression, to the publication of Pascal's *Pensées* or of Bergson's *Creative Evolution*, to the psychology of Freud and the art of D. H. Lawrence, to the Expressionists, to the Nudists, to the scientists, to the war. But whatever its cause, there is little doubt that a mistrust of the intellect has been let loose in the world, and especially among the intellectuals.

It touches unexpected spheres of influence, from the evangelical revivalism known as the Group Movement, to the restless intellectualism of Aldous Huxley. "The heart has its reasons which the intellect knows not of," declared Pascal, and Huxley, Santayana, General Goering and Mr. Buchman, in their varying modes, agree.

It finds political expression in revived enthusiasm for Nationalism, in contempt for democracy, in an outcry for a leader. Throughout the work of D. H. Lawrence, the self-appointed poet and prophet of the movement, that demand for leadership recurs. " 'Men,' says Lilly to Aaron in *Aaron's Rod*, 'must submit to the greater soul in a man for their guidance: and women must submit to the positive power-soul in man for their being.'

" 'You'll never get it,' said Aaron.

" 'You will, when all men want it. All men say, they want a leader. Then let them in their souls *submit* to some greater soul than theirs. At present, when they say they want a leader, they mean they want an instrument, like Lloyd George. A mere instrument for their use. But it's more than that. It's the reverse. It's the deep fathomless submission to the heroic soul in a greater man.' "

Compare that demand to General Goering's affirmation in his book *Germany Reborn.*

In Hitler we have the rare combination of a keen logical thinker, a really profound philosopher and an iron-willed man of action, tenacious to the highest degree. . . . For more than a decade I have stood at his side, and every day spent with him is a new and wonderful experience. From the first moment that I saw and heard him I belonged to him body and soul, and to many of my comrades the same thing has happened. I passionately pledged myself to his service and have followed him unswervingly. In the past months I have received many titles and honours, but no title or honour has so filled me with pride as the title which the German people have given me: "The most loyal lieutenant of our Leader."

All over the world to-day, men and women, fatigued by the austere struggle to serve ideas, are seeking for a man to whom they can surrender their wills—for "the submission to the heroic soul in a greater man." And in Germany, Italy, Turkey, Poland perhaps, Russia while Lenin lived, they have found one. The worship of Lenin had just this difference. He himself was high priest of a religion of rationalism; Marxian communism survived his death.

But a world of hero-worshippers is a world in which women are doomed to subordination. Very rare exceptions, a Queen Elizabeth or Joan of Arc may capture men's imagination. For the most part society takes care to see that the Leader is masculine. The peculiar nature of this cult demands it. Virility, combativeness, physical endurance, power to impress all types of person, are the qualities demanded, and since quite sixty per cent. of humanity is at present irremediably predisposed against submission to a woman, the odds are enormous.

Socially the cult expresses itself in the lauding of the instincts and the emphasis of "biological," "natural," or "traditional" values. Since reason and the intellect have fallen into disfavour, the instincts are accounted as of higher importance than the mind. Passion, which Hegel called "a sort of instinct, almost animal, by which man applies his energies to a single cause," becomes associated almost exclusively with physical desire, and the difference between the sexes is necessarily exaggerated.

Since what has happened in Germany is not unique, it may be worth while to consider the attitude of our most conspicuous English candidate for the dictatorship. Sir Oswald Mosley in 1932 devoted a short section of his statement on policy, *The Greater Britain,* to "Women's Work."

"It has been suggested," he began modestly, "that in our political organisation we have hitherto concentrated on the organisation of men. This was not because we underrate the importance of women in the world. . . . The part of woman in our future organisation will be important, but different from that of men; *we want men who are men and women who are women.*" The italics are Sir Oswald's; they are, I think, important. They illustrate that emphasis upon sexual difference characteristic of a creed which places instinct above reason. "Fascism," he continues, "would treat the normal wife and mother as one of the main pillars of the State," and he is gently sportive about "professional spinster politicians," whose one idea is to escape from "the normal sphere of woman." Professional bachelor politicians like Herr Hitler presumably do not escape from the normal sphere of man. It is man's "natural" sphere to dominate. From that state of exaltation which Mr. Wyndham Lewis writing before Hitler's ascendancy described among his followers as "a true bodily solidarity, identical rhythms in the arteries and muscles and in the effective neural instrument," women are excluded. The blood-brotherhood leaves them outside, quiescent, passive, waiting obediently to refresh the tired warrior.

They have been cast, in the functional state, for the rôle of wives, mothers, expectant and desirous mistresses. The whole force of the Freudian revelation, the "modern" morality and the fashionable insistence upon nerves rather than reasons, lies behind that choice. They have been told that without complete physical satisfaction they will remain dwarfed and crippled. They have been taught that the ubiquitous Eye in the once familiar Scriptural text "Thou God seest me" is blind and merciful in comparison to the jealous watchfulness of the frustrated subconscious. Jehovah the all Terrible might forgive; the instincts have no mercy. There is no appeal from their inexorable judgment.

Therefore let them take their appointed place in society and be satisfied.

It is true that they will be cut off from a hundred fields of action. It is true that they will be separated from their friends and lovers by a gulf of sexual difference. If no bridge of reason is considered trustworthy, if no shared experience of all those vast areas of life unaffected by sexual distinction may unite them, then indeed the ways of men and women become strange to one another. Woman remains a "mystery"; man an inscrutable "power," and though mystery may have its fascination, the comradeship of sympathy and understanding is destroyed.

But this is part of the new gospel, and women must take comfort from the traditionalists who tell them that—save for mad moments of irresponsible experiment—this has always been so.

For to reinforce their arguments, the anti-rationalists envoke tradition. . . .

But tradition is against equality. If in the future we are to rely only upon what has happened in the past, experiment is closed to us. The adventures of the mind must be abandoned. The attempt to create communities where men and women alike share the full stature of humanity is an attempt to do something which has not been done before, and which can only be achieved under certain conditions. And one of these is the acceptance of reason as a guide in human conduct. If we choose an anti-rational philosophy, in this quest, at least, we are defeated. The enemies of reason are inevitably the opponents of "equal rights."

109. Virginia Woolf (1938)

Let us turn to the public press and see if we can discover from the opinions aired there any hint that will guide us in our attempt to decide the delicate and difficult question as to the aroma, the atmosphere that surrounds the word "Miss" in Whitehall. We will consult the newspapers. First:

I think your correspondent . . . correctly sums up this discussion in the observation that woman has too much liberty. It is probable that this so-called liberty came with the war, when women assumed responsibilities so far unknown to them. They did splendid service during those days. Unfortunately, they were praised and petted out of all proportion to the value of their performances.

That does very well for a beginning. But let us proceed:

I am of the opinion that a considerable amount of the distress which is prevalent in this section of the community [the clerical] could be relieved by the policy of employing men instead of women, wherever possible. There are today in Government offices, post offices, insurance companies, banks and other offices, thousands of women doing work which men could do. At the same time there are thousands of qualified men, young and middle-aged, who cannot get a job of any sort. There is a large demand for woman labour in the domestic arts, and in the process of re-grading a large number of women who have drifted into clerical service would become available for domestic service.

The odour thickens, you will agree.
Then once more:

I am certain I voice the opinion of thousands of young men when I say that if men were doing the work that thousands of young women are now doing the men would be able to keep those same women in decent homes. Homes are the real places of the women who are now compelling men to be idle. It is time the Government insisted upon employers giving work to more men, thus enabling them to marry the women they cannot now approach.

There! There can be no doubt of the odour now. The cat is out of the bag; and it is a Tom.

After considering the evidence contained in those three quotations, you will agree that there is good reason to think that the word "Miss," however delicious its scent in the private house, has a certain odour attached to it in Whitehall which is disagreeable to the noses on the other side of the partition; and that it is likely that a name to which "Miss" is attached will, because of this odour, circle in the lower spheres where the salaries are small rather than mount to the higher spheres where the salaries are substantial. As for "Mrs.," it is a contaminated word; an obscene word. The less said about that word the better. Such is the smell of it, so rank does it stink in the nostrils of Whitehall, that Whitehall excludes it entirely. In Whitehall, as in heaven, there is neither marrying nor giving in marriage.

Odour then—or shall we call it "atmosphere"?—is a very important element in professional life, in spite of the fact that like other important elements it is impalpable. It can escape the noses of examiners in examination rooms, yet penetrate boards and divisions and affect the senses of those within. Its bearing upon the case before us is undeniable. For it allows us to decide in the case of *Baldwin* v. *Whitaker* that both the Prime Minister and the *Almanack* are telling the truth. It is true that women civil servants deserve to be paid as much as men; but it is also true that they are not paid as much as men. The discrepancy is due to atmosphere.

Atmosphere plainly is a very mighty power. Atmosphere not only changes the sizes and shapes of things; it affects solid bodies, like salaries, which might have been thought impervious to atmosphere. An epic poem might be written about atmosphere, or a novel in ten or fifteen volumes. But since this is only a letter, and you are pressed for time, let us confine ourselves to the plain statement that atmosphere is one of the most powerful, partly because it is one of the most impalpable, of the enemies with which the daughters of educated men have to fight. If you think that statement exaggerated, look once more at the samples of atmosphere contained in those three quotations. We shall find there not only the reason why the pay of the professional woman is still so small, but something more dangerous, something which, if it spreads, may poison both sexes equally. There, in those quotations, is the egg of the very same worm that we know under other names in other countries. There we have in embryo the creature, Dictator as we call him when he is Italian or German, who believes that he has the right, whether given by God, Nature, sex or race is immaterial, to dictate to other human beings how they shall live; what they shall do. Let us quote again: "Homes are the real places of the women who are now compelling men to be idle. It is time the Government insisted upon employers giving work to more men, thus enabling them to marry the women they cannot now approach." Place beside it another quotation: "There are two worlds in the life of the nation, the world of men and the world of women. Nature has done well to entrust the man with the care of his family and the nation. The woman's world is her family, her husband, her children, and her home." One is written in English, the other in German. But where is the difference? Are they not both saying the same thing? Are they not both the voices of Dictators, whether they speak English or German, and are we not all agreed that the dictator when we meet him abroad is a very dangerous as well as a very ugly animal? And he is here among us, raising his ugly head, spitting his poison, small still, curled up like a caterpillar on a leaf, but in the heart of England. Is it not from this egg, to quote Mr. Wells again, that "the practical obliteration of [our] freedom by Fascists or Nazis" will spring? And is not the woman who has to breathe that poison and to fight that insect, secretly and without arms, in her office, fighting the Fascist or the Nazi as surely as those who fight him with arms in the limelight of publicity? And must not that fight wear down her strength and exhaust her spirit? Should we not help her to crush him in our own country before we ask her to help us to crush him abroad? And what right have we, Sir, to trumpet our ideals of freedom and justice to other countries when we can shake out from our most respectable newspapers any day of the week eggs like these? . . .

What were they working for in the nineteenth century—those queer dead women in their poke bonnets and shawls? The very same cause for which we are working now. "Our claim was no claim of women's rights only;"—it is Josephine Butler who speaks—"it was larger and deeper; it was a claim for the rights of all—all men and women—to the respect in their persons of the great principles of Justice and Equality and Liberty."

The words are the same as yours; the claim is the same as yours. The daughters of educated men who were called, to their resentment, "feminists" were in fact the advance guard of your own movement. They were fighting the same enemy that you are fighting and for the same reasons. They were fighting the tyranny of the patriarchal state as you are fighting the tyranny of the Fascist state. Thus we are merely carrying on the same fight that our mothers and grandmothers fought; their words prove it; your words prove it. But now with your letter before us we have your assurance that you are fighting with us, not against us. That fact is so inspiring that another celebration seems called for. What could be more fitting than to write more dead words, more corrupt words, upon more sheets of paper and burn them—the words, Tyrant, Dictator, for example? But, alas, those words are not yet obsolete. We can still shake out eggs from newspapers; still smell a peculiar and unmistakable odour in the region of Whitehall and Westminster. And abroad the monster has come more openly to the surface. There is no mistaking him there. He has widened his scope. He is interfering now with your liberty; he is dictating how you shall live; he is making distinctions not merely between the sexes, but between the races. You are feeling in your own persons what your mothers felt when they were shut out, when they were shut up, because they were women. Now you are being shut out, you are being shut up, because you are Jews, because you are democrats, because of race, because of religion. It is not a photograph that you look upon any longer; there you go, trapesing along in the procession yourselves. And that makes a difference. The whole iniquity of dictatorship, whether in Oxford or Cambridge, in Whitehall or Downing Street, against Jews or against women, in England, or in Germany, in Italy or in Spain is now apparent to you. But now we are fighting together. The daughters and sons of educated men are fighting side by side. That fact is so inspiring, even if no celebration is yet possible, that if this one guinea could be multiplied a million times all those guineas should be at your service without any other conditions than those that you have imposed upon yourself. Take this one guinea then and use it to assert "the rights of all—all men and women—to the respect in their persons of the great principle of Justice and Equality and Liberty." Put this penny candle in the window of your new society, and may we live to see the day when in the blaze of our common freedom the words tyrant and dictator shall be burnt to ashes, because the words tyrant and dictator shall be obsolete.

Economic Resurgence and the Boost to Women's Employment

SOURCES

110. International Council of Women, *The Economic Status of Women* (Brussels, May 1938): "Conclusion," pp. 43-44.

111. International Labour Office, *The Law and Women's Work* (Geneva, 1939): "Regulation of the Right to Employment," pp. 346-48.

112. Alva Myrdal, *Nation and Family* (London, 1945), pp. 402-3, 414, 416-18. Originally published in Swedish, in Stockholm, 1940.

The end of the 1930's demonstrated once again how economic changes primed public policy decisions regarding women's labor force participation. The first two selections, from reports of two international organizations, summarize the status of women in public employment, especially in the civil service. These reports contrast the nominal legal position with the actual position of women in the labor force. Both reports argued that the Depression of the early 1930's had allowed deep-seated prejudices to surface, especially against married women, that jeopardized working women's rights as individuals as well as their need to support themselves and their families in times of economic stress. Both selections mention the contemporary increase in the number of European women employed and the likelihood of further increases in professional and employment gains by women by the end of the decade. As we have seen, these increases were linked closely to international developments: to Hitler's rearmament of Germany and international reaction to the threat of fascist imperialism; and to state intervention in socio-economic policy in the democracies, as exemplified by the New Deal in the United States and the realization of a social welfare state in Sweden.

The 1938 report of the International Council of Women on the Economic Status of Women was edited by the head of their Standing Committee on Trades and Professions, M. Cecile Matheson. This report, based on information from twenty-two countries (whose National Councils of Women collaborated in the survey), corroborated the analysis of Virginia Woolf (Doc. 109) that a wide discrepancy existed between claims of the British government on the one hand and the statistical evidence (gathered by *Whitaker's Almanac*) on the other. The gap between theory and practice regarding women's employment in the middle and higher levels of government service applied not only in Britain, but also in all countries included in the survey.

The second selection, from a report by the League of Nations' International Labour Office (ILO) in Geneva, offers an acute analysis of the reasons for the fluctuations in women's employment in the labor market. The ILO had a mandate, from its founding in 1918, to deal explicitly with the matter of women's labor, and espoused what for centuries had been regarded as a dissenting point of view. This was due in no small measure to strong pressure brought to bear at the Versailles Peace Conference, by the International Women's League for Peace and Freedom. Although most of the bureaucrats of both the League of Nations and the International Labour Office were men, the participation of women in delegations and decision making was, indeed, strongly and formally encouraged.

The third selection focuses on a novel solution to women's problems in the work force. In the 1930's, Sweden's Social Democratic Workers' Party adopted and publicized Gunnar and Alva Myrdal's unusual combination of pro-natalist and socialist suggestions for reform, which in fact ensured the party's political success.

While starting from a socialist base, the Myrdals were nevertheless able to take into account the national anxiety over depopulation. Drawing on the ideas of the earlier Swedish author, Ellen Key (Docs. 26, 48), who had emphasized women's maternal as well as intellectual and professional drives, they presented a new point of view in their book, *Crisis in the Population Question* (1933). Sociologist, author, politician, diplomat, and Nobel laureate (1982), Alva Reimer Myrdal (b.

1902) was educated at the universities of Stockholm and Uppsala. She married the economist Gunnar Myrdal in 1924, and together they revolutionized the ideas of both Swedish socialists and the Swedish women's movement. Like France, Sweden had (for a variety of reasons, including extensive emigration) experienced severe problems of population replacement since the end of the nineteenth century. Meanwhile, Social Democrats had advocated the spread of birth-control information, in order to improve the living standards of the poor—a policy opposed by many who feared further depopulation. Alva Myrdal reversed the view commonly held in the socialist movement—that married women should be permitted to remain in the labor force—by insisting that women workers should be aided, not penalized, if they married and bore children. In order to implement such a policy, a support system for women including family planning, child care, sex education, and modification of domestic labor and even of domestic architecture would, she believed, have to be instituted by the state.

As a result the Swedish government set up a Population Commission and appointed Alva Myrdal secretary of the Government Committee on Women's Work. In that capacity, from 1935 to 1938, Alva Myrdal was able to realize enactment of many of her ideas, with help from her husband, who was a guiding member of the Population Commission. In her book *Nation and Family*, excerpted below, Alva Myrdal documented both the evolving ideology and the Swedish government's implementation of her plan to facilitate a dual role for women—as participants in the work force and as mothers of families.

---

110. International Council of Women (1938)

All students of recent and contemporary history are probably familiar with the main features of the long struggle for so-called "Women's Rights"—the fight to secure opportunities for service of all kinds, for economic and political freedom, the whole story a chapter of the age-long effort of mankind to evolve an organisation of society that shall be fair to every individual, giving fair scope to talents, reasonable protection in times of weakness and distress and a training that shall be a true preparation for life.

There have been outstanding women in every clime throughout the ages, but less than a century ago the mass of womenkind was condemned to walk in obscure paths, often victims of oppression and greed, generally ill-educated, the protected rich suffering from ignorance and a wearisome seclusion, the poor too often overworked and, with their families, struggling in almost unbelievable conditions of poverty, disease and ignorance, and that not their own ignorance alone.

The changes that have taken place are almost marvellous, and women emerged from the horrors of the great war with fresh opportunities, increased freedom and a broadened experience and greater knowledge of their own powers, a knowledge that they at last had an opportunity of sharing with the world around them. Ancient barriers were swept aside, in country after country they received at last the responsibilities of full citizenship, and while their gains in the "old countries" were considerable, in the countries that were being newly organised, they achieved at a bound a position that had taken generations to build up elsewhere, and the recognition of their claims in the Covenant of the League of Nations seemed, as it were, to put the seal on the new position.

Was the advance too rapid? There came the so-called "crisis" when new-found prosperity threatened to vanish and fear and bewilderment overcast men's minds and obscured their vision. The tide of success was on the ebb, and the old fears of women's inroad into so-called men's spheres, and the forces of tradition and prejudice were revealed once more. They had been submerged but not washed away. Hence reactions over the whole working world, attacks on women's right to work, on the liberty of the married woman, dismissals and exclusions and the need of constant watchfulness and often of protest on the part of the women's societies. Probably most of these reverses must not be taken too seriously. The tide will turn again, but let us not forget the dangers of the ebb, lest they recur. . . .

111. International Labour Office (1939)

While the legislative measures specifically applicable to women which have been analysed in the preceding chapter regulate various features of women's employment, their essential purpose is to preserve health. Some of them are positive measures designed to improve the welfare of women, and others are restrictive measures to shield them from some danger, but all are based on considerations of individual or social health.

The measures dealt with in the present chapter are of quite another kind. They are directly concerned with the position of women on the employment market, their purpose being in some cases to restrict, in others to maintain or to widen, women's opportunities for gainful employment.

They may be classified in three distinct groups: those designed to restrict women's opportunities for gainful employment, those designed either to guarantee to women an opportunity to compete for employment, or to mitigate the effects of measures taken by private employers to exclude women from employment, and, finally, those designed to increase women's opportunities of earning a living by giving them a privileged claim to certain kinds of employment.

The measures which may be classified into these three groups have been inspired by two conflicting tendencies of public opinion and reflect the prevalence of one or the other. And since public opinion is influenced by forces that are often transitory and sometimes make for sharp fluctuations, none of the three groups of measures shows that process of continuous development which is usual in labour legislation. Sudden changes of direction are noticeable not only in the legislation of individual countries, but in the prevailing trend of legislation throughout the world.

This peculiarity is due to causes that can only be described very briefly here; for if an attempt were made, as in previous chapters, to bring out deep-seated causes and particularly those that have their roots in the past, it would be necessary to go into the whole history of feminism and anti-feminism and to analyse very diverse philosophical and sociological conceptions of women's place in the family and in society, tracing the constant mutual reactions of innovation and tradition both with the passage of time and as respectively controlling practice in different places during the same periods. It would also be necessary to note the many compromises made between theory and practice under the pressure of individual and social needs.

No such attempt will be made here. But, to avoid being confused by the inconsistencies appearing in national systems of legislation, the reader will do well to remember the existence of these fundamental trends, which are not always apparent in the arguments advanced by legislators for the adoption of given legislation, and also the compelling influence of the basic causes of employment of women, namely the needs of the women who work and of the society which wants the product of their labour.

Personal and family needs occasioned by many social changes have caused large numbers of women to undertake gainful employment. Their individual need of employment has received legal recognition, through a gradual and almost continuous extension of the fields of activity open to women. The pressure of social needs has also exerted an influence, but because of the great variations to which those needs are subject, social pressure is not continuous and may even operate in different directions at different times. It nevertheless plays an important part in bringing about changes in the law respecting the employment of women.

Women's work, manual and professional, constitutes a reserve of labour on which both the State and private employers draw freely during periods of exceptional activity, whether that activity is due to the demands of national defence or of social reconstruction schemes, or simply to a phase of the economic cycle which brings a brisk demand for consumption goods. When a special demand for labour no longer exists, it seems natural to many that women's work should be dispensed with, and, of the two trends referred to above, that which is unfavourable to the employment of women outside their homes becomes the stronger, because it is in harmony with the practical needs of the moment.

All these factors were at work, in combination, throughout the acute economic depression that nearly every country experienced during the past few years, but the arguments in favour of confining women to domestic activities and excluding them from the labour market found an especially ready hearing. A number of regulations were issued during the depression to restrict the employment of women in order to make their jobs available to men; more were proposed, but not adopted; and during this period the promulgation of regulations opening new fields of activity to women substantially declined.

A reversal of the economic trend is now taking place and consequently a reversal in the trend of legislation.

112. Alva Myrdal (1940)

The ideological fight over the married woman's right to work had been carried on for decades in Sweden as in other countries. On one side were the women's organizations, fighting for the liberty of women to decide about their own lives, i.e., fighting for the married woman's work as a human right. On the other side were most of the members of the Conservative party as well as substantial proportions in all other political parties. Their principal argument was centered on preservation of the family institution. Their auxiliary reason was that married women, who should rightly be supported by their husbands, should cede their supposed rights "to double positions" instead of competing with unemployed family supporters. Those attacks increased in Sweden during the depression of the early thirties until in 1934 at least nine motions were presented in the Riksdag demanding restrictions on married women's right to work. Parliament demanded an investigation. Women were thus definitely placed on the defensive after a long period of steady progress.

The situation became more explosive when the population crisis focused attention on married women as deficient propagators. To understand fully how dangerous this constellation was it is only necessary to recall that the population and family argument had for several decades been effectively utilized against job-seeking married women. The principal reason why their work was considered unwholesome for society was that it was supposed to break up the family and particularly to prevent the bearing and rearing of children. In this situation anything could have happened. The remarkable thing is that in this crucial moment the population argument was wrenched out of the hands of the antifeminists and instead used as a new and formidable weapon for the emancipation ideals. The old debate on married women's right to work was turned into a fight for the working woman's right to marry and have children. The change in public opinion concerning women's problems brought about by this reformulation of the issue was tremendous. It should be noted that in the beginning the feminists themselves were merely bewildered, as their past experiences had made them suspicious of the very term "population policy." The gain was purely a gift to them. Only gradually did they come to appreciate their new strategic situation.

In the chaos out of which the new family ideology was created much of the success undoubtedly depended on seizing the initiative. Another initiation of the population debate might have made all the difference, but the turn of the issue was not the result of any trick or accident. Otherwise the far-reaching effect would not be explainable in this fairly rational political milieu. The economic irrationality from a national point of view of not utilizing the productive resources available, often invested with costly training, was first pointed out. Also, it was shown that remunerative work for the wife, sometimes only for a few stabilizing years in the beginning of marriage, must be thought of as a precondition for marriage in many cases, particularly among young people. The fertility of working wives might be low but nobody should think that these wives would bear more children if they were compelled to stay at home and the families were deprived of part of their incomes. From a population point of view the demand should rather be greater security for working women against dismissal because of marriage or childbirth and, in addition, organizational devices which would make it easier for them to bear and rear children.

The victory on the ideological plane was quick and complete. The attacks on the married woman's right to work were defeated. In fact this right was set forth in legal statutes against willful employers. For the first time the women's movement got a quiet frontier on the legal border and could indulge in constructive long-range planning. The wider societal reforms necessary for materializing the working women's asserted right to have children are still for the most part in the discussion stage. It may well be that the social engineering involved in the new family policy is up against its real test of effectiveness. . . .

The general conclusions of this investigation, demanded by the Swedish Parliament because of repeated private bills to restrict women's right to work, were summarized by the Committee in the following uncompromising terms:

Even if married women in some regards are a relatively new phenomenon on the labor market, our investigation has not found any support for the hypothesis that this factor should fall outside the ordinary framework for the present social and economic organization of cultural progress. After having gone into intensive factual studies of the matter, it seems far more evident to this Committee that the gainful work of married women can neither be spared nor ought to be restricted. The organization of society will instead have to adjust itself to the new situation which is caused by the more general participation of women in work outside the home. At the same time, however, the possibility for mothers to devote time to children during their infancy ought to be regained through social reorganization.

With regard to various proposals suggested for investigation the Committee wants to give the following summarization of its opinions:

1. All attempts legally to restrict married women's right to retain or obtain gainful employment, just as all other restrictive measures against such work, must be firmly rejected.

2. Gratuities, marriage loans, bulk payment of earned pensions, premature pensioning and similar economic encouragements for voluntary retirement on marriage cannot be considered as serving any social aim.

3. Possibilities for obtaining part-time work and temporary positions ought increasingly to be provided both for married women and other persons who for approved reasons want shorter work hours.

4. Possibilities for married couples to get positions in the same locality ought, if they do not damage legitimate interests of other persons, to be provided to some extent.

5. The question of the legal right for married women to retain their own surname ought to be given renewed consideration.

6. Social measures for alleviating the mother's care of small children ought to be instituted and given economic support, but they ought to the same extent to satisfy the needs of mothers engaged both in employment and in homework. . . .

The new law protecting the working woman's right to marry or have children as she pleased was nearly more than women had asked for. The Commission on Women's Work had not expressly called for it, and several women's organizations expressed their misgivings lest the new protection should become a boomerang, hurting women's interest on the labor market more than serving it. Their argument was that some employers might avoid difficulties by not engaging women at all. As a matter of fact, some such results were recognized during the very first months as was also the employers' expression of irritation by withdrawing certain benefits earlier paid to women leaving positions on account of marriage. These difficulties seem, however, to have been of a transitional character. The benefits may be lost; they were in any case not widespread. And in so far as they were solace for dismissal, women can obviously not continue to count on them when dismissal no longer threatens. Utilization of female labor could by and large not be forsaken on account of an issue of such comparatively slight economic importance to the employer. Any eventual curtailment of opportunities for women by some few employers will probably be more than offset by the prevailing tendency on the part of women to join unions and thus attain direct power in labor negotiations. It is even possible that this solidarity and urge to organize will become psychologically fortified if women face the fact that employers are endeavoring to curb such fundamental human rights as marrying and bearing children.

The victories for Swedish women have been won on that one ideological alignment which alone can make the position of the working mother accepted by all as a matter of course, that her marrying and her childbearing are to be encouraged and not discouraged by society. So expressed, her rights coincide with the interests of society. In other words, what is protected is women's right to have those very children that society also wants. That more children can be expected from working wives when they feel free to follow their own desires has been demonstrated in the degree to which these rights have been vindicated and also in some factual experience among the group of women in civil service who already in 1936 had their family rights better safeguarded.

The right of working women to comply with sanctioned social rules and enter marriage when in love is protected. Earlier, the attitudes on the part of the employers had so directly encouraged premarital sex relations that they were more and more excused and justified. Even some clergymen of the state church had found themselves compelled by their consciences to sanction such liaisons. There were also some attempts to legitimatize the practice whereby a couple notified the world of betrothal or even had the banns for marriage published and then openly lived together, sacrificing nothing but the marriage ceremony (and the children). Such a makeshift might have been fairly easily brought about in Sweden with its sex attitudes looking more to hearts than to formalities. But it is difficult to see how such a development could have been preferred by those who caused it, as it was inconsistent with their rationalizations about protecting the family. It is nevertheless a fact that extramarital sex relations, illegitimacy, and abortions had followed the efforts to enforce celibacy rules on the "modern nuns" in offices and banks. Thus, radical as may have appeared the Population Commission's desire to give freedom to work to married women, it ultimately served the truly conservative goals of protecting the formal marriage rites and of facilitating childbearing for a growing group of women.

There were never any attempts to exclude unmarried mothers from the protection. The Population Commission expressed the opinion that unmarried women, who did not seek the easy way out through abortion, were to be honored and not dishonored. It further pointed out that they needed protection even more than married mothers. Even if the new regulations were contrary to the feelings in many quarters, nobody dared to voice any opposition.

Although the ideological battle has been fought and won, many practical difficulties remain to be overcome before the dilemma of the working mother is solved. Legally the dilemma is now abolished in Sweden. Also the condemning attitudes are being gradually vanquished. But this does not conjure away the very real troubles of an economic, institutional, and psychological nature standing in the working mother's way. The difficulties here touched upon go deep down to the fundamental problems of modern marriage itself; they concern women's fate as such, the purposiveness of their lives, and the inherent doubt as to how to plan them. It would be futile even to try to specify a practical solution of these basic problems in any truly realistic terms. The only thing that can be attempted is a sort of check list of still open problems.

Has the wage-earning mother found any sensible solution to her home organization problem? Has she found some satisfactory adjustment to the traditional demands upon her time by husband and children? Have women on the whole found some means of harmonizing investment in training and vocational ambitions with the incidence of marriage? Does marriage serve as a break in their life plans or are the life plans even of the spinsters arranged mainly with marriage in view, or is a rational balance possible?

The feminine sex is a social problem. Whether a woman is young or old, whether she is married or not, whether a wife works or not, she is likely to be a problem. This problem is largely economic in origin as marriage and family are as yet poorly adjusted to the new economic order. This is of vital importance to the individual and society as the family is the essential societal relationship.

Stalinism and the Woman Question in Soviet Russia

SOURCES
113. The Soviet Code on Marriage and Divorce, the Family, and Guardianship, decree of the All-Russian Central Executive Committee, 19 November 1926.

Translated and reprinted in *The Family in the U.S.S.R.*, ed. Rudolf Schlesinger (London, 1949), pp. 155-57.

114. Leon Trotsky, "Thermidor in the Family," from *The Revolution Betrayed*, translated by Max Eastman (New York, 1937), pp. 144-46, 147-50, 151-52, 156. Originally published in Russian, 1936.

115. A. Orlov, "On the Education of Boys and Girls Apart in Separate Schools," *Izvestiya*, 10 August 1943. Reprinted in *The Family in the U.S.S.R.*, pp. 363-66.

116. The Soviet Family Law of 8 July 1944, decree of the Praesidium of the Supreme Soviet of the U.S.S.R. Translated and reprinted in *The Family in the U.S.S.R.*, pp. 367-72.

Seldom has the fragility of new, unpopular ideas under the pressures of tradition and crisis been more evident than during the first decades of the communist experiment in the Soviet Union, when the institution of the patriarchal family was progressively refortified at the expense of women's freedom and equality. Under Lenin, Soviet law had institutionalized some of the more controversial "dissenting" proposals of the last hundred years, intending to enhance the status of women through radical modification of the laws on marriage, abortion, and education. We have also seen how the challenge posed by the Russian Revolution to age-old tradition reverberated throughout the Western world, eliciting harsh and highly emotional reactions from the Vatican, from conservative crypto-fascist publications like the *Woman Patriot* in the United States, and from the proponents of fascism through Europe.

Even the "most revolutionary" Soviet innovation—the 1918 Marriage Code—was, however, rooted in certain traditional values. Responsibility for the welfare of the family members remained within the family; it was not transferred to the state. The Soviet marriage law did require spousal economic support. However, only those marriages registered with the civil authorities came under the purview of the law; in fact, many couples had unregistered "de facto" marriages. Meanwhile, the New Economic Policy (NEP), initiated in 1921 to mitigate the famine and economic chaos that resulted from revolution and civil war, in fact allowed partial capitalism and free enterprise. In the wake of such socio-economic dislocation, many urban women workers lost their jobs. Their situation was aggravated by the fact that many of them had been abandoned by their common-law husbands and were attempting to support themselves and raise their children alone.

By the mid-1920's, therefore, women's unemployment under post-civil war conditions was such that a new marriage and divorce law, emphasizing protection of the "weaker" party (women), was debated by 1925 and promulgated in 1926.

By this time Lenin was dead and the struggle for the succession of Soviet leadership was taking place between Leon Trotsky (1877-1940), who was more openly progressive on women's issues, and Joseph Stalin (1879-1953), whose position on the woman question was far more repressive. Meanwhile, economic scarcity and continuing national disorder hampered the creation of proposed state child-care institutions, substitutes for domestic service, and various other proposals whose origins dated back to the Saint-Simonian and Fourierist discussions of the 1830's. The Marriage Law of 1926 (excerpted in our first selection) reasserted the responsibility of the family toward its members, even in case of divorce. In theory, the employed spouse of either sex was expected to pay alimony to the other. In practice, this upgraded the status of "registered" as opposed to unregistered "de facto" marriages, and evolved more stringent procedures for divorce, such as courtroom discussion and testimony by witnesses, all of which was designed to "protect" mothers who were less likely than men to be able to support themselves and their children.

The second selection, from Leon Trotsky's *Revolution Betrayed*, was written during his exile in Norway, after he had been forced to leave Russia following Stalin's seizure of power. Born into an atypical Russian family, his father a Jewish land-owning farmer, his mother of the assimilated Russian Jewish middle class, Trotsky had been educated at the University of Odessa. He had early become a revolutionary and is still considered one of the outstanding revolutionary theorists and leaders of all time. His commitment to internationalism and to freedom of expression, debate, and criticism conflicted with Stalin's Great Russian chauvinism and dictatorial methods. In *The Revolution Betrayed* (1936) Trotsky analyzed the "problem of problems"—his expression for freeing women from domesticity—in the context of the highly bureaucratic Stalinist Soviet state of the 1930's.

Stalin's violent repression of dissent, climaxing in the Soviet purges of the 1930's, repelled many of the earlier adherents to the communist cause. The legal and sexual freedom of Soviet women, championed by Kollontai (Doc. 83) was severely challenged during the same period. For example, the law of 1936 (discussed here by Trotsky) abolished abortion on demand, which had been legal since 1920 (Doc. 82), and tightened the restrictions on divorce still further. The undercutting of progressive developments that furthered women's freedom and equality as individuals was characteristic in Soviet development under Stalin; this is dramatically illustrated by the abolition in 1943 of coeducation in the ten-year schools of 176 cities, and by the Family Law of 1944. Hitler's attack on Soviet Russia in 1941, and the ensuing war and catastrophic depopulation of the Soviet nation, provided ample pretext for passage of these wartime laws.

The abolition of coeducation (that most basic of egalitarian principles urged by philosophers ever since Plato advocated it in *The Republic*) marked the explicit repudiation of earlier ideals by the Soviet government. The third selection, an article by A. Orlov, director of the Moscow Municipal Department of National Education, published in the daily paper *Izvestiya*, explains this wartime move, which was clearly aimed at redeveloping century-old gender-specific cultural characteristics in Russian schoolchildren, in order to create male warriors and female nurturers. Orlov's statement is not far removed from that of Napoleon (Vol. I, Doc. 23) establishing the girls' school at Écouen in 1807.

The fourth selection, from the Family Law of 1944, decreeing medals to honor mothers of large families, "motherhood glory," and "heroine mothers," on the other hand, resembles the French decree of 1920 (Doc. 84), and the later decrees in the same vein issued by Hitler and Mussolini. All these efforts harked back to measures established by the Roman Emperor Augustus in the first century A.D.— measures all too congenial to rulers who required masses of soldiers to implement expansionist aims.

With this series of laws, the Soviet Union legislated an emphatically biological definition of women's role. Even though (with the Family Law of 1944) the Soviet state did shoulder the entire responsibility for children born to unmarried mothers—a seemingly revolutionary acceptance by the Soviet government of the once-radical proposals advocated by Dr. Blanche Edwards-Pilliet and others in France in 1900 and by the German Mutterschutz Bund in 1907 (Docs. 32, 33)—this move can also be understood as a patriarchal government's attempt to assure re-population and man-power in a period of military and demographic crisis.

---

113. The Soviet Code on Marriage and Divorce (1926)

Rights and Duties of Husband and Wife

7. On registering a marriage the contracting parties may declare it to be their wish to have a common surname, either that of the husband or of the wife, or to retain their antenuptial surnames.

8. On the registration of a marriage between a person who is a citizen of the R.S.F.S.R. and a person who is a foreign citizen, each party retains his or her respective citizenship. Change in citizenship of such persons may be effected in the simplified manner provided for by the Union laws. . . .

9. Both husband and wife enjoy full liberty in the choice of their respective trades and occupations. The manner in which their joint household is conducted is determined by the mutual agreement of the two contracting parties. A change of residence by either husband or wife does not oblige the other marriage partner to follow the former.

10. Property which belonged to either husband or wife prior to their marriage remains the separate property of each of them. Property acquired by husband and wife during continuance of their marriage is regarded as their joint property. The share belonging to either husband or wife shall, in case of dispute, be determined by the court.

Note.—The rights of either husband or wife in regard to the use of land and in regard to property used in common and forming part of a peasant household are defined by Sections 66 and 67 of the Land Code and by the enactments published to supplement the same.

11. Section 10 of the present code extends also to the property of persons married *de facto* though not registered, provided such persons recognize their mutual status of husband and wife, or their marital relationship is established as a fact by a court on the basis of the actual conditions under which they live.

12. Proof of joint cohabitation is sufficient for the court to establish marital cohabitation in cases where the marriage has not been registered, provided that in addition to proof of joint cohabitation proof of a common household be adduced and that statements have been made to third persons either in personal correspondence or in other documents tending to prove the existence of marital relations, taking also into consideration such circumstances as the presence or absence of mutual material support, joint raising of children, and the like.

13. The husband and wife may enter into any contractual relations with each other regarding property provided they are lawful. Agreements between husband and wife intended to restrict the property rights of the wife or of the husband are invalid and are not binding on third parties or on the husband or wife, who may at any time refuse to carry them out.

14. When either husband or wife is in need and unable to work he or she is entitled to receive alimony from the other conjugal partner, if the court finds that the latter is able to support the former. A husband or wife in need of support but able to work is likewise entitled to alimony during the period of his or her unemployment.

15. The right of a husband or wife in need and unable to work to receive alimony from the other conjugal partner continues even after the dissolution of the marriage until there has been a change in the conditions which according to Section 14 of the present code serve as a basis for the receipt of alimony, but not for a period exceeding one year from the time of the dissolution of the marriage. The amount of alimony to be paid to a needy unemployed husband or wife in case of dissolution of the marriage is fixed by the court for a period not exceeding six months and shall not exceed the corresponding amount of Social Insurance relief.

16. The right to receive alimony both during marriage and after its dissolution extends also to persons who are married *de facto*, though not registered, provided they fall within the purview of Sections 11 and 12 of the present code.

17. A marriage is dissolved by the death of one of the parties to it or by a declaration of the presumptive death of either the husband or the wife through a notary public or court. . . .

18. During the lifetime of both parties to a marriage the marriage may be dissolved either by the mutual consent of both parties to it or upon the *ex parte* application of either of them.

19. During the lifetime of both parties, the dissolution of a marriage (divorce) may be registered at the Civil Registrar's Office, whether the marriage was registered or unregistered, provided that in the latter case it had been established as a fact by the court in accordance with Section 12 of the present code.

20. The fact that a marriage has been dissolved may also be established by a court, if the divorce was not registered.

114. Leon Trotsky (1936)

The October Revolution honestly fulfilled its obligations in relation to woman. The young government not only gave her all political and legal rights in equality with man, but, what is more important, did all that it could, and in any case incomparably more than any other government ever did, actually to secure her access to all forms of economic and cultural work. However, the boldest revolution, like the "all-powerful" British Parliament, cannot convert a woman into a man—or, rather, cannot divide equally between them the burden of pregnancy, birth, nursing, and the rearing of children.

The revolution made a heroic effort to destroy the so-called family hearth—that archaic, stuffy, and stagnant institution in which the woman of the toiling classes performs galley labor from childhood to death. The place of the family as a shut-in petty enterprise was to be occupied, according to the plans, by a finished system of social care and accommodation: maternity houses, child-care centers, kindergartens, schools, social dining rooms, social laundries, first-aid stations, hospitals, sanatoria, athletic organizations, moving-picture theaters, etc. The complete absorption of the housekeeping functions of the family by institutions of the socialist society, uniting all generations in solidarity and mutual aid, was to bring to woman, and thereby to the loving couple, a real liberation from the thousand-year-old fetters.

Up to now this problem of problems has not been solved. The forty million Soviet families remain in their overwhelming majority nests of medievalism, female slavery and hysteria, daily humiliation of children, feminine and childish superstition. We must permit ourselves no illusions on this account. For that very reason, the consecutive changes in the approach to the problem of the family in the Soviet Union best of all characterize the actual nature of Soviet society and the evolution of its ruling stratum.

It proved impossible to take the old family by storm—not because the will was lacking, and not because the family was so firmly rooted in men's hearts. On the contrary, after a short period of distrust of the government and its child-care facilities, kindergartens, and like institutions, the working women, and after them the more advanced peasants, appreciated the immeasurable advantages of the collective care of children as well as the socialization of the whole family economy. Unfortunately society proved too poor and little cultured. The real resources of the state did not correspond to the plans and intentions of the Communist Party. You cannot "abolish" the family; you have to replace it. The actual liberation of women is unrealizable on a basis of "generalized want." Experience soon proved this austere truth which Marx had formulated eighty years before.

During the lean years the workers, wherever possible, and in part their families, ate in the factory and other social dining rooms, and this fact was officially regarded as a transition to a socialist form of life. There is no need of pausing again upon the peculiarities of the different periods: military communism, the NEP, and the first five-year plan. The fact is that from the moment of the abolition of the food-card system in 1935, all the better-placed workers began to return to the home dining table. It would be incorrect to regard this retreat as a condemnation of the socialist system, which in general was never tried out. But so much the more withering was the judgment of the workers and their wives upon the "social feeding" organized by the bureaucracy. The same conclusion must be extended to the social laundries, where they tear and steal linen more than they wash it. Back to the family hearth!

But home cooking, and the home washtub, which are now half shame-facedly celebrated by orators and journalists, mean the return of the workers' wives to their pots and pans—that is, to the old slavery. It is doubtful if the resolution of the Communist International on the "complete and irrevocable triumph of socialism in the Soviet Union" sounds very convincing to the women of the factory districts! . . .

The number of children in kindergartens rose during the five years 1930-35 from 370,000 to 1,181,000. The lowness of the figure for 1930 is striking, but the figure for 1935 also seems only a drop in the ocean of Soviet families. A further investigation would undoubtedly show that the principal and, in any case, the better part of these kindergartens appertain to families of the administration, the technical personnel, the Stakhanovists, etc.

The same Central Executive Committee was not long ago compelled to testify openly that the "resolution on the liquidation of homeless and uncared-for children is being weakly carried out." What is concealed behind this dispassionate confession? Only by accident, from newspaper remarks printed in small type, do we know that in Moscow more than a thousand children are living in "extraordinarily difficult conditions." . . . How many children in "extraordinarily difficult conditions" remained unrecorded? In what do *extraordinarily* difficult conditions differ from *simply* difficult ones? Those are the questions which remain unanswered. A vast amount of the homelessness of children, obvious and open as well as disguised, is a direct result of the great social crisis in the course of which the old family continues to dissolve far faster than the new institutions are capable of replacing it.

From these same accidental newspaper remarks and from episodes in the criminal records, the reader may find out about the existence in the Soviet Union of prostitution—that is, the extreme degradation of woman in the interests of men who can pay for it. In the autumn of the past year [1935] *Izvestiya* suddenly informed its readers, for example, of the arrest in Moscow of "as many as a thousand women who were secretly selling themselves on the streets of the proletarian capital." Among those arrested were 177 working women, ninety-two clerks, five university students, etc. What drove them to the sidewalks? Inadequate wages, want, the necessity to "get a little something for a dress, for shoes."

We should vainly seek the approximate dimensions of this social evil. The modest bureaucracy orders the statistician to remain silent. But that enforced silence itself testifies unmistakably to the numerousness of the "class" of Soviet prostitutes. Here there can be essentially no question of "relics of the past"; prostitutes are recruited from the younger generation. No reasonable person, of course, would think of placing special blame for this sore, as old as civilization, upon the Soviet regime. But it is unforgivable in the presence of prostitution to talk about the triumph of socialism. The newspapers assert, to be sure—insofar as they are permitted to touch upon this ticklish theme—that "prostitution is decreasing." It is possible that this is really true by comparison with the years of hunger and decline (1931-33). But the restoration of money relations which has taken place since then, abolishing all direct rationing, will inevitably lead to a new growth of prostitution as well as of homeless children. Wherever there are privileged, there are pariahs!

The mass homelessness of children is undoubtedly the most unmistakable and most tragic symptom of the difficult situation of the mother. On this subject even the optimistic *Pravda* is sometimes compelled to make a bitter confession: "The birth of a child is for many women a serious menace to their position." It is just for this reason that the revolutionary power gave women the right to abortion, which in conditions of want and family distress, whatever may be said upon this subject by the eunuchs and old maids of both sexes, is one of her most important civil, political, and cultural rights. However, this right of women too, gloomy enough in itself, is under the existing social inequality being converted into a privilege. Bits of information trickling into the press about the practice of abortion are literally shocking. Thus through only one village hospital in one district of the Urals, there passed in 1935 "195 women mutilated by midwives"—among them thirty-three working women, twenty-eight clerical workers, sixty-five collective farm women, fifty-eight housewives, etc. This Ural district differs from the majority of other districts only in that information about it happened to get into the press. How many women are mutilated every day throughout the extent of the Soviet Union?

Having revealed its inability to serve women who are compelled to resort to abortion with the necessary medical aid and sanitation, the state makes a sharp change of course and takes the road of prohibition. And just as in other situations, the bureaucracy makes a virtue of necessity. One of the members of the highest Soviet court, Soltz, a specialist on matrimonial questions, bases the forthcoming prohibition of abortion on the fact that in a socialist society where there are no unemployed, etc., etc., a woman has no right to decline "the joys of motherhood." The philosophy of a priest endowed also with the powers of a gendarme. We just heard from the central organ of the ruling party that the birth of a child is for many women, and it would be truer to say for the overwhelming majority, "a menace to their position." We just heard from the highest Soviet institution that "the liquidation of homeless and uncared for children is being weakly carried out," which undoubtedly means a new increase of homelessness. But here the highest Soviet judge informs us that in a country where "life is happy" abortion should be punished with imprisonment—just exactly as in capitalist countries where life is grievous.

It is clear in advance that in the Soviet Union as in the West those who will fall into the claws of the jailer will be chiefly working women, servants, peasant wives, who find it hard to conceal their troubles. . . .

The triumphal rehabilitation of the family, taking place simultaneously—what a providential coincidence!—with the rehabilitation of the ruble, is caused by the material and cultural bankruptcy of the state. Instead of openly saying, "We have proven still too poor and ignorant for the creation of socialist relations among men, our children and grandchildren will realize this aim," the leaders are forcing people to glue together again the shell of the broken family, and not only that, but to consider it, under threat of extreme penalties, the sacred nucleus of triumphant socialism. It is hard to measure with the eye the scope of this retreat. . . .

One of the very dramatic chapters in the great book of the Soviets will be the tale of the disintegration and breaking up of those Soviet families where the husband as a party member, trade unionist, military commander, or administrator, grew and developed and acquired new tastes in life, and the wife, crushed by the family, remained on the old level. The road of the two generations of the Soviet bureaucracy is sown thick with the tragedies of wives rejected and left behind. The same phenomenon is now to be observed in the new generation. The greatest of all crudities and cruelties are to be met perhaps in the very heights of the bureaucracy, where a very large percentage are parvenus of little culture, who consider that everything is permitted to them. Archives and memoirs will someday expose downright crimes in relation to wives, and to women in general, on the part of those evangelists of family morals and the compulsory "joys of motherhood" who are, owing to their position, immune from prosecution.

No, the Soviet woman is not yet free. . . .

115. A. Orlov (1943)

In the ensuing school year, our organs of national education and our schools are confronted with a task of great national importance: as from September 1, 1943, separate education for boys and girls in all forms from the first to the tenth will be introduced in the incomplete and complete secondary schools of the provinces, of district towns, of capitals of the Union and Autonomous Republics and of large industrial towns, as soon as separate schools for boys and girls have been organized in these towns.

Co-education in the schools was proclaimed and put into practice by the Soviet government in 1918, and has played a positive historical rôle in the development of Soviet schools. More than half of all scholars in the higher educational institutions are women. This is a great achievement of the Soviet government, of Soviet culture.

But now we find that co-education in the schools has given rise to a number of inconveniences. In co-education, neither the peculiarities of the physical development of boys and girls, nor the different requirements of their vocational training, practical activities, preparation for leadership and military service can receive proper attention.

In the schools of Moscow, where during the past school year separate education has already been partially introduced as from the fifth form, experience has proved that the collectives of pupils have become more organized and their interests more homogeneous. Discipline in the schools has improved considerably and the activities of the pupils have increased as well. The syllabuses for boys and girls have been differentiated, and thus the necessary conditions have been created for the physical and military training—primary and pre-conscription—of both.

In consequence, remarkable progress has been achieved by pupils in the schools.

The significance of the primary and pre-conscription training of the pupils consists not only in imparting to them elementary facts and notions concerning the established order, the military organization, materials, weapons and so on, but also in providing a genuine military education for our youth. It will be possible to achieve this aim only when these elements of military education are inculcated in our youth from early childhood. Therefore separate education in all incomplete and complete secondary schools will be introduced, beginning in the first form, because the syllabus of physical training and military training, primary and pre-conscription, is different for boys and girls, and this programme can be carried out properly only under conditions of separate education.

For the current year, the instruction in the schools for boys and girls must follow the existing programme. But for the future, the programme of education and the curriculum for boys' schools and girls' schools can be and must be differentiated. It is essential to introduce in girls' schools such additional subjects as pedagogics, needlework, courses in domestic science, personal hygiene and the care of children. In boys' schools, training in handicrafts must become a part of the curriculum. At the end of their school career, those who attend boys' schools must have acquired practical habits, they must be able to cope with simple repairs to electrical installations and heating systems, and with the repair of household objects. The syllabus of boys' schools must also be different for such subjects as geography. It is necessary that the future warrior and commander should be able to use a map and be absolutely reliable, to understand topography, to find his way by means of a map and to apply a map to the locality. . . .

It is not our objective to erect some "Chinese wall" between boys and girls—boys and girls walking on different pavements—what we aim at is only the separate *education* of boys and girls. This is the main thing. We must not imagine that once separate education has been introduced, there will be no association between boys and girls. They will come together in the "pioneer houses," in institutions outside the school, in the theatres, at "school evenings," and so on. A danger exists, nevertheless, in an absurd misinterpretation of the essential meaning of separate education, such as found expression in various memoranda presented to the All-Russian Conference on National Education during the discussion of the problem of separate education.

There is a great deal of work to be done by the organs of national education in selecting the managing body—the principals and directors of studies and the teaching staff. It is clear that both kinds of school have their peculiarities and that the selection of the teachers for boys and girls must take these peculiarities into account. In boys' schools, the principal should as a rule be a man, and in girls' schools a woman. Where in any instance this rule is not observed, it should be regarded as a temporary expedient.

The choice of buildings for boys' and girls' schools should also take these peculiarities into account. Boys' schools should have proper grounds for military training and for carrying out technical manœuvres. They must have a gymnasium and a specially organized military department in accordance with the programme of military education. In girls' schools, the military department should serve the purposes of training for sanitary work, intelligence, and so on.

There should also be a differentiation by the national educational bodies in their management of the schools for boys and girls. It will also be necessary, as a practical measure, to conduct separate headmasters' and headmistresses' conferences. There is a great deal of work to be done in forming pupils' collectives.

The schools of Moscow are at an advantage in this task, as they have already had some small experience of separate education, and at present a great deal of preparatory work is being carried on with a view to school reform. A network of schools for boys and girls has been established, principals and directors of studies have been selected. The body of teachers has been built up. . . .

The introduction of separate education for boys and girls in the incomplete and complete secondary schools marks the achievement of a definite stage in the development of our Soviet schools and will raise the school system to an even higher stage of development.

116. The Soviet Family Law of 8 July 1944

Decree of the Presidium of the Supreme Soviet of the U.S.S.R. on increase of State aid to pregnant women, mothers with many children and unmarried mothers; on strengthening measures for the protection of motherhood and childhood; on the establishment of the title "Heroine Mother"; and on the institution of the order "Motherhood Glory" and the "Motherhood Medal"

Care for children and mothers and the strengthening of the family have always been among the most important tasks of the Soviet State. In safeguarding the interests of mother and child, the State is rendering great material aid to pregnant women and mothers for the support and upbringing of their children. During and after the War, when many families face more considerable material difficulties, a further extension of State aid measures is necessary.

With a view to increasing the material assistance to pregnant women, mothers with many children, and unmarried mothers, and to encouraging large families and providing increased protection for motherhood and childhood the Presidium of the Supreme Soviet of the U.S.S.R. Decrees:

SECTION I

*On the Increase of State Aid to Mothers with Many
Children and Unmarried Mothers*

It is Decreed:

ARTICLE I

That in place of the existing regulation which gives State aid to mothers with six children at the birth of the seventh and of each subsequent child, State assistance shall be given to mothers (either with husbands or widowed) who have two children, on the birth of the third and of each subsequent child.

ARTICLE 2

Payment of State assistance to mothers with several children shall take place in the following manner and amounts:

Mothers.	Non-Recurring Payment. (Rubles.)	Monthly Payment. (Rubles.)
With 2 children on birth of 3rd	400	—
With 3 children on birth of 4th	1,300	80
With 4 children on birth of 5th	1,700	120
With 5 children on birth of 6th	2,000	140
With 6 children on birth of 7th	2,500	200
With 7 children on birth of 8th	2,500	200
With 8 children on birth of 9th	3,500	250
With 9 children on birth of 10th	3,500	250
With 10 children on birth of each subsequent child	5,000	300

. . . On the birth of each subsequent child after publication of the present Decree, assistance is paid out in the manner and to the amount laid down in the present article of this Decree.

In assessing the amount of State assistance to mothers with many children, those children who perished or disappeared without trace on the fronts of the Patriotic War are included.

ARTICLE 3

To establish State assistance to single (unmarried) mothers for support and upbringing of children born after the publication of the present Decree, in the following amounts:

100 rubles monthly for 1 child
150   "   "   for 2 children
200   "   "   for 3 or more children

State assistance to unmarried mothers is paid until the children reach 12 years of age.

Unmarried mothers with 3 or more children receive the State assistance laid down in the present article, in addition to the regular assistance to mothers with many children which is received in accordance with article 2 of the present Decree.

When an unmarried mother marries, the right to assistance laid down in the present article is retained by her.

Mothers who receive alimony for children born before the publication of the present Decree retain their right to receive alimony until the child grows up, and do not receive the assistance laid down in the present article.

Mothers of children born in 1944, before the publication of the present Decree, and not receiving alimony for them, have the right to receive the assistance provided by the present article.

ARTICLE 4

If an unmarried mother wishes to place a child to which she has given birth in a children's institution for its upbringing, the children's institution is obliged to accept the child, to support and bring it up entirely at the expense of the State.

The mother of the child has the right to remove her child from the children's institution and to bring it up herself.

While the child is in the children's institution, State assistance for the child is not paid.

ARTICLE 5

To increase the size of the lump sum assistance paid out for each new-born child from the Social Insurance Fund and Mutual Assistance Funds of the co-operative *artels* from 45 to 120 rubies. To establish that the sale of a layette for the new-born child to the amount of the sum provided shall be assured.

SECTION II

On the Increase of Privileges for Pregnant Women and Mothers and on Measures to Extend the Network of Institutions for the Protection of Motherhood and Childhood

ARTICLE 6

To increase the leave of absence for pregnancy and childbirth for women workers and women office employees from 63 calendar days to 77 calendar days, establishing the length of the leave of absence at 35 calendar days before the birth and 42 calendar days after the birth, assistance to be given during this period at the expense of the State to the amount previously laid down. In cases of difficult births or the birth of twins, leave of absence after birth is increased to 56 calendar days.

To instruct the directors of factories and offices to provide pregnant women with their regular leave of absence, at a suitable time in relation to the leave of absence for pregnancy and birth.

ARTICLE 7

Pregnant women from the 4th month of pregnancy not to be put on overtime work in factories and offices, and women with children at the breast not to be put on nightwork during the period the child is breast-fed.

ARTICLE 8

To double the normal ration of supplementary food for pregnant women, beginning with the 6th month of pregnancy, and for nursing mothers for four months of the nursing period.

ARTICLE 9

To instruct the directors of factories and offices to give aid to pregnant women and nursing mothers in the form of supplementary foodstuffs from their auxiliary farms.

ARTICLE 10

To reduce by 50 per cent. the fees for places in crèches and kindergartens for:

Parents with 3 children and earning up to 400 rubles a month.
Parents with 4 children and earning up to 600 rubles a month.
Parents with 5 or more children irrespective of earnings.

ARTICLE 11

To instruct the Council of People's Commissars of the U.S.S.R.:

(*a*) To confirm the plan for the organization in Republics and Regions of additional Homes for Mother and Child and also of special rest homes for unmarried women needing them and for weakened nursing mothers, the women resting there to be given work in them according to their strength.

(*b*) To confirm the plan for extending the network of children's institutions under the People's Commissariats and departments, with a view to covering fully all children needing such institutions; to provide for extension of the network of children's consulting centres and milk kitchens, organization of crèches for breast-fed children, of evening groups in the kindergartens and maternity institutions in the districts liberated from the German invaders.

(*c*) To provide for the compulsory organization in factories and offices employing women on a mass scale of crèches, kindergartens, rooms for the feeding of breast-fed children, and personal hygiene rooms for women.

(*d*) To instruct the People's Commissariats to include in their plans of industrial construction the building of children's institutions (crèches, kindergartens, Mother and Child Rooms), calculated to cover fully all the children of the women workers and office employees of the given enterprise who require such services.

(*e*) To confirm measures for the considerable expansion of the production of children's clothing, footwear, sanitary and hygienic articles for children, and other articles required by children both for children's institutions and for sale to the population, and measures also for the extension of the network of children's clothing factories and of the network of Mother and Child shops.

SECTION III

*On the Institution of the "Motherhood Medal" and the Order
"Motherhood Glory," and Establishment of the Title of
Honour "Heroine Mother"*

ARTICLE 12

To institute a "Motherhood Medal"—1st and 2nd class—for award to mothers who have given birth to and brought up:

5 children .... 2nd class medal
6 children .... 1st class medal

ARTICLE 13

To establish the Order "Motherhood Glory"—1st, 2nd and 3rd class—for award to mothers who have given birth to and brought up:

7 children .... 3rd class
8 children .... 2nd class
9 children .... 1st class

ARTICLE 14

To establish that mothers who have given birth to and brought up 10 children shall receive the title of honour "Heroine Mother" with award of the Order Heroine Mother and certificate of the Presidium of the Supreme Soviet of the U.S.S.R. . . .

SECTION IV

On Taxes on Bachelors, Single Citizens, and Citizens of the U.S.S.R. with Small Families

ARTICLE 16

As a modification of the Decree of the Presidium of the Supreme Soviet of the U.S.S.R. dated November 21, 1941, "On taxes on bachelors, single and childless citizens of the U.S.S.R.," to establish that a tax is paid by citizens—men between the ages of 20 and 50 years, and women between the ages of 20 and 45 years—having no children and citizens having 1 or 2 children.

CHAPTER 12

An End or a Beginning?

Politics

SOURCES
117. Alva Myrdal, *Nation and Family* (London, 1945), pp. 423-26. Originally published in Swedish, Stockholm, 1940.
118. Pope Pius XII, "Woman's Dignity: Political and Social Obligations" (Questa granade vostra adunata). Broadcast from Vatican City, 21 October 1945; reprinted in *Vital Speeches*, 12 (November 1, 1945), pp. 42-45.

The following selections contrast two documents from the 1940's that foreshadow the post-world-war debate on women. The first is a matter-of-fact analysis by Alva Myrdal (Doc. 112) based on the recent experience of Swedish women. Myrdal's Sweden had successfully preserved its neutrality during the war and had therefore been able to consider the business of designing a better society for women and men in accordance with existing realities. The second is taken from a broadcast by Pope Pius XII, entitled "Woman's Dignity"; it represents the Catholic Church's effort to restate and reinforce traditional Christian values in a social order that appeared to many to be disintegrating.

Myrdal spelled out the basic "psychological dilemma" of twentieth-century Western women, a dilemma that is still with us today: how to improve the status of women as individuals in societies that persist in raising and educating girls for dependence on men, thereby hampering their functioning as independent adult women. Myrdal's intent was, of course, to promote a social democratic program that would offer state support to an enlightened and well-integrated family policy. She put forward, and Swedish legislators tried to address, a plan to eliminate childhood indoctrination to sex roles. Although Myrdal's book encompassed ideas evolved in the 1930's, it first appeared in English in 1945: thus, Myrdal's work and the Pope's pronouncement appeared in the English-speaking world in the same year.

Pius XII (1876-1958) came from an upper-class Italian family with a long tradition of legal and ecclesiastical service; his reputation for astute political diplomacy, particularly in the early 1930's, contributed significantly to his election to the papacy. He had long been noted for embracing new ideas and for his personal drive to keep up with the times; in 1936 Pius XII became the first pope to fly across the Atlantic and to visit the United States. However, his prescriptions for women do not reflect his willingness to consider new ideas in other areas; indeed, his depiction of "woman reigning as queen in her home"—to the exclusion of other activities—reveals that Pius XII echoed mid-nineteenth-century prevailing wisdom on the woman question. Pius was preoccupied with fortifying the Christian family against the intrusiveness of the godless totalitarian state, and especially against Italian communism. He feared that women who were committed to activities in the industrial and political world would be unable to educate their daughters and to train them for marriage, motherhood, and—perhaps not coincidentally—obedience to the discipline of the church.

Pius XII's expression of concern in 1945 coincided with the enfranchisement of Italian women at the end of the Second World War. Although Communist women, including Teresa Noce (Doc. 102), did not enter the Italian Chamber of Deputies until 1948, the strength of the party and its support among women in 1945 was sufficient to cause the Vatican grave concern. However, the pope's alarm at socialist professions of social equality and freedom for women (as expressed in international communist manifestos) seems unjustified when one examines the actual course of family legislation undertaken during these years by the Soviet totalitarian regime under Stalin (Docs. 115, 116); indeed, in Russia, the Communists had accommodated to a persistently recurring patriarchalism, with its emphasis on female domesticity that was not far removed from what the Roman Catholic Church, further to the West, had long espoused.

---

117. Alva Myrdal (1940)

To rectify the organizational forms of housekeeping to take cognizance of the fact that for some women the tie between marriage and homework is dissolved will take both decades and tremendous courage and open-mindedness. The relations between husband and wife when both are engaged in gainful work will probably take still longer to settle harmoniously. Looking at it practically, however, an improvement in this psychological adjustment could really be effected through reforms in verbalisms concerning the family, in the deeply propagandistic advertisements and comics, and in the teachings of home, school, and church about the natural superiority of men and their duty of being sole supporters. As it now is, few are educated or mentally prepared for the new mode of family living.

Within the homes the change to be expected is a mutually helpful division of the laborious family tasks which cannot be farmed out to paid persons. This is already taking place, although no country in the Old World can yet compete with the New World in the domestic helpfulness of its men. The proposals in Sweden, by both the Population Commission and the Committee on Women's Work, that boys be given courses in home economics and family relations is one important step in that direction. These proposals are being indefatigably pushed by the powerful organizations of housewives, of women teachers, and of professional women. Such instruction will be valuable not only for the practical help in the home but even more for changing popular attitudes concerning sex and marriage and the role of women.

The psychological relation of the working mother to her children, finally, is not necessarily a difficult one. But as a certain tension is observable, it may be that some subtle changes in public opinion are needed, so that real companionship and not only number of hours spent in common shall become most highly valued in the relation between parents and children.

The most disquieting questions as to psychological satisfaction are not those concerning the working mothers. Given time, a practical will to reform less important details in life and some adaptation to the new partnership marriages will probably result in the emergence of a fairly stable organization for family life. What is more puzzling to the young woman considering her future married life is her status if a homemaker. What was called the economic dilemma of the homemaker also has a psychological aspect. When the homemaker chooses the lot of dependence, she chooses dependence on some one individual. How will that dependence work out in terms of mental tensions and satisfactions? How long is a woman going to accept the fact that when young so much of her life is organized just to "catch" a man and become married? Could her life be rearranged so as to give her a more clearly definable status? Could marriage be made to require real "man-sized" tasks of women? How are women to endure the lack of a schematic network of daily work routine, such as characterizes other strata of life? How are they going to stand that time distribution which scatters much of their work when the rest of the world is at leisure and gives them leisure at odd hours when nobody else has it? How are they going to adjust to the fact that they have the hardest job and the least freedom of movement when young and when they are so close to the period when they were freely playing around? How are they going to get help in their job of caring for the children when small? And how are they going to get some tasks to put meaning into their lives when the children are gone? How are they going to avoid aging too early, when their life-chosen tasks of marriage and childbearing so often end in their early forties or fifties? How can security be gained and equality reached if only the man is going to be incorporated in the complex economic world? Can that sort of life still be made truly personal and filled with primary satisfactions or will it have to decline into a life secondary in character, thus breeding secret dissatisfaction?

These problems may seem willfully exaggerated, but they are already at work in the subconscious of wives and of all women. They play an indubitable, even if indefinable, role in attitudes with regard to childbearing among women today. As they have been listed here, they give hints of a complicated pattern of brooding over riddles, never solved and rarely even openly expressed. Introducing a new form of marriage where most of the determinants causing troubles and questions are done away with will by comparison expose the problems of the more old-fashioned family. Reviewing all discussions on the problem, "Should married women work?" this seems to be the fundamental dilemma: that *the very existence of one type of marriage begs the question as to the other type.* This criticism works both ways, making both kinds of wives unduly uncertain of themselves. The irritation noticeable in all the discussion about the working mother may in the last instance be attributable to that very threat which men and women feel against the marriage type so long taken for granted.

That such uncertainty exists with regard to the whole field of married women's status is of tremendous importance for the population problem itself. This was the implication drawn by some women members of the Population Commission who published as a separate appendix an analysis and an accusation called "The Crisis of Women." If it is true, and it seems to be from the wealth of discussion in fiction, magazines, and books on the subject, that mothers are in danger of becoming a mentally malcontent group, no population program can remain indifferent. It might then happen that, despite all income equalization for children, despite all of society's solicitude for mothers and children, the whole population program might fail because women are fundamentally dissatisfied with the status defined for them. There is in the end the danger that it might be one day said of the Swedish Population Commission that it failed to tackle the very problems of marriage itself.

Summarizing what may be expected from these women themselves in regard to the future of Swedish population, it is believed that the reforms called into being in Sweden will help them better to combine motherhood and remunerative work. The practical difficulties are so numerous, however, that there will probably be a long transitional period when women will either have to shun too heavy maternal responsibilities or give up their gainful work. The risk is great that society will proceed so slowly in solving these problems of women's existence that new and even more desperate crises may invade the whole field of women, family, and population.

118. Pius XII (1945)

It is beyond dispute that for a long time past the political situation has been evolving in a manner unfavorable to the real welfare of the family and women. Many political movements are turning to woman to win her for their cause. Some totalitarian systems dangle marvelous promises before her eyes of equality of rights with men, care during pregnancy and childbirth, public kitchens and other communal services to free her from some of her household cares, public kindergartens and other institutions maintained and administered by government which relieve her of her maternal obligations toward her own children, free schools and sick benefit.

It is not meant to deny the advantages that can accrue from one and the other of these social services if properly administered. Indeed we have on a former occasion pointed out that for the same work output a woman is entitled to the same wages as a man. But there still remains the crucial point of the question to which we already referred. Has woman's position been thereby improved? Equality of rights with man brought with it her abandonment of the home, where she reigned as queen, and her subjection to the same work strain and working hours. It entails depreciation of her true dignity and the solid foundation of all her rights which is her characteristic feminine role and the intimate coordination of the two sexes. The end intended by God for the good of all human society, especially for that of the family, is lost sight of. In the concessions made to woman one can easily see not respect for her dignity or her mission but an attempt to foster the economic and military power of the totalitarian state to which all must inexorably be subordinated.

On the other hand, can a woman perhaps hope for her real well-being from a regime dominated by capitalism? We do not need to describe to you now the economic and social results that issue from it. You know its characteristic signs, and you yourselves are bearing its burden: Excessive concentration of populations in cities, the constant, all-absorbing increase of big industries, the difficult and precarious state of others, notably those of artisan and agricultural workers, and the disturbing increase of unemployment.

To restore as far as possible the honor of the woman's and mother's place in the home—that is the watchword one hears now from many quarters like a cry of alarm, as if the world were awakening terrified by the fruits of material and scientific progress of which it before was so proud. . . .

Shall we conclude then that you Catholic women and girls must show yourselves adverse to a movement which willy-nilly carries you with it in social and political life? Certainly not.

In the face of theories and practice which by different ways are tearing a woman from her mission and, with a flattering promise of unbridled freedom or, in reality, of hopeless misery, are depriving her of her personal dignity, her dignity as a woman, we have heard the cry of fear which calls for her active presence as far as possible in the home.

A woman is, in fact, kept out of the home not only by her so-called emancipation but often, too, by the necessities of life, by the continuous anxiety about daily bread. It would be useless then to preach to her to return to the home while conditions prevail which constrain her to remain away from it. And this brings us to the first aspect of your mission in the social and political life which opens up before you. Your entry to public life came about suddenly as a result of social upheavals which we see around us. It does not matter. You are called upon to take part. Will you perhaps leave to others, to those who sponsor or collaborate in the ruin of some monopoly of social organization of which the family is the primary factor in its economic, juridical, spiritual and moral unity? The fate of the family, the fate of human relations are at stake. They are in your hands (Tua res agitur). Every woman has then, mark it well, the obligation, the strict obligation in conscience, not to absent herself but to go into action in a manner and way suitable to the condition of each so as to hold back those currents which threaten the home, so as to oppose those doctrines which undermine its foundations, so as to prepare, organize and achieve its restoration.

To this powerful motive which impels a Catholic woman to enter upon a way that now is opened to her to activity there is added another, her dignity as a woman. She has to collaborate with man toward the good of the State, in which she is of the same dignity as he. Each of the two sexes must take the part that belongs to it according to its nature, special qualities and physical, intellectual and moral aptitude. Both have the right and duty to cooperate toward the total good of society and of their country. But it is clear that if man is by temperament more drawn to deal with external things and public affairs, woman has, generally speaking, more perspicacity and a finer touch in knowing and solving delicate problems of domestic and family life which is the foundation of all social life. This does not exclude the possibility of some woman giving genuine proof of great talent in all fields of public activity.

All this is a question, not so much of distinct assignments as of the manner of judging and coming to concrete practical conclusions. Let us take the case of civil rights: These are at present the same for both, but with how much more discernment and efficacy will they be utilized if man and woman come to complement one another. The sensitiveness and fine feeling proper to woman, which might lead her to judge by her impressions and would thus involve the risk of impeding clarity and breadth of vision, serenity of judgment and forethought for remote consequences, are, on the contrary, of immense help when it is a question of throwing light on the needs, aspirations and dangers that touch domestic, public welfare or religious spheres.

Woman's activity is concerned in great part with the labors and occupations of domestic life which contribute to a greater and more beneficial extent than generally is thought to the true interests of social relations. But these interests also call for a group of women who can dispose of more time so as to devote themselves to them more directly and more entirely.

Who then can these women be if not especially (we certainly do not mean exclusively) those whom we referred to a little while ago; those on whom unavoidable circumstances bestowed a mysterious vocation, whom events destined to solitude which was not in their thoughts or desires and which seemed to condemn them to a selfishly futile and aimless life?

Today, on the contrary, their mission is unfolded: multifarious, militant, calling for all their energies and such that few others, held down by cares of family or education or children, or subject to the holy yoke of rule, have equal opportunities of fulfilling.

Up to now some of those women dedicated their lives with a zeal often wonderful to parochial works; others of ever larger views consecrated themselves to moral and social activity of great consequence. Their numbers as a result of the war and the calamities which followed it are considerably increased. Many brave men have fallen in the dreadful war; others returned invalids. Many young women will therefore wait in vain for the return of a husband and the flowering of new lives in their solitary home. But at the same time new needs created by the entry of woman into civil and political life have arisen to claim their assistance. Is it just a strange coincidence or are we to see in it the disposition of divine Providence?

Thus it is a vast field of activity which now lies open to woman, and it can be, corresponding to the mentality or character of each, either intellectual or actively practical. To study and expound the place and role of woman in society, her rights and duties to become a teacher-guide to one's sisters and to direct ideas, dissipate prejudices, clarify obscure points, explain and diffuse the teachings of the Church in order more securely to discredit error, illusion and falsehood, in order to expose more effectively the tactics of those who oppose Catholic dogma and morals is an immense work and one of impelling necessity without which all the zeal of the apostolate could obtain but precarious results. But direct action, too, is indispensable if we do not want sane doctrines and solid convictions to remain, if not entirely of academic interest, at least of little practical consequence.

This direct participation, this effective collaboration in social and political activity does not at all change the normal activity of woman. Associated with men in civil institutions, she will apply herself especially to those matters which call for tact, delicacy and maternal instinct rather than administrative rigidity. Who better than she can understand what is needed for the dignity of woman, the integrity and honor of the young girl and the protection and education of the child? And in all these questions how many problems call for study and action on the part of governments and legislators. Only a woman will know, for instance, how to temper with kindness, without detriment to its efficacy, legislation to repress licentiousness. She alone can find the means to save from degradation and to raise in honesty and in religious and civil virtues the morally derelict young. She alone will be able to render effective the work of protection and rehabilitation for those freed from prison and for fallen girls. She alone will re-echo from her own heart the plea of mothers from whom the totalitarian state, by whatever name it be called, would will to snatch the education of their children.

We outlined a program of woman's duties. Its practical aim is twofold: Her preparation and formation for social and political life and the evolution and activation of this social and political life in private and in public.

It is clear that woman's task thus understood cannot be improvised. Motherly instinct is in her a human instinct not determined by nature down to the details of its application. It is directed by free will and this in turn is guided by intellect. Hence comes its moral value and its dignity but also imperfection which must be compensated for and redeemed by education.

Education proper to her sex of the young girl, and not rarely also of the grown woman, is therefore a necessary condition of her preparation and formation for a life worthy of her. The ideal would evidently be that this education should begin with infancy in the intimacy of the Catholic home under the direction of the mother. It is not, unfortunately, always the case, not always possible. However, it is possible to supply at least in part for this deficiency by securing for the young girl who of necessity must work outside the home one of those occupations which are to some extent a training ground and a noviceship for the life for which she is destined. To such a purpose also serve those schools of domestic economy which aim at making of the child and the young girl of today the wife and mother of tomorrow.

How worthy of praise and encouragement are such institutions! They are one of the forms of activity in which your motherly sense and weal can have ample scope and influence and one, too, of the most precious because the good that you do propagates itself to infinity, preparing your pupils to pass on to others in the family or out of it the good which you have done them. What should we say, besides, of many other kindly offices by which you come to the aid of mothers of families in what regards their intellectual and religious formation and in the sad and difficult circumstances in which their life moves?

But in your social and political activity much depends on the legislation of the State and the administration of local bodies. Accordingly, the electoral ballot in the hands of the Catholic woman is an important means toward the fulfillment of her strict duty in conscience, especially at the present time. The State and politics have, in fact, precisely the office of securing for the family of every social class conditions necessary for them to exist and evolve as economic, juridical and moral units. Then the family will really be the vital nucleus of men who are earning honestly their temporal and eternal welfare. All this, of course, the real woman easily understands. But what she does not understand and cannot is that by politics is meant domination by one class of others and the ambitious striving for ever more extensive economic and national empire on whatever pretended motive such ambition be based. For she knows that such a policy paves the way to hidden or open civil war, to the ever growing accumulation of armaments and to the constant danger of war. She knows from experience that in any event this policy is harmful to the family, which must pay for it at a high price in goods and blood. Accordingly, no wise woman favors a policy of class struggle or war. Her vote is a vote for peace. Hence in the interest and for the good of the family, she will hold to that norm, and she will always refuse her vote to any tendency, from whatever quarter it hails, to the selfish desires of domination, internal or external, of the peace of the nation.

Courage then, Catholic women and girls. Work without ceasing, without allowing yourselves ever to be discouraged by difficulties or obstacles. May you be under the standard of Christ the King, under the patronage of His wonderful Mother, restorers of home, family and society. May divine favors descend on you in a copious stream: favors in token of which we impart to you with all the affection of our paternal heart an apostolic benediction.

Philosophy: *"Otherness" versus Complementarity*

SOURCES

119. Simone de Beauvoir, *The Second Sex*, tr. H. M. Parshley (New York, 1953), pp. xv-xxi, xxvii-xxix. Originally published as *Le Deuxième Sexe* in Paris, 1949.

120. Margaret Mead, *Male and Female: A Study of the Sexes in a Changing World* (New York, 1967), pp. 7-10, 381-84. First published in 1949. (Based on the Jacob Gimbel Lectures in Sex Psychology under the auspices of Stanford University and the University of California in San Francisco, November 1946.)

Soon after the end of the Second World War two women, each drawing on her own professional expertise and her lived experiences as a woman, published provocative analyses of women's position. Both believed that women's individual gifts were being wasted, in a world sadly in need of human resources. Both considered that women were the prisoners of their culture and addressed the perplexing topic of how their subordination in Western culture had come to be, but their approaches and their conclusions differed widely.

Philosopher and novelist Simone de Beauvoir (b. 1908) received a traditional Catholic upbringing in Paris. Her father lived on his investments and dabbled in the law and the theater. The family's financial reverses during the war, however, meant that no funds were available to provide her with a dowry. Thus her parents reluctantly allowed her to study for a teaching career, despite their continued bourgeois belief that women should not be professionally employed and lost social status if they were. During her studies for the *agrégation* (state teaching examination) in Paris, Beauvoir became closely associated with her fellow student Jean-Paul Sartre, who was to become one of the best-known existentialist philosophers of the twentieth century and her life-companion. Beauvoir decided in her student days (as she wrote in her autobiography), "I didn't care two pence for respectability, and in those cases where love could be disassociated from marriage, it seemed to me better to stake everything on love, and to hell with domesticity."

Despite her show of independence and her revolt against both marriage and her traditional Catholic bourgeois upbringing, Beauvoir was deeply influenced by Sartre's thought and personal world view. Her own analysis of the female condition as developed in her brilliant and powerful book *Le Deuxième Sexe*, written when she was about forty years old, is based upon Sartre's existential dichotomies. For example, Beauvoir, like Sartre, employs polarized notions of "the one and the other," "for itself and in itself," "transcendence and immanence," "doing and being." Even more radicalizing was her attempt to grapple with the phallic categories of Freudian psychoanalysis while Sartre was writing about female sexuality in his book *L'Etre et le Néant* (*Being and Nothingness*) in terms of "slime" and "holes." The combination of these ideas resulted in Beauvoir's angry analysis in *Le Deuxième Sexe* (1949) of woman as "other," who could only overcome her inferiority by striving to become active like man, and thereby transcend her "otherness." To do anything else, she believed, was to experience "demission"—a regression into immanence.

Although *Le Deuxième Sexe* was almost immediately translated into English in the early 1950's, the book only gained the status of an international classic following the resurgence of domesticity that women experienced in the decade after World War II. Thereafter the printing history of the book records fantastic leaps—attesting the importance of its message in many languages to millions of female readers. Beauvoir's view that women could not form an independent political group because of their continued sexual—and economic—dependence on men has inspired, angered, and stimulated women in all Western nations to disprove her thesis. Her words provoked them to politicize as a group and to attempt to find a *façon de vivre*, both with men and without them, as economic and professional peers, as companions, as heterosexual lovers, or in lesbian relationships.

Beauvoir's impassioned synthesis of philosophy, history and literary criticism, psychoanalysis and personal experience offers a striking contrast to the conclusions of Margaret Mead, who coupled her own personal experience with the findings from her professional anthropological field work. Mead (1901-1978), whose father took the professionalism of both his own mother and his wife for granted, was raised in an academic milieu in Pennsylvania. Educated at DePauw and Barnard, she became a member of the celebrated group of women graduate students who studied in the 1920's under the distinguished anthropologist Franz Boas at Columbia University. For more than forty years she held an appointment as curator of ethnology at the American Museum of Natural History and remained associated with Columbia University, where she directed various research projects. Her articles in scholarly and popular magazines brought her ideas to a wide American and international audience. Married three times and the mother, with anthropologist Gregory Bateson, of a daughter, Mead confronted her scholarly findings with her personal experience. She was one of the first women to study the cultures of the Pacific islands. Her field work in Samoa, the Admiralty Islands, and New Guinea in the 1920's provided the evidence for her assertion that not only women but men also are the victims of socially imposed gender roles. "The growing boy," she said, "is shaped to a local and special emphasis as inexorably as the local girl." She viewed differences in sex roles as almost arbitrary cultural developments whereby in one society females or males—in another, males or females—may respectively perform certain tasks or exhibit certain traits.

In this selection from her *Male and Female*, Mead insisted on the universality of a sexual division of labor in human societies. In a review of the English version of *The Second Sex* (1953), Mead criticized Beauvoir for failing to acknowledge women's creative contribution as mothers, and disagreed fundamentally with Beauvoir's envious glorification of "transcendent" male characteristics, recognizing such characteristics to be the combined result of personal and cultural history and differing from one culture to another.

---

119. Simone de Beauvoir (1949)

A man would never get the notion of writing a book on the peculiar situation of the human male. But if I wish to define myself, I must first of all say: "I am a woman"; on this truth must be based all further discussion. A man never begins by presenting himself as an individual of a certain sex; it goes without saying that he is a man. The terms *masculine* and *feminine* are used symmetrically only as a matter of form, as on legal papers. In actuality the relation of the two sexes is not quite like that of two electrical poles, for man represents both the positive and the neutral, as is indicated by the common use of *man* to designate human beings in general; whereas woman represents only the negative, defined by limiting criteria, without reciprocity. In the midst of an abstract discussion it is vexing to hear a man say: "You think thus and so because you are a woman"; but I know that my only defense is to reply: "I think thus and so because it is true," thereby removing my subjective self from the argument. It would be out of the question to reply: "And you think the contrary because you are a man," for it is understood that the fact of being a man is no peculiarity. A man is in the right in being a man; it is the woman who is in the wrong. It amounts to this: just as for the ancients there was an absolute vertical with reference to which the oblique was defined, so there is an absolute human type, the masculine. Woman has ovaries, a uterus; these peculiarities imprison her in her subjectivity, circumscribe her within the limits of her own nature. It is often said that she thinks with her glands. Man superbly ignores the fact that his anatomy also includes glands, such as the testicles, and that they secrete hormones. He thinks of his body as a direct and normal connection with the world, which he believes he apprehends objectively, whereas he regards the body of woman as a hindrance, a prison, weighed down by everything peculiar to it. "The female is a female by virtue of a certain *lack* of qualities," said Aristotle; "we should regard the female nature as afflicted with a natural defectiveness." And St. Thomas for his part pronounced woman to be an "imperfect man," an "incidental" being. This is symbolized in Genesis where Eve is depicted as made from what Bossuet called "a supernumerary bone" of Adam.

Thus humanity is male and man defines woman not in herself but as relative to him; she is not regarded as an autonomous being. Michelet writes: "Woman, the relative being. . . ." And Benda is most positive in his *Rapport d'Uriel*: "The body of man makes sense in itself quite apart from that of woman, whereas the latter seems wanting in significance by itself. . . . Man can think of himself without woman. She cannot think of herself without man." And she is simply what man decrees; thus she is called "the sex," by which is meant that she appears essentially to the male as a sexual being. For him she is sex—absolute sex, no less. She is defined and differentiated with reference to man and not he with reference to her; she is the incidental, the inessential as opposed to the essential. He is the Subject, he is the Absolute—she is the Other.

The category of the *Other* is as primordial as consciousness itself. In the most primitive societies, in the most ancient mythologies, one finds the expression of a duality—that of the Self and the Other. This duality was not originally attached to the division of the sexes; it was not dependent upon any empirical facts. It is revealed in such works as that of

Granet on Chinese thought and those of Dumézil on the East Indies and Rome. The feminine element was at first no more involved in such pairs as Varuna-Mitra, Uranus-Zeus, Sun-Moon, and Day-Night than it was in the contrasts between Good and Evil, lucky and unlucky auspices, right and left, God and Lucifer. Otherness is a fundamental category of human thought.

Thus it is that no group ever sets itself up as the One without at once setting up the Other over against itself. If three travelers chance to occupy the same compartment, that is enough to make vaguely hostile "others" out of all the rest of the passengers on the train. In small-town eyes all persons not belonging to the village are "strangers" and suspect; to the native of a country all who inhabit other countries are "foreigners"; Jews are "different" for the anti-Semite, Negroes are "inferior" for American racists, aborigines are "natives" for colonists, proletarians are the "lower class" for the privileged.

Lévi-Strauss, at the end of a profound work on the various forms of primitive societies, reaches the following conclusion: "Passage from the state of Nature to the state of Culture is marked by man's ability to view biological relations as a series of contrasts; duality, alternation, opposition, and symmetry, whether under definite or vague forms, constitute not so much phenomena to be explained as fundamental and immediately given data of social reality." These phenomena would be incomprehensible if in fact human society were simply a *Mitsein* or fellowship based on solidarity and friendliness. Things become clear, on the contrary, if, following Hegel, we find in consciousness itself a fundamental hostility toward every other consciousness; the subject can be posed only in being opposed—he sets himself up as the essential, as opposed to the other, the inessential, the object.

But the other consciousness, the other ego, sets up a reciprocal claim. The native traveling abroad is shocked to find himself in turn regarded as a "stranger" by the natives of neighboring countries. As a matter of fact, wars, festivals, trading, treaties, and contests among tribes, nations, and classes tend to deprive the concept *Other* of its absolute sense and to make manifest its relativity; willy-nilly, individuals and groups are forced to realize the reciprocity of their relations. How is it, then, that this reciprocity has not been recognized between the sexes, that one of the contrasting terms is set up as the sole essential, denying any relativity in regard to its correlative and defining the latter as pure otherness? Why is it that women do not dispute male sovereignty? No subject will readily volunteer to become the object, the inessential; it is not the Other who, in defining himself as the Other, establishes the One. The Other is posed as such by the One in defining himself as the One. But if the Other is not to regain the status of being the One, he must be submissive enough to accept this alien point of view. Whence comes this submission in the case of woman?

There are, to be sure, other cases in which a certain category has been able to dominate another completely for a time. Very often this privilege depends upon inequality of numbers—the majority imposes its rule upon the minority or persecutes it. But women are not a minority, like the American Negroes or the Jews; there are as many women as men on earth. Again, the two groups concerned have often been originally independent; they may have been formerly unaware of each other's existence, or perhaps they recognized each other's autonomy. But a historical event has resulted in the subjugation of the weaker by the stronger. The scattering of the Jews, the introduction of slavery into America, the conquests of imperialism are examples in point. In these cases the oppressed retained at least the memory of former days; they possessed in common a past, a tradition, sometimes a religion or a culture.

The parallel drawn by Bebel between women and the proletariat is valid in that neither ever formed a minority or a separate collective unit of mankind. And instead of a single historical event it is in both cases a historical development that explains their status as a class and accounts for the membership of *particular individuals* in that class. But proletarians have not always existed, whereas there have always been women. They are women in virtue of their anatomy and physiology. Throughout history they have always been subordinated to men, and hence their dependency is not the result of a historical event or a social change—it was not something that *occurred*. The reason why otherness in this case seems to be an absolute is in part that it lacks the contingent or incidental nature of historical facts. A condition brought about at a certain time can be abolished at some other time, as the Negroes of Haiti and others have proved; but it might seem that a natural condition is beyond the possibility of change. In truth, however, the nature of things is no more immutably given, once for all, than is historical reality. If woman seems to be the inessential which never becomes the essential, it is because she herself fails to bring about this change. Proletarians say "We"; Negroes also. Regarding themselves as subjects, they transform the bourgeois, the whites, into "others." But women do not say "We," except at some congress of feminists or similar formal demonstration; men say "women," and women use the same word in referring to themselves. They do not authentically assume a subjective attitude. The proletarians have accomplished the revolution in Russia, the Negroes in Haiti, the Indo-Chinese are battling for it in Indo-China; but the women's effort has never been anything more than a symbolic agitation. They have gained only what men have been willing to grant; they have taken nothing, they have only received.

The reason for this is that women lack concrete means for organizing themselves into a unit which can stand face to face with the correlative unit. They have no past, no history, no religion of their own; and they have no such solidarity of work and interest as that of the proletariat. They are not even promiscuously herded together in the way that creates community feeling among the American Negroes, the ghetto Jews, the workers of Saint-Denis, or the factory hands of Renault. They live dispersed among the males, attached through residence, housework, economic condition, and social standing to certain men—fathers or husbands—more firmly than they are to other women. If they belong to the bourgeoisie, they feel solidarity with men of that class, not with proletarian women; if they are white, their allegiance is to white men, not to Negro women. The proletariat can propose to massacre the ruling class, and a sufficiently fanatical Jew or Negro might dream of getting sole possession of the atomic bomb and making humanity wholly Jewish or black; but woman cannot even dream of exterminating the males. The bond that unites her to her oppressors is not comparable to any other. The division of the sexes is a biological fact, not an event in human history. Male and female stand opposed within a primordial *Mitsein*, and woman has not broken it. The couple is a fundamental unity with its two halves riveted together, and the cleavage of society along the line of sex is impossible. Here is to be found the basic trait of woman: she is the Other in a totality of which the two components are necessary to one another.

One could suppose that this reciprocity might have facilitated the liberation of woman. When Hercules sat at the feet of Omphale and helped with her spinning, his desire for her held him captive; but why did she fail to gain a lasting power? To revenge herself on Jason, Medea killed their children; and this grim legend would seem to suggest that she might have obtained a formidable influence over him through his love for his offspring. In *Lysistrata* Aristophanes gaily depicts a band of women who joined forces to gain social ends through the sexual needs of their men; but this is only a play. In the legend of the Sabine women, the latter soon abandoned their plan of remaining sterile to punish their ravishers. In truth woman has not been socially emancipated through man's need—sexual desire and the desire for offspring—which makes the male dependent for satisfaction upon the female.

Master and slave, also, are united by a reciprocal need, in this case economic, which does not liberate the slave. In the relation of master to slave the master does not make a point of the need that he has for the other; he has in his grasp the power of satisfying this need through his own action; whereas the slave, in his dependent condition, his hope and fear, is quite conscious of the need he has for his master. Even if the need is at bottom equally urgent for both, it always works in favor of the oppressor and against the oppressed. That is why the liberation of the working class, for example, has been slow.

Now, woman has always been man's dependent, if not his slave; the two sexes have never shared the world in equality. And even today woman is heavily handicapped, though her situation is beginning to change. Almost nowhere is her legal status the same as man's, and frequently it is much to her disadvantage. Even when her rights are legally recognized in the abstract, long-standing custom prevents their full expression in the mores. In the economic sphere men and women can almost be said to make up two castes; other things being equal, the former hold the better jobs, get higher wages, and have more opportunity for success than their new competitors. In industry and politics men have a great many more positions and they monopolize the most important posts. In addition to all this, they enjoy a traditional prestige that the education of children tends in every way to support, for the present enshrines the past—and in the past all history has been made by men. At the present time, when women are beginning to take part in the affairs of the world, it is still a world that belongs to men—they have no doubt of it at all and women have scarcely any. To decline to be the Other, to refuse to be a party to the deal—this would be for women to renounce all the advantages conferred upon them by their alliance with the superior caste. Man-the-sovereign will provide woman-the-liege with material protection and will undertake the moral justification of her existence; thus she can evade at once both economic risk and the metaphysical risk of a liberty in which ends and aims must be contrived without assistance. Indeed, along with the ethical urge of each individual to affirm his subjective existence, there is also the temptation to forgo liberty and become a thing. This is an inauspicious road, for he who takes it—passive, lost, ruined—becomes henceforth the creature of another's will, frustrated in his transcendence and deprived of every value. But it is an easy road; on it one avoids the strain involved in undertaking an authentic existence. When man makes of woman the *Other*, he may, then, expect her to manifest deep-seated tendencies toward complicity. Thus, woman may fail to lay claim to the status of subject because she lacks definite resources, because she feels the necessary bond that ties her to man regardless of reciprocity, and because she is often very well pleased with her role as the *Other*.

But it will be asked at once: how did all this begin? It is easy to see that the duality of the sexes, like any duality, gives rise to conflict. And doubtless the winner will assume the status of absolute. But why should man have won from the start? It seems possible that women could have won the victory; or that the outcome of the conflict might never have been decided. How is it that this world has always belonged to the men and that things have begun to change only recently? Is this change a good thing? Will it bring about an equal sharing of the world between men and women?

These questions are now new, and they have often been answered. But the very fact that woman *is the Other* tends to cast suspicion upon all the justifications that men have ever been able to provide for it. . . .

But it is doubtless impossible to approach any human problem with a mind free from bias. The way in which questions are put, the points of view assumed, presuppose a relativity of interest; all characteristics imply values, and every objective description, so called, implies an ethical background. Rather than attempt to conceal principles more or less definitely implied, it is better to state them openly at the beginning. This will make it unnecessary to specify on every page in just what sense one uses such words as *superior, inferior, better, worse, progress, reaction*, and the like. If we survey some of the works on woman, we note that one of the points of view most frequently adopted is that of the public good, the general interest; and one always means by this the benefit of society as one wishes it to be maintained or established. For our part, we hold that the only public good is that which assures the private good of the citizens; we shall pass judgment on institutions according to their effectiveness in giving concrete opportunities to individuals. But we do not confuse the idea of private interest with that of happiness, although that is another common point of view. Are not women of the harem more happy than women voters? Is not the housekeeper happier than the workingwoman? It is not too clear just what the word *happy* really means and still less what true values it may mask. There is no possibility of measuring the happiness of others, and it is always easy to describe as happy the situation in which one wishes to place them.

In particular those who are condemned to stagnation are often pronounced happy on the pretext that happiness consists in being at rest. This notion we reject, for our perspective is that of existentialist ethics. Every subject plays his part as such specifically through exploits or projects that serve as a mode of transcendence; he achieves liberty only through a continual reaching out toward other liberties. There is no justification for present existence other than its expansion into an indefinitely open future. Every time transcendence falls back into immanence, stagnation, there is a degradation of existence into the *"en-soi"*—the brutish life of subjection to given conditions—and of liberty into constraint and contingence. This downfall represents a moral fault if the subject consents to it; if it is inflicted upon him, it spells frustration and oppression. In both cases it is an absolute evil. Every individual concerned to justify his existence feels that his existence involves an undefined need to transcend himself, to engage in freely chosen projects.

Now, what peculiarly signalizes the situation of woman is that she—a free and autonomous being like all human creatures—nevertheless finds herself living in a world where men compel her to assume the status of the Other. They propose to stabilize her as object and to doom her to immanence since her transcendence is to be overshadowed and forever transcended by another ego (*conscience*) which is essential and sovereign. The drama of woman lies in this conflict between the fundamental aspirations of every subject (ego)—who always regards the self as the essential—and the compulsions of a situation in which she is the inessential. How can a human being in woman's situation attain fulfillment? What roads are open to her? Which are blocked? How can independence be recovered in a state of dependency? What circumstances limit woman's liberty and how can they be overcome? These are the fundamental questions on which I would fain throw some light. This means that I am interested in the fortunes of the individual as defined not in terms of happiness but in terms of liberty.

Quite evidently this problem would be without significance if we were to believe that woman's destiny is inevitably determined by physiological, psychological, or economic forces. Hence I shall discuss first of all the light in which woman is viewed by biology, psychoanalysis, and historical materialism. Next I shall try to show exactly how the concept of the "truly feminine" has been fashioned—why woman has been defined as the Other—and what have been the consequences from man's point of view. Then from woman's point of view I shall describe the world in which women must live; and thus we shall be able to envisage the difficulties in their way as, endeavoring to make their escape from the sphere hitherto assigned them, they aspire to full membership in the human race.

120. Margaret Mead (1949)

The differences between the two sexes is one of the important conditions upon which we have built the many varieties of human culture that give human beings dignity and stature. In every known society, mankind has elaborated the biological division of labour into forms often very remotely related to the original biological differences that provided the original clues. Upon the contrast in bodily form and function, men have built analogies between sun and moon, night and day, goodness and evil, strength and tenderness, steadfastness and fickleness, endurance and vulnerability. Sometimes one quality has been assigned to one sex, sometimes to the other. Now it is boys who are thought of as infinitely vulnerable and in need of special cherishing care, now it is girls. In some societies it is girls for whom parents must collect a dowry or make husband-catching magic, in others the parental worry is over the difficulty of marrying off the boys. Some peoples think of women as too weak to work out of doors, others regard women as the appropriate bearers of heavy burdens, "because their heads are stronger than men's." The periodicities of female reproductive functions have appealed to some peoples as making women the natural sources of magical or religious power, to others as directly antithetical to those powers; some religions, including our European traditional religions, have assigned women an inferior rôle in the religious hierarchy, others have built their whole symbolic relationship with the supernatural world upon male imitations of the natural functions of women. In some cultures women are regarded as sieves through whom the best-guarded secrets will sift; in others it is the men who are the gossips. Whether we deal with small matters or with large, with the frivolities of ornament and cosmetics or the sanctities of man's place in the universe, we find this great variety of ways, often flatly contradictory one to the other, in which the rôles of the two sexes have been patterned.

But we always find the patterning. We know of no culture that has said, articulately, that there is no difference between men and women except in the way they contribute to the creation of the next generation; that otherwise in all respects they are simply human beings with varying gifts, no one of which can be exclusively assigned to either sex. We find no culture in which it has been thought that all identified traits—stupidity and brilliance, beauty and ugliness, friendliness and hostility, initiative and responsiveness, courage and patience and industry—are merely human traits. However differently the traits have been assigned, some to one sex, some to the other, and some to both, however arbitrary the assignment must be seen to be (for surely it cannot be true that women's heads are both absolutely weaker—for carrying loads—and absolutely stronger—for carrying loads—than men's), although the division has been arbitrary, it has always been there in every society of which we have any knowledge.

So in the twentieth century, as we try to re-assess our human resources, and by taking thought to add even a jot or a tittle to the stature of our fuller humanity, we are faced with a most bewildering and confusing array of apparently contradictory evidence about sex differences. We may well ask: Are they important? Do real differences exist, in addition to the obvious anatomical and physical ones—but just as biologically based—that may be masked by the learnings appropriate to any given society, but which will nevertheless be there? Will such differences run through all of men's and all of women's behaviour? Must we expect, for instance, that a brave girl may be very brave but will never have the same kind of courage as a brave boy, and that the man who works all day at a monotonous task may learn to produce far more than any woman in his society, but he will do it at a higher price to himself? Are such differences real, and *must* we take them into account? Because men and women have always in all societies built a great superstructure of socially defined sex differences that obviously cannot be true for all humanity—or the people just over the mountain would not be able to do it all in the exactly opposite fashion—must *some* such superstructures be built? We have here two different questions: Are we dealing not with a *must* that we dare not flout because it is rooted so deep in our biological mammalian nature that to flout it means individual and social disease? Or with a *must* that, although not so deeply rooted, still is so very socially convenient and so well tried that it would be uneconomical to flout it—a *must* which says, for example, that it is easier to get children born and bred if we stylize the behaviour of the sexes very differently, teaching them to walk and dress and act in contrasting ways and to specialize in different kinds of work? But there is still the third possibility. Are not sex differences exceedingly valuable, one of the resources of our human nature that every society has used but no society has as yet begun to use to the full?

We live in an age when every inquiry must be judged in terms of urgency. Are such questions about the rôles and the possible rôles of the sexes academic, peripheral to the central problems of our times? Are such discussions querulous fiddling while Rome burns? I think they are not. Upon the growing accuracy with which we are able to judge our limitations and our potentialities, as human beings and in particular as human societies, will depend the survival of our civilization, which we now have the means to destroy. Never before in history has mankind had such momentous choices placed in its hands. . . .

But from men, society has also asked and received something more than this. For thousands of generations men have been asked to do something more than be good lovers and husbands and fathers, even with all that that involved of husbandry and organization and protection against attack. They have been asked to develop and elaborate, each in terms of his own ability, the structure within which the children are reared, to build higher towers, or wider roads, to dream new dreams and see new visions, to penetrate ever farther into the secrets of nature, to learn new ways of making life more human and more rewarding. And within the whole adventure there has been a silent subtle division of labour, which had its roots perhaps in a period of history when the creativeness of bearing children outweighted in splendour every act that men performed, however they danced and pantomimed their pretence that the novices were really their children after all. In this division of labour, there was the assumption that bearing children is enough for the women, and in the rest of the task all the elaborations belong to men. This assumption becomes the less tenable the more men succeed in those elaborations which they have taken on themselves. As a civilization becomes complex, human life is defined in individual terms as well as in the service of the race, and the great structures of law and government, religion and art and science, become something highly valued for themselves. Practised by men, they become indicators of masculine humanity, and men take great pride in these achievements. To the extent that women are barred from them, women become less human. An illiterate woman is no less human than an illiterate man. As long as few men write and most men cannot, a woman may suffer no loss in her sense of herself. But when writing becomes almost universal—access to books, increased precision of thought, possibilities of communication—then if women cannot learn to write because they are women, they lose in stature, and the whole subtle process begins by which the wholeness of both sexes is undermined. When the women's sense of loss of participation is compensated for by other forms of power, by the iron will of the mother-in-law who has been the docile, home-bound wife—as in China and Japan—then the equilibrating pattern may take the form of covert distortions of human relationships that may persist over centuries. When women's sense of impaired participation in society is expressed directly, in rebellion against the restrictions that it has placed on her, we may find instead the sort of freedom for women that occurred just before the break-down of the Roman Empire, or in the goals of the women's movement of the last century. But whatever the compensatory adjustment within the society, women's belief in their own power to contribute directly to human culture will be subtly and deeply impaired, and men's isolation, either covertly threatened or openly attacked, in a world that they have built alone will increase.

If we once accept the premise that we can build a better world by using the different gifts of each sex, we shall have two kinds of freedom, freedom to use untapped gifts of each sex, and freedom to admit freely and cultivate in each sex their special superiorities. We may well find that there are certain fields, such as the physical sciences, mathematics, and instrumental music, in which men by virtue of their sex, as well as by virtue of their qualities as specially gifted human beings, will always have that razor-edge of extra gift which makes all the difference, and that while women may easily follow where men lead, men will always make the new discoveries. We may equally well find that women, through the learning involved in maternity, which once experienced can be taught more easily to all women, even childless women, than to men, have a special superiority in those human sciences which involve that type of understanding which until it is analyzed is called intuition. If intuition is based, as it seems to be, upon an ability to recognize difference from the self rather than upon one to project the self in building a construct or a hypothesis, it may well be that the greatest intuitive gifts will be found among women. Just as for endless ages men's mathematical gifts were neglected and people counted one, two, two and one, and a dog, or were limited to counting on the fingers of their hands, so women's intuitive gifts have lain fallow, uncultivated, uncivilized.

Once it is possible to say it is as important to take women's gifts and make them available to both men and women, in transmittable form, as it was to take men's gifts and make the civilization built upon them available to both men and women, we shall have enriched our society. And we shall be ready to synthesize both kinds of gifts in the sciences, which are now sadly lop-sided with their far greater knowledge of how to destroy than of how to construct, far better equipped to analyze the world of matter into which man can project his intelligence than the world of human relations, which requires the socialized use of intuition. The mother who must learn that the infant who was but an hour ago a part of her body is now a different individual, with its own hungers and its own needs, and that if she listens to her own body to interpret the child, the child will die, is schooled in an irreplaceable school. As she learns to attend to that different individual, she develops a special way of thinking and feeling about human beings. We can leave these special learnings at the present level, or convert them into a more elaborate part of our civilization. Already the men and women who are working together in the human sciences are finding the greatly increased understanding that comes from the way in which their insights complement each other. We are learning that we pay different prices for our insights: for instance, to understand the way a culture socializes children a man must return in imagination to childhood, but a woman has also another and different path, to learn to understand the mothers of these children. Yet both are necessary, and the skill of one sex gives only a partial answer. We can build a whole society only by using both the gifts special to each sex and those shared by both sexes—by using the gifts of the whole of humanity.

Every step away from a tangled situation, in which moves and countermoves have been made over centuries, is a painful step, itself inevitably imperfect. Here is a vicious circle to which it is not possible to assign either a beginning or an end, in which men's over-estimation of women's rôles, or women's over-estimation of men's rôles, leads one sex or the other to arrogate, to neglect, or even to relinquish part of our so dearly won humanity. Those who would break the circle are themselves a product of it, express some of its defects in their every gesture, may be only strong enough to challenge it, not able actually to break it. Yet once identified, once analyzed, it should be possible to create a climate of opinion in which others, a little less the product of the dark past because they have been reared with a light in their hand that can shine backwards as well as forwards, may in turn take the next step. Only by recognizing that each change in human society must be made by those who carry in every cell of their bodies the very reason why the change is necessary can we school our hearts to the patience to build truly and well, recognizing that it is not only the price, but also the glory, of our humanity that civilization must be built by human beings.

REFERENCE MATTER

SUGGESTED FURTHER READING

THE READINGS suggested here do not represent an attempt to provide comprehensive coverage. Whenever possible, we have suggested recent scholarly works that illuminate attitudes on the woman question or that present divergent interpretations. In many instances, however, the scholarship is still developing, or not yet published, and we have had to resort to general works. In instances where no adequate studies are available, we have included contextual works or, in some cases, source readings. We have chosen works in English whenever possible, even when they are not definitive, and have included works in other languages only when none were available in English, or when foreign works were authoritative.

BASHKIRTSEFF, MARIE (Doc. 4)
   Barrès 1889, 1890; Karageorgevich 1903; Cahuet 1926.
BÄUMER, GERTRUD (Doc. 66)
   Zahn-Harnack 1928; Huber 1970; Hackett 1976.
BEAUVOIR, SIMONE DE (Doc. 119)
   Beauvoir 1958, 1962, 1963; Gennari 1967; Collins & Pierce 1976; Walters 1976; Eisenberg 1978, 1979; McCall 1979; Dijkstra 1980; Felstiner 1980; Fuchs 1980; Le Doeuff 1980.
BELLAMY, EDWARD (Doc. 49)
   Bowman 1958; D. Hayden 1981; Lipow 1982.
BJØRNSON, BJØRNSTJERNE (Doc. 11)
   Brandes 1964; Bredsdorff 1969.
BLUM, LÉON (Doc. 43)
   Colton 1966; Logue 1973.
BRIEUX, EUGÈNE (Doc. 28)
   Shaw 1911; Scheifley 1917; Millstone 1977.
BRION, HÉLÈNE (Doc. 71)
   Dubief 1963; Kriegel 1963; Bouchardeau 1978; Sowerwine 1978, 1979, 1982.
BUND DEUTSCHER FRAUENVEREINE (Doc. 20)
   R. Evans 1976; Hackett 1976.
CATT, CARRIE CHAPMAN (Docs. 60, 64, 68)
   Peck 1944; Kraditor 1965; Flexner 1971; Morgan 1972; Camhi 1973; Whittick 1979; Steinson 1980.
CHEKHOV, ANTON (Doc. 9)
   Hahn 1977.
CROUZET-BENABEN, JEANNE (Doc. 39)
   Crouzet-Benaben 1917, 1971; Charrier 1931; Offen 1973b; Mayeur 1977.

"DECLARATION DES DROITS DE LA FAMILLE" (Doc. 88)
  Talmy 1962.
EDWARDS-PILLIET, BLANCHE (Doc. 32)
  Poirier & Nahon, n.d.
ENGELS, FRIEDRICH (Doc. 13; *see also* Vol. I)
  J. Mitchell 1966; Leacock 1972, 1977; Sacks 1974; Delmar 1976; Lane 1976; Zaretsky 1976; Meyer 1977.
FAWCETT, MILLICENT GARRETT (Docs. 62, 65, 90)
  Fawcett 1925; Strachey 1931; Morgan 1974; Hume 1979.
FRANK, LOUIS (Doc. 24)
  Bueger-Van Lierde 1973.
FRENCH DECREE ESTABLISHING MEDALS FOR MOTHERS (J.-L. Breton) (Doc. 84)
  Gaultier 1956; Talmy 1962; Paillat & Houdaille 1975.
FREUD, SIGMUND (Docs. 92, 94, 99)
  Jones 1961; Rieff 1961; Millet 1969; Balogh 1971; J. Miller 1973; Lasch 1974; Mitchell 1974; Strouse 1974; Chodorow 1978; Bettelheim 1982.
GAY, SUSAN ELIZABETH (Doc. 56)
  Blackburn 1902; Rover 1967.
GILMAN, CHARLOTTE STETSON PERKINS (Doc. 25)
  Degler 1956, 1966; Berkin 1980; Hill 1980; Lane 1980.
GLADSTONE, WILLIAM EWART (Doc. 55)
  Blackburn 1902; Rover 1967; Marlow 1977.
GOLDMARK, JOSEPHINE (Doc. 52)
  Sumner 1910; Bremner 1971.
GRIPENBERG, ALEXANDRA (Doc. 57)
  R. Evans 1977; Jallinoja 1980.
HALL, G. STANLEY (Doc. 37)
  Ross 1972; Shields 1975, 1982.
HALL, RADCLYFFE (Doc. 97)
  Troubridge 1961; Brittain 1968; Cook 1979; Fassler 1979; Faderman 1981; Smith-Rosenberg & Newton 1981; Zimmerman 1981; Franks 1982.
HITLER, ADOLF (Doc. 105)
  Bullock 1953; Schoenbaum 1967; McIntyre 1971; Stephenson 1975; Koonz 1977, 1981; Rupp 1977, 1978, 1980.
HOGGAN, FRANCES (Doc. 47; *see also* Vol. I)
  Reiss 1934; E. Bell 1953; Graveson & Crane 1957; Holcombe 1982.
HOLTBY, WINIFRED (Docs. 87, 104, 108)
  White 1938; Brittain 1940.
HORNEY, KAREN (Doc. 93)
  Bettelheim 1962; Kelman 1967; J. Mitchell 1974; Chodorow 1978; Rubins 1978; Garrison 1981.
IBSEN, HENRIK (Doc. 1)
  Lord 1882; Koht 1954; Brandes 1964; Bredsdorff 1969.
INTERNATIONAL CONGRESS OF WOMEN (Doc. 69)
  Addams 1916. *See also* the following works on Jane Addams and the Women's Peace Party: Degen 1939; Lasch 1965; Farrell 1967; Herman 1969; Conway 1971; Davis 1973.
INTERNATIONAL COUNCIL OF WOMEN (Docs. 18, 110)
  Swanwick 1935; Degen 1939; Lefaucheaux 1966; Herman 1969; Hurwitz 1977.
INTERNATIONAL LABOUR OFFICE (Doc. 111)
  Thibert 1971.

INTERNATIONAL SOCIALIST WOMEN'S CONFERENCE (Doc. 59)
Joll 1955; Braunthal 1967; Honeycutt 1975; Meyer 1977; Quataert 1977, 1979; Rebérioux 1978.
JUNG, CARL GUSTAV (Doc. 98)
Hannah 1976; Brome 1978.
KETTLER, HEDWIG (Doc. 36)
Willich 1960; R. Evans 1976; Hackett 1976; Greven-Aschoff 1981.
KEY, ELLEN (Docs. 26, 48)
Nyström-Hamilton 1913; Anthony 1915.
KOLLONTAI, ALEKSANDRA (Docs. 77, 83)
Farnsworth 1976, 1981; C. Hayden 1976; Stites 1976, 1977, 1978; Lapidus 1978; Bobroff 1979; Clements 1979. *See also* Gasiorowska 1968.
KROPOTKIN, PETER (Doc. 22)
Kropotkin 1899; M. Miller 1976; D. Hayden 1981.
LANGE, HELENE (Docs. 35, 63, 67)
Zahn-Harnack 1928; Hackett 1972, 1976; Twellmann 1972; Fransden 1974; R. Evans 1976; Greven-Aschoff 1981.
LAWRENCE, D. H. (Doc. 95)
Beauvoir 1949; Moore 1951, 1955; Rogers 1966; Millett 1969; Lucas 1973; Green 1974.
LENIN (Doc. 76)
Zetkin 1934; Wolfe 1948; McNeal 1972; Wheeler 1975; Stites 1978.
LEO XIII (Docs. 16, 44)
P. Moon 1921; Werth & Mihanovich 1955; Gargan 1961; Wallace 1966.
LINZEN-ERNST, CLARA (Doc. 33)
R. Evans 1976, 1977, 1980; Hackett 1981; Duden 1981a.
"LOI DE 31 JUILLET 1920" (Doc. 85)
Talmy 1962; Guerrand 1971; Paillat & Houdaille 1975; Ronsin 1980. *See also* McLaren 1978a.
MARTIN, MARIA (Docs. 46, 58)
Dzeh-Djen 1934; Sullerot 1966; Taïeb 1982.
MARX, ELEANOR, AND EDWARD AVELING (Doc. 14)
Tsuzuki 1967; Kapp 1972-76.
MAUGERET, MARIE (Doc. 17)
Bidelman 1981; Hause & Kenney 1981a. *See also* Mayeur & Gadille 1980.
MEAD, MARGARET (Doc. 120)
Klein 1946; Mead 1972; Metraux 1979; Rosenberg 1982.
MJØEN, ALFRED (Doc. 53)
Articles in Norwegian *Who's Who.*
MORRIS, WILLIAM (Doc. 23)
Thompson 1955.
MUSSOLINI, BENITO (Doc. 103)
Sarfatti 1925; Kirkpatrick 1964; Grand 1976; Pieroni-Bortolotti 1978; D. Smith 1982.
MYRDAL, ALVA (Docs. 112, 117)
Herman 1976; Carlson 1974, 1980; Qvist 1980.
NAQUET, ALFRED (Doc. 45)
Naquet 1903, 1939; Blanc du Collet 1939; Desforges 1954; Kanipe 1976.
NIETZSCHE, FRIEDRICH (Doc. 6)
Peters 1962; Hollingdale 1965; Binion 1968; Kaufmann 1968.
NOCE, TERESA (Doc. 102)
Noce 1974, 1978; Cammett 1981.

ORLOV, A. (Doc. 115)
Lapidus 1977, 1978; Rosenhan 1977.
PANKHURST, CHRISTABEL (Doc. 54)
Dangerfield 1931; D. Mitchell 1967, 1977; Rosen 1974.
PANKHURST, E. SYLVIA (Doc. 74)
E. S. Pankhurst 1911; Rosen 1974; Newberry 1977; H. Smith 1978; R. Pankhurst 1979; Braybon 1981; Edmondson 1981.
PANKHURST, EMMELINE (Doc. 61)
Dangerfield 1931; D. Mitchell 1967, 1977; Rosen 1974.
PELLETIER, MADELEINE (Doc. 21)
Kenney 1978; Maignien 1978; Sowerwine 1978, 1980, 1982; Bower 1981; Hause & Kenney 1981b.
PIUS XI (Doc. 86)
Werth & Mihanovich 1955; Noonan 1966.
PIUS XII (Doc. 118)
Faherty 1950; Werth & Mihanovich 1955.
POGNON, MARIA (Doc. 51)
Lehmann 1924; Le Van Kim 1926; Dzeh-Djen 1934; Boxer 1975; Sowerwine 1978, 1982; Zylberberg-Hocquart 1978.
PRÉVOST, MARCEL (Doc. 8)
Marcel Prévost et ses contemporains 1943; Offen 1981.
RATHBONE, ELEANOR (Docs. 89, 91)
Stocks 1950; Stobaugh 1978; Lewis 1973, 1980a and b.
REICHSKOMITEE OF WORKING WOMEN (Doc. 107)
Dokumente 1975; Stephenson 1975; Peterson 1977; Frauengruppe Faschismusforschung 1981; Pore 1981.
REICHSKONGRESS OF WORKING WOMEN, SECOND (Doc. 101)
Dokumente 1975; Stephenson 1975; Peterson 1977; Frauengruppe Faschismusforschung 1981; Pore 1981.
ROOSEVELT, THEODORE (Doc. 30)
Pringle 1931; Gordon 1976; Reed 1978.
ROUSSEL, NELLY (Docs. 29, 42)
Pagès 1971; Guerrand 1971; Albistur & Armogathe 1978a and b, 1979; Ronsin 1980.
ROUSSY, BAPTISTE (Doc. 40)
L. Clark 1977, 1981; Mayeur 1977.
SANGER, MARGARET (Doc. 81)
Fryer 1965; Kennedy 1970; Gordon 1976; Reed 1978; Fee & Wallace 1979.
SCHMAHL, JEANNE-E. (Doc. 19)
Schmahl 1896; Misme 1897; Ernest-Charles 1915.
SCHOLTZ-KLINK, GERTRUD (Doc. 106)
Stephenson 1975; Scholtz-Klink 1978; Schüddekopf 1981; Frauengruppe Faschismusforschung 1981.
SCHREINER, OLIVE (Doc. 3)
Fernando 1967, 1977; Scanlon 1976; Berkman 1979; First & Scott 1980.
SCHWIMMER, ROSIKA (Doc. 68)
Degen 1939; Dubin 1971.
SHAW, ANNA HOWARD (Doc. 31)
Flexner 1959; Kraditor 1965; McGovern 1969/70.
SHAW, GEORGE BERNARD (Doc. 5)
MacKenzie & MacKenzie 1977; Silver 1982; Holroyd (forthcoming).

SOVIET CODE ON MARRIAGE AND DIVORCE (Doc. 113)
Farnsworth 1977; Stites 1977. *See also* J. Evans 1981.
SOVIET DECREE ON THE LEGALIZATION OF ABORTION (Doc. 82)
Semashko 1934; Schlesinger 1949; Juviler 1977.
STRINDBERG, AUGUST (Doc. 2)
Masters & Lea 1964; K. Stern 1965; Bredsdorff 1969; Strindberg Colloquium 1978.
STRITT, MARIE (Doc. 34)
R. Evans 1976, 1977, 1980; Hackett 1976.
STROPP, EMMA (Docs. 73, 79)
Bridenthal 1973, 1977, 1979.
SUTTNER, BERTHA VON (Doc. 12)
Suttner 1910; Kampf 1972.
SWANWICK, HELENA M. (Docs. 70, 75)
Swanwick 1935; Cook 1971; Newberry 1977; Braybon 1981; S. Bell (forthcoming).
THOMAS, M. CAREY (Doc. 38)
Newcomer 1959; Cross 1965; Wein 1974a and b; Dobkin 1979.
TOLSTOY, LEO (Doc. 10)
Benson 1973.
TROTSKY, LEON (Doc. 114)
Wolfe 1948; Deutscher 1954, 1959.
TROTT, MAGDA (Doc. 72)
Bridenthal 1973, 1977, 1979.
TURGEON, CHARLES (Doc. 7)
Offen 1973a, 1981.
WEBB, BEATRICE POTTER (Doc. 50)
Cole 1946; Muggeridge & Adam 1968; MacKenzie & MacKenzie 1977; Chew 1982.
WEDEKIND, FRANK (Doc. 41)
Feuchtwanger 1952; Gittleman 1969; Sander 1971.
WEST, REBECCA (Doc. 96)
Ray 1974; Deakin 1980.
WOMAN PATRIOT (Doc. 78)
Camhi 1973.
WOOLF, VIRGINIA STEPHEN (Doc. 100, 109)
Q. Bell 1972; Showalter 1977; Carroll 1978; Gorsky 1978; Rose 1978; Marcus 1981, 1982.
ZETKIN, CLARA (Doc. 15)
Strain 1964; Dornemann 1973; Thönnessen 1973; Honeycutt 1975, 1976, 1979; Wheeler 1975; Draper & Lipow 1976; R. Evans 1976, 1980, 1981; Sowerwine 1976; Quataert 1977, 1979; Niggemann 1981; Pore 1981.
ZIETZ, LUISE (Doc. 80)
Strain 1964; Thönnessen 1973; Wheeler 1975; Koonz 1976, 1977; Quataert 1979; R. Evans 1980; Niggemann 1981; Pore 1981.
ZOLA, ÉMILE (Doc. 27)
Hemmings 1953, 1977; Bertrand-Jennings 1972-73, 1977; Bagueley 1973; Krakowski 1974; Speirs 1974; Kaczynski 1979.

BIBLIOGRAPHY

Abbott, Edith. 1924. *Women in Industry: A Study in American Economic History*. New York and London.

Acomb, Evelyn M. 1941. *The French Laic Laws (1879-1889), The First Anti-Clerical Campaign of the Third Republic*. New York.

Addams, Jane, Emily G. Balch, and Alice Hamilton. 1916. *Women at The Hague: The International Congress of Women and Its Results*. New York.

Agonito, Rosemary, ed. 1977. *History of Ideas on Woman: A Sourcebook*. New York.

Albistur, Maïté, and Daniel Armogathe. 1978a. *Histoire du féminisme français*. 2 vols. Paris.

———. 1978b. *Le Grief des femmes*. 2 vols. Paris.

———. 1979. *Nelly Roussel, l'éternelle sacrifiée*. Paris.

Anderson, Karen. 1981. *Wartime Women: Sex Roles, Family Relations, and the Status of Women During World War II*. Westport, Conn.

Anthony, Katharine. 1915. *Feminism in Germany and Scandinavia*. New York.

Bagueley, David. 1973. *Fécondité d'Émile Zola: Roman à thèse, évangile, mythe*. Toronto.

Balogh, Penelope. 1971. *Freud: A Biographical Introduction*. New York.

Banks, J. A ., and Olive Banks. 1964. *Feminism and Family Planning in Victorian England*. New York.

Barker-Benfield, G. J. 1976. *The Horrors of the Half-Known Life: Male Attitudes Toward Women and Sexuality in Nineteenth-Century America*. New York.

Barrès, Maurice. 1889. "A Lucerne, Marie B . . . ," in Barrès, *Un Homme libre*, ch. 8. Paris.

———. 1890. "La Légende d'une cosmopolite," in Barrès, *Trois Stations de psychothérapie*. Paris.

Barrow, Margaret. 1981. *Women 1870-1928, A Select Guide to Printed and Archival Sources in the United Kingdom*. London and New York.

Basch, Norma. 1979. "Invisible Women: The Legal Fiction of Marital Unity in Nineteenth-Century America," *Feminist Studies*, 5, no. 2 (Summer 1979), 346-66.

Bauer, Carol, and Lawrence Ritt. 1979. *Free and Ennobled: Source Readings in the Development of Victorian Feminism*. Oxford and New York.

Beard, Mary R. 1946. *Woman as Force in History*. New York. Reprint, 1971.

Beauvoir, Simone de. 1949. *Le Deuxième Sexe*. Paris. Tr. H. M. Parshley, as *The Second Sex*. New York. 1953.

———. 1958. *Memoirs of a Dutiful Daughter*. Tr. James Kirkup. New York and London. Originally published in French, 1958.

———. 1962. *The Prime of Life*. Tr. Peter Green. Cleveland, Ohio. Originally published in Paris, 1960.

———. 1963. *Force of Circumstance*. Tr. Richard Howard. New York and London.

Behlmer, George K. 1982. *Child Abuse and Moral Reform in England, 1870-1908*. Stanford, Calif.

Bell, Enid Hester Chataway Moberly. 1953. *Storming the Citadel: The Rise of the Woman Doctor*. London.

Bell, Quentin. 1972. *Virginia Woolf: A Biography*. New York and London.

Bell, Susan Groag. 1981. "The Green Lawns of Newnham," *University Publishing*, 2 (Spring), 15-24.

———. 1982. "Lady Warwick: Aristocrat, Socialist, Gardener," *San Jose Studies*, 8, no. 1 (Feb.), 38-61.

———. Forthcoming. "Helena Swanwick," *Biographical Dictionary of Modern Peace Leaders*, ed. Harold Josephson. Westport, Conn.

Benson, Ruth Crego. 1973. *Women in Tolstoy: The Ideal and the Erotic*. Urbana, Ill.

Berch, Bettina. 1981. "Rational Housekeeping in the Progressive Era." Paper presented at the Fifth Berkshire Conference on the History of Women, Vassar College.

Berkin, Carol. 1980. "Private Woman, Public Woman; The Contradictions of Charlotte Perkins Gilman," in *Women of America: A History*, ed. Carol Berkin and Mary Beth Norton. Boston, Mass.

Berkman, Joyce Avrech. 1979. *Olive Schreiner: Feminism on the Frontier*. Toronto.

Bertrand-Jennings, Chantal. 1972-73. "Zola féministe?," *Les Cahiers Naturalistes*, no. 44: 172-87; no. 45: 1-22.

———. 1977. *L'Eros et la femme chez Zola*. Paris.

Bettelheim, Bruno. 1962. "The Problem of Generations," *Daedalus* (Winter), 68-96.

———. 1982. "Reflections: Freud and the Soul," *New Yorker*, March 1, pp. 52-94.

Bidelman, Patrick Kay. 1976. "The Politics of French Feminism: Léon Richer and the Ligue Française pour le Droit des Femmes, 1882-1891," *Historical Reflections*, 3, no. 1 (Summer), 93-120.

———. 1981. "Right-Wing Feminism in France: The Theory and Practice of the Association Patriotique du Devoir des Femmes Françaises 1901-1913." Paper presented to the Society for French Historical Studies, Bloomington, Ind.

———. 1982. *Pariahs Stand Up! The Founding of the Liberal Feminist Movement in France, 1858-1889*. Westport, Conn.

Binion, Rudolph. 1968. *Frau Lou: Nietzsche's Wayward Disciple*. Princeton, N.J.

Blackburn, Helen. 1902. *Woman Suffrage*. London.

Blakeley, Brian L. 1981. "Woman and Imperialism: The Colonial Office and Female Emigration to South Africa, 1901-1910," *Albion*, 13, no. 2 (Summer), 131-49.

Blanc du Collet, Charles. 1939. *Contribution à l'histoire du rétablissement du divorce en France en 1884: Étude faite d'après les travaux préparatoires de la Loi Naquet*. Thèse de doctorat. Faculté de Droit, Paris. Digne.

Blom, Ida. 1980. "The Struggle for Woman's Suffrage in Norway, 1885-1913," *Scandinavian Journal of History*, 5, no. 1: 23-35.

Bobroff, Anne. 1974. "Bolsheviks and Working Women, 1905-20," *Soviet Studies*, 26, no. 4 (Oct.), 540-67.

———. 1979. "Aleksandra Kollontai: Feminism, Workers' Democracy, and Internationalism," *Radical America*, 13, no. 6 (Nov.-Dec.), 51-75.

Bouchardeau, Huguette, ed. 1978. *Hélène Brion: La voie féministe*. Paris.

Bowman, Sylvia E. 1958. *The Year 2000; a Critical Biography of Edward Bellamy*. New York.

Boxer, Marilyn Jacoby. 1974. "Foyer or Factory: Working Class Women in Nineteenth Century France," *Proceedings of the Western Society for French History*, 2 (1975), 192-203.

———. 1975. "Socialism Faces Feminism in France: 1879-1913." Ph.D. dissertation, University of California at Riverside.

———. 1977. "French Socialism, Feminism, and the Family," *Third Republic/ Troisième République*, nos. 3-4 (Spring/Fall), 128-67.

———. 1978a. "The Class and Sex Connection: An Introduction," in *Socialist Women: European Socialist Feminism in the Nineteenth and Early Twentieth Centuries*, ed. Marilyn J. Boxer and Jean H. Quataert. New York.

———. 1978b. "Socialism Faces Feminism: The Failure of Synthesis in France, 1879-1914," in *Socialist Women*, ed. Marilyn J. Boxer and Jean H. Quataert. New York.

———. 1981. "When Radical and Socialist Feminism Were Joined: The Extraordinary Failure of Madeleine Pelletier," in *European Women on the Left: Socialism, Feminism, and the Problems Faced by Political Women, 1880 to the Present*, ed. Jane Slaughter and Robert Kern. Westport, Conn.

Branca, Patricia. 1975a. "A New Perspective on Women's Work: A Comparative Typology," *Journal of Social History*, 9, no. 2 (Winter), 129-53.

———. 1975b. *Silent Sisterhood: Middle-Class Women in the Victorian Home*. Pittsburgh, Penn.

Brandes, Georg. 1964. *Henrik Ibsen, A Critical Study: With a 42-page Essay on Bjørnstjerne Bjørnson*. New York.

Braunthal, Julius. 1967. *History of the International*, vol. I: *1864-1914*. Tr. Henry Collins and Kenneth Mitchell. New York. Originally published in German, 1961.

Braybon, Gail. 1981. *Women Workers in the First World War: The British Experience*. London and Totowa, N.J.

Bredsdorff, Elias. 1969. "Moralists versus Immoralists: The Great Battle in Scandinavian Literature in the 1880s," *Scandinavica*, 8:91-111.

Bremner, Robert H. 1971. "Josephine Clara Goldmark," in *Notable American Women*, ed. Edward T. James, Janet Wilson James, and Paul S. Boyer. Cambridge, Mass.

Bridenthal, Renate. 1973. "Beyond Kinder, Küche, Kirche: Weimar Women at Work," *Central European History*, 6, no. 2 (June), 148-66.

———. 1977. "Something Old, Something New: Women Between Two World Wars," in *Becoming Visible: Women in European History*, ed. Renate Bridenthal and Claudia Koonz. Boston, Mass.

———. 1979. "After the Vote: Feminism and Class Conflict in the Weimar Republic." Paper read at the 94th Annual Meeting of the American Historical Association, New York.

Brittain, Vera. 1968. *Radclyffe Hall: A Case of Obscenity?* New York.

———. 1940. *Testament of Friendship: The Story of Winifred Holtby*. Republished with an Afterword by Rosalind Delmar, London, 1980.

Brome, Vincent. 1978. *Jung*. New York.

Brooks, Carol Flora. 1966. "The Early History of the Anti-Contraceptive Laws in Massachusetts and Connecticut," *American Quarterly*, 18, no. 1 (Spring), 3-23.

Bueger-Van Lierde, Francoise de. 1973. "Louis Frank, pionnier du mouvement féministe belge," _Revue Belge d'Histoire Contemporaine_, 4, no. 3-4: 377-92.

Bullock, Alan. 1953. _Hitler, A Study in Tyranny._ New York.

Bullough, Vern, and Martha Voght. 1973. "Women, Menstruation, and Nineteenth-Century Medicine," _Bulletin of the History of Medicine_, 47, no. 1 (Jan.-Feb.), 66-82.

Burrow, John Wyon. 1966. _Evolution and Society: A Study in Victorian Social Theory._ Cambridge, Eng.

Burstyn, Joan N. 1973. "Education and Sex: The Medical Case Against Higher Education for Women in England, 1870-1900," _Proceedings of the American Philosophical Society_, 117:79-89.

———. 1980. _Victorian Education and the Ideal of Womanhood._ Totowa, N.J.

Cahuet, Albéric. 1926. _Moussia; ou la vie et la mort de Marie Bashkirtseff._ Paris.

Calder, Jenni. 1976. _Women and Marriage in Victorian Fiction._ New York.

Camhi, Jane. 1974. "Women Against Women: American Antisuffragism, 1880-1920." Ph.D. dissertation, Tufts University.

Cammett, John M. 1981. "Communist Women and the Fascist Experience," in _European Women on the Left: Socialism, Feminism, and the Problems Faced by Political Women, 1880 to the Present_, ed. Jane Slaughter and Robert Kern. Westport, Conn.

Carlson, Allan C. 1974. "The Roles of Alva and Gunnar Myrdal in the Development of a Social Democratic Response to Europe's Population Crisis, 1928-1938." Ph.D. dissertation, University of Ohio.

———. 1980. "The Myrdals, Pro-Natalism, and Social Democracy." Paper presented at the 95th Annual Meeting of the American Historical Association, Washington, D.C.

Carroll, Berenice A. 1978. " 'To Crush Him in Our Own Country': The Political Thought of Virginia Woolf," _Feminist Studies_, 4, no. 1 (Feb.), 99-131.

Chafe, William H. 1972. _The American Woman: Her Changing Social, Economic, and Political Role, 1920-1970._ New York.

Charrier, Edmée. 1931. _L'Evolution intellectuelle féminine._ Paris.

Chew, Ada Nield. 1982. _Ada Nield Chew: The Life and Writings of a Working Woman_, Remembered and collected by Doris Nield Chew with a foreword by Anna Davin. London.

Chodorow, Nancy. 1978. _The Reproduction of Mothering._ Berkeley, Los Angeles, and London.

Clark, Frances Ida. 1937. _The Position of Women in Contemporary France._ London.

Clark, Linda L. 1977. "The Molding of the _Citoyenne_: The Image of the Female in French Educational Literature, 1880-1914," _Third Republic/ Troisième République_, no. 3-4 (Spring/Fall), 74-104.

———. 1981. "The Primary Education of French Girls: Pedagogical Prescriptions and Social Realities, 1880-1940," _History of Education Quarterly_, 21, no. 4 (Winter), 411-28.

Clements, Barbara Evans. 1979. _Bolshevik Feminist. The Life of Aleksandra Kollontai._ Bloomington, Ind., and London.

———. 1982. "Working-Class and Peasant Women in the Russian Revolution, 1917-1923," _SIGNS: Journal of Women in Culture and Society_, 8, no. 2 (Winter), 215-35.

Cole, Margaret. 1946. _Beatrice Webb._ London and New York.

Collins, Margery L., and Christine Pierce. 1976. "Holes and Slime: Sexism in Sartre's Psychoanalysis," in *Women and Philosophy: Toward a Theory of Liberation*, ed. Carol C. Gould and Marx W. Wartofsky. New York.

Colton, Joel. 1966. *Léon Blum: Humanist in Politics*. New York.

Cominos, Peter T. 1973. "Innocent Femina Sensualis in Unconscious Conflict," in *Suffer and Be Still: Women in the Victorian Age*, ed. Martha Vicinus. Bloomington, Ind., and London.

Conway, Jill. 1971. "The Woman's Peace Party and the First World War," in *War and Society in North America*, ed. J. L. Granatstein and R. D. Cuff. Toronto.

Cook, Blanche Wiesen. 1971. Introduction to Helena Swanwick's *Essays on Women and War*. Reprint, New York.

———. 1979. "'Women Alone Stir My Imagination': Lesbianism and the Cultural Tradition," *SIGNS: Journal of Women in Culture and Society*, 4, no. 4 (Summer), 718-39.

Cross, Barbara M., ed. 1965. *The Educated Woman in America: Selected Writings of Catharine Beecher, Margaret Fuller, and M. Carey Thomas*. New York.

Crouzet-Benaben, Jeanne. 1917. "Monographie d'une éducation masculine de femme," *Revue universitaire*, 26, pt. 1: 331-40.

———. 1971. *Souvenirs d'une jeune fille bête: souvenirs autobiographiques d'une des premières agrégées de France*. Paris.

Cunningham, A. R. 1973. "The 'New Woman' Fiction of the 1890s," *Victorian Studies*, 17, no. 2 (Dec.), 177-86.

Cunningham, Gail. 1978. *The New Woman in the Victorian Novel*. London and New York.

Dahl, Kathleen. 1975. "The Feminist-Literary Movement in 19th Century Scandinavia." Unpublished manuscript.

Dangerfield, George. 1931. *The Strange Death of Liberal England 1910-1914*. London. Reprint, 1961.

Davidoff, Lenore. 1973. *The Best Circles: Society, Etiquette, and the Season*. London.

———, Jean L'Esperance, and Howard Newby. 1976. "Landscape with Figures: Home and Community in English Society," in *The Rights and Wrongs of Women*, ed. Juliet Mitchell and Ann Oakley. London.

Davin, Anna. 1978. "Imperialism and Motherhood," *History Workshop*, no. 5 (Spring), 9-65.

———. 1979. "Mind You Do as You Are Told," *Feminist Review*, 3-A: 89-98.

Davis, Allen F. 1973. *American Heroine: The Life and Legend of Jane Addams*. New York and London.

Deakin, Motley F. 1980. *Rebecca West*. Boston.

Degen, Marie Louise. 1939. *History of the Women's Peace Party*. Baltimore, Md. Reprint edition, with introduction by Blanche Wiesen Cook, New York, 1972.

Degler, Carl N. 1956. "Charlotte Perkins Gilman on the Theory and Practice of Feminism," *American Quarterly*, 8, no. 1 (Spring), 21-39.

———. 1966. Introduction to Charlotte Perkins Gilman, *Women and Economics*, ed. Carl N. Degler. New York.

———. 1980. *At Odds: Woman and Family in America from the Revolution to the Present*. Oxford and New York.

Delmar, Rosalind. 1976. "Looking Again at Engels's 'Origins of the Family, Private Property and the State'," in *The Rights and Wrongs of Women*, ed. Juliet Mitchell and Ann Oakley. London.

Derruppé, Jean. 1954. "L'Évolution du droit français de la famille, du début du siècle à la guerre de 1939," in *Renouveau des idées sur la famille*, ed. Robert Prigent. Paris.

Desforges, Jacques. 1954. "La Loi Naquet," in *Renouveau des idées sur la famille*, ed. Robert Prigent. Paris.

Deutscher, Isaac. 1954. *The Prophet Armed, Trotsky: 1879-1921*. Oxford.

———. 1959. *The Prophet Unarmed, Trotsky: 1921-1929*. Oxford.

Digeon, Claude. 1959. *La Crise allemande de la pensée française*. Paris.

Dijkstra, Sandra. 1980. "Simone de Beauvoir and Betty Friedan: The Politics of Omission," *Feminist Studies*, 6, no. 2 (Summer), 290-303.

Ditzion, Sidney. 1955. *Marriage, Morals, and Sex in America: A History of Ideas*. New York. Expanded ed., 1978.

Dobkin, Marjorie Housepian. 1979. *The Making of a Feminist: Early Journals and Letters of M. Carey Thomas*. Kent, Ohio.

Dokumente der revolutionären deutschen Arbeiterbewegung zur Frauenfrage, 1848-1974: Auswahl. 1975. Leipzig.

Dornemann, Luise. 1973. *Clara Zetkin: Leben und Wirken*. Rev. ed., East Berlin.

Drachkovich, Milorad, ed. 1966. *The Revolutionary Internationals, 1864-1943*. Stanford, Calif.

Draper, Hal, and Anne G. Lipow. 1976. "Marxist Women Versus Bourgeois Feminism," in *The Socialist Register 1976*, ed. John Saville and Ralph Miliband. London.

Dübeck, Inger. 1980. "Female Trade Unions in Denmark: Freedom of Association, the Law of Association, and Women's Trade Unions in Denmark in the Second Half of the Nineteenth Century," *Scandinavian Journal of History*, 5, no. 1: 23-35.

Dubief, Henri. 1963. "Hélène Brion," *Le Mouvement social*, no. 44 (July-Sept.), 93-97.

Dubin, Martin David. 1971. "Rosika Schwimmer," in *Notable American Women*, ed. Edward T. James and Janet Wilson James. Cambridge, Mass.

Duden, Barbara. 1981a. "Unwed Motherhood and the State in 19th-Century Germany." Paper presented at the Fifth Berkshire Conference on the History of Women, Vassar College.

———. 1981b. "Unwed Mothers: Pronatalism and Working Mothers in Industry at the End of the Last War in Britain," *History Workshop*, no. 11 (Spring), 59-118.

Duffin, Lorna. 1978. "Prisoners of Progress: Women and Evolution," in *The Nineteenth-Century Woman, Her Cultural and Physical World*, ed. Sara Delamont and Lorna Duffin. London and New York.

Duncan, Carol. 1973. "Virility and Domination in Early 20th Century Vanguard Painting," *Artforum*, 12 (Dec.), 30-39. Reprinted in *Feminism and Art History: Questioning the Litany*, ed. Norma Broude and Mary D. Garrard. New York, 1982.

Dyhouse, Carol. 1976. "Social Darwinistic Ideas and the Development of Women's Education in England, 1880-1920," *History of Education* (London), 5, no. 1 (Feb.), 41-58.

———. 1977. "Good Wives and Little Mothers: Social Anxieties and Schoolgirls' Curriculum, 1890-1920," *Oxford Review of Education*, 3, no. 1: 21-35.

———. 1981. *Girls Growing Up in Late Victorian and Edwardian England*. Boston, Mass.

Dzeh-Djen, Li. 1934. *La Presse féministe en France de 1869 à 1914*. Paris.

Edmondson, Linda. 1976. "Russian Feminists and the First All-Russian Congress of Women," *Russian History*, 3, pt. 2: 123-49.

―――. 1981. "Sylvia Pankhurst: Suffragist, Feminist, or Socialist," *European Women on the Left: Socialism, Feminism, and the Problems Faced by Political Women, 1880 to the Present*, ed. Jane Slaughter and Robert Kern. Westport, Conn.

Ehrenreich, Barbara, and Deirdre English. 1978. *For Her Own Good: 150 Years of the Experts' Advice to Women*. Garden City, N.Y.

Eisenberg, Helene Lamour. 1978. "The Theme of Demission in the Works of Simone de Beauvoir." Ph.D. dissertation, University of California, Berkeley.

―――. 1979. "Existentialism in 'The Second Sex': Its Influence on Modern Feminism." Unpublished essay.

Eisenstein, Zillah R., ed. 1979. *Capitalist Patriarchy and the Case for Socialist Feminism*. New York.

―――. 1980. *The Radical Future of Liberal Feminism*. New York.

Engel, Barbara. 1978. "From Separatism to Socialism: Women in the Russian Revolutionary Movement of the 1870's," in *Socialist Women*, ed. Marilyn J. Boxer and Jean H. Quataert. New York.

―――. 1983. *Mothers and Daughters: Women of the Radical Intelligentsia in Nineteenth Century Russia*. Cambridge, Eng.

Ernest-Charles, J. 1915. "Mme J. Schmahl et le féminisme de demain," *L'Opinion*, May 22, p. 333.

Evans, Janet. 1981. "The Communist Party of the Soviet Union and the Women's Question: The Case of the 1936 Decree 'In Defence of Mother and Child,'" *Journal of Contemporary History*, 16, no. 4 (Oct.), 757-75.

Evans, Richard J. 1976. *The Feminist Movement in Germany 1894-1933*. London.

―――. 1977. *The Feminists: Women's Emancipation Movements in Europe, America, and Australasia, 1840-1920*. London and New York.

―――. 1979. *Sozialdemokratie und Frauenemanzipation im deutschen Kaiserreich*. Bonn-Bad Godesberg.

―――. 1980. "Bourgeois Feminists and Women Socialists in Germany, 1894-1914: Lost Opportunity or Inevitable Conflict," *Women's Studies International Quarterly*, 3, no. 4: 355-76.

―――. 1981. "Politics and the Family: Social Democracy and the Working-class Family in Theory and Practice Before 1914," in *The German Family: Essays on the Social History of the Family in Nineteenth- and Twentieth-Century Germany*, ed. Richard J. Evans and W. R. Lee. London and Totowa, N.J.

Faderman, Lillian. 1981. *Surpassing the Love of Men: Romantic Friendship and Love Between Women from the Renaissance to the Present*. New York.

Faherty, William B. 1950. *The Destiny of Modern Women in the Light of Papal Teaching*. Westminster, Md.

Farnsworth, Beatrice Brod. 1976. "Bolshevism, the Woman Question, and Aleksandra Kollontai," *American Historical Review*, 81, no. 2 (Apr.), 292-316.

―――. 1977. "Bolshevik Alternatives and the Soviet Family: The 1926 Marriage Law Debate," in *Women in Russia*, ed. Dorothy Atkinson, Alexander Dallin, and Gail Lapidus. Stanford, Calif.

―――. 1981. *Aleksandra Kollontai: Socialism, Feminism, and the Bolshevik Revolution*. Stanford, Calif.

Farrell, John. 1967. *Beloved Lady: A History of Jane Addams' Ideas on Reform and Peace*. Baltimore, Md.

Fassler, Barbara. 1979. "Theories of Homosexuality as Sources of Bloomsbury's Androgyny," *SIGNS: Journal of Women in Culture and Society*, 5, no. 2 (Winter), 237-51.

Fawcett, Millicent Garrett, 1925. *What I Remember*. London. Reprint, Westport, Conn. 1975.

Fee, Elizabeth, and Michael Wallace. 1979. "The History and Politics of Birth Control: A Review Essay," *Feminist Studies*, 5, no. 1 (Spring), 201-15.

Felstiner, Mary Lowenthal. 1980. "Seeing *The Second Sex* Through the Second Wave," *Feminist Studies*, 6, no. 2 (Summer), 247-76.

Ferguson, Neal A. 1979. "Women in Twentieth-Century England," in *The Women of England from Anglo-Saxon Times to the Present: Interpretive Bibliographical Essays*, ed. Barbara Kanner. Hamden, Conn.

Fernando, Lloyd. 1967. "Radical Ideology of the New Woman," *Southern Review, An Australian Journal of Literary Studies*, 2, no. 3: 206-22.

———. 1977. *"New Women" in the Late Victorian Novel*. University Park, Penn., and London.

Feuchtwanger, Lion. 1952. Introduction to Frank Wedekind, *Five Tragedies of Sex*. New York.

Figes, Eva. 1970. *Patriarchal Attitudes*. London and Greenwich, Conn.

Finnegan, Frances. 1979. *Poverty and Prostitution: A Study of Victorian Prostitutes in York*. Cambridge, Eng., and New York.

First, Ruth, and Ann Scott. 1980. *Olive Schreiner*. London and New York.

Fletcher, Sheila. 1980. *Feminists and Bureaucrats: A Study in the Development of Girls' Education in the 19th Century*. Cambridge, Eng., and New York.

Flexner, Eleanor. 1959. *Century of Struggle: The Woman's Rights Movement in the United States*. Cambridge, Mass. New edition, 1972.

———. 1971. "Carrie Chapman Catt," in *Notable American Women*, ed. Edward T. James and Janet Wilson James. Cambridge, Mass.

Franks, Claudia Stilman. Forthcoming. "Stephen Gordon, Novelist: A Reevaluation of Radclyffe Hall's *Well of Loneliness*," *Tulsa Studies of Women's Literature*, 1, no. 1.

Fransden, Dorothea. 1974. *Helena Lange*. Hanover, Germany.

Frauengruppe Faschismusforschung. 1981. *Mutterkreutz und Arbeitsbuch: Zur Geschichte der Frauen in der Weimarer Republik und im Nationalsozialismus*. Frankfurt a.M.

Frederiksen, Elke, ed. 1981. *Die Frauenfrage in Deutschland, 1865-1915: Texte und Dokumente*. Stuttgart.

Freedman, Estelle B. 1974. "The New Woman: Changing Views of Women in the 1920's," *Journal of American History*, 61, no. 2 (Sept.), 372-93.

Fryer, Peter. 1965. *The Birth Controllers*. London.

Fuchs, Jo-Ann P. 1980. "Female Eroticism in *The Second Sex*," *Feminist Studies*, 6, no. 2 (Summer), 304-13.

Fulford, Roger. 1956. *Votes for Women: The Story of a Struggle*. London.

Gargan, Edward T., ed. 1961. *Leo XIII and the Modern World*. New York.

Garrison, Dee. 1981. "Karen Horney and Feminism," *SIGNS: Journal of Women in Culture and Society*, 6, no. 4 (Summer), 672-91.

Gasiorowska, Xenia. 1968. *Women in Soviet Fiction, 1917-1964*. Madison, Wisc.

Gaultier, Jean-Patrice. 1956. "Un législateur familial; Jules-Louis Breton," *Pour la Vie: Revue d'études démographiques et familiales*, no. 66 (Sept. 1956), 225-53, 335-53.

Gennari, Geneviève. 1967. *Simone de Beauvoir.* Rev. ed. Paris.

Giffen, Frederick C. 1968. "The Prohibition of Night Work for Women and Young Persons: The Russian Factory Law of June 3, 1885," *Canadian Slavic Studies,* 2, no. 2 (Summer), 208-18.

Gilbert, Sandra M., and Susan Gubar. 1980. *The Madwoman in the Attic.* New Haven, Conn., and London.

Gittleman, Sol. 1969. *Frank Wedekind.* New York.

Glickman, Rose L. 1977. "The Russian Factory Woman, 1880-1914," in *Women in Russia,* ed. Dorothy Atkinson, Alexander Dallin, and Gail Lapidus. Stanford, Calif.

Goliber, Sue Helder. 1975. "The Life and Times of Marguerite Durand: A Study in French Feminism." Ph.D. dissertation, Kent State University, Kent, Ohio.

Gollancz, Victor, ed., 1917. *The Making of Women: Oxford Essays in Feminism.* London.

Goode, John. 1976. "Woman and the Literary Text," in *The Rights and Wrongs of Women,* ed. Juliet Mitchell and Ann Oakley. London.

Gordon, Linda. 1976. *Woman's Body, Woman's Right: A Social History of Birth Control in America.* New York.

Gorham, Deborah. 1982. *The Victorian Girl and the Feminine Ideal.* Bloomington, Ind., and London.

Gorsky, Susan Rubinow. 1978. *Virginia Woolf.* New York.

Gould, Stephen Jay. 1981. *The Mismeasure of Man.* New York.

Grand, Alexander de. 1976. "Women under Italian Fascism," *Historical Journal,* 19, no. 4: 947-68.

Graveson, R. H., and F. R. Crane. 1957. *A Century of Family Law, 1857-1957.* London.

Green, Martin. 1974. *The Von Richtofen Sisters: The Triumphant and Tragic Modes of Love.* New York.

Greene, John C. 1959. "Biology and Social Theory in the Nineteenth Century: Auguste Comte and Herbert Spencer," in *Critical Problems in the History of Science,* ed. Marshall Clagett. Madison, Wisc.

Greven-Aschoff, Barbara. 1981. *Die bürgerliche Frauenbewegung in Deutschland, 1894-1933.* Göttingen, Germany.

Guerrand, Roger. 1971. *La Libre Maternité, 1896-1969.* Tournai, Belgium.

Hackett, Amy Kathleen. 1972. "The German Women's Movement and Suffrage, 1890-1914: A Study of National Feminism," in *Modern European Social History,* ed. Robert Bezucha. Lexington, Mass.

———. 1975. "Feminism and Liberalism in Wilhelmine Germany, 1890-1918," in *Liberating Women's History,* ed. Berenice Carroll. Urbana, Ill.

———. 1976. "The Politics of Feminism in Wilhelmine Germany 1890-1918." 2 vols. Ph.D. dissertation, Columbia University.

———. 1981. "Helene Stoecker: Left Wing Intellectual and Sex Reformer Between Empire and Republic." Paper presented at the Annual Meeting of the American Historical Association, Los Angeles.

Hahn, Beverly. 1977. *Chekhov: A Study of the Major Stories and Plays.* Cambridge, Eng.

Hall, Ruth. 1977. *Marie Stopes, A Biography.* London.

Hannah, Barbara. 1976. *Jung: His Life and Work—A Biographical Memoir.* New York.

Harrison, Brian. 1978. *Separate Spheres: The Opposition to Women's Suffrage in Britain.* London and New York.

Hartmann, Susan M. 1978. "Prescriptions for Penelope: Literature on Women's Obligations to World War II Veterans," *Women's Studies*, 5, no. 3: 223-39.

Hatje, Ann-Katrin. 1974. *The Population Question and Welfare*. Stockholm.

Hause, Steven C. 1977. "The Rejection of Women's Suffrage by the French Senate in November 1922: A Statistical Analysis," in *Third Republic/Troisième République*, no. 3-4 (Spring/Fall), 205-37.

———, and Anne R. Kenney. 1979. "Women Who Rallied to the Tricolor: The Effects of World War I on the French Women's Suffrage Movement," *Proceedings of the Western Society for French History*, 6: 371-78.

———. 1981a. "The Development of the Catholic Women's Suffrage Movement in France, 1896-1922," *Catholic Historical Review*, 67, no. 1 (Jan.), 11-30.

———. 1981b. "The Limits of Suffragist Behavior: Legalism and Militancy in France, 1876-1922," *American Historical Review*, 86, no. 4 (Oct.), 781-806.

Hausen, Karin. 1981. "Family and Role Division: The Polarization of Sexual Stereotypes in the 19th Century—An Aspect of the Dissociation of Work and Family Life," in *The German Family: Essays on the Social History of the Family in 19th and 20th Century Germany*, ed. Richard J. Evans and W. R. Lee. London and New York.

Hayden, Carole Eubanks. 1976. "The Zhenotdel and the Bolshevik Party," *Russian History*, 3, pt. 2: 150-73.

Hayden, Dolores. 1981. *The Grand Domestic Revolution: A History of Feminist Designs for American Homes, Neighborhoods, and Cities*. Cambridge, Mass., and London.

Hays, H. R. 1964. *The Dangerous Sex: The Myth of Feminine Evil*. New York.

Heilbrun, Carolyn. 1974. *Toward a Recognition of Androgyny*. New York.

Hellerstein, Erna Olafson, Leslie Parker Hume, and Karen M. Offen. 1981. *Victorian Women: A Documentary Account of Women's Lives in Nineteenth-Century England, France, and the United States*. Stanford, Calif.

Hemmings, F. W. J. 1953. *Émile Zola*. Oxford.

———. 1977. *The Life of Émile Zola*. New York.

Herman, Sondra R. 1969. *Eleven Against War: Studies in American Internationalist Thought*. Stanford, Calif.

———. 1973. "Loving Courtship or the Marriage Market? The Ideal and Its Critics, 1871-1911," *American Quarterly*, 25, no. 2 (May), 235-52.

———. 1976. "Sweden: A Feminist Model?" in *Women in the World: A Comparative Study*, ed. Lynne B. Iglitzin and Ruth Ross. Santa Barbara, Calif.

Herrmann, Elizabeth Rütschi, and Edna Huttenmaier Spitz. 1978. *German Women Writers of the Twentieth Century*. Oxford and New York.

Heymann, Lida Gustava. 1972. *Erlebtes—Erschautes, Deutsche Frauen kämpfen für Freiheit Recht und Frieden, 1850-1940*, ed. Margrit Twellmann. Meisenheim-am-Glan, Germany.

Hill, Mary A. 1980. *Charlotte Perkins Gilman: The Making of a Radical Feminist, 1860-1896*. Philadelphia.

Holcombe, Lee. 1973. *Victorian Ladies at Work*. Hamden, Conn.

———. 1977. "Victorian Wives and Property: Reform of the Married Women's Property Law, 1857-1882," in *A Widening Sphere*, ed. Martha Vicinus. Bloomington, Ind.

———. 1982. *Wives and Property: Reform of the Married Women's Property Law in Nineteenth-Century England*. Toronto.

Hollingdale, R. J. 1965. *Nietzsche: The Man and the Philosophy*. Baton Rouge, La.

Hollis, Patricia. 1979. *Women in Public, 1850-1900; Documents of the Victorian Women's Movement.* London.

Holroyd, Michael. Forthcoming. *George Bernard Shaw.*

Honeycutt, Karen. 1975. "Clara Zetkin: A Left-Wing Socialist and Feminist in Imperial Germany." Ph.D. dissertation, Columbia University.

———. 1976. "Clara Zetkin: A Socialist Approach to the Problem of Women's Oppression," *Feminist Studies,* 3, nos. 3-4 (Spring-Summer), 131-44.

———. 1979. "Socialism and Feminism in Imperial Germany," *SIGNS: Journal of Women in Culture and Society,* 5, no. 1 (Autumn), 30-41.

Huber, Werner. 1970. "Gertrud Bäumer: Eine politische Biographie." Ph.D. dissertation, University of Munich.

Hume, Leslie Parker. 1979. "The National Union of Women's Suffrage Societies, 1897-1914." Ph.D. dissertation, Stanford University.

Hurwitz, Edith F. 1977. "The International Sisterhood," in *Becoming Visible,* ed. Renate Bridenthal and Claudia Koonz. Boston.

Inman, Peggy. 1957. *Labour in the Munitions Industries.* London.

Jallinoja, Ritta. 1980. "The Women's Liberation Movement in Finland: The Social and Political Mobilisation of Women in Finland, 1880-1910," *Scandinavian Journal of History,* 5, no. 1: 37-49.

Janssen-Jurreit, Marielouise. 1981. *Sexism: The Male Monopoly on History and Thought.* New York.

Jenkins, William D. 1979. "Housewifery and Motherhood: The Question of Role Change in the Progressive Era," in *Woman's Being, Woman's Place,* ed. Mary Kelley. Boston.

Johansson, Sheila Ryan. 1979. "Demographic Contributions to the History of Victorian Women," in *The Women of England from Anglo-Saxon Times to the Present: Interpretive Bibliographical Essays,* ed. Barbara Kanner. Hamden, Conn.

John, Angela V. 1980. *By the Sweat of Their Brow: Women Workers at Victorian Coal Mines.* London.

Johnson, Richard L. 1976. "Nazi Feminists: A Contradiction in Terms," *Frontiers: A Journal of Women's Studies,* 1, no. 3 (Winter), 55-62.

Joll, James. 1955. *The Second International, 1889-1914.* New York. Reprint, 1966.

Jones, Ernest. 1961. *The Life and Work of Sigmund Freud,* ed. and abr. Lionel Trilling and Steven Marcus. New York.

Juliver, Peter H. 1977. "Women and Sex in Soviet Law," in *Women in Russia,* ed. Dorothy Atkinson, Alexander Dallin, and Gail Lapidus. Stanford, Calif.

Kaczynski, Mieczyslaw. 1979. "*Les Quatre Evangiles" d'Émile Zola, entre la vision catastrophique et la vision utopique.* Lublin, Poland.

Kamm, Josephine. 1965. *Hope Deferred: Girls' Education in English History.* London.

Kampf, Beatrix. 1972. *Suffragette for Peace: The Life of Bertha von Suttner.* Tr. R. W. Last. London.

Kanipe, Esther Sue. 1976. "The Family, Private Property, and the State in France, 1870-1914." Ph.D. dissertation, University of Wisconsin, Madison.

Kanner, S. Barbara. 1973. "The Women of England in a Century of Social Change, 1815-1914: A Select Bibliography, Part I," in *Suffer and Be Still: Women in the Victorian Age,* ed. Martha Vicinus. Bloomington, Ind., and London.

———. 1977. "The Women of England in a Century of Social Change, 1815-

1914: A Select Bibliography, Part II," in *A Widening Sphere: Changing Roles of Victorian Women*, ed. Martha Vicinus. Bloomington, Ind., and London.

———. 1979. *The Women of England from Anglo-Saxon Times to the Present: Interpretive Bibliographical Essays*. Hamden, Conn.

Kaplan, Marion A. 1976. "Bertha Pappenheim: Founder of German-Jewish Feminism," in *The Jewish Woman*, ed. Elizabeth Koltun. New York.

———. 1979. *The Jewish Feminist Movement in Germany: The Campaigns of the Jüdischer Frauenbund, 1904-1938*. Westport, Conn.

———. 1981. "Double Jeopardy: The Entry of Jewish Women into the Public Worlds of Work and Higher Education of Imperial Germany." Paper presented at the 96th Annual Meeting of the American Historical Association, Los Angeles.

Kapp, Yvonne Mayer. 1972-76. *Eleanor Marx*. 2 vols. London.

Karageorgevich, Prince. 1903. "Marie Bashkirtseff et la légende," *Revue Mondiale*, October 1, pp. 90-97.

Kaufmann, Walter. 1968. *Nietzsche: Philosopher, Psychologist, Antichrist*. 3rd ed. Princeton, N.J.

Kelley, Mary, ed. 1979. *Woman's Being, Woman's Place: Female Identity and Vocation in American History*. Boston.

Kelman, Harold. 1967. Introduction to Karen Horney, *Feminine Psychology*. New York.

Kennedy, David M. 1970. *Birth Control in America: The Career of Margaret Sanger*. New Haven, Conn.

Kenney, Anne R. 1978. "A Militant Feminist in France: Dr. Madeleine Pelletier, Her Ideas and Actions." Paper presented at the Fourth Berkshire Conference on Women's History, Mount Holyoke College.

Kessner, Carole S. 1976. "Ghetto Intellectuals and the 'New Woman,'" *Yiddish*, 2, no. 2-3 (Winter-Spring), 23-31.

Kirkpatrick, Ivone. 1964. *Mussolini: A Study in Power*. New York.

Klaus, Patricia Otto. 1979. "Women in the Mirror: Using Novels to Study Victorian Women," in *The Women of England from Anglo-Saxon Times to the Present: Interpretive Bibliographical Essays*, ed. Barbara Kanner. Hamden, Conn.

Klein, Viola. 1946. *The Feminine Character: History of an Ideology*. London. New ed., New York, 1972.

Knibiehler, Yvonne, and Catherine Fouquet. 1980. *L'Histoire de mères du Moyen Age à nos jours*. Paris.

Koht, Halvdan. 1954. "Women and Society: A Doll's House (1878-79)," ch. 31, in Koht, *Life of Ibsen*. New York. Reprint, 1971.

Koonz, Claudia. 1976. "Conflicting Allegiances: Political Ideology and Women Legislators in Weimar Germany," *SIGNS: Journal of Women in Culture and Society*, 1, no. 3, pt. 1 (Spring), 663-83.

———. 1977. "Mothers in the Fatherland: Women in Nazi Germany," in *Becoming Visible: Women in European History*, ed. Renate Bridenthal and Claudia Koonz. Boston.

———. 1981. "German Women Between God and the Führer." Paper presented at the Fifth Berkshire Conference on the History of Women, Vassar College.

Kraditor, Aileen S. 1965. *The Ideas of the Woman Suffrage Movement, 1890-1920*. New York.

Krakowski, Anna. 1974. *La Condition de la femme dans l'oeuvre d'Émile Zola*. Paris.

Kriegel, Annie. 1963. "Procès de guerre—procès Brion," *Le Mouvement Social,* no. 44 (July-Sept.), 97-99.

Kropotkin, Peter. 1899. *Memoirs of a Revolutionist.* London, Boston, and New York.

Lafleur, Ingrun. 1975. "Adelheid Popp and Working Class Feminism in Austria," *Frontiers,* 1, no. 1 (Fall), 86-105.

———. 1978. "Five Socialist Women: Traditionalist Conflicts and Socialist Visions in Austria, 1893-1934," in *Socialist Women: European Socialist Feminism in the Nineteenth and Early Twentieth Centuries,* ed. Marilyn J. Boxer and Jean H. Quataert. New York.

Lane, Ann J. 1976. "Women in Society: A Critique of Frederick Engels," in *Liberating Women's History,* ed. Berenice Carroll. Urbana, Ill.

———. 1980. Introduction to the *Charlotte Perkins Gilman Reader,* ed. A. J. Lane. New York.

Lapidus, Gail Warshofsky. 1977. "Sexual Equality in Soviet Policy: A Developmental Perspective," in *Women in Russia,* ed. Dorothy Atkinson, Alexander Dallin, and Gail Lapidus. Stanford, Calif.

———. 1978. *Women in Soviet Society: Equality, Development, and Social Change.* Berkeley, Los Angeles, and London.

Lasch, Christopher, ed. 1965. *The Social Thought of Jane Addams.* Indianapolis, Ind.

———. 1974. "Freud and Women," *New York Review of Books,* October 3, pp. 12-17.

———. 1977. *Haven in a Heartless World: The Family Besieged.* New York.

———. 1978. *The Culture of Narcissism: American Life in an Age of Diminishing Expectation.* New York.

LaVigna, Claire. 1978. "The Marxist Ambivalence Toward Women: Between Socialism and Feminism in the Italian Socialist Party," in *Socialist Women,* ed. Marilyn J. Boxer and Jean H. Quataert. New York.

Leach, William R. 1980. *True Love and Perfect Union: The Feminist Reform of Sex and Society.* New York.

Leacock, Eleanor Burke. 1972. Introduction to F. Engels, *The Origin of the Family, Private Property, and the State.* New York.

———. 1977. "Women in Egalitarian Societies," in *Becoming Visible,* ed. Renate Bridenthal and Claudia Koonz. Boston.

Lederer, Wolfgang. 1968. *The Fear of Women.* New York.

Le Doeuff, Michèle. 1980. "Simone de Beauvoir and Existentialism," *Feminist Studies,* 6, no. 2 (Summer), 277-89.

Lefaucheux, Marie-Hélène. 1966. *Women in a Changing World: The Dynamic Story of the International Council of Women Since 1888.* London.

Leff, Mark H. 1973. "Consensus for Reform: The Mothers' Pension Movement in the Progressive Era," *Social Science Review,* 47, no. 3 (Sept.), 397-417.

Lehmann, Andrée. 1924. *De la Réglementation légale du travail féminin (Etude de législation comparée).* Paris.

Lemons, J. Stanley. 1973. *The Woman Citizen; Social Feminism in the 1920s.* Urbana, Ill.

Le Van Kim. 1926. *Féminisme et travail féminin dans les doctrines et dans les faits.* Paris.

Lewenhawk, Sheila. 1980. *Women and Work.* New York.

Lewis, Jane. 1973. "Beyond Suffrage: English Feminism During the 1920s," *The Maryland Historian,* 6, no. 1: 1-17.

————. 1980a. "In Search of a Real Equality: Women Between the Wars," in *Class, Culture, and Social Change: A New View of the 1930s*, ed. Frank Gloversmith. Brighton, Eng., and Totowa, N.J.

————. 1980b. *The Politics of Motherhood: Child and Maternal Welfare in England, 1900-1939*. London and Montreal.

Liddington, Jill, and Jill Norris. 1978. *One Hand Tied Behind Us: The Rise of the Women's Suffrage Movement*. London.

Linder, Doris H. 1980. "Elise Ottesen-Jensen and Sexual Enlightenment in Social Democratic Sweden, 1932-1948." Paper presented at the 95th Annual Meeting of the American Historical Association, Washington, D.C.

————. 1982. "Elise Ottesen-Jensen, Advocate of Sexual Enlightenment." Paper presented at the Western Association of Women Historians, San Marino, Calif.

Lipow, Arthur. 1982. *Authoritarian Socialism in America: Edward Bellamy and the National Movement*. Berkeley, Calif.

Logue, William. 1973. *Léon Blum: The Formative Years*. De Kalb, Ill.

Lord, Henrietta Frances. 1882. "Life of Henrik Ibsen," preface to Ibsen's *A Doll's House*, tr. H. F. Lord. New York.

Lucas, Robert. 1973. *Frieda Lawrence: The Story of Frieda von Richthofen and D. H. Lawrence*. Tr. Geoffrey Skelton. New York. Originally published in German, Munich, 1972.

McCall, Dorothy Kaufmann. 1979. "Simone de Beauvoir, *The Second Sex*, and Jean-Paul Sartre," *SIGNS: Journal of Women in Culture and Society*, 5, no. 2 (Winter), 209-21.

McDougall, Mary Lynn. 1977. "Working Class Women During the Industrial Revolution, 1780-1914," in *Becoming Visible*, ed. Renate Bridenthal and Claudia Koonz. Boston.

McFarland, C. K., and Nevin E. Neal. 1974. "The Reluctant Reformer: Woodrow Wilson and Woman Suffrage, 1913-1920," *Rocky Mountain Social Science Journal*, 11, no. 2 (Apr.), 33-43.

McGovern, James R. 1969/70. "Anna Howard Shaw: New Approaches to Feminism," *Journal of Social History*, 3, no. 2 (Winter), 135-53.

McIntyre, Jill. 1971. "Women and the Professions in Germany, 1930-1940," in *German Democracy and the Triumph of Hitler*, ed. Anthony Nicholls and Erich Mathias. Oxford.

MacKenzie, Norman, and Jeanne MacKenzie. 1977. *The Fabians*. New York.

McLaren, Angus. 1978a. "Abortion in France: Women and the Regulation of Family Size, 1800-1914," *French Historical Studies*, 10, no. 3 (Spring), 461-85.

————. 1978b. *Birth Control in Nineteenth-Century England*. London.

McMillan, James E. 1981. *Housewife or Harlot: The Place of Women in French Society, 1870-1940*. New York and London.

McNeal, Robert H. 1972. *Bride of the Revolution: Krupskaya and Lenin*. Ann Arbor, Mich.

Magnus-Hausen, Frances. 1922. "Ziel und Weg in der deutschen Frauenbewegung des XIX Jahrhunderts," in *Deutscher Staat und deutsche Parteien: Beiträge zur deutschen Partei- und Ideensgeschichte, Friedrich Meinecke zum 60. Geburtstag dargebracht*, ed. Paul Wentzcke. Munich. Reprint, Aalen, 1973.

Maier, Charles S. 1975. *Recasting Bourgeois Europe.* Princeton, N.J.

Maignien, Claude, ed. 1978. *Madeleine Pelletier: L'Éducation féministe des filles et autres textes*. Paris.

Marandon, Sylvaine. 1967. *L'Image de la France dans l'Angleterre victorienne, 1848-1900*. Paris.

Marcel Prévost et ses contemporains: Un demi-siècle de littérature française, 1887-1941. 1943. 2 vols. Paris.

Marcus, Jane, ed. 1981. *New Feminist Essays on Virginia Woolf*. Lincoln, Nebr.

————. 1982. "Storming the Toolshed," *SIGNS: Journal of Women in Culture and Society*, 7, no. 3 (Spring), 622-40.

Marlow, Joyce. 1977. *Mr. and Mrs. Gladstone: An Intimate Biography*. London. Published in New York as *The Ivy and the Oak*.

Marwick, Arthur. 1977. *Women at War, 1914-1918*. London.

Masters, R. E. L., and Eduard Lea. 1964. *The Anti-Sex: The Belief in the Natural Inferiority of Women. Studies in Male Frustration and Sexual Conflict*. New York.

Mayeur, Françoise. 1977. *L'Enseignement secondaire des jeunes filles sous la Troisième République*. Paris.

————, and Jacques Gadille, eds. 1980. *Éducation et images de la femme chrétienne en France au début du XXème siècle*. Lyons.

Mead, Margaret. 1972. *Blackberry Winter: My Earlier Years*. New York.

Metraux, Rhoda, ed. 1979. *Margaret Mead: Some Personal Views*. New York.

Meyer, Alfred G. 1977. "Marxism and the Women's Movement," in *Women in Russia*, ed. Dorothy Atkinson, Alexander Dallin, and Gail Lapidus. Stanford, Calif.

Middleton, Lucy. 1977. *Women in the Labour Movement: The British Experience*. London and Totowa, N.J.

Milkman, Ruth. 1976. "Women's Work and Economic Crisis: Some Lessons of the Great Depression," *Review of Radical Political Economics*, 8 (Spring), 73-97.

Miller, Jean B. 1973. *Psychoanalysis and Women: Contributions to New Theory and Therapy*. New York.

Miller, Martin A. 1976. *Kropotkin*. Chicago.

Millett, Kate. 1969. *Sexual Politics*. New York.

Millstone, Amy Blythe. 1977. "Feminist Theatre in France: 1870-1914." Ph.D. dissertation, University of Wisconsin, Madison.

Minor, Iris. 1978. "Working-class Women and Matrimonial Law Reform, 1890-1914," in *Ideology and the Labour Movement, Essays Presented to John Saville*, ed. David E. Martin and David Rubinstein. London.

Misme, Jane. 1897. "Madame Jeanne E. Schmahl," *Revue Bleue*, January 23, pp. 119-22.

Mitchell, David J. 1966. *Women on the Warpath*. London.

————. 1967. *The Fighting Pankhursts*. London.

————. 1977. *Queen Christabel: A Biography of Christabel Pankhurst*. London.

Mitchell, Juliet. 1966. "Women: The Longest Revolution," *New Left Review*, 40 (Dec.), 11-37.

————. 1971. *Woman's Estate*. New York.

————. 1974. *Psycho-Analysis and Feminism: Freud, Reich, Laing, and Women*. New York and London.

————. 1976. "Women and Equality," in *The Rights and Wrongs of Women*, ed. Juliet Mitchell and Ann Oakley. London.

Mohr, James C. 1978. *Abortion in America*. Oxford and New York.

Moon, Parker T. 1921. *The Labor Problem and the Social Catholic Movement in France: A Study in the History of Social Politics*. New York.

Moore, Harry T. 1951. *D. H. Lawrence: His Life and Works.* New York. 2nd rev. ed., 1971.

———. 1955. *The Intelligent Heart.* New York.

Morgan, David. 1972. *Suffragists and Democrats: The Politics of Woman Suffrage in America.* East Lansing, Mich.

———. 1974. *Suffragists and Liberals: The Politics of Woman Suffrage in England.* Totowa, N.J.

Mosedale, Susan Sleeth. 1978. "Science Corrupted: Victorian Biologists Consider 'The Woman Question,'" *Journal of the History of Biology,* 11, no. 1 (Spring), 1-55.

Mosse, George Lachmann. 1961. *The Crisis of German Ideology: Intellectual Origins of the Third Reich.* New York.

Muggeridge, Kitty, and Ruth Adam. 1968. *Beatrice Webb; A Life, 1858-1943.* New York.

Naquet, Alfred. 1903. *La Loi de divorce.* Paris.

———. 1939. *Alfred Naquet: Autobiographie,* ed. Emile Pillias. Paris.

Nathan, Peter Wilfred. 1943. *The Psychology of Fascism.* London.

Neff, Wanda Fraiken. 1929. *Victorian Working Women.* New York.

Neumann, Robert P. 1974. "The Sexual Question and Social Democracy in Imperial Germany," *Journal of Social History,* 7, no. 3 (Spring), 271-86.

Newberry, Jo Velacott. 1977. "Anti-War Suffragists," *History,* 62 (Oct.), 411-25.

Newcomer, Mabel. 1959. *A Century of Higher Education for American Women.* New York.

Niggemann, Heinz. 1981. *Emanzipation zwischen Sozialismus und Feminismus: die sozialdemokratische Frauenbewegung im Kaiserreich.* Wuppertal, Germany.

Noce, Teresa. 1974. *Revoluzionaria professionale.* Milan.

———. 1978. *Vivere in piedi.* Milan.

Noonan, John T., Jr. 1966. *Contraception, a History of its Treatment by the Catholic Theologians and Canonists.* Cambridge, Mass.

Nyström-Hamilton, Louise Sofia. 1913. *Ellen Key, Her Life and Her Work.* New York.

Offen, Karen M. 1973a. "The 'Woman Question' as a Social Issue in Republican France Before 1914." Unpublished manuscript.

———. 1973b. "A Feminist Challenge to the Third Republic's Public Education for Girls: The Campaign for Equal Access to the *Baccalauréat,* 1880-1924." Paper presented at the American Historical Association, San Francisco.

———. 1977. "The 'Woman Question' as a Social Issue in Nineteenth-Century France: A Bibliographical Essay," *Third Republic/Troisième République,* no. 3-4 (Spring/Fall), 238-99.

———. 1981. "Depopulation, Nationalism, and Feminism in Belle-Epoque France." Paper presented at the Society for French Historical Studies, Bloomington, Ind.

———. 1982a. "First Wave Feminism in France: New Work and Resources," *Women's Studies International Forum,* 5, no. 6: 685-89.

———. 1982b. Reviews of McMillan 1981 and Smith 1981, *SIGNS: Journal of Women in Culture and Society,* 8, no. 2 (Winter), 372-76.

Okin, Susan Moller. 1979. *Women in Western Political Thought.* Princeton, N.J.

O'Neill, William L. 1969a. *Everyone was Brave: The Rise and Fall of Feminism in America.* Chicago, Ill.

———. 1969b. *The Woman Movement: Feminism in the United States and England.* London. Chicago edition, 1971.

———. 1973. *Divorce in the Progressive Era*. New York.

———. 1975. "Divorce as a Moral Issue: A Hundred Years of Controversy," in *Remember the Ladies*, ed. Carol V. R. George. Syracuse, N.Y.

Osborne, Martha Lee, ed. 1979. *Woman in Western Thought*. New York.

Pagès, Jeanne. 1971. *Le Contrôle des naissances en France et à l'étranger*. Paris.

Paillat, Paul, and Jacques Houdaille. 1975. "Legislation Directly or Indirectly Influencing Fertility in France," in *Law and Fertility in Europe*, ed. Maurice Kirk, Alassimo Livi-Bacci, and Egon Szabady. Dolhain, Belgium.

Pankhurst, E. Sylvia. 1911. *The Suffragette: The History of the Women's Militant Suffrage Movement, 1905-1910*. London.

———. 1930. *Save the Mothers*. London.

Pankhurst, Emmeline. 1914. *My Own Story*. London. Reprint, New York, 1970.

Pankhurst, Richard K. P. 1979. *Sylvia Pankhurst, Artist and Crusader: An Intimate Portrait*. London and New York.

Peck, Mary Gray. 1944. *Carrie Chapman Catt: A Biography*. New York. Reprint, 1975.

Peters, H. F. 1962. *My Sister, My Spouse: A Biography of Lou Andreas Salomé*. New York.

Peterson, Brian. 1977. "The Politics of Working Class Women in the Weimar Republic," *Central European History*, 10, no. 2 (June), 87-111.

Petrie, Glen. 1971. *A Singular Iniquity: The Campaigns of Josephine Butler*. New York and London.

Pieroni-Bortolotti, Franca. 1963. *Alle origini del movimento femminile in Italia, 1848-1892*. Turin. Reprint, 1975.

———. 1978. *Femminismo e partiti politici in Italia, 1919-1926*. Rome.

Pivar, David J. 1973. *Purity Crusade: Sexual Morality and Social Control, 1868-1900*. Westport, Conn.

Poirier, J., and R. Nahon. 1978. "L'Accession des femmes à la carrière médicale (à la fin du XIXe siècle)" in *Médicine et philosophie à la fin du XIXe siècle*, ed. J. and J.-L. Poirier. Cahier de l'Institut de Recherche Universitaire d'Histoire de la Connaissance, des Idées et des Mentalités, no. 2, University of Paris XII (Val de Marne).

Pope, Barbara Corrado. 1977. "Angels in the Devil's Workshop: Leisured and Charitable Women in Nineteenth-Century England and France," in *Becoming Visible*, ed. Renate Bridenthal and Claudia Koonz. Boston.

Pore, Renate. 1981. *A Conflict of Interest: Women in German Social Democracy, 1919-1933*. Westport, Conn.

Prévost, Marcel. See *Marcel Prévost . . .*

Pringle, Henry F. 1931. *Theodore Roosevelt; A Biography*. New York.

Prochaska, F. K. 1980. *Women and Philanthropy in 19th Century England*. Oxford and New York.

Puckett, Hugh Wiley. 1930. *Germany's Women Go Forward*. New York.

Pugh, Martin D. 1974. "Politicians and the Woman's Vote, 1914-1918," *History*, 59 (Oct.), 358-74.

Quataert, Jean H. 1977. "Feminist Tactics in German Social Democracy 1890-1914: A Dilemma," in *Internationale Wissenschaftliche Korrespondenz*, 13 (1977), 49-65.

———. 1978. "Unequal Partners in an Uneasy Alliance: Women and the Working Class in Imperial Germany," in *Socialist Women*, ed. Marilyn J. Boxer and Jean H. Quataert. New York.

———. 1979. *Reluctant Feminists in German Social Democracy, 1885-1917*. Princeton, N.J.

———— and Marilyn J. Boxer. 1978. "The Class and Sex Connection: An Intro-duction," in *Socialist Women*, ed. Marilyn J. Boxer and Jean H. Quataert. New York.

Qvist, Gunnar. 1980. "Policy Towards Women and the Women's Struggle in Swe-den," *Scandinavian Journal of History*, 5, no. 1: 51-73.

Ray, Gordon N. 1974. *H. G. Wells and Rebecca West*. New Haven, Conn.

Rebérioux, Madeleine. 1978. "La Questione femminile nei dibattiti della Sec-onda Internazionale," in *Anna Kuliscioff e l'eta del riformismo: Atti del Con-vegno di Milano-dicembre 1976*. Rome.

Reed, James. 1978. *From Private Vice to Public Virtue: The Birth Control Move-ment and American Society Since 1830*. New York.

Reilly, Catherine W., ed. 1981. *Scars Upon My Heart: Women's Poetry and Verse of the First World War*. London.

Reiss, Erna. 1934. *The Rights and Duties of Englishwomen: A Study in Law and Public Opinion*. Manchester, Eng.

Rieff, Philip. 1961. *Freud: The Mind of the Moralist*. New York.

Riley, Denise. 1981. "The Free Mothers: Pronatalism and Working Mothers in Industry at the End of the Last War in Britain," *History Workshop*, no. 11 (Spring), 59-118.

Rogers, Katharine M. 1966. *The Troublesome Helpmate*. Seattle, Wash.

Ronsin, Francis. 1980. *La Grève des ventres, propagande néo-malthusienne et baisse de la natalité francaise (XIX-XXe siècles)*. Paris.

Rose, Phyllis. 1978. *Woman of Letters: A Life of Virginia Woolf*. Oxford and New York.

Rosen, Andrew. 1974. *Rise Up, Women! The Militant Campaign of the Women's Social and Political Union, 1903-14*. London.

Rosenberg, Rosalind. 1982. *Beyond Separate Spheres: Intellectual Roots of Mod-ern Feminism*. New Haven, Conn.

Rosenhan, Mollie Schwartz. 1977. "Images of Male and Female in Children's Readers," in *Women in Russia*, ed. Dorothy Atkinson, Alexander Dallin, and Gail Lapidus. Stanford, Calif.

————. 1981. "*Women's Place and Cultural Values in Soviet Children's Readers: An Historical Analysis of the Maintenance of Role Division by Gender, 1920s and 1970s*." Ph.D. dissertation, University of Pennsylvania.

Ross, Dorothy. 1972. *G. Stanley Hall: The Psychologist as Prophet*. Chicago.

Rossi, Alice S., ed. 1973. *The Feminist Papers, from Adams to De Beauvoir*. New York.

Roszak, Theodore. 1969. "The Hard and the Soft: The Force of Feminism in Modern Times," in *Masculine/Feminine: Readings in Sexual Mythology and the Liberation of Women*, ed. Betty Roszak and Theodore Roszak. New York.

Rothman, Sheila M. 1978. *Woman's Proper Place: A History of Changing Ideals and Practices, 1870 to the Present*. New York.

Rover, Constance. 1967. *Women's Suffrage and Party Politics in Britain, 1866-1914*. London.

————. 1970. *Love, Morals, and the Feminists*. London.

Rowbotham, Sheila. 1972. *Women, Resistance, and Revolution: A History of Women and Revolution in the Modern World*. London. New York, 1973.

————. 1973. *Hidden from History: Rediscovering Women in History from the 17th Century to the Present*. London; New York ed., 1974.

Royle, Edward. 1974. *Radicals, Secularists, and Republicans: Popular Free-thought in Britain, 1866-1915*. Manchester, Eng.

Rubins, Jack L. 1978. *Karen Horney: Gentle Rebel of Psychoanalysis*. New York.

Rupp, Leila J. 1977. "Mother of the Volk: The Image of Women in Nazi Ideology," *SIGNS: Journal of Women in Culture and Society*, 3, no. 2 (Winter), 362-79.

———. 1978. *Mobilizing Women for War: German and American Propaganda, 1939-1945*. Princeton, N.J.

———. 1980. "'I Don't Call That *Volksgemeinschaft*': Women, Class, and War in Nazi Germany," in *Women, War, and Revolution*, ed. Carol R. Berkin and Clara M. Lovett. New York.

Ryan, Mary P. 1975. *Womanhood in America*. New York.

Sacks, Karen. 1974. "Engels Revisited: Women, the Organization of Production, and Private Property," in *Women, Culture, and Society*, ed. Michelle Rosaldo and Louise Lamphere. Stanford, Calif.

Salleron, Claude. 1954. "La Littérature au XIXe siècle et la famille," in *Renouveau des idées sur la famille*, ed. Robert Prigent. Paris.

Sander, Margaret. 1971. Introduction to Frank Wedekind, *Frühlings Erwachen, eine Kindertragödie*. Waltham, Mass.

Sarfatti, Margherita Grassini. 1925. *The Life of Benito Mussolini*. Tr. Frederic Whyte. New York.

Sargent, Lydia, ed. 1981. *Women and Revolution: A Discussion of the Unhappy Marriage of Marxism and Feminism*. Boston, Mass.

Sartre, Jean-Paul. 1972. *Being and Nothingness*. Tr. Hazel Barnes. New York. Originally published in French, 1943.

Scanlon, Leone. 1976. "The New Woman in the Literature of 1883 to 1909," *University of Michigan, Papers in Women's Studies*, 2, no. 2: 133-59.

Scharf, Lois. 1980. *To Work and to Wed: Female Employment, Feminism and the Great Depression*. Westport, Conn.

Scheifley, William H. 1917. *Brieux and Contemporary French Society*. New York.

Schlesinger, Rudolf, ed. 1949. *The Family in the U.S.S.R.* London.

Schmahl, Jeanne-E. 1896. "Progress of the Women's Rights Movement in France," *Forum*, 22 (Sept.), 79-92.

Schneir, Miriam, 1972. *Feminism: The Essential Historical Writings*. New York.

Schoenbaum, David. 1967. *Hitler's Social Revolution: Class and Status in Nazi Germany*, ch. 6: "The Third Reich and Women." New York.

Scholtz-Klink, Gertrud. 1978. *Die Frau im Dritten Reich*. Tübingen, Germany.

Schroeder, Hannelore. 1981. *Die Frau ist frei geboren: Texte zur Frauenemanzipation*, II: *1870-1918*. Munich.

Schüddekopf, Charles, ed. 1981. *Der alltägliche Faschismus: Frauen im Dritten Reich*. Berlin and Bonn.

Schwartz, Gudrun. 1981. "The Single Woman, Berlin 1900-1920." Paper presented at the Fifth Berkshire Conference on the History of Women, Vassar College.

Semashko, P. 1934. *Health Protection in the U.S.S.R.* London.

Shaw, George Bernard. 1911. Preface, to *Three Plays by Brieux*, ed. G. B. Shaw. New York.

Shields, Stephanie A. 1975. "Functionalism, Darwinism, and the Psychology of Women: A Study in Social Myth," *American Psychologist*, 30, no. 7 (July), 739-54.

———. 1982. "The Variability Hypothesis: The History of a Biological Model of Sex Differences in Intelligence," *SIGNS: Journal of Women in Culture and Society*, 7, no. 4 (Summer), 769-97.

Shorter, Edward. 1973. "Female Emancipation, Birth Control, and Fertility in European History," *American Historical Review*, 78, no. 3 (June), 605-40.

Showalter, Elaine. 1975. "Literary Criticism: A Review Essay." *SIGNS: Journal of Women in Culture and Society*, 1, no. 1 (Winter), 435-60.

———. 1977. *A Literature of Their Own: British Women Novelists from Brontë to Lessing*. Princeton, N.J.

Silver, Arnold. 1982. *Bernard Shaw: The Darker Side*. Stanford, Calif.

Simmel, Monika. 1980. *Erziehung zum Weibe: Mädchenbildung im 19. Jahrhundert*. Frankfurt a.M.

Skold, Karen Beck. 1980. "The Job He Left Behind: American Women in the Shipyards During World War II," in *Women, War, and Revolution*, ed. Carol R. Berkin and Clara M. Lovett. New York.

Smith, Bonnie G. 1981. *Ladies of the Leisure Class: The Bourgeoises of Northern France in the Nineteenth Century*. Princeton, N.J.

Smith, Denis Mack. 1982. *Mussolini*. New York.

Smith, Harold. 1978. "The Issue of 'Equal Pay for Equal Work' in Great Britain, 1914-1919," *Societas*, 8, no. 1 (Winter), 39-51.

———. 1981. "The Problem of 'Equal Pay for Equal Work' in Great Britain during World War II," *Journal of Modern History*, 53, no. 4 (Dec.), 652-72.

Smith-Rosenberg, Carroll, and Charles Rosenberg. 1973. "The Female Animal: Medical and Biological Views of Women in Nineteenth-Century America," *Journal of American History*, 60, no. 2 (Sept.), 332-56.

Smith-Rosenberg, Carroll, and Esther Newton. 1981. "Male Mythologies and Their Internalization of Deviance from Krafft-Ebing to Radclyffe Hall." Paper presented at the Fifth Berkshire Conference on the History of Women, Vassar College.

Sohn, Anne-Marie. 1972. "*La Garçonne* face à l'opinion publique; type littéraire ou type social des années 20?," *Le Mouvement Social*, no. 80: 3-27.

Soloway, Richard Allan. 1983. *Birth Control and the Population Question in England, 1877-1930*. Chapel Hill, N.C.

Sowerwine, Charles. 1975. "Le Groupe féministe socialist, 1899-1902," *Le Mouvement Social*, no. 90 (Jan.-Mar.), 87-120.

———. 1976. "The Organization of French Socialist Women, 1880-1914; A European Perspective for Women's Movements," *Historical Reflections*, 3, no. 2 (Winter), 3-24.

———. 1977. "Women, Socialism, and Feminism, 1872-1922: A Bibliography," *Third Republic/Troisième République*, no. 3-4 (Spring/Fall), 300-366.

———. 1978. *Les Femmes et le Socialisme*. Paris.

———. 1979. "Women Against the War: A Feminine Basis for Internationalism and Pacifism?" *Proceedings of the Western Society for French History*, 6: 361-70.

———. 1980. "Socialism, Feminism, and Violence: The Analysis of Madeleine Pelletier." Paper presented at the Western Society for French History, Eugene, Oregon.

———. 1981. "Workers and Women in France Before 1914: The Debate over the Couriau Affair." Unpublished manuscript.

———. 1982. *Sisters or Citizens? Women and Socialism in France Since 1876*. Cambridge, Eng., and New York.

Speirs, Dorothy. 1974. "État présent des études sur 'Les quatre evangiles,'" *Les Cahiers Naturalistes*, no. 48: 215-35.

Stage, Sarah. 1981. "From Domestic Science to Political Housekeeping: Home Economics as a Rationale for Progressivism." Paper presented at the Fifth Berkshire Conference on the History of Women, Vassar College.

Stanton, Elizabeth Cady. 1898. *Eighty Years and More: Reminiscences, 1815-1897.* New York. Reprint, 1971.

Stanton, Theodore, ed. 1884. *The Woman Question in Europe.* New York.

Stearns, Peter N. 1979. *Be a Man! Males in Modern Society.* New York.

Steinson, Barbara J. 1980. "'The Mother Half of Humanity': American Women in the Peace and Preparedness Movements in World War I," in *Women, War, and Revolution,* ed. Carol R. Berkin and Clara M. Lovett. New York.

Stephenson, Jill. 1975. *Women in Nazi Society.* London.

Stern, Fritz. 1961. *The Politics of Cultural Despair: A Study in the Rise of the Germanic Ideology.* Berkeley, Calif. Reprint, 1965.

Stern, Karl. 1965. *The Flight from Woman.* New York.

Stites, Richard. 1976. "Zhenodtel: Bolshevism and Russian Women, 1917-1930," *Russian History,* 3, pt. 2: 174-93.

———. 1977. "Women and the Russian Intelligentsia: Three Perspectives," in *Women in Russia,* ed. Dorothy Atkinson, Alexander Dallin, and Gail Lapidus. Stanford, Calif.

———. 1978. *The Women's Liberation Movement in Russia: Nihilism, Feminism, and Bolshevism, 1860-1930.* Princeton, N.J.

Stobaugh, Beverly Parker. 1978. *Women and Parliament, 1918-1970.* New York.

Stock, Phyllis. 1978. *Better than Rubies: A History of Women's Education.* New York.

Stocks, Mary D. 1950. *Eleanor Rathbone: A Biography.* London.

Strachey, Ray. 1928. *The Cause: A Short History of the Women's Movement in Great Britain.* London. Reprinted, with a new introduction, 1978.

———. 1931. *Millicent Garrett Fawcett.* London.

Strain, Jacqueline. 1964. "*Feminism and Political Radicalism in the German Social Democratic Movement, 1890-1914.*" Ph.D. dissertation, University of California, Berkeley.

Strouse, Jean, ed., 1974. *Women and Analysis: Dialogues on Psychoanalytic Views of Femininity.* New York.

Sullerot, Evelyne. 1966. *Histoire de la presse féminine en France, des origines à 1848.* Paris.

———. 1968. *Histoire et sociologie du travail féminin.* Paris.

Sumner, Helen L. 1910. *History of Women in Industry in the United States.* Washington, D.C. Reprint, 1974.

Sussman, George D. 1977. "The End of the Wet-Nursing Business in France, 1874-1914," *Journal of Family History,* 2, no. 3 (Fall), 237-58.

———. 1982. *Selling Mothers' Milk: The Wet-Nursing Business in France, 1715-1914.* Champaign, Ill.

Suttner, Bertha Felicie Sophia von. 1910. *Memoirs of Bertha von Suttner; the Record of an Eventful Life.* Boston and London. Originally published in German, Stuttgart, 1909.

Swanwick, Helena M. 1913. *The Future of the Women's Movement.* London.

———. 1935. *I Have Been Young.* London.

Swart, Koenraad W. 1964. *The Sense of Decadence in Nineteenth Century France.* The Hague.

Taïeb, Edith, ed., 1982. *Hubertine Auclert: La Citoyenne, 1848-1914.* Paris.

Talmy, Robert. 1962. *Histoire du mouvement familial en France (1896-1939).* 2 vols. Paris.

Thibert, Marguerite. 1971. "Discours." *Les Pionnières du féminisme: Réunion du Cercle des femmes républicaines, 24 mars 1971.* Paris.

Thompson, E. P. 1955. *William Morris—Romantic to Revolutionary*. London. Reprint with new postscript, 1977.

Thönnessen, Werner. 1973. *The Emancipation of Women: The Rise and Decline of the Women's Movement in German Social Democracy, 1863-1933*. Tr. Joris de Bres. London. Originally published in German, Frankfurt, 1969.

Thorne, Barrie, with Marilyn Yalom. 1982. *Rethinking the Family: Some Feminist Questions*. New York.

Tilly, Louise A., and Joan W. Scott. 1978. *Women, Work and Family*. New York.

Tilly, Louise A., Joan W. Scott, and Miriam Cohen. 1976. "Women's Work and European Fertility Patterns," *Journal of Interdisciplinary History*, 6, no. 3 (Winter), 447-76.

Timasheff, Nicholas S. 1960. "The Attempt to Abolish the Family in Russia," in *A Modern Introduction to the Family*, ed. N. W. Bell and E. V. Vogel. Glencoe, Ill.

Troubridge, Una. 1961. *The Life of Radclyffe Hall*. London.

Tsuzuki, Chushichi. 1967. *The Life of Eleanor Marx, 1855-1898: A Socialist Tragedy*. Oxford.

Twellmann, Margrit. 1972. *Die deutsche Frauenbewegung im Spiegel repräsentativer Frauenzeitschriften, ihre Anfänge und erste Entwicklung*. 2 vols. Meisenheim-am-Glan, Germany.

U.S. Army Center of Military History. 1978. *Women in Combat and as Military Leaders: A Survey*. Washington, D.C.

Van Herik, Judith. 1982. *Freud on Femininity and Faith*. Berkeley, Calif.

Vicinus, Martha. 1981. "Students and Faculty in British Women's Colleges." Paper presented at the Fifth Berkshire Conference on the History of Women, Vassar College.

Walkowitz, Judith R. 1980. *Prostitution and Victorian Society: Women, Class, and the State*. Cambridge, Eng., and New York.

Wallace, Lillian Parker. 1966. *Leo XIII and the Rise of Socialism*. Durham, N.C.

Walsh, Mary Roth. 1977. *"Doctors Wanted: No Women Need Apply": Sexual Barriers in the Medical Profession, 1835-1975*. New Haven, Conn.

Walters, Margaret. 1976. "The Rights and Wrongs of Women: Mary Wollstonecraft, Harriet Martineau, Simone de Beauvoir," in *The Rights and Wrongs of Women*, ed. Juliet Mitchell and Ann Oakley. London.

Wandersee, Winifred D. 1981. *Women's Work and Family Values, 1920-1940*. Cambridge, Mass.

Ware, Susan. 1981. *Beyond Suffrage: Women in the New Deal*. Cambridge, Mass.

Wein, Roberta. 1974a. "Educated Women and the Limits of Domesticity, 1830-1918." Ph.D. dissertation, New York University.

———. 1974b. "Women's Colleges and Domesticity, 1875-1918," in *Liberating Women's History*, ed. Berenice Carroll. Urbana, Ill.

Weiner, Lynn. 1980. "Subsidized Motherhood: The Mothers' Pension Movement in the United States." Paper presented to the American Historical Association, Washington, D.C.

Werth, Alvin, and Clement S. Mihanovich, comps. 1955. *Papal Pronouncements on Marriage and the Family from Leo XIII to Pius XII (1878-1954)*. Milwaukee, Wisc.

Weston, Elisabeth. 1979. "Prostitution in Paris in the Later Nineteenth Century: A Study in Political and Social Ideology." Ph.D. dissertation, State University of New York, Buffalo.

Wheeler, Robert F. 1975. "German Women and the Communist International: The Case of the Independent Social Democrats," *Central European History*, 8, no. 2 (June), 113-39.

White, Evelyne. 1938. *Winifred Holtby As I Knew Her: A Study of the Author and Her Works*. London.

Whittick, Arnold. 1979. *Woman into Citizen*. Santa Barbara, Calif.

Willich, Hans. 1960. "Hedwig Kettler," *Niedersächsische Lebensbilder* (Hildesheim), 4: 155-71.

Wisenthal, J. L. 1979. *Shaw and Ibsen: Bernard Shaw's 'The Quintessence of Ibsenism' and Related Writings*. Toronto.

Wolfe, Bertram D. 1948. *Three Who Made a Revolution: A Biographical History*. New York.

Zahn-Harnak, Agnes. 1928. *Die Frauenbewegung, Geschichte, Probleme, Ziele*. Berlin.

Zaretsky, Eli. 1976. *Capitalism, the Family, and Personal Life*. New York.

———. 1982. "The Place of the Family in the Origins of the Welfare State," in *Rethinking the Family: Some Feminist Questions*, ed. Barrie Thorne with Marilyn Yalom. New York.

Zetkin, Clara. 1934. *Lenin on the Woman Question*. 2nd ed. New York.

Zimmerman, Bonnie. 1981. "What Has Never Been: An Overview of Lesbian Feminist Literary Criticism," *Feminist Studies*, 7, no. 3 (Fall), 451-75.

Zylberberg-Hocquard, Marie-Hélène. 1978. *Féminisme et Syndicalisme en France*. Paris.

ACKNOWLEDGMENTS

Simone de Beauvoir, *The Second Sex*, trans. H. M. Parshley. Copyright © 1952 by Alfred A. Knopf, Inc. Selections reprinted by permission of Alfred A. Knopf, Inc., and Jonathan Cape, Ltd.

Bjørnstjerne Bjørnson, *A Gauntlet*, trans. R. Farquharson Sharp. Copyright © 1912 by J. M. Dent & Sons, Ltd. Selections reprinted by permission of J. M. Dent & Sons, Ltd.

Eugène Brieux, *Maternity*, in *Three Plays by Brieux*, ed. and introduced by Bernard Shaw, trans. Mrs. Bernard Shaw. Copyright © 1911 by Charlotte Frances Shaw. Selection reprinted by permission of the Bank of Ireland, trustees for the estate of Mrs. Bernard Shaw.

Anton Chekhov, "The Darling," in *The Darling and Other Stories*, trans. Constance Garnett. Copyright © 1916 by the Macmillan Publishing Co., Inc. Selections reprinted by permission of the Macmillan Publishing Co., Inc., and A. P. Watt, Ltd., for the estate of Constance Garnett and for Chatto & Windus, Ltd.

Friedrich Engels, *The Origin of the Family, Private Property, and the State, in the Light of the Researches of Lewis H. Morgan*, trans. Alick West. Copyright © 1941 by Lawrence & Wishart, Ltd. Selections reprinted by permission of Lawrence & Wishart, Ltd.

Sigmund Freud, "Some Psychological Consequences of the Anatomical Distinction Between the Sexes," in *The Standard Edition of the Complete Psychological Works of Sigmund Freud*, ed. James Strachey; "Femininity," in *New Introductory Lectures on Psychoanalysis*, trans. and ed. James Strachey; and *Civilization and Its Discontents*, trans. James Strachey. Copyright © 1964; 1965; 1962 by Sigmund Freud Copyrights, Ltd. Selections reprinted by permission of Sigmund Freud Copyrights, Ltd.

Radclyffe Hall, *The Well of Loneliness*. Copyright © 1928 by Radclyffe Hall. Copyright renewed © 1956 by Una, Lady Troubridge. Selections reprinted by permission of Brandt & Brandt Literary Agents, Inc.

Winifred Holtby, *Women and a Changing Civilization*. Copyright © 1934 by Bodley Head, Ltd. Selections reprinted by permission of Paul Berry, literary executor for Winifred Holtby.

Karen Horney, "The Flight from Womanhood: The Masculinity Complex in Women as Viewed by Men and Women," *International Journal of Psycho-Analysis*, 7, pts. 3 and 4 (July and October 1926). Copyright © 1926 by the *International Journal of Psycho-Analysis*. Selections reprinted by permission of the *International Journal of Psycho-Analysis* and the heirs of Karen Horney.

International Socialist Women's Conference, Resolution on woman suffrage (1907), trans. Alfred G. Meyer, in *Women in Russia*, ed. Dorothy Atkinson,

Alexander Dallin, and Gail Lapidus. Copyright © 1977 by Stanford University Press. Reprinted by permission of Stanford University Press.

Carl Gustav Jung, "Woman in Europe," in *Contributions to Analytical Psychology*, trans. H. G. and Cary C. Baynes. Copyright © 1928 by Princeton University Press. Reprinted by permission of Princeton University Press and Routledge & Kegan Paul, Ltd.

Aleksandra Kollontai, "The Labour of Women in the Evolution of the Economy," in *The Family in the U.S.S.R.*, ed. Rudolf Schlesinger. Copyright © 1949 by Routledge & Kegan Paul, Ltd. Selections reprinted by permission of Routledge & Kegan Paul, Ltd.

Margaret Mead, *Male and Female*. Copyright © 1949, 1967 by Margaret Mead. Selections reprinted by permission of William Morrow & Company, Inc., and Victor Gollancz, Ltd.

Alva Myrdal, *Nation and Family: The Swedish Experiment in Democratic Family and Population Policy*. Copyright © 1941 by Harper & Row, Inc. Selections reprinted by permission of Harper & Row, Inc.

Friedrich Nietzsche, *Beyond Good and Evil*, in *Basic Writings of Nietzsche*, trans. Walter Kaufmann. Copyright © 1968 by Random House, Inc. Selections reprinted by permission of Random House, Inc.

A. Orlov, "On the Education of Boys and Girls Apart in Separate Schools," in *The Family in the U.S.S.R.*, ed. Rudolf Schlesinger. Copyright © 1949 by Routledge & Kegan Paul, Ltd. Selections reprinted by permission of Routledge & Kegan Paul, Ltd.

Eleanor Rathbone, *The Disinherited Family*. Copyright © 1927 by Edward Arnold, Ltd. Selections reprinted by permission of Edward Arnold, Ltd.

Bernard Shaw, *The Quintessence of Ibsenism*. Copyright © 1891 by Bernard Shaw. Selections reprinted by permission of the Society of Authors on behalf of the Bernard Shaw Estate.

The Soviet Code on Marriage and Divorce (1926), in *The Family in the U.S.S.R.*, ed. Rudolf Schlesinger. Copyright © 1949 by Routledge & Kegan Paul, Ltd. Selections reprinted by permission of Routledge & Kegan Paul, Ltd.

The Soviet Decree on the Legalization of Abortion (1920), in N. A. Semashko, *Health Protection in the U.S.S.R.* Copyright © 1934 by Victor Gollancz, Ltd. Selection reprinted by permission of Victor Gollancz, Ltd.

The Soviet Family Law of 8 July 1944, in *The Family in the U.S.S.R.*, ed. Rudolf Schlesinger. Copyright © 1949 by Routledge & Kegan Paul, Ltd. Selections reprinted by permission of Routledge & Kegan Paul, Ltd.

Leo Tolstoy, "Tolstoy's Criticism on 'The Darling,'" in Anton Chekhov, *The Darling and Other Stories*, trans. Constance Garnett. Copyright © 1916 by the Macmillan Publishing Co., Inc. Selections reprinted by permission of the Macmillan Publishing Co., Inc., and A. P. Watt, Ltd., for the estate of Constance Garnett and for Chatto & Windus, Ltd.

Leon Trotsky, "Thermidor in the Family," in *The Revolution Betrayed*, trans. Max Eastman. Copyright © 1937 by Merit Publishers. Selections reprinted by permission of Merit Publishers.

Beatrice Webb, *Women and the Factory Acts*, Fabian Tract No. 67. Copyright © 1896 by the Fabian Society. Selection reprinted by permission of the Fabian Society, London.

Rebecca West, *The Judge*. Copyright © 1922 by Rebecca West. Selections reprinted by permission of A. D. Peters & Co., Ltd.

Virginia Woolf, *Three Guineas*. Copyright © 1938 by Harcourt Brace Jovanovich, Inc. Copyright renewed © 1966 by Leonard Woolf. Selections reprinted by permission of Harcourt Brace Jovanovich, Inc., and the Hogarth Press, Ltd.

INDEX

Abortion, 172, 175f, 255, 260, 299-302, 309f, 366, 383, 397, 404; legalization of, 302
Adam, Juliette, 100
Addams, Jane, 11, 251, 263f
Alimony, 370
All-Russian Congress of Women, 287
Anderson, Elizabeth Garrett, 190, 233
Andreas-Salomé, Lou, 46
Androgyny, 355
Anthony, Katharine, 98
Anthony, Susan B., 137, 292
Antifeminism, 3n
Aquinas, Thomas, 95, 313
Aragon, Catherine of, 181
Acton, Lord, 242
Auclert, Hubertine, 1, 73, 228
Augustus (Roman Emperor), 253, 399
Autonomy, 2f, 7, 14, 148f, 220f, 256, 258, 313f, 318
Aveling, Edward, 73-74, 81-87

Bachofen, Johann-Jakob, 5, 46, 73, 76, 78, 257
Balch, Emily G., 263
Baring, Evelyn (Lord Cromer), 2
Barnard College, 421
Barney, Natalie, 343
Barrès, Maurice, 11
Bashkirtseff, Marie, 32, 39-41, 43f
Bateson, Gregory, 421
Bäumer, Gertrud, 144, 259f, 261-62
Beauvoir, Simone de, 251, 258, 420f, 421-28
Bebel, August, 73, 81f, 85
Beecher, Catharine, 150
Bell, Julian, 356

Bell, Vanessa, 355
Bellamy, Edward, 118, 200f, 202-5
Bergson, Henri, 384
Bernays, Martha, 328
Bettelheim, Bruno, 330, 331n
Binion, Rudolph, 46
Biography, 7
Birth control, 2, 13, 123, 130, 136, 139-40, 148, 172, 256, 327, 391, 394-97; as a moral issue, 123, 299-317; contraception, 130, 144, 299, 307, 310; clinics, 299, 306f; legalization of, 306. *See also* Family planning
Birthrate, 8f, 129, 142, 166, 168, 254, 256, 322; statistics, 6, 136, 139
Bjørnson, Bjørnstjerne, 64-65, 65-68, 118
Blackwell, Elizabeth, 5
Blum, Léon, 13, 172f, 179-80
Boas, Franz, 421
Bonald, Louis de, 181
Brandeis, Louis, 202
Breast-feeding, *see under* Motherhood
Breton, Jules Louis, 306f, 308-9
Brieux, Eugène, 3n, 14, 129f, 132-34, 172, 177
Brion, Hélène, 252, 263f, 273-75
Brittain, Vera, 307
Broca, Paul, 5
Brontë, Charlotte, 162
Browning, Elizabeth Barrett, 162
Bund Deutscher Frauenvereine, 97f, 102-4, 144, 260
Burckhardt, Jacob, 5
Butler, Josephine, 382

121, 124; as duty to the state, 120-21, 123, 137-40, 252, 286, 290f, 303-6, 308-9, 322f, 365, 374f; unwed, 130, 132-35, 146f, 200, 254, 307, 325, 342, 399, 407-11; education for, 152, 157, 159, 162; medals for, 252, 255, 306, 308-9, 407, 410-11; insurance for, 103, 145-47, 254, 297; allowance for, 318-22; fertility, 130-32, 136, 394f; pregnancy, 219; child bearing, 135f, 177, 308f, 321f, 383, 395, 397; breast-feeding, 161, 305; maternity benefits, 108, 144, 297f; mothers as educators, 11, 103-4, 118, 122, 150, 167; working mothers, 391, 394-97
Mother-right, 78
Mott, Lucretia, 222
Mussolini, Benito, 253, 307f, 355f, 363f, 369-70, 374, 399
Myrdal, Alva, 250, 256, 390f, 394-97, 412, 413-15
Myrdal, Gunnar, 390f

Napoleon I, 399
Napoleon III, 187
Naquet, Alfred, 180f, 187-89
National Consumers' League, 202
National Service Duty, *see* *Dienstpflicht*
National Socialist Workers' Party (Nazi Party), 253-55, 365, 373ff, 382f
National Union of Societies for Equal Citizenship (NUSEC, British), 318, 326f
National Union of Woman Suffrage Societies (NUWSS, British), 16, 233, 240-41, 259f, 318
National Woman Suffrage Association (U.S.), 97, 99, 137
National Women's Party of America, 372
Nationalism, 3, 6, 8, 136-43, 255
Nature/culture dichotomy, 7
Nazi Party, *see* National Socialist Workers' Party
Neomalthusianism, 148f. *See also* Birth control
Neumann, Erich, 330

New Economic Policy (Soviet), 398, 402
"New Feminism," 317-27
"New Woman," 12, 17-56, 342
Nietzsche, Friedrich, 12, 45-46, 47-50
Nineteenth Amendment (U.S. Constitution), 234
Nobel, Alfred, 65
Noce, Teresa, 363f, 366-69, 413

Oedipus complex, 257, 329-34, 336-42
Orlov, A., 398f, 405-7
"Otherness" of woman, 422-28

Pacifism, 8, 99, 251-52, 260, 263-70, 361
Pankhurst, Christabel, 13, 216f, 219-20, 232, 239, 276
Pankhurst, E. Sylvia, 216, 239, 276f, 280-82
Pankhurst, Emmeline, 16, 216, 233, 236-39, 276
Pankhurst, Richard, 233
Pascal, Blaise, 384
Passivity of women, 7, 47, 301, 329
Patriarchy, 1, 3, 7, 17f, 79-80, 91, 95, 129-30, 250, 255, 258, 317-20, 329, 355, 362, 382; and education, 150, 359
Paul, Alice, 234
Pedestal theory, 4, 5, 314, 413, 417
Pelletier, Madeleine, 97f, 105-6
Penis envy, 157, 329, 331-41
Pestalozzi, Johann H., 150, 152, 162
Physical strength, arguments from, 9, 95, 203, 271; and college women, 165
Pius IX, 4, 91, 92-95
Pius XI, 256-57, 306f, 310-14
Pius XII, 412-13, 415-20
Pizan, Christine de, 88n, 251
Plato, 324
Pognon, Maria, 13, 200f, 211-13
Population Commission (Swedish), 413-15
Population policy, 13, 14n, 129-49, 156, 218, 255-56, 306, 327, 390f, 394-97, 399-400
Prévost, Marcel, 46f, 51-56
Prostitution, 2, 9f, 86, 144, 216f,